The Paganism Reader

"If you're wondering why people want to be Pagans today – or want to be one yourself – this book provides you with a rich variety of Pagan voices: guiding, feeling, thinking, arguing. Clifton and Harvey have given Pagans a voice and an understanding of themselves – with enviable sympathy and authority."

Ken Dowden, Professor of Classics, University of Birmingham and author of *European Paganism*

"The Pagan revival of the nineteenth and twentieth centuries endeavoured to revitalise ancient Pagan symbols and traditions into a meaningful spirituality for the contemporary West. *The Paganism Reader* is the first to bring together some of the formative writings that have given birth to the Pagan revival and gives readers a fascinating insight into influences on contemporary Pagan thought."

Vivianne Crowley, Heythrop College

Paganism is one of the world's fastest-growing religions, practiced in a huge variety of ways. *The Paganism Reader* provides a definitive collection of key sources in Paganism, ranging from its ancient origins to its twentieth-century reconstruction and revival. Chronologically organized sections include extracts from ancient Greek, Norse, and Celtic literature, inspirational texts from the early twentieth century, writings by leaders of the Pagan revival, and newer perspectives showing the diversity of Paganism today. Witchcraft, nature religion, shamanism, and Goddess worship are represented, as are influential feminist and environmental viewpoints. Fully introduced by the editors, and containing dedicated prefaces to all extracts and suggestions for further reading, this comprehensive book is an invaluable guide to Paganism and to critical issues in its study.

Chas S. Clifton lectures at Colorado State University Pueblo. He is editor of *The Pomegranate: The Journal of Pagan Studies* and a former editor of *Gnosis* and *Witchcraft Today*. His books include *Living Between Two Worlds* (1996) and *Sacred Mask, Sacred Dance* (1997). **Graham Harvey** is Lecturer in Religious Studies at the Open University, UK. He is editor of *Shamanism: A Reader* (Routledge, 2002), co-editor with Charlotte Hardman of *Pagan Pathways* (2001), and author of *Listening People, Speaking Earth: Contemporary Paganism* (1997).

The Paganism Reader

Edited by

Chas S. Clifton and Graham Harvey

Routledge
Taylor & Francis Group

NEW YORK AND LONDON

First published 2004
by Routledge
270 Madison Ave, New York, NY 10016

Simultaneously published in the UK
by Routledge
2 Park Square, Milton Park, Abingdon, Oxon OX14 4RN

Reprinted 2006

Routledge is an imprint of the Taylor & Francis Group

Typeset in Bell Gothic and Perpetua by
Florence Production Ltd, Stoodleigh, Devon
Printed and bound in Great Britain by
TJ International Ltd, Padstow, Cornwall

Library of Congress Cataloging in Publication Data
A catalog record for this book has been requested

British Library Cataloguing in Publication Data
A catalogue record for this book is available from the British Library

ISBN 0–415–30352–4 (hbk)
ISBN 0–415–30353–2 (pbk)

Contents

Acknowledgements

The author and publishers would like to thank the following for their permission to reproduce material:

'The Hymn to the Mother of the Gods' and 'The Hymn to the Moon', from *The Homeric Hymns*, Charles Boer Translation, Spring Publications, Putnam, CT. Copyright 1970 Charles Boer, Sixth printing 2003. Reprinted by permission of Spring Publications. Apuleius, 'Isis' speech', pp. 262–6, from *The Golden Ass*, translated by Robert Graves, New York: Farrar, Straus & Giroux, 1951. Copyright © 1951, renewed 1979 by Robert Graves. Reprinted by permission of Carcanet Press Limited. Pliny the Elder, 'Mistletoe', pp. 549, 551, reprinted by permission of the publishers and the Trustees of the Loeb Classical Library from *Pliny*, Volume IV, Loeb Classical Library Volume L370, translated by H. Rackham, Cambridge, MA: Harvard University Press, 1945, 1968. The Loeb Classical Library ® is a registered trademark of the President and fellows of Harvard College. 'Fragment of Julian the Hellene, Letter to a Priest', pp. 299–39, reprinted by permission of the publishers and the Trustees of the Loeb Classical Library from *Julian*, Volume II, Loeb Classical Library Volume L29, translated by Wilmer C. Wright, Cambridge, MA: Harvard University Press, 1913. The Loeb Classical Library ® is a registered trademark of the President and fellows of Harvard College. 'The Thunder: Perfect Mind', pp. 297–303, from *The Nag Hammadi Library in English*, 3rd edn, completely revised ed. James M. Robinson, Editor. Copyright © 1978, 1988 by E.J. Brill, Leiden, The Netherlands. Reprinted, on pp. 34–9 of this book, by permission of HarperCollins Publishers Inc. and Brill Academic Publishers. *Hávámal*, stanzas 1 to 20 and 138 to 145 from *The Poetic Edda* (1996), translated by Carolyne Larrington, by permission of Oxford University Press. 'The seeress', pp. 206–9, from

Einar Ólafur Sveinsson and Matthías Þorðarson (eds), *Íslenzk Fornrit*: Vol. 4: *Eyrbyggja saga*, Reykjavik: University of Iceland, 1935. Excerpt translated by Phil Cardew (Quality Assurance Agency for Higher Education, UK). Reproduced by permission of Phil Cardew. 'Math Son of Mathonwy', pp. 110–17, from *The Mabinogion*, translated by Jeffrey Gantz, London: Penguin Classics, 1976. Translation copyright © Jeffrey Gantz, 1976. Reproduced by permission of Penguin Books Ltd. Excerpt from *Over Nine Waves* by Marie Heaney. Copyright © 1994 by Marie Heaney. Reprinted by permission of Faber and Faber, Inc., an affiliate of Farrar, Straus and Giroux, LLC, and Faber and Faber. Geoffrey of Monmouth, 'The tower, the pool and the dragon', pp. 168–9, from *The History of the Kings of Britain*, translated by Lewis Thorpe, London: Penguin Classics, 1966. Translation copyright © Lewis Thorpe, 1966. Reproduced by permission of Penguin Books Ltd. Charles Leland, 'How Diana gave birth to Aradia (Herodias)', pp. 127–33 and 355–63, from *Aradia, Or the Gospel of the Witches*, translated by Mario Pazzaglini and Dina Pazzaglini, Blaine, Washington, DC: Phoenix Publishing, 1998. Reprinted by permission of Phoenix Publishing, Inc. Aleister Crowley, *The Book of the Law*, London, 1906, reprinted by permission of Ordo Templi Orientis. Rudyard Kipling, 'A tree song', from *Puck of Pook's Hill*, London: Macmillan, 1906, reprinted by permission of A.P. Watt Ltd on behalf of the National Trust for Places of Historical Interest or Natural Beauty. Kenneth Grahame, 'The Piper at the Gates of Dawn', pp. 115–30, from *The Wind in the Willows*, London: Puffin Books, 1994. Margaret Murray, 'Witchcraft', reprinted with permission from *Encyclopedia Britannica*, 14th edition, vol. 23, © 1929 by Encyclopaedia Britannica, Inc. C.R.F. Seymour, 'The Old Gods', pp. 143–86, from *The Forgotten Mage: The Magical Lectures of Colonel C.R.F. Seymour*, Wellingborough: The Aquarian Press Ltd. Robert Graves, 'The triple muse', pp. 383–408, from *The White Goddess*, New York: Farrar, Straus & Giroux, 1948. Copyright © 1948, renewed 1975 by Robert Graves. Reprinted by permission of Carcanet Press Limited. Gerald Gardner, 'Living witchcraft', pp. 17–30, from *Witchcraft Today*, Secaucus, New Jersey: Citadel Press, 1973. Robert Heinlein, 'Thou art God', pp. 133–40, from *Stranger in a Strange Land*, revised edition by Robert A. Heinlein, copyright © 1961 by Robert A. Heinlein, renewed © 1989 by Virginia Heinlein. Revised edition © 1991 by Virginia Heinlein. Used by permission of G.P. Putnam's Sons, a division of Penguin Group (USA) Inc. and International Scripts. Paul Huson, 'Preliminary preparations', pp. 38–62, from *Mastering Witchcraft* by Paul Huson, copyright © 1970 by Paul Huson. Used by permission of G.P. Putnam's Sons, a division of Penguin Group (USA) Inc. Copyright © 1970 by Paul Huson. Reprinted by permission of William Morris Agency, Inc. on behalf of the author. Hans Holzer, 'Isis and Ishtar: the comeback of ancient cults', pp. 85–123, from *The New Pagans*, Garden City, New York: Doubleday, 1972. Copyright © Hans Holzer. Reprinted by permission of the author. Raymond Buckland, 'As it was: as it will be', from *Witchcraft from the Inside* by Raymond Buckland, © 1971. All rights reserved. Llewellyn Worldwide, Ltd, PO Box 64383, St. Paul, MN 55164. Reprinted by permission of Llewellyn Worldwide Ltd. Doreen Valiente, 'Working with Gerald' and 'Robert Cochrane, Magister', pp. 49–52 and 117–36, from *The Rebirth of Witchcraft*, London: Robert Hale, 1989.

Reprinted by permission of Robert Hale Books. Evan John Jones and Doreen Valiente, 'The nature of the rites', pp. 47–68, from *Witchcraft: A Tradition Renewed*, London: Robert Hale, 1990. Reprinted by permission of Robert Hale Books. June Johns, 'A magic childhood', pp. 18–26, from *King of the Witches: The World of Alex Sanders*, New York: Coward-McCann Inc., 1969. Michael McNierney, 'The Stoic way of nature: a Pagan spiritual path', pp. 13–27, in *The Pomegranate* 7 (February 1999), copyright © Michael McNierney. Reprinted by permission of the author. Heather O'Dell, 'The solo witch', pp. 133–47, from *Witchcraft Today, Book One*. Copyright © 1992 by Chas S. Clifton. All rights reserved. Llewellyn Worldwide, Ltd, PO Box 64383, St. Paul, MN 55164. Reprinted by permission of Llewellyn Worldwide Ltd. Judy Harrow, 'Initiation by ordeal: military service as a passage into adulthood', pp. 129–63, from *Witchcraft Today, Book Two*. Copyright © 1993 by Chas S. Clifton. All rights reserved. Llewellyn Worldwide Ltd, PO Box 64383, St Paul, MN 55164. Reprinted by permission of Llewellyn Worldwide Ltd. Tony Kelly, all pages copyright © 1999–2002 by Herb Mitchell for The Online Georgian Council of Elders. Asphodel Long, 'The Goddess movement in Britain today', pp. 11–39, in *Feminist Theology*, 5, 1994. Reprinted by permission of The Continuum International Publishing Group Ltd. Marion Bradley, 'Initiations', from *The Mists of Avalon*, Harmondsworth: Penguin, 1984, pp. 157–8, 202–3. Copyright © 1984 by Marion Bradley. Reproduced by permission of Penguin Books. Wren Sidhe, 'Drawing down the Moon', and 'Candlemas ritual cake', reprinted by permission of the author. Chas S. Clifton, 'Nature religion for real', pp. 16–20, in *Gnosis Magazine* 48 (Summer 1998). Reprinted by permission of *Gnosis*, PO Box 14820, San Francisco, CA 94114 www.gnosismagazine.com. Chas S. Clifton, 'What happened to Western shamanism?', pp. 73–91, from *Witchcraft Today, Book Three*. Copyright © 1994 by Chas S. Clifton. All rights reserved. Llewellyn Worldwide Ltd, PO Box 64383, St. Paul, MN 55164. Reprinted by permission of Llewellyn Worldwide Ltd. Barry Patterson, 'Finding your way in the woods: the art of conversation with the *Genius Loci*', copyright © Barry Patterson self-published: 1st edn 1991, 4th edn 1999 from http://www.redsandstonehill.net/esprit/woods-fulltxt.html. Reprinted by permission of Barry Patterson. Gordon MacLellan, 'Entertaining faeries', originally published in *White Dragon* 19: pp. 4–7, Beltane 1998. Reprinted by permission of the author.

Introduction

Chas S. Clifton and Graham Harvey

PAGANISM IS AN UMBRELLA term for various religions, or spiritual movements, whose practitioners are inspired by the indigenous, pre-Christian, traditions of Europe, and engagement with other indigenous religious traditions, to evolve satisfying and respectful ways of celebrating human relationships with the wider, other-than-human world. The creators of contemporary Paganism have drawn upon sources ranging from the earliest religious documents of the Classical world to the ceremonial magic of the Renaissance to the works of recent poets and novelists. Indeed, the list could be expanded far beyond the contents of this book, particularly into the realms of speculative fantasy writing: Robert Heinlein's *Stranger in a Strange Land* is included in this collection, but Andre Norton, Evangeline Walton, Charles DeLint, Margaret St. Clair, Neil Gaiman, and others might well be. In other words, Paganisms make explicit and engage many of the most interesting tendencies of the contemporary world. In doing so, they challenge any attempt at neat categories such as pre-modern, modern and post-modern. By drawing on hymns to Classical Greek deities or trance practices suggested in Norse sagas, blending these with modern romantic ascriptions of value to "nature," reclaiming the authority of women, and challenging all hierarchy with the essential plurality of self-constructing individuals and societies—and so on—Paganisms transgress many established boundaries.

The people who created and re-created Paganism in the mid-twentieth century were motivated largely by religious goals, and they looked to the past for models of animistic, polytheistic, and shamanic religious practices. The initial impulse was self-consciously religious, and the texts researched from the Classical period and from pre-Christian Europe were largely those labelled as "religious." Later, Pagans were influenced by second-wave feminism and by the growing environmental movement.

Therefore, this *Reader* includes selected excerpts from literature that influenced Paganism's development during the twentieth century — including ancient sources, practitioner narratives, and insightful observation. The ways in which such sources led to the evolution of a diversity of Pagan "traditions" will also be made clear in those excerpts that illustrate those emerging variations. Editorial introductions will situate each entry in its literary and historical context, but are particularly interested in the significance of entries in the development and expression of Paganism. Beyond providing a valuable resource of narratives that build a complex picture of Paganism as it has developed, the *Reader* will direct attention to critical academic debates, theories, and perspectives. Guidance towards significant creative works (novels, films, poetry, etc.) will permit a richer engagement with a religious tradition which tends not to present itself in dogmatic or systematic form. Reference to further sources will also suggest ways in which an issue has been elaborated by other Pagans or in other Pagan traditions.

For these reasons, and many more, Paganisms are popular both in the sense of widespread (indeed, fashionable in some places), non-elite, and accessible. At the same time, and for the same reasons, Paganisms are of increasing interest to academics in a variety of disciplines, especially Religious Studies, Anthropology, History, Sociology, and Cultural Studies. Other disciplines as diverse as Heritage and Tourism Studies, Environmental Ethics, Gender Studies, and Media Studies have been interested in Paganisms and their various engagements with the world. Paganisms are already approached using the finest and most incisive scholarly methods and this promises to contribute to their further refinement and use. Study of Paganisms is at the forefront of the academic study of religion and might serve as both a model and an invitation to the study of any and all religions and spiritualities. It is arguable, of course, that all religions benefit from the application of inter- and multi-disciplinary methods and approaches. Indeed, it is precisely that point that inspires the collaborative effort of the editors and other scholars interested in Paganisms and in other religions.

This *Reader* aims to contribute to these dialogues and explorations by increasing the availability of texts that cover and discuss significant themes and trends. It also aims to contribute to increased understanding of and debate about Paganism, utilizing excerpts from sources of significance in the revival and development of contemporary Paganisms as the foundation for critical reflection and discussion.

The *Reader* is divided into three Parts that place material in broad historical blocks. It is important to stress the arbitrary nature of these divisions and structuring. In reality, these texts can be read synchronically. That is, each of them can be read as inspirations for contemporary thought and practice. They might have been written today or, at least, in the early days of the Pagan revival. This is not to say that Pagans are uncritical. In fact, many are deeply interested in history and wish to understand what the authors meant in their own time and what they were saying to their contemporaries. Pagans do not tend to simplistically appropriate material that seems to support their own experientially gained understanding or justify any preconceived ideas. However, they are inspired by accounts of ancient invocations and rituals. They re-tell stories learnt from ancient bards as well as those told by friends and companions. Material in each of the three Parts might, then, be considered for what it reveals about contemporary Paganisms. While each chapter is prefaced by a short editorial introduction, the following notes may provide some further broad understanding of what each Part of this *Reader* entails.

Classical texts

Part One includes a series of Classical texts drawn from the literatures of ancient Israel, Greece, Rome, Egypt, Wales, Ireland, and Iceland. These are clearly not all alike and it would be difficult to make them proclaim the same message. Already these readings indicate the positive value of plurality and diversity. They suggest one reason for the existence of different ways of being Pagan, different Paganisms rather than one systematised religion. They are also different from one another in the way in which they communicate. They include a letter, an autobiographical account, an historical or ethnographic account, stories, and poems. Again, the difficulty of systematizing such material is indicative of Pagan resistance to dogmatism and the security of strong boundaries. These texts include descriptions and/or discussion of what might be called rituals and myths. It has become easy to dismiss these as meaningless or bizarre behaviors and childish or silly stories. In fact, however, Pagan performance of ceremonies and (re-)telling of stories are evidence of the inadequacy of such criticism or denigration. Many people find it helpful and even necessary to recognize certain moments, places, experiences, and persons as having more significance than others. Everyday modes of action and speech might not be sufficient to the task of paying and drawing attention to these matters. Much that is specific to Pagan being in the world is wrapped up in these texts. On the other hand, it is important not to overplay the enchanted and other-worldly aspects of Paganisms. One of the most important concerns that motivate Pagans—and a recurrent theme in people's accounts of why they identify themselves as Pagan—is the celebration of the ordinary, physical, mundane, everyday world.

Proto-revival texts

If the word "Pagan" and its cognate "Heathen" derive from ancient literatures, they began to be reinvented as nature (both worldly and human) was increasingly and variously re-valued from the eighteenth through the twentieth centuries. From being the occasion of temptation to sin, the imprisoning limitation constraining progress, the location of primitive and sensual oppositions to culture, "nature" slowly came to be valued as the location of truth, beauty, harmony, and balance. As urbanization and industrialization increased, so too did the positive value of nature. Trends that underlay phenomena as diverse as the popularity of Romanticism and the creation of wilderness reserves also led to a re-evaluation of the meaning and associations of the word "pagan." Such re-evaluations of nature, physicality, materialism, embodiment, and so on are part of what underlies the revival and/or re-creation of

Paganisms in the twentieth century. This, in turn, sometimes went hand in hand with a rediscovery of ancient deities and other persons of power who might be encountered out there beyond the cities and civilization. Once again, poetry and myth along with ritual might be more adequate ways of engaging with such persons and notions than either religious dogma or scientific theory.

The texts included in Part Two not only illustrate the reimagination of nature and the re-enchantment of the world, but also engage with the reconfiguration of what the word "witch" might mean. In almost every language there is a word for people who do harm by magical means (although the words "magic" and "harm" themselves require some debate too). In English that word was "witch." However, it was commonly thought among nineteenth-century folklorists and anthropologists that it was possible to retrieve knowledge about popular religion and culture of all previous ages from what elite texts and folk custom provided in a more garbled form. From the records of the early modern witch trials such scholars claimed to be able to recover the truth about a pagan fertility cult that had somehow survived and even thrived on the margins of society. This understanding may have been hotly contested among scholars but it gained rapid popularity among those who were already rediscovering ways of being pagan again. Some such, therefore, chose to identify themselves not only as Pagans but as Witches.

Another root and source of the Pagan revival is illustrated here. Alongside the celebration of nature and the reimagination of magic as foundations of the new Paganisms was a long tradition of esotericism. Modes of discourse and performance that enabled the expression and experience of greater than individual human perception and knowledge had been enshrined in traditions as various but cohesive as astrology, alchemy, kabala, tarot, and meditation. Societies such as the Golden Dawn brought together those in quest of ways to understand and benefit from the connections between "the above" and "the below." Among such groups can be found the origins of much that is recognizable among Pagan groups now. But they are not alone: New Age too grows out of earlier esoteric movements. Reflection on the similarities and differences, the divergences and confluences of these spiritualities (and others) can be rewarding.

Revival and diversification texts

Part Three of this *Reader* provides a selection of texts that illustrate the diverse forms and interests of the Paganisms that arose in the twentieth century. The majority of these are practitioners' accounts, works written by and for Pagans. They derive from Witches, Druids, Shamans, Goddess Feminists, Eco-activist and shamanic Pagans, and others. Certainly these texts are not sufficient for an understanding of all the diverse groups and styles of Paganism. They do not pretend to be all-embracing. They do, however, illustrate some of the tendencies and tensions among Pagans. Some of the debates about matters of contention and importance are embedded in these texts. Will Paganisms be religions of nature or of personal self-discovery? Will they be priest-centered traditions or religions of experience?

How will they construct and perform gender and relationships with others? Will they be pacifist? There are many other topics and questions of importance. The texts selected will, with some reflection, lead to a better understanding of Paganisms and the many ways in which they engage with the wider human and other-than-human world.

Conclusion

It is not the purpose of this (or any) *Reader* to indicate firm conclusions. Rather, it is their purpose to seduce and entice readers into further reflection and study. Even more fundamentally, it is the purpose of a *Reader* to enhance the value of other available literature and resources. We anticipate that this book will be used along-side other books that focus attention on particular issues of importance in the study of Paganisms and other religious movements. The final chapter is a guide to further reading and provides some suggestions about the current state of the study of Paganisms. This is not intended to be an exhaustive list of everything published on the subject. It refers to important texts for those who want to think more about the history and pre-history of Paganisms and how they came to be as they are now. It refers to texts on the various sociological structures that have been found to fit the thoughts and experiences Pagans have of the world. It mentions some books that provide ethnographies of particular kinds of Paganism on the understanding that only attention to these lived realities is worthy of being identified as the proper study of Paganisms. Reference is made to encyclopedias and journals that inform and debate Paganisms. The editors hope that this *Reader* and its guide to further reading will not only say something about how Paganisms came to be what they are today but will provoke and enable further study. We are excited by the possibilities that become available when people engage fully and critically with existing sources of knowledge and understanding.

PART ONE

Classical texts

Chapter 1

Jeremiah

CAKES FOR THE QUEEN OF HEAVEN

■ Jeremiah 44:15–19, trans. Graham Harvey, from the Hebrew text of the **BIBLIA HEBRAICA STUTTGARTENSIA**, Stuttgart, 1967/77, p. 871

O FFERINGS OF CAKE AND libations of wine to the Queen of Heaven – known by many names in different places throughout time – have been a standard feature not only of popular spirituality and polytheistic social action, but also of polemic and invective against 'nature religions'. In this passage (Jeremiah 44:15–19), the congregation of Judean refugees living in Egypt after the defeat of Judah by Babylon (sometime in the seventh century BCE) answer the prophet Jeremiah who has been threatening that God will destroy them for trusting Egypt and honouring 'foreign deities'. Their response is clear: Israel's religion is not monotheistic, the Goddess deserves veneration as well as the God. Moreover, they assert that when they did make offerings and libations to the Queen of Heaven, life was good. While this should not be taken for a verbatim report of what actual Goddess worshippers once said – after all, this is a polemic about wickedness and infidelity – it does provide an interesting insight into what the writer thinks is important to many fellow Judeans.

The Bible provides other examples of what it considers 'foreign religion', but may often be read as evidence of popular Israelite engagement with a community of deities who were also (like the Lord YHWH) interested in the lives and well-being of those who lived in the land of Israel. Such passages have been used by later polemicists to attack 'false religion' and 'inappropriate behaviour' – whether in Europe or in encounters with indigenous peoples worldwide. More recently, such material has been inspirational to those seeking resources for a more ecologically-centred religion and life-style.

For a classic study of Israel's Goddess, see Patai (1978). Among the contemporary Goddess literature and iconography, see Gadon (1990). Many other Goddess/ Feminist Spirituality and Wiccan books attend to the Queen of Heaven too.

Another biblical text that has been of some significance in understanding Paganism is the notorious line 'You shall not suffer a witch to live' (Exodus 22:17). Since the text, and the Bible, never say what a 'witch', *mekassefah*, actually is or does, or even looks like, it has been up to each generation to use this decree as they will. In fact, the traditional European image of the witch (ugly crone dressed in dark ragged clothes, haunting graveyards and harming people, crops and animals by magic) derives from pagan Roman sources such as Lucan's *Civil War* (vi. 499–568). For further discussion of biblical references to witches, see Harvey (1995).

Graham Harvey

References

Gadon, Elinor W. (1990) *The Once and Future Goddess*. San Francisco: Harper and Row.

Harvey, Graham (1995) 'The suffering of witches and children: uses of the witchcraft passages in the Bible', in Jon Davies, Graham Harvey and Wilfred G.E. Watson (eds) *Words Remembered, Texts Renewed: Festschrift for Prof. John F.A. Sawyer*. Sheffield: Sheffield Academic Press, pp. 113–34.

Patai, Raphael (1978) *The Hebrew Goddess*. New York: Avon Books.

A LL THE MEN WHO knew that their wives made offerings to other deities, and all the women present, a large congregation, and all the people who lived in Pathros in Egypt, answered Jeremiah,

> We will not listen to the things you've said to us in the name of YHWH. On the contrary, we will certainly do all that we've vowed. We will make offerings to the Queen of Heaven, and pour libations to her as we used to do – we and our ancestors, our kings and princes in the towns of Judah and in the streets of Jerusalem – because then we had plenty of bread and we were satisfied, and suffered no misfortune. But since we ceased making offerings to the Queen of Heaven and pouring libations to her, we have lacked everything and have been consumed by sword and famine. And when we make offerings to the Queen of Heaven and pour libations to her, is it without our husbands' approval that we make cakes in her likeness and pour libations to her?

Chapter 2

Anonymous

THE HYMN TO THE MOTHER OF THE GODS AND THE HYMN TO THE MOON

■ from **THE HOMERIC HYMNS**, trans. Charles Boer, Chicago, 1970, pp. 144–5

THERE IS MORE TO CONTEMPORARY Paganism than Wicca, of course. Contemporary Greek and Roman Reconstructionist Pagans are fortunate in having many ancient religious texts to study and to model their own practices upon. As translator Charles Boer (1970) notes, the Homeric hymns, composed over many centuries but attributed in ancient times to the author of the *Iliad* and the *Odyssey*, demonstrate "a dynamic relationship between man and the gods they sing of," the same type of relationship sought by Pagans today. Consequently, the Homeric hymns are found on the reading lists of every Greek and Roman Reconstructionist group today. (Other favorite poetic models of religious speech are the poet Sappho's invocation of Aphrodite and Chryses' invocation of Apollo in Book One of the *Iliad*.)

"Apollonius Sophistes," creator of The Stele, a website devoted to Greek and Roman Paganism, notes that contemporary Pagans do not view such texts as dogma even though they are held in high regard.

> How then do we find out about the Gods, if we don't have a book to tell us what to believe about Them? By studying the opinions of ancient Pagans, and evaluating them through our personal experience of the Gods, through meditation, divination, rituals, visions and mystical experiences.

The tone of the Homeric hymns varies considerably, from the devotional to the comic, but the two selected here are among the more devotional, Goddess-focused selections. In the words of Drew Campbell (2000), a Greek Reconstructionist Pagan priest, the Homeric hymns count among the foundations of "religious understanding and cultural literacy."

Chas S. Clifton

References

Boer, Charles (trans.) (1970) *The Homeric Hymns*. Chicago: Swallow Press.
Campbell, Drew (2000) *Old Stones, New Temples*. Philadelphia, PA: Xlibris.
The Stele. http://www.cs.utk.edu/~mclennan/OM/

The Hymn to the Mother of the Gods

Chant your hymn for me
                    this time,
                                Muse,
        clearly,
                        daughter of great Zeus,
                                to the mother of all the gods,
                                the mother of all men
            She loves the sound
                            of castanets
                the sound of kettle-drums
            and on top of this noise
                            she loves the shouts
                                            of flutes
                and the clamor of wolves
                and the cries of bright-eyed lions

    and hill echoes
                    and wood hollows
            she loves them

                    And that's
        how I greet you, goddess,
        and all the other goddesses
                        with this song

The Hymn to the Moon

Go on,
    Muses,
    and sing the Moon with her big wings,
                        daughters of Zeus,
                            son of Cronos,

in your sweet voices,
   you technicians
      of song

Off her immortal head
      a brightness,
   pointed from heaven,
         encircles earth,
and from this brightness
      great beauty,
and the air
   that was unlighted before
glows
   with her golden crown,
and her rays spring out
when the goddess
         Selene
has washed her beautiful body
in Ocean,
and put on her clothes
         that shine so far
and yoked her flashing horses
   with their strong necks,
and when she speeds these horses on
   in their beautiful hair,
at evening,
in the middle of the month

      Her great orb is full then
and her rays, as she is
         increasing,
become brightest

      And she becomes
         an assurance
         a sign
               to men

There was once a time
when she made love
      to Zeus
         in bed
She became pregnant
and had a daughter,
         Pandia,
         who had a particular beauty
         among the immortal gods

Greetings, lady
                    goddess with white arms
                    divine Selene
                    kind Selene
                         with your beautiful hair

          I began with you
          but now I will sing
                    the fame of those men who are
                              half divine,
                    those men whose works
                    have been made famous by
                    the lovely mouths of singers
                              who are themselves
                              only servants of the Muses

Chapter 3

Apuleius

ISIS' SPEECH

■ from **THE GOLDEN ASS**, trans. Robert Graves, New York, 1951, pp. 262–6

THE *METAMORPHOSES* OF APULEIUS, better known by its alternative title, *The Golden Ass*, is the only intact surviving novel from ancient Rome. Its protagonist, Lucius, spies on a Greek witch, is turned into a donkey in revenge, and undergoes various adventures until he is returned to human shape by the goddess Isis. The book was written in the 2nd century CE, by the poet and philosopher Apuleius, born abut 123 CE in Roman North Africa (present-day Libya). Amid its tales of witches, lovers, and bandits, Apuleius' book incorporates some older material, including the story of Eros (Love) and Psyche (Soul), which philosophers told as the descent of the soul into matter and its redemption by love.

The worship of Isis, the great mother goddess of Egypt, had grown in Rome as Rome's ties with Egypt increased, and it lasted into the Christian era. Although her worship began in Egypt and carried Egypt's ancient religious prestige, her followers covered the spectrum of peoples of the Roman Empire. As the Great Goddess of the Roman Empire, she was viewed as incorporating all other goddesses, but her worship also included special initiations and, unusual in the Classical world, a full-time professional priesthood. Her emblems included the sistrum (a metallic rattle) and a ship. (Model ships dedicated to her were often launched on the Mediterranean as offerings at the beginning of each summer sailing season.) After his return to human form, Lucius himself continues living at the temple of Isis and eventually takes holy orders in her priesthood: "The brotherhood accepted me almost as one of themselves, a loyal devotee of the Great Goddess."

But before that can occur, Lucius as the donkey must escape from near-certain death among wild beasts in the Roman amphitheatre. Alone at the seashore to which he was run, he prays to the Great Goddess and is rewarded with a vision in which she explains her many manifestations in terms reminiscent of the Wiccan "Charge of the Goddess." "I am Nature, the universal mother," she tells Lucius,

adding, "Above all, have faith: do not think that my commands are hard to obey."
In this statement, suggests historian Ronald Hutton (1999), we find the literary
forerunner of the "thealogy" of much contemporary Paganism.

In fact, some Pagan writers have argued that Apuleius' writing directly inspired
an alleged early nineteenth-century Pagan revival among undergraduates at Cambridge
University, while others have seen in it the direct inspiration for "The Charge of the
Goddess." The "Charge's" main author, Doreen Valiente, said that she found her literary inspiration in Charles Leland's *Aradia*, however. More typically, the Wiccan
author Vivianne Crowley (1996) refers to Isis of the Roman period as "the Goddess as
worshipped in Wicca; immanent, transcendent and mysterious" and describes her cult,
the same which Apuleius entered, as sharing many features with Wicca today, combining "religion, magic, the processes of spiritual growth and healing."

For further discussion of Apuleius' world and work, see Gollnick (1999).

Chas S. Clifton

References

Crowley, Vivianne (1996) *Wicca: The Old Religion in the New Millennium*. London:
    Thorsons.
Gollnick, James (1999) *The Religious Dreamworld of Apuleius' 'Metamorphoses':
    Recovering a Religious Hermeneutic*. Waterloo, Ontario: Wilfred Laurier
    University Press.
Graves, Robert (trans.) (1951) *Apuleius, The Golden Ass*, New York: Farrar, Straus &
    Giroux.
Hutton, Ronald (1999) *Triumph of the Moon: A History of Modern Pagan Witchcraft*.
    London: Oxford.

NOT LONG AFTERWARDS I awoke in sudden terror. A dazzling full
moon was rising from the sea. It is at this secret hour that the Moon-goddess,
sole sovereign of all mankind, is possessed of her greatest power and majesty. She
is the shining deity by whose divine influence not only beasts, wild and tame, but
all inanimate things as well, are invigorated; whose ebbs and flows control the
rhythm of all bodies whatsoever, whether in the air, on earth, or below the sea. Of
this I was well aware, and therefore resolved to address the visible image of the
goddess, imploring her help; for Fortune seemed at last to have made up her mind
that I had suffered enough and to be offering me a hope of release.

Jumping up and shaking off my drowsiness, I went down to the sea to purify
myself by bathing in it. Seven times I dipped my head under the waves—seven,
according to the divine philosopher Pythagoras, is a number that suits all religious
occasions—and with joyful eagerness, though tears were running down my hairy
face, I offered this soundless prayer to the supreme Goddess:

'Blessed Queen of Heaven, whether you are pleased to be known as Ceres, the
original harvest mother who in joy at the finding of your lost daughter Proserpine
abolished the rude acorn diet of our forefathers and gave them bread raised from the
fertile soil of Eleusis; or whether as celestial Venus, now adored at sea-girt Paphos,
who at the time of the first Creation coupled the sexes in mutual love and so

contrived that man should continue to propagate his kind for ever; or whether as Artemis, the physician sister of Phoebus Apollo, reliever of the birth pangs of women, and now adored in the ancient shrine at Ephesus; or whether as dread Proserpine to whom the owl cries at night, whose triple face is potent against the malice of ghosts, keeping them imprisoned below earth; you who wander through many sacred groves and are propitiated with many different rites—you whose womanly light illumines the walls of every city, whose misty radiance nurses the happy seeds under the soil, you who control the wandering course of the sun and the very power of his rays—I beseech you, by whatever name, in whatever aspect, with whatever ceremonies you deign to be invoked, have mercy on me in my extreme distress, restore my shattered fortune, grant me repose and peace after this long sequence of miseries. End my sufferings and perils, rid me of this hateful four-footed disguise, return me to my family, make me Lucius once more. But if I have offended some god of unappeasable cruelty who is bent on making life impossible for me, at least grant me one sure gift, the gift of death.'

When I had finished my prayer and poured out the full bitterness of my oppressed heart, I returned to my sandy hollow, where once more sleep overcame me. I had scarcely closed my eyes before the apparition of a woman began to rise from the middle of the sea with so lovely a face that the gods themselves would have fallen down in adoration of it. First the head, then the whole shining body gradually emerged and stood before me poised on the surface of the waves. Yes, I will try to describe this transcendent vision, for though human speech is poor and limited, the Goddess herself will perhaps inspire me with poetic imagery sufficient to convey some slight inkling of what I saw.

Her long thick hair fell in tapering ringlets on her lovely neck, and was crowned with an intricate chaplet in which was woven every kind of flower. Just above her brow shone a round disc, like a mirror, or like the bright face of the moon, which told me who she was. Vipers rising from the left-hand and right-hand partings of her hair supported this disc, with ears of corn bristling beside them. Her many-coloured robe was of finest linen; part was glistening white, part crocus-yellow, part glowing red and along the entire hem a woven bordure of flowers and fruit clung swaying in the breeze.[1] But what caught and held my eye more than anything else was the deep black lustre of her mantle. She wore it slung across her body from the right hip to the left shoulder, where it was caught in a knot resembling the boss of a shield; but part of it hung in innumerable folds, the tasselled fringe quivering. It was embroidered with glittering stars on the hem and everywhere else, and in the middle beamed a full and fiery moon.

In her right hand she held a bronze rattle, of the sort used to frighten away the God of the Sirocco; its narrow rim was curved like a sword-belt and three little rods, which sang shrilly when she shook the handle, passed horizontally through it. A boat-shaped gold dish hung from her left hand, and along the upper surface of the handle writhed an asp with puffed throat and head raised ready to strike. On her divine feet were slippers of palm leaves, the emblem of victory.

All the perfumes of Arabia floated into my nostrils as the Goddess deigned to address me: 'You see me here, Lucius, in answer to your prayer. I am Nature, the universal Mother, mistress of all the elements, primordial child of time, sovereign of all things spiritual, queen of the dead, queen also of the immortals, the single manifestation of all gods and goddesses that are. My nod governs the shining heights of Heaven, the wholesome sea-breezes, the lamentable silences of the world below. Though I am worshipped in many aspects, known by countless names, and propitiated with all manner of different rites, yet the whole round earth venerates me. The primeval Phrygians call me Pessinuntica, Mother of the gods; the Athenians, sprung from their own soil, call me Cecropian Artemis; for the islanders of Cyprus I am Paphian Aphrodite; for the archers of Crete I am Dictynna; for the trilingual Sicilians, Stygian Proserpine; and for the Eleusinians their ancient Mother of the Corn.

'Some know me as Juno, some as Bellona of the Battles; others as Hecate, others again as Rhamnubia, but both races of Aethiopians, whose lands the morning sun first shines upon, and the Egyptians who excel in ancient learning and worship me with ceremonies proper to my godhead, call me by my true name, namely, Queen Isis. I have come in pity of your plight, I have come to favour and aid you. Weep no more, lament no longer; the hour of deliverance, shone over by my watchful light, is at hand.

'Listen attentively to my orders.

'The eternal laws of religion devote to my worship the day born from this night. Tomorrow my priests offer me the first-fruits of the new sailing season by dedicating a ship to me: for at this season the storms of winter lose their force, the leaping waves subside and the sea becomes navigable once more, You must wait for this sacred ceremony, with a mind that is neither anxious for the future nor clouded with profane thoughts; and I shall order the High Priest to carry a garland of roses in my procession, tied to the rattle which he carries in his right hand. Do not hesitate, push the crowd aside, join the procession with confidence in my grace. Then come close up to the High Priest as if you wished to kiss his hand, gently pluck the roses with your mouth and you will immediately slough off the hide of what has always been for me the most hateful beast in the universe.

'Above all, have faith: do not think that my commands are hard to obey. For at this very moment, while I am speaking to you here, I am also giving complementary instructions to my sleeping High Priest; and tomorrow, at my commandment, the dense crowds of people will make way for you. I promise you that in the joy and laughter of the festival nobody will either view your ugly shape with abhorrence or dare to put a sinister interpretation on your sudden return to human shape. Only remember, and keep these words of mine locked tight in your heart, that from now onwards until the very last day of your life you are dedicated to my service. It is only right that you should devote your whole life to the Goddess who makes you a man again. Under my protection you will be happy and famous, and when at the destined end of your life you descend to the land of ghosts, there too in the subterrene hemisphere you shall have frequent occasion to adore me. From the Elysian fields you will see me as queen of the profound Stygian realm, shining through the darkness of Acheron with a light as kindly and tender as I show you now. Further, if you are found to deserve my divine protection by careful obedience to the ordinances of my religion and by perfect chastity, you will become aware that I, and I alone, have power to prolong your life beyond the limits appointed by destiny.'

With this, the vision of the invincible Goddess faded and dissolved.

Note

1   Part of this sentence has been displaced in the Latin text and an early editor has corrected it unintelligently.

Chapter 4

Pliny the Elder

MISTLETOE

■ from **NATURAL HISTORY**, 16.249–51, trans. Graham Harvey
from the Latin text available on-line at http://www.ukans.edu/history/
index/europe/ancient_rome/L/Roman/Texts/Pliny_the_Elder/16*.html

P LINY'S *NATURAL HISTORY* (16.249) seems to provide a foundational, perhaps even fundamental, description of the Druids of Gaul. Here are
the white-robed priests ascending venerable oaks to cut mistletoe with a golden
pruning hook, offering sacrifice and linked to healing and the good of their people.
Certainly this text has been significant in the many and various versions of Druidry
that have emerged since the Roman conquest of Europe supplanted them. There are,
however, problems. It is not only that the now typical Druid outfit of a long white
robe seems entirely unsuited to climbing oak trees while carrying a golden pruning
hook. Nor is it the erasure of sacrifice from later rituals that otherwise claim to
continue the Druidic association with oaks and mistletoe. More than that, historians
have raised doubts about the veracity of Pliny's etymology and the accuracy of his
description. However, what is of interest is precisely the classic image. Druid writers
regularly re-visit the text to find what their chosen name means. Often they blend
Pliny's oak etymology with others that link Druids with knowledge and truth or trust-
worthiness. Perhaps oak trees symbolize or demonstrate these virtues and attributes
by their longevity and strength. At any rate, Pliny's authority is cited by those who
evolve ceremonies utilizing oak groves and mistletoe in midwinter. Some are true to
Pliny's insistence that, for the Druids (but not himself), mistletoe is sacred only if
it has grown on oaks, others are happy to buy sprigs from the market (in which case,
in England at least, it is likely to have come from French apple or poplar trees).
    Historical discussions of ancient Druidry include Hutton (1991), Berresford
Ellis (1994), and Raoult (1988). Hutton (2003) is an invaluable and incomparable
discussion of the recent history of the Druidic movements.
    Among the many introductions to the diverse groups (usually called 'Orders'),
interests and engagements of contemporary Druidry, see Carr-Gomm (2002a).

Carr-Gomm (2003) contains excellent discussions of the Druidic revival in America, Ireland, and Brittany, as well as considerations of much else of importance to Druids now. Carr-Gomm (2002b) explores the relationship between Wicca and Druidry. Many of the Druid Orders also have websites which should be consulted.

Graham Harvey

References

Berresford Ellis, Peter (1994) *The Druids*. London: Constable.

Carr-Gomm, Philip (2002a) *Druid Mysteries*. London: Rider.

Carr-Gomm, Philip (2002b) *Druidcraft*. London: Thorsons.

Carr-Gomm, Philip (ed.) (2003) *The Rebirth of Druidry*. London: Element.

Hutton, Ronald (1991) *The Pagan Religions of the Ancient British Isles*. Oxford: Blackwell.

Hutton, Ronald (2003) *Witches, Druids and King Arthur*. London: Hambledon and London.

Raoult, Michael (1988) *Les Druides*. Monaco: Editions du Rocher.

THE DRUIDS, AS THEY call their magicians, consider nothing more sacred than the mistletoe and the tree on which it grows, provided that it is an oak. They select a particular grove of oaks and perform no sacred rites without oak leaves. It is from this custom they seem to have been called Druids, based on the Greek interpretation of that word [i.e. relating to the Greek *drys*, oak]. They reckon that whatever grows on these trees is sent down from heaven as a proof that the particular tree is chosen by a God. But mistletoe is very rarely found on an oak, but when found is gathered with considerable ceremony, especially on the sixth day of the moon (from which they count their months, years and periods of thirty years). At this time although the moon is still waxing, it has attained considerable vigour. They call it [mistletoe] All-Heal in their language. They prepare a ritual sacrifice and feast beneath the tree, and lead up to it two white bulls whose horns are then bound for the first time. A priest attired in a white vestment climbs the tree and, using a golden sickle, cuts the mistletoe which is caught in a white cloak. Next they sacrifice the bulls praying that the God will make his gift propitious to its recipients. They believe that if given in drink the mistletoe will give fecundity to any sterile animal, and that it is effective against all poisons. This is typical of the way people surround frivolous things with religiosity.

Chapter 5

Julian the Hellene

FRAGMENT OF A LETTER TO A PRIEST

■ from W.C. Wright (ed.) **THE WORKS OF THE EMPEROR JULIAN II**, Cambridge, MA, 1932, pp. 299–39

THE EMPEROR JULIAN, WHOSE full name was Flavius Claudius Julianus, was born in Constantinople in 331 CE. His uncle Constantine "the Great" had moved the seat of the Roman Empire from Rome to that city and converted to Christianity on his deathbed, after murdering various of his relatives, a pattern that was continued by his successors. Julian's father, eldest brother, and cousins were all killed in subsequent family infighting, but Julian, although kept under house arrest for six years as a boy, was later allowed to study Greek literature and philosophy at Nicomedea and at Athens. Although he had been raised a Christian, his surroundings, his readings, and his teachers reconverted him to a form of Paganism highly influenced by Neoplatonic philosophy. During his time in Athens, he was initiated in the Mysteries of the goddess Demeter at Eleusis.

In 355 Julian was sent to Milan. Facing another attempted *coup d'état*, the Emperor Constantius, who had executed Julian's brother Gallus for treason five years before, now promoted him to "Caesar," or regional ruler, of the western portion of the empire, since by this point there were no other men to carry on the dynasty of the Constantii. A marriage was arranged to the emperor's sister, Helena, who was 30 to Julian's 24. Suddenly the quiet student of philosophy was ruler, at least in name, of Britain, Iberia, and Gaul. He traveled to Paris, where he assumed command of a campaign underway against the German and Frankish tribes. Julian studied the craft of war from veteran officers and won several victories in the field, which enhanced his popularity among the legionnaires and the inhabitants of Roman Gaul.

Unfortunately, his military success made the emperor jealous. To reduce Julian's power, Constantius ordered him to send his best six legions to join an expedition against the Persian empire. The soldiers, many of them Celts who had been promised that they could serve nearer their homes, mutinied and proclaimed Julian as emperor, threatening yet another Roman civil war. In 361 both leaders began moving their forces towards an inevitable confrontation. Constantius, however, fell ill and died in Syria, leaving Julian to march in triumph into Constantinople in December.

His reign was short but eventful. The young philosopher emperor reduced the splendor of the imperial court and issued edicts of religious toleration. Not only did he permit Pagans and Christians their religious practices equally, but he stopped the Christian clergy's government salaries and refused to intervene in their disputes over heresy. Another decree stipulated that Pagan temple property confiscated under Constantine and his successors be returned to its original owners. Most importantly, however, Julian attempted to give Pagan religions an improved theological footing and a social conscience, thus permitting them to compete more effectively with Christianity both among intellectuals and among the urban masses. He urged the remaining Pagan clergy to lead pure lives, avoiding taverns and popular amusements.

Julian's efforts to hinder Christianity and restore the old gods in a Neoplatonic synthesis with himself as *pontifex maximus*, a sort of Pagan pope, ended in 363. Continuing Constantius' campaign against the Persian emperor Sapor, he was killed in a victorious engagement with Persian forces somewhere in what is now northern Iraq. Christian leaders saw his death as divinely willed: a century later, a myth developed that the well-known bishop Basil (later canonized as St. Basil, an important figure in Orthodox monasticism) dreamed the night before the battle that Christ (or in other versions, Mary) called up the second-century martyr St. Mercurius to invisibly guide the Persian soldier's lance and slay the apostate emperor. (A medieval painting depicting the St. Mercurius myth may be seen in Winchester cathedral.) Another Christian myth spread in subsequent centuries was that on his deathbed, Julian had cried, "Thou hast conquered, Galilaean," a reference to Jesus. Pagan chroniclers close to the emperor claimed that he discussed philosophical issues with his adviser Maximus until losing consciousness from loss of blood.

The beginning of Julian's letter to the Pagan priest has been lost. The surviving text, probably written in the city of Antioch while the Roman army was assembling for the expedition against Persia, begins abruptly with an apparent denunciation of Christian monks who remove themselves from civil society, thus making themselves prey to evil demons in their lonely hermitages. Julian goes on to exhort his reader(s) to lead holy and philosophical lives and to serve as moral exemplars to the people. In imitation of the Christians, he suggests that Pagan temples should also be centers of philanthropy (a function previously left to one's family, fellow clansmen, or villagers), offering aid to the needy around them. Priests themselves should lead well-regulated lives, performing regular ritual purifications and worship with all the magnificence possible, yet when they move in society outside their temples they should put on modest clothing. Priests should avoid drunkenness, gambling, and attendance at chariot races or lascivious theatrical performances—in other words, they should follow Julian's own example. He also defends the use of divine images even while admitting that the bodiless gods themselves have no need of sacrifices, for the gods will still reward their pious worshipers. Furthermore, he suggests that statues of the gods, while not divine themselves, will nevertheless bring delight to pious Pagans.

Julian's religious concerns naturally make him an emblematic figure to today's Pagans, particularly those interested in reconstructing and updating Classical Paganisms. The Julian Society, founded in the late 1960s in the United States, was among the first manifestations of non-Wiccan revived Paganism, and it continues today, chiefly in cyberspace. Pagan artisans continue to create images of the emperor and jewelry based upon coins minted under his reign. And as modern Pagan congregations increasingly seek legal recognition, their clergy may, after sixteen centuries, be carrying out Julian's recommendations to organize "congregations" somewhat in imitation of the Christian model.

For further discussion and evocations of Julian's life and significance, see Athanassiadi (1992), Browning (1976), Head (1976), Vidal (1964), and The Julian Society's website.

Chas S. Clifton

References

Athanassiadi, Polymnia (1992) *Julian: An Intellectual Biography*. London: Routledge.
Browning, Robert (1976) *The Emperor Julian*. Berkeley, CA: University of California Press.
Head, Constance (1976) *The Emperor Julian*. Boston: Twayne.
Vidal, Gore (1964) *Julian: A Novel*. Boston: Little, Brown.
The Julian Society http://www.juliansociety.org

T HOUGH JUST CONDUCT IN accordance with the laws of the state will evidently be the concern of the governors of cities, you in your turn will properly take care to exhort men not to transgress the laws of the gods, since those are sacred. Moreover, inasmuch as the life of a priest ought to be more holy than the political life, you must guide and instruct men to adopt it. And the better sort will naturally follow your guidance. Nay I pray that all men may, but at any rate I hope that those who are naturally good and upright will do so; for they will recognise that your teachings are peculiarly adapted to them.

You must above all exercise philanthropy, for from it result many other blessings, and moreover that choicest and greatest blessing of all, the good will of the gods. For just as those who are in agreement with their masters about their friendships and ambitions and loves are more kindly treated than their fellow slaves, so we must suppose that God, who naturally loves human beings, has more kindness for those men who love their fellows. Now philanthropy has many divisions and is of many kinds. For instance it is shown when men are punished in moderation with a view to the betterment of those punished, as schoolmasters punish children; and again in ministering to men's needs, even as the gods minister to our own. You see all the blessings of the earth that they have granted to us, food of all sorts, and in an abundance that they have not granted to all other creatures put together. And since we were born naked they covered us with the hair of animals, and with things that grow in the ground and on trees. Nor were they content to do this simply or off-hand, as Moses tells us men took coats of skins,[1] but you see how numerous are the gifts of Athene the Craftswoman. What other animals use wine, or olive oil? Except indeed in cases where we let them share in these things, even though we do not share them with our fellowmen. What creature of the sea uses corn, what land animal uses things that grow in the sea? And I have not yet mentioned gold and bronze and iron, though in all these the gods have made us very rich; yet not to the end that we may bring reproach on them by disregarding the poor who go about in our midst, especially when they happen to be of good character—men for instance who have inherited no paternal estate, and are poor because in the greatness of their souls they have no desire for money. Now the crowd when they see such men blame the gods. However, it is not the gods who are to blame for their poverty, but rather the insatiate greed of us men of property becomes the cause of this false conception of the gods among men, and besides of unjust blame of the gods. Of what use, I ask, is it for us to pray that God will rain gold on the poor as he did on the people of Rhodes?[2] For even though this should come to pass, we should forthwith set our slaves underneath to catch it, and put out vessels everywhere, and drive off all corners so that we alone might seize upon the gifts of the gods meant for all in common. And anyone would naturally think it strange if we should ask for this, which is not in the nature of things, and is in every way unprofitable, while we do not do what is in our power. Who, I ask, ever became poor by giving to his neighbours? Indeed I myself, who have often given lavishly to those in need, have recovered my gifts again many times over at the hands of the gods, though I am a poor man of business; nor have I ever repented of that lavish giving. And of the present time I will say nothing, for it would be altogether irrational of me to compare the expenditure of private persons with that of an Emperor; but when I was myself still a private person I know that this happened to me many times. My grandmother's estate for instance was kept for me untouched, though others had taken possession of it by violence, because from the little that I had I spent money on those in need and gave them a share.

We ought then to share our money with all men, but more generously with the good, and with the helpless and poor so as to suffice for their need. And I will assert, even though it be paradoxical to say so, that it would be a pious act to share our clothes and food even with the wicked. For it is to the humanity in a man that we give, and not to his moral character. Hence I think that even those who are shut up in prison have a right to the same sort of care; since this kind of philanthropy will not hinder justice. For when many have been shut up in prison to await trial, of whom some will be found guilty, while others will prove to be innocent, it would be harsh indeed if out of regard for the guiltless we should not bestow some pity on the guilty also, or again, if on account of the guilty we should behave ruthlessly and inhumanly to those also who have done no wrong. This too, when I consider it, seems to me altogether wrong; I mean that we call Zeus by the title "God of Strangers," while we show ourselves more inhospitable to strangers than are the very Scythians. How, I ask, can one who wishes to sacrifice to Zeus, the God of Strangers, even approach his temple? With what conscience can he do so, when he has forgotten the saying "From Zeus come all beggars and strangers; and a gift is precious though small"?[3]

Again, the man who worships Zeus the God of Comrades, and who, though he sees his neighbours in need of money, does not give them even so much as a drachma, how, I say, can he think that he is worshipping Zeus aright? When I observe this I am wholly amazed, since I see that these titles of the gods are from the beginning of the world their express images, yet in our practice we pay no attention to anything of the sort. The gods are called by us "gods of kindred," and Zeus the "God of Kindred," but we treat our kinsmen as though they were strangers. I say "kinsmen" because every man, whether he will or no, is akin to every other man, whether it be true, as some say, that we are all descended from one man and one woman, or whether it came about in some other way, and the gods created us all together, at the first when the world began, not one man and one woman only, but many men and many women at once. For they who had the power to create one man and one woman, were able to create many men and women at once; since the manner of creating one man and one woman is the same as that of creating many men and many women. And[4] one must have regard to the differences in our habits and laws, or still more to that which is higher and more precious and more authoritative, I mean the sacred tradition of the gods which has been handed down to us by the theurgists of earlier days, namely that when Zeus was setting all things in order there fell from him drops of sacred blood, and from them, as they say, arose the race of men. It follows therefore that we are all kinsmen, whether, many men and women as we are, we come from two human beings, or whether, as the gods tell us, and as we ought to believe, since facts bear witness thereto, we are all descended from the gods. And that facts bear witness that many men came into the world at once, I shall maintain elsewhere, and precisely, but for the moment it will be enough to say this much, that if we were descended from one man and one woman, it is not likely that our laws would show such great divergence; nor in any case is it likely that the whole earth was filled with people by one man; nay, not even if the women used to bear many children at a time to their husbands, like swine. But when the gods all together had given birth to men, just as one man came forth, so in like manner came forth many men who had been allotted to the gods who rule over births; and they brought them forth, receiving their souls from the Demiurge from eternity.[5]

It is proper also to bear in mind how many discourses have been devoted by men in the past to show that man is by nature a social animal. And shall we, after asserting this and enjoining it, bear ourselves unsociably to our neighbours? Then let everyone make the basis of his conduct moral virtues, and actions like these, namely reverence towards the gods, benevolence towards men, personal chastity; and thus let him abound in pious acts, I mean by endeavouring always to have pious thoughts about the gods, and by regarding the temples and images of the gods with due honour and veneration, and by worshipping the gods as though he saw them actually present. For our fathers established images and altars, and the maintenance of undying fire, and, generally speaking, everything of the sort, as symbols of the presence of the gods, not that we may regard such things as gods, but that we may worship the gods through them. For since being in the body it was in bodily wise that we must needs perform our service to the gods also, though they are themselves without bodies; they therefore revealed to us in the earliest images the class of gods next in rank to the first, even those that revolve in a circle about the whole heavens. But since not even to these can due worship be offered in bodily wise—for they are by nature not in need of anything[6]—another class of images was invented on the earth, and by performing our worship to them we shall make the gods propitious to ourselves.

For just as those who make offerings to the statues of the emperors, who are in need of nothing, nevertheless induce goodwill towards themselves thereby, so too those who make offerings to the images of the gods, though the gods need nothing, do nevertheless thereby persuade them to help and to care for them. For zeal to do all that is in one's power is, in truth, a proof of piety, and it is evident that he who abounds in such zeal thereby displays a higher degree of piety; whereas he who neglects what is possible, and then pretends to aim at what is impossible, evidently does not strive after the impossible, since he overlooks the possible. For even though God stands in need of nothing, it does not follow that on that account nothing ought to be offered to him. He does not need the reverence that is paid in words. What then? Is it rational to deprive him of this also? By no means. It follows then that one ought not to deprive him either of the honour that is paid to him through deeds, an honour which not three years or three thousand years have ordained, but all past time among all the nations of the earth.

Therefore, when we look at the images of the gods, let us not indeed think they are stones or wood, but neither let us think they are the gods themselves; and indeed we do not say that the statues of the emperors are mere wood and stone and bronze, but still less do we say they are the emperors themselves. He therefore who loves the emperor delights to see the emperor's statue, and he who loves his son delights to see his son's statue, and he who loves his father delights to see his father's statue. It follows that he who loves the gods delights to gaze on the images of the gods, and their likenesses, and he feels reverence and shudders with awe of the gods who look at him from the unseen world. Therefore if any man thinks that because they have once been called likenesses of the gods, they are incapable of being destroyed, he is, it seems to me, altogether foolish; for surely in that case they were incapable of being made by men's hands. But what has been made by a wise and good man can be destroyed by a bad and ignorant man. But those beings which were fashioned by the gods as the living images of their invisible nature, I mean the gods who revolve in a circle in the heavens, abide imperishable for all time. Therefore let no man disbelieve in gods because he sees and hears that certain persons have profaned their images and temples. Have they not in many cases put good men to death, like Socrates and Dio and the great Empedotimus?[7] And yet I am very sure that the gods cared more for these men than for the temples. But observe that since they knew that the bodies even of these men were destructible, they allowed them to yield to nature and to submit, but later on they exacted punishment from their slayers; and this has happened in the sight of all, in our own day also, in the case of all who have profaned the temples.

Therefore let no man deceive us with his sayings or trouble our faith in a divine providence. For as for those who make such profanation a reproach against us, I mean the prophets of the Jews, what have they to say about their own temple, which was overthrown three times and even now is not being raised up again? This I mention not as a reproach against them, for I myself, after so great a lapse of time, intended to restore it, in honour of the god whose name has been associated with it. But in the present case I have used this instance because I wish to prove that nothing made by man can be indestructible, and that those prophets who wrote such statements were uttering nonsense, due to their gossiping with silly old women. In my opinion there is no reason why their god should not be a mighty god, even though he does not happen to have wise prophets or interpreters. But the real reason why they are not wise is that they have not submitted their souls to be cleansed by the regular course of study, nor have they allowed those studies to open their tightly closed eyes, and to clear away the mist that hangs over them. But since these men see as it were a great light through a fog, not plainly or clearly, and since they think that what they see is not a pure light but a fire, and they fail to discern all that surrounds it, they cry with a loud voice "Tremble, be afraid, fire, flame, death, a dagger, a broad-sword!" thus describing under many names the harmful might of fire. But on this subject it will be better to demonstrate separately how much inferior to our own poets are these teachers of tales about the gods.

It is our duty to adore not only the images of the gods, but also their temples and sacred precincts and altars. And it is reasonable to honour the priests also as officials and servants of the gods; and because they minister to us what concerns the gods, and they lend strength to the gods' gift of good things to us; for they sacrifice and pray on behalf of all men. It is therefore right that we should pay them all not less, if not indeed more, than the honours that we pay to the magistrates of the state. And if any one thinks that we ought to assign equal honours to them and to the magistrates of the state, since the latter also are in some sort dedicated to the service of the gods, as being guardians of the laws, nevertheless we ought at any rate to give the priests a far greater share of our good will. The Achaeans, for instance, enjoined on their king[8] to reverence the priest, though he was one of the enemy, whereas we do not even reverence the priests who are our friends, and who pray and sacrifice on our behalf.

But since my discourse has come back again to the beginning as I have so long wished, I think it is worth while for me to describe next in order what sort of man a priest ought to be, in order that he may justly be honoured himself and may cause the gods to be honoured. For as for us, we ought not to investigate or enquire as to his conduct, but so long as a man is called a priest we ought to honour and cherish him, but if he prove to be wicked we ought to allow his priestly office to be taken away from him, since he has shown himself unworthy of it. But so long as he sacrifices for us and makes offerings and stands in the presence of the gods, we must regard him with respect and reverence as the most highly honoured chattel[9] of the gods. For it would be absurd for us to pay respect to the very stones of which the altars are made, on account of their being dedicated to the gods, because they have a certain shape and form suited to the ritual for which they have been fashioned, and then not to think that we ought to honour a man who has been dedicated to the gods. Perhaps someone will object—"But suppose he does wrong and often fails to offer to the gods their sacred rites?" Then indeed I answer that we ought to convict a man of that sort, so that he may not by his wickedness offend the gods; but that we ought not to dishonour him until he has been convicted. Nor indeed is it reasonable that when we have set our hands to this business, we should take away their honour not only from these offenders but also from those who are worthy to be honoured. Then let every priest, like every magistrate, be treated with respect, since there is also an oracle to that effect from the Didymaean god:[10] "As for men who with reckless minds work wickedness against the priests of the deathless gods and plot against their privileges with plans that fear not the gods, never shall such men travel life's path to the end, men who have sinned against the blessed gods whose honour and holy service those priests have in charge."[11] And again in another oracle the god says: "All my servants from harmful mischief——;"[12] and he says that on their behalf he will inflict punishment on the aggressors.

Now though there are many utterances of the god to the same effect, by means of which we may learn to honour and cherish priests as we ought, I shall speak on this subject elsewhere at greater length. But for the present it is enough to point out that I am not inventing anything offhand, since I think that the declaration made by the god and the injunction expressed in his own words are sufficient. Therefore let any man who considers that as a teacher of such matters I am worthy to be believed show due respect to the god and obey him, and honour the priests of the gods above all other men. And now I will try to describe what sort of man a priest himself ought to be, though not for your especial benefit. For if I did not already know from the evidence both of the high priest and of the most mighty gods that you administer this priestly office aright—at least all matters that come under your management— I should not have ventured to confide to you a matter so important. But I do so in order that you may be able from what I say to instruct the other priests, not only in the cities but in the country districts also, more convincingly and with complete freedom; since not of your own self do you alone devise these precepts and practise them, but you have me also to give you support, who by the grace of the gods am known as sovereign pontiff, though I am indeed by no means worthy of so high an office; though I desire, and moreover constantly pray to the gods that I may be worthy. For the gods, you must know, hold out great hopes for us after death; and we must believe them absolutely. For they are always truthful, not only about the future life, but about the affairs of this life also. And since in the superabundance of their power they are able both to overcome the confusion that exists in this life and to regulate its disorders and irregularities, will they not all the more in that other life where conflicting things are reconciled, after the immortal soul has been sepa- rated from the body and the lifeless body has turned to earth, be able to bestow all those things for which they have held out hopes to mankind? Therefore since we know that the gods have granted to their priests a great recompense, let us make them responsible in all things for men's esteem of the gods, displaying their own lives as an example of what they ought to preach to the people.

The first thing we ought to preach is reverence towards the gods. For it is fitting that we should perform our service to the gods as though they were themselves present with us and beheld us, and though not seen by us could direct their gaze, which is more powerful than any light, even as far as our hidden thoughts. And this saying is not my own[13] but the god's, and has been declared in many utterances, but for me surely it is sufficient, by bringing forth one such utterance, to illustrate two things in one, namely how, the gods see all things and how they rejoice in god- fearing men: "On all sides extend the far-seeing rays of Phoebus. His swift gaze pierces even through sturdy rocks, and travels through the dark blue sea, nor is he unaware of the starry multitude that passes in returning circuit through the unwea- ried heavens for ever by the statutes of necessity; nor of all the tribes of the dead in the underworld whom Tartarus has admitted within the misty dwelling of Hades, beneath the western darkness. And I delight in god-fearing men as much even as in Olympus."[14]

Now in so far as all soul, but in a much higher degree the soul of man, is akin to and related to the gods, so much the more is it likely that the gaze of the gods should penetrate through his soul easily and effectively. And observe the love of the god for mankind when he says that he delights in the disposition of god-fearing men as much as in Olympus most pure and bright. How then shall he not lead up our souls from the darkness and from Tartarus, if we approach him with pious awe? And indeed he has knowledge even of those who have been imprisoned in Tartarus—for not even that region falls outside the power of the gods,—and to the god-fearing he promises Olympus instead of Tartarus. Wherefore we ought by all means to hold fast to deeds of piety, approaching the gods with reverence, and neither saying nor listening to anything base. And the priests ought to keep themselves pure not only from impure or shameful acts, but also from uttering words and hearing speeches of that character. Accordingly we must banish all offensive jests and all licentious intercourse. And that you may understand what I mean by this, let no one who has been consecrated a priest read either Archilochus or Hipponax[15] or anyone else who writes such poems as theirs. And in Old Comedy let him avoid everything of that type—for it is better so—and indeed on all accounts philosophy alone will be appropriate for us priests; and of philosophers only those who chose the gods as guides of their mental discipline, like Pythagoras and Plato and Aristotle, and the school of Chrysippus and Zeno. For we ought not to give heed to them all nor to the doctrines of all, but only to those philosophers and those of their doctrines that make men god-fearing, and teach concerning the gods, first that they exist, secondly that they concern themselves with the things of this world, and further that they do no injury at all either to mankind or to one another, out of jealousy or envy or enmity. I mean the sort of thing our poets in the first place have brought themselves into disrepute by writing, and in the second place such tales as the prophets of the Jews take pains to invent, and are admired for so doing by those miserable men who have attached themselves to the Galilaeans.

But for us it will be appropriate to read such narratives as have been composed about deeds that have actually been done; but we must avoid all fictions in the form of narrative such as were circulated among men in the past, for instance tales whose theme is love, and generally speaking everything of that sort. For just as not every road is suitable for consecrated priests, but the roads they travel ought to be duly assigned, so not every sort of reading is suitable for a priest. For words breed a certain sort of disposition in the soul, and little by little it arouses desires, and then on a sudden kindles a terrible blaze, against which one ought, in my opinion, to arm oneself well in advance.

Let us not admit discourses by Epicurus or Pyrrho; but indeed the gods have already in their wisdom destroyed their works, so that most of their books have ceased to be. Nevertheless there is no reason why I should not, by way of example, mention these works too, to show what sort of discourses priests must especially avoid; and if such discourses, then much more must they avoid such thoughts. For an error of speech is, in my opinion, by no means the same as an error of the mind, but we ought to give heed to the mind first of all, since the tongue sins in company with it. We ought to learn by heart the hymns in honour of the gods— and many and beautiful they are, composed by men of old and of our own time—though indeed we ought to try to know also those which are being sung in the temples. For the greater number were bestowed on us by the gods them- selves, in answer to prayer, though some few also were written by men, and were composed in honour of the gods by the aid of divine inspiration and a soul inaccessible to things evil.

All this, at least, we ought to study to do, and we ought also to pray often to the gods, both in private and in public, if possible three times a day, but if not so often, certainly at dawn and in the evening. For it is not meet that a consecrated priest should pass a day or a night without sacrifice; and dawn is the beginning of the day as twilight is of the night. And it is proper to begin both periods with sacrifice to the gods, even when we happen not to be assigned to perform the service. For it is our duty to maintain all the ritual of the temples that the law of our fathers prescribes, and we ought to perform neither more nor less than that ritual; for eternal are the gods, so that we too ought to imitate their essential nature in order that thereby we may make them propitious.

Now if we were pure soul alone, and our bodies did not hinder us in any respect, it would be well to prescribe one sort of life for priests. But since what he should practise when on duty concerns the individual priest alone, not priests absolutely, what should we concede to a man who has received the office of priest, on occasions when he is not actually engaged in service in the temples? I think that a priest ought to keep himself pure from all contamination, for a night and a day, and then after purifying himself for another night following on the first, with such rites of purification as the sacred laws prescribe, he should under these conditions enter the temple and remain there for as many days as the law commands. (Thirty is the number with us at Rome, but in other places the number varies.) It is proper then, I think, that he should remain throughout all these days in the sacred precincts, devoting himself to philosophy, and that he should not enter a house or a market-place, or see even a magistrate, except in the precincts, but should concern himself with his service to the god, overseeing and arranging everything in person; and then, when he has completed the term of days, he should retire from his office in favour of another. And when he turns again to the ordinary life of mankind, he may be allowed to visit a friend's house, and, when invited, to attend a feast, but not on the invitation of all but only of persons of the highest character. And at this time there would be nothing out of the way in his going occasionally to the market-place and conversing with the governor or the chief magistrate of his tribe, and giving aid, as far as lies in his power, to those who have a good reason for needing it.

And it is in my opinion fitting for priests to wear the most magnificent dress when they are within the temple performing the services, but when they are outside the sacred precincts to wear ordinary dress, without any extravagance. For it is not rational that we should misuse, in empty conceit and vain ostentation, what has been given to us for the honour of the gods. And for this reason we ought in the market place to abstain from too costly dress and from outward show, and in a word from every sort of pretentiousness. For consider how the gods, because they admired the perfect moderation of Amphiaraus,[16] after they had decreed the destruction of that famous army—and he, though he knew that it would be so, went with the expedition and therefore did not escape his fated end,—the gods I say transformed him completely from what he had been, and removed him to the sphere of the gods. For all the others who were in the expedition against Thebes engraved a device on their shields before they had conquered the enemy, and erected trophies to celebrate the downfall of the Cadmeans; but he, the associate of the gods, when he went to war had arms with no device; but gentleness he had, and moderation, as even the enemy bore witness. Hence I think that we priests ought to show moderation in our dress, in order that we may win the goodwill of the gods, since it is no slight offence that we commit against them when we wear in public the sacred dress and make it public property, and in a word give all men an opportunity to stare at it as though it were something marvellous. For whenever this happens, many who are not purified come near us, and by this means the symbols of the gods are polluted. Moreover what lawlessness it is, what arrogance towards the gods for us ourselves when we are not living the priestly life to wear the priestly dress! However, of this too I shall speak more particularly in another place; and what I am writing to you at the moment is only a mere outline of the subject.

No priest must anywhere be present at the licentious theatrical shows of the present day, nor introduce one into his own house; for that is altogether unfitting. Indeed if it were possible to banish such shows absolutely from the theatres so as to restore to Dionysus those theatres pure as of old, I should certainly have endeavoured with all my heart to bring this about; but as it is, since I thought that this is impossible, and that even if it should prove to be possible it would not on other accounts be expedient, I forebore entirely from this ambition. But I do demand that priests should withdraw themselves from the licentiousness of the theatres and leave them to the crowd. Therefore let no priest enter a theatre or have an actor or a chariot-driver for his friend; and let no dancer or mime even approach his door. And as for the sacred games, I permit anyone who will to attend those only in which women are forbidden not only to compete but even to be spectators. With regard to the hunting shows with dogs which are performed in the cities inside the theatres, need I say that not only priests but even the sons of priests must keep away from them?

Now it would perhaps have been well to say earlier from what class of men and by what method priests must be appointed; but it is quite appropriate that my remarks should end with this. I say that the most upright men in every city, by preference those who show most love for the gods, and next those who show most love for their fellow men, must be appointed, whether they be poor or rich. And in this matter let there be no distinction whatever whether they are unknown or well known. For the man who by reason of his gentleness has not won notice ought not to be barred by reason of his want of fame. Even though he be poor and a man of the people, if he possess within himself these two things, love for God and love for his fellow men, let him be appointed priest. And a proof of his love for God is his inducing his own people to show reverence to the gods; a proof of his love for his fellows is his sharing cheerfully, even from a small store, with those in need, and his giving willingly thereof, and trying to do good to as many men as he is able.

We must pay especial attention to this point, and by this means effect a cure. For when it came about that the poor were neglected and overlooked by the priests, then I think the impious Galilaeans observed this fact and devoted themselves to philanthropy. And they have gained ascendancy in the worst of their deeds through the credit they win for such practices. For just as those who entice children with a cake, and by throwing it to them two or three times induce them to follow them, and then, when they are far away from their friends cast them on board a ship and sell them as slaves, and that which for the moment seemed sweet, proves to be bitter for all the rest of their lives—by the same method, I say, the Galilaeans also begin with their so-called love-feast, or hospitality, or service of tables,—for they have many ways of carrying it out and hence call it by many names,—and the result is that they have led very many into atheism. . . .[17]

Notes

1   *Genesis* 3. 21.
2   Pindar, *Olympian Ode* 7 49; this became a Sophistic commonplace. Cf. Menander (Spengel) 3. 362; Aristides 1. 807; Libanius 31. 6, Foerster; Philostratus, *Imagines* 2. 270.
3   *Odyssey* 6. 207.
4   The connection of the thought is not clear, and Petavius thinks that something has been lost.
5   Julian here prefers the Platonic account of the creation in the *Timaeus* to the Biblical narrative.
6   Cf. St. Paul, *Acts* 17. 25, "neither is he worshipped with men's hands, as though he needed anything."
7   Of Syracuse, whose claim to be immortal was accepted by the Sicilians.
8   Agamemnon; *Iliad* 1. 23.
9   Cf. Plato, *Phaedo* 62 C; *Letter to the Athenians* 276 B.
10   Apollo.
11   An oracle from an unknown source: these verses occur again in *Epistle* 62. 451 A.
12   *Sc.* I will protect.
13   Euripides, *fr.* 488 Nauck; cf. 197 C, 358 D, 387 B, 391 this phrase became a proverb; cf. Lucian, *Hermotimus* 789.
14   An oracle from an unknown source.
15   Hipponax of Ephesus, a scurrilous poet who wrote in choliambics (the skazon) and flourished about the middle of the sixth century B.C.; cf. Horace, *Epodes* 6. 12.
16   Cf. Aeschylus, *Seven Against Thebes*; Euripides, *Phoenissae* 1118
    ὁ μάντις Ἀμφιάραος οὐ σημεῖ᾽ ἔχων
    ὑβρισμέν᾽, ἀλλὰ σωφρόνως ἄσημ᾽ ὅπλα.
17   The conclusion is lost, and may have been suppressed by Christian copyists.

Chapter 6

Anonymous

THE THUNDER: PERFECT MIND

■ from James M. Robinson (ed.) **THE NAG HAMMADI LIBRARY IN ENGLISH**, 3rd edn, San Francisco, 1990, pp. 297–303

I N 1945 AN EGYPTIAN farmer digging for mineral fertilizer unearthed a large clay jar full of ancient books, which came to be known as the "Nag Hammadi library," after a nearby village. When translated, they were found to contain fifty-two individual works, of which "The Thunder: Perfect Mind" was one. Many were hitherto unknown Christian gospels (the best known was the *Gospel According to Thomas*, see Guillaumont *et al.*, 1959), but "The Thunder, Perfect Mind" stands alone as a poem spoken by a goddess or priestess in paradoxical language: "I am the honored one and the scorned one / I am the wife and the virgin," and so on.

Other Nag Hammadi texts speak of Mary Magdalene as a close disciple of Jesus. For example, the Gospel of Mary (Robinson, 1990) speaks of her as loved by Jesus more than the male disciples, and in it she describes a typically Gnostic ascent of the soul through seven levels after death. Popular Christian tradition has often described her as a reformed prostitute, although she is never directly so labeled in the four canonical gospels. Alternatively, some biblical scholars see her as a wealthy woman who not only followed Jesus but helped to finance his ministry. But followers of Goddess religion frequently see her as a follower or even avatar of the Middle Eastern triple goddess Mari-Anna-Ishtar, claiming that the "prostitute" label actually meant she was a temple priestess or sacred prostitute. In this reading, popularized in *The Woman with the Alabaster Jar* (Starbird, 1993, also see Blanca, 2002), her relationship with Jesus was a sacred marriage between a representative of the Goddess and her consort. Her cult is often linked with the cult of the Black Madonna perpetuated in southern France.

In that reading of Mary Magdalene's story, therefore, "The Thunder: Perfect Mind" becomes the inspired invocation of the temple priestess as she incarnates the Triple Goddess. Certainly the text perplexes biblical scholars: translator

George W. MacRae described it as containing "no distinctively Christian, Jewish, or Gnostic allusions . . . [it] does not seem clearly to presuppose any particular Gnostic myth" (in Robinson, 1990) but noted that the text has some structural similarity to inscriptions describing the goddess Isis (see Apuleius, Chapter 3). Other scholars, however, have suggested that the speaker is Eve or else Sophia, the Gnostic personification of divine wisdom.

Note: page and line numbers and breaks from the original codex have been removed to improve the readability of the text. For these, refer to the critical edition from which this version is extracted.

Chas S. Clifton

References

Blanca, Luna (2002) "Mary as Goddess: Mary Magdalene." http://www.thewhitemoon. com/mary/magdalene.html (accessed 10 November 2002).

Guillaumont, Antoine *et al.* (eds) (1959) *The Gospel According to Thomas*. Leiden: E.J. Brill.

Qualls-Corbett, Nancy (1988) *The Sacred Prostitute: Eternal Aspect of the Feminine*. Toronto: Inner City Books.

Robinson, James M. (ed.) (1990) *The Nag Hammadi Library in English*. 3rd edition. San Francisco: HarperCollins.

Starbird, Margaret (1993) *The Woman with the Alabaster Jar: Mary Magdalen and the Holy Grail*. Santa Fe, New Mexico: Bear & Co.

I was sent forth from [the] power,
    and I have come to those who reflect upon me,
    and I have been found among those who seek after me.
Look upon me, you (pl.) who reflect upon me,
    and you hearers, hear me.
    You who are waiting for me, take me to yourselves.
And do not banish me from your sight.
And do not make your voice hate me, nor your hearing.
    Do not be ignorant of me anywhere or any time. Be on your guard!
    Do not be ignorant of me.

For I am the first and the last.
I am the honored one and the scorned one.
I am the whore and the holy one.
I am the wife and the virgin.
I am <the mother> and the daughter.
I am the members of my mother.
I am the barren one
    and many are her sons.
I am she whose wedding is great,
    and I have not taken a husband.

I am the midwife and she who does not bear.
I am the solace of my labor pains.
I am the bride and the bridegroom,
    and it is my husband who begot me.
I am the mother of my father
    and the sister of my husband,
    and he is my offspring.
I am the slave of him who prepared me.
I am the ruler of my offspring.
    But he is the one who [begot me] before the time on a birthday.
    And he is my offspring [in] (due) time,
    and my power is from him.
I am the staff of his power in his youth,
    [and] he is the rod of my old age.
    And whatever he wills happens to me.
I am the silence that is incomprehensible
    and the idea whose remembrance is frequent.
I am the voice whose sound is manifold
    and the word whose appearance is multiple.
I am the utterance of my name.

Why, you who hate me, do you love me
    and hate those who love me?
You who deny me, confess me,
    and you who confess me, deny me.
You who tell the truth about me, lie about me,
    and you who have lied about me, tell the truth about me.
You who know me, be ignorant of me,
    and those who have not known me, let them know me.

For I am knowledge and ignorance.
I am shame and boldness.
I am shameless; I am ashamed.
I am strength and I am fear.
I am war and peace.
Give heed to me.
I am the one who is disgraced and the great one.
Give heed to my poverty and my wealth.
Do not be arrogant to me when I am cast out upon the earth,
    [and] you will find me in [those that] are to come.
And do not look [upon] me on the dung-heap
    nor go and leave me cast out,
    and you will find me in the kingdoms.
And do not look upon me when I am cast out among those who
    are disgraced and in the least places,
    nor laugh at me.
And do not cast me out among those who are slain in violence.
But I, I am compassionate and I am cruel.

Be on your guard!
Do not hate my obedience
    and do not love my self-control.
In my weakness, do not forsake me,
    and do not be afraid of my power.
For why do you despise my fear
and curse my pride?
But I am she who exists in all fears
    and strength in trembling.
I am she who is weak,
    and I am well in a pleasant place.
    I am senseless and I am wise.

Why have you hated me in your counsels?
For I shall be silent among those who are silent,
    and I shall appear and speak.
Why then have you hated me, you Greeks?
    Because I am a barbarian among [the] barbarians?
For I am the wisdom [of the] Greeks
    and the knowledge of [the] barbarians.
I am the judgment of [the] Greeks and of the barbarians.
[I] am the one whose image is great in Egypt
    and the one who has no image among the barbarians.
I am the one who has been hated everywhere
    and who has been loved everywhere.
I am the one whom they call Life,
    and you have called Death.
I am the one whom they call Law,
    and you have called Lawlessness.
I am the one whom you have pursued,
    and I am the one whom you have seized.
I am the one whom you have scattered,
    and you have gathered me together.
I am the one before whom you have been ashamed,
    and you have been shameless to me.
I am she who does not keep festival,
    and I am she whose festivals are many.
I, I am godless,
    and I am the one whose God is great.
I am the one whom you have reflected upon,
    and you have scorned me.
I am unlearned,
    and they learn from me.
I am the one whom you have despised,
    and you reflect upon me.
I am the one whom you have hidden from,
    and you appear to me.

But whenever you hide yourselves,
    I myself will appear.
For [whenever] you [appear],
    I myself [will hide] from you.
Those who have . . . to it . . . senselessly . . .

Take me [. . . understanding] from grief,
    and take me to yourselves from understanding [and] grief.
And take me to yourselves from places that are ugly and in ruin,
    and rob from those which are good even though in ugliness.
Out of shame, take me to yourselves shamelessly;
    and out of shamelessness and shame, upbraid my members in
        yourselves.
And come forward to me, you who know me
    and you who know my members,
    and establish the great ones among the small first creatures.
Come forward to childhood,
    and do not despise it because it is small and it is little.
And do not turn away greatnesses in some parts from the smallnesses,
    for the smallnesses are known from the greatnesses.

Why do you curse me and honor me?
You have wounded and you have had mercy.
Do not separate me from the first ones whom you have [known].
[And] do not cast anyone [out nor] turn anyone away
    . . . turn you away and [. . . know] him not.
    . . . .
    What is mine . . .
I know the [first ones] and those after them [know] me.

But I am the mind of . . . and the rest of . . .
I am the knowledge of my inquiry,
    and the finding of those who seek after me,
    and I the command of those who ask of me,
    and the power of the powers in my knowledge
        of the angels, who have been sent at my word,
    and of gods in their seasons by my counsel,
    and of spirits of every man who exists with me,
        and of women who dwell within me.
I am the one who is honored, and who is praised,
    and who is despised scornfully.
I am peace,
    and war has come because of me.
And I am an alien and a citizen.
I am the substance and the one who has no substance.

Those who are without association with me are ignorant of me,
    and those who are in my substance are the ones who know me.
Those who are close to me have been ignorant of me,
    and those who are far away from me are the ones who have known
        me.
On the day when I am close to [you],
     [you] are far away [from me],
    [and] on the day when I [am far away] from you,
      [I am close] to you.

[I am . . .] within.
[I am . . .] of the natures.
I am . . . of the creation of the [spirits].
. . . request of the souls.
[I am] control and the uncontrollable.
I am the union and the dissolution.
I am the abiding and I am the dissolution.
I am the one below,
    and they come up to me.
I am the judgment and the acquittal.
I, I am sinless,
    and the root of sin derives from me.
I am lust in (outward) appearance,
    and interior self-control exists within me.
I am the hearing which is attainable to everyone
    and the speech which cannot be grasped.
I am a mute who does not speak,
    and great is my multitude of words.

Hear me in gentleness, and learn of me in roughness.
I am she who cries out,
    and I am cast forth upon the face of the earth.
I prepare the bread and my mind within.
I am the knowledge of my name.
I am the one who cries out,
    and I listen.
I appear and . . . walk in . . . seal of my . . ..
I am . . . the defense . . ..
I am the one who is called Truth,
    and iniquity . . ..

You honor me . . . and you whisper against [me].
You [who] are vanquished,
judge them (who vanquish you) before they give judgment against you,
    because the judge and partiality exist in you.
If you are condemned by this one, who will acquit you?
    Or if you are acquitted by him, who will be able to detain you?

For what is inside of you is what is outside of you,
  and the one who fashions you on the outside
    is the one who shaped the inside of you.
  And what you see outside of you,
    you see inside of you;
    it is visible and it is your garment.

Hear me, you hearers,
  and learn of my words, you who know me.
I am the hearing that is attainable to everything;
  I am the speech that cannot be grasped.
I am the name of the sound
  and the sound of the name.
I am the sign of the letter
  and the designation of the division.
And I . . ..
. . . light . . ..
. . . hearers . . . to you
. . . the great power.
And . . . will not move the name.
. . . to the one who created me.
  And I will speak his name.
Look then at his words
  and all the writings which have been completed.
Give heed then, you hearers
  and you also, the angels and those who have been sent,
  and you spirits who have arisen from the dead.
For I am the one who alone exists,
  and I have no one who will judge me.

For many are the pleasant forms which exist in
  numerous sins,
  and incontinencies,
  and disgraceful passions,
  and fleeting pleasures,
    which (men) embrace until they become sober
  and go up to their resting-place.
And they will find me there,
  and they will live,
  and they will not die again.

Chapter 7

Anonymous

SAYINGS OF THE HIGH ONE

■ from Carolyne Larrington (trans.) **THE POETIC EDDA**, Oxford, 1996, pp. 14–17, 34–5

THE HIGH ONE (ODIN, Woden or whatever else he might call himself) reveals the means by which he gained knowledge of the runes and powerful spells (or words of power), in the *Hávámal*. But he does this only beginning in stanza 138 of a poem that begins by offering advice about social etiquette and wisdom.

The few stanzas detailing Odin's self-sacrifice to gain runes and magical wisdom are probably better known than his social wisdom. Whether they should really be separated is debatable, but all religions offer the temptation of other-worldly mysteries that might lure attention away from the everyday concerns of feeding guests and honouring hosts. Equally, all religions regularly reiterate the call to root knowledge of transcendent matters in improved everyday living. Thus, the following extracts from the *Hávámal* (or Sayings of the High One) do not leap immediately to the stanzas about Odin's nine night long hanging in a tree, wounded and suffering, but ultimately achieving wisdom. It begins with stanza 1, advice about entering new places. As the arch-traveller, and sometime trickster, Odin knows all the pleasures and pains of visiting and the vagaries of hospitality. Such knowledge is continuous with whatever might be gained from runes and word-craft. (Note that in the full version this extract is followed by further references to runic knowledges, spells and word-craft.) Both require experiential engagement and hard work. Both are rooted in and rewarded by further self-knowledge. Quite what this might mean to those who buy their runes ready made and neatly packaged is hard to say. The Pagan revival has drawn on many sources and resources. The *Hávámal*, like other sources, may repay many return visits, many queries and quests. It also repays reading alongside other Norse, Icelandic, and Anglo-Saxon material. It is most obviously of importance, alongside other material in the Eddas, sagas and similar Icelandic, Norse, Germanic, and Anglo-Saxon sources, within Heathenry.

For further discussion and a translation of the complete text, see Larrington (1996).

Graham Harvey

Reference

Larrington, Carolyne (1996) *The Poetic Edda*. Oxford: Oxford University Press.

1   All the entrances, before you walk forward,
       you should look at,
       you should spy out;
       for you can't know for certain where enemies are sitting
       ahead in the hall.

2   Blessed be the givers! A guest has come in,
       where is he going to sit?
       He's in great haste, the one who by the hearth
       is going to be tested out.

3   Fire is needful for someone who's come in
       and who's chilled to the knee;
       food and clothing are necessary for the man
       who's journeyed over the mountains.

4   Water is needful for someone who comes to a meal,
       a towel and a warm welcome,
       a disposition, if he can get it, for good words
       and silence in return.

5   Wits are needful for someone who travels widely,
       anything will do at home;
       he becomes a laughing-stock, the man who knows nothing
       and sits among the wise.

6   About his intelligence no man should be boastful,
       rather cautious of mind;
       when a wise and silent man comes to a homestead
       seldom does shame befall the wary;
       for no more trustworthy a friend can any man get
       than a store of common sense.

7   The careful guest, who comes to a meal,
       keeps silent with hearing finely attuned;
       he listens with his ears, and looks about with his eyes;
       so every wise man informs himself.

8   This man is fortunate who can get for himself
       praise and good will;
       very difficult it is when a man lays claim
       to what's in another's heart.

9   That man is fortunate who, in himself,
       keeps his reputation and wits while he lives;

for men have often received bad advice
from another's heart.

10 No better burden can a man carry on the road
than a store of common sense;
better than riches it will seem in an unfamiliar place,
such is the resort of the wretched.

11 No better burden can a man carry on the road
than a store of common sense;
a worse journey-provisioning he couldn't carry over the land
than to be too drunk on ale.

12 It isn't as good as it's said to be,
ale, for the sons of men;
for the more he drinks,
the less he knows about the nature of men.

13 The heron of forgetfulness hovers over the ale-drinking;
he steals men's wits;
with the feathers of this bird I was fettered in the court of Gunnlod. [1]

14 Drunk I was, I was more than drunk
at wise Fialar's; [2]
that's the best sort of ale-drinking when afterwards
every man gets his mind back again.

15 Silent and thoughtful a prince's son should be
and bold in fighting;
cheerful and merry every man should be
until he waits for death.

16 The foolish man thinks he will live for ever,
if he keeps away from fighting;
but old age won't grant him a truce
even if the spears do.

17 The fool gapes when he comes on a visit,
he mutters to himself or keeps silent;
but it's all up with him if he gets a swig of drink;
the man's mind is exposed.

18 Only that man who travels widely
and has journeyed a great deal knows
what sort of mind each man has in his control;
he who's sharp in his wits.

19 A man shouldn't hold onto the cup but drink mead in moderation,
it's necessary to speak or be silent;
no man will blame you for impoliteness
if you go early to bed.

20 The greedy man, unless he guards against this tendency
will eat himself into lifelong trouble;
often he's laughed at when he comes among the wise,
the man who's foolish about his stomach.

. . .

138 I know that I hung on a windy tree[3]
     nine long nights,
     wounded with a spear, dedicated to Odin,
     myself to myself,
     on that tree of which no man knows from where its roots run.

139 No bread did they give me nor a drink from a horn,
     downwards I peered;
     I took up the runes, screaming I took them,
     then I fell back from there.

140 Nine mighty spells I learnt from the famous son
     of Bolthor, Bestla's father,[4]
     and I got a drink of the precious mead,
     poured from Odrerir.

141 Then I began to quicken and be wise,
     and to grow and to prosper;
     one word found another word for me,
     one deed found another deed for me.

142 The runes you must find and the meaningful letter,
     a very great letter,
     a very powerful letter,
     which the mighty sage stained
     and the powerful gods made
     and the runemaster of the gods carved out.

143 Odin for the Æsir, and Dain for the elves,
     Dvalin for the dwarfs,
     Asvid for the giants,
     I myself carved some.

144 Do you know how to carve, do you know how to interpret,
     do you know how to stain, do you know how to test out,
     do you know how to ask, do you know how to sacrifice,
     do you know how to dispatch, do you know how to slaughter?

145 Better not to pray, than to sacrifice too much,
     one gift always calls for another;
     better not dispatched than to slaughter too much.
     So Thund carved before the history of nations,[5]
     where he rose up, when he came back.

146 I know those spells which a ruler's wife doesn't know,[6]
     nor any man's son;
     'help' one is called,
     and that will help you
     against accusations and sorrows
     and every sort of anxiety.

Notes

1 *Gunnlod*: this alludes to the story of the winning of the mead of poetry, told in full
   in Snorri, *Eddas*, pp. 61–4. The mead originally belonged to two dwarfs, Fialar

and Gialar, and was stolen by the giants. Odin had worked for a year as a thrall for the brother of Suttung, the giant who had the mead. When the year was up he went to Suttung (here confusingly called Fialar) to claim his reward of mead. By seducing Gunnlod, Suttung's daughter, he gained her help and escaped with the mead back to Asgard. The story is told in fuller detail in vv. 104–10 [of the *Hávámal*].

2   *Fialar*: here a mistake for Suttung, owner of the mead.

3   *I hung on a windy tree*: Odin performs a sacrifice by hanging for nine nights on the tree Yggdrasill, pierced with a spear in order to gain knowledge of the runes. The parallels with the Crucifixion are marked, though interpretation is controversial. The motif of the Hanged God is widespread in Indo-European and ancient Near Eastern religion, however, so direct Christian influence need not be present here.

4   *Bolthor*: Odin's maternal grandfather; Bolthor's son is therefore Odin's mother's brother, a particularly close relationship in Germanic society.

5   *Thund*: an Odinic name.

6   *spells*: the spells which Odin alludes to here broadly match those magical skills listed for him in *Ynglinga saga*, Chapters 2 and 6.

Chapter 8

Anonymous

THE SEERESS

■ from *Eiríks saga rauða* (based on Einar Ólafur Sveinsson and Matthías
Þorðarson (eds) **ÍSLENZK FORNRIT: VOL. 4: EYRBYGGJA SAGA**,
Reykjavik, 1935, pp. 206–9, trans. Phil Cardew

A ROUND A THOUSAND YEARS ago, a seeress (*spákona*) visited a farm
in Greenland and was asked about its future. *The Saga of Eirík the Red* not only
describes what Þorbjörg, the seeress, wore and carried, it also tells us how she acted
towards the community and how she set about ascertaining the answer to their question. The method by which she entered trance required the help of others, especially
someone to chant for her. Only one woman claims to know the required chant, but
she performs so well that she is thanked warmly. The chapter details Þorbjörg's costume, behaviour and performance. There are, as ever, gaps in our knowledge of what
took place. The chant is not provided, and the precise processes of entrancement and
enquiry are invisible. These gaps, however, provide the spaces in which creative
research and experimentation can occur. Contemporary Heathens have found this a
rich resource from which to initiate engagements with powerful persons – 'spirits'
perhaps, but certainly ancestors, deities and land-guardians – who might participate
in the recovery of similar knowledge-seeking practices. Blain (2002) is the most complete and interesting discussion of contemporary Heathen 'neo-shamanry' to date. It
is well worth comparing her discussion of *seidr*, the specifically Heathen form of
shamanry, with that arising and evolving in other Pagan communities. Clifton (1994)
and Wallis (2003) are most helpful in this direction. There is, of course, a vast literature on shamans, indigenous and new/Western (see Harvey, 2002), much of it
proffering interesting parallels and differences from that described in this extract.

None of the above is to suggest that the Saga's depiction of the seer's regalia,
accoutrements and activities must be taken as a straightforward description of the
historical reality. Catharina Raudvere, for example, discusses the role of this part
of the narrative in portraying Greenland as backward and primitive in continuing
to hold, albeit with some contest, to ancestral religious practices (2002: 121–7).

However, contemporary Heathens are themselves engaged in parallel processes of imagination, narration and contestation. In all these the Sagas make interesting and at times complex reading.

Graham Harvey

References

Blain, Jenny (2002) *Nine Worlds of Seid-Magic: Ecstasy and Neo-Shamanism in North European Paganism*. London: Routledge.

Clifton, Chas S. (ed.) (1994) *Witchcraft and Shamanism*. St. Paul, MN: Llewellyn.

Harvey, Graham (ed.) (2002) *Shamanism: A Reader*. London: Routledge.

Raudvere, Catharina (2002) 'Trolldómr in early medieval Scandinavia', in K. Jolly, C. Raudvere and E. Peters, *Witchcraft and Magic in Europe*. London: Athlone.

Sveinsson, Einar Ólafur and Þorðarson, Matthías (eds) (1935) *Íslenzk Fornrit: Vol. 4: Eyrbyggja saga*. Reykjavik: University of Iceland Press.

Wallis, Robert (2003) *Shamans / Neo-Shamans: Ecstasy, Alternative Archaeologies and Contemporary Pagans*. London: Routledge.

A T THAT TIME [THERE] was a great famine in Greenland; those men who had gone on fishing expeditions caught little (and some did not return). That woman was there in the village, who was called Þorbjörg; she was a prophetess and was called 'little völva'.[1] She had had nine sisters, and all were prophetesses, but she alone [of them] was then living. It was Þorbjörg's habit during [the] winter that she went to feasts and those men welcomed her most at [their] home[s] who were eager to know their destiny or [that of the] season; and because Þorkell was then the most powerful farmer it seemed his duty to find out when this bad season, which beset [them], might finish. Þorkell invites the prophetess home, and she is given a good welcome, as the custom was, when a woman of this kind is received. The high seat was made ready for her and a cushion laid under her; there should be hens' feathers in[side it]. And when she came during the evening together with that man, who was sent to meet her, then was she so dressed, that she had over her a blue cloak with a strap, and [it] was set [with] stones all [over the] skirts; she had glass beads on her neck, a black lambskin kerchief (with white catskin inside) on her head; and she had a staff in [her] hand, and [there] was a knob on [it]; it was ornamented with brass and stones [were] set below the knob; she had a belt about her and a large skin purse was on it, and she preserved therein her charms, those which she needed to have [for her] magic. She had calfskin shoes on [her] feet, and long thongs on [them] and large tin knobs on the end [of them]. She had catskin gloves on her hands and [they] were white inside and hairy. And when she came in, it seemed to all people [that they] should accord her honourable greetings. She received them, [the] people were agreeable to her. Þorkell the farmer took her by the hand and led her to that seat which was prepared for her. Þorkell asked her to run her eyes over household and herd and thus [his] home. She was reticent about everything. A table was set up during the evening, and from this [it] is [possible] to relate what was cooked for the prophetess. A porridge of kid's milk was prepared for her, and [the] hearts out of all [kinds of] living beasts cooked, those that were available there. She had a brass spoon and a knife with a handle of walrus tusk, mounted with a double ring of brass, and [it] was broken at the point. And when the table was set up, then Þorkell the farmer went before Þorbjörg and asked, how that [all] seemed

to her, or how agreeable to her are the home or the people's manners or how speedily she would know that [which would] happen, which he had asked her and [all] men
are most curious to know. She declared that she would not say anything until the
morning after, when she had first slept through the night. And the next day, towards
the end of day, that equipment was brought to her, which she needed to have in order
to perform the spells. She asked them to find her those women, who knew that lore
which was necessary for the spell and is called Varðlokur. But they were not able to
find [such] women. Then [it] was sought out throughout the farm, if anyone knew [the
lore]. Then Guðríðr says: 'Neither am I skilled in magic nor a wise-woman, but yet
Halldís, my foster mother, taught me in Iceland that song which she called Varðlokur.'
Þorkell says: 'Then you are wise in season.' She says: 'This is that kind of action, that
I intend never to be of help to, because I am a Christian woman.' Þorbjörg says: 'It
might so happen, that you become a person of help in this [matter], and you would be
then a woman no worse than before. And yet I shall ask Þorkell to get those things,
of which I have need.' Þorkell now pressed Guðríðr hard and she said she would do
as he wished. Women then formed a ring around the dais that Þorbjörg sat upon.
Guðríðr sang the song so fairly and [so] well that none there at that time thought [they
had] heard the song sung by a fairer voice. The prophetess thanked her [for] the song
and said many of those spirits now to have sought [them] and considered [it] fair to listen [to], when the song was so well sung – 'who before wished to separate [them-
selves from] us and never grant us obedience. But now many [of] those things are
apparent to me, which before were hidden [from] me, and many others. And I am
able to say to you, Þorkell, that this famine will not hold out longer than through [the]
winter and the season shall be mended with the coming of spring. The sickness, which
has lain over [you] shall be made better sooner than hoped for. And to you, Guðríðr,
shall I repay that assistance, which we have received from you, because your fate is
now completely clear to me. You will make a match here in Greenland, that who is
most honourable, though that will not become of long duration to you, because your
way lies out towards Iceland, and shall there come from you both a great and good
family line, and over your pedigree shines bright rays and I have been able to know
exactly [how they] are set; to end [with] fare you now well and hale, daughter.'
Afterwards people went to the prophetess and asked each then that which [they] were
most curious to know. She was liberal with her information; and little of that which
she said was not fulfilled. Next those were come after her from another farm; then
she went thither. Then Þorbjörn was sent for, because he did not wish to be at home
whilst such idolatry was practised. The bad weather swiftly got better, as Þorbjörg had
said. Þorbjörn prepared his ship and then travelled out until he came to Brattahlíð.
Eiríkr greeted him well, with joy, and said it was good that he was come. Þorbjörn
was with him and his family during the winter, but they found lodgings for the oars-
men with [other] farmers. Later during the spring Eiríkr gave Þorbjörn land in
Stokkaness, and a magnificent dwelling was built there, and he lived there afterwards.

Note

1   The Norse term 'völva' is often translated as 'sibyl'; however, this term has clas-
     sical overtones which seem inappropriate to the more domesticated nature of
     Þorbjörg's role within this section of the saga. Therefore the Norse term has been
     retained.

Chapter 9

Anonymous

MATH SON OF MATHONWY

■ from Jeffrey Gantz (trans.) **THE MABINOGION**, Harmondsworth, 1976, pp. 110–17

IN THIS EXTRACT FROM 'Math Son of Mathonwy' in *The Mabinogion*, magic and passion, death and rebirth, judgement and memory are all entangled. Many Pagans take the tales of *The Mabinogion* to be retellings of stories first told in the pre-Roman Iron Age of ancient Britain. Even if this now seems unlikely, and a new interest in medieval bards and troubadours is rising, this and other *Mabinogion* tales are not only re-told but have also inspired a number of songs and stories that are regularly incorporated into Pagan seasonal festivals. 'Math Son of Mathonwy' blends a series of transformations that suggest an intimate kinship between all living persons – divine, human, animal and plant. In the following excerpt, Math and Gwydyon make a woman out of flowers and name her Blodeuedd. Left by her husband, Lleu, she finds solace with Goronwy and (somewhat like the biblical Delilah) betrays the secret that protects Lleu. His transformation into a badly injured eagle initiates another transformative quest, ending in the death of Goronwy, and Blodeuedd becoming an owl. Apart from the pleasure of the tale and its telling, lessons may be derived about life and death, magic and power, trust and tricks, and more.

The extract is included here principally because it has been used in the Pagan revival, inspiring bardic arts and suggesting understandings of the way of the world. The transformative abilities of powerful beings, and the amoral (at least) actions of Tricksters, invite dialogue with and consideration of similar themes in indigenous religious traditions.

Graham Harvey

THEN GWYDYON AND LLEU went to Math and made the most persistent complaints ever against Aranrhod, telling him how Gwydyon had obtained arms for Lleu, and Math said, 'Let us use our magic and enchantments to conjure up a woman out of flowers.' By then Lleu had the stature of a man and was the hand-somest lad anyone had seen. Math and Gwydyon took the flowers of oak and broom and meadowsweet and from these conjured up the loveliest and most beautiful girl anyone had seen; they baptized her with the form of baptism that was used then, and named her Blodeuedd.[1]

After the couple had slept together at the wedding-feast Gwydyon said, 'It is not easy for a man with no land to support himself.' 'Very well,' said Math, 'I will give him the best cantrev there is for a young man to have.' 'Which cantrev is that?' 'The cantrev of Dinoding,' said Math. (lit is now called Eivyonydd and Ardudwy.) Lleu set up his court in the place called Mur Castell,[2] in the hills of Ardudwy; he settled there and governed the land, and all were content with his rule.

One day he left for Caer Dathal to visit Math. The day of his departure his wife was stirring about the court when she heard a horn blown and saw an exhausted stag going by with dogs and hunters in pursuit, followed by a company of men on foot. 'Send a lad to find out who these people are,' she said, so the lad went out and asked what lord they served; 'Goronwy the Staunch, Lord of Penllyn,' was the answer, and the lad reported that to Blodeuedd. Goronwy pursued the stag until he over-took it at Avon Gynvael,[3] and there he killed it, and what with killing the stag and feeding his dogs he was there until night closed in. As day ended and night drew, near he came to the gate of the court.

'God knows, we will be disgraced for letting this chieftain go elsewhere at this hour and not asking him in,' said Blodeuedd. 'God knows, lady, we should ask him in,' said her attendants. Messengers were sent, and Goronwy was glad to accept the invitation; he entered the court and she came to welcome and greet him. 'Lady, God reward you for this welcome,' he said, and then they changed and went to sit down. Blodeuedd looked at Goronwy, and as she looked there was no part of her that was not filled with love for him; he returned her gaze, and the feeling that had overcome her overcame him also. He could not conceal his love for her and so he told her; this made her very happy, and their talk that night was of the love and affection they felt for each other. Nor did they hesitate to embrace – that night they slept together.

The next day Goronwy made to leave, but Blodeuedd said, 'God knows, you must not go from me tonight,' so they spent that night together also, planning how they might stay together. 'There is only one way,' said Goronwy, 'you must try to learn from your husband how his death might be brought about – you can do so by feigning concern for his well-being.' The next day Goronwy made to leave, but Blodeuedd said, 'God knows, I do not advise you to leave me today.' 'God knows, since you feel that way, I will not go. Though I am considering the danger that the chief whose court this is will return.' 'All right, I will let you go tomorrow.' The next day he prepared to leave and she did not hinder him. 'Now remember what I told you,' he said, 'speak privately with him, feign affection, and learn how he can be killed.'

That night Lleu returned home. He and his wife spent the day singing and carousing and talking, and at night they went to sleep together, and he spoke to her, and then a second time, but not one word did he get in reply. 'What has happened to you – are you all right?' he asked. 'I am thinking of something you would not expect from me,' she answered, 'that is, I am worried about your death, about your going before I do.' 'Well, God reward you for your concern,' said he. 'But unless God strikes me down, it will not be easy for anyone to kill me.' 'Then for God's sake and mine, tell me how you can be killed, for my memory is a better safeguard than yours.' 'Gladly. It will not he easy for anyone to strike me, since he would have to spend a year working on the spear, and no work may be done except when people are at Mass on Sundays.' 'Are you certain of that?' 'I am. I cannot be killed indoors or out of doors, on horse or on foot.'[4] 'Then how can you be killed?' 'I will tell you. Make a bath for me on a river bank, with a good snugly thatched roof over the tub; then bring a buck goat and put it alongside the tub. If I put one foot on the goat's back and the other on the edge of the tub, whoever struck me then would bring about my death.' 'Well, I thank God for that,' she said, 'for this can easily be avoided.'

No sooner had Blodeuedd obtained the information than she sent it to Goronwy the Staunch. Goronwy worked over the spear until, at the end of the year, it was ready, and he told Blodeuedd that very day. 'Lord,' she said to her husband, 'I am thinking of how what you told me earlier might come about. If I prepare the bath, will you show me how you would stand on the goat and the edge of the tub?' 'I will,' said Lleu, whereupon she sent for Goronwy and told him to wait in the shadow of the hill now called Brynn Kyvergyr, on the bank of Avon Gynvael; then she had men gather all the goats they could find in the cantrev and bring them to the far side of the river, the side facing Brynn Kyvergyr. The next day she said, 'Lord, I have had the roof and the bath prepared, and everything is ready.' 'Then let us go and look,' said Lleu. The next day they came to look at the bath. 'Will you step into the bath, lord?' she asked. 'Gladly,' he said. 'Lord, here are those animals you said were called buck goats.' 'Then have them catch one and bring it here.' The goat was brought; Lleu rose from the bath and put on his trousers, then put one foot on the edge of the tub and the other on the goat's back. At once from the hill called Brynn Kyvergyr Goronwy rose to one knee and cast the poisoned spear at Lleu and struck him in the side so that the shaft stuck out but the head stayed in. Lleu flew up in the form of an eagle and gave a horrible scream, and he was not seen again.

As soon as he had disappeared Goronwy and Blodeuedd set off for the court, and that night they slept together. The next day Goronwy rose and subdued Ardudwy and ruled over it, so that both Ardudwy and Penilyn were in his power. Upon hearing of this Math was grieved and heavy-hearted, and Gwydyon was sadder still. 'Lord, I cannot rest until I get news of my nephew,' said he, and Math replied, 'Go then, and God be your strength.' Gwydyon set out on his journey; he searched Gwynedd and every part of Powys, and after looking everywhere he came to Arvon and stopped at a peasant's house in the stronghold of Pennardd, where he dismounted and spent the night. When the man of the house and his household entered, the swineherd came last, and the master said to his swineherd, 'Lad, has your sow come in this evening?' 'She has just come in to the swine.' 'What sort of journey does this sow make?' asked Gwydyon. 'Every day when the sty is opened she goes out; no one can hold her, nor do we know where she goes any more than if she went into the earth.' 'Will you do something for me?' asked Gwydyon. 'Do not open the sty until I am standing by.' 'I will do that,' said the swineherd.

They went to sleep that night, and when the swineherd saw the light of day he woke Gwydyon, who rose and dressed and went out and stood by the sty. The swineherd opened the sty, and at once the sow bolted out and raced away, with Gwydyon in pursuit. She headed upstream and made for the valley which is now called Nantlleu, and there she halted and began to feed. Gwydyon walked under the tree to see what she was feeding on, and he found her eating rotten flesh and maggots. Then he looked up into the top of the tree and there was an eagle; when the eagle shook, worms and rotten flesh fell away and the sow would eat. Gwydyon thought that the eagle was Lleu, so he sang this englyn:

> An oak[5] grows between two lakes,
> Dark sky and glen.
> If I speak truly
> This comes from Lleu's feathers.

At that the eagle dropped into the middle of the tree. Gwydyon then sang another englyn:

> An oak grows on a high plain;
> Rain soaks it no more than does putrefaction.[6]
> It has supported twenty crafts;[7]
> In its branches is Lleu Skilful Hand.

At that the eagle dropped down into the lowest branch of the tree, and Gwydyon sang still another englyn:

> An oak grows on a slope,
> The refuge of a handsome prince.
> If I speak truly
> Lleu will come to my lap.

At that the eagle dropped down onto Gwydyon's knee, and Gwydyon struck him with his magic wand so that he regained human form. No one had ever seen such a pitiful sight of a man – he was nothing but skin and bone. Gwydyon took him to Caer Dathal; all the good doctors in Gwynedd were brought, and well before the end of the year he was cured.

Lleu then said to Math, 'Lord, it is time to demand compensation from the man who did me this injury.' 'God knows, he cannot continue to keep it from you,' said Math. 'Well, the sooner I receive compensation the better I will feel.' So they mustered the forces of Gwynedd and made for Ardudwy, and Gwydyon rode ahead to Mur Castell. When Blodeuedd heard that they were coming she took her women with her and made across Avon Gynvael to a court which was on the mountain; these women, however, were so afraid that they would only advance with their faces turned backwards, and so they knew nothing until they had fallen into the lake and drowned, all but Blodeuedd. Gwydyon overtook her and said, 'I will not kill you, but I will do what is worse: I will let you go in the form of a bird. Because of the shame you have brought on Lleu Skilful Hand, you are never to show your face to the light of day, rather you shall fear other birds; they will be hostile to you, and it will be their nature to maul and molest you wherever they find you. You will not lose your name but will always be called Blodeuwedd.[8] (Blodeuwedd means owl in the language of our day, and therefore birds are hostile to the owl.)

Goronwy the Staunch set out for Penllyn, from where he sent messengers to ask Lleu Skilful Hand if he would accept land or territory or gold or silver for the injury. 'I swear by my confession to God, I will not,' said Lleu. 'He must come to where I was when he cast the spear at me, while I am standing where he was, and must let me throw a spear at him. That is the least I will accept.' This was told to Goronwy, who replied, 'Well, I must do that. Nobles, troops, foster-brothers, will any of you take the blow in my stead?' 'God knows, we will not,' they all said, and because of their refusal to stand and take the blow for their lord they were known as one of the Three Disloyal Companies.

'Then I must take the blow,' said Goronwy. The two men went to the bank of Avon Gynvael; Goronwy stood where Lleu had been when the spear was thrown, and Lleu where Goronwy had been. But Goronwy went to Lleu and said, 'Lord, since it was through a woman's bad influence that I struck you, I beg this of you in God's name. I see a stone by the river bank – let me put that between myself and the blow.' 'God knows I will not refuse you that,' said Lleu. 'God reward you,' said Goronwy, and he took up the stone and put it between himself and the blow. Then Lleu threw the spear and pierced both the stone and Goronwy; Goronwy's back was broken and he was killed. The stone still stands on the bank of Avon Gynvael in Ardudwy, with the spear through it, and so it is called Llech Oronwy.[9] But Lleu Skilful Hand subdued the land a second time and ruled over it prosperously, and according to the storytellers he was Lord of Gwynedd thereafter. So ends this Branch of the Mabinogi.

Notes

1   Blodeu: flowers.
2   Mur Castell: castle wall.
3   Avon: river.
4   When he is killed, Lleu is also standing neither on dry land (the goat's back) nor in water (the edge of the tub).
5   oak: one of the flowers from which Blodeuedd was made.
6   Lleu's rotting flesh falls like rain.
7   Lug is master of many crafts – perhaps that is the significance of the twenty crafts mentioned here.
8   Blodeuwedd: flower face.
9   Llech Oronwy: stone of Goronwy.

Chapter 10

Marie Heaney

OVER NINE WAVES

■ from **OVER NINE WAVES**, London, 1994

THERE ARE TWO ASPECTS of this excerpt from Ireland's *Mythological Cycle* (and more specifically *The Book of Conquests of Ireland*) that are of particular interest to Pagans. First, the story involves the Tuatha De Danaan (pronounced *too*-ha day *dan*-an). Second, it includes a recitation by Amergin that resonates with other initiatory and transformational poems. Of course, the story can be read for sheer pleasure too.

In the excerpt, the Tuatha De Danaan are defeated by the invading Milesians and Gaels who become the ancestors of later inhabitants of Ireland. The Tuatha, however, do not disappear. Rather, they 'went underground to inhabit the mounds and earthworks known as *sidhes* that are scattered all over the country'. Indeed, many people now refer to the Tuatha as *sidhe* (pronounced 'shee') and consider them to be the equivalent of the faerie peoples, other-than-human persons who would not have given up the land merely to force of weapons. The story might be read as an explanation of the mounds scattered across Ireland and elsewhere – mounds now commonly interpreted as the burial places of earlier peoples. However, they can still be treated as places where this world and the 'Otherworld' interpenetrate one another, making access possible, if dangerous.

Amergin's poem is the kind of powerful utterance which might give someone access to considerable power. It links them to the forces of nature and to powerful other-than-human persons. It is often considered to be derived from initiation practices in which people enter trance in ways akin to shamans elsewhere.

Gordon the Toad's 'Entertaining Faeries' is included later in this collection (Chapter 37) as a fine example of contemporary Pagan engagement with those who, tradition suggests, should not be named too often. Terry Pratchett's *Lords and Ladies* (1995) not only borrows a traditional circumlocution for names that might otherwise invite presence, but also powerfully renews a traditional understanding diminished by Victorian fantasies about cute gossamer-winged flower-dwellers. Amergin's poem is a significant source for John Matthews' (1991) creation of a Celtic Shamanism.

Graham Harvey

References

Matthews, John (1991) *Taliesin: Shamanism and the Bardic Mysteries in Britain and Ireland*. London: Aquarian.
Pratchett, Terry (1995) *Lords and Ladies*. New York: HarperCollins.

A GREAT HOST OF PEOPLE, Milesians and Gaels, assembled in Brigaton, chiefs and warriors and with them ordinary people, men and women both.

They set sail in a huge fleet, sixty-five ships in all, and on the day before the first day of May they saw the island rise slowly out of the sea ahead of them. Then they raced each other, sailing and rowing with all their strength, to see who would be first to set foot in Ireland.

This time the Tuatha De Danaan were expecting them. They hurried to the shore and watched helplessly as the Milesian fleet approached with great speed. The De Danaans had made no armed preparations for war so their leaders asked their magicians to use their druidic powers to halt the approach of the invaders.

The druids began to work their spells and the outline of the shore began to shimmer and waver, until the Milesians saw land and sea swirling together in one confusing mass. The approaching ships were completely engulfed in a mist. Cloud closed round them and the sailors lost their bearings completely. Three times they circled the island, frightened and helpless. At last, through a break in the fog, they saw an inlet into which the fleet could sail and here they anchored.

Disembarking quickly, glad to be ashore, they began to march to Tara to confront the three De Danaan kings. On the way they met the three queens of Ireland, Eiriu, Fodla and Banba, who prophesied to them that the island of Ireland would belong to them and to their children for ever. This gave the Milesians encouragement and they pressed on with renewed will. At Tara, they found the three kings who had killed Ith in council. The Milesians chose Amergin, a poet and one of their leaders, to meet the De Danaan kings and give them an ultimatum. Amergin went into the hail where the kings were in council and told them the choices they had: to give over their country peacefully, or to fight to keep it. The loss of their homeland was the price they would have to pay for the murder of Ith.

Though they were not ready for battle, the Tuatha De Danaan had no notion of handing over their land without a struggle, so they played for time. 'Let your poets and wise men make an offer,' they said, 'but it must be a fair offer, otherwise our druids will kill you with their spells.'

So Amergin made his offer.

'We will go back to our boats and retreat from the shore over the distance of nine waves. Then we will come back over the nine waves, disembark and take this island by force if need be. But if you can prevent us setting foot on the shore, we will turn our boats homewards and we will never trouble you again.'

The Tuatha De Danaan were pleased with this offer. They were sure that their druids' power was strong enough to prevent the Milesians landing, so they agreed to the terms.

Amergin and his companions put out to sea over the space of nine waves and then turned to approach the shore. Immediately a huge storm blew up and gravel on the sea bed rose to the surface with the force of the wind. Waves rose in front of the boats as tall as the cliffs along the strand. In the tempestuous breakers the boats were pitched and tossed. They lost sight of each other in the deep troughs and were driven westward and scattered in every direction until they were exhausted. Many, many boats foundered in the boiling sea.

Amergin and the other leaders knew that the storm was not a natural one, but one called up by the power of the druids. They did not know how far from land they had been driven, so Amergin's brother climbed to the top of the mast to see if land was visible over the towering waves. He was flung from the mast by a fierce gust of wind and crashed to his death on the deck below. The people in the boat were terrified and angry. They ranted at Amergin and begged him to use his powers to calm the sea and save them. Amergin, buffeted by the winds and waves, made his way forward and clinging to the prow, his voice rising above the roar of the waves, he invoked the spirit of the land of Ireland, calling out to it, praising its beauty. Instantly there was a lull in the wind, the dreadful noise ceased and the sea became calm. Swiftly the boat headed for land over the nine waves, with Amergin like a figurehead leaning forward in the prow. As soon as the keel of the boat touched bottom, Amergin jumped out and waded ashore. He put his right foot on dry land at Inver Sceine and then, standing on the shore of Ireland, he chanted this poem,

'I am the wind on the sea.
I am the wave of the ocean.
I am a powerful bull.
I am an eagle on the rock.
I am the brightness of the sun.
I am a fierce wild boar.
I am a salmon in the pool.
I am the wisdom of art.
I am a spear, sharp in battle.
I am the god that puts fire in the brain.'

Other ships pulled ashore and the men and women who had survived the storm disembarked. They were grateful to be alive and more willing than before to fight the Tuatha De Danaan whose magical powers had cost them so many lives. They fell into formation and marched to meet their enemy.

The Tuatha De were dismayed to see the Milesians land in spite of their druids' efforts and they hastily marshalled their forces. Then they too marched to battle.

The first skirmish was won by the Gaels and Milesians but the Tuatha De mustered again and on the plain of Tailtinn faced the invaders. It was a fierce battle. The Milesians, remembering Ith and their lost kinsmen, fought fiercely. The Tuatha De Danaan, knowing their territory was at stake, fought to the death. The three De

Danaan kings and their three queens were killed in the battle and when their followers saw this happen they lost heart. They were pushed back to the sea by the triumphant Milesians. They too had suffered losses, but they had won the battle for the land.

Then the Milesians divided Ireland into provinces: Ulster in the north, Munster in the south, Leinster in the east and Connacht in the west and, at the centre, Tara. Each province had its own king, chiefs and champions, but the High King, who lived in Tara, ruled the country, helped by the provincial kings and chiefs.

As for the Tuatha De Danaan, though they had been defeated by the Milesians at the battle of Tailtinn, they did not leave Ireland. They went underground to inhabit the mounds and earthworks known as *sidhes* that are scattered all over the country. Above them, in the upper kingdom, the human inhabitants of Ireland, the descendants of the Milesians and Gaels, lived and died, helped and sometimes hindered by the People of the Sidhe. From time to time, down through the ages, these mysterious, imperishable people entered the world of mortals. Sometimes they fell in love with human beings and at other times they held humans in thrall with their beauty and their haunting music. But their kingdom was that Happy Otherworld under the earth and they always went back there to the Land of the Ever Young.

Chapter 11

Geoffrey of Monmouth

THE TOWER, THE POOL AND THE DRAGONS

■ from Lewis Thorpe (trans.) **GEOFFREY OF MONMOUTH: THE HISTORY OF THE KINGS OF BRITAIN**, Harmondsworth, 1966, pp. 168–9

MERLIN AND OTHER ANCIENT magicians have been of some significance to Pagans of various kinds – from ceremonial magicians to Wiccans and Druids, and including Goddess devotees.

This chapter briefly introduces Merlin as wise child. Merlin's contest with the king's flattering magician-advisers has some obvious parallels with biblical and classical stories, but it is also rooted in medieval bardic contests. The attempt to build a tower is also echoed in many other narratives, including more recent folk tales that seem to demand respectful interactions with spirits of a place.

Merlin is a powerful presence wherever he appears – including in fantasy literature, films, poems, ceremonies and even claimed hierophanies and reincarnations. These are too many to list fully, and would be certain to miss the reader's favourite version of a Merlin tale. However, Merlin is not hard to discern in the character, demeanour and actions of Tolkien's Gandalf and J.K. Rowling's Dumbledore. Geoffrey of Monmouth's Merlin is, like many others, an ambiguous character, who foils bad magicians but is himself, finally, part of the old age that must give way to more civilized, noble and (most importantly) Christian virtues and pursuits. However, his departure to other-worldly realms does not absolutely bar him from contact with succeeding generations. Pagan traditions suggest that his acquiescence to the rise of Christianity was only a temporary withdrawal – and thereby make space to tell their own stories. In turn, these varied expressions of Merlin's renewed popularity are emblematic of the renewal of Paganism itself – whether as a magical, ecological or feminist spirituality. Marion Bradley's *The Mists of Avalon* (1984) is an interesting and popular example of this trend.

Graham Harvey

Reference

Bradley, Marion Z. (1984) *The Mists of Avalon*. London: Sphere.

WHEN HE HAD LISTENED to all this, Merlin went up to the King and asked: 'Why have my mother and I been brought into your presence?' 'My magicians have advised me,' answered Vortigern, 'that I should look for a fatherless man, so that my building can be sprinkled with his blood and thus stand firm.' 'Tell your magicians to appear in front of me,' answered Merlin, 'and I will prove that they have lied.'

The King was amazed at what Merlin said. He ordered his magicians to come immediately and sit down in front of Merlin. 'Just because you do not know what is obstructing the foundations of the tower which these men have begun,' said Merlin to the magicians, 'you have recommended that my blood should be sprinkled on the mortar to make the building stand firm. Tell me, then, what lies hidden under the foundation. There is certainly something there which is preventing it from holding firm.'

The magicians, who were terrified, said nothing. Merlin, who was also called Ambrosius,[1] then went on: 'My Lord King, summon your workmen. Order them to dig in the earth, and, underneath, you will find a pool. That is what is preventing the tower from standing.' This was done. A pool was duly found beneath the earth, and it was this which made the ground unsteady.

Ambrosius Merlin went up to the magicians a second time and said: 'Tell me, now, you lying flatterers. What lies beneath the pool?' They remained silent, unable to utter a single sound. 'Order the pool to be drained,' said Merlin, 'and at the bottom you will observe two hollow stones. Inside the stones you will see two Dragons which are sleeping.'

The King believed what Merlin said, for he had told the truth about the pool. He ordered the pool to be drained. He was more astounded by Merlin than he had ever been by anything. All those present were equally amazed at his knowledge, and they realized that there was something supernatural about him.

Note

1   The words '*qui et Ambrosius dicebatur*' have all the air of being a gloss.

PART TWO

Proto-revival texts

Charles Leland

HOW DIANA GAVE BIRTH TO ARADIA (HERODIAS)

■ from **ARADIA: OR THE GOSPEL OF THE WITCHES**, Blaine, Washington, DC, 1899, 1998, pp. 127–33, 355–63. Reprinted by Phoenix Publishing, Inc.

T HE JUXTAPOSITION OF THE words "witches" and "gospel" might seem strange to contemporary readers, but evidently they did not seem so to Charles Godfrey Leland (1824–1903), a multifaceted Philadelphian whose avocational research into Italian folklore and magic would provide the later Wiccan religion with some vital textual inspiration. Ironically, Leland regarded his collecting and editing of Italian (and English Gypsy and Native American) lore as a sort of salvage operation, sure that such practices would die out in the new twentieth century.

As a boy, Leland was encouraged by his parents to read widely. He attended Princeton University, showing an early interest in mysticism and Neoplatonic philosophy, and after his graduation his father financed further study at Heidelberg, where the six-foot four-inch (190 cm) Leland also immersed himself in the world of German university dueling clubs, then briefly participated in the Parisian street fighting of the 1848 revolution.

Back home, he studied law but found himself more at home in journalism, eventually becoming editor of a leading political magazine where, as the Civil War loomed, he strongly supported President Lincoln's hard line against Southern secession and became one of the president's unofficial advisers. After the war, through his own earnings and an inheritance, he was able to leave journalism in favor of world travel, writing, and research. Anthropology did not yet exist as an academic discipline, so Leland became one of many late Victorian amateur ethnographers, proudest perhaps of his knowledge of the Romany (Gypsy) language and his acceptance in Romany society. He was the first president of the Gypsy-Lore Society, founded in London in 1888. (For discussion of Leland's engagement with Native American religions, see Parkhill, 1997.)

But by the 1880s, Leland and his wife were spending more and more time in Florence than in London. In 1886 he met an Italian witch named "Maddalena", who became his chief informant and point of entry into *la vecchia religione*, the Old Religion—for Leland was convinced that an unbroken secret tradition connected these late nineteenth-century sorcerers with Etruscan and Roman Paganism of millennia before. Through her and her acquaintances he hastened to collect spells, chants, legends, and other material, convinced that with the dawn of a more secular age, "both priest and wizard are vanishing now with incredible rapidity."

Leland wrote several books based on his Italian experiences, particularly *Etruscan Roman Remains* (1892) and *Aradia* (1899), which together laid out his evidence for survivals of Classical Paganism in popular culture. In the 1950s, Leland's work was important to the creation of Gardnerian Wicca. Doreen Valiente, who created many of Wicca's ritual texts, called Leland "the first major influence [on witchcraft] in relatively modern times" (Valiente, 1989: 2). One of these, the "Charge of the Goddess," was directly inspired by the lines beginning, *Quando io saro partita da questa mondo*. Likewise, the Gardnerian insistence on ritual nudity was buttressed by Leland's translation, "Ye shall be naked in your rites."

The first Gardnerian witches often used Aradia as a name for their goddess, and Raymond Buckland, the first Gardnerian high priest in the United States, published his own edition of *Aradia* in 1968, the first in seventy years. The question of the "gospel's" origin remains open, however; Leland himself supposed that Maddalena had written down what were chiefly oral texts, and then he combined her text with other material that he had collected. The annotated centennial edition, cited below, includes a retranslation by a native of the region.

Chas S. Clifton

References

Leland, Charles G. ([1892] 1999) *Etruscan Roman Remains*. Blaine, Washington, DC: Phoenix Publishing.

Leland, Charles G. ([1899] 1998) *Aradia: or the Gospel of the Witches*. Blaine, Washington, DC: Phoenix Publishing.

Parkhill, Thomas C. (1997) *Weaving Ourselves into the Land: Charles Godfrey Leland, "Indians," and the Study of Native American Religions*. Albany, NY: State University of New York Press.

Valiente, Doreen (1989) *The Rebirth of Witchcraft*. London: Robert Hale.

"It is Diana! Lo!
She rises crescented."
         — Keats' *Endymion*

"Make more bright
The Star Queen's crescent on her marriage night."
         — *Ibid*.

This is the Gospel (*Vangelo*) of the Witches:

Diana greatly loved her brother Lucifer, the god of the Sun and of the Moon, the god of Light (*Splendor*), who was so proud of his beauty, and who for his pride was driven from Paradise.

Diana had by her brother a daughter, to whom they gave the name of Aradia [*i.e.* Herodias].

In those days there were on earth many rich and many poor.

The rich made slaves of all the poor.

In those days were many slaves who were cruelly treated; in every palace tortures, in every castle prisoners.

Many slaves escaped. They fled to the country: thus they became thieves and evil folk. Instead of sleeping by night, they plotted escape and robbed their masters, and then slew them. So they dwelt in the mountains and forests as robbers and assassins, all to avoid slavery.

Diana said one day to her daughter Aradia:

1. E vero che tu sei uno spirito,
2. Ma tu sei nata per essere ancora,
3. Mortale, e tu devi andare
4. Sulla terra e fare da maestra
5. A donne e a' uomini che avranno
6. Volentà di inparare la tua scuola
7. Che sara composta di stregonerie.

8. Non devi essere come la figlia di Caino,
9. E della razza che sono devenuti
10. Scellerati infami a causa dei maltrattamenti,
11. Come Giudei e Zingari,
12. Tutti ladri e briganti,
13. Tu non divieni . . .

14. Tu sarai (sempre) la prima strega,
15. La prima strega divenuta nel mondo,
16. Tu insegnerai l'arte di avvelenare,
17. Di avvelenare (tutti) i signori,
18. Di farli morti nei loro palazzi,

19. Di legare il spirito del oppressore,
20. E dove si trova un contadino ricco e avaro,
21. Insegnare alle strege tue alunne,
22. Come rovinare suo raccolto
23. Con tempesta, folgore e balen,
24. Con grandine e vento.

25. Quando un prete ti fara del male,
26. Del male colle sue bene di'Zioni,
27. Tu le farei (sempre) un doppio male

28. Col mio nome, col nome di *Diana*,
29. Regina delle streghe . . .

30. Quando i nobili e prete vi diranno
31. Dovete credere nel Padre, Figlio,
32. E Maria, rispondete gli sempre,
33. "IL vostro dio Padre e Maria
34. Sono tre diavoli . . .

35. "Il vero dio Padre non e il vostro—
36. Il vostro dio—io sono venuta
37. Per distruggere la gente cattiva
38. E la distruggero. . . .

39. "Voi altri poveri soffrite anche la fame,
40. E lavorato malo e molte volte;
41. Soffrite anche la prigione;
42. Mapero avete una anima,
43. Una anima più buona, e nell'altra,
44. Nell'altra mondo voi starete bene,
45. E gli altri male." . . .

Translation

'Tis true indeed that thou a spirit art,
But thou wert born but to become again
A mortal; thou must go to earth below
To be a teacher unto women and men
Who fain would study witchcraft in thy school

Yet like Cain's daughter thou shalt never be,
Nor like the race who have become at last
Wicked and infamous from suffering,
As are the Jews and wandering Zingari,
Who are all thieves and knaves; like unto them
Ye shall not be. . . .

And thou shalt be the first of witches known;
And thou shall be the first of all i' the world;
And thou shalt teach the art of poisoning,
Of poisoning those who are great lords of all;
Yea, thou shalt make them die in their palaces;
And thou shalt bind the oppressor's soul (with power);[1]
And when ye find a peasant who is rich,
Then ye shall teach the witch, your pupil, how
To ruin all his crops with tempests dire,

With lightning and with thunder (terrible),
And the hail and wind. . . .

And when a priest shall do you injury
By his benedictions, ye shall do to him
Double the harm, and do it in the name
Of me, *Diana*, Queen of witches all!

And when the priests or the nobility
Shall say to you that you should put your faith
In the Father, Son, and Mary, then reply:
"Your God, the Father, and Maria are
Three devils. . . .

"For the true God the Father is not yours;
For I have come to sweep away the bad,
The men of evil, all will I destroy!

"Ye who are poor suffer with hunger keen,
And toil in wretchedness, and suffer too
Full oft imprisonment; yet with it all
Ye have a soul, and for your sufferings
Ye shall be happy in the other world,
But ill the fate of all who do ye wrong!"

Now when Aradia had been taught, taught to work all witchcraft, how to destroy the evil race (of oppressors), she (imparted it to her pupils) and said unto them:

46. Quando io saro partita da questo mondo,
47. Qualunque cosa che avrete bisogna,
48. Una volta al mese quando la luna
49. E piena . . .
50. Dovete venire in luogo deserto,
51. In una selva tutte insieme,
52. E adorare lo spirito potente
53. Di mia madre Diana, e chi vorra
54. Imparare la stregonerie,
55. Che non la sopra,
56. Mia madre le insegnera,
57. Tutte cose . . .
58. Sarete liberi della schiavitù!
59. E cosi diverrete tutti liberi!
60. Pero uomini e donne
61. Sarete tutti nudi, per fino.
62. Che non sara morto l'ultimo
63. Degli oppressori e morto,

64. Farete il giuoco della moccola
65. Di Benevento, e farete poi
66. Una cena cosi:

Translation

When I shall have departed from this world,
Whenever ye have need of anything,
Once in the month, and when the moon is full,
Ye shall assemble in some desert place,
Or in a forest all together join
To adore the potent spirit of your queen,
My mother, great *Diana*. She who fain
Would learn all sorcery yet has not won
Its deepest secrets, them my mother will
Teach her, in truth all things as yet unknown.
And ye shall all be freed from slavery,
And so ye shall be free in everything;
And as the sign that ye are truly free,
Ye shall be naked in your rites, both men
And women also: this shall last until
The last of your oppressors shall be dead;
And ye shall make the game of Benevento,
Extinguishing the lights, and after that
Shall hold your supper thus:

Acknowledgement

This extract (pp. 127–33 and 355–63) from *Aradia, Or the Gospel of the Witches*, translated by Mario Pazzaglini and Dina Pazzaglini, Blaine, Washington, DC: Phoenix Publishing, 1998. Reprinted by permission of Phoenix Publishing, Inc.

Note

1   *Legare*, the binding and paralysing of human faculties by means of witchcraft.

Chapter 13

Aleister Crowley

THE BOOK OF THE LAW

■ from *The Book of the Law*, London, 1906

I F PAGANISMS CAN BE defined by the centrality of their celebration of nature – understood in various ways – there are myriad ways in which such celebration might be expressed. Pagans might look to classical Roman, Greek, Celtic or Norse texts for descriptions and understandings of how to show respect to deities, woodland groves, and so on. They might also look to contemporary indigenous religionists in North America, Asia, Africa and elsewhere for other ceremonial practices. However, the common ground of Pagan ritual is certainly built on the foundations laid by esoteric or high ritual magical movements of previous centuries. Such sources provide inspiration for, among other matters, the casting of circles, the greeting of the directions, the use of magical symbols and tools, invocations, and understandings of magical acts and ethics. Hanegraaff (1996) is a particularly useful and important discussion of the development of such esotericism. Aleister Crowley's role both in esoteric movements (e.g. the Golden Dawn) and in the re-creation of Paganism is colourful and sometimes controversial. As Ronald Hutton writes, Crowley 'amalgamated pagan deities, Hebrew demons and redeveloped Christian ritual to produce a personal set of rites and beliefs linked by what may be termed therapeutic blasphemy'. But, he continues, 'as in all documented ceremonial magic of this period, the central impulse was not essentially religious; it was not to worship or honour supernatural beings so much as to gain personal power from them' (Hutton, 1996: 5). That is, Crowley's magick (as he preferred to spell the word), writings and other pursuits were not yet entirely Pagan. Or, rather, they prefigure only some aspects of what Paganism became. It is also important to note that Crowley's influence on the Pagan revival is primarily through two fairly distinct roots. There are Pagans whose performance of magic(k) continues in Crowley's tradition, some identifying themselves as thelemic 'left hand path' or 'tantric' magickians (see Sutcliffe, 1996). Crowley's more pervasive influence is filtered through his friendship with Gerald Gardner and others (see Hutton, 1999). A prime example is the re-working of the most commonly remembered phrase from *The Book of the Law*, namely 'Do what thou wilt shall be the whole of the Law' (itself deriving from Augustine's 'Love and do what you will') into the Wiccan 'rede' (or counsel), 'An it harm none, do what thou wilt'. There are other elements of Wiccan and Pagan ritual and cosmology that have obvious sources in Crowley and other high ritual or ceremonial magicians in the longer esoteric tradition. Joanne Pearson (2002) provides a slightly more detailed introduction to these influences and engagements.

The Book of the Law is included in its entirety. It comprises a series of statements, sometimes 'laws', that Crowley insisted derived from three visionary experiences. Careful reading will reveal themes of significance to broader Paganisms, but the most obvious value of the *Book* is in relation to magic(k)al groups and practices within Paganism and beyond.

Graham Harvey

References

Hanegraaff, Wouter (1996) *New Age Religion and Western Culture: Esotericism in the Mirror of Secular Thought*, Leiden: E. J. Brill.

Hutton, Ronald (1996) 'The roots of modern Paganism', in Graham Harvey and Charlotte Hardman (eds) *Paganism Today*. London: Thorsons, pp. 3–15.

Hutton, Ronald (1999) *The Triumph of the Moon*. Oxford: Oxford University Press.

Pearson, Joanne (2002) 'The history and development of Wicca and Paganism', in Joanne Pearson (ed.) *Belief Beyond Boundaries*. Aldershot: Ashgate.

Sutcliffe, Richard (1996) 'Left-hand path ritual magick', in Graham Harvey and Charlotte Hardman (eds) *Paganism Today*. London: Thorsons, pp. 109–37.

I.

1. Had! The manifestation of Nuit.
2. The unveiling of the company of heaven.
3. Every man and every woman is a star.
4. Every number is infinite; there is no difference.
5. Help me, o warrior lord of Thebes, in my unveiling before the Children of men!
6. Be thou Hadit, my secret centre, my heart & my tongue!
7. Behold! it is revealed by Aiwass the minister of Hoor-paar-kraat.
8. The Khabs is in the Khu, not the Khu in the Khabs.
9. Worship then the Khabs, and behold my light shed over you!
10. Let my servants be few & secret: they shall rule the many & the known.
11. These are fools that men adore; both their Gods & their men are fools.
12. Come forth, o children, under the stars, & take your fill of love!
13. I am above you and in you. My ecstasy is in yours. My joy is to see your joy.

14.   Above, the gemmèd azure is
           The naked splendour of Nuit;
           She bends in ecstasy to kiss
           The secret ardours of Hadit.
           The wingèd globe, the starry blue,
           Are mine, O Ankh-af-na-khonsu!

15.   Now ye shall know that the chosen priest & apostle of infinite space is the prince-priest the Beast; and in his woman called the Scarlet Woman is all power given. They shall gather my children into their fold: they shall bring the glory of the stars into the hearts of men.

16.   For he is ever a sun, and she a moon. But to him is the winged secret flame, and to her the stooping starlight.

17.   But ye are not so chosen.

18.   Burn upon their brows, o splendrous serpent!

19.   O azure-lidded woman, bend upon them!

20.   The key of the rituals is in the secret word which I have given unto him.

21.   With the God & the Adorer I am nothing: they do not see me. They are as upon the earth; I am Heaven, and there is no other God than me, and my lord Hadit.

22.   Now, therefore, I am known to ye by my name Nuit, and to him by a secret name which I will give him when at last he knoweth me. Since I am Infinite Space, and the Infinite Stars thereof, do ye also thus. Bind nothing! Let there be no difference made among you between any one thing & any other thing; for thereby there cometh hurt.

23.   But whoso availeth in this, let him be the chief of all!

24.   I am Nuit, and my word is six and fifty.

25.   Divide, add, multiply, and understand.

26.   Then saith the prophet and slave of the beauteous one: Who am I, and what shall be the sign? So she answered him, bending down, a lambent flame of blue, all-touching, all penetrant, her lovely hands upon the black earth, & her lithe body arched for love, and her soft feet not hurting the little flowers: Thou knowest! And the sign shall be my ecstasy, the consciousness of the continuity of existence, the omnipresence of my body.

27.   Then the priest answered & said unto the Queen of Space, kissing her lovely brows, and the dew of her light bathing his whole body in a sweet-smelling perfume of sweat: O Nuit, continuous one of Heaven, let it be ever thus; that men speak not of Thee as One but as None; and let them speak not of thee at all, since thou art continuous!

28.   None, breathed the light, faint & færy, of the stars, and two.

29.   For I am divided for love's sake, for the chance of union.

30.   This is the creation of the world, that the pain of division is as nothing, and the joy of dissolution all.

31.   For these fools of men and their woes care not thou at all! They feel little; what is, is balanced by weak joys; but ye are my chosen ones.

32.   Obey my prophet! follow out the ordeals of my knowledge! seek me only! Then the joys of my love will redeem ye from all pain. This is so: I swear it

by the vault of my body; by my sacred heart and tongue; by all I can give, by all I desire of ye all.

33. Then the priest fell into a deep trance or swoon, & said unto the Queen of Heaven; Write unto us the ordeals; write unto us the rituals; write unto us the law!

34. But she said: the ordeals I write not: the rituals shall be half known and half concealed: the Law is for all.

35. This that thou writest is the threefold book of Law.

36. My scribe Ankh-af-na-khonsu, the priest of the princes, shall not in one letter change this book; but lest there be folly, he shall comment thereupon by the wisdom of Ra-Hoor-Khu-it.

37. Also the mantras and spells; the obeah and the wanga; the work of the wand and the work of the sword; these he shall learn and teach.

38. He must teach; but he may make severe the ordeals.

39. The word of the Law is Θελημα.

40. Who calls us Thelemites will do no wrong, if he look but close into the word. For there are therein Three Grades, the Hermit, and the Lover, and the man of Earth. Do what thou wilt shall be the whole of the Law.

41. The word of Sin is Restriction. O man! refuse not thy wife, if she will! O lover, if thou wilt, depart! There is no bond that can unite the divided but love: all else is a curse. Accursèd! Accursèd be it to the æons! Hell.

42. Let it be that state of manyhood bound and loathing. So with thy all; thou hast no right but to do thy will.

43. Do that, and no other shall say nay.

44. For pure will, unassuaged of purpose, delivered from the lust of result, is every way perfect.

45. The Perfect and the Perfect are one Perfect and not two; nay, are none!

46. Nothing is a secret key of this law. Sixty-one the Jews call it; I call it eight, eighty, four hundred & eighteen.

47. But they have the half: unite by thine art so that all disappear.

48. My prophet is a fool with his one, one, one; are not they the Ox, and none by the Book?

49. Abrogate are all rituals, all ordeals, all words and signs. Ra-Hoor-Khuit hath taken his seat in the East at the Equinox of the Gods; and let Asar be with Isa, who also are one. But they are not of me. Let Asar be the adorant, Isa the sufferer; Hoor in his secret name and splendour is the Lord initiating.

50. There is a word to say about the Hierophantic task. Behold! there are three ordeals in one, and it may be given in three ways. The gross must pass through fire; let the fine be tried in intellect, and the lofty chosen ones in the highest. Thus ye have star & star, system & system; let not one know well the other!

51. There are four gates to one palace; the floor of that palace is of silver and gold; lapis lazuli & jasper are there; and all rare scents; jasmine & rose, and the emblems of death. Let him enter in turn or at once the four gates; let him stand on the floor of the palace. Will he not sink? Amn. Ho! warrior, if thy servant sink? But there are means and means. Be goodly therefore: dress ye all in fine apparel; eat rich foods and drink sweet wines and wines that foam! Also,

take your fill and will of love as ye will, when, where and with whom ye will! But always unto me.

52. If this be not aright; if ye confound the space-marks, saying: They are one; or saying, They are many; if the ritual be not ever unto me: then expect the direful judgments of Ra Hoor Khuit!

53. This shall regenerate the world, the little world my sister, my heart & my tongue, unto whom I send this kiss. Also, o scribe and prophet, though thou be of the princes, it shall not assuage thee nor absolve thee. But ecstasy be thine and joy of earth: ever To me! To me!

54. Change not as much as the style of a letter; for behold! thou, o prophet, shalt not behold all these mysteries hidden therein.

55. The child of thy bowels, *he* shall behold them.

56. Expect him not from the East, nor from the West; for from no expected house cometh that child. Aum! All words are sacred and all prophets true; save only that they understand a little; solve the first half of the equation, leave the second unattacked. But thou hast all in the clear light, and some, though not all, in the dark.

57. Invoke me under my stars! Love is the law, love under will. Nor let the fools mistake love; for there are love and love. There is the dove, and there is the serpent. Choose ye well! He, my prophet, hath chosen, knowing the law of the fortress, and the great mystery of the House of God. All these old letters of my Book are aright; but j is not the Star. This also is secret: my prophet shall reveal it to the wise.

58. I give unimaginable joys on earth: certainty, not faith, while in life, upon death; peace unutterable, rest, ecstasy; nor do I demand aught in sacrifice.

59. My incense is of resinous woods & gums; and there is no blood therein: because of my hair the trees of Eternity.

60. My number is 11, as all their numbers who are of us. The Five Pointed Star, with a Circle in the Middle, & the circle is Red. My colour is black to the blind, but the blue & gold are seen of the seeing. Also I have a secret glory for them that love me.

61. But to love me is better than all things: if under the night-stars in the desert thou presently burnest mine incense before me, invoking me with a pure heart, and the Serpent flame therein, thou shalt come a little to lie in my bosom. For one kiss wilt thou then be willing to give all; but whoso gives one particle of dust shall lose all in that hour. Ye shall gather goods and store of women and spices; ye shall wear rich jewels; ye shall exceed the nations of the earth in splendour & pride; but always in the love of me, and so shall ye come to my joy. I charge you earnestly to come before me in a single robe, and covered with a rich headdress. I love you! I yearn to you! Pale or purple, veiled or voluptuous, I who am all pleasure and purple, and drunkenness of the inner-most sense, desire you. Put on the wings, and arouse the coiled splendour within you: come unto me!

62. At all my meetings with you shall the priestess say—and her eyes shall burn with desire as she stands bare and rejoicing in my secret temple—To me! To me! calling forth the flame of the hearts of all in her love-chant.

63. Sing the rapturous love-song unto me! Burn to me perfumes! Wear to me jewels! Drink to me, for I love you! I love you!
64. I am the blue-lidded daughter of Sunset; I am the naked brilliance of the voluptuous night-sky.
65. To me! To me!
66. The Manifestation of Nuit is at an end.

II.

1. Nu! the hiding of Hadit.
2. Come! all ye, and learn the secret that hath not yet been revealed. I, Hadit, am the complement of Nu, my bride. I am not extended, and Khabs is the name of my House.
3. In the sphere I am everywhere the centre, as she, the circumference, is nowhere found.
4. Yet she shall be known & I never.
5. Behold! the rituals of the old time are black. Let the evil ones be cast away; let the good ones be purged by the prophet! Then shall this Knowledge go aright.
6. I am the flame that burns in every heart of man, and in the core of every star. I am Life, and the giver of Life, yet therefore is the knowledge of me the knowledge of death.
7. I am the Magician and the Exorcist. I am the axle of the wheel, and the cube in the circle. "Come unto me" is a foolish word: for it is I that go.
8. Who worshipped Heru-pa-kraath have worshipped me; ill, for I am the worshipper.
9. Remember all ye that existence is pure joy; that all the sorrows are but as shadows; they pass & are done; but there is that which remains.
10. O prophet! thou hast ill will to learn this writing.
11. I see thee hate the hand & the pen; but I am stronger.
12. Because of me in Thee which thou knewest not.
13. For why? Because thou wast the knower, and me.
14. Now let there be a veiling of this shrine: now let the light devour men and eat them up with blindness!
15. For I am perfect, being Not; and my number is nine by the fools; but with the just I am eight, and one in eight: Which is vital, for I am none indeed. The Empress and the King are not of me; for there is a further secret.
16. I am The Empress & the Hierophant. Thus eleven, as my bride is eleven.
17. Hear me, ye people of sighing!
    The sorrows of pain and regret
    Are left to the dead and the dying,
    The folk that not know me as yet.
18. These are dead, these fellows; they feel not. We are not for the poor and sad: the lords of the earth are our kinsfolk.
19. Is a God to live in a dog? No! but the highest are of us. They shall rejoice, our chosen: who sorroweth is not of us.
20. Beauty and strength, leaping laughter and delicious languor, force and fire, are of us.

21. We have nothing with the outcast and the unfit: let them die in their misery. For they feel not. Compassion is the vice of kings: stamp down the wretched & the weak: this is the law of the strong: this is our law and the joy of the world. Think not, o king, upon that lie: That Thou Must Die: verily thou shalt not die, but live. Now let it be understood: If the body of the King dissolve, he shall remain in pure ecstasy for ever. Nuit! Hadit! Ra-Hoor-Khuit! The Sun, Strength & Sight, Light; these are for the servants of the Star & the Snake.

22. I am the Snake that giveth Knowledge & Delight and bright glory, and stir the hearts of men with drunkenness. To worship me take wine and strange drugs whereof I will tell my prophet, & be drunk thereof! They shall not harm ye at all. It is a lie, this folly against self. The exposure of innocence is a lie. Be strong, o man! lust, enjoy all things of sense and rapture: fear not that any God shall deny thee for this.

23. I am alone: there is no God where I am.

24. Behold! these be grave mysteries; for there are also of my friends who be hermits. Now think not to find them in the forest or on the mountain; but in beds of purple, caressed by magnificent beasts of women with large limbs, and fire and light in their eyes, and masses of flaming hair about them; there shall ye find them. Ye shall see them at rule, at victorious armies, at all the joy; and there shall be in them a joy a million times greater than this. Beware lest any force another, King against King! Love one another with burning hearts; on the low men trample in the fierce lust of your pride, in the day of your wrath.

25. Ye are against the people, O my chosen!

26. I am the secret Serpent coiled about to spring: in my coiling there is joy. If I lift up my head, I and my Nuit are one. If I droop down mine head, and shoot forth venom, then is rapture of the earth, and I and the earth are one.

27. There is great danger in me; for who doth not understand these runes shall make a great miss. He shall fall down into the pit called Because, and there he shall perish with the dogs of Reason.

28. Now a curse upon Because and his kin!

29. May Because be accursèd for ever!

30. If Will stops and cries Why, invoking Because, then Will stops & does nought.

31. If Power asks why, then is Power weakness.

32. Also reason is a lie; for there is a factor infinite & unknown; & all their words are skew-wise.

33. Enough of Because! Be he damned for a dog!

34. But ye, o my people, rise up & awake!

35. Let the rituals be rightly performed with joy & beauty!

36. There are rituals of the elements and feasts of the times.

37. A feast for the first night of the Prophet and his Bride!

38. A feast for the three days of the writing of the Book of the Law.

39. A feast for Tahuti and the child of the Prophet—secret, O Prophet!

40. A feast for the Supreme Ritual, and a feast for the Equinox of the Gods.

41. A feast for fire and a feast for water; a feast for life and a greater feast for death!

42. A feast every day in your hearts in the joy of my rapture!

43. A feast every night unto Nu, and the pleasure of uttermost delight!

44. Aye! feast! rejoice! there is no dread hereafter. There is the dissolution, and eternal ecstasy in the kisses of Nu.
45. There is death for the dogs.
46. Dost thou fail? Art thou sorry? Is fear in thine heart?
47. Where I am these are not.
48. Pity not the fallen! I never knew them. I am not for them. I console not: I hate the consoled & the consoler.
49. I am unique & conqueror. I am not of the slaves that perish. Be they damned & dead! Amen. (This is of the 4: there is a fifth who is invisible, & therein am I as a babe in an egg.)
50. Blue am I and gold in the light of my bride: but the red gleam is in my eyes; & my spangles are purple & green.
51. Purple beyond purple: it is the light higher than eyesight.
52. There is a veil: that veil is black. It is the veil of the modest woman; it is the veil of sorrow, & the pall of death: this is none of me. Tear down that lying spectre of the centuries: veil not your vices in virtuous words: these vices are my service; ye do well, & I will reward you here and hereafter.
53. Fear not, o prophet, when these words are said, thou shalt not be sorry. Thou art emphatically my chosen; and blessed are the eyes that thou shalt look upon with gladness. But I will hide thee in a mask of sorrow: they that see thee shall fear thou art fallen: but I lift thee up.
54. Nor shall they who cry aloud their folly that thou meanest nought avail; thou shall reveal it: thou availest: they are the slaves of because: They are not of me. The stops as thou wilt; the letters? change them not in style or value!
55. Thou shalt obtain the order & value of the English Alphabet; thou shalt find new symbols to attribute them unto.
56. Begone! ye mockers; even though ye laugh in my honour ye shall laugh not long: then when ye are sad know that I have forsaken you.
57. He that is righteous shall be righteous still; he that is filthy shall be filthy still.
58. Yea! deem not of change: ye shall be as ye are, & not other. Therefore the kings of the earth shall be Kings for ever: the slaves shall serve. There is none that shall be cast down or lifted up: all is ever as it was. Yet there are masked ones my servants: it may be that yonder beggar is a King. A King may choose his garment as he will: there is no certain test: but a beggar cannot hide his poverty.
59. Beware therefore! Love all, lest perchance is a King concealed! Say you so? Fool! If he be a King, thou canst not hurt him.
60. Therefore strike hard & low, and to hell with them, master!
61. There is a light before thine eyes, o prophet, a light undesired, most desirable.
62. I am uplifted in thine heart; and the kisses of the stars rain hard upon thy body.
63. Thou art exhaust in the voluptuous fullness of the inspiration; the expiration is sweeter than death, more rapid and laughterful than a caress of Hell's own worm.
64. Oh! thou art overcome: we are upon thee; our delight is all over thee: hail! hail: prophet of Nu! prophet of Had! prophet of Ra-Hoor-Khu! Now rejoice! now come in our splendour & rapture! Come in our passionate peace, & write sweet words for the Kings!
65. I am the Master: thou art the Holy Chosen One.

66. Write, & find ecstasy in writing! Work, & be our bed in working! Thrill with the joy of life & death! Ah! thy death shall be lovely: whoso seeth it shall be glad. Thy death shall be the seal of the promise of our agelong love. Come! lift up thine heart & rejoice! We are one; we are none.

67. Hold! Hold! Bear up in thy rapture; fall not in swoon of the excellent kisses!

68. Harder! Hold up thyself! Lift thine head! breathe not so deep—die!

69. Ah! Ah! What do I feel? Is the word exhausted?

70. There is help & hope in other spells. Wisdom says: be strong! Then canst thou bear more joy. Be not animal; refine thy rapture! If thou drink, drink by the eight and ninety rules of art: if thou love, exceed by delicacy; and if thou do aught joyous, let there be subtlety therein!

71. But exceed! exceed!

72. Strive ever to more! and if thou art truly mine—and doubt it not, an if thou art ever joyous!—death is the crown of all.

73. Ah! Ah! Death! Death! thou shalt long for death. Death is forbidden, o man, unto thee.

74. The length of thy longing shall be the strength of its glory. He that lives long & desires death much is ever the King among the Kings.

75. Aye! listen to the numbers & the words:

76. 4 6 3 8 A B K 2 4 A L G M O R 3 Y X 24 89 R P S T O V A L. What meaneth this, o prophet? Thou knowest not; nor shalt thou know ever. There cometh one to follow thee: he shall expound it. But remember, o chosen one, to be me; to follow the love of Nu in the star-lit heaven; to look forth upon men, to tell them this glad word.

77. O be thou proud and mighty among men!

78. Lift up thyself! for there is none like unto thee among men or among Gods! Lift up thyself, o my prophet, thy stature shall surpass the stars. They shall worship thy name, foursquare, mystic, wonderful, the number of the man; and the name of thy house 418.

79. The end of the hiding of Hadit; and blessing & worship to the prophet of the lovely Star!

III.

1. Abrahadabra; the reward of Ra Hoor Khut.

2. There is division hither homeward; there is a word not known. Spelling is defunct; all is not aught. Beware! Hold! Raise the spell of Ra-Hoor-Khuit!

3. Now let it be first understood that I am a god of War and of Vengeance. I shall deal hardly with them.

4. Choose ye an island!

5. Fortify it!

6. Dung it about with enginery of war!

7. I will give you a war-engine.

8. With it ye shall smite the peoples; and none shall stand before you.

9. Lurk! Withdraw! Upon them! this is the Law of the Battle of Conquest: thus shall my worship be about my secret house.

10. Get the stélé of revealing itself; set it in thy secret temple—and that temple is already aright disposed—& it shall be your Kiblah for ever. It shall not fade, but miraculous colour shall come back to it day after day. Close it in locked glass for a proof to the world.

11. This shall be your only proof. I forbid argument. Conquer! That is enough. I will make easy to you the abstruction from the ill-ordered house in the Victorious City. Thou shalt thyself convey it with worship, o prophet, though thou likest it not. Thou shalt have danger & trouble. Ra-Hoor-Khu is with thee. Worship me with fire & blood; worship me with swords & with spears. Let the woman be girt with a sword before me: let blood flow to my name. Trample down the Heathen; be upon them, o warrior, I will give you of their flesh to eat!

12. Sacrifice cattle, little and big: after a child.

13. But not now.

14. Ye shall see that hour, o blessèd Beast, and thou the Scarlet Concubine of his desire!

15. Ye shall be sad thereof.

16. Deem not too eagerly to catch the promises; fear not to undergo the curses. Ye, even ye, know not this meaning all.

17. Fear not at all; fear neither men nor Fates, nor gods, nor anything. Money fear not, nor laughter of the folk folly, nor any other power in heaven or upon the earth or under the earth. Nu is your refuge as Hadit your light; and I am the strength, force, vigour, of your arms.

18. Mercy let be off: damn them who pity! Kill and torture; spare not; be upon them!

19. That stélé they shall call the Abomination of Desolation; count well its name, & it shall be to you as 718.

20. Why? Because of the fall of Because, that he is not there again.

21. Set up my image in the East: thou shalt buy thee an image which I will show thee, especial, not unlike the one thou knowest. And it shall be suddenly easy for thee to do this.

22. The other images group around me to support me: let all be worshipped, for they shall cluster to exalt me. I am the visible object of worship; the others are secret; for the Beast & his Bride are they: and for the winners of the Ordeal x. What is this? Thou shalt know.

23. For perfume mix meal & honey & thick leavings of red wine: then oil of Abramelin and olive oil, and afterward soften & smooth down with rich fresh blood.

24. The best blood is of the moon, monthly: then the fresh blood of a child, or dropping from the host of heaven: then of enemies; then of the priest or of the worshippers: last of some beast, no matter what.

25. This burn: of this make cakes & eat unto me. This hath also another use; let it be laid before me, and kept thick with perfumes of your orison: it shall become full of beetles as it were and creeping things sacred unto me.

26. These slay, naming your enemies; & they shall fall before you.

27. Also these shall breed lust & power of lust in you at the eating thereof.

28. Also ye shall be strong in war.
29. Moreover, be they long kept, it is better; for they swell with my force. All before me.
30. My altar is of open brass work: burn thereon in silver or gold!
31. There cometh a rich man from the West who shall pour his gold upon thee.
32. From gold forge steel!
33. Be ready to fly or to smite!
34. But your holy place shall be untouched throughout the centuries: though with fire and sword it be burnt down & shattered, yet an invisible house there standeth, and shall stand until the fall of the Great Equinox; when Hrumachis shall arise and the double-wanded one assume my throne and place. Another prophet shall arise, and bring fresh fever from the skies; another woman shall awake the lust & worship of the Snake; another soul of God and beast shall mingle in the globèd priest; another sacrifice shall stain the tomb; another king shall reign; and blessing no longer be poured To the Hawk-headed mystical Lord!
35. The half of the word of Heru-ra-ha, called Hoor-pa-kraat and Ra-Hoor-Khut.
36. Then said the prophet unto the God:
37. I adore thee in the song—
     I am the Lord of Thebes, and I
        The inspired forth-speaker of Mentu;
     For me unveils the veilèd sky,
        The self-slain Ankh-af-na-khonsu
     Whose words are truth. I invoke, I greet
        Thy presence, O Ra-Hoor-Khuit!

     Unity uttermost showed!
        I adore the might of Thy breath,
     Supreme and terrible God,
        Who makest the gods and death
     To tremble before Thee:—
        I, I adore thee!

     Appear on the throne of Ra!
        Open the ways of the Khu!
     Lighten the ways of the Ka!
        The ways of the Khabs run through
     To stir me or still me!
        Aum! let it fill me!
38. So that thy light is in me; & its red flame is as a sword in my hand to push thy order. There is a secret door that I shall make to establish thy way in all the quarters, (these are the adorations, as thou hast written), as it is said:
     The light is mine; its rays consume
        Me: I have made a secret door
           Into the House of Ra and Tum,
              Of Khephra and of Ahathoor.
           I am thy Theban, O Mentu,
              The prophet Ankh-af-na-khonsu!

> By Bes-na-Maut my breast I beat;
>> By wise Ta-Nech I weave my spell.
> Show thy star-splendour, O Nuit!
>> Bid me within thine House to dwell,
> O wingèd snake of light, Hadit!
>> Abide with me, Ra-Hoor-Khuit!

39. All this and a book to say how thou didst come hither and a reproduction of this ink and paper for ever—for in it is the word secret & not only in the English—and thy comment upon this the Book of the Law shall be printed beautifully in red ink and black upon beautiful paper made by hand; and to each man and woman that thou meetest, were it but to dine or to drink at them, it is the Law to give. Then they shall chance to abide in this bliss or no; it is no odds. Do this quickly!

40. But the work of the comment? That is easy; and Hadit burning in thy heart shall make swift and secure thy pen.

41. Establish at thy Kaaba a clerk-house: all must be done well and with business way.

42. The ordeals thou shalt oversee thyself, save only the blind ones. Refuse none, but thou shalt know & destroy the traitors. I am Ra-Hoor-Khuit; and I am powerful to protect my servant. Success is thy proof: argue not; convert not; talk not overmuch! Them that seek to entrap thee, to overthrow thee, them attack without pity or quarter; & destroy them utterly. Swift as a trodden serpent turn and strike! Be thou yet deadlier than he! Drag down their souls to awful torment: laugh at their fear: spit upon them!

43. Let the Scarlet Woman beware! If pity and compassion and tenderness visit her heart; if she leave my work to toy with old sweetnesses; then shall my vengeance be known. I will slay me her child: I will alienate her heart: I will cast her out from men: as a shrinking and despised harlot shall she crawl through dusk wet streets, and die cold and an-hungered.

44. But let her raise herself in pride! Let her follow me in my way! Let her work the work of wickedness! Let her kill her heart! Let her be loud and adulterous! Let her be covered with jewels, and rich garments, and let her be shameless before all men!

45. Then will I lift her to pinnacles of power: then will I breed from her a child mightier than all the kings of the earth. I will fill her with joy: with my force shall she see & strike at the worship of Nu: she shall achieve Hadit.

46. I am the warrior Lord of the Forties: the Eighties cower before me, & are abased. I will bring you to victory & joy: I will be at your arms in battle & ye shall delight to slay. Success is your proof; courage is your armour; go on, go on, in my strength; & ye shall turn not back for any!

47. This book shall be translated into all tongues: but always with the original in the writing of the Beast; for in the chance shape of the letters and their position to one another: in these are mysteries that no Beast shall divine. Let him not seek to try: but one cometh after him, whence I say not, who shall discover the Key of it all. Then this line drawn is a key: then this circle squared in its failure is a key also. And Abrahadabra. It shall be his child & that strangely. Let him not seek after this; for thereby alone can he fall from it.

48. Now this mystery of the letters is done, and I want to go on to the holier place.
49. I am in a secret fourfold word, the blasphemy against all gods of men.
50. Curse them! Curse them! Curse them!
51. With my Hawk's head I peck at the eyes of Jesus as he hangs upon the cross.
52. I flap my wings in the face of Mohammed & blind him.
53. With my claws I tear out the flesh of the Indian and the Buddhist, Mongol and Din.
54. Bahlasti! Ompehda! I spit on your crapulous creeds.
55. Let Mary inviolate be torn upon wheels: for her sake let all chaste women be utterly despised among you!
56. Also for beauty's sake and love's!
57. Despise also all cowards; professional soldiers who dare not fight, but play; all fools despise!
58. But the keen and the proud, the royal and the lofty; ye are brothers!
59. As brothers fight ye!
60. There is no law beyond Do what thou wilt.
61. There is an end of the word of the God enthroned in Ra's seat, lightening the girders of the soul.
62. To Me do ye reverence! to me come ye through tribulation of ordeal, which is bliss.
63. The fool readeth this Book of the Law, and its comment; & he understandeth it not.
64. Let him come through the first ordeal, & it will be to him as silver.
65. Through the second, gold.
66. Through the third, stones of precious water.
67. Through the fourth, ultimate sparks of the intimate fire.
68. Yet to all it shall seem beautiful. Its enemies who say not so, are mere liars.
69. There is success.
70. I am the Hawk-Headed Lord of Silence & of Strength; my nemyss shrouds the night-blue sky.
71. Hail! ye twin warriors about the pillars of the world! for your time is nigh at hand.
72. I am the Lord of the Double Wand of Power; the wand of the Force of Coph Nia—but my left hand is empty, for I have crushed an Universe; & nought remains.
73. Paste the sheets from right to left and from top to bottom: then behold!
74. There is a splendour in my name hidden and glorious, as the sun of midnight is ever the son.
75. The ending of the words is the Word Abrahadabra.

The Book of the Law is Written
and Concealed.
Aum. Ha.

Chapter 14

Rudyard Kipling

A TREE SONG

■ from **PUCK OF POOK'S HILL**, London, 1906

ALTHOUGH MOST CONTEMPORARY PAGANS would not share his authoritarian and emotionally imperialistic views (see Seymour-Smith, 1989), a verse of one of Rudyard Kipling's poems, "A Tree Song," also known as "Oak and Ash and Thorn," has found its way into many Beltane (May Day) ritual celebrations. The poem comes from his 1906 collection of stories, *Puck of Pook's Hill*, written ostensibly for his children Elsie and John when the family lived in Sussex. The tales appeared to be for children to read, Kipling himself later commented, "before people realised that they were meant for grown-ups." Featuring the fairy Puck, the last "Old Thing" in England (which is "a bad country for Gods"), an improbably wise countryman, Hobden, and two children like Kipling's own, the stories create a myth of England's history from its days as Roman province to more recent centuries. A second book, *Rewards and Fairies*, continues the tales.

Kipling's idealized countryside, in which the aristocrats were (usually) generous and the peasants were (usually) wise and both were sensitive to the energies of wood and brook, appealed to the creators of the Pagan revival, as did such lines as "Oh, do not tell the Priest our Plight, / Or he would call it a sin;" with their suggestion that country customs did indeed carry on a pre-Christian Paganism. Consequently, all or parts of a "A Tree Song" have been incorporated into more recent ritual texts (e.g. StoneCreed Grove's website), and it is often the case that Kipling's authorship has been forgotten and the poem regarded as an authentic relic of pre-Christian religion. For example, the verse appears as part of the Rudemas (May Eve) Sabbat ritual in one version of the *Book of Shadows* published in the United States in 1971 but of English origin (Lady Sheba, 1971).

Chas S. Clifton

References

Lady Sheba (1971) *The Book of Shadows*. St. Paul, Minnesota: Llewellyn Publications.

Seymour-Smith, Martin (1989) *Rudyard Kipling: A Biography*. New York: St. Martin's.

StoneCreed Grove, ADF. "Oak & Ash & Thorn," Druid Beltaine Mayday Songbook. http://www.stonecreed.org/songbook/beltaine/oak-and-ash.html (accessed 14 January 2003).

Of all the trees that grow so fair,
Old England to adorn,
Greater are none beneath the Sun,
Than Oak and Ash and Thorn.
Sing Oak and Ash and Thorn, good Sirs
(All of a Midsummer morn)!
Surely we sing no little thing,
In Oak and Ash and Thorn!

Oak of the Clay lived many a day,
Or ever Aeneas began;
Ash of the Loam was a lady at home,
When Brut was an outlaw man;
Thorn of the Down saw New Troy Town
(From which was London born);
Witness hereby the ancientry
Of Oak and Ash and Thorn!

Yew that is old in churchyard mould,
He breedeth a mighty bow;
Alder for shoes do wise men choose,
And beech for cups also.
But when ye have killed, and your bowl is spilled,
And your shoes are clean outworn,
Back ye must speed for all that ye need,
To Oak and Ash and Thorn!

Ellum she hateth mankind, and waiteth
Till every gust be laid,
To drop a limb on the head of him
That anyway trusts her shade:
But whether a lad be sober or sad,
Or mellow with ale from the horn,
He will take no wrong when he lieth along
'Neath Oak and Ash and Thorn!

Oh, do not tell the Priest our plight,
Or he would call it a sin;

But — we have been out in the woods all night,
A-conjuring Summer in!
And we bring you news by word of mouth —
Good news for cattle and corn —
Now is the Sun come up from the South,
With Oak and Ash and Thorn!

Sing Oak and Ash and Thorn, good Sirs
(All of a Midsummer morn)!
England shall bide till Judgement Tide,
By Oak and Ash and Thorn!

Chapter 15

Kenneth Grahame

THE PIPER AT THE GATES OF DAWN

■ from **THE WIND IN THE WILLOWS**, London, 1908, 1994, pp. 115–30

A S MANY BRITISH HISTORIANS have noted, by the end of the nine-teenth century, England in particular had shifted from being a largely rural society to a largely urban one. Several notable Edwardian writers looked back to an "eternal," unmodernized countryside, portrayed as linked to pre-Christian times and containing the very soul of the nation—a sentiment that would, fifty years later, find its way into Wicca. Like Rudyard Kipling, Arthur Machen, and Saki (H.H. Munro) at about the same time, Kenneth Grahame personified Nature in the form of the horned god Pan, who intervenes at times of need in his fictional society of clothes-wearing, boat-rowing, small animals who fill the pages of his 1908 book *The Wind in the Willows*. They are small animals, yes, but with more emotional range than A.A. Milne's Winnie the Pooh and his companions, though they fill certain roles: Toad, the vainglorious *nouveau-riche* country gentleman, Rat, the adept boatman, Mole, the good fellow and spiritual pilgrim, and Badger, not a predator, but a sort of village constable. The book's animals form a sort of peaceful village society under the noses of human society, yet they too have their irruptions of the sacred into mundane life, and 'The Piper at the Gates of Dawn' is one of these.

For further discussion, see Kuznets (1987) and Wullschläger (1995).

Chas S. Clifton

References

Kuznets, Lois R. (1987) *Kenneth Grahame*. Boston: Twayne.

Wullschläger, Jackie (1995) *Inventing Wonderland: The Lives and Fantasies of Lewis Carroll, Edward Lear, J.M. Barrie, Kenneth Grahame, and A.A. Milne*. New York: Free Press.

THE WILLOW-WREN WAS twittering his thin little song, hidden himself
in the dark selvedge of the river bank. Though it was past ten o'clock at
night, the sky still clung to and retained some lingering skirts of light from the
departed day; and the sullen heats of the torrid afternoon broke up and rolled away
at the dispersing touch of the cool fingers of the short midsummer night. Mole lay
stretched on the bank, still panting from the stress of the fierce day that had been
cloudless from dawn to late sunset, and waited for his friend to return. He had
been on the river with some companions, leaving the Water Rat free to keep an
engagement of long standing with Otter; and he had come back to find the house
dark and deserted, and no sign of Rat, who was doubtless keeping it up late with his
old comrade. It was still too hot to think of staying indoors, so he lay on some cool
dock-leaves, and thought over the past day and its doings, and how very good they
all had been.

The Rat's light footfall was presently heard approaching over the parched grass.
'O, the blessed coolness!' he said, and sat down, gazing thoughtfully into the river,
silent and preoccupied.

'You stayed to supper, of course?' said the Mole presently.

'Simply had to,' said the Rat. 'They wouldn't hear of my going before. You
know how kind they always are. And they made things as jolly for me as ever they
could, right up to the moment I left. But I felt a brute all the time, as it was clear
to me they were very unhappy, though they tried to hide it. Mole, I'm afraid they're
in trouble. Little Portly is missing again; and you know what a lot his father thinks
of him, though he never says much about it.'

'What, that child?' said the Mole lightly. 'Well, suppose he is; why worry about
it? He's always straying off and getting lost, and turning up again; he's so adventurous. But no harm ever happens to him. Everybody hereabouts knows him and
likes him, just as they do old Otter, and you may be sure some animal or other will
come across him and bring him back again all right. Why, we've found him
ourselves, miles from home, and quite self-possessed and cheerful!'

'Yes; but this time it's more serious,' said the Rat gravely. 'He's been missing
for some days now, and the Otters have hunted everywhere, high and low, without
finding the slightest trace. And they've asked every animal, too, for miles around,
and no one knows anything about him. Otter's evidently more anxious than he'll
admit. I got out of him that young Portly hasn't learnt to swim very well yet, and
I can see he's thinking of the weir. There's a lot of water coming down still, considering the time of the year, and the place always had a fascination for the child. And
then there are – well, traps and things – *you* know. Otter's not the fellow to be
nervous about any son of his before it's time. And now he is nervous. When I left,
he came out with me – said he wanted some air, and talked about stretching his legs.
But I could see it wasn't that, so I drew him out and pumped him, and got it
all from him at last. He was going to spend the night watching by the ford. You
know the place where the old ford used to be, in bygone days before they built
the bridge?'

'I know it well,' said the Mole. 'But why should Otter choose to watch there?'

'Well, it seems that it was there he gave Portly his first swimming lesson,'
continued the Rat. 'From that shallow, gravelly spit near the bank. And it was there

he used to teach him fishing, and there young Portly caught his first fish, of which he was so very proud. The child loved the spot, and Otter thinks that if he came wandering back from wherever he is – if he *is* anywhere by this time, poor little chap – he might make for the ford he was so fond of; or if he came across it he'd remember it well, and stop there and play, perhaps. So Otter goes there every night and watches – on the chance, you know, just on the chance!'

They were silent for a time, both thinking of the same thing – the lonely, heart-sore animal, crouched by the ford, watching and waiting, the long night through – on the chance.

'Well, well,' said the Rat presently, 'I suppose we ought to be thinking about turning in.' But he never offered to move.

'Rat,' said the Mole, 'I simply can't go and turn in, and go to sleep, and *do* nothing, even though there doesn't seem to be anything to be done. We'll get the boat out, and paddle upstream. The moon will be up in an hour or so, and then we will search as well as we can – anyhow, it will be better than going to bed and doing *nothing.*'

'Just what I was thinking myself,' said the Rat. 'It's not the sort of night for bed anyhow; and daybreak is not so very far off, and then we may pick up some news of him from early risers as we go along.'

They got the boat out, and the Rat took the sculls, paddling with caution. Out in midstream there was a clear, narrow track that faintly reflected the sky; but wherever shadows fell on the water from bank, bush, or tree, they were as solid to all appearance as the banks themselves, and the Mole had to steer with judgement accordingly. Dark and deserted as it was, the night was full of small noises, song and chatter and rustling, telling of the busy little population who were up and about, plying their trades and vocations through the night till sunshine should fall on them at last and send them off to their well-earned repose. The water's own noises, too, were more apparent than by day, its gurglings and 'cloops' more unexpected and near at hand; and constantly they started at what seemed a sudden clear call from an actual articulate voice.

The line of the horizon was clear and hard against the sky, and in one particular quarter it showed black against a silvery climbing phosphorescence that grew and grew. At last, over the rim of the waiting earth the moon lifted with slow majesty till it swung clear of the horizon and rode off, free of moorings; and once more they began to see surfaces – meadows widespread, and quiet gardens, and the river itself from bank to bank, all softly disclosed, all washed clean of mystery and terror, all radiant again as by day, but with a difference that was tremendous. Their old haunts greeted them again in other raiment, as if they had slipped away and put on this pure new apparel and come quietly back, smiling as they shyly waited to see if they would be recognized again under it.

Fastening their boat to a willow, the friends landed in this silent, silver kingdom, and patiently explored the hedges, the hollow trees, the runnels and their little culverts, the ditches and dry water-ways. Embarking again and crossing over, they worked their way up the stream in this manner, while the moon, serene and detached in a cloudless sky, did what she could; though so far off, to help them in their quest; till her hour came and she sank earthwards reluctantly, and left them, and mystery once more held field and river.

Then a change began slowly to declare itself. The horizon became clearer, field and tree came more into sight, and somehow with a different look; the mystery began to drop away from them. A bird piped suddenly, and was still; and a light breeze sprang up and set the reeds and bulrushes rustling. Rat, who was in the stern of the boat, while Mole sculled, sat up suddenly and listened with a passionate intentness. Mole, who with gentle strokes was just keeping the boat moving while he scanned the banks with care, looked at him with curiosity.

'It's gone!' sighed the Rat, sinking back in his seat again. 'So beautiful and strange and new! Since it was to end so soon, I almost wish I had never heard it. For it has roused a longing in me that is pain, and nothing seems worth while but just to hear that sound once more and go on listening to it for ever. No! There it is again!' he cried, alert once more. Entranced, he was silent for a long space, spellbound.

'Now it passes on and I begin to lose it,' he said presently. 'O, Mole! the beauty of it! The merry bubble and joy, the thin, clear happy call of the distant piping! Such music I never dreamed of, and the call in it is stronger even than the music is sweet! Row on, Mole, row! For the music and the call must be for us.'

The Mole, greatly wondering, obeyed. 'I hear nothing myself,' he said, 'but the wind playing in the reeds and rushes and osiers.'

The Rat never answered, if indeed he heard. Rapt, transported, trembling, he was possessed in all his senses by this new divine thing that caught up his helpless soul and swung and dandled it, a powerless but happy infant in a strong sustaining grasp.

In silence Mole rowed steadily, and soon they came to a point where the river divided, a long backwater branching off to one side. With a slight movement of his head Rat, who had long dropped the rudder-lines, directed the rower to take the backwater. The creeping tide of light gained and gained, and now they could see the colour of the flowers that gemmed the water's edge.

'Clearer and nearer still,' cried the Rat joyously. 'Now you must surely hear it! Ah – at last – I see you do!'

Breathless and transfixed the Mole stopped rowing as the liquid run of that glad piping broke on him like a wave, caught him up, and possessed him utterly. He saw the tears on his comrade's cheeks, and bowed his head and understood. For a space they hung there, brushed by the purple loosestrife that fringed the bank; then the clear imperious summons that marched hand-in-hand with the intoxicating melody imposed its will on Mole, and mechanically he bent to his oars again. And the light grew steadily stronger, but no birds sang as they were wont to do at the approach of dawn; and but for the heavenly music all was marvellously still.

On either side of them, as they glided onwards, the rich meadow-grass seemed that morning of a freshness and a greenness unsurpassable. Never had they noticed the roses so vivid, the willow-herb so riotous, the meadow-sweet so odorous and pervading. Then the murmur of the approaching weir began to hold the air, and they felt a consciousness that they were nearing the end, whatever it might be, that surely awaited their expedition.

A wide half-circle of foam and glinting lights and shining shoulders of green water, the great weir closed the backwater from bank to bank, troubled all the quiet surface with twirling eddies and floating foam-streaks, and deadened all other sounds with its solemn and soothing rumble. In midmost of the stream, embraced in the weir's shimmering arm-spread, a small island lay anchored, fringed close with willow and silver birch and alder. Reserved, shy, but full of significance, it hid whatever it might hold behind a veil, keeping it till the hour should come, and, with the hour, those who were called and chosen.

Slowly, but with no doubt or hesitation whatever, and in something of a solemn expectancy, the two animals passed through the broken, tumultuous water and moored their boat at the flowery margin of the island. In silence they landed, and pushed through the blossom and scented herbage and undergrowth that led up to the level ground, till they stood on a little lawn of a marvellous green, set round with Nature's own orchard-trees – crab-apple, wild cherry, and sloe.

'This is the place of my song-dream, the place the music played to me,' whispered the Rat, as if in a trance. 'Here, in this holy place, here if anywhere, surely we shall find Him!'

Then suddenly the Mole felt a great Awe fall upon him, an awe that turned his muscles to water, bowed his head, and rooted his feet to the ground. It was no panic terror – indeed he felt wonderfully at peace and happy – but it was an awe that smote and held him and, without seeing, he knew it could only mean that some august Presence was very, very near. With difficulty he turned to look for his friend, and saw him at his side cowed, stricken, and trembling violently. And still there was utter silence in the populous bird-haunted branches around them; and still the light grew and grew.

Perhaps he would never have dared to raise his eyes, but that, though the piping was now hushed, the call and the summons seemed still dominant and imperious. He might not refuse, were Death himself waiting to strike him instantly, once he had looked with mortal eye on things rightly kept hidden. Trembling he obeyed, and raised his humble head; and then, in that utter clearness of the imminent dawn, while Nature, flushed with fullness of incredible colour, seemed to hold her breath for the event, he looked in the very eyes of the Friend and Helper; saw the backward sweep of the curved horns, gleaming in the growing daylight; saw the stern, hooked nose between the kindly eyes that were looking down on them humorously, while the bearded mouth broke into a half-smile at the corners; saw the rippling muscles on the arm that lay across the broad chest, the long supple hand still holding the pan-pipes only just fallen away from the parted lips; saw the splendid curves of the shaggy limbs disposed in majestic ease on the sward; saw, last of all, nestling between his very hooves, sleeping soundly in entire peace and contentment, the little, round, podgy, childish form of the baby otter. All this he saw, for one moment breathless and intense, vivid on the morning sky; and still, as he looked, he lived; and still, as he lived, he wondered.

'Rat!' he found breath to whisper, shaking. 'Are you afraid?'

'Afraid?' murmured the Rat, his eyes shining with unutterable love, 'Afraid! Of *Him*? O, never, never! And yet – and yet – O, Mole, I am afraid!'

Then the two animals, crouching to the earth, bowed their heads and did worship.

Sudden and magnificent, the sun's broad golden disc showed itself over the horizon facing them; and the first rays, shooting across the level water-meadows, took the animals full in the eyes and dazzled them. When they were able to look once more, the Vision had vanished, and the air was full of the carol of birds that hailed the dawn.

As they stared blankly, in dumb misery deepening as they slowly realized all they had seen and all they had lost, a capricious little breeze, dancing up from the surface of the water, tossed aspens, shook the dewy roses, and blew lightly and caressingly in their faces, and with its soft touch came instant oblivion. For this is the last best gift that the kindly, demigod is careful to bestow on those to whom he has revealed himself in their helping: the gift of forgetfulness. Lest the awful remembrance should remain and grow, and overshadow mirth and pleasure, and the great haunting memory should spoil all the after-lives of little animals helped out of difficulties, in order that they should be happy and lighthearted as before.

Mole rubbed his eyes and stared at Rat, who was looking about him in a puzzled sort of way. 'I beg your pardon; what did you say, Rat?' he asked.

'I think I was only remarking,' said Rat slowly, 'that this was the right sort of place, and that here, if anywhere, we should find him. And look! Why, there he is, the little fellow!' And with a cry of delight he ran towards the slumbering Portly.

But Mole stood still a moment, held in thought. As one wakened suddenly from a beautiful dream, who struggles to recall it, and can recapture nothing but a dim sense of the beauty of it, the beauty! Till that, too, fades away in its turn, and the dreamer bitterly accepts the hard, cold waking and all its penalties; so Mole, after struggling with his memory for a brief space, shook his head sadly and followed the Rat.

Portly woke up with a joyous squeak, and wriggled with pleasure at the sight of his father's friends, who had played with him so often in past days. In a moment; however, his face grew blank, and he fell to hunting round in a circle with pleading whine. As a child that has fallen happily asleep in its nurse's arms, and wakes to find itself alone and laid in a strange place, and searches corners and cupboards, and runs from room to room, despair growing silently in its heart, even so Portly searched the island and searched, dogged and unwearying, till at last the black moment came for giving it up, and sitting down and crying bitterly.

The Mole ran quickly to comfort the little animal; but Rat, lingering, looked long and doubtfully at certain hoof-marks deep in the sward.

'Some – great – animal – has been here,' he murmured slowly and thoughtfully; and stood musing, musing; his mind strangely stirred.

'Come along, Rat!' called the Mole. 'Think of poor Otter, waiting up there by the ford!'

Portly had soon been comforted by the promise of a treat – a jaunt on the river in Mr Rat's real boat; and the two animals conducted him to the water's side, placed him securely between them in the bottom of the boat, and paddled off down the backwater. The sun was fully up by now, and hot on them, birds sang lustily and without restraint, and flowers smiled and nodded from either bank, but somehow – so thought the animals – with less of richness and blaze of colour than they seemed to remember seeing quite recently somewhere – they wondered where.

The main river reached again, they turned the boat's head upstream, towards the point where they knew their friend was keeping his lonely vigil. As they drew near the familiar ford, the Mole took the boat in to the bank, and they lifted Portly out and set him on his legs on the towpath, gave him his marching orders and a friendly farewell pat on the back, and shoved out into midstream. They watched the little animal as he waddled along the path contentedly and with importance; watched him till they saw his muzzle suddenly lift and his waddle break into a clumsy amble as he quickened his pace with shrill whines and wriggles of recognition. Looking up the river, they could see Otter start up, tense and rigid, from out of the shallows where he crouched in dumb patience, and could hear his amazed and joyous bark as he bounded up through the osiers on to the path. Then the Mole, with a strong pull on one oar, swung the boat round and let the full stream bear them down again whither it would, their quest now happily ended.

'I feel strangely tired, Rat,' said the Mole, leaning wearily over his oars as the boat drifted. 'It's being up all night, you'll say, perhaps; but that's nothing. We do as much half the nights of the week, at this time of the year. No; I feel as if I had been through something very exciting and rather terrible, and it was just over; and yet nothing particular has happened.'

'Or something very surprising and splendid and beautiful,' murmured the Rat, leaning back and closing his eyes. 'I feel just as you do, Mole; simply dead tired, though not body-tired. It's lucky we've got the stream with us, to take us home. Isn't it jolly to feel the sun again, soaking into one's bones! And hark to the wind playing in the reeds!'

'It's like music – far-away music,' said the Mole, nodding drowsily.

'So I was thinking,' murmured the Rat, dreamful and languid. 'Dance-music – the lilting sort that runs on without a stop – but with words in it, too – it passes into words and out of them again – I catch them at intervals – then it is dance-music once more, and then nothing but the reeds' soft thin whispering.'

'You hear better than I,' said the Mole sadly. 'I cannot catch the words.'

'Let me try and give you them,' said the Rat softly, his eyes still closed. 'Now it is turning into words again – faint but clear – *Lest the awe should dwell – And turn your frolic to fret – You shall look on my power at the helping hour – But then you shall forget!* Now the reeds take it up – *forget, forget*, they sigh, and it dies away in a rustle and a whisper. Then the voice returns –

'*Lest limbs be reddened and rent – I spring the trap that is set – As I loose the snare you may glimpse me there – For surely you shall forget!* Row nearer, Mole, nearer to the reeds! It is hard to catch, and grows each minute fainter.

'*Helper and healer, I cheer – Small waifs in the woodland wet – Strays I find in it, wounds I bind in it – Bidding them all forget!* Nearer, Mole, nearer! No, it is no good; the song has died away into reed-talk.'

'But what do the words mean?' asked the wondering Mole.

'That I do not know,' said the Rat simply. 'I passed them on to you as they reached me. Ah! now they return again, and this time full and clear! This time, at last, it is the real, the unmistakable thing, simple – passionate – perfect –'

'Well, let's have it, then,' said the Mole, after he had waited patiently for a few minutes, half dozing in the hot sun.

But no answer came: He looked, and understood the silence. With a smile of much happiness on his face, and something of a listening look still lingering there, the weary Rat was fast asleep.

Chapter 16

Margaret Murray

WITCHCRAFT

■ first published in **ENCYCLOPEDIA BRITANNICA**, vol. 23 (1929),
pp. 686–8

M ARGARET MURRAY DID NOT set out to be an expert on medieval
witchcraft. Born in 1863, she was a true pioneer, both as a female scholar
and as an Egyptologist, her chosen field of study. The outbreak of World War I,
however, forced her to leave Egypt and return to England, where, according to her
autobiography, an acquaintance suggested to her that the victims of the Renaissance
and Early Modern witch trials were members of a surviving Pagan religion. She
pursued the idea, and in 1921 her book *The Witch Cult in Western Europe* set out
the idea of a surviving Pagan fertility religion, complete with underground organization and the tacit protection of the Plantagenet dynasty. She supported this thesis
with evidence from the witch-trial records; later scholars, such as Elliot Rose
(1962), accused her of selective quotation and of ignoring evidence that did not fit
her thesis.

Her second, more popular book, *The God of the Witches*, published in 1933,
asserted that the Horned God (Pan, Cernunnos, etc.) was the universal deity of
witches in the Middle East and Europe. But it was on the strength of *The Witch
Cult* that Murray was asked to write a new 'Witchcraft' entry for the *Encyclopedia
Britannica*'s 1929 edition. Here she not only asserted her thesis about the universal
"Old Religion," but she also attempted to link "witch" etymologically with "to
know," a connection which, while popular with contemporary witches (as in "Craft
of the Wise"), is not generally supported by scholars.

Most of the elements of the 1950s' Wiccan revival are here: the division of the
year into holidays called "sabbaths" (actually a medieval slur against Jews), the
coven of thirteen, and the idea that the Old Religion persisted under the nose of
Christian authorities. Consequently, it is not surprising that when Gerald Gardner,
chief figure of 1950s' revived Witchcraft, wrote his own *Witchcraft Today* (1954),

that Murray was pleased to write its introduction, in which she praises "Dr" Gardner for finding contemporary evidence of her theories in the form of a purported actual coven of the Old Religion.

For further discussion, see Hutton (1999).

Chas S. Clifton

References

Gardner, Gerald ([1954] 1973) *Witchcraft Today*. Secaucus, NJ: Citadel.

Hutton, Ronald (1999) *The Triumph of the Moon: A History of Modern Pagan Witchcraft*. Oxford: Oxford University Press.

Murray, Margaret ([1921] 1962) *The Witch Cult in Western Europe*. Oxford: Clarendon Press.

Murray, Margaret ([1933] 1970) *The God of the Witches*. London: Oxford University Press.

Rose, Elliot (1962) *A Razor for a Goat*. Toronto: University of Toronto Press.

WITCHCRAFT. THE ACTUAL MEANING of this word appears to be the art or craft of the wise, as the word "witch" is allied with "wit," *to know*. From about the 15th century the word has been almost exclusively applied to workers of magic, whether male or female. Magicians and sorcerers are known in all parts of the world; among savage communities they are usually credited with supernatural powers by their fellow-tribesmen (*see* MAGIC). Divination (*q.v.*) or foretelling the future is one of the commonest forms of witchcraft; when this is done in the name of the deity of one of the established religions it is called prophecy; when, however, the divination is in the name of a pagan god it is mere witchcraft. This distinction is very clear in the account of the contest between Moses and Pharaoh's magicians as given in Exodus; but in the demotic story, which appears to give the Egyptian version of the incident, the wise priest of Egypt defeats the miserable foreign sorcerer whom he had saved from the water when a child.

Mediaeval Witches.—In England the legal definition of a witch is, according to Lord Coke, "a person who hath conference with the Devil to consult with him or to do some act."

The word "devil" (*q.v.*) is a diminutive from the root "div," from which we also get the word "divine." It merely means "little god." It is a well-known fact that when a new religion is established in any country, the god or gods of the old religion becomes the devil of the new.

When examining the records of the mediaeval witches, we are dealing with the remains of a pagan religion which survived, in England at least, till the 18th century, 1,200 years after the introduction of Christianity. The practices of this ancient faith can be found in France at the present day, though with the name of the deity changed; and in Italy *la vecchia religione* still numbers many followers in spite of the efforts of the Christian Church.

The number of the witches put to death by the inquisitors and other persecutors in the 16th and 17th centuries is a proof of the obstinate paganism of Europe. Whole villages followed the beliefs of their ancestors; and in many cases the priests, drawn from the peasant class, were only outwardly Christian and carried on the ancient rites; even the bishops and other high ecclesiastics took part. As civilization increased and Christianity became more firmly rooted, the old religion retreated to the less frequented parts of the country and was practised by the more ignorant members of the community. This is very noticeable in the innumerable trials of the 15th to the 18th centuries.

The Witch-cult—The religion consisted of a belief in a god incarnate in a human being or an animal, and thus resembled in many ways the religions of numerous primitive peoples of the present day. This god, who was always called the Devil by the Christian recorders of the trials, appeared to his worshippers disguised in various animal forms or dressed inconspicuously in black. The earliest form of the animal disguise is the figure of the man clothed in a stag's skin with antlers on his head, which is among the palaeolithic paintings in a cave in Ariège in southern France. Another early example is carved on a slate palette of the prehistoric period of Egypt; in this case the man is disguised as a jackal. The goat disguise is not found in Great Britain though common in France and Germany, where it is probably the survival of the god Cernunnos. In the British Isles the usual forms were the bull, the dog and the cat.

The rites with which this god was worshipped are known to all students of primitive or savage religions, ancient and modern. The sacred dances, the feasts, the chants in honour of the god, the liturgical ritual, and above all the ceremonies to promote fertility, occurred at public assemblies as now in the islands of the Pacific or in Africa. The fertility rites attracted the special attention of the recorders of the legal trials. But to the followers of the old god these rites were as holy as the sacred marriage was to the ancient Greeks; to them, as to the Greeks, it was the outward and visible sign of the fertility of crops and herds which should bring comfort and wealth and life itself.

The assemblies or "Sabbaths" took place four times a year; on Feb. 2 (Candlemas), May-eve (known later as Roodmas), Aug. 1 (Lammas), and November-eve (All Hallow E'en). To these joyous meetings came all the worshippers, from far and near, to the number of many hundreds, old and young, men, women and children, till the scene was like a great fair with dancing and singing and feasting. The celebrations began in the evening, lasted all night, and ended at dawn. These were the great Sabbaths, and the dates show that the year was divided at May and November. This division shows that the religion dates back to a primitive period, probably before the introduction of agriculture though after the domestication of animals, for the festivals emphasize the seasons of the breeding of animals. There were, however, smaller meetings (known in France as "*esbats*"), which took place weekly or at short irregular intervals. To these came the principal members of the cult, who held a position analogous to the priesthood. There were in each district a band of such persons, in number 13, *i.e.*, a chief or "devil" and 12 members. This band was known as a "Coven." They celebrated the religious rites, they practised as healers under the leadership and instruction of their divine master, and were the consultants in all cases where "witchcraft" was required. The earliest record of a Coven is in the *Handlyng Synne*, a work of the early 14th century, in which the (Christian) priest's daughter and 12 "fools" danced in the churchyard as a *coueyne*. The next record is in the 15th century in the trial of Gilles de Rais, where it is apparent that he and his associates were 13 in number in the practice of their rites. In the later trials the word Coven is continually used, and the number in a Coven is always 13.

One of the most impressive and important rites was the sacrifice of the god, which took place at intervals of seven or nine years. The accounts suggest that the sacrifice was by fire (for similar sacrifices *see* Frazer's *Golden Bough*).

The Familiars.—There are two kinds of familiars, the divining familiar and the domestic familiar. The divining familiar is common to the whole of Europe and is found in all records of the trials. In ancient Rome divination by animals, especially by birds, was known as "Augury" (*q.v.*), and was considered a legitimate means of learning the future, but when it was practised by "witches" in the 16th and 17th centuries their persecutors claimed that they were inspired by the Devil. As a rule the witches were instructed by their chief in the method of divining by animals, and he usually appointed the class of animal which each witch was to use. Thus Agnes Sampson of North Berwick divined by dogs, so also did Elizabeth Style in Somerset; John Walsh of Netherberry in Dorset had "a gray blackish culver," and Alexander Hamilton in Lothian divined by a "corbie" or a cat. In France the familiar was always a toad, which was consulted before going on a journey or undertaking any enterprise.

Spell, and Charms (*q.v.*).—Forms of words with manual gestures are used in all countries and in all periods to produce results which cannot be obtained by physical means. They may be used for good or evil purposes, for the benefit of the user or for the benefit of someone else. A good harvest, a good catch of fish, a favourable wind for a ship, victory over an enemy, could all be obtained by formulae of words addressed to the appropriate power. But as the power was always incomprehensible, not to say freakish, it was necessary that it should be approached by those who knew the right methods. Sacrifice (*q.v.*) in the temples of the ancient civilization was among the means to propitiate the god and render him favourable to the petitions of his worshippers. When, however, there was more than one god, it is obvious that if a prayer were ineffectual in one temple nothing could be easier than to petition another deity.

Among the ritual methods to destroy an enemy one of the most ancient as well as the most dramatic was the making of an image, generally in wax, to represent the enemy, and gradually destroying it. The earliest record of this charm is in the trial of some women and officers of the harem of Rameses III. in Egypt, about 1100 B.C. They made wax images of the Pharaoh with magical incantations, but unfortunately the record gives only the outline of the trial without details.

Transformation into Animals (*see* LYCANTHROPY).—The belief that certain persons can transform themselves into animals is common to all parts of the world. The power belongs to the *shaman* or priest. A wound inflicted on a human being when in animal shape is believed to be visible when the person resumes his human form. The method of transformation was by putting on the skin of the animal, as did Sigmund the Volsung when he became a wolf. This being the case, it is obvious that the wounds received by the transformed person must certainly have remained when he returned to his proper shape.

The Suppression of Witchcraft.—In comparing the witches and witch-cult of the middle ages with the rites and beliefs of pagan religions, whether ancient or modern, it becomes abundantly clear that in Europe traces of the ancient heathenism survived the adoption of Christianity. It was only when the new religion had gained sufficient strength that it ventured to try conclusions with the old. Backed by the civil law, it overcame the old religion, not only by persuasion but by the use of force, just as it destroyed the ancient religion of Egypt and in later times the religion of the Aztecs. That the old religion was not an ordinary heresy is clearly shown by the fact that in England, Scotland, France, Germany, Italy, Switzerland, the Netherlands and in New England, in the days of Cotton Mather, certain ministers of some Christian bodies were as zealous as the priests of the Roman Church in hunting down and bringing to trial and death persons suspected of witchcraft.

BIBLIOGRAPHY.—For general works, *see* N. Remy, *Daemonolatrie* (Lyons, 1595); Lecky's *Hist. of Rationalism* in *Europe*, vol. 1. (new ed, 1950); H. Williams, *Superstitions of Witchcraft* (1865); J. Baissac, *Les grands Jours de la Sorcellerie* (1890); W. G. Soldan, *Gesch. der Hexenprozesse* (new ed., 1910); E. B. Tylor, *Primitive Culture* (new ed., 1920); M. A. Murray, *Witchcraft in West. Europe* (1921); J. W. Wickwar, *Witchcraft and the Black Art* (1925); M. Summers, *Hist. of Witchcraft and Demonology* (1926), *Geog. of Witchcraft* (1927) and (ed.), J. Sprenger and H. Institoris, *Malleus Maleficarum* (1928). For ENGLAND, *see* J. Glanvil, *Sadducismus Triumphatus* (1681); R. Scot, *Discoverie of Witchcraft* (1584); W. Notestein, *Hist. of Witchcraft in England* (1911); SCOTLAND: Pitcairn, *Criminal Trials* (4 vols., 1930–33); FRANCE: Boguet, *Discours des Sorciers* (1608); P. de Lancre, *Tableau de l'Inconstance des mauvais Anger* (1612) and *l'Incridulité et Mescréance du Sortilège* (1622); Bodin, *Fléau des Demons* (1616); J. Garinet, *Hist. de la Magie en France* (1818); BELGIUM: Cannaert, *Procis des Sorcières en Belgique* (1847); ITALY: C. G. Leland, *Aradia* (1899); AMERICA: Burr (ed.), *Narrative of the Witchcraft Cases* (1914).

Chapter 17

C.R.F. Seymour

THE OLD GODS

■ from Dolores Ashcrof-Nowicki (ed.) **THE FORGOTTEN MAGE**, Wellingborough, 1986, pp. 143–86

C HARLES RICHARD FOSTER SEYMOUR (1880–1943) was one of several significant British occultists ("very much the ex-colonel," one biographer called him) who was both soldier and magician. As a writer he connected twentieth-century ceremonial magic with Classical Neoplatonism while also prefiguring the Pagan revival that sprang up after his death. As a magician he played a key role in the Fraternity (now Society) of the Inner Light, an organization derived in spirit from the highly influential Order of the Golden Dawn. He also inspired one or two characters in the novels written by the Fraternity's founder, Dion Fortune, most notably the Priest of the Moon in her book *The Sea Priestess* (1957).

Seymour's active military career ended in 1930, after service in the Boer War and World War I, followed by postings in Iraq and Russia. Already a Freemason, he was drawn to the more esoteric and Qabalistic teachings of the Fraternity of the Inner Light and rapidly became one of its stars, editing its monthly magazine. Articles and essays flowed from his pen during the 1930s, with "The Old Gods" being written between 1936 and 1937. In his work, the occult currents of Egypt, Greece, Rome, and the Celtic West all intermingled, as they continue to do today. In this excerpt from Seymour's writing, we can see how he combines almost all the elements of contemporary Paganism—in the 1930s.

For further information, see Richardson (1985).

Note: in the edition from which this extract is taken, the symbols are not shown. Readers are referred to the Thoth edition, 1999, ISBN 1–870450–39–6, to see the symbols.

Chas S. Clifton

References

Fortune, Dion (1957) *The Sea Priestess*. London: Aquarian.
Richardson, Alan (1985) *Dancers to the Gods: The Magical Records of Charles Seymour and Christine Hartley 1937–1939*. Wellingborough: Aquarian Press.

Part 1

WHO OR WHAT WERE the Old Gods? Pause for a moment and reflect on this, then note what pictures float up from memory's storehouse as the conscious mind focuses attention on the question. The answer will show, to some extent, what religion you hold. An atheist might well dismiss the whole question as meaningless, holding that there is no God and no gods. He is probably right and certainly not altogether wrong.

The Westerner brought up in an atmosphere of so-called Christianity will usually dismiss the gods of pagan religions as nonsense, or, he may admit to their existence, in the past of course, and attribute them to Satan.

It has been written that: 'An honest God is the noblest work of man.' Turning over the sacred books of mankind and considering their claims, it would appear that man is not yet an expert craftsman. The student is here recommended to read J. M. Robertson's book *A Short History of Christianity*, published by the Thinker's Library. It is widely read and to meet this type of thinker on his own territory one should have a sound knowledge of this type of literature. Do hold in mind, however, that the Church historians start with the assumption that the pagan religions were false, and on this basis they exalt the Christian religion as being the only true faith. Robertson starts with the same assumption and shows clearly that there is nothing in the theology or rites of Christianity that was not in the various pagan religions, and on this he bases his conclusion that Christianity is also a false religion.

Both these outlooks are false for they ignore the fact that all theology and all rites are of human fabrication. All religions contain some small portion of the truth mixed with much error for they are all the result of man's inner and personal religious experience. Paul, not Jesus, is the founder of modern Christianity, for it is a religion *about* Jesus and not the religion *of* Jesus.

It is often forgotten that religion, *per se*, is a matter of personal experience which is valid only for the person experiencing it. Since this is so, religions should be systems for the obtaining of that experience. They would then avoid the dogma which has crippled modern Christianity, and the need for a privileged class of priests claiming to be mediators between man and God would disappear. Naturally this will antagonize vested interests.

It is a universal principle that to appreciate a thing one must share the mental attitude of its creator. Once able to enter into its spirit we can reproduce in our own souls the same quality of life which called that thing into existence. To understand paganism we must enter into the spirit of paganism. What answer then can be given to the question asked at the beginning? Let us see what the pagans themselves had to say. Seneca wrote:

The wisest among men understand him whom we call Jove to be the Guardian and ruler, spirit and soul of the universe, the Lord and Maker of this mundane sphere, to whom every name is applicable. Dost wish to call him Fate? Thou wilt not err. He it is on whom all things are dependent . . . Dost wish to call him Providence, rightly wilt thou do so; for by his counsel . . . provision is made for this world so that it may proceed in an orderly fashion, and unfold his deeds to our view. Dost thou wish to call him Nature? Thou wilt commit no sin; for he it is from whom all things are sprung and by whose spirit we breathe life. Dost wish to call him the World? Thou wilt not be mistaken, for he . . . is all infused in its parts.

Over a temple at Sais in nothern Egypt was the inscription, 'I am all that was, and is, and is to come.' An Orphic teaching runs, 'One is the Self Begotten, and all things were derived from this same one.' The Egyptians called God *Ua Neter*, the One God, they were as much monotheists as the Jews, the Arabs and the Christians who officially believe in saints, archangels and jinnee.

Proclus in his *Elements of Theology* gives the same teachings, as the following will show, related to the Qabalistic Tree of Life.

(A)	The One Originative Principle of the Universe	The Qabalistic Unmanifest, called by Proclus The One and the Good. The First Principle. It is Unparticipated, and is Unparticipable.
(B)	The Many or High Gods	The Qabalistic Manifest. The ten Sephiroth in Atziluth.

The high gods are the 'Participated' and the 'Participable' as well as the source of all that participates. They are above being, life and intelligence. These gods are divine henads or unities, the outshinings of the One and the Good. They are the Ten Holy Sephiroth, and are derivative terms proceeding from the first principle. Their attributes pre-subsist them in a unitary and supra-existential mode.

In connection with the above and with the aid of the Tree of Life consider the implications which are contained in the following propositions of Proclus.

Prop. 126. A God is more universal as he is nearer to the One, more specific in proportion to His remoteness from it.

Prop. 128. Every God, when participated by beings of an order relatively near to Him, is participated directly; when participated by those more remote, indirectly, through a varying number of intermediate principles.

These propositions when studied in the light of the descent of life force through the Four Worlds of the Qabalists give a clue to the use of god-forms, and to the varying functions of certain gods, like Osiris, Thoth and Isis.

To the uninitiated the pagan systems look chaotic, but there is a clue. It goes by function and not by name. So to answer the question posed at the opening of this chapter we may say that for an initiated pagan, the gods, as distinguished from God, represented divine intelligences and hierarchies of intelligences who were, and are, living out a form of experience which is other than man's experience. They were, and are, undergoing this experience of living on the various planes of consciousness in this universe in much the same way that man undergoes the experience of living on this earth.

The atheist believes he is the highest type of intelligence the universe can produce, which conceit explains why he is an atheist. The average Christian is little better, for he usually repudiates all the unseen that stands between God and man. He may give lip-service via the prayer book to the angels and archangels, but he is secretly ashamed of them as being ancient and unscientific. The Catholics are a little wiser, they at least acknowledge the existence of the archangels, angels and saints, and teach their followers how to get in touch with them.

We can divide these intelligences and hierarchies into three main classes, which in turn have many subdivisions. There are the high gods which correspond largely with the Qabalistic names of God, the archangels and lesser gods corresponding to the great devas, jinnee and angels, and the humanized gods such as Osiris, Orpheus, Im-hotep, etc., which are somewhat similar in conception to the Christian saints.

Behind these high gods are unmanifested divine aspects which are not usually personalized, and are named as the Unmanifest, Chaos, Old Night, etc. They could be said to correspond to the Unmanifest and the Three Veils of Negative Existence as used in the Mystery schools of the Western Tradition.

Within the above classification there is another and smaller one: that of the sun-gods, the underworld- and moon-gods, the earth-gods and the mind-gods. This last is important for it contains the 'principles' which were and are used by the pagans for the practical working of their rites and for meditation work.

The first classification gives us the broad background of paganism. The second gives us the foreground of the stage on which the action takes place in the pagan Mystery dramas. Therefore, for the pagan both past and present the gods as a class represent the type of experience of which it has been said, 'I do not believe that our experience is the highest form extant in the universe.'

The gods were personalized and named by the initiates in the same way, and for the same reason, that modern science names certain types of experience as electromagnetic, radioactive, etc. The Old God names are labels for certain types of divine experience which the initiates of old met up with in the course of their researches into the nature of the unseen. To sum up we may say, by using methods similar to those used centuries ago we can get similar experiences of the divine, for the old classifications still hold good. This again means the message which the Egyptian Thamus gave to the islanders of Palodes is false.

Part 2

In the study of religions it soon becomes evident that each one has its inner and its outer section. Christianity denies this and protests that all its goods are in the shop window. At first sight this appears to be so. But even a perfunctory glance at Roman Catholicism shows that its priesthood forms an inner section and the laity its outer. The priesthood, too, has the same inner and outer sections, and this division rests not upon the secret dogmatic teachings which the 'inner' keeps from the 'outer', but upon the use of secret methods of spiritual, mental and emotional training.

The Roman Church says that it has no secret dogmas which are kept from the faithful that support it with money and votes. This is probably correct. But the priesthood, the monastic orders, the enclosed orders and the higher grades of the hierarchy have methods of training which are not readily available to the general public. The expression 'religious vocation' had for the highly trained Roman priesthood a meaning of which the Protestant laity has little suspicion. The highly trained priest bothers little about dogmas, for he knows it is the method not the dogma that really matters.

The great difference between the Church of England and the Church of Rome is that the former base their faith on a regard for the Thirty-Nine Articles, and the latter upon that special religious experience that Mother Church provides for those who are capable of using it.

The intent of celibacy and monasticism is, *au fond*, magical, and their community life prevents worry about the earning of their daily bread. With no financial worry, discipline, celibacy and a highly developed system of mental training, the efficacious evocation of the 'real presence' becomes an easy matter of daily religious routine. This explains why almost all the Roman Catholic churches are centres of magical power, and those of the Protestant have all the charm and warmth of an empty lecture hall. The Roman Catholic is said to call Protestant churches temples. This is the one thing they are not.

The reason why the Roman Church has this magical power is that it works, in a modified form, the old magical system that it took over from paganism. The Protestant divine is in most cases totally ignorant of, and hostile to, magic, which is why the spiritual and devotional atmosphere is lacking in his church. Such churches are not temples, for a temple is the dwelling place of the god and is ensouled by him. Instead they are places for the teaching of an ethic tinged with a decorous emotionalism. The magical element is absent from their rituals, the ministers are teachers, not priestly magicians as are the Roman Catholic clergy.

The Mystery schools based their training methods on the maxim, 'As above, so below.' They taught that man is a replica of the Great Cosmos, he is the little cosmos. The ancient teaching of Hermes is the method to be followed in this exposition of paganism, and it takes 'mind' in its various forms as the working basis of its training methods.

It postulates that mind is everywhere and directs everything. For example: the earth is the outward symbol of an indwelling intelligence in a manner analogous to a man's body, which should also be the outer symbol of an indwelling intelligence. This intelligence incarnates to gain experience as does man.

All upon the earth lives, moves and has its being and is dependent upon this intelligence, called the Earth Soul or Earth Mother. These indwelling cosmic intelligences are graded. The grade above that which controls the earth, is that of the sun. This intelligence controls the whole solar system, which in its outer spatial form is its body. The planets and all they contain live, move and have their being within the all-inclusive being of this solar intelligence, considered to be the Great Father and giver of life to the Earth Mother.

The same idea holds good with regard to these vast transcendental intelligences which control the systems of solar intelligences and even the cosmos itself. Each god lives, moves and has its being within the vaster intelligence of the grade above it, the grade above fertilizing the grade below it. If you wish to study this more deeply you will find the ideas developed more fully in Proclus, *The Elements of Theology*, Propositions 113–17.

These ideas are worth bringing into the sphere of everyday life. For example think of the multitude of little lives that have their being within the vaster life, being and intelligence of a man. Study the living contents of your next boil with a micro-scope, then meditate by analogy on man and the gods, and the cosmos, keeping in mind the axiom, 'As above, so below.'

Compared with man these cosmic gods are superior and perfect, while man is inferior and imperfect. The object of the initiated pagan was to gain conscious touch with these superior beings in whom he had his own beingness. He based his methods on the psychological maxim, 'As a man thinks, so he becomes.'

The second great hypothesis on which they based their training was, 'The mind gains conscious touch with that upon which it broods.' The method of Loyola depends upon this, and his system is one of the most successful that Christianity has produced and is essentially magical in its methods and results.

It now becomes necessary to define the word 'pagan'. According to the *Oxford Dictionary*, it means 'heathen, unenlightened person', yet Socrates, Plato and all the great intellects of the ancient world were pagans. Jesus ben Joseph was the flower of a pagan civilization. The word comes from the Latin, *paganus*, meaning in, or of, the country. When Christianity came to power it was used to denote those who worshipped the old gods at their shrines on the hills and in the vales, in contradis-tinction to the Christians, who were mainly town-dwellers.

The modern pagan, too, is a lover of open air, one who worships God made manifest in nature. In Qabalistic terminology he worships Adonai Ha Atretz, the Lord of the Earth. He sees God most clearly in the countryside and finds Him in the open spaces. He knows that God is just as present in the stuffy chapel, and the slum dwellings, and in the public houses as He is in the wooded vale and the dim forest glade.

For him the approach is not via a priesthood for every pagan is his own priest or priestess, he is the master of his own soul, and his own saviour, he has no belief in a supreme personal God. He denies all that the Church holds dear, including bishops, priests and even deacons. However, he remembers gratefully the great pagan mystic who walked and taught in Galilee, a man who, when he was tired of working in the towns and slums, went out into the hills to commune with his Father, Adonai, to obtain by meditation refreshment for body and soul from the open spaces and night skies. He learned to draw near to the Great Mother and to be at One with Her.

Jesus was essentially a pagan whose home was the *paganus*. It was the city-dwelling Saul who founded that which we call Christianity. The communism of the Galilean pagan was put to one side and its place filled with a teaching *about* Jesus, which made of him a God to be worshipped. Thus the very real dangers of communism were averted by deifying this Arch Communist and turning attention from an inconvenient teaching to the person of the teacher.

It has been said that *real* Christianity has never been tried. It might equally be said that the supposed founder of Christianity was the greatest of the ancient pagans.

As with Jesus, so with the modern pagan; communion with nature is his means of worship and of rest, of refreshment for body and soul and spirit. Religion is for him a conscious linking of phenomenon with noumenon. Once this has been mastered the pagan is his own high priest, and he is independent of the priesthood as Jesus was independent of the Temple and the priests in Jerusalem. The third great hypothesis upon which modern initiation bases its system of training is, every man can become his own priest by right of *function*.

Part 3: The background of paganism

> The mind of Man is this world's true dimension,
> And knowledge is the measure of the mind:
> And as the mind, in her vast comprehension,
> Contains more worlds than all the world can find,
> So knowledge doth itself far more extend
> Than all the minds of man can comprehend.
>
> Rupert Brooke

The cosmic background to pagan religious thought is formed by the idea of the 'oversoul' or 'world soul', which Plotinus calls the Divine Creative World Soul, and which he describes thus:

> First let every soul consider that it is the World Soul which created all things, breathing into them the breath of life – into all living things which are on Earth, in the air, and in the sea, and the stars in heaven, the Sun, and the great heaven itself. The Creative World Soul sets them in their order and directs their motions, keeping *itself* apart from the things which it orders and moves and causes to *live*.

It will be seen from this quotation (*Enneads*) that the Divine Creative World Soul is the ultimate form of creative energy to which the mind of man can reach. The other great and divine souls, such as that of the solar logos, our sun, of the great Earth Mother, of the various stellar logoi, are born and persist as this Oversoul grants them life . . . but this oversoul lives for ever and ever and never ceases to be *itself*. This is not the Earth Soul, which is of a lesser grade.

To use the terminology of the Qabalah, in its first manifestation this creative oversoul is the Supernal Triad of Kether, Chokmah and Binah, and *as such*, it is the primal manifestation of that Unmanfest which the Qabalists call the Ain, the One, the Absolute; that which has its own mode of being behind that purely human convention which is called the Three Veils of the Unmanifest. The Ain thus corresponds to the *itself* of the passage quoted above.

Emerson, as the prophet of modern paganism, in his work *Oversoul*, writes with regard to man, the microcosm: 'The Soul of man is not an organ, but animates, and exercises all the organs: it is not a function like the power of memory, of calculation . . . it is not a faculty . . . it is the background of our being in which all faculties lie.'

'As above so below.' The ancient initiates, recognizing the limitations of human thinking and of human methods for expressing their thinking, postulated as a working hypothesis the theory of the Divine Oversoul, analogous to the Soul of man. And this theory of a Divine Creative Oversoul which is analogous in its working to the Soul of man, and with which the human soul can get conscious communion, is the background of both ancient and modern Mystery school training.

We can divide up the Mystery systems of the Western Esoteric Tradition of today into six groups – Qabalistic, Chaldean, Egyptian, Greek, Celtic and Norse. It is not easy to decide which of these is the oldest. When educated people thought of human history as beginning in about 5,000 BC, it was generally considered that the Egyptian system was the oldest and that Egypt was the Mother of civilized religions. Today this assumption is considered a doubtful one. There are schools which think that the Druidic branch of the Celtic religion and the Egyptian Mystery systems are both offshoots from a common and still more primitive religion which they call Iberian, a system which was in vogue between 10,000 and 5,000 BC. If this theory is true it will explain the likeness as well as the curious differences between the British Druidic systems and the Mystery religions of ancient Egypt. The Celts themselves are not Iberians, but in their wanderings conquered or displaced the more ancient Iberian tribes and added their predecessors' religious practices to their own.

It must here be remembered that these ancient religious systems were not collections of dogmatic teachings which are supposed to be capable of demonstration by, and to, reasoning minds. They were practical systems for obtaining 'religious experience', in its widest sense; and as most of them were based upon a technique for using the subconscious mind, they could not be rationalized or made reasonable in the modern sense of that term.

The ancient initiates found these systems reasonable because their sole religious criterion was that of utility. A system was valid if it produced religious experiences. If it did, all well and good – if not, the priest died! Invaders coming into a new country found that the old power centres were easier to work, and the old and local methods often gave more satisfactory results than their own. This is why so many of the old centres have remained in use for religious purposes down to the present day. Many Christian churches are sited upon old pagan centres that have been in use from time immemorial.

From a practical point of view it is far easier to open up, and gradually modify an ancient centre of religious power, than to start a new centre and a new system that is alien to the country, to the oversoul of the place and to the race. Looked at from the pagan initiate's point of view the key idea is this: that man can get into intimate touch – almost at will – with the world soul once he has realized that the mind touches that which it constantly and sympathetically thinks about.

Part 4: General classification of the gods

The object of this section is to classify the gods of the pagan initiates from the practical point of view. This classification may not recommend itself to the historian or to the scholar. In the first place it is limited. In the second place it deals with deities which are unlike those of the classical religions and philosophies. And, finally, it is according neither to popular historical importance nor to the conventions of esoteric religion, but to the efficiency of gods when they are used in accordance with a certain technique.

The reader may say here: 'What does this mean? Can I for example see, hear and touch the Great God Pan?' Certainly. You can make Pan your constant companion and you can bring the 'Pan within' to life in exactly the same way that the orthodox Christian saint by a certain technique brings to birth the 'Christ within'. But you are not recommended to do this without safeguards, for the pagan who has called into over-activity the 'Pan within' can be as unbalanced a person as the Christian saint who has roused into undue activity those forces which are sometimes called the Christ Within.

If you are a monotheist, and not that much-abused person, the dualist, you must, logically, recognize that Pan and Christ are but two aspects of the same thing, which temporarily, for the sake of convenience, will be called God. Both aspects are good – in the right place and in the right proportions. Both are harmful when misplaced in time, or space, or both. Spiritual adultery is just as common as physical and in the long run it is even more undesirable.

In *The Mystical Qabalah* by Dion Fortune there is given the system for the classification of the pagan gods which is used by the initiates of a number of modern schools. Briefly, it divides all the gods of the pantheons into ten classes, called the Sephiroth, and presupposes that they emanate from an unmanifested state of being which is the source of all that has been, is, or will be. The Neo-Platonists call it the One, as opposed to the Many. These ten classes are:

1.	The space – time-gods	— Kether
2.	The all-fathers	— Chokmah
3.	The great mothers	— Binah
4.	The builders	— Chesed
5.	The destroyers	— Geburah
6.	The sun-gods	— Tipareth
7.	The virgin nature-gods	— Netzach
8.	The wisdom-gods	— Hod
9.	The underworld- and the moon-gods	— Yesod
10.	The earth-gods	— Malkuth

From the practical point of view the student need, for the present, concentrate only upon numbers 1, 6, 9, 10 and 8, which reduces his classification to the space- or time-gods, sun-gods, moon- and underworld-gods, earth-gods and the gods of wisdom.

The more common types of symbols for these cosmic intelligences are:

1.   The space-gods. The point within the circle. 'The Serpent that
     devoured his tail.'   ,   and occasionally   .
     The signs   and   are also used for Chokmah
     and Binah respectively as the positive and nega-
     tive functions of the Kether space – time gods.
     The zodiac is also a symbol for Chokmah.
2.   The sun-gods: .
3.   The moon-gods: .
4.   The signs of the Four Elements are used for various elemental
     deities:
        fire;   air;   water;   earth.
5.   The sign   for the gods of wisdom.

A short comparative list of the more common forms is:

1.   Space-gods:

     Qabalah   – –   Eheieh.
     Greek   – –   Chaos, Nox and Eros.
                      Zeus, Jupiter as sky-gods.
     Egyptian   – –   The Eight Gods of
                      Hermopolis with Thoth at
                      their head; Amen and Ptah;
                      Nu and Nun.
     Chaldean   – –   Apsu, Mommu and Tiamath.
                      Anu as the All-Father.
     Celtic   – –   Lir and Beli.
     Nordic   – –   Odin or Tiwaz or Tyr.

2.   Sun-gods:

     Qabalah   – –   Aloah va Daath.
     Greek   – –   Apollo and Helios.
     Egyptian   – –   Ra, Horus and Osiris.
     Chaldean   – –   Shamash, Asshur, Enlil,
                      Merodach or Bel.
     Celtic   – –   Lugh or Angus Og, Dagda,
                      Bile and Hu.
     Norse   – –   Balder.

3.   Moon-gods and the underworld-gods.

     Qabalah   – –   Shaddai El Hai.
     Greek   – –   Semele, Pluto, Persephone.
     Egyptian   – –   Isis of the Moon and Thoth as
                      Tehuti, Khensu and Osiris.
     Chaldean   – –   Nin-gal and Sin. Ishtar. Allatu
                      and Nergal.
     Celtic   – –   Celi as the husband of
                      Keredwen. Midir and Etain

of the Fairies. Bile, Manannan
Manawyddan Mab Llyr the
Welsh Lord of Hades. Brigid
and Gwynn ap Nudd.

Nordic   –– Mani the moon-god. Ran and
Hel the Goddesses of Death.

4.   Earth-gods:

Qabalah   –– Adonai.

Greek   –– Demeter, Gaea as Earth
Mother and Ceres.

Egyptian   –– Isis.

Chaldean   –– Ishtar. Tiamath as Earth
Mother.

Celtic   –– Keridwen and Dana (Irish),
Brigantia. Cernunnos.

Nordic   –– Rinda. Thor and Sif, the God
and Goddess of Crops.

5.   Gods of wisdom:

Qabalah   –– Hermes, Thoth.

Greek   –– Hermes. Pallas Athene.

Egyptian   –– Thoth.

Chaldean   –– Nabu or Nebo, and Sin.

Celtic   –– Ogmios and Briganda. Ogma
(Irish), Myrddin (English).
Dagda ('The Lord of Great
Knowledge').

Nordic   –– Odin, with Loki as the God
of Evil Wisdom.

This list is a brief one, and it refers only to the cosmic intelligences, i.e. to the type of beings that Iamblichus in his book *The Egyptian Mysteries* calls 'the gods'.

In the Mystery schools of Egypt and the Gnostic schools at Alexandria, the 'many' gods were considered to be the emanations or the 'outshinings' of the 'One' God who was the super-essential deity, or, as we should say, the Unmanifest Cause of All. Iamblichus divides the divine hierarchy into the gods and the superior races, and it is clear that he considered the former as representing or personifying qualities in the Divine Mind rather than as personalities or individuals.

For the ancient initiate, mind was 'the leader and King of the things that actually are'. Thus we can best understand these pagan gods by thinking about them as the great directing minds of this universe.

When studying these deities, the student, in the course of meditations made with some degree of proficiency in the technique of the Mystery school method, is bound to come across certain curious phenomena which have been described as the Memory of the Earth. A.E. in *The Candle of Vision* (p. 56) has dealt with this subject and the student is advised to study this great writer's theories. But for the present we may take the 'Memory of the Earth' as a working hypothesis. The *modus operandi* will be discussed later, and if the student will tentatively accept this theory, he will save himself a good deal of worry about details, and this will result in accelerated progress.

The student is advised to read and re-read these classifications of the gods. He may not agree with them. If he has been educated in what is called the classical tradition he will probably disagree heartily. But it must be called to mind that we are not dealing with the classical pantheons. The criteria of the classical records are not the same as the criteria that are applied to results obtained from the recovery of Earth Memories. The latter are empirical; the former are not. The main object is to get a working process that can be relied upon to give adequate results when recovering the past.

The more these gods are reflected upon in solitary meditations, the more such meditations pass inwards into sympathetic contemplation and the easier it becomes to develop, from latent existence in the subconscious mind, the long-hidden memories of the ancient Wisdom religions.

Part 5: The gods and their functions

> The souls came hither[1] not by sending, and not of their own will, or at least their will is no deliberate choice, but a prompting of nature . . . The Intelligence which is before the World contains the destiny of our abiding yonder[2] no less than of our sending forth; the individual is 'sent' forth as falling under the general ordinance. For the universal is implicit in each, and not by authority from without does the ordinance enforce itself; it is inherent in those who shall obey it and they carry it always within them. And when their season is come, that which it will is brought to pass by those in whom it resides; bearing it within them, they fulfil it of their own accord; the ordinance prevails because the ordinance has its seat in them, as it were pressing upon them weightily, awakening in them an impulse, a yearning, to go to that place whither the indwelling voice seems to bid them go.
>
> (Dodds, *Select Passages Illustrating Neoplatonism*)

When striving to unravel the complexities of the numerous pantheons it is necessary to call to mind the fact that the gods are but symbols for certain manifestations of divine force. Their names are the X, Y and Z which enable the theurgist to work out this system of divine algebra and to function as a priest.

Isis, for example, is a man-made personification of a certain type of divine force. Again X may stand for many things which are not of this physical plane. Isis too stands for many non-material things. There is Isis as the Earth Mother, as the Virgin Lady of Nature, as the Queen of Heaven, as the Moon, as the Cosmic Mother, and so on.

There are many forms in which electricity can be used – as a motor agent, as light, as heat, as a curative agent, or as a means for executing a criminal. What electricity is *per se* we do not know, but we do know how to make use of it in various particular ways. What the gods are *per se* we do not know, but the theurgist does know how to bring into function a god-form, i.e. a divine symbol – in many particularized ways.

From a practical point of view this is all that really matters. The divine within reaches out to the divine that is without, the contact is made, and the divine machinery is set in motion upon the plane of consciousness that is required. But if there is no Isis within your own soul, you will call in vain to this goddess. You must seek within yourself for the starting-handle.

To understand what the pagan was trying to do one must imagine, as he did, that divine all-embracing power which welling up under pressure from the unmanifest is ever seeking to express itself more and more fully, more and more perfectly. It has been well said that 'God is pressure.'

This pressure is often called Spirit, or Life. In reality it is all these things, and more, for there is the transcendent aspect to this power which the Chaldeans called the Great Silence, as well as the imminent aspect which is the Great Sea. In order to exist – this universal power must differentiate itself into particular units. The One must become the many – the High Gods.

The Qabalists use the system of the Tree of Life to explain, the process by which the One becomes the Many. They divide divine manifestation into four worlds or states of consciousness. The most subtle of these worlds is Atziloth, which might be called the world of pure spirit, the Archetypal World, the sphere of the divine archetypal ideas, the plane of the High Gods, or the world of the ten Divine Names. All these things, and many others, it has been called, but it must be remembered that in itself the world of Atziloth is beyond our comprehension. It can be described only by means of analogy and by the use of symbols. Neo-Platonism, as a system, gives a full and very vivid teaching concerning this sphere of the divine activity. But the modern student must not forget that these ancient initiates were carefully trained in the pure dialectical method, a subject little studied today.

The best line of intellectual approach to the comprehension of ideas concerning the world of Atziloth is a study of mystical theology. This art reaches out to the supreme goal by the use of analogy and paradox, by blending the *Via Affirmativa* and the *Via Negativa*, until the super-essential Darkness which is the Ultimate Light of Light is reached in a contemplation that ends in *Agnosia*. One can study these methods even if one cannot use them. A study of Neo-Platonism can take the competently taught student by an ancient, well-trodden road to identification with the 'One and the Many'. But competently taught students are extremely rare for the world has seen few such teachers as Plotinus, Ammonius Saccas or Lao-tzu. These teachers are themselves living embodiments of the divine wisdom-gods. By sympathy they have become 'at one' with the divine wisdom. By their 'at-one-ment' they are able, at least temporarily, to lift the prepared student up to the metaphysical heights of the Light beyond all Lights – the Transcendental One, or to take him down to that abyss beyond all abysses.

The experiences which these teachers produce in the student's soul are evanescent. Yet something remains in memory for the hand of the Initiator has been laid upon the neophyte. When Height has challenged Height, and Deep has called to Deep, one is never quite the same.

The second sphere of the divine outpouring is called the world of Briah, a word derived from the Hebrew verb meaning to create, to produce. The divine ideals have, as it were, become the divine ideas. In Qabalistic terminology this is the world of the archangels, of the creating gods and the all-mothers of the ancient pantheons.

It is the world of the great devas of the Eastern systems. In modern language we might call it the sphere of the abstract mind, or the world of abstract thought and ideas.

The third world is called Yetzirah. Now the Hebrew word Yatzar (Yod, Tzaddi, Resh) has several significant (from our point of view) meanings. It means to form in the mind, to plan, to fashion as an artist, and in certain cases to destine for a particular purpose. Now the initiates conceive the physical world to be crystallized astral matter, the astral world to be crystallized mind-stuff; and mind-stuff to be crystallized spirit. The same thing but varying in, shall we say, density.

In this third sphere of being, ideas take form, and the etheric moulds that hold dense matter in its physical form as we know it are fashioned by the divine artists; for Yetzirah is the sphere of the greater localized divinities, and the student will find a good deal given in Chapters 3–6 of *The Egyptian Mysteries* by Iamblichus. In modern terminology Yetzirah may be called the astro-mental world, though one must remember that there is no hard and fast line between the various spheres of being; they shade off imperceptibly one into the other. Dividing them up is like dividing the human mind into the descriptive sections that are used by psychologists. This is convenient for teaching and description, but these hard and fast lines of distinction exist only in textbooks.

The fourth sphere or world is that of Assiah. It corresponds to the physical world in its most subtle form. It is the densest form of the etheric world. In this sphere of the subtle pre-matter of existence are to be found the nature spirits, elementals, and the children of Dana, of the Great Earth Mother, the divinities of mountains, streams and woods.

If we bear in mind the ancient Mystery teaching that 'all the gods are one god, all the goddesses are one goddess, and there is one Initiator', it will be seen that in the system of the Tree of Life as expounded in *The Mystical Qabalah* there is developed a perfectly logical sequence of cause and effect. From the human point of view the Tree of Life works as a system for enabling a human being to obtain contact with divine things, and again using the analogy of electricity, to put himself in circuit with the power-house of the universe.

Once more the student is warned that he must distinguish between 'the order of that which is' and 'the order of ideas concerning that which is'. One is not now trying to describe a chemical experiment. How these things that have just been described by analogy and by symbol may appear to minds superior to our human minds, we have no idea. To such minds our explanations are certainly childishly inadequate even if they are not entirely inaccurate. But this Qabalistic system of describing and using the mind fulfils the following fundamental conditions for obtaining results. First there is the power. Then there are individuals of various grades in all four worlds of manifestation who understand how to use this (divine) power. And, lastly, there is a method, or rather methods, for using this power in so far as mankind can become aware of it.

The divine life or power – like electricity – is not generated by the individual. The individual uses power which is already existing and the specializing of the divine energy which alone leads to manifestation must take place through individuals, human or otherwise. In theurgy this is a matter of experience as well as of common sense.

The pagans taught that every man is a distributor of this all-embracing, originating divine spirit or power. The initiate, however, was a trained man who, understanding the nature of the divine power, was able to transform it at will. He was a well-trained engineer, and he got his training in the same way that an electrical engineer gets his today – by working practically in an electrical power station. The initiate worked in the power-house of nature after having been taught the theory of his craft in a Mystery school. Then he took his practical training in the sphere of Yesod, which is the unmanifested element of the Four Elements of the physical world, the aether of the wise, the astral light of the ancients.

Thus it will be clear that the pagan initiate looked upon life from a rather different point of view from that of the ordinary man. The ambitious self-reliant man of the world strives to make himself a forceful personality and to get things done by his own driving power. He is his own power-house, and he supplies – or thinks he does – his own energy. The pagan, however, grasped the idea of 'Spirit' as the fountain head of a great 'forming power' which he received into himself. Then he proceeded to manifest it in accordance with the Law of Harmony and by means of a technique that he had been taught.

The various gods and their hierarchies are specialized functional types of this omnipresent divine energy. For example, Venus is the personification of the divine activity that is called attraction; Mars is that of repulsion, the divine destructive force; and Jupiter is a constructive mode of action. Again the religions of the mother and the daughter – Demeter and Persephone for example – are not so much family relationships as psychological stages in the life of the soul. From this point of view, the doctrine of the identity of Kore the Maid and her mother is obvious. The Maid is the psychological parent of the mother, and so the confusion of the persons disappears – the mother is the virgin and vice versa. The One God has become many gods, and each god functions as the head of a divine hierarchy with aspects that are spiritual, mental and astral. Each hierarchy in its turn carries further into manifestation the cosmic principle of the One, which becomes the Many. And each plane of manifestation has its own standard of truth and its own ethic, and these standards are by no means identical.

Cosmically, every man is a unit, but he is also a multiplicity, a hierarchy of divine lives, and in his activities proper to himself he manifests the same principles as the One and the Many. The virgin is the parent of the mother(!) psychologically if not physically. The virgin goddess renews her virginity every winter solstice. This becomes clear if we study the Babylonian Ishtar, who is called 'the Virgin', 'the Holy Virgin' and 'the Virgin Mother' by her worshippers. Yet this virgin goddess says of herself, 'A harlot compassionate am I.' Among the ancient Jews and Babylonians a veil was the mark of both virgins and prostitutes – Ishtar in certain aspects wears the veil. And Genesis 38: 14–15 throws a curious light on this custom. Also, the word *Parthenos*, upon which so much theology has been founded, is worth looking up in a *modern* Greek dictionary, for in ancient days bastards were called *Parthenioi*, virgin-born.

To sum up we may say that in this universe there is an ever-descending stream of divine power and life welling up under pressure from an unmanifested state of being and pouring down into manifestation. The various gods, each on their own plane and functioning according to their own degree, manifest and specialize this life force on planes of being which are more subtle than the plane of physical matter. The pagan by taking conscious thought of the gods can draw through himself the specialized life force of the gods or god with whom he is most in sympathy. Thus by a conscious effort man can forward evolution by increasing his capacity to distribute and to specialize this divine life power.

Again, by the study of the inner aspects of man's existence before conception draws him back into the realms of matter, the identity of Kore becomes manifest, for Kore is the Virgin Mother, the higher self in man; and every man – in terms of his lower self, and excluding the physical body – is one of the *parthenioi*. For the ancients, the moon-mother is a virgin, yet Demeter, curiously enough is the goddess who presides over divorce. (Harding, *Women's Mysteries*, p. 78.) The doctrines of the virgin who has a child, of the perpetual virginity of the mother, of the renewal of the mother's virginity with the death of the child, will yield much spiritual food for thoughtful meditation.

There are many curious paradoxes to be found in the psychological teachings of these ancient myths when once we begin to study the 'Great Silence'. For, as the 'Great Sea' is the root of things that are in matter, so the 'Great Silence' is the root of thoughts that are in mind – divine mind. As the Chaldeans taught, the 'Great Silence' and the 'Great Sea' are cosmic yoke-fellows. They are the duad of the monad which, on each plane of being, forms a divine triad – such as woman, saint, butterfly; Zeus, Apollo, Dionysius; Chaos, Erebus, Nox. Does not the picture of Nox, crowned with poppies or stars, with large dark wings and flying robes, riding in a chariot drawn by two black horses, touch the very depths of your being with a feeling that is subtle and mysterious?

The key to 'understanding' is sympathy, which is strong feeling carefully directed. Once sympathy has been aroused, the soul feels the truth of a 'mythos', not because it is in any way reasonable, but because something in the depths of one's innermost being has been touched. Pre-natal memories of a divine knowledge that the soul once had long ago – a knowledge temporarily lost while wandering in the realms of mortal generation – begin to stir. By meditation these memories of a lost understanding can be recovered; for in the long dead past, perhaps, one may have known something of the Egyptian, Chaldean, Orphic and Pythagorean systems.

Part 6: The Earth Mother

26
Oh, come with old Khayyam and leave the Wise
To talk; one thing is certain that life flies:
One thing is certain and the rest is lies;
The flower that once has blown for ever dies.

27
Myself when young did eagerly frequent
Doctor and Saint and heard great argument
About it and about: but ever more
Came out by the same Door as in I went.

(*Roses of Parnassus*, Number One)

The modern man with his childhood mind shaped by the dogmas of Christianity, his youthful mind filled with the facts of modern science, and his mature mind discarding both, is often apt to let religion slide. If there is life after death he just hopes for the best. And so we find that among the more thoughtful men of this type an intense pleasure is sometimes taken in Fitzgerald's 'Omar Khayyam'. Consider the first verse just quoted. Can, so far as human experience goes, anything be more certain than these facts and this conclusion? Can anything be more satisfying to the average logically trained mind than stanza 26?

Christianity and science alike consider that the earth is a soulless ball of mud, following natural laws which condemn it to float for aeons through apparently boundless space. Man's body is part of it, man's mind is – and here please read stanza 27, for it describes the situation as regards this last point perfectly.

The greatest of the Masters told us much about that inner reality which lies just beyond appearances. He called it the Kingdom of the Heavens. It is within man himself; men have got to become as little children to enter it; it is possible to know the hidden things of this inner kingdom of the heavens, and that those who think that they are 'learned' and the 'sanctimonious' cannot enter it themselves, and will even try to prevent others from entering.

The pagan initiates who lived at the time of Jesus knew that the earth is not soul-less. They knew of the greater reality that underlies the actuality of outward physical manifestation. They could enter this Kingdom of the Heavens at will. They would not have contradicted any of these statements of Jesus.

There is no reason why the student of this ancient paganism should not follow in the footsteps of these initiated pagans if he wants to do so, and if he knows what to do. And the knowing what to do is perfectly simple; all that is required is to get in touch with the earth soul consciously instead of subconsciously. For the subcon-scious mind is always in touch with the earth soul, even when the conscious mind denies the earth soul's existence.

There is an ancient proverb which runs: 'Any fool can tell you what to do: only a wise man can tell you how to do it.' Having, I hope, achieved the first of these things, let me try so far as lies in my power to do the second.

Speaking generally, it is unwise to try to take the Kingdom of the Heavens, i.e. the inner worlds of nature, by force. For the average man, the only safe and reason-able way is to train under a competent teacher in a Mystery school which is functioning under a duly authorized authority. There he will be taught, and guarded, and later on, guided. The difficulty does not lie in opening the gates – that is easy – but in closing them after your return, which is quite another matter.

There are many who are by temperament what is called nature mystics. These persons seem to have an innate right of entry into those kingdoms of nature that substand the outer form of the Great Mother Nature. The process comes so easily to them that they are almost unaware of the fact that a technique is needed. And the very facility with which they are able to function makes them unsafe as teachers. They are unaware of the many and dangerous pitfalls which await persons less gifted than themselves; and so they can do little to help or guide their pupils in time of trouble.

The number of desirable students who can attend a Mystery school is limited. The number of schools which can teach under duly constituted authority is exceedingly limited. What then can be done by the would-be enquirer who cannot, as yet, attend a school in order to learn the 'How' to which reference has just been made?

He can do a great deal in safety if he sets about the long preliminary preparation methodically. If he determines to get in touch with an authorized school, it is curious how the way will open for a really determined student.

In the preliminary stage one can get in touch with the Earth Mother by taking a pre-determined line of thought and sticking to it. Also, it helps to store the mind with ancient symbols, and with the myths and folklore of the pagans, studying their pantheons as a record of psychological processes which are both human and cosmic. Here the Tree of Life makes a good filing system, and it is an aid to their analysis, classification and synthesis.

There are two distinct aspects to this method of study, and for convenience we will call them the 'out of doors' and the 'indoors' methods. The student must remember that unless he is a nature mystic of a very high type, one who has recovered from his subconscious mind the knowledge that we once had before the darkness of the Middle Ages fell upon Europe, he must work these two methods in a harmonized proportion while waiting for the opportunity of joining a Mystery school, an opportunity which will come fairly quickly *when* he is ready.

The minor details of this out of doors method for regaining touch with the soul of the Great Mother must vary widely. No two individuals are alike, no one method will completely suit all comers. But the following generalized methods are suggested, not because they are specially valuable, but because they have been tried out and found to be adequate even if elementary.

Next time you are alone in the country or by the seaside, get into a quiet place and note carefully all that you can see, hear and *feel* of the nature happenings that occur within a hundred yards of where you are sitting. Be sure to limit your awareness strictly to the things that happen within this circle, and do not go outside it. Later, with practice, you will be able to limit your sphere of sensation further, to, say, a single tree or a bed of flowers.

Below is an example of how the method works. Remember that in actual practice you make the experience intensely personal until you find that your consciousness of yourself is merging into something that is wider, greater, and more intense than you are: also it is of a beauty more vivid than that of your own imaginings at their best. This sensation of merging is the test of success; by it you can tell whether or not you are at heart a pagan, i.e. a member by right of function of the *paganus*, of the countryside.

Example of the Method

You are lying on a cliff face on the coast of Devon; the sun is hot and bright, and the cliffs are covered with sea-pinks and small yellow flowers. The sea, a hundred feet below, is blue and very still. It is late spring or early summer, and the young gulls in their brown plumage keep the old ones busy. They scream and mew. It is lovely and warm lying on the red-brown earth, and no one is near. A large gull floats up, balances for a moment, looks at you seriously out of bright, intelligent, but soulless eyes and then slides swiftly to the left and out of sight. The warm air, the warm earth, the soft murmur of the summery waves, produce a feeling as of sleep, and slowly one begins to slide down that slope that leads to unconsciousness and to slumber.

Now comes the critical moment if you want to gain touch with the earth soul. You must slide down until you come almost to the slumber line. Then by an effort you bring your focus of consciousness to a fixed point and watch in an active and yet detached manner, the impressions that are coming in upon the inner senses and recording themselves in your mind. And here the student had better note that this is much easier said than done.

This last stage must not be allowed to develop into passivity. It is a simple form of semi-physical contemplation. The mind and the inner senses are intensely active, while the bodily functions have passed out of the focus of consciousness. The soul of man can then consciously draw nearer to the soul of the Earth Mother. What this exercise tries to do is turn a subconscious into a conscious contact: and this takes time and much earnest practice. Constant *daily* practice is necessary. This need not be always in the same place, though it undoubtedly helps to have one favourite spot for this type of meditation. What may we expect to get from this exercise? At first very little. In any event the conscious result is small even when a careful daily record is kept. But the object is not factual knowledge; instead, it is the conscious opening up of latent powers within the soul itself that is aimed at. And this slowly leads to a heightening of some inner sense of awareness, to some inner sensing of the beauty and harmony of the unseen side of nature. The focus of consciousness is very carefully being transferred from the Malkuth of Earth to that inner kingdom of life and strength and beauty which lies just beyond this visible physical plane. And in times of weakness and weariness the trained soul can draw consciously on the life forces of these 'inner kingdoms' for renewed health and strength.

The next stage in this process comes when the holiday is ended. Suppose one is back in town and that the noise, and smells, and asphalt have cut one off from earth contacts, then indeed the Earth Mother can seem very far away. The past is as a dream, vague, distorted and lifeless. The initiated pagan, however, does not let this worry him. He settles comfortably in the easy chair he uses for his daily meditation in the privacy of his own room. His thoughts turn inwards and he seeks the Kingdom of the Heavens that is within himself. He goes into that inner chamber as that great man Jesus ben Joseph told his disciples to do. By means of the technique that his school teaches he is, in thought, *in feeling* and in action, back in Devon. Again he is lying on that cliff, he sees the sea-pinks, he hears the sea-birds; once more the big gull with its bright eyes floats up, hovers for a moment, and then slides away. More and more the focus of consciousness turns within until suddenly a contact is clearly *felt* between the soul of the initiate and the living earth soul. Then once more he is in the loving arms of the great Earth Mother. Her life flows into him until every cell and nerve is bathed in it. The joy becomes almost an agony of ecstasy. The Chalice of the Soul is full to overflowing. Later the contact is cut deliberately. Grateful thanks are given, and the pagan initiate returns to his daily round, rested, strengthened and refreshed with the Elixir of Life.

Heidrun supplied Odin with the heavenly mead, the drink of the gods of the Norsemen; this supply is still available for those who can earn it; for the high gods never die. It is man who foolishly forgets that they are powers immanent within his own soul.

But one must have understanding if one is to earn this sacred drink of the gods, be it called Soma, Haomo or the Heavenly Mead; and the indoor training of the nature mystic aims at producing this understanding. For few educated persons today are content with 'rule of thumb' methods for attaining to glimpses of that Truth, Harmony and Beauty which are aspects of that Infinite Unity which we know as Nature, the Earth Mother.

The first question that has to be answered is 'What is nature?' It has been said by modern philosophers that, as a man sees things, nature is 'a concept of order', also that nature is 'an empirical reality in space'. The nature mystic would say that these concepts are undoubtedly true, and they are useful so far as they go. But they do not go far enough; for, from the mystical point of view, they do not cover the whole of man's experience, even though they may cover the whole of some men's experience. It can fairly truthfully be said that many people regard the existence of nature as a self-evident fact, and say 'why worry about asking "What is nature?" Is it not obvious that nature is just naturally nature? Why bother about the obvious?'

Looking at this question solely from the point of view of the nature mystic, there are three ways of approaching the study of nature: the way of materialism; the way that some philosophers call spiritualism (this way has nothing to do with ghosts and mediums, but refers to ideas and not to so-called psychical manifestations); and the way of the initiates of the Ancient Mysteries. The wise student will study all three with strict impartiality, for all are true, none is all the truth, and one learns most by combining them in that harmonized proportion which suits your own mental make-up. Study most the aspect you like least in order to obtain balance.

Some of the most modern materialists deal only with nature as an 'empirical reality in space and time'. The late Professor J. B. S. Haldane describes this attitude of mind thus:

> To many persons in modern times, it seems that the only reality is what can be interpreted in terms of the physical sciences, with the addition, however, that certain physical processes occurring in the brain are mysteriously accompanied by consciousness, the quality of which depends on the nature of these processes. This belief is known as materialism, and for those holding it, religion is necessarily no more than an illusion based on ignorance . . .
>
> For traditional physical science the visible and tangible world of our experience is interpreted as consisting of self-existent material units reacting in space and time with one another in such a way that the energy represented in mutual movements and reactions remains constant. Any apparent co-ordination or unity which exists in the physical world is regarded as accidental to the unit of which it consists, and ultimately a mere matter of chance as far as our knowledge goes . . .
>
> If we disregard the fact of life, and of our own relations to the universe around us, it undoubtedly seems to behave in such a manner as physical science assumes . . . If we assume this interpretation then anything that we can really be conscious of can only consist of isolated impressions in our brains, these impressions being somehow put together to form a picture which is really subjective, and only simulating a surrounding universe.

These extracts from one of Professor Haldane's last lectures are worthy of close attention. Materialism from the nature mystic's point of view is a true and very valuable belief so long as it is remembered that here is a partial and not an integral or complete view of nature as the mystic apprehends it. For him Nature is more than her physical manifestation in time and space.

As regards philosophical spiritualism, which is the foundation of all religions, Professor Hocking in his extremely useful book *Types of Philosophy* (p. 28) has summarized it as follows:

> There exists another world than this world shown us by the senses. This other world is somehow veiled from our ordinary perceptions; and yet is is continuous with Nature; and of easy access in either direction if one has the right path. It is the residence of powers or agencies which we distinguish as divine; they always know how to get at us; we are not so clear as to how to get at them.

In these seven short statements there is given us a very different conception of nature; and yet it is one which is the complement and not the contradiction of materialism. For when both are taken together, a more complete and satisfactory view of Nature and man's relationship to Nature is obtained than when either is taken singly and the importance of the other ignored or decried, or denied.

Now let us turn to the third way – that of the initiates of the Ancient Mysteries. How did they touch the inner realms over which rules Rhea, the Tower-Crowned Phrygian Mother of All?

One way is shown in the celebrated romance of *The Golden Ass* by Lucius Apuleius, a well-known writer and philosopher who lived in the early part of the second century. This book, while suited to grave students, advanced in years and learning and above all in understanding, should not be left lying around indiscreetly, lest a prudish and priggish ignorance mock at that which it cannot understand.

Some 400 years ago, Apuleius was familiar to classical students and was used by discerning theologians. The student of the Mysteries will remember that the 'ass' is the symbol of the Typhonic aspect of human nature. This is the key to the inner meaning of the first ten books, for nature mysticism may, in an ill-balanced soul, stir up that aspect of human nature which is here depicted in the adventures of the 'ass'.

In the eleventh book Apuleius turns to the Goddess of Nature, to Isis of the Sea, of the Moon, and of the Earth, imploring her to save him from himself for the forces that he has, by mistaken methods, evoked from within himself threaten to destroy him. In this, the last book, we have in carefully veiled language the story of his initiation into the Lesser Mysteries. The scene by the seashore depicts, in the curious symbolism of 2,000 years ago, the first step that must be taken by those who seek this ancient way into the adytum of Pessinuntia, who is the mother of the gods. With the coming of this divine vision that, star-crowned and moon-girt, rises from the hushed sea of man's subconscious nature, the great adventure of religion begins, for this is the inner way to vision.

Without this vision, and without the direct summons of that Tower-Crowned One whom the ancients adored under many forms as Aphrodite Pandemos (seeing her veiled in the symbols of the Moon, of the Star that rises from the twilight sea, and of the 'Rosa Mystica') there is for the would-be initiate no road to those unseen realms that are concealed within the soul of the great and fruitful Earth Mother, Queen Isis.

Part 7: The Door and the Bowl

Stanza XXXII
There was a door to which I found no Key:
There was a Veil past which I could not see:
Some little talk awhile of Me and Thee
There seem'd – and then no more of Thee and Me.

Stanza XXXV
Then to this Earthen Bowl did I adjourn
My lip the secret Well of Life to learn:
And lip to lip it murmur'd – 'While you live
Drink – for once dead you never shall return.'
(Omar Khayyam)

Reference has been made to that peculiar phenomenon which A.E. in *The Candle of Vision* calls 'The Memory of the Earth'. He says:

> We experience the romance and delight of voyaging upon uncharted seas when the imagination is released from the foolish notion that the images seen in reverie and dream are merely images of memory refashioned; and in tracking to their originals the forms seen in vision we discover for them a varied ancestry, as that some come from the minds of others, and of some we cannot surmise another origin than that they are portions of the memory of Earth which is accessible to us. We soon grow to think our memory but a portion of that Eternal memory *and that we in our lives are gathering an innumerable experience for a mightier being than our own.* The more vividly we see with the inner eye the more swiftly do we come to this conviction. Those who see vaguely are satisfied with vague explanations which those who see vividly at once reject as inadequate.

This quotation with regard to the earth memory should be carefully studied. It reveals ideas concerning the nature of experience which are much the same as those which William James expressed when he wrote: 'I do not believe that our experience is the highest form of experience extant in the Universe.' It lays stress on seeing vividly with the inner eye, and upon the fact that those who have not this gift strongly developed are really not in a position to offer criticism of a constructive nature. How can you criticize that of which you are ignorant? In order to see, you must visualize the veil until the intentness of your gaze renders it transparent; you must knock long and loud upon the unseen door until an unseen hand presses the key upon you. When your lips touch the bowl that some call the Grail, and some the Cauldron, the Goddess will Herself impart to you the riddle of the secret well of life. Omar Khayyam had the solution of that secret, though Edward Fitzgerald did not.

If the student with aptitude and energy takes up the study of these ancient pagan systems, he is bound, in time, to come across things unpleasant as well as pleasant, and it is well to warn the enquirer that he may, unexpectedly and without any previous preparations, touch pages of the 'Earth Memory' congruous to hidden records buried deep in his own subconscious mind. This experience may leave him badly shaken mentally and physically. By working in a group with trained teachers and obeying the rules, this shock can be minimized and no permanent harm is done; but working alone, groping blindly in the dark, using a half-understood technique drawn from the books of those who pretend to have been able to betray the secrets of the Mysteries, is folly. The genuine secrets of the Mysteries cannot be betrayed. Would Judas have betrayed Jesus if he had really understood the source of his Master's power and could have used it himself? Jesus taught nothing new; and even Judas, the intimate companion, the treasurer of the inner group, one of the Twelve, could not betray the secret of the power of Jesus for he could not *realize* it, or use it. Judas only betrays because he does not understand.

The student working alone is advised to read and to ponder deeply on the symbols of the ancient pagan systems, on their gods, on their teachings, on their folklore and myths. This work is preparatory to the real inner work that is developed in a Mystery school. He must not expect from these articles anything except hints as to how he must best prepare himself for the coming of a teacher. When the neophyte is ready, the Master will see that he is called to the Temple. This sentence – an ancient one – is written from personal experience, and from seeing again and again this same experience happen to others.

As the Memory of the Earth is one of the chief clues to the Mysteries of the pagans, it is worthy of examination as a working hypothesis and in order to familiarize oneself with this somewhat unusual concept. Beyond, behind, within and yet without (one has to use spatial terms) transcendent to and yet immanent in man's body, is the soul of man. Man is triune: spirit, soul and body. The soul, as the instrument for gaining experience, has faculties which are called the will, the memory, the imagination, the emotions, the reason, the instincts, etc. If the student will accept the hypothesis that the earth is the body of a great entity whose soul may be thought of as being in certain respects analogous to the soul of man, he can pursue the following methods of study with the prospect of getting a mental and spiritual training that will enable him one day to come prepared to the Temple. If he cannot accept this working hypothesis then he had better go off and play golf, where foozling – even if it leads him into blasphemy, will not take him, and others, into serious trouble.

The Earth Mother has many names. In Egypt the initiates called her Isis, and they thought of her as veiled in green. In Ireland they called her Dana or Danu, and in that country, which was one of the world's greatest spiritual centres, the Tuatha de Danaan, the Tribe of the Goddess Dana, can be communicated with – given the right conditions – more easily than is usual elsewhere. The veil between the actual and the real, the phenomenal and the noumenal, the seen and the unseen, the sensible and the intelligible, is less dense in Ireland than it is in stolid, bovine England. This fact, probably, is the true explanation of the curious characteristics of the Irish, and of the 'more Irish than the Irish' sentiments of certain Sassenachs that settle there. Ireland can stir strangely the deeper strata of the souls of certain Englishmen. It can charm, it can also annoy. It can produce love and hate, seldom indifference.

In England the Great Mother is Keredwen, and from the Welsh point of view Snowdon is her most sacred district. But the true Englishman can get in touch with the Great Mother at Glastonbury where Christianity has metamorphosed the goddess Brigantia into Saint Brigid. On the Tor and at the Well are nature-worship centres which are inferior to no other. Brigantia is as potent for better or for worse as is the Greek Athene.

The classical tradition has had its effects on the group soul of England, and the gods of Greece and Rome must not be neglected. Demeter was the best-known name of the Earth Mother in Greece, and her chief centre was Eleusis, the centre of the Eleusinian Mysteries. In Asia Minor and Babylonia she was known as Astarte, Ishtar and Astoreth, the Earthly Venus-Aphrodite. The student must never forget that while names seem to divide, functions bind the pantheon into an intelligible religious unity. Here is a valuable clue.

Before we start meditation, it is wise to examine facts and to avoid fancies. So let us take this list of names – Dana, Keredwen, Isis, Demeter, Ishtar, Astarte – and see what we can find out about them when we consider them as symbols of the unknown power which we call the Earth Mother, the great Fertile Mother. Go to the monumental works of Sir James George Frazer. Read if you can the twelve volumes of *The Golden Bough: A Study in Magic and Religion*, and see what is to be found. Dana is not mentioned in the general index, neither is Keredwen, though there is a large number of useful references to the other four names. *The Golden Bough* is supposed to be a study in magic for the English-speaking race, but although Sir James may know much about curious and indecent rites which he thinks are magic, he has not made clear to his readers the elementary principle that true magic, like charity, begins at home, in the group soul of the English race.

There is a very interesting book by Dr M. Harding called *Women's Mysteries Ancient and Modern*. In it is an immense amount of information which should set the reader's subconscious mind questing to and fro on a scent which grows warmer and warmer until Chapter 15 is reached. What Chapter 15 means to you will depend entirely upon what you are. It is true this work deals almost entirely with the Moon Mysteries, but, a man's immediate inner self – his anima – is feminine; also it is well to remember that the ancient initiates believed that the earth and the moon shared one 'etheric', and that in this state of cosmic matrimony the moon is the positive and the senior partner – a situation not altogether unknown in the earthly state of so-called holy matrimony, for woman has an animus (masculine aspect) – not an anima – if Jung is correct.

Let us suppose that you have got your supply of facts from your general reading, and that from meditation upon your reading you have built up in your mind a set of living symbols dealing with that Great Mother aspect of the Inner Worlds with which you wish to get in touch. The next step is to specialize in type. So concentrate on Isis, if that suits you best.

Isis is a goddess that is peculiarly attractive to this race. She was worshipped under her own name for a long period of the Roman occupation of Britain. The adoration of the Virgin Mary is the Christianized adaptation of the Egyptian Isis worship, and its introduction in the fourth century was the cause of bitter strife in the Christian Church; so the intense Mariolatry of medieval England has been a blessing for us pagan moderns, for it has kept alive in the great power centres of England those ancient forces which were once called the goddesses Keredwen, Danu, Isis and Briganda – who as a nature goddess is the Catholic St Bride. The modern English pagan owes the great Christian Church of Rome a deep debt of gratitude for preserving for him in working order these ancient shrines of the pagan power deities. In these places are concentrated centres of pagan power, astral, mental and spiritual, of which the Protestants and agnostics in their ignorance have never suspected the existence. In the ranks of the Church of England are many fine scholars, great social organizers, and great ethical teachers, but genuine priests are few.

In Isis, Keredwen, Dana, Briganda, and in their particular symbols of the Cup, the Grail, the Cauldron, the Sword or Spear, and in the young horned moon, low in the southern sky, are the keys of the Mysteries of the English Earth Mother, the One who is veiled in green; yet first you must solve the mystery of the ever-fruitful virgin mother who dwells in the most secret recesses of man's individuality. The cosmic aphorism 'As above, so below' has its counterpart in the psychological aphorism 'As within, so without.' In all the pagan Mystery systems it is clearly taught that the clue to the forces of Mother Nature is hidden within the soul of the worshipper, and it is there that the search for the key must commence. The veil that was impenetrable to the outward-looking eye of Edward Fitzgerald becomes transparent to the inward-looking eye of the trained mind. The Cauldron of the Earth Mother when raised to the lips of the neophyte gives him that ever-flowing inspiration which is from the Secret Well of Life.

Now let us turn to the particular symbols and see what door to the inner realms the moon symbols will open. What does the term 'Diana's Mirror' convey to you? Anything, or nothing? A memory that is almost a feeling. Have you ever seen it cold and black, still and star-lit? The moon-goddesses are regarded as the guardians of water, rivers, wells and springs. The moon-god is the local divinity that inhabits many of the sacred wells of Ireland and England. You can get some vivid emotional reactions by meditation upon the moon shining in a holy well if you have had personal contact with one of these holy wells.

Ishtar was called the All-Dewy-One; she is the ruler of dewponds and springs. There are some curious superstitions in Celtic countries about seeing the moon in wells and springs – confused remnants of ancient teachings and practices. There are, even in modern England, superstitions about seeing the moon in the crystal bowl of a dewpond; there are even more curious myths about the serpent in these moon-consecrated wells and ponds. Even Oxford has its Child's Well and serpent lore, and the serpent in the well is the man in the moon. Jung has told us of the interacting effect of a man's anima and a woman's animus. New Thought and Christian Science tell us of the powers of the directed will acting upon a vivid imagination. Hence the maiden at the moon-well concentrating on what is hidden in the crystal bowl in her imagination.

To the average exoteric Christian who carefully refrains from using his mind in religion, except in church when he concentrates on the task of keeping awake, these things are unknown, uncanny, and not quite nice. Study, for example, Dr Jung's

Psychology of the Unconscious. He gives some examples of moon symbols and their effect on the human mind. Why should this be so? Why should the symbols of the ancient religions live in the hidden recesses of the men and women of this twentieth century? Is this due to the convenient explanation – race memory? Is it due to reincarnation and to the recovery of individual lost memories? Has the earth got a memory, and if so can we recover from it these lost memories? No single theory will explain all the factors. Perhaps all three theories are partially true.

The regular and methodical use of symbols such as those just mentioned, can, in some cases, produce results that are to say the least not dull. Sometimes they can be exciting, far too exciting, and occasionally – and this warning is given from personal experience – they can be rather terrible. A very unpleasant death, died some 2,000 years ago, is still unpleasant if you happen to recover it from what shall we call it? – a race memory, a personal subconscious memory, or the earth memory?

As has been said before, the lore of the Mysteries is not for all and sundry.

Part 8: The Priest and the Moon Bowl

LXXIV
Oh, Moon of my Delight who know'st no wane,
The Moon of Heav'n is rising once again:
How oft hereafter rising shall she look
Through this same Garden after me – in vain!

LXXV
And when myself with shining Foot shall pass
Among the Guests star-scatter'd on the Grass
And in Thy joyous Errand reach the Spot
Where I made one – turn down an empty Glass!

(Iamad Shud)

In research work it is usually considered to be wiser to hunt up the facts and then think out the implications for oneself. Afterwards one can compare results with the standard authorities, and then decide upon one's attitude. In dealing with the great myths such as those of Isis and Osiris, or with the ancient sun and moon myths, the student cannot as a rule follow this method in its entirety. In all cosmic myths there are at least two aspects to be considered, the sensible and the intelligible meanings. In applying a cosmic myth to the microcosm, man, there are also two aspects which have to be taken into account, the objective and the subjective. One must know something of both these aspects before one can realize the implications of the facts one has collected.

So when the anthropological school takes an ancient myth and explains it in terms of corn and oil and water and fruitful soil, it is giving a true explanation, the type of explanation that might suit a rude unlettered child of the soil, the farmer and his labourers. But there are at least two other explanations which can be given, and all three are partially true, though taken singly each is inadequate, for it is but a partial explanation.

In the Isis myth, for example, Osiris can be taken as the life-giving moisture, he is the Nile-Flood: Isis, his wife, is the fertile soil rendered fruitful by the Nile. Set, his adversary and slayer, is the dry heat of the desert which hems in the Nile valley. Nephthys is the ribbon of soil that marks the edge of the fertile land; sometimes the Nile is high enough to render it fertile for a short time, then it lapses into the condition of wasteland. And so we find in this myth that Nephthys has sometimes as her husband Osiris, though she is usually considered to be the wife of the destructive Set. The child of Osiris and Nephthys is Anubis, the jackal-headed god. A fit symbol when we remember that the home of the Jackal is the desert edge and his hunting grounds are the fertile lands where men and their leavings abound.

Osiris is the moon-god who measures the seasons, and regulates the moisture and dew as well as the rise and fall of the Nile. He reigned twenty-eight years; twenty-eight is the moon period. Set cut his body into fourteen pieces, the fourteen days of the waning moon. Horus the younger is his son and is the new moon that reigns in place of the old moon, and so on. Divine numbers and god-names were sometimes keys to the 'inner tides' and their festivals, as are the Christian Golden Number and Dominical Letter.

Isis as the moon-goddess plays a role which can be explained by the growth of plants, fertility, etc. Again, up to a point this explanation is true for she is the Lady of Nature, and hers are the moon-powers which influence the physical life of the mothering sex. These ideas may be considered satisfactory when looked at from the point of view of the farmyard, but there were minds in the olden days which had progressed beyond the rather rustic level of modern anthropologists; not that their views are either new or modern. Plutarch, an initiate who lived at the time when St Paul was laying the foundations of Christianity, writes (LXV.):

> And we shall also get our hands on the dull crowd who take pleasure in associating the mystic recitals about these Gods either with changes of the atmosphere according to the seasons, or the generation of corn and sowings and ploughings, and in saying that Osiris is buried when the sown corn is hidden by the earth, and comes to life and shows himself again when the corn begins to sprout.

Plutarch, as one who was initiated into the Osiriaca at Delphi, knew that the true initiate of Isis is one who must for ever look for hidden reasons that substand the things said and done 'in the sacred rites' (III.5). But a true Isiac is one who, when he by law receives them, searches out by reason (Logos) the Mysteries shown and done concerning these gods and meditates upon the truth in them. This last sentence tells us where to look for the cosmic solutions of these ancient myths. For meditation is the process that links the microcosmic mind of man with the cosmos through the mind side of nature, that is with Isis, the Lady of Nature, the teacher, the nurse, the mother, the slayer of all.

Another solution of these problems of the ancient myths is psychological. It deals with the relationship between the subjective in man and the objective mind side of nature. The priest must look within the brimming circle of his moon bowl, for this solution is a matter of interpreting symbols that have an effect on the subconscious mind of man. It is not merely a matter of ancient history of kings and queens, nor of natural phenomena.

Psychologically, Isis is within the soul of man, and from one aspect we may call her the subconscious mind. Osiris, too, has his place in man's soul; he is focused consciousness. Both the Isis within and the Osiris within have a relationship to the Isis without and the Osiris without – that is, with the objective, mind side of nature, the dual-natured world – Isis and the world Osiris. Or in terms of the Chaldean myths, with Ishtar and Sin, the moon-god.

Isis had many names and so too have Osiris and Sin. The initiate of the Ancient Mysteries selected the aspect of Isis or of Sin that he intended to meditate upon with exactly the same care with which a watchmaker selects the tools that he is going to use. Also, a thing that is often forgotten today, the initiate of that day had to know his times and his seasons. It is no good seeking the Black Isis when it is the rising tide of the Lady that is veiled in green. When the silver moon rides high in the blue-black night sky, and when she is seen shining brightly in the crystal vase, waste not a tide that is flowing strongly in your favour.

Osiris too has his black and green and golden moments, and Sin also is a triune god; but it is only within the pylon gates that this detailed knowledge is given to the student. Still, the methodical worker who is able to measure the rise and fall of the tides within his own psyche, and who is prepared to note the times and seasons at the head of his daily meditation record and to analyse and synthesize and correlate results, can work out a practical table for himself. It will not take him very far, but it will save him quite a lot of time that would otherwise be wasted. For how many novices remember that in the Ancient Mysteries the moon is not only the sphere of generation, but it also the place of the dead, and the sphere of regeneration?

Again, the moon-man ever attends upon the moon goddess who sails in the 'Ship of Life'. It is often forgotten that it takes two to make a pair, for the sphere of manifestation is the sphere of duality, and while we are in these realms of duality it takes two to complete the functional unit, whether that unit is in the sphere of generation or in the sphere of intellection. There is always the subject and the object, the within and the without, the subjective and the objective, the worshipper and his deity. Nine-tenths of students' failures are due to neglect of these commonplace hackneyed truisms. How many keep in their daily record a note of their inner states and feelings during meditations? There is a direct relationship between these inner feelings and the so-called superstitions of the myths, for both have reference to the impalpable, immaterial substance which has been well called 'the plastic material of life'.

There is an ancient saying that a goddess cannot indwell her shrine unless there is a priest to offer the acceptable sacrifice. This is true of the cosmos, and it is also true in psychology. 'As above, so below.' All women are Isis; and a woman is most feminine and most like her true self when the priest invokes the inner nature of the goddess. But, whether it be Great Isis above, or one of her human incarnations here below, the priest has to be acceptable by right of function. So waste not 'here' or 'yonder' the propitious seasons; be true to 'instinct' when working in the realms of the moon deities.

When in solitary meditation a man sits in the Temple of the Goddess who nurses, mothers, slays and gives life, if he is to win through to that inner sanctuary where sits Isis, Astarte, Aphrodite or the Great Mountain Mother – the names matter not, for all the goddesses are one goddess – and to find his own regeneration, he must see himself as the priest who bears the sacrifice. That sacrifice is himself. He must face himself, his own instincts; and above all his own emotions. He must experience the latter to the utmost. There is no need for him, today, to become one of the Galloi, but there must be no mental reservations. It is 'all or nothing'. *Do ut des* is a fundamental principle when one is seeking to evoke the appearance of the Goddess.

Isis will come only to the favoured few. Always she, and she only, selects her own priest; and she will come only when the postulant for the ordeal of the priestly initiations has reached his limit.

It is here that the role of Typhon or Set, as the story is told by Plutarch, rounds off and completes the dual role of Isis and Osiris. The great gods of the cosmos and of the souls of men are always triune in their nature. Osiris is the brother of Set, neither is complete and neither can function without the other, as Apuleius shows in the story of the 'Golden Ass'. It is after the Typhonic ordeal that the postulant is given the 'Roses of Isis', and attains to the power of a moon initiate. But a moon priest the initiate cannot become until he has been called yet again by the goddess of Perfect Intelligence.

Sin as the moon-god is triune, and we know from the cuneiform inscriptions, as translated by Rawlinson, that Sin is Three Persons but one god; and these Persons are Anu, En-lil and Ea. As the inscription runs: 'The moon is during the period of his visibility, in the first five days, the god Anu; from the sixth to the tenth day, the god Ea; from the eleventh to the fifteenth day, the god En-lil.'

Look up in a mythological dictionary the essential natures of these three gods, the God of Heaven, the God of the Primeval Deep, and the Lord of the Golden Age. Then you will understand, through your meditations, why the moon priest has to undergo three initiations and has to make three sacrifices before he can drink from the moon bowl the draft of conscious immortality that will make him a priest of Isis or Ishtar, the Lord of the Three Worlds; for the moon-goddess is 'Goddess of Heaven, Goddess of Earth, and Goddess of the Underworld'.

Always there are these three moon initiations, whether the rites are those of Isis, of Sin and Ishtar, or of the Celtic Briganda. In terms of psychology this means that the initiate has gained the knowledge of the subconscious mind as the past, as the source, as the origin of things that are and that will be. 'I am all that has been and is and shall be, And no mortal has ever revealed my robe!' said Great Isis.

When the moon priest has drunk from the moon bowl, the mortal has become immortal, and that which the robe hides is revealed; the Veil has been parted, and the goddess within leaves the shadows of the sanctuary and becomes the regnatrix that dwells within the soul of that man. The Light of the Goddess is rising once again and is enwombed in the psyche of the moon priest.

The moon priest and the moon priestess become one, for the man has found his anima. And once the moon that lights the inner life has risen there is no need to seek in the garden of psyche in vain! There is no need to 'turn down an empty glass'! The bowl is filled with a living water and those who drink of it shall thirst no more – for it is ever flowing, and it is within – for ever. The goddess, incarnation after incarnation, will call her own back to her temple.

Part 9: The Moon Virgin and the Snake of Wisdom

'The Maiden's First Love Song'

What can I do, what can I begin?
That shuddering thing:
There it crackles within
And coils in a ring.
It must be poisoned.
Here it crawls around
Blissfully I feel as it worms
Itself into my Soul
And kills me finally.

(Mörike, quoted in Jung, *Psychology of the Unconscious*, p. 5.)

The snake was a symbol for the divine wisdom. It was a dual symbol, the White Serpent of Yetsirah and the Dark Serpent of the World of Assiah, two aspects of the same principle.

If one thinks for a few moments on the nature of human wisdom it can be divided into three main divisions or faculties. There is first of all that which has been called the estimative faculty, or the wisdom of the children of this world. It deals chiefly with the mundane business of living well, and with that type of concept and opinion which man's mind formulates as the result of experiences met with in what the ancient mystics called the 'sensible' world. Plato calls this faculty *pistis* . . . faith in the aspect of trust. He considered it to be a non-reasoning faculty because it depends upon the opinions of others and on the testimony of the senses. It is a faculty that when highly developed leads to success in things mundane. It can always be distinguished from reason because though it knows that a thing *is*, it cannot explain *why* it is. Many of those who take their opinions ready-made mistake this particular faculty of the mind for reason. But when the student has begun to study 'religion', then he commences to suspect that much of his supposed religious and philosophical knowledge is based upon an authority external to himself and not upon that personal reasoning faculty which Mother Nature has implanted in every man's mind. Meditation upon the fundamentals of the estimative faculty will lead man to the next main division – reason.

In the Ancient Mysteries each of the moon-goddesses was looked upon as the giver of wisdom, as man's protectress during life upon earth, and as offering worldly success to diligent devotees.

In terms of modern psychology it may be said that the moon deities rule over the estimative faculty of the human soul. They were the goddesses of instinct and of instinctive reaction, and they were the rulers of the powerful subconscious mind. In terms of the Qabalah, they function in the sphere of Yesod. Again, if we study these ancient myths, we shall find that these moon-goddesses were taught by the cosmic wisdom-gods. For example Thoth as the Logos or Divine Reason taught Isis, and there are somewhat similar myths in most of the other great religions.

In the Neo-Platonic system of psychology, reason, which Plato called *dianoia*, is that faculty of the soul which addresses itself to those intelligible principles upon which all sensible nature depends. In the mysteries based upon Plato's teachings, pure reason was described as the faculty that enables the *mystae* to know and to apply those abstract and divine ideas which the ancient form of 'Idealism', as a philosophy, holds to be innate in the human soul. Their Mystery initiations aimed rather at educing these innate divine ideals by means of the cult's meditation technique than at teaching a special and novel kind of concrete knowledge. Reason is innate in the human soul, though often it appears to be almost completely dormant, as is clearly shown by the difficulty some people have in following an argument when put formally as logic, or in comprehending abstract ideas. How many people can study with pleasure the science of logic?

Thoth, Nabu or Nebo, Hermes, Sin (or Enzu) as the 'Lord of Wisdom', the Celtic Dagda and Myrddin, all are, to a greater or lesser degree, gods of that Divine Wisdom which is typified by the White Snake. As such they are the teachers of the moon-goddesses, who represent that type of divine wisdom which some of the Gnostics called the fallen Sophia. As moon-gods they gave their 'syzygy' the divine knowledge which ensures power over the creations of the great creator-gods such as Ra.

'As above, so below'; and turning to the microcosm and to psychology we find reason as the positive mental faculty controlling, organizing and often repressing those power-supplying instincts that lie behind and energize the somewhat feminine and less positive estimative faculty. In the Egyptian Mysteries Thoth's syzygy is Maat, who is a form of Isis. Nabu's wife was Tashmetu – 'she who hears', an exact description of the rather negative faculty, that is, the lower reason.

Thoth as the god of reason guides the 'Ship of Life', that is to say, Isis, who is psychologically the subconscious mind of man and of Nature, according to the teaching of these Ancient Mystery systems.

In addition to *pistis* and *dianoia* there was also a third faculty – intuition. This Plato called *noesis*, and it was thought of as the highest expression of all the human mental faculties when working as a well-trained team. It is often confused with instinct and with feeling. We all know the person who says: 'I have an intuition; I feel it in my bones.' But the *noesis* of the Ancient Mysteries was something much more than this for it was a faculty of comprehending those 'great universal ideas of which the manifested universe is a differentiated and objective expression'. It is the unfallen Sophia; it is a wisdom that is beyond all earthly wisdom.

Bearing in mind this psychological background, which may seem strange to us moderns, one can comprehend the importance of understanding clearly the use of the snake as an explanatory symbol. Some of the goddesses are shown holding snakes or attended by snakes; to the initiated this explained the phase of the goddess that he was expected to concentrate upon. The snake, or pair of snakes, stood for a partic-ular aspect of sacred knowledge; and there were many special kinds of this knowledge that the ancient gods and goddesses could impart to their devotees through meditation, contemplation and ritual. They knew that one must focus and restrict if power is to be generated in mental work.

Man's greatest task is the finding of himself and his purpose in life. And man can only find these two things by using himself for the conscious and concentrated expression of life (Isis with the Ankh) according to his own personal potentialities.

In this lies the dual wisdom of the divine snakes as they climb the sacred rod of Hermes, or the Paths of the Tree of Life. In finding himself man is working in the sphere ruled by the cosmic gods of wisdom, the realm of ideals. He becomes an initiate, or better, a devotee of the Great Hermes Trismegistus. But for the expression of his life purpose, man must serve the moon-goddess, for she and not a male god rules in the realm of actuality. The dark snake rules in Assiah, the sphere of the form-giving mother, Mut of ancient Thebes.

Wisdom, like most other things in cosmic manifestation, is dual in its nature. There is the wisdom of the Ibis-headed Thoth, who has been described as the Logos of Plato. There is also the wisdom of Isis of the throne, and of dark Nephthys of the Cup. Always there is the Wisdom of the Inner and the Outer, of the Sensible and the Intelligible.

The parable of the unjust steward, who was, we are often told, an unworldly visionary and not really a thief, explains this; and the steward's lord commends him for learning the earthly wisdom before trying to master the Wisdom of the Children of Light. In terms of the Mystery initiations, you must serve Isis before you can ascend to the eight steps that lead to the Throne of Khemennu in the House of the Net. For in ancient Egypt there were the Lesser Mysteries and the Greater Mysteries. There was also the Mystery that was taught in 'the House of the Net' at Hermopolis.

For those who care to seek it, there is divine as well as human symbolism in that love song of Mörike which begins:

> What is in the net?
> Behold,
> But I am afraid,
> Do I grasp a sweet eel,
> Do I seize a snake?

In this section the reader has been given a series of mental pictures, a number of mythological images which have to be meditated upon frequently in order to get at their inner meaning. They are not meant to teach the conscious mind anything. The hard-headed man of the world will find them incoherent and unreasonable. Up to a point he is right. They are incoherent, that is to say, they are not easily followed. But their meanings can be grasped if you will follow the example of Theseus and carry Ariadne's thread with you when, in meditation, you enter the labyrinth that is your own subconscious mind. Again they are, of course, unreasonable! 'Love', that seizes a snake, 'is a blind fisherwoman'. But these mythic images are most certainly not untrue to your own inner nature. Try them and see what comes to you in the still moments of deep meditation; or better still, try to dream about them at night.

Have you ever read 'The Song of Solomon' translated accurately into modern English? Moffat's translation is as good as any other. Try reading the verse given below, and see what comes. Your conscious mind may seek to give you one set of meanings, and they are reasonable. But the pictures that will rise from the depths of your subconscious mind when it is stilled in meditation on this jewel of ancient wisdom may not be reasonable, yet they may not be the less true. For 'The Song of

Solomon' deals with the snakes of wisdom and it pertains to a moon-virgin and to the moon-goddess. Get at the subconscious meaning of the following:

> 5. I am dark, but I am a beauty,
>   Maidens of Jerusalem,
>   Dark as the tents of the Blackmen,
>   Beautiful as curtains of a Solomon.

> 6. Scorn me not for being dark . . .

When the subconscious mind is as still as the dark windless surface of the high-flying, star-lit mountain lake that is at the foot of the five white glaciers, you may enter in safety the labyrinth and rely on the thread that Ariadne (intuition) has given Theseus (yourself).

As Adam and Solomon discovered long ago, there is a close connection between 'the Woman' and the Snake of Wisdom. Today Jung teaches that a man's inner self is an anima not an animus. Here is your Ariadne's thread — if you can use it.

October 1936 to September 1937

Notes

1   'Hither' is a technical term for the material world. (Seymour).
2   'Yonder' is a technical term for the unseen world. (Seymour).

Chapter 18

Robert Graves

THE TRIPLE MUSE

■ from **THE WHITE GODDESS**, New York, 1948, pp. 383–408

ROBERT GRAVES SUBTITLED *THE* White Goddess, 'A Historical
Grammar of Poetic Myth'. But in 1955 he is said to have written to a stranger:
'Some day scholars will sort out the White Goddess grain from the chaff. It's a crazy
book and I didn't mean to write it' (Seymour-Smith, 1982: 405). In fact, scholars
(especially classicists, historians and folklorists) have not received the book well.
Poets, playwrights and Pagans, however, have mined it for materials to use both as
foundations and adornments in their own works. Perhaps inspiration works this way.
The themes and motifs that most resonate with Pagan interests (perhaps inspiring
some of them) are Graves' elaboration of a 'tree calendar' and his reverence for a
triple Goddess. The former underlies various recent versions of tree and ogham (rune-
like characters) calendars, as well as divinatory and meditative systems (e.g. Murray
and Murray, 1989; Matthews, 2001) popular among Druids. The latter is pervasive
among Wiccans and many other Pagans.

The excerpt included here is Chapter 22: 'The Triple Muse'. Here, Graves
discusses three forms of the Goddess in ways instantly recognizable and thoroughly
familiar to many Pagans. In palaeolithic painting, classical statues and myths,
Christian Marian devotion, European witch accusations, English folklore and
Victorian royalist poetry, Graves discerns a prevailing devotion to a Goddess who
is virgin, mother and crone – or youthful, mature and elderly. He also notes that
in each phase the Goddess is attended to by Gods who match her life-cycle.
Transformations between these phases link the Goddess with bards, magicians and
others of importance in the rest of *The White Goddess*.

Taking Graves' mature conclusion, we might reject the historicity of his schema
while being inspired by the passionate devotion to a deity who is sufficiently like us
to enchant our everyday lives and sufficiently different to inspire us to improve on

the present. Certainly the triple Goddess and her consort are central to initiatory Wicca and foundational of much Goddess/Feminist Spirituality. Later chapters in this *Reader* illustrate the later and continuing attraction of Graves' Goddess.

Graham Harvey

References

Matthews, Caítlin (2001) *Celtic Wisdom Sticks*. London: Connections.
Murray, Liz and Murray, Colin (1989) *The Celtic Tree Oracle*. London: Rider.
Seymour-Smith, Martin (1982) *Robert Graves: His Life and Work*. London: Hutchinson.

WHY DO POETS invoke the Muse?

Milton in the opening lines of *Paradise Lost* briefly summarizes the Classical tradition, and states his intention, as a Christian, of transcending it:

> *Sing, heav'nly Muse, that on the secret top*
> *Of Oreb, or of Sinai, didst inspire*
> *That shepherd, who first taught the chosen seed*
> *In the beginning how the Heav'ns and Earth*
> *Rose out of Chaos: Or if Sion hill*
> *Delight thee more, and Siloa's brook that flow'd*
> *Fast by the oracle of God: I thence*
> *Invoke thy aid to my advent'rous song*
> *That with no middle flight intends to soar*
> *Above th'Aonian mount, while it pursues*
> *Things unattempted yet in prose or rhime.*

The Aonian Mount is Mount Helicon in Boeotia, a mountain a few miles to the east of Parnassus, and known in Classical times as 'the seat of the Muses'. The adjective 'Aonian' is a reminiscence of a memorable line from Virgil's Georgics:

> *Aonio rediens deducam vertice Musas*

which is spoken by Apollo, the God of poetry, who by Virgil's time was also recognized as the Sun-god. The line means 'On my return I shall lead the Muses down from the top of Mount Helicon'. Apollo is referring to the transplanting of the worship of the Muses from Ascra, a town on a ridge of Helicon, to Delphi, on Mount Parnassus, a place which had become sacred to himself. On Helicon rose the spring named Hippocrene, 'The Horse Well', which was horse-shoe shaped. The legend was that it had been struck by the hoof of the horse Pegasus, whose name means 'of the springs of water'. Poets were said to drink of Hippocrene for inspiration. Hence John Skelton's lines (*Against Garnesche*):

> *I gave him of the sugryd welle*
> *Of Eliconys waters crystallyne.*

But it may be supposed that Hippocrene and Aganippe were originally struck by the moon-shaped hoof of Leucippe ('White Mare'), the Mare-headed Mother herself, and that the story of how Bellerophon son of Poseidon mastered Pegasus and then destroyed the triple-shaped Chimaera is really the story of an Achaean capture of the Goddess's shrine: Pegasus, in fact, was originally called Aganippe. *Aganos* is a Homeric adjective applied to the shafts of Artemis and Apollo, meaning 'giving a merciful death'; so Aganippe would mean: 'The Mare who destroys mercifully.' This supposition is strengthened by the Greek legend of the pursuit of Demeter, the Barley Mother, by the Achaean god Poseidon. Demeter, to escape his attentions, disguised herself as a mare and concealed herself among the horses of Oncios the Arcadian, but Poseidon became a stallion and covered her; her anger at this outrage was said to account for her statue at Onceum, called Demeter Erinnus—the Fury.

Demeter as a Mare-goddess was widely worshipped under the name of Epona, or 'the Three Eponae', among the Gallic Celts, and there is a strange account in Giraldus Cambrensis's *Topography of Ireland* which shows that relics of the same cult survived in Ireland until the twelfth century. It concerns the crowning of an Irish petty-king at Tyrconnell, a preliminary to which was his symbolic rebirth from a white mare. He crawled naked towards her on all fours as if he were her foal; she was then slaughtered, and her pieces boiled in a cauldron. He himself entered the cauldron and began sucking up the broth and eating the flesh. Afterwards he stood on an inauguration stone, was presented with a straight white wand, and turned about three times from left to right, and then three times from right to left—'in honour of the Trinity'. Originally no doubt in honour of the Triple White Goddess.

The horse, or pony, has been a sacred animal in Britain from pre-historic times, not merely since the Bronze Age introduction of the stronger Asiatic breed. The only human figure represented in what survives of British Old Stone Age art is a man wearing a horse-mask, carved in bone, found in the Derbyshire Pin-hole Cave; a remote ancestor of the hobby-horse mummers in the English 'Christmas play'. The Saxons and Danes venerated the horse as much as did their Celtic predecessors, and the taboo on eating horse-flesh survives in Britain as a strong physical repugnance, despite attempts made during World War II to popularize hippophagism; but among the Bronze Age British the taboo must have been lifted at an annual October horse-feast, as among the Latins. In mediaeval Denmark the ecstatic three-day horse-feast, banned by the Church, survived among the heathenish serf-class; a circumstantial description is given by Johannes Jensen in his *Fall of the King*. He mentions that the priest first sprinkled bowls of the horse's blood towards the South and East—which explains the horse as an incarnation of the Spirit of the Solar Year, son of the Mare-goddess.

In the *Romance of Pwyll, Prince of Dyfed* the Goddess appears as Rhiannon mother of Pryderi. Rhiannon is a corruption of Rigantona ('Great Queen') and Dyfed consisted of most of Carmarthen and the whole of Pembrokeshire and included St. David's; its central point was called 'The Dark Gate', an entrance to the Underworld. When Pwyll ('Prudence') first sees Rhiannon and falls in love with her, he pursues her on his fastest horse but cannot overtake her; evidently in the original story she took the form of a white mare. When at last she consents to be overtaken, and marries him twelve months later, she bears him a son afterwards called Pryderi ('Anxiety') who disappears at birth; and her maids falsely accuse her of having devoured him, smearing her face with the blood of puppies. As a penance she is ordered to stand at a horse-block outside Pwyll's palace, like a mare, ready to carry guests on her back.[1] The life of her son Pryderi is closely connected with a magical foal which has been rescued from a harpy; all the previous foals of the same mare have been snatched off on May Eve and never seen again. Pryderi, a Divine Child of the sort that is taken away from its mother—like Llew Llaw, or Zeus, or Romulus—is later, as usual, given a name and arms by her, mounts the magical horse and eventually becomes a Lord of the Dead. Rhiannon is thus seen to be a Mare-goddess, but she is also a Muse-goddess, for the sirens that appear in the *Triads*, and also in the *Romance of Branwen*, singing with wonderful sweetness are called 'The Birds of Rhiannon'. The story about the puppies recalls the Roman habit of sacrificing red puppies in the Spring to avert the baleful influence of the Dog-star on their grain; the sacrifice was really to the Barley-mother who had the Dog-star as her attendant. Rhiannon, in fact, is the Mare-Demeter, a successor of the Sow-Demeter Cerridwen. That the Mare-Demeter devoured children, like the Sow-Demeter, is proved by the myth of Leucippe ('White Mare') the Orchomenan, who with her two sisters ran wild and devoured her son Hippasus ('foal'); and by the myth recorded by Pausanias, that when Rhea gave birth to Poseidon she offered her lover Cronos a foal to eat instead of the child, whom she gave secretly into the charge of the shepherds of Arcadian Arne.

Mount Helicon was not the earliest seat of the Muse Goddesses, as their title 'The Pierians' shows; the word Muse is now generally derived from the root *mont*, meaning a mountain. Their worship had been brought there in the Heroic Age during a migration of the Boeotian people from Mount Pieria in Northern Thessaly. But to make the transplanted Muses feel at home on Helicon, and so to preserve the old magic, the Boeotians named the geographical features of the mountain—the springs, the peaks and grottoes—after the corresponding features of Pieria. The Muses were at this time three in number, an indivisible Trinity, as the mediaeval Catholics recognized when they built the church of their own Holy Trinity on the site of the deserted shrine of the Heliconian Muses. The appropriate names of the three Persons were Meditation, Memory and Song. The worship of the Muses on Helicon (and presumably also in Pieria) was concerned with incantatory cursing and incantatory blessing; Helicon was famous for the medicinal herbs which supplemented the incantations—especially for the nine-leaved black hellebore used by Melampus at Lusi as a cure for the Daughters of Proetus, which could either cause or cure insanity and which has a stimulative action on the heart like *digitalis* (fox-glove). It was famous also for the erotic fertility dances about a stone herm at Thespiae, a town at its foot, in which the women-votaries of the Muses took part. Spenser addresses the Muses as 'Virgins of Helicon'; he might equally have called them 'witches', for the witches of his day worshipped the same White Goddess—in *Macbeth* called Hecate—performed the same fertility dances on their Sabbaths, and were similarly gifted in incantatory magic and knowledge of herbs.

The Muse priestesses of Helicon presumably used two products of the horse to stimulate their ecstasies: the slimy vaginal issue of a mare in heat and the black membrane, or *hippomanes*, cut from the forehead of a new-born colt, which the mare (according to Aristotle) normally eats as a means of increasing her mother-love. Dido in the *Aeneid* used this *hippomanes* in her love-potion.

Skelton in his *Garland of Laurell* thus describes the Triple Goddess in her three characters as Goddess of the Sky, Earth and Underworld:

> *Diana in the leavës green,*
> *Luna that so bright doth sheen,*
> *   Persephone in Hell.*

As Goddess of the Underworld she was concerned with Birth, Procreation and Death. As Goddess of the Earth she was concerned with the three seasons of Spring, Summer and Winter: she animated trees and plants and ruled all living creatures, As Goddess of the Sky she was the Moon, in her three phases of New Moon, Full Moon, and Waning Moon. This explains why from a triad she was so often enlarged to an ennead. But it must never be forgotten that the Triple Goddess, as worshipped for example at Stymphalus, was a personification of primitive woman—woman the creatress and destructress. As the New Moon or Spring she was girl; as the Full Moon or Summer she was woman; as the Old Moon or Winter she was hag.

In a Gallo-Roman '*allée couverte*' burial at Tressé near St. Malo in Brittany two pairs of girls' breasts are sculptured on one megalithic upright, two maternal pairs of breasts on another; the top of a third upright has been broken off, but V. C. C. Collum who excavated the burial suggests that it pictured a third pair—probably the shrunken breasts of the Hag. A very interesting find in this same burial, which can be dated by a bronze coin of Domitian to the end of the first century A.D., was a flint arrow-head of the usual willow-leaf shape with an incised decoration of half-moons. The willow, as we have seen, was sacred to the Moon, and in the Beth-Luis-Nion is *Saille*, the letter S. The most primitive character of the Greek letter S is C, which is borrowed from the Cretan linear script. Sir Arthur Evans in his *Palace of Minos* gives a table showing the gradual development of the Cretan characters from ideograms, and the sign C is there explained as a waning moon—the Moon-goddess as hag. The arrow-head, which in Roman Brittany was as completely out of date, except for ritual uses, as the Queen's sword of state, or the Archbishop's crozier is now, must be an offering to the third person of the female Trinity.[2] V. C. C. Collum took the trouble to have an analysis made of the charcoal found under the uprights, apparently the remains of the funerary pyre on which the dead man had been cremated. It was willow, oak and hazel charcoal, expressive of the sequence: enchantment, royalty, wisdom.

In Europe there were at first no male gods contemporary with the Goddess to challenge her prestige or power, but she had a lover who was alternatively the beneficent Serpent of Wisdom, and the beneficent Star of Life, her son. The Son was incarnate in the male demons of the various totem societies ruled by her, who assisted in the erotic dances held in her honour. The Serpent, incarnate in the sacred serpents which were the ghosts of the dead, sent the winds. The Son, who was also called Lucifer or Phosphorus ('bringer of light') because as evening-star he led in the light of the Moon, was reborn every year, grew up as the year advanced, destroyed the Serpent, and won the Goddess's love. Her love destroyed him, but from his ashes was born another Serpent which, at Easter, laid the *glain* or red egg which she ate; so that the Son was reborn to her as a child once more. Osiris was a Star-son, and though after his death he looped himself around the world like a serpent, yet when his fifty-yard long phallus was carried in procession it was topped with a golden star; this stood for himself renewed as the Child Horus, son of Isis, who had been both his bride and his layer-out and was now his mother once again. Her absolute power was proved by a yearly holocaust in her honour as 'Lady of the Wild Things', in which the totem bird or beast of each society was burned alive.

The most familiar icon of Aegean religion is therefore a Moon-woman, a Star-son and a wise spotted Serpent grouped under a fruit-tree—Artemis, Hercules and Erechtheus. Star-son and Serpent are at war; one succeeds the other in the Moon-woman's favour, as summer succeeds winter, and winter succeeds summer; as death succeeds birth and birth succeeds death. The Sun grows weaker or stronger as the year takes its course, the branches of the tree are now loaded and now bare, but the light of the Moon is invariable. She is impartial: she destroys or creates with equal passion. The conflict between the twins is given an ingenious turn in the Romance of *Kilhwych and Olwen*: Gwyn ('White') and his rival Gwythur ap Greidawl ('Victor, son of Scorcher') waged perpetual war for Creiddylad (*alias* Cordelia), daughter of Lludd (*alias* Llyr, *alias* Lear, *alias* Nudd, *alias* Nuada, *alias* Nodens), each in turn stealing her from the other, until the matter was referred to King Arthur. He gave the ironical decision that Creiddylad should be returned to her father and that the twins should 'fight for her every first of May, until the day of doom', and that whichever of them should then be conqueror should keep her.

There are as yet no fathers, for the Serpent is no more the father of the Star-son than the Star-son is of the Serpent. They are twins, and here we are returned to the single poetic Theme. The poet identifies himself with the Star-son, his hated rival is the Serpent; only if he is writing as a satirist, does he play the Serpent. The Triple Muse is woman in her divine character: the poet's enchantress, the only theme of his songs. It must not be forgotten that Apollo himself was once a yearly victim of the Serpent: for Pythagoras carved an inscription on his tomb at Delphi, recording his death in a fight with the local python—the python which he was usually supposed to have killed outright. The Star-son and the Serpent are still mere demons, and in Crete the Goddess is not even pictured with a divine child in her arms. She is the mother of all things; her sons and lovers partake of the sacred essence only by her grace.

The revolutionary institution of fatherhood, imported into Europe from the East, brought with it the institution of individual marriage. Hitherto there had been only group marriages of all female members of a particular totem society with all members of another; every child's maternity was certain, but its paternity debatable and irrelevant. Once this revolution had occurred, the social status of woman altered: man took over many of the sacred practices from which his sex had debarred him, and finally declared himself head of the household, though much property still passed from mother to daughter. This second stage, the Olympian stage, necessitated a change in mythology. It was not enough to introduce the concept of fatherhood into the ordinary myth, as in the Orphic formula quoted by Clement of Alexandria, 'The Bull that is the Serpent's father, the Serpent that is the Bull's.' A new child was needed who should supersede both the Star-son and the Serpent. He was celebrated by poets as the Thunder-child, or the Axe-child, or the Hammer-child. There are different legends as to how he removed his enemies. Either he borrowed the golden sickle of the Moon-woman, his mother, and castrated the

Star-son; or he flung him down from a mountain top; or he stunned him with his axe so that he fell into perpetual sleep. The Serpent he usually killed outright. Then he became the Father-god, or Thunder-god, married his mother and begot his divine sons and daughters on her. The daughters were really limited versions of herself— herself in various young-moon and full-moon aspects. In her old-moon aspect she became her own mother, or grandmother, or sister, and the sons were limited revivals of the destroyed Star-son and Serpent. Among these sons was a God of poetry, music, the arts and the sciences: he was eventually recognized as the Sun-god and acted in many countries as active regent for his senescent father, the Thunder-god. In some cases he even displaced him. The Greeks and the Romans had reached this religious stage by the time that Christianity began.

The third stage of cultural development—the purely patriarchal, in which there are no Goddesses at all—is that of later Judaism, Judaic Christianity, Mohammedanism and Protestant Christianity. This stage was not reached in England until the Commonwealth, since in mediaeval Catholicism the Virgin and Son—who took over the rites and honours of the Moon-woman and her Star-son—were of greater religious importance than God the Father. (The Serpent had become the Devil; which was appropriate because Jesus had opposed fish to serpent in *Matthew, VII, 10,* and was himself symbolized as a fish by his followers.) The Welsh worshipped Virgin and Son for fifty years longer than the English; the Irish of Eire still do so. This stage is unfavourable to poetry. Hymns addressed to the Thunder-god, however lavishly they may gild him in Sun-god style—even Skelton's magnificent *Hymn to God the Father*—fail as poems, because to credit him with illimitable and unrestrained power denies the poet's inalienable allegiance to the Muse; and because though the Thunder-god has been a jurist, logician, declamator and prose-stylist, he has never been a poet or had the least understanding of true poems since he escaped from his Mother's tutelage.

In Greece, when the Moon-woman first became subordinated to the Thunder-god as his wife, she delegated the charge of poetry to her so-called daughter, her former self as the Triple Muse, and no poem was considered auspicious that did not begin with an appeal to the Muse for inspiration. Thus the early ballad, *The Wrath of Achilles*, which introduces the *Iliad* of Homer, begins: 'Sing, Goddess, of the destructive anger of Achilles, son of Peleus.' That Achilles is styled 'son of Peleus' rather than 'son of Thetis' proves that the patriarchal system was already in force, though totem society lingered on as a social convenience, Achilles being a sacred king of the Myrmidons of Thessaly, apparently an Ant clan subject to the Goddess as Wryneck; but the Goddess is clearly the Triple Muse, not merely one of the nine little Muses, mentioned in a less primitive part of the *Iliad*, whom Apollo later led down from Helicon, and up to Parnassus when, as recorded in the *Hymn to Pythian Apollo*, he superseded the local Earth-goddess in the navel-shrine at Delphi. Apollo ('Destroyer or Averter') was at this time considered to be a male twin to the daughter-goddess Artemis; they were represented as children of the Thunder-god, born on Quail Island, off Delos, to the Goddess Latona the Hyperborean, daughter of Phoebe and Coieus ('Moonlight and Initiation').

The myths get confused here because Latona, being a newcomer to Delos, was not at first recognized by the local Triple Goddess; and because Artemis, the name of Apollo's twin, had previously been a Greek title of the Triple Goddess herself.

Artemis probably means 'The Disposer of Water' from *ard-* and *themis*. Apollo, one may say, was securing his position by persuading his twin to take over the emblems and titles of her predecessor: he himself adopted the titles and emblems of a Pelasgian 'Averter' or 'Destroyer', in one aspect (as his title Smintheus proves) a Cretan Mouse-demon. Apollo and Artemis then together took over the charge of poetry from the Triple Muse (in this context their mother Latona); but Artemis soon ceased to be an equal partner of Apollo's, though she continued to be a Goddess of magical charms and eventually was credited with evil charms only. So Tatian records in his *Address to the Greeks*: 'Artemis is a poisoner, Apollo performs cures.' In Ireland, similarly, the Goddess Brigit became overshadowed by the God Ogma. In Cormac's *Glossary* it was necessary to explain her as: 'Brigit, daughter of The Dagda, the poetess, that is, the goddess worshipped by the poets on account of the great and illustrious protection afforded them by her.' It was in her honour that the ollave carried a golden branch with tinkling bells when he went abroad.

About the eighth century B.C. the Muse triad became enlarged under Thraco-Macedonian influence to three triads, or an ennead. Here the nine orgiastic priestesses of the Island of Sein in West Brittany, and the nine damsels in the *Preiddeu Annwm* whose breaths warmed Cerridwen's cauldron, will be recalled. A ninefold Muse was more expressive of the universality of the Goddess's rule than a threefold one; but the Apollo priesthood who ruled Greek Classical literature soon used the change as a means of weakening her power by a process of departmentalization. Hesiod writes of the Nine Daughters of Zeus, who under Apollo's patronage were given the following functions and names:

> *Epic poetry, Calliope.*
> *History, Clio.*
> *Lyric poetry, Euterpe.*
> *Tragedy, Melpomene.*
> *Choral dancing, Terpsichore.*
> *Erotic poetry and mime, Erato.*
> *Sacred Poetry, Polyhymnia.*
> *Astronomy, Urania.*
> *Comedy, Thaleia.*

Calliope ('beautiful face') was a name of the original Muse, in her full-moon aspect; so were Erato 'the beloved one'; and Urania 'the heavenly one'. The first mention of Erato in Greek myth is as the Oak-queen to whom Arcas was married; he gave his name to Arcadia and was the son of Callisto the She-bear and father of Atheneatis. The other names apparently refer to the several functions of the Muses. It will be observed that though the Muses of Helicon still had erotic tendencies, their chief function, that of healing and cursing by incantation, had been taken away from them under Olympianism. It had passed to Apollo himself and a surrogate, his physician son Aesculapius.

Apollo, though the God of Poetry and the leader of the Muses, did not yet, however, claim to inspire poems: the inspiration was still held to come to the poet from the Muse or Muses. He had originally been a mere Demon[3] whom his Muse mother had inspired with poetic frenzy; now he required that, as the Ninefold Muse, she should inspire individual poets in his honour—though not to the point of ecstasy. These poets, if they proved to be his faithful and industrious servants, he rewarded with a garland of laurel—in Greek, *daphne*. The connexion of poetry with laurel is not merely that laurel is an evergreen and thus an emblem of immortality: it is also an intoxicant. The female celebrants of the Triple Goddess at Tempe had chewed laurel leaves to induce a poetic and erotic frenzy, as the Bacchanals chewed ivy— *daphne* maybe a shortened form of *daphoine*, 'the bloody one', a title of the Goddess—and when Apollo took over the Delphic oracle the Pythian priestess who continued in charge learned to chew laurel for oracular inspiration. The laurel had become sacred to Apollo—his legendary pursuit of the nymph Daphne records his capture of the Goddess's shrine at Tempe near Mount Olympus—but he was now the God of Reason with the motto 'nothing in excess', and his male initiates wore the laurel without chewing at it; Empedocles, as Pythagoras's semi-divine successor, held laurel-chewing in as great horror as bean-eating. Poetry as a magical practice was already in decline.

The Romans conquered Greece and brought Apollo with them to Italy. They were a military nation, ashamed of their own rude poetic tradition, but some of them began to take up Greek poetry seriously as part of their education in political rhetoric, an art which they found necessary for consolidating their military conquests. They studied under the Greek sophists and understood from them that major poetry was a more musical and more philosophical form of rhetoric than could be achieved by prose and that minor poetry was the most elegant of social accomplishments. True poets will agree that poetry is spiritual illumination delivered by a poet to his equals, not an ingenious technique of swaying a popular audience or of enlivening a sottish dinner-party, and will think of Catullus as one of the very few poets who transcended the Graeco-Roman poetic tradition. The reason perhaps was that he was of Celtic birth: at any rate, he had a fearlessness, originality and emotional sensitivity entirely lacking in the general run of Latin poets. He alone showed a sincere love of women; the others were content to celebrate either comrade-loyalty or playful homosexuality. His contemporary, Virgil, is to be read for qualities that are not poetic in the sense that they invoke the presence of the Muse. The musical and rhetorical skill, the fine-sounding periphrases, and the rolling periods, are admired by classicists, but the *Aeneid* is designed to dazzle and over-power, and true poets do not find it consistent with their integrity to follow Virgil's example. They honour Catullus more, because he never seems to be calling upon them, as posterity, to applaud a demonstration of immortal genius; rather, he appeals to them as a contemporary: 'Is this not so?' For Horace as the elegant verse-writer they may feel affection, and admire his intention of avoiding extremes of feeling and the natural Roman temptation to be vulgar. But for all his wit, affability and skilful gleemanship they can hardly reckon him a poet, any more than they can reckon, say, Calverley or Austin Dobson.

To summarize the history of the Greek Muses:

The Triple Muse, or the Three Muses, or the Ninefold Muse, or Cerridwen, or whatever else one may care to call her, is originally the Great Goddess in her poetic or incantatory character. She has a son who is also her lover and her victim, the Star-son, or Demon of the Waxing Year. He alternates in her favour with his tanist Python, the Serpent of Wisdom, the Demon of the Waning year, his darker self.

Next, she is courted by the Thunder-god (a rebellious Star-son infected by Eastern patriarchalism) and has twins by him, a male and a female—in Welsh poetry called Merddin and Olwen. She remains the Goddess of Incantation, but forfeits part of her sovereignty to the Thunder-god, particularly law-making and the witnessing of oaths.

Next, she divides the power of poetic enchantment between her twins, whose symbols are the morning star and the evening star, the female twin being herself in decline, the male a revival of the Star-son.

Next, she becomes enlarged in number, though reduced in power, to a bevy of nine little departmental goddesses of inspiration, under the tutelage of the former male twin.

Finally, the male twin, Apollo, proclaims himself the Eternal Sun, and the Nine Muses become his ladies-in-waiting. He delegates their functions to male gods who are himself in multiplication.

(The legendary origin of Japanese poetry is in an encounter between the Moon-goddess and the Sun-god as they walked around the pillar of the world in opposite directions. The Moon-goddess spoke first, saying in verse:

> *What Joy beyond compare*
> *To see a man so fair!*

The Sun-god was angry that she had spoken out of turn in this unseemly fashion; he told her to return and come to meet him again. On this occasion he spoke first:

> *To see a maid so fair—*
> *What joy beyond compare!*

This was the first verse ever composed. In other words, the Sun-god took over the control of poetry from the Muse, and pretended that he had originated it—a lie that did Japanese poets no good at all.)

With that, poetry becomes academic and decays until the Muse chooses to reassert her power in what are called Romantic Revivals.

In mediaeval poetry the Virgin Mary was plainly identified with the Muse by being put in charge of the Cauldron of Cerridwen. D. W. Nash notes in his edition of the Taliesin poems:

> The Christian bards of the thirteenth and fourteenth centuries repeatedly refer to the Virgin Mary herself as the cauldron or source of inspiration—to which they were led, as it seems, partly by a play on the word *pair*, a cauldron, and the secondary form of that word, on assuming the soft form of its initial *mair*, which also means Mary. Mary was *Mair*, the mother of Christ, the mystical receptacle of the Holy Spirit, and *Pair* was the cauldron or receptacle and fountain of Christian inspiration. Thus we have in a poem of Davydd Benfras in the thirteenth century:
> *Crist mab Mair am Pair par vonhedd.*
> Christ, son of Mary, my cauldron of pure descent.

In mediaeval Irish poetry Mary was equally plainly identified with Brigit the Goddess of Poetry: for St. Brigit, the Virgin as Muse, was popularly known as 'Mary of the Gael'. Brigit as a Goddess had been a Triad: the Brigit of Poetry, the Brigit of Healing and the Brigit of Smithcraft. In Gaelic Scotland her symbol was the White Swan, and she was known as Bride of the Golden Hair, Bride of the White Hills, mother of the King of Glory. In the Hebrides she was the patroness of childbirth. Her Aegean prototype seems to have been Brizo of Delos, a moon-goddess to whom votive ships were offered, and whose name was derived by the Greeks from the word *brizein*, 'to enchant'. Brigit was much cultivated in Gaul and Britain in Roman times, as numerous dedications to her attest, and in parts of Britain Saint Brigit retained her character of Muse until the Puritan Revolution, her healing powers being exercised largely through poetic incantation at sacred wells. Bridewell, the female penitentiary in London, was originally a nunnery of hers.[4]

A Cornish invocation to the local Brigit Triad runs:

> *Three Ladies came from the East,*
> *One with fire and two with frost,*
> *Out with thee, fire, and in with thee, frost.*

It is a charm against a scald. One dips nine bramble leaves in spring water and then applies them to the scald; the charm must be said three times to each leaf to be effective. For the bramble is sacred both to the Pentad and Triad of seasonal Goddesses, the number of leaves on a single stalk varying between three and five—so that in Brittany and parts of Wales there is a strong taboo on the eating of blackberries. In this charm the Goddesses are clearly seasonal, the Goddess of Summer bringing fire, her sisters bringing frost. A fourth rhyming line is usually added, as a sop to the clergy: *In the name of the Father, Son and Holy Ghost.*

The mediaeval Brigit shared the Muse-ship with another Mary, 'Mary Gipsy' or St. Mary of Egypt, in whose honour the oath 'Marry' or 'Marry Gyp!' was sworn. This charming Virgin with the blue robe and pearl necklace was the ancient pagan Sea-goddess Marian in transparent disguise—Marian,[5] Miriam, Mariamne ('Sea Lamb') Myrrhine, Myrtea, Myrrha,[6] Maria or Marina, patroness of poets and lovers and proud mother of the Archer of Love. Robin Hood, in the ballads, always swore by her. She was swarthy-faced, and in a mediaeval *Book of the Saints* she is recorded to have worked her passage to the Holy Land, where she was to live for years as a desert anchorite, by offering herself as a prostitute to the whole crew of the only vessel sailing there; so, once in Heaven, she showed particular indulgence to carnal sins.

A familiar disguise of this same Marian is the merry-maid, as 'mermaid' was once written. The conventional figure of the mermaid—a beautiful woman with a round mirror, a golden comb and a fish-tail—expresses 'The Love-goddess rises from the Sea'. Every initiate of the Eleusinian Mysteries, which were of Pelasgian origin, went through a love rite with her representative after taking a cauldron bath in Llew Llaw fashion. The round mirror, to match the comb, may be some bygone artist's mistaken substitute for the quince, which Marian always held in her hand as a love-gift; but the mirror did also form part of the sacred furniture of the Mysteries, and probably stood for 'know thyself'. The comb was originally a plectrum for plucking lyre-strings. The Greeks called her Aphrodite ('risen from sea-foam') and used the tunny, sturgeon, scallop and periwinkle, all sacred to her, as aphrodisiacs. Her most famous temples were built by the sea-side, so it is easy to understand her symbolic fish-tail. She can be identified with the Moon-goddess Eurynome whose statue at Phigalia in Arcadia was a mermaid carved in wood. The myrtle, murex and myrrh tree were also everywhere sacred to her; with the palm-tree (which thrives on salt), the love-faithful dove, and the colours white, green, blue and scarlet. Botticelli's *Birth of Venus* is an exact icon of her cult. Tall, golden-haired, blue-eyed, pale-faced, the Love-goddess arrives in her scallop-shell at the myrtle-grove, and Earth, in a flowery robe, hastens to wrap her in a scarlet gold-fringed mantle. In English ballad-poetry the mermaid stands for the bitter-sweetness of love and for the danger run by susceptible mariners (once spelt 'merriners') in foreign ports: her mirror and comb stand for vanity and heartlessness.

Constantine, the first Christian Emperor, officially abolished Mary-worship, but much of the ancient ritual survived within the Church: for example among the Collyridians, an Arabian sect who used to offer the same cake and liquor at her shrine as they had formerly offered to Ashtaroth. Myrrh, too, but this was more orthodox because St. Jerome had praised the Virgin as *Stilla Maris*, 'Myrrh of the Sea'. St. Jerome was punning on the name 'Mary', connecting it with Hebrew words *marah* (brine) and *mor* (myrrh) and recalling the gifts of the Three Wise Men.

When the Crusaders invaded the Holy Land, built castles and settled down, they found a number of heretical Christian sects living there under Moslem protection, who soon seduced them from orthodoxy. This was how the cult of Mary Gipsy came to England, brought through Compostella in Spain by poor pilgrims with palm-branches in their hands, copies of the Apocryphal Gospels in their wallets and Aphrodite's scallop-shells stitched in their caps—the palmers, celebrated in Ophelia's song in *Hamlet*. The lyre-plucking, red-stockinged troubadours, of whom King Richard Lion-Heart is the best remembered in Britain, ecstatically adopted the Marian cult. From their French songs derive the lyrics by 'Anon' which are the chief glory of early English poetry; as the prettiest carols derive from the Apocryphal Gospels, thanks to the palmers. The most memorable result of the Crusades was to introduce into Western Europe an idea of romantic love which, expressed in terms of the ancient Welsh minstrel tales, eventually transformed the loutish robber barons and their sluttish wives to a polished society of courtly lords and ladies. From the castle and court good manners and courtesy spread to the country folk; and this explains 'Merry England' as the country most engrossed with Mary-worship.

In the English countryside Mary Gipsy was soon identified with the Love-goddess known to the Saxons as 'The May Bride' because of her ancient association with the may-tree cult brought to Britain by the Atrebates in the first century B.C. or A.D. She paired off with Merddin, by this time Christianized as 'Robin Hood', apparently a variant of Merddin's Saxon name, *Rof Breoht Woden*, 'Bright Strength of Woden', also known euphemistically as 'Robin Good-fellow'. In French the word *Robin*, which is regarded as a diminutive of Robert but is probably pre-Teutonic, means a ram and also a devil. A *robinet*, or water-faucet, is so called because in rustic fountains it was shaped like a ram's head. The two senses of ram and devil are combined in the illustration to a pamphlet published in London in 1639: *Robin Goodfellow, his mad pranks and merry gests*. Robin is depicted as an ithyphallic god of the witches with young ram's horns sprouting from his forehead, ram's legs, a witches' besom over his left shoulder, a lighted candle in his right hand. Behind him in a ring dance a coven of men and women witches in Puritan costume, a black dog adores him, a musician plays a trumpet, an owl flies overhead. It will be recalled that the Somersetshire witches called their god Robin, and 'Robin son of Art' was the Devil of Dame Alice Kyteler, the famous early fourteenth-century witch of Kilkenny, and used sometimes to take the form of a black dog. For the Devil as ram the classical instance is the one whom in 1303 the Bishop of Coventry honoured with, a Black Mass and saluted with a posterior kiss. In Cornwall 'Robin' means phallus. 'Robin Hood' is a country name for red campion ('campion' means 'champion'), perhaps because its cloven petal suggests a ram's hoof, and because 'Red Champion' was a title of the Witch-god. It may be no more than a coincidence that 'ram' in Sanscrit is *huda*. 'Robin', meaning 'a ram', has become mythologically equated with Robin (latin: *rubens*), meaning the red-breast.

Here the story becomes complicated. The merry exploits of one Robin Hood, the famous outlaw of Sherwood Forest—whom J. W. Walker[7] has now proved to have been a historical character, born at Wakefield in Yorkshire between the years 1285 and 1295, and in the service of King Edward II in the years 1323 and 1324—became closely associated with the May Day revels. Presumably this was because the outlaw happened to have been christened Robert by his father Adam Hood the forester, and because during the twenty-two years that he spent as a bandit in the greenwood he improved on this identification of himself with Robin by renaming his wife Matilda 'Maid Marian'. To judge from the early ballad, *The Banished Man*, Matilda must have cut her hair and put on male dress in order to belong to the outlaw fraternity, as in Albania to this day young women join male hunting parties, dress as men and are so treated—Atalanta of Calydon who took part in the hunt of the Calydonian Boar was the prototype. The outlaw band then formed a coven of thirteen with Marian acting as the *pucelle*, or maiden of the coven; presumably she wore her proper clothes in the May Day orgies as Robin's bride. By his successful defiance of the ecclesiastics Robin became such a popular hero that he was later regarded as the founder of the Robin Hood religion, and its primitive forms are difficult to recover. However, 'Hood' (or Hod or Hud) meant 'log'—the log put at the back of the fire—and it was in this log, cut from the sacred oak, that Robin had once been believed to reside. Hence 'Robin Hood's steed', the wood-louse which ran out when the Yule log was burned. In the popular superstition Robin himself escaped up the chimney in the form of a Robin and, when Yule ended, went out as Belin against his rival Bran, or Saturn—who had been 'Lord of Misrule' at the Yule-tide revels. Bran hid from pursuit in the ivy-bush disguised as a Gold Crest Wren; but Robin always caught and hanged him. Hence the song:

> *'Who'll hunt the Wren?' cries Robin the Bobbin.*

Since 'Maid Marian' had been acting as Lady of Misrule in the Yule-tide revels and deserting Robin for his rival, it is easy to see how she earned a bad name for inconstancy. Thus 'Maud Marian' was often written for 'Maid Marian': 'Maud' is Mary Magdalene the penitent. In *Tom o' Bedlam's Song* she is Tom's Muse—'Merry Mad Maud'.

Christmas was merry in the middle ages, but May Day was still merrier. It was the time of beribboned Maypoles, of Collyridian cakes and ale, of wreaths and posies, of lovers' gifts, of archery contests, of merritotters (see-saws) and merribowks (great vats of milk-punch) But particularly of mad-merry marriages 'under the greenwood tree', when the dancers from the Green went off, hand in hand, into the greenwood and built themselves little love-bowers and listened hopefully for the merry nightingale. 'Mad Merry' is another popular spelling of 'Maid Marian', and as an adjective became attached to the magician Merlin (the original 'Old Moore' of the popular almanacks) whose prophetic almanacks were hawked at fairs and merrimakes. Merlin was really Merddin, as Spenser explains in the *Faerie Queene*, but Robin Hood had taken his place as the May Bride's lover, and he had become an old bearded prophet. The 'merritotter' is perhaps called after the scales (representing the Autumn equinox) in the hand of the Virgin in the Zodiac, who figured in the Mad Merry Merlin almanack: devoted readers naturally identified her with St. Mary Gipsy, for true-lovers' fates tottered in her balance, see-sawing up and down.

Many of these greenwood marriages, blessed by a renegade friar styled Friar Tuck, were afterwards formally confirmed in the church-porch. But very often 'merrybegots' were repudiated by their fathers. It is probably because each year, by old custom, the tallest and toughest village lad was chosen to be Little John (or 'Jenkin') Robin's deputy in the Merry Men masque, that Johnson, Jackson and Jenkinson are now among the commonest English names—Little John's merrybegots. But Robin did as merrily with Robson, Hobson, Dobson (all short for Robin), Robinson, Hodson, Hudson and Hood; Greenwood and Merriman were of doubtful paternity. The Christmas 'merrimake' (as Sir James Frazer mentions in *The Golden Bough*) also produced its crop of children. Who knows how many of the Morrises and Morrisons derive their patronymics from the amorous 'morrice-men',[8] Marian's 'merry-weathers'? Or how a many 'Princes', 'Lords' and 'Kings' from the Christmas King, or Prince, or Lord, of Misrule?

The Christmas merry-night play was an important part of the English Yule-tide festivities: seven or eight versions survive. The principal incidents are the beheading and restoration to life of the Christmas King, or Christmas Fool. This is one of the clearest survivals of the pre-Christian religion, and ultimately derives from ancient Crete. Firmicus Maternus in his *On the Error of Profane Religion* tells how Cretan Dionysus (Zagreus) was killed at Zeus's orders, boiled in a cauldron and eaten by the Titans. The Cretans, he says, celebrated an annual funeral feast, in which they played out the drama of the boy's sufferings—and his shape-shifting—eating a live bull as his surrogate. Yet he did not die for, according to Epimenides, quoted by St. Paul, Minos made a panegyric over him:

Thou diest not, but to eternity thou livest and standest.

St. Paul quoted a similar passage from the poet Aratus:

In thee we live, move, and have our being.

At Athens, the same festival, called the Lenaea ('Festival of the Wild Women'), was held at the winter solstice, and the death and rebirth of the harvest infant Dionysus were similarly dramatized. In the original myth it was not the Titans but the wild women, the nine representatives of the Moon-goddess Hera, who tore the child in pieces and ate him. And at the Lenaea it was a yearling kid, not a bull, that was eaten; when Apollodorus says that Dionysus was transformed into a kid, Eriphos, to save him from the wrath of Hera, this means that Hera once ate him as a human child, but that when men (the Titans or tutors) were admitted to the feast a kid was substituted as victim.

The most ancient surviving record of European religious practice is an Aurignacian cave-painting at Cogul in North-Eastern Spain of the Old Stone Age Lenaea. A young Dionysus with huge genitals stands unarmed, alone and exhausted in the middle of a crescent of nine dancing women, who face him. He is naked, except for what appear to be a pair of close-fitting boots laced at the knee; they are fully clothed and wear small cone-shaped hats. These wild women, differentiated by their figures and details of their dress, grow progressively older as one looks clock-wise around the crescent. The row begins with three young girls, the first two in long skirts, on the right and ends with two thin dark elderly women on the left and an emaciated crone on the far side; the crone has a face like the old moon and is dancing widdershins. In between are three vigorous golden-haired women, one of them in a short, bright party-frock. They clearly represent the New Moon, Old Moon and Full Moon triads—the crone being Atropos, the senior member of the Old Moon triad.

In front of the senior member of the New Moon triad is an animal whose fore-quarters are concealed by her skirt—it seems to be a black pig. And in the foreground of the picture, bounding away behind the backs of the Full Moon triad, is the very creature that Oisin saw in his vision when being conveyed by Niamh of the Golden Hair to the Land of Youth: a hornless fawn. Balanced erect on the fawn's neck, and facing backwards, is a boyish-looking imp or sprite, as clearly as anything the escaping soul of the doomed Dionysus. For the wild women are closing in on him and will presently tear him in bloody morsels and devour him. Though there is nothing in the painting to indicate the season, we can be sure that it was the winter solstice.

So we get back once more to the dramatic romance of Gwion—the boy who was eaten by the wild hag Cerridwen and reborn as the miraculous child Taliesin— and to the dispute between Phylip Brydydd and the 'vulgar rhymesters' . . . as to who should first present a song to their prince on Christmas Day. The *Romance of Taliesin* is a sort of Christmas play, in which the sufferings of the shape-shifting child are riddlingly presented. This is the elder version, reflecting the religious theory of early European society where woman was the master of man's destiny: pursued, was not pursued; raped, was not raped—as may be read in the faded legends of Dryope and Hylas, Venus and Adonis, Diana and Endymion, Circe and Ulysses. The danger of the various islands of women was that the male who ventured there might be sexually assaulted in the same murderous way as, according to B. Malinowski in *The Sexual Life of Savages*, men of North-Western Melanesia are punished for trespasses against female privilege. At least one coven of nine wild women seems to have been active in South Wales during early mediaeval times: old St. Samson of Dol, travel-ling with a young companion, was unlucky enough to trespass in their precinct. A frightful shriek rang out suddenly and from a thicket darted a grey-haired, redgarmented hag with a bloody trident in her hand. St. Samson stood his ground; his companion fled, but was soon overtaken and stabbed to death. The hag refused to come to an accommodation with St. Samson when he reproached her, and informed him that she was one of the nine sisters who lived in those woods with their mother—apparently the Goddess Hecate. Perhaps if the younger sisters had reached the scene first, the young man would have been the victim of a concerted sexual assault. Nine murderous black-garbed women occur in the Icelandic saga of Thidrandi, who one night opened his door to a knock, though warned against the consequences, and saw them riding against him from the north. He resisted their attack with his sword for awhile, but fell mortally wounded.

The transformations of Gwion run in strict seasonal order: hare in the autumn coursing season, fish in the rains of winter; bird in the spring when the migrants return, finally grain of corn in the summer harvest season, The Fury rushes after him in the form first of greyhound bitch, then of bitch-otter, then of falcon, finally overtakes him in the shape of a high-crested black hen—red comb and black feathers show her to be the Death Goddess. In this account the solar year ends in the winnowing season of early autumn, which points to an Eastern Mediterranean origin of the story. In Classical times the Cretan, Cyprian and Delphic years, and those of Asia Minor and Palestine, ended in September.

However, when the victory of the patriarchal Indo-Europeans revolutionized the social system of the Eastern Mediterranean, the myth of the sexual chase was reversed. Greek and Latin mythology contains numerous anecdotes of the pursuit and rape of elusive goddesses or nymphs by gods in beast disguise: especially by the two senior gods, Zeus and Poseidon. Similarly in European folk-lore there are scores of variants on the 'Two Magicians' theme, in which the male magician, after a hot chase, out-magics the female and gains her maidenhead. In the English ballad of *The Coal Black Smith*, a convenient example of this altered form of chase, the correct seasonal order of events is broken because the original context has been forgotten. She becomes a fish, he an otter; she a hare, he a greyhound; she becomes a fly, he a spider and pulls her to his lair; finally she becomes a quilt on his bed, he a coverlet and the game is won. In a still more debased French variant, she falls sick, he becomes her doctor; she turns nun, he becomes her priest and confesses her night and day; she becomes a star, he a cloud and muffles her.

In the British witch-cult the male sorcerer was dominant—though in parts of Scotland Hecate, or the Queen of Elfin or Faerie, still ruled—and *The Coal Black Smith* is likely to have been the song sung at a dramatic performance of the chase at a witches' Sabbath; the association of smiths and horned gods is as ancient as Tubal Cain, the Kenite Goat-god. The horned Devil of the Sabbath had sexual connexion with all his witch attendants, though he seems to have used an enormous artificial member, not his own. Anne Armstrong, the Northumbrian witch already mentioned, testified in 1673 that, at a well-attended Sabbath held at Allansford, one of her companions, Ann Baites of Morpeth, successively transformed herself into cat, hare, greyhound and bee, to let the Devil—'a long black man, their protector, whom they call their God'—admire her facility in changes. At first I thought that he chased Ann Baites, who was apparently the Maiden, or female leader of the coven, around the ring of witches, and that she mimicked the gait and cry of these various creatures in turn while he pursued her, adapting his changes to hers. The formula in *The Coal Black Smith* is 'he became a greyhound dog', or 'he became an otter brown', 'and fetched her home again'. 'Home again' is used here in the technical sense of 'to her own shape', for Isobel Gowdie of Auldearne at her trial in 1662, quoted the witch formula for turning oneself into a hare:

> *I shall go into a hare*
> *With sorrow and sighing and mickle care,*
> *And I shall go in the Devil's name*
> *Aye, till I come home again.*

It is clear from her subsequent account that there was no change of outward shape, but only of behaviour, and the verse suggests a dramatic dance. I see now that Ann Baites gave a solo performance, alternately mimicking the pursued and the pursuer, and that the Devil was content merely to applaud her. Probably the sequence was seasonal—hare and greyhound, trout and otter, bee and swallow, mouse and cat— and inherited from the earlier form of chase, with the pursuer as the Cat-Demeter finally destroying the Sminthean mouse on the threshing-floor in the winnowing season. The whole song is easy to restore in its original version.[9]

An intermediate form of the 'Two Magicians' myth, quoted by Diodorus Siculus, Callimachus in his *Hymn to Artemis* and Antoninus Liberalis, the second-century A.D. mythographer, in his *Transformations*, who all refer it to different regions, is that the Goddess Artemis, *alias* Aphaea, Dictynna, Britomart or Atergatis, is unsuccessfully pursued and finally escapes in fish form. Callimachus makes Minos of Crete the erotic pursuer and Britomart the chaste pursued, and relates that the pursuit lasted for nine months from the early flood season to the winnowing season. The myth is intended to explain the fish-tail in the statues of the goddess at Ascalon, Phigalia, Crabos, Aegina, Cephallenia, Mount Dictynnaeum in Crete and elsewhere, and to justify her local devotees in remaining faithful to their pre-Hellenic rites and marital customs. Fishermen figure prominently in the story—Dictynna means a net—and fishermen are notoriously conservative in their beliefs. In the Philistine version from Ascalon, quoted by Athenaeus, the Goddess was Derketo and the pursuer was one Moxus or Mopsus: perhaps this should be Moschus the ancestor of King Midas's tribe who defeated the Hittites. Cognate with this myth is the fruit-less attempt by Apollo on the maidenhead of the nymph Daphne.

The love-chase is, unexpectedly, the basis of the Coventry legend of Lady Godiva. The clue is provided by a miserere-seat in Coventry Cathedral, paralleled elsewhere in Early English grotesque wood-carving which shows what the guide-books call 'a figure emblematic of lechery': a long-haired woman wrapped in a net, riding sideways on a goat and preceded by a hare. Gaster in his stories from the Jewish *Targum*, collected all over Europe, tells of a woman who when given a love-test by her royal lover, namely to come to him 'neither clothed nor unclothed, neither on foot nor on horseback, neither on water nor on dry land, neither with or without a gift' arrived dressed in a net, mounted on a goat, with one foot trailing in the ditch, and releasing a hare. The same story with slight variations, was told by Saxo Grammaticus in his late twelfth-century *History of Denmark*. Aslog, the last of the Volsungs, Brynhild's daughter by Sigurd, was living on a farm at Spangerejd in

Norway, disguised as a sooty-faced kitchen-maid called Krake (raven). Even so, her beauty made such an impression on the followers of the hero Ragnar Lodbrog that he thought of marrying her, and as a test of her worthiness told her to come to him neither on foot nor riding, neither dressed nor naked, neither fasting nor feasting, neither attended nor alone. She arrived on goatback, one foot trailing on the ground, clothed only in her hair and a fishing-net, holding an onion to her lips, a hound by her side.

If the two stories are combined into a picture, the 'figure emblematic of lechery' has a black face, long hair, a raven flying overhead, a hare running ahead, a hound at her side, a fruit to her lips, a net over her and a goat under her. She will now be easily recognized as the May-eve aspect of the Love-and-Death goddess Freya, *alias* Frigg, Holda, Held, Hilde, Goda, or Ostara. In neolithic or early Bronze Age times she went North from the Mediterranean, where she was known as Dictynna (from her net), Aegea (from her goat), Coronis (from her raven), also Rhea, Britomart, Artemis and so on, and brought the Maze Dance with her.

The fruit at her lips is probably the apple of immortality and the raven denotes death and prophecy—Freya's prophetic raven was borrowed from her by Odin, just as Bran borrowed Danu's and Apollo Athene's. The Goddess was established in Britain as Rhiannon, Arianrhod, Cerridwen, Blodeuwedd, Danu or Anna long before the Saxons, Angles and Danes brought very similar versions of her with them. Hilde was at home in the Milky Way, like Rhea in Crete and Blodeuwedd (Olwen) in Britain, both of whom were connected with goats; and in the Brocken May-eve cere-mony a goat was sacrificed in her honour. As Holda she was mounted on a goat with a pack of twenty-four hounds, her daughters running beside her—the twenty-four hours of May Eve—and was sometimes shown as piebald to represent her ambiva-lent character of black Earth-mother and corpse-like Death—Holda and Hel. As Ostara, the Saxon Goddess after whom Easter is named, she attended a May-eve Sabbath where a goat was sacrificed to her. The hare was her ritual animal: it still 'lays' Easter eggs. The goat spelt fertility of cattle; the hare, good hunting; the net, good fishing; the long hair, tall crops.

The May-eve goat, as is clear from the English witch ceremonies and from the Swedish May-play, 'Bükkerwise', was mated to the goddess, sacrificed and resur-rected: that is to say, the Priestess had public connexion with the annual king dressed in goatskins, and either he was then killed and resurrected in the form of his successor, or else a goat was sacrificed in his stead and his reign prolonged. This fertility rite was the basis of the highly intellectualized 'Lesser Mysteries' of Eleusis, performed in February, representing the marriage of Goat-Dionysus to the Goddess Thyone, 'the raving queen', his death and resurrection.[10] At Coventry, she evidently went to the ceremony riding on his back, to denote her domination of him—as Europa rode on the Minos bull, or Hera on her lion.

The hare . . . was sacred both in Pelasgian Greece and Britain because it is swift, prolific and mates openly without embarrassment. I should have mentioned in this context that the early British tabu on hunting the hare, the penalty for a breach of which was to he struck with cowardice, was originally lifted on a single day in the year—May-eve—as the tabu on hunting the wren was lifted only on St. Stephen's Day. (Boadicea let loose the hare during her battle with the Romans in the hope, pre-sumably, that the Romans would strike at it with their swords and so lose courage.)

The hare was ritually hunted on May-eve, and the miserere-seat 'figure of lechery'—which is a fair enough description of the Goddess on this occasion—is releasing the hare for her daughters to hunt. The folk-song *If all those young men* evidently belongs to these May-eve witch frolics:

> *If all those young men were like hares on the mountain*
> *Then all those pretty maidens would get guns, go a-hunting.*

'Get guns' is eighteenth-century; one should read 'turn hounds'. There are other verses:

> *If all those young men were like fish in the water*
> *Then all those pretty maidens would soon follow after.*

With nets? As we know from the story of Prince Elphin and Little Gwion, May-eve was the proper day for netting a weir, and the Goddess would not bring her net to the Sabbath for nothing.

> *If all those young men were like rushes a-growing*
> *Then all those pretty maidens would get scythes go a-mowing.*

The love-chase again: the soul of the sacred king, ringed about by orgiastic women, tries to escape in the likeness of hare, or fish, or bee; but they pursue him relentlessly and in the end he is caught, torn in pieces and devoured. In one variant of the folk-song, the man is the pursuer, not the pursued:

> *Young women they run like hares on the mountain*
> *If I were but a young man I'd soon go a-hunting.*

The story of Lady Godiva, as recorded by Roger of Wendover, a St. Albans chronicler, in the thirteenth century, is that shortly before the Norman Conquest the Saxon Lady Godiva (Godgifu) asked her husband Leofric Earl of Mercia to relieve the people of Coventry from oppressive tolls. He consented on condition that she rode naked through the crowded market on a fair-day; and she did so with a knight on either side, but preserved her modesty by covering herself with her hair, so that only her 'very white legs' showed underneath. The story, which is also told of the Countess of Hereford and 'King John' in connexion with the distribution of bread and cheese at St. Briavel's in Gloucestershire, cannot be historically true, because Coventry in Lady Godiva's day was a village without either tolls or fairs. But it is certain that in 1040 she persuaded Leofric to build and endow a Benedictine monastery at Coventry, and what seems to have happened is that after the Conquest the monks disguised a local May-eve procession of the Goddess Goda, during which all pious Christians were at first required to keep indoors, with an edifying anecdote about their benefactress Lady Godiva, modelling the story on Saxo's. The fraud is given away by the 'Lady Godiva' procession of Southam (twelve miles south of Coventry and included in Leofric's earldom), where two figures were carried, one white and one black—the Goddess as Holda and Hel, Love and Death. The story of Peeping Tom the Tailor is not mentioned by Roger of Wendover, but may be a genuine early tradition. The St. Briavel's ceremony which took place, like the Southam and Coventry processions, on Corpus Christi, a date associated both at York and Coventry with mystery plays, is said to have commemorated the freeing of the people from a tax on the gathering of fire-wood in the neighbouring forest; Corpus Christi always falls on a Friday, the Goddess's own day, and corresponds roughly with May Eve; thus, it seems that the mystery-play has its origin in the May Eve festivities, Bükkerwise, in honour of Goda, the Bona Dea. If there was a prohibition against men witnessing the procession, as there was at Rome in the Bona Dea ceremonies, and as there was in Celtic Germany according to Tacitus (*Germania*, chap. 40) against any man witnessing Hertha's annual bath after her progress back to her sacred grove, and as there was in Greece in the days of Actaeon, when Diana took her woodland bath, Peeping Tom may record the memory of this.

The British are a mixed race, but the non-Teutonic goddess-worshipping strains are the strongest. This explains why the poets' poetry written in English remains obstinately pagan. The Biblical conception of the necessary supremacy of man over woman is alien to the British mind: among all Britons of sensibility the rule is 'ladies first' on all social occasions. The chivalrous man dies far more readily in the service of a queen than of a king: self-destruction is indeed the recognized proof of grand passion:

And for bonnie Annie Laurie
I wad lay me doon and dee.

There is an unconscious hankering in Britain after goddesses, if not for a goddess so dominant as the aboriginal Triple Goddess, at least for a female softening of the all-maleness of the Christian Trinity. The male Trinity corresponds increasingly less with the British social system, in which woman, now that she has become a property owner and a voter, has nearly regained the position of respect which she enjoyed before the Puritan revolution. True, the male Trinity antedated the Puritan revolution but it was a theological not an emotional concept: as has been shown, the Queen of Heaven with her retinue of female saints had a far greater hold in the popular imagination between the Crusades and the Civil War than either the Father or the Son. And one of the results of Henry VIII's breach with Rome was that when his daughter Queen Elizabeth became head of the Anglican Church she was popularly regarded as a sort of deity: poets not only made her their Muse but gave her titles— Phoebe, Virginia, Gloriana—which identified her with the Moon-goddess, and the extraordinary hold that she gained on the affections of her subjects was largely due to this cult.

The temporary reinstatement of the Thunder-god in effective religious sovereignty during the Commonwealth is the most remarkable event in modern British history: the cause was a mental ferment induced by the King James Bible among the mercantile classes of the great towns and in parts of Scotland and England where Celtic blood ran thinnest. The first Civil War was fought largely between the chivalrous nobility with their retainers and the anti-chivalrous mercantile classes with their artisan supporters. The Anglo-Saxon-Danish south-east was solidly Parliamentarian and the Celtic north-west as solidly Royalist. It was therefore appropriate that at the Battle of Naseby, which decided the war, the rival battle cries were, for the Parliamentary army, 'God our Strength' and for the Royalist army 'Queen Marie'.

Queen Marie was a Catholic and her name evoked the Queen of Heaven and of Love. The Thunder-god won the day, and vented his spite not only on the Virgin and her retinue of saints, but on Maid Marian and her maypole retinue, and on the other Triple Goddess cult which still survived secretly in many parts of the British Isles— the witch cult. But his triumph was short-lived because after gaining the victory he had removed the King,[11] his chief representative. He was therefore temporarily ousted at the Restoration and when he returned in 1688 with a Protestant King as his representative, his thunderous fury had been curbed. He gained a second access of strength in the enthusiastic religious revival, fostered by the merchant class, which accompanied the Industrial Revolution; but lost ground again at the beginning of the present century.

Elizabeth was the last Queen to play the Muse. Victoria, like Queen Anne, preferred the part of War-goddess in inspiring her armies, and proved an effective substitute for the Thunder-god. In the reign of her grandson the 88th Carnatics of the Indian Army were still singing:

> Cooch parwani
> *Good time coming!*
> *Queen Victoria*
> *Very good man!*
> *Rise up early*
> *In the morning.*
> *Britons never, never*
> *Shall be slave . . .*

But Victoria expected the women of England to reverence their husbands as she had reverenced hers and displayed none of the sexual coquetry or interest in love-poetry and scholarship that serve to make a queen into a Muse for poets. Queen Anne and Queen Victoria both gave their names to well-known periods of English poetry, but the name of Queen Anne connotes passionless decorum in writing, and that of Victoria didacticism and rococo ornament.

The British love of Queens does not seem to be based merely on the common-place that 'Britain is never so prosperous as when a Queen is on the Throne': it reflects, rather, a stubborn conviction that this is a Mother Country not a Father Land—a peculiarity that the Classical Greeks also noted about Crete—and that the King's prime function is to be the Queen's consort. Such national apprehensions or convictions or obsessions are the ultimate source of all religion, myth and poetry, and cannot be eradicated either by conquest or education.

Notes

1   This magical tradition survived in the Northern witch-cult. In 1673 Anne Armstrong the Northumbrian witch confessed at her trial to having been temporarily transformed into a mare by her mistress Ann Forster of Stockfield, who threw a bridle over her head and rode her to a meeting of five witch-covens at Riding Mill Bridge End.

2   Insufficient notice has yet been taken of the shape of flint arrow-heads as having a magical rather than a utilitarian origin. The tanged arrow-head of fir-tree shape, for example, needs explanation. It must have been very difficult to knap without breaking off either one of the tangs or the projecting stem between them, and has no obvious advantage in hunting over the simple willow-leaf or elder-leaf types. For though a narrow bronze arrow-head with four tangs cannot be easily drawn out through a wound, because the flesh closes up behind, the broad two-tanged flint one would not be more difficult to draw out than an elder-leaf or willow-leaf one shot into a beast with equal force. The fir-tree shane seems therefore to be magically intended: an appeal to Artemis Elate—Diana the Huntress, Goddess of the Fir-tree—to direct the aim. The point was probably smeared with a paralysant poison—a 'merciful shaft' of the sort with which the Goddess was credited. An Irish fir-tree arrow-head in my possession, taken from an Iron Age burial, cannot have been seriously intended for archery. The chip of white flint from which it has been knapped is awkwardly curved, and it has so large a 'bulb of percussion' and so short a stem as to prevent it from being spliced to admit an arrow-shaft: it is clearly for funerary use only.

3   The ancients were well aware of Apollo's frequent changes of divine function. Cicero in his essay *On the Nature of the Gods* distinguishes four Apollos in descending order of antiquity: the son of Hephaestos; the son of the Cretan Corybantes; the Arcadian Apollo who gave Arcadia its laws; and lastly the son of Latona and Zeus. He might have enlarged his list to twenty or thirty.

4   The fourteenth-century Swedish St. Brigid, or Birgit, who founded the Order of St. Brigid was not, of course, the original saint, though some houses of the Order reverted merrily to paganism.

5   The earliest spelling of the Virgin's name in English is Marian—not Mariam which is the Greek form used in the Gospels.

6   She was the mother of Adonis; hence the Alexandrian grammarian Lycophron calls Byblos 'The City of Myrrha'.

7   *Yorkshire Archaeological Journal*, No. 141, 1944.

8   This same word 'morris', as the prefix to 'pike', is first written 'maris': so it is likely that the morris-men were Mary's men, not *moriscoes* or Moorish men, as is usually supposed. The innocent word 'merry' has deceived the editors of the *Oxford English Dictionary*. They trace it back to an Indo-Germanic root *murgjo* meaning 'brief', arguing that when one is merry, time flies; but without much confidence, for they are obliged to admit that *murgjo* does not take this course in any other language.

9   Cunning and art he did not lack
But aye her whistle would fetch him back.

O, I shall go into a hare
With sorrow and sighing and mickle care,
And I shall go in the Devil's name
Aye, till I be fetchèd hame.
      —Hare, take heed of a bitch greyhound
      Will harry thee all these fells around,
      For here come I in Our Lady's name
      All but for to fetch thee hame.
Cunning and art, etc.

Yet I shall go into a trout
With sorrow and sighing and mickle doubt,
And show thee many a merry game
Ere that I be fetchèd hame.
　　　——Trout, take heed of an otter lank
　　　Will harry thee close from bank to bank,
　　　For here I come in Our Lady's name
　　　All but for to fetch thee hame.
Cunning and art, etc.
Yet I shall go into a bee
With mickle horror and dread of thee,
And flit to hive in the Devil's name
Ere that I be fetchèd hame.
　　　——Bee, take heed of a swallow hen
　　　Will harry thee close, both butt and ben,
　　　For here I come in Our Lady's name
　　　All but for to fetch thee hame.
Cunning and art, etc.

Yet I shall go into a mouse
And haste me unto the miller's house,
There in his corn to have good game
Ere that I be fetchèd hame.
　　　——Mouse, take heed of a white tib-cat
　　　That never was baulked of mouse or rat,
　　　For I'll crack thy bones in Our Lady's name:
　　　Thus shalt thou be fetchèd hame.
Cunning and art, etc.

10　In the corresponding ancient British mysteries there seems to have been a formula in which the Goddess teasingly promised the initiate who performed a sacred marriage with her that he would not die 'either on foot or on horseback, on water or on land, on the ground or in the air, outside a house or inside, shod or unshod, clothed or unclothed,' and then, as a demonstration of her power, manoeuvred him into a position where the promise was no longer valid—as in the legend of Llew Llaw and Blodeuwedd, where a goat figures in the murder scene. Part of the formula survives in the Masonic initiation ritual. The apprentice 'neither naked nor clothed, barefoot nor shod, deprived of all metals, hood winked, with a cable-tow about his neck is led to the door of the lodge in a halting moving posture.'

11　It is a strange paradox that Milton, though he had been the first Parliamentary author to defend the execution of Charles I and was the Thunder-god's own Laureate, fell later under the spell of 'the Northern Muse', Christina of Sweden, and in his *Second Defense of the English People* his flattery of her is not only as extravagant as anything that the Elizabethans wrote about Elizabeth, but seems wholly sincere.

PART THREE

Revival and diversification texts

Chapter 19

Gerald Gardner

LIVING WITCHCRAFT

■ from **WITCHCRAFT TODAY**, Secaucus, New Jersey, 1954, 1973, pp. 17–30

IN THIS CHAPTER FROM *Witchcraft Today*, published originally in 1954, Gerald B. Gardner (1884–1964), a civil servant retired to England after a career in the Far East, presents himself as a disinterested anthropologist (self-taught) studying a surviving group of witches. It is more probable, however, that he himself was in the thick of *creating* the mystery religion now known as Wicca, or at the very least, giving it much of its present form. Today, historians of Wicca such as Ronald Hutton (1999) are more likely to portray him as co-founder of a new religion.

Gardner here writes in the voice of a "participant observer," giving the reader the impression that he accepted initiation into "a dying cult" in order to record its knowledge, teachings, and practices. Following in the spirit of Margaret Murray, Gardner suggests that "the cult" is linked to a surviving Western European Paganism that during the period of persecution had wrongly been described as satanic. He also links it with such topics as parapsychology, yoga, and Spiritualism, including all these under the banner of Western magic, much as did Aleister Crowley.

Most importantly, Gardner here draws a picture of Wicca as an alternative religion, one suited for those with "an attraction for the occult, a sense of wonder, a feeling that you can slip for a few minutes out of this world into the other world of faery." Those words have proven to be prophetic indeed.

For further discussion, see Heselton (2000), Hutton (1999), Kelly (1991), Valiente (1989) and Davis's website.

Chas S. Clifton

References

Davis, Morgan. *Gerald Gardner: The History of Wicca*. http://www.geraldgardner.com
Heselton, Philip (2000) *Wiccan Roots: Gerald Gardner and the Modern Witchcraft Revival*. Chievely: Capall Bann Publishing.
Hutton, Ronald (1999) *The Triumph of the Moon: A History of Modern Pagan Witchcraft*. Oxford: Oxford University Press.
Kelly, Aidan (1991) *Crafting the Art of Magic: A History of Modern Witchcraft 1939-1964*. St. Paul, MN: Llewellyn Publications.
Valiente, Doreen (1989) *The Rebirth of Witchcraft*. London: Robert Hale.

> Some books on witchcraft—the author is permitted to write about witches "from the inside"—primitive initiations akin to witchcraft—the witch power exudes from the body, hence nudity—author's theory of an electro-magnetic field—certain rites increase clairvoyance—the author refutes Mr. Pennethorne Hughes' view that witchcraft is a cult of evil—witch rituals—witches are not disappointed perverts—their belief that their ancestors came from the east and that their paradise is in the north—ceremony to cause rebirth of the sun—the cauldron of regeneration and the dance of the wheel—the nature of the witch's circle to keep in power—denial of the use of skulls, etc.—witches have nothing to do with the Black Mass—initiation in witchcraft develops certain powers known collectively as magic—"inside the circle they are between the worlds"—necessity for a partner.

There have been many books written on witchcraft. The early ones were mostly propaganda written by the various Churches to discourage and frighten people from having any connections with what was to them a hated rival—for witchcraft is a religion. Later there were books setting out to prove that this craft had never existed. Some of these books may have been inspired or even written by witches themselves. Latterly there have been many books dealing in a scientific way with witchcraft by such writers as Dr. Margaret Murray, R. Trevor Davis, Christine Hoyle, Arne Runeberg, Pennethorne Hughes and Montague Summers. Mr. Hughes in his most scholarly book on witchcraft has, I think, clearly proved what many knew: that the Little People of the heaths, called fairies or elves at one period, were called witches in the next, but to my mind all these books have one fault. Though their authors know that witches exist, none of them seems to have asked a witch for her[1] views on the subject of witchcraft. For after all, a witch's opinions should have some value, even though they may not fit in with preconceived opinions.

Of course there are good reasons for this reticence. Recently I was talking to a very learned Continental professor who was writing up some witch trials of two hundred years ago, and he told me that he had obtained much information from witches. But, though invited, he had been afraid to go to their meetings. Religious feeling was very strong in his country and if it were known that he was in communication with witches he would be in danger of losing his professorship. Moreover, witches are shy people, and publicity is the last thing they want. I asked the first one I knew: "Why do you keep all this wonderful knowledge secret? There is no persecution nowadays." I was told: "Isn't there? If it were known in the village what I am, every time anyone's chickens died, every time a child became sick, I should be blamed. Witchcraft doesn't pay for broken windows !"

Now I am an anthropologist, and it is agreed that an anthropologist's job is to investigate what people do and believe, and not what other people say they should do and believe. It is also part of his task to read as many writings as possible on the matter he is investigating, though not accepting such writings uncritically, especially when in. conflict with the evidence as he finds it. Anthropologists may draw their own conclusions and advance any theories of their own, but they must make it clear that these are their own conclusions and their own theories and not proven facts; and this is the method I propose to adopt. In dealing with native races one records their folklore, the stories and religious rites on which they base their beliefs and actions. So why not do the same with English witches?

I must first explain why I claim to speak of things not generally known. I have been interested in magic and kindred subjects all my life, and have made a collection of magical instruments and charms. These studies led me to spiritualist and other societies, and I met some people who claimed to have known me in a past life. Here I must say that, though I believe in reincarnation, as most people, do who have lived in the East, I do not remember any past lives, albeit I have had curious experiences. I only wish I did. Anyhow, I soon found myself in the circle and took the usual oaths of secrecy which bound me not to reveal any secrets of the cult. But, as it is a dying cult, I thought it was a pity that all the knowledge should be lost, so in the end I was permitted to write, as fiction, something of what a witch believes in the novel *High Magic's Aid*.[2] This present volume has the same purpose, but deals with the subject in a factual way.

Many people ask me how I can believe in magic. If I explain what I believe magic to be, I go a long way towards an answer. My view is that it is simply the use of some abnormal faculty. It is a recognized fact that such faculties exist. So-called calculating boys are famous, and very many people have the faculty under hypnotic control to calculate time most accurately. While asleep they are ordered to do something at, say, the end of a million seconds; they will know nothing of this order in their normal state, but their inner consciousness calculates it and at the end of the millionth second they obey the order without knowing why. Try to calculate a million seconds in your waking state, and say when it is up, without a watch, and you will see what I mean. The powers used are utterly unlike any mental powers we know. And exercising them is normally impossible. So, if there are some people with some abnormal powers, why should there not be other people who have other forms of abnormal powers and unusual ways of inducing them?

I am continually being asked various questions regarding the witch cult, and I can only answer: Nearly all primitive people had initiation ceremonies and some of these were initiation into priesthoods, into magic powers, secret societies and mysteries. They were usually regarded as necessary for the welfare of the tribe as well as for the individual, They usually included purification and some test of courage and fortitude—often severe and painful—terrorization, instruction in tribal lore, in sexual knowledge, in the making of charms, and in religious and magical matters generally, and often a ritual of death and resurrection.

Now I did not cause the primitive people to do these things; I simply hold that witches, being in many cases the descendants of primitive people, do in fact do many of them. So when people, for example, ask me: "Why do you say that witches work naked?" I can only say: "Because they do." "Why?" is another question, the easy reply being that their ritual tells them they must. Another is that their practices are the remnants of a Stone Age religion and they keep to their old ways. There is also the Church's explanation: "Because witches are inherently wicked." But I think the witches' own explanation is the best: "Because only in that way can we obtain power."

Witches are taught and believe that the power resides within their bodies which they can release in various ways, the simplest being dancing round in a circle, singing or shouting, to induce a frenzy; this power they believe exudes from their bodies, clothes impeding its release. In dealing with such matters it is, of course, difficult to say how much is real and how much imagination.

As in the case of dowsing, if a man believes that when insulated from the ground by rubber insoles he cannot find water, this belief inhibits him, even though the insoles contain no rubber, whilst wearing insoles made of rubber—though he didn't know it—he can find water, as many experiments prove.

It is easy to imagine that a witch who firmly believes that it is essential to be naked could not whip up the final effort to attain the ecstasy without being naked. Another, however, who did not share this belief might, though partially clothed, exert sufficient energy to force power through her face, shoulders, arms and legs, to produce some result; but who can say that she could not have produced twice the power with half the effort had she been in the traditional nakedness? All we can be sure of is that in ancient times it was recognized that witches did so and even journeyed to their meetings in that costume; but in later times the Church, and more especially the Puritans, tried to hush this up and invented the story of the foul old woman on a broomstick, to replace the story told at so many witch trials of wild dances in the moonlight by beautiful young witches.

Personally I am inclined to believe that while allowing for imagination there is something in the witches' belief. I think that there is something in the nature of an electro-magnetic field surrounding all living bodies, and that this is what is seen by some people who call it the aura. I can sometimes see it myself, but only on bare flesh, so clothes evidently obstruct its functioning; this, however, is simply my own private belief. I think a witch by her formulae stimulates it, or possibly creates more of it. They say that witches by constant practice can train their wills to blend this nerve force, or whatever it is, and that their united wills can project this as a beam of force, or that they can use it in other ways to gain clairvoyance, or even to release the astral body. These practices include increasing and quickening the blood supply, or in other cases slowing it down, as well as the use of will-power; so it is reasonable to believe that it does have some effect. I am not stating that it does. I only record the fact that they attempt these effects, and believe that sometimes they succeed. The only way to find the truth or falsity of this would be to experiment. (I should think that slips or Bikinis could be worn without unduly causing loss of power. It would be interesting to try the effect of one team in the traditional nude and one in Bikinis.) At the same time one might heed the witches' dictum: "You must be this way always in the rites, 'tis the command of the Goddess," You must be this way so that it becomes second nature; you are no longer naked, you are simply natural and comfortable.

The cult, whether in England or elsewhere, starts with several advantages. First, it usually obtains recruits very young and slowly trains them so that they come to have the sense of mystery and wonder, the knowledge that they have an age-old tradition behind them. They have probably seen things happen and know they can happen again: instead of mere curiosity and a pious belief that "something may happen", inhibited by an unacknowledged but firm belief that "it will never happen to me".

What it comes to, then, is this: certain people were born with clairvoyant powers. They discovered that certain rites and processes increased these powers, thus they became useful to the community. They performed these rites, and obtained benefits, and being lucky and successful were looked at with envy and dislike by others, and so they began to perform their rites in secret. Power which can be used for good can be used for evil, and they were tempted perhaps to use this power against their opponents, and thus become more unpopular. As a result calamities would be laid at their doors, and people would be tortured till they confessed to causing them. And who can blame the children of some of those thus tortured to death for making a wax image of their oppressors?

That, in brief, is the truth about witchcraft. In mid-Victorian days it would have been shocking, but in these days of nudist clubs is it so very terrible? It seems to me more or less like a family party trying a scientific experiment according to the text-book.

I should like at this stage to deal with the view, not infrequently held, that witchcraft has connections with diabolism. Mr. Summers himself appears to think the question is settled because the Roman Catholic Church said the cult was diabolic, and Mr. Pennethorne Hughes's book also gives the impression that witchcraft is a cult of evil. Mr. Hughes says (page 128):

"As the cult declined, any sort of common practice must have been lost, until by the nineteenth century the indoor practitioners of self-conscious diabolism merely conducted the Black Mass of inverted Catholicism. At the time of the trials there was clearly some sort of formal service quite apart from the crescendo of the fertility dance. It would, in a Catholic Age, be very like the known pageantry of the Church's own celebrations, with candles, vestments and a parody of the sacrament. It might be conducted by an unfrocked priest using hosts with the devil's name stamped on them instead of Jesus, and the defiling of the Crucifix—to insult Christians and please the Devil. The Devil himself received praise and homage. A liturgy of evil would be repeated, there would be a mock sermon and absolution made with the left hand and an inverted cross."

Those who attended these meetings he dismisses in the following way (page 131):

"Some were perhaps dissipated perverts and had shame or guilty pride; some were just members of a primitive stock, already disappearing, but still following the ways of their fathers, knowing the Church disapproved yet finding physical and psychological satisfaction. Some were ecstatic, 'The Sabbat,' said one, 'is the true Paradise.'"

Mr. Hughes does not say why he thinks they should have given up their own rites, which were made for a definite purpose and which produced definite results simply to parody those of an alien faith. I have attended many of these cult rites, and I declare that most of what he says is simply not true. There may be a fertility dance, but the other rites are simple, and with a purpose, and in no way resemble those of the Roman Catholic or any other Church that I know. True, sometimes there is a short ceremony when cakes and wine are blessed and eaten. (They tell me that in the old days mead or ale was often used.) This may be in imitation of the early Christian Agape, the Love Feast, but there is no suggestion that the cakes turn into flesh and blood. The ceremony is simply intended as a short repast, though it is definitely religious.

The priestess usually presides. Candles are used, one to read the book by and others set round the circle. This does not in any way resemble the practice of any other religious sect I know. I do not think that can be called "imitation of the Church's pageantry".

There are no crucifixes, inverted or otherwise, no sermons, mock or otherwise, and no absolution or hosts save for the cake and wine mentioned. Incense is used, but this has a practical purpose. There is no praise or homage to the Devil, no liturgy, evil or otherwise, nothing is said backwards, and there are no gestures with the left hand; in fact with the exception that it is a religious service and all religious services resemble one another, the rites are not in any way an imitation of anything I have ever seen. I do not say there have never been diabolists. I only say that, as far as I know, witches do not do the things of which they have been accused, and knowing what I do of their religion and practices I do not think they ever did.

Naturally it is impossible to speak for all of them. I have seen in print that priests and clergymen have been convicted of every crime there is in British law, and in the Isle of Man priests have been convicted of singing psalms of destruction against people (*vide* the *Isle of Man N. M. &A. Soc. Proceedings*, vol. v, 1946), which is a new crime to me at least; but this does not mean that the majority of priests and clergymen are criminals. Nor do I think it fair to call witches disappointed perverts. They may truly be said to be followers of a primitive religion, already disappearing; they are following the ways of their fathers, knowing the Church disapproves of their practices, but finding physical and psychological satisfaction. And cannot the same be said of the Buddhists or Shintoists? They have ancient, and to them good rites, and they are not in the least concerned if others disapprove. All that matters to them is, are they on the Path? I have learnt tolerance in the many years I spent in the East and if anyone finds true paradise in the Buddhist rites, the Sabbat, or the Mass, I am well content.

If I were permitted to disclose all their rituals, I think it would be easy to prove that witches are not diabolists; but the oaths are solemn and the witches are my friends. I would not hurt their feelings. They have secrets which to them are sacred. They have good reason for this secrecy. I am, however, permitted to give one sample of their rites. It tells little, for, apart from the rites, they themselves know little. For one reason or another they keep the names of their god and goddess a secret. To them the cult has existed unchanged from the beginning of time, though there is also a vague notion that the old people came from the East, possibly as a result of the Christian belief that the East is the holy place whence everything came. In this connection it should be noted that witches start in the East when forming the circle, and the representative of the god or goddess usually stands in the East. This may simply be because the sun and moon rise in the East, because of the position of the altar, or for some unknown reason, since actually the main invocations are towards the North. I have been given no reason for this; but I have an idea that in the old days they thought their paradise lay in the North, as they hold that the Northern Lights are the lights of their paradise, though this is usually thought of as being underground, or in a hollow hill. It is worth noting, too, that Scandinavian mythology makes the North the dwelling-place of the gods, and that in Gaelic myth the South, often camouflaged as "Spain", is evil or hell. Presumably, therefore, its opposite, the North, is paradise.

I have seen one very interesting ceremony: the Cauldron of Regeneration and the Dance of the Wheel, or Yule, to cause the sun to be reborn, or summer to return. This in theory should be on December 22, but nowadays it is held on the nearest day to that date that is convenient for the members. The ceremony starts in the usual way. The circle is cast and purified, the celebrants also being purified in the usual manner, and the ordinary business of the cult is done. Then the small ceremony is performed (sometimes called "Drawing down the Moon") so that the High Priestess is regarded as the incarnation of the goddess. The Cakes and Wine ceremony follows. Then a cauldron (or something to represent one) is placed in the middle of the circle, spirit is put in and ignited. Various leaves, etc., are cast in. Then the Priestess stands by it in the pentacle (goddess) position. The High Priest stands on the opposite side of the cauldron, leading the chant. The others stand round in a circle with torches. They are lighted at the burning cauldron and they dance round in the "sunwise" direction, i.e. clockwise. The chant I heard was as follows, but others are sometimes used:

> "Queen of the Moon, Queen of the Sun,
> Queen of the Heavens, Queen of the Stars,
> Queen of the Waters, Queen of the Earth
> Bring to us the Child of Promise![3]
>
> It is the great mother who giveth birth to him,
> It is the Lord of Life who is born again.
> Darkness and tears are set aside
> When the Sun shall come up early.
>
> Golden Sun of the Mountains,
> Illumine the Land, Light up the World,
> Illumine the Seas and the Rivers,
> Sorrows be laid, Joy to the World.
>
> Blessed be the Great Goddess,
> Without beginning, without end,
> Everlasting to eternity.
> I.O. EVO.HE Blessed Be."

They dance round furiously, crying:

> "I. O. EVO.HE
> Blessed Be I. O. EVO.HE Blessed Be."

Sometimes couples join hands and jump over the blazing cauldron, as I have seen for myself. When the fire had burnt itself out the Priestess led the usual dances. This was followed by a feast.

Is there anything very wicked or awful in all this? If it were performed in a church, omitting the word goddess or substituting the name of a saint, would anyone object?

Other rites I am forbidden to give because they are definitely magical, though otherwise they are no more harmful than this. But they do not wish it to be known how they raise power. The dances that follow are more like children's games than modern dances—they might be called boisterous and noisy, with much laughter. In fact, they *are* more or less children's games performed by grown-ups, and like children's games they have a story, or are done for a certain definite purpose other than mere enjoyment.

I am also permitted to tell for the first time in print the true reason why the important thing in all their ceremonies is "Casting the Circle". They are taught that the circle is "between the worlds", that is, between this world and the next, the dominions of the gods.

The circle such as it is shown in pictures may or may not be used. It is most convenient to mark it with chalk, paint or otherwise, to show where it is; but marks on the carpet may be utilized. Furniture may be placed to indicate the bounds. The only circle that matters is the one drawn before every ceremony with either a duly consecrated Magic Sword or a Knife, the latter being the Witches' Athame or Black-Hilted Knife, with magic signs on the hilt, and this is most generally used. The circle is usually nine feet in diameter, unless made for some very special purpose. There are two outer circles, each six inches apart, so the third circle has a diameter of eleven feet. When drawn, this circle is carefully purified, as also are all who celebrate the rites. Witches attach great importance to this, for within the circle is the gods' domain.

It is necessary to distinguish this clearly from the work of the magician or sorcerer, who draws a circle on the ground and fortifies it with mighty words of power and summons (or attempts to summon) spirits and demons to do his bidding, the circle being to prevent them from doing him harm, and he dare not leave it.

The Witches' Circle, on the other hand, is to *keep in* the power which they believe they can raise from their own bodies and to prevent it from being dissipated before they can mould it to their own will. They can and do step in and out if they wish to, but this involves some loss of power, so they avoid doing so as much as possible.

People try to make me say that in the rites skulls and other repulsive things are used. I have never seen such things; but they tell me that in the old days sometimes, when the High Priest was not present, a skull and crossbones was used to represent the god, death and resurrection (or reincarnation). Nowadays the High Priestess stands in a position representing the skull and crossbones, or death, and moves to another position, a pentacle, representing resurrection, during the rites. I expect the old village herbalist type of witch may have used skulls and bones and other things to impress people because they were expected to. They were good psychologists, and if a patient was convinced that only a nasty-tasting medicine would do him good, then the witches' draught was sure to taste horrible—and consequently it cured. If the people firmly believed that mumbo-jumbo with skulls and bones gave the witch power to cure or kill, then the skulls and bones would be there, for witches are consummate leg-pullers; they are taught it as part of their stock-in-trade.

It is often thought that the performance of the Black Mass is part of the tradition of witchcraft; but to use the late Dr. Joad's words, "it all depends on what you mean" by the Black Mass. I understand it to be a blasphemous parody of the Catholic

Mass. I have neither seen nor heard of this in connection with the cult, and I do not believe it ever existed as one of their rites. Rites are performed for certain purposes. These take time, but when they are finished the assembly have a little meal, then dance and enjoy themselves. They have no time or inclination for indulging in blasphemy. Has anyone ever heard of people wasting time in troubling themselves to go through a parody of a Buddhist or Mohammedan rite?

Another thing I have always understood is that to perform a Black Mass you needed a Catholic priest who would perform a valid transubstantiation: God so present in the Host would then be desecrated. Unless it were a valid communion there could be no desecration. I should be surprised to find a Catholic priest among witches nowadays, though in the past many are said to have been members of the cult. It has been suggested that witches did not really celebrate the Black Mass but that people become witches by obtaining hosts, either by stealing the reserved sacrament from the churches or by receiving the communion and keeping it under their tongues and then putting it in their pockets; this was then taken to the rites and desecrated. During my lifetime there has been much trouble because priests and missionaries have destroyed or desecrated figures of heathen gods, and I also believe that some eminent Nonconformist churchmen have obtained consecrated hosts and held them up to ridicule. But I have never heard that so doing made them witches, and I do not think that witches ever do it or did it. On the other hand, there have been many instances of consecrated hosts being made use of in unorthodox ways by people who were not witches; to stop fires or volcanic eruptions, for instance, or to wear round the neck as personal charms, to bring good fortune, avert evil and, especially, to checkmate attacks by vampires; but all this was done by believers. A witch would not do these things, since she believes she can fabricate much more powerful charms of her own.

I believe, however, that sometimes the Black Mass *is* performed. Once I doubted it; but in February, 1952, I was in Rome and was told that some unfrocked priests and nuns celebrated it at times. My informants said they could arrange for me to see it done properly by these unfrocked priests and nuns, but that it would cost me about £20; I had not enough foreign exchange or else I would have gone, so as to settle the question to my own satisfaction. I think it was probably a show put on for the tourists, though I was assured by responsible people that it was not.

In short, I believe that people may perform Black Masses at times for a thrill, or with evil intent; but I do not believe that these people are witches, or know anything about witchcraft. Incidentally, I met more than one witch in Rome, though witches have to keep underground, and they knew nothing of this Black Mass.

Being initiated into the witch cult does not give a witch supernatural powers as I reckon them, but instructions are given, in rather veiled terms, in processes which develop various clairvoyant and other powers, in those who naturally possess them slightly. If they have none they can create none. Some of these powers are akin to magnetism, mesmerism and suggestion, and depend on the possibility of forming a sort of human battery, as it were, of combined human wills working together to influence persons or events at a distance. They have instructions in how to learn to do this by practice. It would take many people a long time, if I understand the directions aright. If these arts were more generally practised nowadays, we should call most of them spiritualism, mesmerism, suggestion, E.S.P., Yoga or perhaps Christian Science; to a witch it is all MAGIC, and magic is the art of getting results.

To do this certain processes are necessary and the rites are such that these processes may be used. In other words, they condition you. This is the secret of the cult.

I do not say that these processes are the only way to develop these powers. I presume that professional clairvoyants, for instance, have some method of teaching or training to bring out the powers which they naturally possess. It is possible that their method may be superior to that of witchcraft; possibly they know the witches' system and all the teaching it involves and keep it as a trade secret. Witches are also taught that in some mysterious way "inside the circle they are between the worlds" (this world and the next), and "that which happens between the worlds does not concern this world". To form this battery of wills, male and female intelligences are necessary in couples. In practice these are usually husband and wife, but there are younger people who often form attachments which usually end in marriage. There are also, of course, some unattached people, or some whose respective spouses are for some reason or other not members of the cult. I have heard fierce purists declare that no married man or woman should belong to, or attend, any club or society to which their respective partners did not also belong; but such strict views are not part of witchcraft.

Witchcraft was, and is, not a cult for everybody. Unless you have an attraction towards the occult, a sense of wonder, a feeling that you can slip for a few minutes out of this world into the other world of faery, it is of no use to you. By it you can obtain peace, the soothing of jangled nerves and many other benefits, just from the companionship, but to obtain the more fundamental effects you must attempt to develop any occult power you may have. But it is no use trying to develop these powers unless you have time and a suitable partner, and it is no place to take your maiden aunt, even if she is romantic; for witches, being realists, have few inhibitions and if they want to produce certain effects they do so in the most simple way. Although most of their activities have been for good, or have at least been harmless, certain aspects gave the Church in England and the Puritans the chance to accuse them of all kinds of immoralities, Devil-worship and cannibalism, as I have shown. Torture sometimes made poor wretches confess to these impossibilities, in order to lead the questioning away from the truth. The fact that their god had horns caused him to be identified with the Devil. The fact that witches were often people of some property worth looting supplied the incentive; rack and branding iron did the rest. Christian fear and Christian fire prevailed. The few remaining members of the cult dived underground and have remained secretive ever since. They are happy practising their lovely old rites. They do not want converts: converts mean talk: talk means bother and semi-persecution. All they desire is peace.

Notes

1   Witches are as often men as women, but in English a witch is always called "she", so I will use that word, and the reader must understand it to mean either male or female.
2   Published by Michael Houghton, 49 Museum Street, London, W.C.1.
3   The Sun, thought of as being reborn.

Chapter 20

Robert Heinlein

THOU ART GOD

■ from **STRANGER IN A STRANGE LAND**, New York, 1961, pp. 133–40

PUBLISHED IN 1961, ROBERT Heinlein's science-fiction novel *Stranger in a Strange Land* is intimately connected with the American Pagan movement, for it inspired the creation of The Church of All Worlds (CAW) later in that decade. Still in existence, CAW is organized in "nests," a term taken from Heinlein's work.

To borrow from the cover blurb of the 1968 edition (the 36th printing of this wildly popular signature 1960s' novel), *Stranger* is "the story of Valentine Michael Smith, born and educated [by Martians] on Mars, who arrives on our planet super-human in abilities and ignorant of sex as we know it." Surely Smith's utopian and paradisiacal attitude towards sex was responsible for much of the book's popularity: *Stranger* was perhaps the first science-fiction novel to deal openly with sex. In our excerpt, Jubal Harshaw, a rich writer—and spokesman for Heinlein's point of view—is attempting to explain the concept of "religion" to Smith, who has been raised by nonhumans, is incapable of lying, but who can "grok," or acquire new knowledge wholly and intuitively. His exclamation, "Thou art God!" modified to "Thou art God/dess," became a byword of the pantheistic Church of All Worlds.

Stranger in a Strange Land has also been more darkly credited with also inspiring Charles Manson's "family" of serial killers in the late 1960s. (Heinlein considered filing a libel suit against the newspaper that made the connection between his book and Manson, but let the matter drop after his own lawyer interviewed Manson in prison, who professed no knowledge of the book.)

The year of its publication, it was read by two undergraduates at Westminster College in Fulton, Missouri: Timothy Zell (now known as Oberon Zell-Ravenheart) and Richard Lance Christie, who immediately lifted the name "Church of All Worlds" (CAW) from its pages and created their own pantheistic religion, which later added influences from other forms of contemporary Paganism and ecological spirituality (see the CAW website). Zell, in fact, credits himself with coining (or at least popularizing) the term "Neo-Pagan." To judge from a letter Heinlein wrote to *Green Egg*, the Church of All Worlds' magazine from the late 1960s through 2001 (perhaps the most influential American Pagan magazine in those years), the author viewed the CAW with friendly detachment.

For further discussion of Heinlein, see Slusser (1977) and Stover (1989).

Chas S. Clifton

References

Church of All Worlds. http://www.caw.org

Slusser, George Edgar (1977) *Robert A. Heinlein, Stranger in His Own Land*. San Bernardino, CA: Borgo Press.

Stover, Leon (1989) *Robert Heinlein*. Boston: Twayne Publishers.

J UBAL FOUND THAT THE MAN FROM Mars was still in front of him, quiet as a sculptured figure. Sculpture? Uh— Jubal searched his memory. Michelangelo's "David"! Yes, even the puppyish hands and feet, the serenely sensual face, the tousled, too-long hair. "That was all, Mike."

"Yes, Jubal."

But Mike waited, Jubal said, "Something on your mind, son?"

"About what I was seeing in that goddam-noisy-box. You said, 'But talk to me later.'"

"Oh." Harshaw recalled the Fosterite broadcast and winced. "Yes, but don't call that thing a 'goddam noisy box.' It is a stereovision receiver."

Mike looked puzzled. "It is not a goddam-noisy-box? I heard you not rightly?"

"It is indeed a goddam noisy box. But *you* must call it a stereovision receiver."

"I will call it a 'stereovision-receiver.' Why, Jubal? I do not grok."

Harshaw sighed; he had climbed these stairs too many times. Any conversation with Smith turned up human behavior which could not be justified logically, and attempts to do so were endlessly time-consuming. "I do not grok it myself, Mike," he admitted, "but Jill wants you to say it that way."

"I will do it, Jubal. Jill wants it."

"Now tell me what you saw and heard—and what you grok of it."

Mike recalled every word and action in the babble tank, including all commercials. Since he had almost finished the encyclopedia, he had read articles on "Religion," "Christianity," "Islam," "Judaism," "Confucianism," "Buddhism," and related subjects. He had grokked none of this.

Jubal learned that: (a) Mike did not know that the Fosterite service was religious; (b) Mike remembered what he had read about religions but had filed such for future meditation, not having understood them; (c) Mike had a most confused notion of what "religion" meant, although he could quote nine dictionary definitions; (d) the Martian language contained no word which Mike could equate with *any* of these definitions; (e) the customs which Jubal had described to Duke as Martian "religious ceremonies" were not; to Mike such matters were as matter-of-fact as grocery markets were to Jubal; (f) it was not possible to separate in the Martian tongue the human concepts: "religion," "philosophy," and "science"—and, since Mike thought in Martian, it was not possible for him to tell them apart. All such matters were "learnings" from the "Old Ones." Doubt he had never heard of, nor of research (no Martian word for either); the answers to any questions were available from the Old Ones, who were omniscient and infallible, whether on tomorrow's weather or cosmic teleology. Mike had seen a weather forecast and had assumed that this was a message from human "Old Ones" for those still corporate. He held a similar assumption concerning the authors of the Encyclopedia Britannica.

But last, and worst to Jubal, Mike had grokked the Fosterite service as announcing impending discorporation of two humans to join the human "Old Ones"—and Mike was tremendously excited. Had he grokked it rightly? Mike knew that his English was imperfect; he made mistakes through ignorance, being "only an egg." But had he grokked *this* correctly? He had been waiting to meet the human "Old Ones," he had many questions to ask. Was this an opportunity? Or did he require more learnings before he was ready?

Jubal was saved by the bell; Dorcas arrived with sandwiches and coffee. Jubal ate silently, which suited Smith as his rearing had taught him that eating was a time for meditation. Jubal stretched his meal while he pondered—and cursed himself for letting Mike watch stereo. Oh, the boy had to come up against religions—couldn't be helped if he was going to spend his life on this dizzy planet. But, damn it, it would have been better to wait until Mike was used to the cockeyed pattern of human behavior . . . and not *Fosterites* as his first experience!

A devout agnostic, Jubal rated all religions, from the animism of Kalahari Bushmen to the most intellectualized faith, as equal. But emotionally he disliked some more than others and the Church of the New Revelation set his teeth on edge. The Fosterites' flat-footed claim to gnosis through a direct line to Heaven, their arrogant intolerance, their football-rally and sales-convention services—these depressed him. If people must go to church, why the devil couldn't they be dignified, like Catholics, Christian Scientists, or Quakers?

If God existed (concerning which Jubal maintained neutrality) and if He wanted to be worshipped (a proposition which Jubal found improbable but nevertheless possible in the light of his own ignorance), then it seemed wildly unlikely that a God potent to shape galaxies would be swayed by the whoop-te-do nonsense the Fosterites offered as "worship."

But with bleak honesty Jubal admitted that the Fosterites might own the Truth, the exact Truth, nothing but the Truth. The Universe was a silly place at best . . . but the least likely explanation for it was the no-explanation of random chance, the conceit that abstract somethings "just happened" to be atoms that "just happened" to get together in ways which "just happened" to look like consistent laws and some configurations "just happened" to possess self-awareness and that two "just happened" to be the Man from Mars and a bald-headed old coot with Jubal inside.

No, he could not swallow the "just-happened" theory, popular as it was with men who called themselves scientists. Random chance was not a sufficient explanation of the Universe—random chance was not sufficient to explain random chance; the pot could not hold itself.

What then? "Least hypothesis" deserved no preference; Occam's Razor could not slice the prime problem, the Nature of the Mind of God (might as well call it that, you old scoundrel; it's an Anglo-Saxon monosyllable not banned by four letters—and as good a tag for what you don't understand as any).

Was there any basis for preferring any sufficient hypothesis over another? When you did not understand a thing: *No!* Jubal admitted that a long life had left him not understanding the basic problems of the Universe.

The Fosterites might be right.

But, he reminded himself savagely, two things remained: his taste and his pride. If the Fosterites held a monopoly on Truth, if Heaven were open only to Fosterites, then he, Jubal Harshaw, gentleman, preferred that eternity of pain-filled damnation promised to "sinners" who refused the New Revelation. He could not see the naked Face of God . . . but his eyesight was good enough to pick out his social equals—and those Fosterites did not measure up!

But he could see how Mike had been misled; the Fosterite "going to Heaven" at a selected time did sound like the voluntary "discorporation" which, Jubal did not doubt, was the practice on Mars. Jubal suspected that a better term for the Fosterite practice was "murder"—but such had never been proved and rarely hinted. Foster had been the first to "go to Heaven" on schedule; dying at a prophesied instant; since then, it had been a Fosterite mark of special grace . . . it had been years since any coroner had had the temerity to pry into such deaths.

Not that Jubal cared—a good Fosterite was a dead Fosterite.

But it was going to be hard to explain.

No use stalling, another cup of coffee wouldn't make it easier—"Mike, who made the world?"

"Beg pardon?"

"Look around you. All this. Mars, too. The stars. Everything. You and me and everybody. Did the Old Ones tell you who made it?"

Mike looked puzzled. "No, Jubal."

"Well, have you wondered? Where did the Sun come from? Who put the stars in the sky? Who started it? All, everything, the whole world, the Universe . . . so that you and I are here talking." Jubal paused, surprised at himself. He had intended to take the usual agnostic approach . . . and found himself compulsively following his legal training, being an honest advocate in spite of himself, attempting to support a religious belief he did not hold but which was believed by most human beings. He found that, willy-nilly, he was attorney for the orthodoxies of his own race against—he wasn't sure what. An unhuman viewpoint. "How do your Old Ones answer such questions?"

"Jubal, I do not grok . . . that these are '*questions.*' I am sorry."

"Eh? I don't grok your answer."

Mike hesitated. "I will try. But words are . . . are *not* . . . rightly. Not 'putting.' Not 'mading.' A *now*ing. World is. World was. World shall be. *Now.*"

" 'As it was in the beginning, so it now and ever shall be, World without end—' "

Mike smiled happily. "You grok it!"

"I don't grok it," Jubal answered gruffly, "I was quoting something, uh, an 'Old One' said." He decided to try another approach; God the Creator was not the aspect of Deity to use as an opening—Mike did not grasp the idea of Creation. Well, Jubal wasn't sure that he did, either—long ago he had made a pact with himself to postulate a created Universe on even-numbered days, a tail-swallowing eternal-and-uncreated Universe on odd-numbered days—since each hypothesis, while paradoxical, avoided the paradoxes of the other—with a day off each leap year for sheer solipsist debauchery. Having tabled an unanswerable question he had given no thought to it for more than a generation.

Jubal decided to explain religion in its broadest sense and tackle the notion of Deity and Its aspects later.

Mike agreed that learnings came in various sizes, from little learnings that a nestling could grok on up to great learnings which only an Old One could grok in fullness. But Jubal's attempt to draw a line between small learnings and great so that "great learnings" would have the meanings of "religious questions" was not successful; some religious questions did not seem to Mike to be questions (such as "Creation") and others seemed to him to be "little" questions, with answers obvious to nestlings—such as life after death.

Jubal dropped it and passed on to the multiplicity of human religions. He explained that humans had hundreds of ways by which "great learnings" were taught, each with its own answers and each claiming to be the truth.

"What is 'truth'?" Mike asked.

("What is Truth?" asked a Roman judge, and washed his hands. Jubal wished that he could do likewise.) "An answer is truth when you speak rightly, Mike. How many hands do I have?"

"Two hands. I see two hands," Mike amended.

Anne glanced up from reading. "In six weeks I could make a Witness of him."

"Quiet, Anne. Things are tough enough. Mike, you spoke rightly; I have two hands. Your answer is truth. Suppose you said that I had seven hands?"

Mike looked troubled. "I do not grok that I could say that."

"No, I don't think you could. You would not speak rightly if you did; your answer would not be truth. But, Mike—listen carefully—each religion claims to be truth, claims to speak rightly. Yet their answers are as different as two hands and, seven hands. Fosterites say one thing, Buddhists say another, Moslems still another—many answers, all different."

Mike seemed to be making great effort. "All speak rightly? Jubal, I do not grok."

"Nor I."

The Man from Mars looked troubled, then suddenly smiled. "I will ask the Fosterites to ask your Old Ones and then we will know, my brother. How will I do this?"

A few minutes later Jubal found, to his disgust, that he had promised Mike an interview with some Fosterite bigmouth. Nor had he been able to dent Mike's assumption that Fosterites were in touch with human "Old Ones." Mike's difficulty was that he didn't know what a lie was—definitions of "lie" and "falsehood" had been filed in his mind with no trace of grokking. One could "speak wrongly" only by accident. So he had taken the Fosterite service at its face value.

Jubal tried to explain that *all* human religions claimed to be in touch with "Old Ones" one way or another; nevertheless their answers were all different.

Mike looked patiently troubled. "Jubal my brother, I try . . . but I do not grok how this can be right speaking. With my people, Old Ones speak always rightly. Your people—"

"Hold it, Mike."

"Beg pardon?"

"When you said, 'my people' you were talking about Martians. Mike, you are not a Martian; you are a man."

"What is 'Man'?"

Jubal groaned. Mike could, he was sure, quote the dictionary definitions. Yet the lad never asked a question to be annoying; he asked always for information—and expected Jubal to be able to tell him. "I am a man, you are a man, Larry is a man."

"But Anne is not a man?"

"Uh . . . Anne is a man, a female man. A woman."

("Thanks, Jubal."—"Shut up, Anne.")

"A baby is a man? I have seen pictures—and in the goddam-noi—in stereovision. A baby is not shaped like Anne . . . and Anne is not shaped like you . . . and you are not shaped like I. But a baby is a nestling man?"

"Uh . . . yes, a baby is a man."

"Jubal . . . I think I grok that my people—'Martians'—are man. Not shape. Shape is not man. Man is grokking. I speak rightly?"

Jubal decided to resign from the Philosophical Society and take up tatting! What was "grokking"? He had been using the word for a week—and he didn't grok it. But what was "Man"? A featherless biped? God's image? Or a fortuitous result of "survival of the fittest" in a circular definition? The heir of death and taxes? The Martians seemed to have defeated death, and they seemed not to have money, property, nor government in any human sense—so how could they have taxes?

Yet the boy was right; shape was irrelevant in defining "Man," as unimportant as the bottle containing the wine. You could even take a man out of his bottle, like that poor fellow whose life those Russians had "saved" by placing his brain in a vitreous envelope and wiring him like a telephone exchange. Gad, what a horrible joke! He wondered if the poor devil appreciated the humor.

But *how*, from the viewpoint of a Martian, did Man differ from other animals? Would a race that could levitate (and God knows what else) be impressed by engineering? If so, would the Aswan Dam, or a thousand miles of coral reef, win first prize? Man's self-awareness? Sheer conceit, there was no way to prove that sperm whales or sequoias were not philosophers and poets exceeding any human merit.

There was one field in which man was unsurpassed; he showed unlimited ingenuity in devising bigger and more efficient ways to kill off, enslave, harass and in all ways make an unbearable nuisance of himself to himself. Man was his own grimmest joke on himself. The very bedrock of humor was—

"Man is the animal who laughs," Jubal answered.

Mike considered this. "Then I am not a man."

"Huh?"

"I do not laugh. I have heard laughing and it frighted me. Then I grokked that it did not hurt. I have tried to learn——" Mike threw his head back and gave out a raucous cackle.

Jubal covered his ears. "*Stop!*"

"You heard," Mike agreed sadly. "I cannot rightly do it. So I am not man."

"Wait a minute, son. You simply haven't learned yet . . . and you'll never learn by trying. But you will, I promise you. If you live among us long enough, one day you will see how funny we are—and you will laugh."

"I will?"

"You will. Don't worry, just let it come. Why, son, even a Martian would laugh once he grokked us."

"I will wait," Smith agreed placidly.

"And while you are waiting, don't doubt that you are man. You are. Man born of woman and born to trouble . . . and some day you will grok its fullness and laugh—because man is the animal that laughs at himself. About your Martian friends, I do not know. But I grok that they may be 'man.'"

"Yes, Jubal."

Harshaw thought that the interview was over and felt relieved. He had not been so embarrassed since a day long gone when his father had explained the birds and the bees and the flowers—*much* too late.

But the Man from Mars was not yet done. "Jubal my brother, you were ask me [sic], 'Who made the World?' and I did not have words why I did not grok it rightly to be a question. I have been thinking words."

"So?"

"You told me, 'God made the World.'"

"No, no!" Harshaw said. "I told you that, while religions said many things, most of them said, 'God made the World.' I told you that I did not grok the fullness, but that 'God' was the word that was used."

"Yes, Jubal," Mike agreed. "Word is 'God.'" He added, "You grok."

"I must admit I don't grok."

"You grok," Smith repeated firmly. "I am explain. I did not have the word. You grok. Anne groks. I grok. The grasses under my feet grok in happy beauty. But I needed the word. The word is God."

"Go ahead."

Mike pointed triumphantly at Jubal. "*Thou art God!*"

Jubal slapped a hand to his face. "Oh, Jesus H.—— *What have I done?* Look, Mike, take it easy! You didn't understand me. I'm sorry. I'm very sorry! Just forget what I've said and we'll start over another day. But——"

"Thou art God," Mike repeated serenely. "That which groks. Anne is God. I am God. The happy grasses are God. Jill groks in beauty always. Jill is God. All shaping and making and creating together——"

He croaked something in Martian and smiled.

Chapter 21

Paul Huson

PRELIMINARY PREPARATIONS

■ from **MASTERING WITCHCRAFT**, New York, 1970, pp. 38–62

B ORN IN 1942 IN London, Paul Huson came from an artistic family. He attended the Slade School of Fine Art and worked as an art director for BBC television and Columbia Pictures, UK, before emigrating to the United States in 1968. Although employed primarily as a television writer and producer, Huson also wrote several books on witchcraft and magic, most notably *Mastering Witchcraft*, subtitled "A Practical Guide for Witches, Warlocks, and Covens."

Huson's writing in *Mastering Witchcraft* shows a bent towards ceremonial magic rather than revived Pagan religion, which can be explained by his instruction, beginning at age 17, in the Society of the Inner Light and then another group based on the Order of the Golden Dawn, both highly intellectual ceremonial orders founded much earlier—the Golden Dawn dates from the late nineteenth century.

Once in the United States, Huson had some initial difficulty finding employment in films, so he turned to writing. His timing was good, as the late 1960s and early 1970s saw an explosion in "occult" publishing that included even mainstream publishers. Witchcraft was trendy but far from respectable in those days, Huson recalls: "The Craft was something that was only trotted out each Halloween, and only then with a nudge and a wink."

Chas S. Clifton

Your witch name

A SSUMING, YOU HAVE EMBARKED on your career as a practitioner of the Black Arts, you will have to take a new, magical name to supplement your old, mundane one. Some unkind critics have called this the *nom du Diable*. It is nothing of the sort; at least, not in the sense they mean it. It is, in fact, an important part of your newly burgeoning witch personality, and henceforth you will be known chiefly by it to your fellow practitioners.

Many witches or warlocks choose to take a name which is intimately connected with magic and the supernatural, the favorites being the names of other, legendary practitioners of the Black Arts.

For instance, if you are male, you may choose the name of a legendary sorcerer such as Zyto, Balaam, Elymas, or Cyprian; or, alternatively, maybe Merlin, Althotas, Vergilius, or Vandermast.

A witch might well choose Morgana, Armida, Vivienne, or Melusina; Brisen, Nimue, Hellawes, or Fredegonda, Nocticula, Bensozia, Sidonia, or even Urganda!

Or you might choose a name of more classical inspiration like Apollonius, Medea, or Circe; or ancient Egyptian like Nectanebo or Arnuphis, or maybe something really complicated like Diancecht, Osmandine, or Ansuperomin!

The choice is yours. You must find one that appeals to you, that calls forth your feeling for the unseen world, gives you a thrill, and frankly makes you feel considerably powerful and no less sinister! Should you not wish to use a name from legend, you may try toying with those of the gods and demigods of mythology. Greek, Roman, Norse, Celtic—whichever you wish. A very good lead in these matters can be provided by finding out your astrological birth sign and planet and looking up the legends that surround them. For instance, if you are an artist or craftsman born under the sign of Taurus, you may well decide on the name of Daedalus, being that of the wizard-craftsman of King Minos, leader of the Cretan Bull Cult, thus linking with Taurus the Bull. Or, alternatively, if you are a female witch born under Taurus, ruled by Venus, you may decide that the name "Ariadne," daughter of King Minos and Theseus' bride, would be suitable, especially as she is indeed a form of Aradia, one of the chief spirit powers of the witch world.

A third method which can yield results is the numerological one. Add up all the digits which compose the name you are best known by, using this scheme to allocate the letters to numbers:

1	2	3	4	5	6	7	8	9
A	B	C	D	E	F	G	H	I
J	K	L	M	N	O	P	Q	R
S	T	U	V	W	X	Y	Z	

Keep adding the resultant numbers together till they form a single digit, thus:

$$\begin{array}{ccccccccc} J & O & H & N & & S & M & I & T & H \\ 1 + & 6 + & 8 + & 5 & & 1 + & 4 + & 9 + & 2 + & 8 \\ & = 20 & & & + & & = 24 & & & = 44 = 4 + 4 = 8 \end{array}$$

Now numerologically speaking the digits have the following traditional planetary attribution:

    1 The Sun
    2 The Moon
    3 Mars
    4 Mercury
    5 Jupiter
    6 Venus
    7 Saturn
    8 Uranus
    9 Neptune

In John Smith's case, his name planet will be Uranus. His next step would be to consult a book of classical myth and legend, on the subject matter surrounding Uranus. There will be ample material to select a name from, especially if the book is one of comparative mythology, showing the interrelations of legends among different cultures.

Should none of these methods yield results or appeal to you, then you should just go ahead and evolve a name that "feels right," cooking it up for yourself out of the blue, using your intuition to guide you. This in fact is ultimately the only criterion; the preceding methods are merely indicators and helps.

So mull over a selection of names in your mind. Ponder them in reverie if you can and let your deep mind send up some hints if possible. This really is the best way, as in the final analysis the deep mind is what we are really concerned with here. The witch name is basically designed to be an indication of the *true* nature of you as you really are deep down! There exists a coven of witches in England today whose female members only use witch names of a floral derivation, Rosemary, Japonica, Aubretia, Flora, and so on!

Some witches like to take worthy mottoes in Latin like *Sapiens dominabitur astris* or *Omnia vincam*, maybe a bit ecclesiastical in tone, but quite legitimate, though to my mind again less effective than the considerably more evocative names of legend.

Just choose one that satisfies you. It may take a bit of time; but it is worth considering well since once you inscribe it on your magical instruments, you are stuck with it.

Having settled on your witch name, you must keep it very, very secret, as it will eventually become one of the keys to your deep mind. You will be using it whenever you wish to "switch on" to perform a spell; this will be partly accomplished by pronouncing the name silently to yourself whenever you begin your use of the pyramid powers.

You should only divulge it to others who are close witch friends, preferably when you are closely bound together with them in the form of a group, or coven.

And as already mentioned, you will *also* write it on all your magical witch tools, using special witch runes to do so. Which brings me to my next topic.

The witch runes

These are, in fact, the letters of your witches' alphabet. Whenever you write your name on one of your magic instruments, you will use them. They are quite easy to learn, and with a little practice, you will soon be able to write them speedily. They are variously called by practitioners the Runes of Honorious or Theban Script, although this latter name does not necessarily imply a Greek or Egyptian derivation. Some witches believe that they are relics of Atlantean days, while others think that they have a connection with the Cabalistic "Enochian Script" of the Elizabethan astrologer and magician Dr. John Dee. Whatever the case, they are very ancient and have been used from time immemorial by witches as their magical alphabet in which spells and inscriptions were written.

Not only will you use these runes to write your witch name on your magical tools, but also to write it on your witch jewels.

Signs of identification

All witches and warlocks usually possess items that are often known by occult ritualists as jewels; in a witch's case these are items worn like jewelry signifying witchdom to those that have eyes to see, often bearing in runes the witch's name, the symbol adopted by her coven (should she belong to one), and her rank in it if it possesses a hierarchy of any sort. They usually serve three purposes—that of providing a means of recognition between members of different covens; a talismanic "link" with the collective mind of their own group by means of which they "plug in" to the elemental powers drawn down at the Sabbats; and third, sometimes as a means of "Fascination," that is to provide a reflective surface of the same sort often made use of by hypnotists when they wish to throw their subjects into a trance. The ring and pendant, which often contain gemstones, are generally the only jewels which are put to the latter use, however. One jewel which definitely does not fit into this latter category, however, being hidden mostly and only revealed at Sabbat meetings, is the garter. This and the girdle cord I shall consider last.

The witch jewels

The necklace, the bracelet, the ring and pendant, the girdle cord and garter

The necklace: The necklace is worn by women coven members often at Sabbats and Esbats only. It is in all probability of similar derivation to that of the girdle or garter. Some witches say that it has a connection with "Brisingamen," the elven necklace possessed by Freya, the Norse love goddess. Others say that through its occasional use of acorns as beads, it derives from the worship of Diana of Ephesus, whose devotees saw the head of their goddess bound with a coil of hair in the shape of the acorn itself. The number of beads for the necklace often consists of multiples of nine or thirteen. Acorns aside, however, the beads may be made of any material you please—metal, stone or wood—the only qualification being that they be fairly large and chunky. Amber is a favorite, as also are turquoise and jet. Many witches like to string their own, after exorcising the beads with fire and water initially and charging them in their own witch name, like any other magical tool, when they finish. (For instructions on general exorcisms by fire and water as well as magical "charging," see further on in this chapter.)

The bracelet: This is usually made of copper or silver and is worn by witches of either sex, again as a form of identity sign. However, unlike the necklace, it is engraved with the witch name of the bearer, the coven symbol (which is often an animal such as an owl, cat, or serpent), and his rank in it. There are usually only two "degrees" of rank, that of the triangle and the more advanced one of the pentacle. If male, the leader of the coven is sometimes known as the magister or master, the female as the high priestess. These are generally honorary ranks and titles, however, and simply indicate seniority of membership for the most part. Very occasionally are they indications of power. . . . Sometimes coven members will wear the bracelet to signify the triangle, and the garter, the pentacle grade.

Should you not belong to a properly formed coven, your name in witch runes will be all you need to have, plus any other amuletic symbols of good luck you may choose, such as your zodiac birth sign and planet.

Similar to the bracelet are the *ring and the pendant*. These are usually the only witch jewels bar the necklace that actually possess gems or stones set into them. These are the primary "fascination" jewels, and the more intricate and unusual the jewel, the better it serves its purpose. As to its composition and monetary value, it is completely a matter of individual taste and economy. The best magical witch stones are traditionally the sapphire and the opal. However, most precious and semiprecious stones do just as well, especially those which traditionally are held efficacious *against* the evil eye and fascination! These, in fact, are excellent accumulators of witch power, and as such, if you have ever worn one as a good-luck charm, has provided you, albeit unwittingly maybe, with an equal and opposite means of fascinating others or casting your own evil eye! In effect, you will be fighting fire with fire!

Here is a list, in alphabetical order, of some of those stones you may care to use as the bezel of your ring or pendant:

FASCINATION GEMS

Amber	Diamond	Onyx
Beryl	Emerald	Peridot
Bloodstone	Jade	Sardonyx
Carbuncle	Jasper	Staurotides (Cross-stone)
Carnelian	Jet	Ruby
Cat's-eye	Lapis Lazuli	Turquoise
Coral	Moonstone	Zircon

You may have your witch name engraved upon the ring or pendant—either on the reverse surface or around the stone itself. Sometimes the zodiac birth signs are also engraved, occasionally even a Cabalistic word of power such as Ararita, Tetragrammaton, Mehafelon, Ananizapta, or Shemhamphorash.

Incidentally, a very good idea which some witches resort to is to use a poison ring as their jewel. The inner cavity of the ring itself is very well suited for concealing either written charms to be carried about the person or philter powders to be slipped warily into some unsuspecting person's drink! The metal of which the ring or pendant is made can be any you wish—the following are used by witches to magically stimulate the following traits in their witch character:

> Gold — energy and general success
> Silver — intuitiveness and magical ability
> Copper — success in love
> Brass or fixed mercury — mental agility
> Tin — expansiveness and generosity
> Iron — courage and aggressive instincts
> Lead — stability

Sometimes an amalgam is made of some or all of them, depending on the orientation required. The resulting alloy is then known as magical electrum. But this is specialist stuff. Gold, silver, or copper is the usual choice.

Like the other jewels, the ring or pendant will always be exorcised and consecrated with fire and water in the waxing moon, and named with the possessor's name.

Finally, we come to a consideration of the concealed signs, the witch's *girdle cord and garter*. The girdle cord, often red in color, is used for several practical purposes, the least of which is to hold in your tabard, or ritual witch's robe. It is made of a specified length with certain knots tied in it, and is also used to measure the diameter of your magic circle when you cast one. Some practitioners also use it as a type of ritual rosary when they are performing a spell with a lot of repetitions in it, telling the knots in it like beads; I shall describe its manufacture later in the chapter under the heading of "Your Witches' Working Tools."

The garter is perhaps the most unusual piece of insignia carried by witches and, as such, is concealed and worn openly only at coven meetings. The other jewels can pass as regular items in the eyes of the uninitiated, and as such can usually be worn openly.

There are many styles of witch garters in existence. The traditional color is bright red, though black, blue, and green ones are to be seen. Often a female practitioner will have her garter made of velvet and backed with silk, the male variants being snakeskin, crocodile, or soft leather of some sort backed with blue silk. The garters are fastened by means of gold or silver gilt buckles. Sometimes tiny gold or silver bells are also sewn on, reminiscent of those worn by English Morris dancers.

On the outer surface of the garter are embroidered the witch name, coven symbol, and coven rank, if any. Sometimes the same signs that are inscribed upon the Athamé are also added.

Garters are always worn above the left knee, and let me reiterate, *only* on coven occasions or during the casting of spells.

The garter concludes the list of witch jewels. Most of them are optional, except for the necklace in the case of women. Why this latter exception should be made, I do not know. However, it is traditional coven practice, and as such should be complied with by any female witch, if she really wishes to obey the letter of the law.

Manner of dress

This is a matter over which there is much controversy in the witch world. Many practitioners claim that the best way to work magic is the traditional way: nude.

Others, equally tradition-minded, claim that this is not necessarily the case, and that ritual robes, or tabards, should be worn. The rationale behind nudity, apart from the sheer fun of it, is that clothing inhibits the emanation of your witch power. As an explanation or justification of the belief, I have never felt it held much water. Witch power is not easily impeded by mere clothing. It passes through walls and traverses wide distances easily enough, so why should a few flimsy garments prove such a barrier to it?

No, the chief reason for the nudity is a psychological one, the state of release from tension, mundane cares, and sexual inhibition is the aim being striven for here.

So if you feel that wearing no clothes may put you in the frame of mind where your magic will work all the better, then that is what you must indeed do. Careful though! Remember prying mother-in-law. Lock the door!

However, for those who live in chilly climates or who aren't enchanted by the idea of naked frolics, the tabard is the alternative. This at its simplest is a long piece of fairly heavy black material, folded double, with a hole for the head cut at the top, poncho-wise; the sides are sewn up to within about nine inches of the top, leaving holes for the arms to pass through. The completed garment hangs to the ankles. It is belted with the girdle cord.

Many practitioners, however, prefer more complicated or flattering garments, in varying colors such as blue, violet, red, green, or white, often with the addition of a hood, or cowl, to be drawn over the head for greater impersonality during a ritual. Special sandals may be worn or the feet left bare, again as you will. However, let me advise you here, should you form a coven, a certain uniformity of dress is desirable—often zealous witches will possess *two* robes for that very reason; a uniform one for Sabbats and Esbats, and a more individualistic one for private use.

Again your witch name and appropriate signs may be embroidered on the hem or breast of the garment if you desire, but this really isn't necessary. Indeed the tabard itself is not entirely necessary. It is merely a psychological prop to put you in the right frame of mind for magic, and all the rituals and processes can be as easily performed wearing your ordinary, everyday clothes—just as long as they don't work to your disadvantage by bringing you back down to earth again with a bump, that is.

Your witches' working tools

In order to perform any act of successful ritual witchcraft, you must have your set of basic traditional working tools. Without them, all but the most powerful born-witch or warlock is powerless when working at a distance from his victim. They are the tools of your trade, as much as an easel and brushes are of the artist.

The magical act is a cumulative one. You start from scratch with newly purchased substances, ritually purify or demagnetize them with salt, water, and incense, and then recharge them with your concentrated witch power. From these charged substances, you then fashion your implements, and with these implements, you cast your first spells.

The basic witch tools themselves are five in number; the full complement eight. There are many lesser ones which merit the designation more of common household implements that you keep specially for your witchcraft. For instance, needles for sewing, scissors for cutting, a white-hilted knife, and so on. I shall list the important ones at the end of this chapter along with other useful things you will need in your witches' cupboard.

These are your basic working tools, however:

> *The Witches' Knife* — also known as an Athamé or Bolline.
> *The Witches' Cord* — already mentioned, known variously as a girdle cord,
> or cingulum.
> *The Witches' Censer* — the incense burner or chafing dish, also known as
> the thurible.
> *The Witches' Cup* — also known as the chalice.
> *The Witches' Spellbook* — known variously as a witches' Bible, workbook,
> *Liber spirituum*, or Book of Shadows.

With these simple though basic tools you will be able to manufacture all the other magical artifacts that are mentioned in the following pages; the wand, the speculum, the candlesticks, the pentacle, the mandragore, and the alraun, and all the talismans, philters, incenses, images, and amulets that will be your general stock in trade. The ways and means to manufacture such things will be discussed under the specific headings throughout the book as we come to them.

To make your working tools, the first thing you must do is to learn how to purify and consecrate all your raw materials (or exorcise them, as we call it) by means of salt, water, and incense.

Theoretically, the salt, water, and incense stand for the four elements of the Wise—earth, water, and fire, together with air—symbolically constituting the basis for the material universe, in the language of alchemy and witchcraft. By exorcising anything, you are in effect symbolically using these four basic constituents to "wash" the article of all extraneous vibrations, prior to recharging it with your own will and concentrated witch power. Before, in fact, transforming it into a servant to accomplish a given magical task. Throughout the following pages I will refer to this process of purification as either exorcism or "passing something through fire and water."

Formula of exorcism by salt, water, and incense

Basically, any form of words can be used to exorcise something, ranging from a long ecclesiastical-sounding Latin invocation to a simple jingle. Witches generally prefer the latter. Here are two charms that can be used for exorcism, and which partake of the nature of jingles:

Taking a small handful of new salt and casting it into a bowl of fresh water, *breathe* these words onto the water's surface, mentally visualizing—and this is the important thing—with all the faith, will, and imagination you can muster, a dim bluish light beginning to hover over it as you do.

> Water and earth
> Where you are cast
> No spell nor adverse purpose last
> Not in complete accord with me.
> As my word, so mote it be!

This is now your charged salt and water of exorcism which you will use to make your working tools.

Similarly, casting a few grains of good-quality church incense onto a glowing charcoal block contained in an ashtray, chant as you hold your hand outstretched over it:

> Creature of fire
> this charge I lay,
> no phantom in thy presence stay.
> Here my will addressed to thee;
> and as my word, so mote it be!

Again, strongly visualize the coals radiating that strange blue light as you speak. With this charged fire, you will complete the exorcism of your raw materials.

Now the first working tools you should make are the cup and the thurible. In fact, as soon as you have made these you will be using them to contain the water and fire respectively, rather than relying on the services of any handy bowl and ashtray.

The witches' cup

The witches' cup is a variant of the cauldron of Ceridwen. This, in turn, was a Celtic development of early Prytanic myth which later became the central theme of all the legends concerning the Holy Grail, that mysterious relic which is woven inextricably into the Arthurian romances.

The cauldron, bowl, or cup symbolizes the receptive passivity of the great womb of nature, out of which all things are born and to which all return. It is seen as female in nature and is analogous with night, darkness, space, and, of course, the all-encompassing sea. Water is the traditional element of the Wise related to it.

The cup or chalice is used to contain the salt water of exorcism or, alternatively, the wine of libation. This is the sacramental wine which is consumed in some ceremonies, and also used to consecrate things at times. The cup is also used to compose philters in.

During persecution times the use of the chalice or cup was generally discontinued, owing to the fact that should a witch or warlock be found in possession of one, it usually led to an immediate bout of prolonged torture, the reason being, of course, that church authorities inevitably suspected the cup to have been used for heretical and blasphemous perversions of the Mass. In their eyes they were undoubtedly justified, as there is indeed a ceremonial feast at the Sabbat, wherein witches consume cakes and wine in much the same manner as the early church did in its Agape, or love feast. It is a rite common to many cults.

In order to make your own cup, you must first buy, *without bargaining over the price* (this will apply to anything you use in your spells), a goblet anywhere from three to five inches in diameter. It can be made out of anything you please that isn't porous and will hold a liquid. Some old witch cups are made of animal horn, and others of silver or silver-gilt like the conventional church chalice, or even of tinned copper. If you decide on a brass or copper one, be sure you glaze it well on the inside, since both of these metals can become very poisonous when a reactive liquid like wine is brought into contact with them. Glass and ceramic are also acceptable, but, as I say, a metal or horn one is traditional.

The process of consecration is simple. During the period of the month when the moon is waxing toward full, take some salt water in a bowl and steep in it the following powdered herbs: vervain (verbena), mint, basil, rosemary, Hyssop, lavender, sage, valerian, fennel. Sprinkle some incense on a charcoal block and charge both fire and water with the words I have already given you, mentally putting all your effort of will, faith, and imagination into *seeing* the elements as glowing with vibrant, purifying light. Having done this, sprinkle the cup with the water, then pass it through the incense smoke, chanting words to this effect, and visualizing the blue purifying light flickering around it as you do.

> By water and fire I conjure thee
> That there remain
> within thy frame
> no adverse thought nor enmity.
> Hear my will! Attend to me!
> As my word, so mote it be!

Having done this, paint . . . runes around the cup with a new brush and paint. Black or white enamel or stove-black is best for this. For this ritual you may also mix into it a pinch of your powdered herbs, vervain, *et al.*

As you paint each rune, chant these words, visualizing the signs glowing with magical light as you do: "Blessed be thou cup of water!"

Having done this, paint the runes that spell your witch name around the base of the cup, pronouncing each letter out loud as you do so.

When you finish, chant the words "So mote it be!" and put your completed cup safely away for future use.

The thurible

Again, a simple process. Buy a new metal chafing dish or incense burner, preferably with small legs or a stand to raise its base off the table top to prevent scorching.

Fill it with about an inch of sand. This will provide good insulation from the heat of the burning charcoal. Now, again when the moon is waxing (this will always be the case, unless otherwise stated), exorcise the thurible with charged fire and water in the same way that you did your cup. Then paint the proper symbols around it, chanting the following words with each symbol and again charging them with light. You may mix a little dragon's blood resin with your paint if you like, for added potency. "Blessed be thou creature of fire!"

Paint your witch name around the base, repeating the letters and charging them as you do so, and again terminate the spell with the words "So mote it be!" This is your completed thurible. With it and your cup you will henceforth perform all your water and fire exorcisms.

Now that we are equipped with our main tools of consecration, we shall deal with one of the most important of all the other witch tools:

The Athamé

The Athamé, or witches' black-hilted knife, is the instrument we use to draw magical circles and other diagrams, in the midst of which many of our spells are cast. Some witches, following the Cabalistic tradition of the old magical grimoire, the *Key of Solomon*, also employ a white-hilted knife, in addition, using the former to cast the circle, and the latter for anything that needs to be ritually dug, engraved, cut, or pierced. Most present-day witches, however, refer the white-hilted knife to the ranks of the lesser instruments, and rely entirely upon the Athamé in their operations.

Buy a *steel* knife with a black handle; the blade should be about five or six inches long. When the moon is *waning*, make an infusion in distilled water of any of the *Martial* herbs . . . .. Into this, mix a few drops of blood, either your own, traditionally that of a black cat, but that of a fresh beefsteak, chicken, or lamb chop from your nearest supermarket will do. Your own is best, however.

Exorcise the knife with water from your cup and incense mixed with some of the aforesaid herbs burned in your thurible; then proceed to heat the blade of the knife on the thurible coals until it gets as hot as possible. You will have to stoke up a good heat to do this. When the blade is good and hot, plunge it into your waiting brew, chanting these words, and visualizing the knife glowing with power after each immersion:

> Blade of steel I conjure thee
> to ban such things as named by me.
> As my word, so mote it be!

This process of tempering, or forging as it is called, should be repeated three times.

Having accomplished this, you must now magnetize the blade by stroking it repeatedly with a lodestone or bar magnet. Hold the Athamé in your left hand, the magnet by one end in your right, and beginning at the handle end of the blade, draw the tip of the magnet down the whole length to the very point. Keep this up for a good five minutes, always stroking in the same direction, chanting these words at each stroke:

> Blade of steel, I conjure thee
> attract all things as named by me!
> As my word, so mote it be!

Finally, paint the proper runes upon the handle in white paint, with which you may again mix any of the powdered herbs you used in your previous infusion. Chant the following words to charge each rune: "Blessed be thou knife of art!"

Then paint your witch name on the reverse side of the handle, again spelling the letters out loud to charge them, finishing with your usual words "So mote it be!"

Finally, you must bury the Athamé for three days and three nights in the earth, point down. Your backyard will amply suffice.

At the end of this time, you may dig up your Athamé, and, wrapping it in an exorcised piece of cloth, tuck it safely away, ready for future magical use.

The third of your working tools is:

The cord

otherwise known as the girdle, cingulum, or cable tow. The latter name derives from its use in various initiation rituals . . .. The cord is used basically to measure the radius of your circles, for binding things—and even, on occasions, for binding oneself! . . .

To make the cord, you should ideally spin your own flax or gather your own river rushes. Never mind, though; do as most urban witches do and buy a ball of red ribbon. From this you should measure off three six-foot lengths. When the moon is waxing, exorcise these with water and fire, and knotting the three ends together, start braiding them, chanting the following jingle, binding in the magical light with each twist:

> Made to measure,
> wrought to bind,
> blessed be
> thou cord entwined.

When you finish, make a large firm knot with the free ribbon ends to prevent them from unraveling, and repeat your sealing words, "So mote it be!"

Finally, tie another large knot three feet six inches from the first knot, a further one at four feet, another at four feet six inches, another at five feet, and yet another at five feet six inches. These will be the measurements of the triple radii when you use the cord as a compass cord for your magic circle. Using it to measure by, you can make two different triple circles; a larger one for coven working and a smaller one for solo spells or small groups.

The workbook

Your final major working tool!

In this, you must write all your magical recipes, spells, and rituals before you use them, using a good clear hand which will be legible by candlelight.

Our old friend the tradition-minded witch will insist on making her workbook out of parchment, sewing it herself, and sticking a cover on it.

However, if this seems overcomplicated to you, buy a thick book of good-quality drawing paper, about the size of a large exercise book. Then, when the moon is waxing, cover the back and binding of this book with a material of your own choice. Many practitioners favor velvet or moiré silk. Others prefer a leather or skin, often reptile. The choice of color ranges from black or white to red and green, even an occasional silver or gold!

You should then exorcise the book with water and fire. Then, with a pen and ink specially bought for this purpose, draw in this pentacle and its runes on the front side of the first page and the reverse of the last. As you draw in each rune, chant the following words:

> Book of words,
> book of deeds,
> blessed be
> thou book of art!

The "art" referred to is magical art, needless to say.

Finally, write your own witch name in the center of the pentacles, charging each letter as you do so in the usual way, and sealing again with the words "So mote it be!"

This book, along with your Athamé, will be your most treasured magical possession and should only be shown to other witches and coven members.

How to make your magic circle

This is your first spell of practical witchcraft! To cast it, you will be using all your working tools.

To those familiar with Cabalistic sorcery, the magic circle is generally viewed as a means of defense against hostile spirit entities; to the witch, however, though it may serve this purpose in some of her spells, it has a far more important function usually. This is, in fact, to serve as a lens to focus the witch power she raises in her rituals. It is a sort of magical boiler tank in which the steam is compressed in order to channel it into some useful activity such as driving a piston rod. In this way the witches' circle can be compared very closely with the ground mandala, or dkyilhkhor, used in Indian and Tibetan magic. It has very ancient, pre-Celtic origins.

In Cabalistic magic the circle will usually consist of basically a double or triple concentric circle. In between the lines will be written Hebrew names, divine and angelic, which pertain to the nature of the operation. In the center may often be traced geometrical figures, such as a square or a pentagram whose sides or number of points again correspond numerologically with the type of spell being cast.

To the practicing witch, however, this is all mostly totally irrelevant and unnecessary. Quite apart from the theoretical over-complication, the practical details are much too demanding. Unless one is wealthy enough to possess a house or apartment with sufficient rooms to dedicate one entirely to magical practice, the full-painted floor circle with all its geometrical ramifications is generally quite out of the question.

No, as a witch, your basic requirement for many spells will simply be a triple circle drawn out on the floor or carpet in temporary masking tape if you want. This is advisable for group or coven workings, but when you are operating solo, you can dispense with even that, using an imaginary boundary line, but making quite sure you stick within it. Because of this it is wise to make the circle rims coincide with marks on the carpet or pieces of furniture, so you can maintain a correct visualization. Anyway, here is your method of casting your circle.

Clear a space on your den or living room floor sufficient to draw a nine-foot-diameter circle (eleven-foot for coven working). Now, pin one end of your cord down to the floor in roughly the center of the room with a heavy object—a chair or table leg maybe—or have someone hold it down if you are working in company. Now, stretching the cord out tightly, take your Athamé, and wrapping the cord around its handle at the first knot, the one four feet six inches from the pinned end, trace a nine-foot-diameter circle lightly on the floor with the knife point, keeping the cord taut and using the chair as a pivot.

You must do this in a *clockwise* direction (known as deosil to witches) always turning to the *right*. You must also *begin* your tracing operation standing in the *east* and end up back in the east. For this, you will need the aid of a small pocket direction-finding compass. As you trace the circle, use your witchly imagination to visualize that blue witch fire blasting down your Athamé blade, like an oxyacetelyne blowtorch, leaving a line of flickering violet-colored flames in its wake. Listen to them hiss and crackle; you are surrounding yourself with a circle of magical light!

If you want to memorize the right color of the fire, try igniting a few drops of methylated spirits or brandy in a saucer (careful though!) and observing the resultant flame.

Having drawn your first circle, you must now repeat the operation, shortening your cord by moving your Athamé six inches down it to the second knot, the four-foot one, giving you a circle with an eight-foot diameter. Repeat the operation a third and final time, using the next knot down, the three-feet-six-inch one, which will give you your inner circle of seven-foot diameter.

This is your magic circle. You must now proceed to exorcise the ground inside it by sprinkling and censing to the four quarters—east, south, west, and north—always traveling deosil, and using your usual fire and water exorcism.

Having got this far, you are now standing in a ritually purified witches' circle, and the lens for your witch power is in position. You can now proceed with the spell itself . . . .

Before finishing this chapter, however, I shall list a few of the ingredients and bits and pieces you will find useful in practicing your craft; buy them new, without haggling over the price, of course; keep them apart from your everyday things; and before you use any of them in a spell, simply exorcise them with fire and water.

A witch's initial supplies

1. Charcoal blocks for the thurible. Preferably self-igniting, but the regular kind will do, sprinkled with a few drops of alcohol or cheap cologne to ignite. You can obtain them from most religious supply stores. A lot of shops specializing in the sale of exotic foreign imports also stock them. Be sure to get them *unperfumed*, though.
2. A supply of plain, undecorated white candles about six to nine inches long. Beeswax is excellent, but ordinary tallow or stearin will do well. Candles of other colors such as black or red will be mentioned in the spells, where they are called for.

3.   Salt. Ground rock salt is best, but ordinary table salt will do for exorcisms.
4.   Water. Tap water will do for exorcisms, but distilled water such as used for steam irons will be needed for your philters and elixirs.
5.   White masking tape. Most art suppliers stock this. It is very useful for the temporary marking out of circles or triangles, particularly where group work is concerned.
6.   Good-quality plain white drawing paper for your talismans. Ideally, sheepskin parchment, but this is very expensive and the paper will do just as well.
7.   An elementary schoolboy's geometry set including compasses, protractor, ruler, and set square. This is to draw your talismans and sigils (magical symbols) with.
8.   A small sewing kit containing scissors, needles, and thread.
9.   A dip pen; your "pen of art" (not a ballpoint) for drawing talismans and writing in your workbook.
10.   A good-quality (squirrel or sable) paintbrush for painting runes on your magical tools.
11.   Thick black waterproof ink to use with your dip pen; your "ink of art." To this, you may add a perfume or herb at the time you cast your spell, consonant with its nature, such as powdered basil for love, cinnamon for intelligence, etc.

Tradition-minded witches make their own ink with one of the following two recipes, usually the latter:

Either

Powdered gall-nuts
Roman vitriol or green copperas
Alum or gum Arabic

or

Gum Arabic
Powdered burned peach kernels
Soot or lampblack (hold the back of a spoon over a candle)
Distilled water

12.   A selection of household glues.
13.   Paint, both black and white; your "paint of art." Most witches find a stove enamel is best because it takes on ceramic and glass as well as metal. You will be using it to inscribe the runes on your working tools.
14.   A small square table to practice on, of cardtable size. This throughout the text will be known as the "table of practice" or "altar."
15.   A good assortment of jars and bottles. Little medicine bottles are extremely handy for containing philters and powders. The herb jars sold in various sizes at shops dealing in fancy kitchenware are, of course, ideal.

16. Finally, a generous supply of adhesive labels for easy identification of your preparations. Many a hex powder looks all too similar to a love sachet mixture! Enough said.
17. Finally a sharp, white-hilted knife for preparatory cutting or "Bigraving" (engraving).

These are your basics. You can build up your stock as you go along. Many of the spells . . . call for special herbs or spices, and you can buy them for the one instance, and then store the remainder for future use. Try to keep all your magical things together, preferably locked away in a safe place—perhaps a cupboard or closet reserved for the purpose, best of all a room dedicated to your craft.

Chapter 22

Hans Holzer

ISIS AND ISHTAR
The comeback of ancient cults

■ from **THE NEW PAGANS**, Garden City, New York, 1972, pp. 85–123

T HE SAME BOOM IN "occult" publishing that produced Paul Huson's *Mastering Witchcraft* (1970) also saw the publication of several journalistic books chronicling a mélange of Paganism, Satanism, and parapsychology. Hans Holzer, a New York City-based writer born in 1920, produced three such surveys in close succession: *The Truth about Witchcraft* (1969), *The New Pagans* (1972), and *The Witchcraft Report* (1973). It is significant that the middle book used "Pagans" in its title, for in it Holzer described his visits to several revived Pagan religious groups in the United States that did not consider themselves "Wiccan" or "Craft." He included some Satanists as well. Everybody did: even Margot Adler in her more thorough and respected book *Drawing Down the Moon* (1986) followed much of Holzer's cross-country itinerary.

Contrary to Holzer's speculation, Feraferia never grew much beyond what he describes, although it still exists. Nor have these other groups succeeded in having the impact on the religious landscape that Wicca (broadly defined) has had. The Church of All Worlds has had the broadest reach, helped in large part by its journal *Green Egg*, which during the 1970s, and again in the late 1980s–90s, was probably the most widely distributed Pagan magazine in the United States, until it ceased publication. It is important to understand, however, that the impulse behind the Pagan revival has taken many others forms besides Wicca—Druid, Heathen, and Greco-Roman revival groups are also part of Paganism today.

Chas S. Clifton

References

Adler, Margot ([1979] 1986) *Drawing Down the Moon*. Boston: Beacon Press.
Holzer, Hans (1969) *The Truth about Witchcraft*. New York: Pocket Books.

Holzer, Hans (1973) *The Witchcraft Report.* New York: Ace Books.
Huson, Paul (1970) *Mastering Witchcraft.* New York: G.P. Putnam's Sons.
Roberts, Susan (1971) *Witches U.S.A.* New York: Dell.

"**W**ELCOME TO THE HOUSE OF ISHTAR**," said a female voice in dulcet yet exciting tones. A slight Russian accent made it even more incongruous, for I was standing at the threshold of a modest house on a tree-shaded lane in Pasadena. The year was 1969, the season All Hallows' Eve and the occasion, my long-awaited visit to Feraferia, a unique coven of pagans worshiping in the ancient Greek traditions.

I looked up in the semidarkness and found that the voice belonged to a pretty, dark-haired woman dressed in the flowing robe of a priestess. The material was quite sheer and her pale skin showed through it. An elaborate necklace and headdress, amulets, bracelets, and anklets, all of which were of a kind I had never seen before, completed her costume. The house, an older, very comfortable building, set back somewhat from the quiet street, was ideally suited for a secret ritual. Although I was yet to learn that prying neighbors will always find a way to disrupt that which they cannot understand or participate in, at the time I first met the people of Feraferia all was serene and the night was quiet and warm.

I had originally heard of Fred Adams and his strange pagan sect through a mutual friend, Mark Roberts of Dallas. After some correspondence with the president of Feraferia, Richard Stanewick, I was finally invited to their autumnal ritual. Both Fred and Richard are professional artists. Fred's mate, Svetlana, the lady who had so enticingly greeted me at the door, liked to create jewelry and strange designs, and everything in and about Feraferia, as I was soon to learn, was done by the people themselves in a unique manner based on authentic ancient models and ideas. Feraferia describes itself as "a love culture for wilderness" and ecological concepts were at the core of its teachings long before ecology became a household term in America, long before an alarmed country became finally aware of the need to preserve what is left of our natural heritage. Fred Adams lives and breathes preservation, return to the natural state of living, the planting of new trees, the saving of city areas from destruction, the cleansing and purification of rural areas. Those are as important to him and his group as are the more involved pagan rituals, worshiping the "magic maiden," the symbolic deity representing the female principle in nature, creation, the spark within.

Feraferia does not call itself witchcraft by that name. It is far more. Where Wicca or male-oriented witchcraft groups worship in rites to express their desires symbolically and, through incantations, try to change things for themselves or for others, Feraferia goes beyond the ritual: It enacts what it stands for in actual nature. There are side trips, weather permitting, into the wilderness, where the group communes with nature. There are attempts at restoring neglected areas to their natural appearance, and as a consequence, even the ritual is far more realistic and vital than the rituals of so many intellectually inclined pagan groups.

Promptly at seven-thirty, Richard had called for me at the Hotel Continental in Hollywood. The ride out to Pasadena takes about thirty or forty minutes. We talked very little en route. As we approached Pasadena, Richard said, "You know about our principles, don't you?" I nodded, I had done some reading beforehand and I was fully prepared to learn more firsthand. Of course, I didn't come to this group exactly as a novice. Fred knew that I had been through several high-level pagan initiations before and that I was probably familiar with the ancient Greek aspects of his group since I had originally been a classical archeologist. I didn't know, of course, to what degree I would be welcome tonight. After all, they knew I would write about the group, although I had promised not to disclose anything that would be in violation of their trust in me. There are certain words in all magic rituals that should not be disclosed to anyone other than an actual initiate hearing them for the first time. But there are other things, especially visual descriptions of certain rituals, that can be safely disclosed to outsiders, especially if the purpose is to explain a little-known cult and possibly interest others in studying it. "You have no hangups, do you?" Dick continued. "Some of our rites are done in the nude." I wasn't particularly surprised since most Wicca groups also worship in the nude. I had long learned that being naked did not necessarily mean misbehaving.

There were already six or seven people assembled in the living room of "the house of Ishtar." The lights were not too bright, but they were strong enough to disclose an incredible array of paraphernalia covering literally every inch of space along the walls. There were drawings, paintings, figurines, ritual objects, leaves, wreaths, small altars—much of it the work of Fred Adams himself. All of these objects fitted well together, and turned the room into a kind of outer temple. The inner temple, I was to learn later, was much smaller and quite different. Many of the art objects along the walls represented beautiful young women, since the "magic maiden" of this cult is a young girl about twenty-three years old rather than the Mother Goddess of slightly more mature connotations generally worshiped in other witchcraft cults.

Everything about Feraferia is vibrant and love-orientated. Feraferia does not contain a negative ritual. While there are some protective incantations and spells in Wicca to ward off enemies or evil human beings, Feraferia has none of those. This group believes that the positive force alone will protect them. All ritualistic activity in Feraferia revolves around the ancient Greek calendar, based upon thirteen lunar months of twenty-eight days each. Every moment is carefully charted by Fred Adams in an elaborate and intricate calendar, which he himself has constructed. The inner secret of this pagan group is to be completely in tune with what goes on in nature, to find the right moment for whatever one is undertaking, the right auspices, and not merely a casual glance at the horoscope. This goes far deeper than any astrologer normally does. A rhythmical tying up with nature's own inner movements is the ultimate goal for the men and women in Feraferia. As a result, their lives become wholly attuned to natural living, bringing, Feraferia believes, total immersion, total fulfillment, and a way of life different from the city-bred destructiveness and ill health to which Fred and his friends ascribe so many of today's ills.

Except for the priestess, whose dress apparently required greater preparation, the others were still in their "civilian clothes." There were one couple from a nearby community, who were friends of Fred, a local doctor, a lady whom he had brought, a young girl with long dark hair who seemed to know everyone already, Fred, Dick, and myself. I was the only new person in this gathering. Altogether there were nine people, five men and four women. The room was heavy with incense, and the conversation flowed freely as these people exchanged greetings and brought each other up to date on their doings since the last time they had gathered together.

Promptly at nine o'clock, Fred asked for attention. "We are about ready to begin," he explained. "Ladies can change in the bedroom, gentlemen in the kitchen." Quickly the two sexes repaired to their respective changing quarters and a little later emerged wearing white robes. I had not brought any such garment, so Fred kindly lent me an extra one. The robes are kept in the temple and since some members of the group hadn't come tonight, there was a spare robe available.

After we had filed back into the living room, we were told to lie down on the floor, heads touching in starlike fashion and legs outward bound. As we gazed up at the ceiling, we were to try astral projection together. Actually this was a kind of communal relaxation, in that for a few moments we would forget our worldly problems and try to relate to each other as parts of a larger community. I don't think I flew up to the ceiling and out the window the way I was directed, but I did experience a calm sense of relaxation and it was rather a warm feeling to rub ears with someone you had just met, yet without having any sensation of being close to a stranger.

This was followed by some yoga breathing exercises, which relaxed us even further. As we sat up on the floor on top of what turned out to be a carefully engraved calendar wheel, Fred stepped up to a small altar in the corner, where he was joined by Svetlana. In front of the effigy of the magic maiden, the female goddess Ishtar, or Astar, the priestly couple then intoned the proper ritual prayer requesting that the goddess be present in our undertaking.

To the left of the altar there was an icon of Kore, the Greek name for "the magic maiden" of wildness, while to the right was a similar picture honoring Kouros, her male counterpart, the "magic youth" of wildness. Between them was placed a picture or symbol of Awiya, also called Korythalia, the great tree of the cosmos. According to Feraferia interpretation, this tree is the seat of Sophia, whom Frederick Adams calls "the black goddess of unfathomable mystery, who unites Kore and Kouros in unending love, dance, play, dream fulfillment." In addition to these symbolic representations, to the east of the altar was a musical instrument representing air; to the south, an incense burner representing fire; a mortar and pestle with soil inside representing earth to the west; a container of water placed to the north; some pebbles in the center representing the omphalos—what Adams calls the "earth sky navel" of ritual significance—a bell to call the spirits of nature; and finally various talismans or charms on the ground in front of the altar to mark the four quarters.

A special ritual movement, almost a dance, was performed in front of the altar to open the proceedings. This movement is called phytala, and is enacted by first putting the palms of the hands together, then raising them above one's head, opening the arms wide, bringing them down toward the lower solar plexus, letting the arms hang loose by the sides of the body, and finally lifting them up, palms outward, in an attitude of blessing. During this posturing, a chant up and down the tonal scale is intoned: "Magic maiden, magic maiden, evoe Kore, evoe Kouros, Awiya." *Evoe* means "hail!" There is another chant in honor of Kore that may also be used on this as well as other occasions:

O holy maiden of the kindling quick of merging mist and mazing echo, the innocent bounty of the trees bears your faerie flesh of wildness, wonder, magic, mirth, and love. Your beauty seals our bridal with all life. The dance of your green pulse unfolds all bodies from earth's fragrant form.

Evidently, everyone except me had been through such ceremonies before because they responded immediately with their own "Evoe Kore, evoe Kouros, Awiya! Hail, holy maiden, hail, holy youth, hail, great lady of living cosmos and of eternal wildness and love."

Now the priest motioned us to rise and follow him and the priestess out into the garden, where we would enact an outdoor ceremonial. One by one we walked through the rear door of the house, down a few steps into the rather large garden behind the building. Gently sloping, the fruit trees opened up into a carefully constructed open-air sanctuary. "This is our wilderness henge," Fred explained as we walked toward it. A little like a miniature Stonehenge, the sanctuary consisted of stones marking certain specific moments in the calendar. In fact, the sanctuary was essentially a reproduction of the cosmos, drawn exactly to scale and properly marked so that each step would have parallel meaning in terms of nature, cosmos, and the calendar.

It was getting somewhat cool now, and the thin robe wasn't enough to keep me from shivering, but the excitement of seeing an ancient Greek ritual reenacted precisely as it had been done in ancient Crete, a thousand years before Christ, dispelled all thoughts of catching a cold or being a little uncomfortable.

Since this was the festival of Samhain, better known as Hallowe'en, the appropriate incantations had to be made for that season of the year. The henge, from an old Anglo-Saxon term meaning "to hang," represents the entire cosmos. The boundary path around the henge stands for the horizon of the earth seen from the center, if one were to stand there and look out from it.

After invoking the goddess and the four quarters and in a sense dedicating ourselves to the spirit of nature communion expressed in this ceremony, we proceeded back to the house and assembled once again in the living room. Fred and Svetlana left us there for a while to prepare the temple itself, for the major part of the evening was yet to come.

For the next ten or fifteen minutes we chatted about the need to save what was left of nature in the Los Angeles area from expanding industry and pollution. Then Fred reappeared and beckoned us to follow him. The time was at hand for the mysteries to begin.

In ancient Greek witchcraft, or rather in the religious cult of Artemis, the Diana of the Celtic world, and Dionysos, the services are called mysteries—not in the sense of mystery stories of today, but relating to the term mysticism as we understand it at present.

Some things are veiled and are disclosed to the initiate at the proper time. Others must remain veiled forever. Entering the mysteries is a gradual and emotional experience. In so closely knit a group as Feraferia even the introductory step was not possible until the initiate had been properly prepared through studies and above all through the understanding of the ritual meaning inherent in Feraferia.

The word "Feraferia" is derived from Latin and means wildness festival. In writing of the principles of this group, which was founded in 1967, Fred Adams stated,

> Wildness is the elusive quick of all spontaneous delicately urging life. The only way to reunite mankind is to reunite mankind with nature. Man will become humane toward man only when he becomes humane toward all nature. The inner nature of man has been disastrously severed from the all-enveloping nature of wilderness. The vital link between visionary nature within and ecological nature without is poetry.

As part of tonight's celebration, I was to be initiated so that I might then participate in the celebration called for by that particular season. One by one, we stepped into the adjoining room. It was very dark now as most of the lights had been doused. To the right was the door to the temple, a room so small that even half a dozen people would fill it. This was the inner sanctum of Kore, a room specially prepared by Fred and Svetlana, painted, adorned with sacred icons, altars in all four corners, a chair called "the chair of Demeter," and many ritual objects I am not permitted to describe here.

At the moment, however, that door was closed and I could see only very dim light coming from under it, the kind of light made by one or two candles. Some of the heavy incense being burned inside the temple escaped into the anteroom, and the sweet yet intoxicating smell of the strange aromatic made the entire proceedings even more remote to me. I had long forgotten where I was or that no more than two blocks away the Freeway traffic raced past. I was here to experience, firsthand, a very ancient ritual and to understand the pagan soul in such a way that through my eyes and heart, others might partake of it.

Silently, everyone took off his robe. Then the door to the temple was opened and one by one we slowly stepped into the steaming inner temple. Priest and priestess took their places in the center, standing upon the sacred calendar engraved on the floor, while the others grouped themselves around in a circle. Stepping in last, I was motioned to stand opposite the priest inside the circle. The door was shut tight. A piece of cloth was immediately put over my head, preventing my seeing. Then the priest read the charge, or statement of intent, to me. Following this, there were some unearthly noises and it felt as if monsters were grappling my legs. However, I did not budge or show any fear. I expected this, of course, since I am quite familiar with the ancient mysteries.

After I had thus been symbolically tested, I was welcomed into the fold and permitted to kiss the sacred apple that represents the goddess.

In truth, though the entire initiation ceremony took no more than ten or fifteen minutes, I felt as if I had been away a year. As I stepped back into the adjoining room to return to the present, it seemed as if I were stepping down from Mount Olympus.

As a token of my initiation, I was handed a stone and wood sculpture, the work of Fred Adams, inscribed "Full moon over the mountain." The rest of the evening was social. Somehow Svetlana had managed to prepare cold cuts and wine and coffee, and with all tension gone, the evening was perhaps not so different from other evenings in Pasadena, California.

By midnight I was back in my Hollywood hotel room.

Since the ancient gods are merely various aspects of nature and since within us we have aspects of these gods, there may be many names by which one and the same deity is called. All pagan religions equate nature forces with various deities. In worshiping a seemingly independent deity existing somewhere outside oneself, one is in fact drawing upon one's inner forces, and in so doing, sparkplugs them into performing for oneself.

Kore, by the way, is "the magic maiden" or simply "the goddess." 'When the priestess greeted me with "welcome to the house of Ishtar," she was merely referring to another aspect of the Great Goddess. Just as "the magic maiden" inspires and causes beginnings, so the great "Mother Goddess," the later development of the same principle, attends to fulfillment of that which is promised.

Ishtar exists under one form or another in every religion. In the Old Testament, she is called Ashtorat. She was also known as Semiramis by the Assyrians, and to Greeks and Romans she was Aphrodite and Venus. To Celtic and Anglo-Saxon witches she is "the Queen of Heaven" or simply "the Mother Goddess." Even Christianity has taken some of her aspects in creating the image of the Madonna.

A female deity is very necessary for mankind to understand itself, because the female goddess stands at the beginning of life itself. Dr. Paul M. Vest, in an article called "Ishtar, Goddess of Love," says that "in the days of Ishtar, veneration of sexual phenomena was customary. It was mankind's primal response to the great force which is the direct source of all life. Consequently, adoration of sex and sex symbols was common to many early religions. And broadly speaking, the goddess Ishtar personified sex, fertility, and the female reproductive life force."

No orgies take place in Feraferia. No Psychedelic Venus Church here. The mechanics of sex are not stressed, but, rather, the spiritual unfoldment leading to love and being in tune with nature.

Fred Adams is a marvelously gifted painter. His interpretations of the mystery gods of ancient Greece rank favorably with some of the classical originals. At one point, he was interested in the American nudist movement but later discovered that the motivations of his mystic involvement differed greatly from the health aspects of nudism as it is generally known today. Whereas the shedding of clothes and playing in the sun seemed to be the main objectives of traditional nudism, Adams in Feraferia practices considers this only the first step in the right direction. Once the outer garments have been stripped off, it is necessary to attune the inner man to nature. Walking around a few hours without clothes and then returning to civilization and life as usual is not enough. Only when we readjust our thinking and feeling completely to total naturalness, whether we wear clothes or not, do we hold out hope that our civilization can still be saved from self-destruction.

That, in a nutshell, is the main point of Feraferia's philosophy. "The Feraferian vision includes new inspirations and new combinations from the most ancient wellsprings of the goddess. Innovations there are, but always in continuity with those ancient sources," Fred Adams explains. "You will find in the Feraferian vision no slavish archeological reconstructions, because the new paganism must accommodate all the new developments in human knowledge and awareness that have occurred since the old paganism quite deservedly lost its congregations and crumbled to ruin."

Adams calls the incantations for the days of the week "enchantments." The idea is not to beseech the goddess or to threaten her in order to force her to perform what is wanted, but rather to entice her, enchant her with charm, charisma, expressions of love and devotion. In other words, a positive approach to the goddess, all the way.

Mr. Adams is not only a great classical scholar with an amazing command of ancient Greek, but also quite a poet. The incantations here cited are mainly his work, even though they are based on ancient rituals and verbalizations and in essence express for modern man that which was similarly used by the ancient Greek worshiper in addressing *his* image of the goddess.

Beginning with Saturday, the day sacred to Saturn, the enchantments differ for each day of the week. These are not specific incantations but are rather like morning prayers in the Christian religion. In a way they are requests for guidance and the blessings of the day.

> Ourania-Aphaia-Pheraia-Despoina, I dedicate this day to thee and to thine own land-sky-love-body of deep heaven, all stars, all grounds and matrices of existence, the geosphere, polar icecaps, tundra, and alpine fell.
>
> Blessed be thy faerie realms. They will grow in wildness and love even as they suffuse my presence with joy and wilderness wisdom. Grant all wildlings in these realms thrive, find fulfillment and rebirth. I bestow my genius and love upon these realms and all their wildlings. May the wild realms of Ourania, black goddess of stars, bestow upon me their genius for mystery that divine ground essence, immanence transcendence, lasting value, eternity, wholeness, plurality, magistery, magnanimity, merging field cohesion, peace, cosmic completion, ultimate consummations. May I dance in the endless wedding procession of Ourania and Kronos, of alpine peaks and cone forests, as it winds through mazes of starlight in the nuptial night of the nameless bride! Evoe Kore! Evoe Kouros! Awiya!

After this prayer, whatever particular spells one wishes to make follow. Similar incantations and rituals have been created, or rather recreated, for each day of the week.

According to Mr. Adams, the proper time for cosmic communion is Saturday, the Sabbath and the night of Ourania, at 9:00 P.M. This is also the time for meditation and, of course, the meeting of covens. The second day of the week, Sunday, is sacred to Helios, the sun god. Monday is sacred to Artemis, and it is the third day of the week in the pagan calendar. Tuesday, the fourth day, belongs to Hermes-Pan, and Wednesday is sacred to Aphrodite. Thursday belongs to Ares, the god of war; Friday is dedicated to Kronos-Zeus-Godfather.

It is not my intention to publish here more than a few significant samples of Feraferia's and Fred Adams' poetic incantations. Let those who find in them inspiration gain the knowledge directly when they can immerse themselves in the study and practice of the cult itself.

Nevertheless, in addition to Saturday, the day of the Sabbath, perhaps the day of Diana, Monday, should also be singled out since many pagans who do not have access to Feraferia directly may want to know at least one valid ritual to use in some form of Dianic worship when the occasion arises.

Here, then, is the enchantment for Monday, the third day of the week:

> Dione-Artemis-Selene-Hekate-Faerie-Diana-Aradia! I dedicate this day
> to thee and to thine own land-sky-love-body of waters: oceans, seas,
> lagoons, rivers, lakes, pools, springs, dew, mist, rain and snow; all
> cryptic communities of shade and soil; nocturnal air.
>
> Blessed be thy faerie realms. They will grow in wildness and love
> even as they suffuse my presence with joy and wilderness wisdom. Grant
> all wildlings in these realms thrive, find fulfillment and continued rebirth.
> I bestow my genius and love upon these realms and all their wildlings.
> May the wild realms of Dione-Artemis, of Selene and Hekate, triune
> goddess of whirling dew-veiled night, bestow upon me their genius for:
> desire, imagination, vision, enchantment, inspiration, magic, fascination,
> delicacy, subtlety and wants, quality, influence, assimilation, empathy,
> fertility of soil, resistivity, sensitivity, creativity, poetry, music, Kore-
> care, charisma, tenderness, uniqueness, wonder.
>
> May I forever hail and toast the divine wedding vows of the moon
> and the sun where they clasp each other—burning sands and frothing
> waters—along the far curving back of mighty earth. Evoe Kore! Evoe
> Kouros! Awiya!

This is again followed by the appropriate spells and incantations.

According to Mr. Adams the night of Diana is the proper time for such psychic enterprises as astral-projection, scrying, and magic. Nine P.M. is the proper hour for the circle of members of the coven to lie in star formation on the ground, heads together at the center, arms loosely touching all around. It is also a good time to trance-dance for specific magical purposes.

"The very backbone of the pagan movement is the calendar," Fred Adams explained. This does not mean the calendar in the conventional sense, but rather living completely in tune with the natural rhythm of life, doing whatever is appropriate at any given moment of the calendar and avoiding that which is contrary to its position.

Like all pagan movements, Feraferia celebrates a number of festivals during the calendar year. The beginning of the year, or vernal equinox, falls on March 21. It is called Ostara, and in the sacred circle it represents the East. Ostara celebrates the awakening in nature, the beginning, of the new year, the end of winter. It is a joyous occasion and generally involves outdoor festivities.

Next comes Beltane, May Day, which is celebrated May 1. In Wicca, however, this holiday is marked on May eve, April 30. Beltane is described as "the festival of full flowering; sex crowns the holy nakedness of blossoming flesh. By sex the two are divided only to be molded closer in bliss."

Midsummer or the summer solstice is celebrated on June 21. This represents the longest day of the year and the full union in nature of all that is alive, "both in each," according to the Feraferia calendar.

August 1 is called Lammas or sometimes Lugnasad. This festival represents the height of summer fertility, the culmination of all that which man has strived for during winter and spring.

The autumnal equinox, on September 23, is a celebration of homecoming. It represents the harvesting of the fruit, both in the field and in human experience.

November 1 is the day of Samhain, also called All Souls' Day and in Wicca celebrated the night before as Hallowe'en. Far from being a jolly occasion filled with levity, it is a thought-provoking day of reflection at the beginning of winter. In Wicca the reign of the horned god begins while the Mother Goddess rests. In Feraferia this is a time when new members may be initiated into the coven or when the "dread doors between worlds swing open." It is a time, then, for listening to the voices of the occult, both within and without.

On December 21, a day of thanksgiving is celebrated. It is also called a day of repose, since it signifies the return of the elements into the soil, when nature rests in preparation for the spring to come. The following day, December 22, is the day of Yule, or winter solstice. This is a celebration of first awakening, since at this point the sun turns north again, and heralds the coming of distant spring. Yule, therefore, is a joyous celebration, even though nature still sleeps.

February 10 is the festival of Olmelc, also known as Candlemas. This festival of the lights is called Brigid's Day in some Wicca covens because the prettiest member of the coven is selected to perform the ritual of Brigid, the eternal bride.

At the vernal equinox, March 21, the magic circle is completed and the new year begins.

Since 1967, Frederick Adams has published *Korythalia*, a newsletter of the new pagan movement. With it comes a monthly calendar called "Moon Mansions of the Magic Maiden." Here the twenty-eight days of the lunar month are given with their Greek names, the deities who rule them, and the elements in nature with which they connect. There are drawings of phases of the moon and poetic descriptions of what the moon seems to do to the eye of man. "Ishtar removing her veil" is the description for the new moon, while the full moon signifies "Ishtar removing her navel gem." The newsletter and calendar can be subscribed to for $4 a year from Post Office Box 691, Altadena, California 91001.

Recently Frederick Adams published what he calls the *Oracles of the Faerie Faith*. "The survival of human culture," Mr. Adams postulates, "depends on its psychic identification with ecologically viable styles of cultivation. This, in turn, depends on the creation of a new cultus of nature that stems from prehistoric sources while retaining everything of value that history has produced. Toward this new pagan synthesis of cult, culture, and cultivation in devotion to great nature Feraferia presents the following oracles."

The nine oracles to which Mr. Adams refers are *wildness*, that is to say, to live in nature and in tune with nature as it exists freely and not as it is planted or created; *faerie*, relating to arts and crafts as expressions of man's truly spontaneous genius of creation; *magic*, that which is possible beyond the causality as we know it, that is, poetry, and what Carl Jung has called "acausal synchronicity"; *divinity*, meaning a multitude of divine aspects rather than the solemn god-father image of monotheistic religions; *pantheism*, or the manifestations in nature represented by appropriate gods and goddesses corresponding to similar elements within each human being. To Feraferia these pantheistic deities include the Great Goddess, her two children Kore and Kouros, the seven gods and goddesses linking up with sun, moon, and the five visible planets, the tutelary spirits of specific nature regions, features, forms, and forces, and, finally, the faerie dance of ancestral spirits freely roving about while awaiting reincarnation—what in some occult philosophies are called elementals.

The sixth oracle of the faerie faith, according to Frederick Adams, is *paradise*, a sanctuary which the faith wishes to found where people can live the hesperian or paradisal way of life. These sanctuaries are the antithesis of city living, pollution, industrialization, centralization, and all that makes life miserable today.

How these sanctuaries will come into being and where they will be located, only the future can show. Some of the things representative of the hesperian way of life are organic gardening, concerned mainly with tree crops not grass crops; forestation; a diet of fruit and nuts, raw if possible; reverence for all animal life; freeing of all cattle and even pets; friendship with wild animals as free agents; harmlessness and pacifism; outside living in open-air dwellings made from natural materials, preferably in Southern climates; a maximum of work and play in the nude, using clothes only for protection and adornment, not for modesty; life in small villages with larger groups of people joining only for the celebration of special occasions. Adams has elaborated on this and many other concepts in a book called *The Hesperian Life—The Maiden Way*, first issued in 1957.

The seventh oracle of the faerie faith concerns "*the queendom of the trees.*" Living by and among the great trees is an integral part of this faith, and for that reason reforestation and preservation of existing trees is of prime importance.

The eighth oracle is called "*community is freedom to love.*" Since overpopulation would endanger the paradisal aspects of this visionary community, the fertility of the population would have to be curtailed. It is therefore necessary, Adams reasons, that libido be freed from reproductive applications and directed toward "nonrepressive sublimations of eros." The freedom to love, then, in this sense means fulfillment and enjoyment without fear of consequences.

Finally, the ninth oracle concerns itself with "*education for wildness and love.*" Reeducating those coming from the cities and not yet in tune with the new pagan movement will be a prime requisite. "The arts of eros, especially rhapsodic dancing and singing, will prime each fiber of the body for all of love's delights and for the discharge of immense cosmic energies through magically informed erotic exchanges of every variety, so long as the heterosexual mode of the Divine Lovers predominates and no one is ever victimized." In a sense, this relates to the Wicca dictum, "An' it harm none, do what thou wilt."

In many ways Feraferia's theories are only a little ahead of current mores. In this day, when we speak of group sex and involvement and sensitivity training, that which was taboo not so long ago has become experimental, and what is experimental today may very well be the norm among some of tomorrow's advanced societies. Feraferia's prophet Frederick Adams states, "There is a decided connection between the antipagan waste of man's erotic potential and his laying waste of earth's ecological potential," meaning that frustrated people like to destroy what they cannot possess, while happy people prefer to see a happy world around them. "The fullest expression of kindness depends on the fullest experience of sensual grace. Love clusters of committed persons who constitute themselves experimental families will have the function of developing communal living and sexuality within the paradisal context."

As if to remind the reader of this manifesto that paradise has not yet been established on earth, and that the commonplace is still rampant all around us, there is a footnote at the bottom of this newsletter: "Feraferia so badly, badly, needs a volunteer typist, we will feed the lucky individual who dances forward celery hearts, ripe strawberries, and white wine from the lake of Niagara."

I ask you, who could resist such an invitation?

According to the calculations of the *Dictionary of Astrology* by Nicholas DeVore as interpreted by Feraferia, the last constellation visible before the sun rises on Ostara morning is Aquarius. This makes the Aquarian Age also the beginning of the new pagan era. The Aquarian Age, according to Frederick Adams and of course others, began with a rare celestial event on February 4, 1962. On that day, an eclipse occurred in Aquarius, during which all visible planets were in the same sign within twenty degrees of the exact conjunction of moon and sun.

The time is right, but author W. Holman Keith deplores the lack of great leadership among neo-pagans: "Sectarianism is the bane of the neo-pagan movement. There is freedom, which is all to the good, but unity is lacking." He points out that "no religious movement of thought and worship is more radical and significant for our time and the future than is neo-paganism."

On a practical level, Feraferia believes that physical contact between the skin of man and the natural environment, that is to say, between flesh and plant, in activities they call "play-love-work" and which include sports, playfulness, and love-making, can actually work to the advantage of both. Man derives strength and revitalization from coming in contact with unspoiled wilderness, nature, growing things, plants and trees. Nature, on the other hand, by being touched directly by living bodies, obtains new energies with which to purify itself and to ensure its continued growth.

This conviction is, for instance, expressed in a ritual best undertaken at Beltane, or May Day, for the benefit of improving the landscape. "Some individuals or groups may enchant within actual grass environments at these times. If you make love *for* the grasses *in* the grasses, then you follow the most ancient and venerable precedence and newly initiate the most progressive psycho-religious processes of earth-self integration."

The ritual then continues, "The foreplay may be enjoyed as dance, ranging far and wide over the swards of Ares. As lovers caress each other on the move, clasp and unclasp while running and rolling through grass scapes, they at the same time caress, rub, pummel, and exchange blades and tufts of grass between them. Their beings become saturated with grassiness, until love longing is the very surge of chlorophyll. On the green wave of orgasm, they flow together into the landscape. Land and sky become their fused body of love, their unified land-sky-love-body."

This kind of activity, of course, requires not only privacy but a skin not yet so weakened by civilization that it is bothered by insect bites, pebbles, and sand and such, that prevents the participants from immersing themselves in a truly magnificent union with nature.

According to W. Holman Keith, the author who is frequently quoted as a kind of elder statesman by *Korythalia*, the principal difference between orthodox religions and the neopagan movement is the absence in orthodoxy of three divine principles: polytheism, or plurality of gods, perhaps better the multiple aspect of the deity, for even the pagan ultimately accepts that there is only one eternal divine force in the universe; fascination with its implied eroticism, which in paganism means erotic action, but with divine inspiration and eternal overtones; and exuberance, the wholly positive attitude toward life and all living creatures with its resulting rejection of violence, destruction, war, hunting and fishing, and any form of restriction contrary to natural law, be it spiritual or physical.

Keith rightly points out that the Bible speaks in amazement, "O Lord, how manifold are thy works!" The pagan simply uses different names for the various works of the Lord. He is well aware of the relationship between these various god principles, both toward each other and toward man, but in worshiping one principle, one symbolism, one deity at a time, man can put much more of himself into the ritual. He can visualize, sympathize with, even merge with that principle which he understands and which is responsible for the kind of action he requires or desires at any given moment. There isn't a shred less of divinity in pagan worship than there is in any orthodox religion. To the contrary, to the pagan all nature is holy. God is everywhere. God has many names.

To this Frederick Adams has added, "The primary sacrament and paradigm of cosmic process is the wild play and sweet union of the sexes, which eternizes both the unique and the universal infusion of giving and taking and in the supreme communion, Both in Each. The great divide of gender is the root condition of all being and becoming, and of the uncompromised approximation of the coming to being."

One need only take one good look at the Los Angeles countryside to realize that the building of paradise will require major efforts, either in physical distance or in the removal of existing clutter. But the followers of nature religions need not wait for this somewhat distant moment to enjoy at least some meaningful communion with nature. Many people in Southern California have gardens in back of their houses. Just as the Englishman feels that his home is his castle, so the Feraferian considers his garden his sacred precinct where he can do as he pleases. So far, no intrusion of privacy has occurred where people have worshiped whatever deities they choose to call their own within their houses or gardens. I doubt that even a neighbor's interference could stand up in a court of law unless something along the lines of a public nuisance could be proven. The gentle Feraferians are not only no public nuisances, they are not even private nuisances. Although they are perfectly entitled to conduct those rituals requiring nudity in their gardens, they have not done so in order to avoid any form of controversy.

Fred Adams' wilderhenge need not be the only one, however. Anyone wishing to worship Kore, the magic maiden, can do so in a henge of his own construction. The spot chosen should be appealing for reasons of beauty and have a certain sense of what Fred Adams calls "aliveness."

First one must drive a stake into the center of the chosen area and mark off a circle of at least ten feet in diameter. The circle may be larger, if that is possible. Around this circle one must dig a shallow ditch about eight inches wide and deep, which represents the round river of the sacred year. This is the preliminary step. On the first clear, moonless night one must go out into the garden or back yard and drive a stake into the soil near the inside edge of the shallow ditch representing the round river. The spot is a point where a line drawn from the center of the circle crosses the ditch and thereby seems to connect to Polaris, better known as the North Star.

The following day, a line must be drawn from the Yule point, which is the spot one has marked the previous night, through the center, and onto the midsummer point, or south on the opposite side. There another stake is to be driven into the ground. In similar manner, the east and west points are marked off, with either chains or ropes or tapes, and stakes driven into the soil at the east and west points. Then the four points midway between the cardinal points are marked off in such a way that all eight points by the edge of the round river are an equal distance from each other. Stone or wooden markers called menhirs are then placed on these eight spots and the center.

As far as the spheres of the gods are concerned, Adams explains that these are astral realms surrounding the planets, the sun, and the moon. By a magical extension of the relativity theory, psychic and divine aspects are added to the gravitational field surrounding every heavenly body.

"When pagans prepare their henge or faerie ring for the avocation of wild realms," Fred Adams explains, "by the magic of imagination they witness these planetary spheres converging within the circle, since it is a condensation of earth-in-cosmos."

He refers to these magic operations as eco-psychic, meaning that the spirit of wilderness represented by Kore, from which comes all life, is contained in the totality of the landscape not just in the minds of men, but also in the environment.

"There is a way of laying the planetary spheres on the henge to form a psycho-cosmic tuning dial, equivalent to the sefirah tree of Kabbalah, but more appropriate to newly emerging pagan consciousness." In a sense, the magic henge works on a principle similar to a listening device aimed into outer space to catch the faint signals from distant stars and enlarge them so they can be understood on earth. This system draws upon the emanations from planets and stars and from nature on this planet and pulls these forces into the small area of the henge. The result, of course, is that by being compressed into a relatively small area, these powers become condensed and tremendously effective. When these forces are then enlarged by the human powers within the bodies and minds of the participants in celebrations, we have a considerable reservoir of energy requiring only channeling and direction to become a realistic force capable of accomplishing specific tasks.

The moon is the most powerful influence in the heavens, being closer to us than any other celestial body. Thus, the utilization of the moon's radiation in certain rituals, forms an important part of Feraferia's activities.

The moon has thirty phases, one half of which are waxing, or increasing in size as we see her here on earth, and the other half waning, or decreasing her apparent size. When the moon is waxing, that is to say, during phases one through fourteen, she is sending us cosmic energies, and it is a good time to start projects requiring energy. It is also the best time for rituals. In the thinking of Feraferia, a ritual is an active externalization magic. During the waning phase of the moon, inward activities, such as meditation, are better. Between phases one and eight, until the turn of the moon is reached, ceremonials calling for gaiety, fancy, whimsicality are called for. From phases eight through fourteen, as the moon increases in apparent size, the stimulation of appetite, the deepening of passion, and the maturation of ourselves are best emphasized.

At the time of the full moon, phases fourteen to sixteen, the time of the Sabbath is at hand. At such times, the moon assists, as Adams puts it, "the most vivid and festive exhilarations of love, and the fulfillment of psychosomatic interactions." Contrary to popularly held views concerning the waning moon, that period is not unsuitable for occult practices but merely holds different values. "When the moon is waning," Adams explains, "the mystic intimacy between interstellar distances is waxing. As the white moon diminishes, the black moon unfolds."

The waning power of the moon apparently draws energies out of the earth and sends them toward heaven, thus reversing the flow. During the waning phases, the operator of magic practices would best contact his or her own inner depths, the unconscious, the occult.

Assuming that one has created one's own henge to worship in the pagan manner and is ready to use it, there is still the matter of a proper incantation. How does one approach the sacred precinct for the first time? Through its poetic high priest, Feraferia suggests the following prayer:

> We stand before the temple of Great Nature, mandala of the sacred year, mandala of the sacred self, psycho-cosmic tuning dial of an eternal metamorphosis through perennial sacrament. Hail, Great Goddess. Evoe Kore! Harken to the mythologos of the sacred year. We worship the divine lovers, eternal goddess of nature and containment and perennial god of purpose and penetration. Their union is the pattern of creation. They are the protogenesis of all things. Their celestrial thrones are moon and sun. Their love round of the year is the everlasting religion of nature, the inspired dance of the seasons. Evoe Kore. Evoe Kouros. Awiya!

The purpose of worshiping in the henge is to commune with the reality of whatever divinity or deity is being addressed. "If we open ourselves sufficiently to the landscapes of earth, the divinities residing therein will identify themselves in their characteristic resonances, their sensory and intuitional complexes." The deities worshiped in this manner do exist in reality and are not just symbols, in the view of Feraferia, although one may regard them symbolically as well. But the more one can accept these deities as being real personalities, the stronger will be the relationship between worshiper and deity. The rituals have overtones of the dramatic, the theatrical, because in the view of this cult, the arts and crafts are "handmaidens of religion."

In the summer of 1970, various pagan groups active in the Los Angeles area met for an informal discussion of principles to see whether they could work together under an overall organization. That organization became the Council of Themis and it is still in existence. From the discussions, followed by "small-scale feasting," there emerged eight statements of principle, to which all participating groups could subscribe.

These pagans felt that the two principal "articles of faith" concerned the nature of their deity. The first statement, therefore, concerns polytheism: "Polytheism begins with the female and male principles, the goddess and god, divine lovers, from whose love all creation is derived. The multiplicity of goddess and god individualities are aspects of the infinite variety of creation, stemming from goddess and god. Slightly revising a saying, it may be asserted that the omnipotence of divinity is merely another word for its polytheist unity."

The second most important "article of faith" agreed upon at the conference concerns the principle divinity focus of worship: "Worship focuses on goddess and god as divine lovers, bride and groom, eternal feminine source and perennial masculine quickening, protogenesis of all things: worlds, gods, nature, men, and so forth."

Next came freedom of worship: "Worship, as an essential part of religious practice, is both a venerating of and a communing with divinity. Because people are unique individuals, they differ in their images, conceptions, and experiences of divinity and in their ways of worshiping as well. Therefore, freedom of worship is an indispensable condition of their development and fulfillment as human beings, so long as their worship imposes no undue hardship on others."

Of increasing importance is the next "article of faith" agreed upon by the six participating groups in the Los Angeles area. It concerns the worship of nature and our attitude toward ecology: "Nature is divinity made manifest, the perennial love feast of the divine lovers, goddess and god . . . creativity, continuity, balance, beauty, and truth of life. Of all man's secular studies, ecology comes perhaps closest to bringing him to the threshold of a reverent attitude toward his world and its inhabitants. Ecology not only confirms the wonders of form and function that other secular studies have revealed, but it brings these into organic union with each other as one dynamic, living whole; and it indicates the conditions for the well-being of both this overall unity and the parts that compose it. An intensive realization of these conditions, and of one's own immediate role in their sustainment and development, brings one to the threshold of religious experience. To worship nature, therefore, is to venerate and commune with divinity as the dynamically organic perfection of the whole."

The fifth "article of faith" concerns an area of human expression easily misunderstood or misinterpreted, or, if taken out of context and unduly emphasized, likely to cast a distorted image of paganism as a whole. Eroticism is derived from Eros, a god of love: "Love is the essence of divinity, and is the creative action of the universe. Eroticism in its religious reference, venerates love play in the sexual act as divine, as creative physical expression of our union with nature as we reconcile and unite sexual opposites. Hence, love play and sex are natural and beautiful whenever shared in mutual consent. Sexual freedom in this comprehensive sense is a primary doctrine of many pagan religions. It is the freedom to express love, sensually, to be physically natural, to be at one with nature in the effectual functioning of the physical being, and to be free from guilt due to repressive, antinatural conditioning. To deny or denigrate sexuality in man is to deny or denigrate nature and divinity."

Next comes the subject of violence and aggression: "We try to create in practice a style of living in which violence and the occasion for it are progressively reduced through both our own inner growth and our way of dealing with the outer affairs and conditions of our lives. We deplore and censure all wanton violence and destruction, all murder, all habitual coercion, including habitually punitive attitudes and practices. Defense of home and loved ones against immediate threat of death or severe suffering is a natural reflex. When finesse fails to deflect or thwart such aggression, coercion and/or violence would seem to be the only recourse."

The seventh "article of faith" dealt with the subject of reincarnation or what pagans call "life between death and rebirth": "A vigorous and wholehearted living in *this* life, in *this* time-and-space world, does negate the idea that this life in this world should be submitted as a matter of policy to restraint and chastisement, especially in its sensuous aspects for the supposed benefits of a future, after-death life or condition. Belief is asserted in reincarnation as a periodic flowering of the soul in sensuous flesh, in an objective body among objective surroundings. The quality and direction of our activities are by no means without definite implications for the conditions of a soul's life between bodily death and rebirth."

Finally, the eighth "article of faith" the six pagan groups agreed upon as mutually binding and acceptable to them concerns the sacred myths: "The sacred myths are a tapestry of truths, but are not to be interpreted as reports of historical events. They are a dimension of theological reality, a wondrous and inspired form of religious art."

The myths referred to here are the stories of mythological gods, goddesses and heroes ranging from the ancient Greek and Egyptian pantheons through the Celtic and American Indian mythological canvases into Far Eastern concepts of divinity— in short, all of mankind's mythological distillations and exteriorizations. For it can be seen that there is much duplication and there are many parallels among the mythological concepts of different nationalities, even though these nations may not have had any actual contact with each other. Thus it appears that all this material may very well derive from a common source, a source not as yet fully understood and perhaps forever beyond human reach. What we can grasp, however, are the implications as they concern us, the living, on this planet earth.

When it appeared that I might spend late October of 1970 in the Los Angeles area, I asked Fred whether I might take part in their Hallowe'en ritual. A note from Svetlana informed me that the night of October 30 they would perform a "whole earth invocation." Since this would be performed at night it would in effect be the beginning of Hallowe'en whereas Wicca rituals are generally done the night of Hallowe'en itself.

There were nine of us present. The ritual of invoking the various aspects of Mother Earth was performed mainly outdoors. Everyone wore black robes and, except for me, had his face covered by hoods. My robe, unfortunately, did not have a hood but no one seemed to mind.

In a ritually carefully planned manner the priest and priestess followed by the other participants opened the "astral doors" of the henge. Entering the henge between northeast and east, "they slide giddily down the other side into the Faerie Ring Between Worlds." When each celebrant was at his or her proper station, the spirits of the four quarters were invoked, followed by the spirits of the hours and seasons. After they invoked the elemental spirits, the enchanters had "recreated the universe in eco-psychic terms, that is, in terms of a spiritual relativity respecting man-in-earth."

The priestess was then seated in the center of the ring representing "the nameless bride." At this point the actual ceremonial undertaking began. Carrying a wand, the priestess moved from menhir or subdivision to subdivision speaking the sacred incantations and performing certain ritual dance steps. Finally she returned to the point of departure. This signified that all the Mighty Ones of earth and sky were present around the altar dedicated to Kore and that the further celebration could commence. The entire proceedings took about twenty minutes.

At this point, the priestess followed by the priest and the rest of the congregation made her way back into the house to continue their worship indoors. After a short pause, which gave Fred a chance to prepare the inner temple for the secret ritual that was to follow, the group entered the tiny temple itself. It was very difficult for all of us to get inside, but somehow we managed, standing in a tight circle around the center in which the ritual was being performed by priest and priestess.

We still wore our black robes, but the priestly couple had changed to different robes in keeping with the nature of the occasion. With the help of tarot cards, the priest then evoked, step by step, the various qualities of the goddess, equating forces of nature with parts of her physical body. From time to time, the group would dance around the center as best it could invoking the goddess and stopping abruptly to let the energy thus generated permeate the temple.

With the ceremonial kiss of the sacred apple that represented the goddess, the ritual ended.

I saw Fred Adams again on Candlemas, February 6, 1971. A friend had expressed a desire to be initiated into the preliminary grade. Wearing black robes and cords, we performed the "midwinter" ceremony in keeping with the season. I had given Fred a small terracotta statuette of the goddess Astarte that dated from second-century Egypt. The figure was officially welcomed into the fold and placed ceremoniously upon the western altar of the outer sanctuary.

One of the reasons why some of my experiences and some of the material used in the initiations cannot be published here and must remain reserved for those who become initiates themselves at the proper time is the need for the element of surprise. "It is certainly one of the most effective aspects of any initiation that really 'takes,'" Fred Adams explained somewhat apologetically, "and it helps the mystes or initiate to continue to initiate himself after the formal 'jolt,' much in the same way education becomes a lifelong process of self-actualization after the 'instruments' of this process are obtained from formal curricula."

It was time now for a dedication ceremony indoors honoring Candlemas. Consequently, lights were very prominent, and both priest and priestess carried lighted candles around the sacred circle laid out on the floor of the outer temple. As they moved about ceremoniously, they chanted the poetic reinterpretation of the ancient liturgical invocations, sometimes alternating, sometimes in unison:

"I am the infant sun of Ostara or lady day on the eastern end of the equinox aligned. O full moon, queen of unfurling buds, enchant the Ostara menhir of the East, dawn and spring."

Svetlana continued the incantation alone.

"Onnn," she intoned, and then she continued the incantation: "Here begins the arc of vernal alliance as I am the herald of winds that swirl in my lungs like drafty jets causing the chasm of mountain ranges. . . ."

This was followed by "Evoe ecos," and to the accompaniment of a tambourine she took some ritual dance steps around the circle.

Next, it was Fred who continued: "The new moon is reborn. Evoe kallistos Artemis." About half of the rituals at Feraferia are in the ancient Greek language, which Fred Adams understands perfectly. Artemis, of course, is Diana, goddess of the moon, identified here with the magic maiden and Kore.

"I am the ithyphallic adolescent sun of Beltane, or May Day," Fred went on. "O full moon, queen of voluptuous boons, enchant the Beltane menhir of the Southeast of midmorning and spring season at high tide."

This was followed by the invocation of the other positions of the sun until the original position had once again been reached. Together with the incantations, they performed the ritual steps, taking great care that the candles did not set fire to the house. Quite obviously, this ritual was much easier to do outside, but it was an exceptionally cold night and the neighbors had been curious of late, so Fred had decided to try to do it indoors for a change.

Finally, priest and priestess had gone through the entire invocation and returned to their original positions.

For a few minutes we sat around and chatted, for the impressive ceremony we had just witnessed gave us food for thought. My friend Patricia, for whom all this was entirely new even though she had studied witchcraft and the neopagan religions assiduously prior to being invited, seemed misty-eyed with excitement and the novelty of it all. She is by profession a medical X-ray technician and by avocation a student at the Police Academy, for she wants to become a deputy sheriff. This world was about as far removed from her ordinary surroundings as anything could be.

A little while later the inner temple was ready to receive us and Patricia would now be introduced to the preliminary grade, a kind of novice's rank, in Feraferia. Again, wearing black robes, we entered the inner temple. The new member-to-be was stationed on the perimeter of the calendar design engraved on the floor. I stood across from her on the other side of the calendar.

While Fred invoked various elements as they related to parts of the body, Svetlana coaxed the goddess to descend: "Kore, spirit, now appear in mystery raiment of the year." This was followed by the metallic sound of the sistrum, a musical instrument of Egyptian origin. Striking the sistrum, the priestess then danced around the center as part of the enchantment directed toward the spirit of Kore.

After each round of enchantment, the priest continued the incantation, gradually going through the months of the calendar one by one and correlating them with various parts of the human body. The names of the months are the old Celtic designations, just as the entire Feraferia cult is a strange intermixture of Greek, Celtic, and even American Indian elements. "Month of Quirt, apple month in the biome body of the holy maiden. All broad leaf evergreen forests become our skin and love zones," Fred intoned, "the erogenous zones of the body by skin and erogenous zones of thy perfect body, by grace of magic maiden is conferred upon thee from broad leaf evergreen forests."

A total of twenty-two such descriptive incantations were read by the priest to the new member while, with the twenty-second pronouncement, her "perfect resurrection body" had been conferred on Patricia. All she had to do was just stand there and listen, while the priest and priestess together intoned the closing verses: "O holy maiden of the kindling quick, surging mist and mazing echo, the innocent bounty of the trees bears thy faerie flesh of wildness, wonder, magic, mirth and love. . . ."

Slowly we walked out of the temple back to the living room. After a period of rest Fred summoned me back alone. This time Patricia, the new novice, had to stay behind. Despite the lateness of the hour, I was to be raised to a higher degree of initiation. Seated in the "chair of Demeter," I quietly listened as the priest with the help of the priestess performed the magic ceremony. Then I was given a piece of black cloth in the shape of a veil as a token of the occasion.

I am not at liberty to disclose what was said, but I felt strange and stranger yet after I had left the sacred precincts of the House of Ishtar. It was as if some chord had been struck, a chord that continued to reverberate inside me and imbue me with a greater understanding of nature, both within and without. I haven't been quite the same since. To be sure, my logical thinking, my power of reasoning, and my worldly affairs have in no way been affected. If anything, I am sharper than I was six months ago, but my emotional self seems to have undergone some strange developments. Somehow I am able to feel differently, accept fate more understandingly, and give to others more of myself than I was ever able to before.

It may be years before cults like Feraferia become mass movements, if they ever do. But even sporadic groups working throughout the country and the world might sufficiently change the course of destruction on which most of humanity is now traveling, or at least slow down the end results.

I found my initiation into the mysteries of Feraferia a rewarding and unique experience. It does not conflict with anything else I hold dear, nor with any religion I might practice, whether Christian or pagan. It merely makes them all more meaningful.

Feraferia is not for everyone, nor should everyone think that Feraferia is for him, or that he will be accepted for membership. All ancient mysteries were selective in their admission of new members. This must be so to preserve the power, the integrity, the purpose of the cult. Thinning the blood makes it weaker; spreading the secret truths too far afield lessens their impact where they are most needed.

I mentioned Sára Cunningham when I discussed the heirs of Wicca. When I first met Sára a few years ago she was living in the Hollywood hills in a delightful semidilapidated house that even the most experienced taxi drivers had difficulty locating. The house was filled to the brim with the paraphernalia of witchcraft, ranging from herbs, dried ritual objects, even animals, to books and the tools of her witchcraft trade. For Sàra was then, and is now, a teacher in the ancient art of witchcraft. Her pupils range from students eager to learn the occult through the backdoor, so to speak, rather than at U.C.L.A., to such motion-picture luminaries as Susan Cabot and June Lockhart. These people weren't necessarily practicing witches, but they came to listen to Sàra as friends and because they were interested in the many aspects of the occult in which Sàra Cunningham is an expert.

In the summer of 1970, Sára decided to turn her priestly activities in another direction. Long a student of Egyptian religion and well aware of the Egyptian origins of much of Celtic Wicca, she felt that the Egyptian ritual was more suited to her emotionally at that time in her life. Consequently, she established a temple dedicated to the main Egyptian gods, Iris, Osiris, and Ra. When she heard that I was coming again to Pasadena, she not only invited me to her new temple, but offered to let me film a portion of one of her rituals for my documentary on pagan religions.

The Church of the Eternal Source, as she has called her temple, is the refounded church of ancient Egypt in which the original gods of mankind are worshiped by their original names. "Communication with the gods is practiced through intuitive sciences such as ritual worship, astrology, personal meditation, Yoga, and divination, including the tarot and I Ching," Sára explained.

Thus, the worshiper may get to understand the will of the gods and as a result expand consciousness and evolve spiritually. This, Sára feels, will put one in harmony with divine forces and of course with one's own self. Since ancient Egypt enjoyed a long period of prosperity and peace under these same gods, it is hoped that worshiping them will produce similar conditions in our society.

The problem of polytheistic worship, of having more than one god to pray to, does not faze the Church of the Eternal Source. The high priestess points out that Christianity also worships four distinct deities, the Holy Father, the Holy Mother, the Son, and the Holy Spirit. What she calls the "multiplicity of the godhead" is reached through study and concentration by her students and this in turn leads them to an understanding and acceptance of human diversity.

Everyone seems to be welcome in this group. "As the gods appear to each person solely in respect to his accomplishments in this and past lives, no discrimination on account of ancestry or previous religious or political affiliation is practiced," Sára explains. Psychic and spiritually evolved individuals are particularly welcome in the group. The church is supported by freewill donations, is incorporated in California as a religious institution, and offers a complete educational program "leading ultimately to the doctor of divinity degree and priestly orders." There is a "pyramid of initiation" comprising nine different steps from the lowest, called aspirant, followed by brother or sister, neophyte, zelator, in turn followed by the novitiate, then the proselyte, finally the initiate, priest, and high priest. Distinctive colors, dress, and astrological concepts are attached to each step. Since the church conducts public prayer services, there is nothing secretive about it, at least not in the initial stages.

Unquestionably, the higher degrees are conferred only after serious study and other conditions. Publication of ritual and pledges in this book was not allowed. But the Church of the Eternal Source publishes a kind of newsletter (Post Office Box 2942 in Pasadena, California), and anyone wishing to be an ancient Egyptian rather than a modern Christian has a chance to do so under the sunny skies of Southern California. True, there are no pyramids around and the buildings on main street are far from majestic, but you can forget all that once you are inside Sára's temple.

The temple is located in the upstairs part of a rambling old wooden structure she calls home. It is probably one of the oldest buildings in Pasadena, surrounded by trees and set within a small garden. From the veranda one enters the living room, a comfortable and mystically decorated place. To the left is a room she uses for her classes and lectures. Up the stairs there are two rooms to each side of the landing. To the right is Sára's private study and inner temple where she continues to worship in the Wicca tradition. Acquiring Egyptian ritual in no way forces one to dispose of earlier religious convictions and Sára still rightfully considers herself a high priestess of the Wicca.

To the left of the staircase is her Egyptian temple. Since her priests are all professional artists and she herself is a very fine painter and sculptress, the room is truly magnificent within the context of its size and proportions.

Painstakingly, these people have reproduced the Egyptian designs required for such a place. The altar was handmade from specifications derived from ancient sources. Large, life-size paintings of the gods of ancient Egypt adorn the walls. Even the tools of the Egyptian priesthood have been made by the group themselves including a pipe, sistrum, a bell, and, of course, a large ankh—a large T-shaped cross surmounted by a loop and symbolizing life.

While I was waiting for the temple to be prepared for the ceremony to follow, I admired some of the necklaces Sára makes. Some of these are fertility symbols such as the Blue Goddess, while others are representations of the zodiac. They are strung onto bead necklaces and made up by Sára in small quantities to be sold at very little profit to her friends and those who want to wear a sacred witchcraft necklace.

As a token of good luck for the incipient temple, I had brought along a genuine Egyptian relic dating back to pre-Christian times. The small terracotta ushabti was to be received and installed ceremoniously in another few moments. (An ushabti is the figure of a worker who will do the deceased's work in the world beyond.)

Shortly after, Sára reappeared in heavy Egyptian makeup and wearing her robe of office adorned with jewelry closely copied from Egyptian models that prevailed at the height of Egypt's civilization. Her three male companions, the priests of Osiris, Ra, and Toth, were splendidly attired in white robes. Since I am a professional archeologist and familiar with the traditional outfits worn by worshipers for such occasions, I had brought a white robe myself, though it was simple and in no way comparable to the artistic robes worn by my hosts.

Leaving behind some friends and students who happened to be there that evening, we ascended the stairs, and entered the temple, which was heavily scented with incense. The door was shut and the six of us, two women and four men were ready for the ceremony to welcome the little relic into its new home.

"Omen, omen, omen, omen," the group intoned, breathing in deeply and singing out the sound that was to establish the proper vibrations for the occasion. At the same time, the sistrum was rattled. This was followed by an incantation in ancient Egyptian. Then Sára, in a voice filled with deep emotion, raised her hands to the sky and called out, "Adoration unto thee, O lotus queen of heaven, blessed mother. Hail unto thee, O mighty Isis! May this ritual find favor in thine eyes. Grant thy blessings unto thy children. Be with us this night. Omen, omen."

This was followed by some rattling of the sistrum and further intonation of Egyptian sentences. Then the priest of Amun-Ra approached the altar as Sára stepped to one side. It was now his turn to invoke his particular tutelary deity, and this he did in a mixture of ancient Egyptian and ritual English. Having hailed Ra and asked his presence in our midst, he continued, "Thou art the first and last light; thine eyes are the sun and the moon; we call thee by thy ancient name Hara; thou art Apollo; thou art Mercury; thou art Mars; thou art Christos; thou art light; thou art music; thou art lust; thou art freedom; those who serve, let us serve thee. Divine initiator, help us achieve our aspirations. We call thee by thy true name, Hara."

In most religions, especially the mystery religions, it was considered wrong to call the gods by their proper names. Instead, synonyms or descriptive words were used. "Thou shalt not take the name of thy Lord in vain," the Bible teaches us, and in the orthodox Hebrew religion the name Yahweh or Jehovah is never used. Instead, the term Adonai must be pronounced even though the letters spell Yahweh or Jehovah. This is a very ancient concept. The idea is that one must reserve the actual name of the god for very secret and very important occasions; otherwise his power will be lessened.

It is from that point of view that the Egyptian worshipers at Pasadena pointed out that they were calling to their god by his proper name, thus showing that their mission was an important one and they expected him to come forth and be recognized.

Now the priest of Osiris stepped up to the altar and invoked his god. "Homage to thee, Osiris, lord of eternity, king of gods, whose names are manifold, whose forms are holy. Thou art the beneficial spirit amongst spirits, god of celestial oceans. Drop from thee its waters. Assa, assa, Ra, thou art one. Rebirth." Now the others chimed in with the ritual intonation of "omen, omen, omen!"

After the two others had also stepped up and invoked their respective deities, the little idol was presented to Isis, put into a ceremonial container and properly accepted and blessed. Then the high priestess closed the circle, and one by one we filed out of the temple. In the other room upstairs we changed back into civilian clothes.

Maybe I didn't feel the presence of ancient Egypt's gods within me the way these worshipers may very well feel them since they come here so often and have risen spiritually over a long period of time, but I did feel an almost total alienation from the physical world outside, as if I were indeed enveloped by something other than the already polluted California air. The vibrations at Sára Cunningham's Egyptian temple are genuine whether her magic is Egyptian or Wicca. Perhaps it seems somewhat incongruous for people in the 1970's to go back to ancient Egypt for their religious experience. One might argue that being bizarre compensates for the disappointments and routine assignments of everyday life. Dressing up for the part, the dramatic show-business-like ritual, the strange environment of the temple, would of course create in student or worshiper the feeling of being different from the rest of the community. Since all pagan religions teach that the gods are within oneself as well as on the outside, this would only indicate another form of searching for one's own identity. The absence of the Christian doctrine of original sin and of identification with the suffering of Jesus makes it a joyous religion, creating in turn a more positive personality.

That at least seemed to me the result of taking part in these rituals.

Chapter 23

Raymond Buckland

AS IT WAS: AS IT WILL BE

■ from **WITCHCRAFT FROM THE INSIDE**, St. Paul, MN, 1971, pp. 79–86

T HE WICCAN RELIGION MIGHT be said to have officially arrived in the United States with the immigration of Raymond and Rosemary Buckland, two English witches who moved to Long Island, New York, in 1962. Born in 1934, Raymond Buckland had married Rosemary in 1955, served in the Royal Air Force from 1957 to 1959, and then worked in the airline industry. The Bucklands were initiated into Gardnerian Wicca in the UK in 1963, and from then on, they became Gerald Gardner's official spokespersons in the United States. Queries about Wicca sent to Gardner were forwarded to the Bucklands for response. (It should be noted that Gardner's book *Witchcraft Today* was already available in America and helped to attract people to Wicca.)

During the next nine years, the Bucklands trained and initiated a small but influential group of students. These students greatly influenced the shape of Pagan witchcraft in the United States, particularly its strict Gardnerian faction, who developed a more elaborate manual of laws and rituals (Book of Shadows) than their British progenitors and who zealously guard their privacy and initiatory lineages. In the early 1970s, Raymond and Rosemary Buckland divorced, and leadership of American Gardnerian Wicca passed to another Long Island couple, whose Craft names are Theos and Phoenix. Raymond Buckland now lives in Ohio.

Having started his own tiny "museum of witchcraft" in Long Island, somewhat on the order of Gardner's establishment on the Isle of Man, Buckland also moved into writing and publishing, including producing his own edition of Charles Leland's *Aradia*. *Witchcraft from the Inside*, however, is a snapshot of 1960s' Wicca, whose initiates generally believed in Margaret Murray's thesis of a centuries-old underground Pagan religion, and in Gerald Gardner's contention that "rediscovered" Wicca was its current manifestation. Buckland writes scornfully of "do-it-yourself" witches, "thrill-seekers and deviates." Ironically, a few years after publication of *Witchcraft from the Inside*, when he was no longer the recognized male leader of America's Gardnerian witches (in true matriarchal fashion, their loyalty tended more towards his ex-wife and high priestess), Buckland would reverse his position and write that self-initiation was perfectly valid and that there was more to the Craft than the Gardnerian lineage. Since *Witchcraft from the Inside*, Buckland has written additional books on Witchcraft, magic, and Gypsy lore, as well as several novels.

His concluding paragraph here, however, would still meet the approval of many more conservative American witches who have no desire to form a mass religion. Whether it is an accurate prediction, it is still too early to say.

Chas S. Clifton

References

Buckland, Raymond (1974) *The Tree: The Book of Saxon Witchcraft*. York Beach, Maine: Samuel Weiser.

Buckland, Raymond (1986) *Buckland's Complete Book of Witchcraft*. St. Paul, MN: Llewellyn Publications.

IT IS SAID THAT IMITATION IS the most sincere form of flattery. That witchcraft should be so flattered is surprising. Parody would be understandable, perhaps on the lines that the Hell Fire Club parodied Catholicism; but imitation is unexpected. It says much for the success of Gerald Gardner in obtaining recognition for the Craft as a religion, for its imitators are those who, unable to gain access to a coven, have decided to start their own. These do-it-yourself "witches" would, on the face of it, seem harmless but on closer scrutiny are not so. They are causing considerable confusion to others who, seeking the true, get caught up in the false. The majority of these latter-day "witches" have usually read, or heard of, at least two books—Gardner's *Witchcraft Today*, and Leland's *Aradia*. From these they pick out as much information as they feel is valid and make up whatever is missing. Usually *Aradia* is taken as being the "secret" name of the Wica Goddess—it is not! The God is given any name from *Herne to Pan*. Aleister Crowley's *Magick in Theory and Practise* (as reprinted by Castle Books, New York) provides major parts of the ceremonies for these new "covens". Some rituals are long and rambling, happily mixing Egyptian gods and Celtic goddesses; while others are so short and terse they would surely be considered an insult to any gods.

The majority of these pretenders are in Britain—happily there have been few examples so far in the United States. A spokesman for the Craft in England recently said that a move was being made to "root out of the movement the large number of thrill seekers and deviates. These 'covens', spreading like chicken-pox have no association with the Craft." Why do people start such "covens"? Why not wait and search? For some it is just that they have no patience. They feel so strongly for the Craft that they must participate in some way. By the time they eventually do come in contact with the true Craft it is too late. They are by then so set in their own rites and, unfortunately, have others whom they have led along, that they cannot back down. Some, however, are merely in search of "fame and fortune". Once Gardner had done the groundwork, suffered, and eventually come through the brickbats and abuse, then it was "everyone on the bandwagon". It was found that there was money to be made from claiming to be a witch.

One woman, who ran an antique store, thought it would be a wonderful way to draw customers. She voiced her claim and was then dismayed to find herself evicted by an unsympathetic landlord! Nothing daunted she moved on to the United States where she found she could make a lucrative living with television appearances and lectures. Many and varied were her claims—from being "the only practising witch in England today"[1] to "Chief Witch of England".[2] The fact that there is no such title as "Chief Witch" or "Queen of all the Witches" does not, apparently dismay her. A number of times, in fact, she has said that she was "voted" to her position "by the witches of the world, in 1947". This is a surprising statement for three reasons. Firstly, no one is ever voted into any position in the Craft. Secondly, no true witch in England or the United States acknowledges this woman as leader of anything. And thirdly, in 1947 covens were still in hiding and consequently very few indeed were in touch with others. How, then, could "the witches of the world" get together to vote for this unknown woman? E.S.P. perhaps?

In October 1964 she turned up selling Hallowe'en candy at the New York World's Fair and claiming that she was "one of 80 professional witches in Great Britain" and also, incidentally, that she communicates "with the more than 300 ghosts she keeps around her old beamed cottage".[3] The lady, it seems, has quite a "thing" about figures. By September 1964 she claimed to have starred in "some 926 television shows"[4]; by December of the same year she commanded "800 full-fledged, initiated witches in addition to some 8,000 followers of witchcraft".[5] This same report says that she "boasts that she can trace her witch lineage back some 500 years." She herself claims to be 450 years old[6]—apparently she can remember every single one of her incarnations clearly. The New York Journal American of November 23rd. 1965 put her number of followers at a mere 6,000, and a Reuters report of March 25th. stated that she "claimed recently there were at least 60 covens in Britain."

This woman's tax return would be interesting to see for, while in June 1964 she was an antique dealer; by March 1965 (Reuters) she was "an anthropologist"; November she said "I'm a journalist by trade"[7]; March 1966 "self-proclaimed Queen of England's witches and a spiritualist"[8]; and in July 1966 she was "the British writer and medium".[9] By the beginning of 1966 she had also picked up the "title" of "Dame". Now a Dame of the British Empire is the female equivalent of a knighthood. Since her name does not appear on any of the honors lists over this period it would be interesting to know when, and for what, Her Majesty bestowed this honor? Without troubling with further details it must be said that this woman has said so much nonsense about the Craft; has contradicted herself so frequently, that it is amazing she is still taken seriously by anyone. The one good point is that she does attract many of the previously mentioned "nuts"; but on the other hand she also side-tracks many true seekers.

In England the main status-seeker in the pseudo-"witch" world is a man. He appeared claiming to be "King of England's 30,000 witches".[10] There is, as mentioned, no single leader of all witches. Also the title *King* is not used in witchcraft, The High Priest of a Witch Queen takes the gratuitous title *Magus* only. On December 8th. 1965 this man had a much publicized "witch wedding", claiming it to be "Britain's first in over 200 years".[11] It was certainly not the first—they go on all the time—though it may have been the first ever as it was described, for it bore no resemblance whatsoever to the traditional Wica Handfasting Ceremony. However, the publicity apparently did the trick from the financial point of view, for soon there were articles on, or by, this gentleman appearing in large numbers of the popular Men's Magazines all over England and the United States. They were all basically the same article and frequently used the same photographs. The header picture for *Science and Mechanics* June 1966 was exactly the same as in the nudist magazine *Jaybird* for the same month. The photographs are revealing in several ways. They show the "witches" performing in a circle marked out for Ceremonial Magick—not a Craft circle at all. It may also be noted that the self-styled "King" is himself always clad in a white, monkish outfit while everyone else is skyclad. Never does he appear nude. Does he have something to hide?

On the other side of the coin much good has come out of the revealing of the true picture of witchcraft. A few documentary movies have looked at the subject seriously. There have been many worthwhile magazine and newspaper articles. Schools, colleges and universities are troubling to examine all possible sides of the subject. Witchcraft is now a popular subject, among students, for a term paper. Lectures are even requested by small clubs, societies, even PTAs. A major step forward occurred at the end of October 1965 when the Ecumenical Council in Rome decreed that Catholics pay respect to Islam and other non-Christian religions, and reject any kind of discrimination.[12]

One of the problems that faces a witch, especially one about to set up a coven, is where to get the necessary tools. There are no witch supply stores listed in the telephone directory. A witch must learn to make, and to make do. Athames are not too difficult to find, in the form of hunting knives, and adapt. Even the sword can be got from an antique shop and have the cross-hilt replaced with one of the correct design. A censer is no problem. A horned helmet, for the High Priest, however can present a problem, and then it is up to the initiative of that Priest. In recent times there have emerged one or two businesses which are *almost* Craft supply houses. They sell the usual incense, perfume, lucky charms, etc., but also can supply many items previously unobtainable. One of the finest of these supply houses is in Co. Durham, England, and is run by Miss Margaret Bruce. Miss Bruce goes to a great deal of trouble to ensure that anything she sells is correct according to magickal tradition. Her wands, for instance, are of Hazel wood and are cut from the tree at the "proper" time of the day. Miss Bruce even took lessons from a blacksmith so that she could make athames and swords as they should be made, from virgin metal.

The culmination of the acceptance of the old into the new is perhaps seen in the novel *Sign of the Labrys* by Margaret St. Clair.[13] This is a science-fiction story with a background of the Old Religion. Miss St. Clair is a science-fiction writer who painstakingly researches any subject she may want to use as a background to her novels, giving them an air of authenticity not always found in other similar works. In *Sign of the Labrys* she has excelled herself. The Craft ideas, feelings, beliefs, have been worked into the futuristic story extraordinarily cleverly yet quite unobtrusively. Here the Old Religion has really become a part of the modern world.

Interest in any subject can be gauged fairly accurately by the numbers and types of people who visit a museum devoted to that particular subject. On witchcraft there are two main museums: the Gardner Museum of Magic and Witchcraft on the Isle of Man in Britain, and the Buckland Museum of Witchcraft and Magick on Long Island in the United States. The Buckland Museum was inspired by Dr. Gardner's one, which was probably the first such in the world. Initially visitors to these museums were purely curiosity seekers. But in the last two years there has been a distinct change. More and more people are going to these museums with previous knowledge of the subject and seeking to broaden that knowledge. They have already seen the outline and now want to examine the details. Questions asked are intelligent ones. Groups of students go with their teachers. The museums have become, in effect, centers of research for scholars, anthropologists and students of comparative religion and folklore.

On the other hand the New Religion seems, in a number of ways, to have failed many people. It has worn itself out and some of its followers are claiming a feeling of "having been cheated". In *The Lost Gods of England*[14] Brian Branston sums it up by saying, "Today, organised Christianity is dying a lingering death, smothered under an accretion of man-made dogma and doctrine which is vainly invoked to answer the scientist who (if the truth be known) looks like hoisting himself with his own petard anyway in the shape of the hydrogen bomb: it is only at the main festivals, Christmas and Easter, the birth and the death and re-birth of God, that its adherents show any sign of real religious activity. For the modern Christ has been crucified on the wheels of industry created by science and his body buried under the slag-heap from whose smoke and infertile clinker no growth comes, no resurrection can be expected."

Within the Church itself there is rebellion. Father James Kavanaugh, a family counselor in La Jolla, California, and former parish priest of the Lansing, Michigan, diocese, protests the division which the Catholic Church makes between itself and all others. He says he can only feel ashamed and apologise for the attitude of his church and can only look forward "to the day when my church will have abandoned its arrogance, when it will not offer its Catholic code to force the conscience of the world. Then there will be no 'non-Catholics', there will be only persons, struggling to be honest to themselves. Then I can call you 'brother', not Jew or Protestant or non-Catholic, and hope that you will forgive my narrowness and call me 'brother' too."[15] The nuns, too, are finally seeking freedom. Sister M. Charles Borromeo, in *The New Nuns*, cries "The totally regulated life is not human, especially under pressures built into modern life."[16] Some of these disillusioned people find the Craft and "come home"; the others continue to seek.

What lies ahead for the Wica? Probably not a great deal more than can be found today. Though more and more people are turning to the Craft, finding there many answers to their religious needs, yet the Craft will never become a powerful religion in the way that, for example, Catholicism has. It cannot, by virtue of the smallness of its covens and its lack—despite the various spurious claims—of a single leader. This is, perhaps, a good thing. The Craft is not for everyone, obviously. If it may just be allowed to continue, in peace, worshipping in its own way; that is all that it would ask for itself.

Notes

1   *New York Times*, April 26th. 1964.
2   *Fate Magazine*, June, 1964.
3   *New York Daily News*, October 13th. 1964.
4   *Boston Herald*, September 16th. 1964.
5   *New York Sunday News*, December 6th. 1964.
6   WNEW-TV, June 11th. 1966.
7   *Houston Post*, November 28th. 1966.
8   *Staten Island Sunday Advance*, March 20th. 1966.
9   *New York Sunday News*, July 3rd. 1966.
10 *New York Post*, January 28th. 1966.
11 *New York World Telegram and Sun*, December 8th. 1965.
12 See report by Eleanor Packard, *New York Daily News*, October 29th. 1965.
13 Bantam Books, 1963.
14 Thames and Hudson, London, 1957.
15 *A Modern Priest Looks at His Outdated Church*, Trident Press, New York, 1967.
16 New American Library, 1967.

Chapter 24

Doreen Valiente

WORKING WITH GERALD, AND ROBERT COCHRANE, MAGISTER

■ from **THE REBIRTH OF WITCHCRAFT**, London, 1989, pp. 49–52 and 117–36

DOREEN VALIENTE (1922–99) played a large role in shaping contemporary Pagan witchcraft, first as a student and initiate of Gerald Gardner during the 1950s, and later as a covener of "Robert Cochrane," pseudonym of a young Craft leader who died while only in his mid-thirties. Some describe her as the "mother of modern witchcraft." In these two selections from her 1989 book, *The Rebirth of Witchcraft*, she describes her experience in each coven. Under Gardner's direction, as described, she reworked much of that coven's ritual material, "cutting out the Crowleyanity" and shaping much of the feel of today's "Gardnerian Craft," creative work for which she often was not credited, as she wryly admits. Many modern witches, particularly in North America but also elsewhere were too willing to see Valiente's ritual poetry and invocations as "ancient."

Valiente spent only two years in Cochrane's coven before the latter's death in 1966, but her magical experiences were so profound that they stayed with her for the rest of her life. Cochrane, unlike Gardner, wrote down very little. In fact, a series of letters exchanged with an American student, Joseph Wilson, during 1965, are probably his best-known writings; these letters, widely copied and circulated, helped form what is known in the United States as the "1734" tradition of witchcraft (a mystical numerical combination, not an eighteenth-century date). Much later, another of Cochrane's associates, Evan John Jones, would elaborate on the "magister's" ideas and practices in several books, one of which (1990) is excerpted in this volume. Elsewhere in *The Rebirth of Witchcraft*, Valiente herself asserts that all magic is at base shamanic, and certainly Cochrane, whatever his personal flaws, presented a vision of witchcraft that was at base more shamanic than Gerald Gardner's. Glass (1965) provides further discussion of Cochrane.

Also see the Doreen Valiente memorial website.

Chas S. Clifton

References

Doreen Valiente memorial website: www.doreenvaliente.com
Glass, Justine (1965) *Witchcraft, the Sixth Sense – and Us*. London: Neville Spearman.
Jones, Evan John (1990) *Witchcraft: A Tradition Renewed*. London: Robert Hale.

Working with Gerald

HOW LONG GERALD'S LONDON coven had been working I do not know. However, I believe it to be the subject of a cryptic remark made by a journalist, Peter Hawkins, in the old *Sunday Pictorial* newspaper. In an article entitled 'BLACK MAGIC' (28 October 1951), he states: 'I learned of a nudist camp where at midnight rites were performed with nude devotees of both sexes.' The occasion of the article, apart from the season being close to Hallowe'en, was a claim by a Brighton man, a Mr Michael Glenister, that 'A revival of witchcraft is sweeping the country and people must be warned against it.'

It will be noted that this article appeared long before I had ever met Gerald Gardner. From my own subsequent enquiries some years afterwards, I learned that 'Michael Glenister' (a pseudonym) had been an acquaintance of Madeline Montalban, who was a friend of Gerald's and known to him and others as 'The Witch of St Giles' because she lived in St Giles High Street, London. Madeline Montalban later became well known as a regular contributor to the popular occult magazine *Prediction*. Her real name was Dolores North and I believe her family had some connection with the then Lord Louis Mountbatten's estate, Broadlands, in the New Forest area. Whether she also had any connection with or knowledge of the New Forest coven is tempting to speculate; but, alas, she is no longer with us, and Gerald never said anything to me upon this point. However, it seems probable that Michael Glenister's acquaintance with Madeline Montalban was the source of his statement to the journalist.

Gerald did tell me, however, that it was Dolores North (as he more frequently referred to her, 'Madeline Montalban' being really only her pen-name) who had typed out for him the manuscript of his book *High Magic's Aid*. He told me another very intriguing thing about her, too; namely, that he had first met her in London during the war, when she had been wearing the uniform of an officer in the WRNS. This, he told me, was simply a cover for what she was really doing. According to him, Lord Louis Mountbatten, who knew her because of her family's connection with his estate, had retained her as his personal clairvoyant and psychic adviser.

A very curious account of what may be a magical working with Gerald Gardner and Dolores North appears in a book by Kenneth Grant entitled *Nightside of Eden*. He states that he himself was present at this ritual, which took place in 1949. He refers to a lady called 'Mrs South' who was alleged to be a witch. Five people were to be present at the rite: Kenneth Grant and his wife, Gerald Gardner, 'Mrs South' and another young woman who was also said to be a witch. The ritual involved circumambulating a large sigil inscribed on parchment, which had been drawn by the famous occult artist Austin Osman Spare. Its purpose was to contact an extra-terrestrial intelligence which the sigil was supposed to summon.

Unfortunately, before the initial invocation had been concluded there was an interruption, caused by a ring at the door. The caller was the proprietor of an occult bookshop not far away, who sounds like Michael Houghton, the publisher of *High Magic's Aid*. On learning that Mr Grant was present, the caller declined to come up and drifted off into the November night. However, the spell was effectively broken and the ritual aborted. Soon afterwards, Mr Grant tells us, 'Mrs South' died under mysterious circumstances, the bookshop owner's marriage broke up and he too died, and 'Gerald Gardner was himself not long in following suit.'

Unfortunately for Mr Grant's story, Gerald Gardner did not die until 1964. It was true that Michael Houghton's marriage broke up, although I do not know when he died – he was certainly still alive in the early fifties, because I used to go into his shop. Dolores North died in 1982.

The point of recounting this story here is to show that Gerald was acquainted with witches in London, or people who regarded themselves as witches, as far back as 1949. The ritual described by Mr Grant has more connection with ceremonial magic than with witchcraft, although witches assisted in it. This partnership between witches and ceremonial magicians finds an echo in the story told in *High Magic's Aid*, published in that year.

The year 1949 was an important one for Gerald Gardner. Not only was it then that his novel about witchcraft appeared; I believe that it was also the time at which he first got the idea of calling a witches' book of rituals and magical information 'The Book of Shadows'. This term is not contained in *High Magic's Aid*. In that book, the only thing handed down to the witch heroine from her mother, apart from traditional teaching, is a pair of ritual knives, one with a black hilt and one with a white. Nor is the witches' book, when any reference is made to it in old records, ever referred to as 'The Book of Shadows'. It is sometimes called 'The Black Book', but such references are few. So where did this romantic name, 'The Book of Shadows', come from?

It was only in recent years that I discovered the answer. In the course of one of my favourite occupations, rummaging around in a second-hand bookshop, I came across some back numbers of a magazine called *The Occult Observer*, subtitled 'A Quarterly Journal of Occultism, Art and Philosophy'. They dated back to 1949 and were edited by 'Michael Juste', the pen-name of Michael Houghton. Moreover, they were published from the same address as his bookshop in Museum Street, London, as was *High Magic's Aid*. Turning the pages of the first one, (Volume I, No. 3), I found an advertisement for *High Magic's Aid*, described as 'just published'. But what else was this? An article entitled 'The Book of Shadows'?

Needless to say, I purchased the old magazine and the number next to it, in which the article on 'The Book of Shadows' was continued. However, I discovered that the articles referred not to anything to do with witchcraft but to an ancient manuscript written in Sanskrit. The author of the articles, a well-known palmist called Mir Bashir, had first heard of its existence in Bombay in 1941. The manuscript was reputed to be thousands of years old and to describe a means of foretelling a person's destiny by measuring their shadow. Eventually he discovered an Indian *pundit* (holy man) who possessed a copy of the manuscript. Mir Bashir visited him with a friend and persuaded him to conduct a ceremonial divination by means of the mysterious book. The results, for both his friend and himself, were uncannily accurate, and the author proceeds to tell how the divination worked out in their lives.

Can it possibly be coincidence that this reference to a manuscript called 'The Book of Shadows' appears in a magazine edited by the publisher of Gerald's novel – and in which an advertisement for that novel, 'just published', also appears? Or, as I think, did Gerald see this hitherto unknown (in Britain at any rate) and striking term for a magical manuscript and seize upon it as a good name for a witches' secret book? It was too late to incorporate it in *High Magic's Aid*, because that book was already published; but in future Gerald would make use of it. It would not do to call a witches' book a grimoire, because this was the term used to describe the books of ceremonial magicians, which had associations of black magic. But 'The Book of Shadows' made one think of flickering firelight and candle-flame and of the shadows they cast; of those who had to live in the shadows, in the days when discovery meant torture and death; and of those magical symbols and rituals which are in themselves shadows of a greater reality. It was a good name, and it is a good name still, wherever Gerald found it.

Another interesting and possibly significant point about *High Magic's Aid* is that, although it speaks of witches as worshipping the old gods, it gives only one god-name – Janicot. When I first met Gerald, the name his coven were using for the Goddess was Airdia or Areda, both evidently variants of Aradia. The god-name Cernunnos or Kernunno which they also used, is really a title and means 'the Horned One'. I have a theory that Janicot (the word is spelt in the French fashion and pronounced *Jan*-e-ko) may well be the oldest god-name we have. Was this the god-name used by the old New Forest coven?

My reasons for suggesting this arise from the researches carried out by Michael Harrison and detailed in his book *The Roots of Witchcraft*. Mr Harrison is an expert on the Basque language and has been examining some of the old witch names and words in the light of this specialized knowledge. He notes that the god-name 'Janicot' appears in the records of witch trials given by Pierre de l'Ancre, who was responsible for the trial and condemnation of many witches in the Basque country in the early seventeenth century. Mr Harrison notes the likeness of this name to the Basque word *Jainco*, meaning 'God'. It may be the origin of the old-fashioned exclamation, 'By Jingo!' *Chambers Twentieth Century Dictionary* confirms this derivation and adds that the word first appears as a conjurer's summoning call. There is a further instance of it in the name of an old children's game, the Jingo-ring, in which the players dance round one of their number, singing. The likeness to a witches' rite is obvious. In fact, traces of the Old Religion may be found in many old games and rhymes, which started out in the long ago as rituals and may have been worn down to their present form.

Mr Harrison notes that in the Basque language *Araldia* means 'the reproduction of one's kind, fertility, fruitfulness'. Its likeness to 'Aradia' is surely beyond coincidence. But what is the peculiar significance of these names being in the Basque language? The answer is that Basque is unique among the languages of Europe. It is not related to any other European language and is believed to pre-date them. The Basques themselves say that it is the oldest language in the world. The Basque people are thought to be descended from Cro-Magnon man, the earliest race who are believed to have been able to develop a language at all.

If this theory is correct, Basque is truly a relic of the speech of prehistoric man of the Stone Age, the people of the painted caves and the deities depicted on their walls – deities who consisted of a horned god and a goddess of fertility. Janicot and Aradia are names of awesome antiquity. That they should have survived into the present day is an amazing fact which is proof in itself of the age of the fundamentals of the witch religion.

Let it be at once understood, however, that I am referring to such fundamentals only. No one with any sense would claim, or ever has claimed, that the witch rites of today are the unaltered rituals of our remotest ancestors. On the contrary, witchcraft today is the product of a long period of evolution, in the course of which there have been many changes and accretions. For instance, surely few people today would uphold the retention of the practice of human sacrifice, even if the victim were a willing one? Also, the usages and symbolism of ceremonial magicians such as Cornelius Agrippa (1486–1535) and his successors, often based upon the Hebrew Qabalah, have undoubtedly found their way into witchcraft.

The big question which remains to be answered is, how much of the Gardnerian 'Book of Shadows' represents the rites of the old New Forest coven and how much is Gerald Gardner's own concoction? I braved some hostile criticism from devoted Gardnerians by trying to answer this question when I collaborated with Janet and Stewart Farrar in their book *The Witches' Way*. I remain totally unrepentant, because I too seek the answer and shall continue to do so. There has been too much childish cloak-and-dagger business in the world of the occult, too much of what Aleister Crowley satirized as swearing someone to the most frightful penalties if they betray the secret knowledge and then confiding the Hebrew alphabet to their safe keeping.

The only reason for secrecy today is when witches themselves prefer not to have their identities and their private addresses revealed – and this, oddly enough, is the area in which their fellow-witches tend to be most lax. I remember when a male witch from across the Atlantic seemed to be making a kind of Cook's tour of witches in Europe. For weeks he bombarded me with postcards (having obtained my private address from a fellow-witch), naming and describing the people he had been visiting. Our postman must have had a very interesting time. And then the gentleman was surprised to find that I wasn't very keen on seeing him. Another gentleman from the USA deigned to call upon me one day, unexpected and unannounced – and because, forsooth, I failed to receive him with that deference which he felt to be his due, proceeded on his return home to publish my private address in his own magazine, together with a personal attack upon me. Unfortunately, however, he did not give anyone the opportunity to find out how he liked unexpected and inconvenient callers. His attack upon me was published from his usual box-number.

It became obvious to me as soon as I had been given Gerald's 'Book of Shadows' to copy that it owed a good deal to the works of Aleister Crowley. Moreover, I recognized in one of the chants used in the rituals an adaptation of a poem by Rudyard Kipling called 'A Tree Song' from his book *Puck of Pook's Hill*, which had been a favourite of mine from my childhood. Its words, however, obviously refer to the Old Religion and one wonders how much Kipling knew:

> Oh, do not tell the priest our plight,
> Or he would call it a sin;
> But – we have been in the woods all night,
> A-conjuring summer in!

> And we bring you news by word of mouth –
> Good news for cattle and corn –
> Now is the Sun come up from the South,
> With Oak, and Ash, and Thorn!

Another book which had been drawn upon was the old magical grimoire called *The Key of Solomon*, edited by S. Liddell MacGregor Mathers in 1888. This is particularly interesting, as it is obvious from the illustrations on Plate XIII of that book (page 97) that this is the origin of the markings used on the hilt of the witch's athame (black-hilted knife). However, as I pointed out to Janet and Stewart Farrar and as they quote in *The Witches' Way*, if one compares the different versions of these sigils, a meaning can be drawn from them which is of special significance to the Old Religion. So which came first – the ceremonial magicians' use of them or the witches' use of them? It may be of significance that in the Hebrew version of the *Key of Solomon* called the *Sepher Maphteah Shelomo*, as published by the distinguished Hebrew scholar Hermann Gollancz in 1914, no such version of these sigils appears.

In *High Magic's Aid* Gerald Gardner had quoted a very old and interesting incantation in an unknown language, beginning '*Bagabi lacha bachabe* . . .'. Michael Harrison (*op cit.*) believes this to be in the Basque language and it can be traced back to the works of a thirteenth-century French troubadour called Rutebeuf. However, it also appears in a book called *The History of Magic* by Kurt Seligmann (1948) and in *A Pictorial Anthology of Witchcraft, Magic and Alchemy* by Grillot de Givry (1931). So, while this may well be a genuine witch incantation, at the same time Gerald could have found it in either of these books.

Another tradition which has obviously been laid under tribute by Gerald's rituals is that of Freemasonry. Thanks to the work of such writers as Walton Hannah, the ordinary reader is able to find out a good deal more about Masonic ritual than was generally available before. We can therefore see that there are terms such as 'the Working Tools', the reference to the candidate's being 'properly prepared' for initiation, the 'Charge' which is read to the new initiate, and the existence of three Degrees through which the initiate must advance, which are all very reminiscent of Masonic procedure when one finds them in the witch rituals. Indeed, both Masons and witches today refer to their cult as 'the Craft'. The Third Degree of the witches refers to 'the Five Points of Fellowship', just as the Third Degree of Freemasonry does, though with a rather different meaning. In the First Degree Initiation, the candidate is blindfolded, has a cable-tow placed about the neck and is admitted upon the point of a sharp instrument, in both Gardnerian witchcraft and Freemasonry.

What do these resemblances mean? It has been argued that there was an ancient connection between witch rituals and those of Freemasonry. This may be so; but it is a fact that both Gerald Gardner and Dafo were members of the Co-Masons. Co-Masonry is an offshoot of Freemasonry which permits the admission of women as well as men to the order, something which, of course, the United Grand Lodge of England strictly forbids. It originated in France and spread to Britain in 1902, when its first British Lodge was formed in London. In this Lodge the famous leader of the Theosophical Society, Mrs Annie Besant, was initiated and became the national delegate for Britain. She proceeded to organize Co-Masonry in Britain, and in 1922 Co-Masonry was affiliated to the Grand Orient of France. When Annie Besant died, her daughter, Mrs Mabel Besant-Scott, became the leader of Co-Masonry in Britain – and Mrs Mabel Besant-Scott was Gerald Gardner's neighbour in Highcliffe, near Christchurch, on the edge of the New Forest. She was also a leading member of the Rosicrucian Fellowship of Crotona . . ..

Gerald Gardner was also a close friend of J.S.M. Ward, a leading Freemason and author of a number of learned books on the subject. The story of their friendship is told in his biography *Gerald Gardner: Witch*, which states that the reputed 'witch's cottage' which Gerald purchased and had rebuilt upon some private land near St Albans was obtained from J.S.M. Ward, who was a pioneer in the rescue and conservation of ancient buildings. I have taken part in many witch rituals in this cottage. It had a marvellous atmosphere; but unfortunately that of the land around it was very hostile. It was adjacent to the naturist club referred to previously. Some of the leading members of this club knew what was going on in it and strongly disapproved. One can understand their feelings. Naturism in itself was scandalous enough in those days, without the added scandal of witchcraft being whispered about. So the atmosphere became very tense . . ..

My purpose at the moment is to indicate the possible sources of the Masonic element in the 'Book of Shadows'. The 'Charge of the Goddess' takes its rise from this, as I have already noted. As Gerald originally had it, this was derived partly from Charles Godfrey Leland's *Aradia* and partly from Aleister Crowley's *Liber Legis*. Indeed, the influence of Crowley was very apparent throughout the rituals.

As time went on, I had in practice become Gerald's High Priestess. He had got over his discomfiture at realizing that I could spot all the Crowley material in the rites we used. He explained this to me by saying, firstly, that as the holder of a Charter from Crowley himself to operate a Lodge of the OTO, he was entitled to use it; secondly, that the rituals he had received from the old coven were very fragmentary and that in order to make them workable he had been compelled to supplement them with other material. He had felt that Crowley's writings, modern though they were, breathed the very spirit of paganism and were expressed in splendid poetry. That was why he had used them.

He showed me this OTO Charter, signed by Crowley but otherwise in Gerald's handwriting. It had a large seal upon it but was undated. On the one occasion when I met him, Gerald Yorke, a friend of Crowley's for many years, told me that Gerald Gardner had paid Crowley about £300 for it, which was quite a lot of money in those days. I wonder if this is the origin of the story that Gerald Gardner paid Aleister Crowley for writing the witchcraft rituals? No evidence of this allegation, so far as I know, has ever been produced; yet among some writers on the subject it has been regarded as proven fact. It has also been stated quite confidently that a 'Book of Shadows' in Aleister Crowley's handwriting was among the exhibits in Gerald's museum on the Isle of Man. I have never seen it on any occasion when I visited the Isle of Man and I have never met anyone else who has seen it either. Nor was any such book in Crowley's handwriting found among the papers from this museum which found their way, via Ripley's, across the Atlantic. A very interesting manuscript, 'Ye Booke of Ye Art Magical', is among these papers; but it is in Gerald's handwriting, not Crowley's. Its ritual contents owe a good deal to the OTO; in fact, it is a kind of hybrid between the OTO and witchcraft. Gerald's first draft of it is in my own collection.

As the Charter mentioned above is undated, much speculation has arisen as to when Gerald received it from Crowley. According to my information, it can only have been in the very last years of Crowley's life, when he was residing at the private hotel 'Netherwood' at Hastings. Crowley moved to this address, his last, in January, 1945. My informant on this subject, namely when Crowley and Gardner met, is the late Arnold Crowther, the husband of Patricia Crowther who is a well-known witch and author of *Lid Off the Cauldron*. In this book, Patricia says that Arnold introduced Gerald Gardner to Aleister Crowley in 1946.

Arnold told me the story of this meeting in his own words, and it is rather an amusing one. At that time, Arnold was working as a stage magician and had done a lot of travelling with ENSA, entertaining the troops in World War II. Back in Britain, he was at a party or gathering of some sort when he was introduced to a lady as 'Arnold Crowther, the magician'. The lady recoiled in horror, exclaiming, 'Good heavens – you're not *that* dreadful man?' Arnold was taken aback. He could see no reason why anyone should regard him as a dreadful man and asked the lady what she meant. Eventually the matter was sorted out. The lady had thought he was the notorious 'Great Beast', black magician, etc., etc., Aleister Crowley. Arnold was intrigued. Who was this infamous character he was likely to be mistaken for? He had better set himself to find out.

He began enquiries accordingly, having always been interested in magic of all kinds. Eventually he found the 'Great Beast', who turned out to be just an old gentleman living in retirement in a Hastings guest house and glad to have someone to talk to. Arnold had known Gerald Gardner for years and suggested that the two should meet. Accordingly, one day he took Gerald down to Hastings and introduced him. The two men got on well together, and Gerald repeated the visit a number of times on his own, according to Arnold. It seems that by this time Crowley's occult order, the OTO, existed more on paper than in actuality. Initiation into it seems to have consisted mostly of being given the rituals to read. At any rate, Gerald was made a member by Crowley and given the famous Charter. Crowley died on 1 December 1947, which narrows down the Charter's date to a fairly short period of possible time.

Some people have alleged that Gardner's actual acquaintanceship with Crowley dates back much earlier than this. I can only say that this is Arnold Crowther's personal account of the matter and I have no reason to disbelieve it.

We had a happy working coven in Gerald's old flat in London. I had never felt any objection to working in the nude. On the contrary, it was fun to be free and to dance out the circle in freedom. I disliked the element of flagellation and bondage in the rituals at first; but I came to accept it for one good reason – it worked. It genuinely raised power and enabled one to have flashes of clairvoyant vision. The flagellation was not intended to cause pain but merely to stimulate, which it did. One of the most remarkable relics of ancient pagan initiation, the famous frescoes from the Villa of the Mysteries, which was discovered among the ruins of Pompeii in 1910, depicts a scene of ritual flagellation. This series of pictures runs round the walls of a large hall which was used in the rituals of the Orphic Mysteries. They show the initiation of a young woman into this secret cult, from the beginning, when she arrives draped in a veil, unto the end, when, having passed through the ordeal of flagellation, she dances joyfully naked. So there is a time-honoured precedent for this practice, as there is for ritual nudity.

Contrary to what many people believe, we never took part in sexual intercourse in the presence of other people in the circle. Although the Third Degree taught the ritual and magical uses of sex, the actual rite was always performed in private by those who wished to make use of it. The Great Rite, as we called it, was publicly performed at the Sabbats; but by us it was only 'in token', although we were told that in the old days the High Priest and High Priestess actually celebrated the *hieros gamos* (Sacred Marriage) on the great ritual occasions. We were encouraged to find a partner of the opposite sex within the cult and to be faithful to that partner, working privately with them to perform our own magics, in which we were instructed in the circle and by copying from the 'Book of Shadows'. Nor did we ever use drugs for magical purposes, contrary to another often-repeated allegation. Again, however, we were told that in the old days witches had specialized knowledge of many herbal drugs and could use them to obtain altered states of consciousness; but nowadays such knowledge has been lost and without it experimentation was dangerous. This, of course, was before the days of 'flower power' and the hippy era, which brought about an explosion of activity connected with psychedelic drugs.

One of the favourite ways of celebrating the Great Rite 'in token' has come to be the ceremonial dipping of the athame (the ritual knife) into the cup which holds the wine, which is then passed around and drunk. Gerald seems to have derived this from the Sixth Degree Ritual of the OTO, in which a female officer called the Cup Bearer represents 'the Lady Babalon' and a male officer called the Grand Commander represents the Templars' god Baphomet. The wine is consecrated by having the point of the sacred lance dipped into it. The general nature of the Sixth Degree OTO may be gathered from the letters inscribed upon the ring which is part of its regalia. They are VDSA, which stands for '*Vult Deus Sanctum Amorem*', 'God Wills Holy Love.' (See *The Secret Rituals of the OTO*, edited and introduced by Francis King.)

Gerald's original members, as I have said, were either people who were also members of the naturist club referred to or people who were already witches; but, with the publication of his book *Witchcraft Today* in 1954 and his lectures and appearances on television, more and more people began contacting Gerald and wanting to join. Gerald began to realize that he had a real chance of reviving the Old Religion, and he wanted to gain popular acceptance for it. I pointed out to him that in my opinion he would never succeed in doing this so long as the influence of the late Aleister Crowley was so prevalent and obvious within the cult. Crowley's name stank; not only because of his association in the popular press with black magic but because of the indubitable fact that for years he had lived 'upon involuntary contributions from his friends', as one of them told his biographer, John Symonds. I remember reading a review of Symonds' book which described it as 'How not to be a magician in twelve very difficult lessons'. Most people, both within the occult world and outside it, agreed with the reviewer. Crowley may have been a brilliant writer and a splendid poet but as a person he was simply a nasty piece of work. His great importance in the occult world was that he had wrenched open that treasure chest in which the Order of the Golden Dawn had locked up the secret knowledge of the Western Mystery Tradition, and had invited all to share the treasure.

Gerald's reaction was, 'Well, if you think you can do any better, go ahead.' I accepted the challenge and set out to rewrite the 'Book of Shadows', cutting out the Crowleyanity as much as I could and trying to bring it back to what I felt was, if not so elaborate as Crowley's phraseology, at least our own and in our own words. I felt that the words from *Aradia* qualified in this respect, so I retained them as the basis for my new version of 'The Charge', which I originally wrote in verse as follows:

Mother darksome and divine,
Mine the scourge and mine the kiss.
Five-point star of life and bliss,
Here I charge ye in this sign.

Bow before my spirit bright,
Aphrodite, Arianrhod,
Lover of the Hornèd God,
Queen of witchery and night.

Diana, Brigid, Melusine,
Am I named of old by men;
Artemis and Cerridwen,
Hell's dark mistress, Heaven's Queen.

Ye who ask of me a boon,
Meet ye in some hidden shade,
Lead my dance in greenwood glade,
By the light of the full moon.

Dance about mine altar stone,
Work my holy magistry
Ye who are fain of sorcery,
I bring ye secrets yet unknown.

No more shall ye know slavery,
Who tread my round the Sabbat night.
Come ye all naked to the rite,
In sign that ye are truly free.

Keep ye my mysteries in mirth,
Heart joined to heart and lip to lip.
Five are the points of fellowship
That bring ye ecstasy on earth.

No other law but love I know,
By naught but love may I be known;
And all that liveth is my own,
From me they come, to me they go.

However, people seemed to have some difficulty with this, because of the various goddess-names which they found hard to pronounce. Also, they could not understand the word 'magistry', which I use in the same sense as the famous writer of weird tales, Arthur Machen, used it. So I wrote what has come to be known much better as the prose version of 'The Charge' and which in various versions seems to have been copied all over the world. It may be found in Janet and Stewart Farrar's books *Eight Sabbats for Witches* and *The Witches' Way*, so, instead of repeating it here, I have given the verses above, which I do not think have been accurately published before. Just recently I was very amused to find something evidently based upon them printed in an American book on witchcraft, in which they were attributed to the late Sybil Leek!

Robert Cochrane, Magister

It was in 1964, not long after Gerald Gardner had died, that I first met the man who used the name of Robert Cochrane and claimed to be an hereditary witch. To tell his story here is personally painful to me, because I regard it as one of the most tragic in the annals of present-day witchcraft. Nevertheless, it has to be told as I knew it, in the interests of truth and because the story of the revival of witchcraft would not be complete without it.

I had been told about this man by some mutual acquaintances in the world of the occult who had already met him at a gathering on Glastonbury Tor held by the Brotherhood of the Essenes. Many people who were not members of that Brotherhood attended this gathering, as it was open to the public. Among them were my friends and Robert Cochrane. They were impressed by his personality and told me that I ought to meet him, knowing of my interest in witchcraft. I agreed and we all foregathered later in London.

Robert Cochrane proved to be a strikingly handsome young man, tall and dark and obviously highly intelligent. He was accompanied by his very attractive wife, and we all got on well together at that happy first meeting.

He told me that his coven practised a kind of witchcraft very different from that of Gerald Gardner and that it had been handed down to him by a member of his family now deceased. He had initiated his wife and a number of other people who now formed his coven. They worked, he said, sometimes in the countryside and sometimes at his home. They observed the Sabbats and the Esbats on the same dates as what he called somewhat contemptuously the 'Gardnerian' witches; but they did not follow their practices of ritual nudity and flagellation. Instead, they wore hooded black robes and were consequently known as a 'robed' coven. Most of their raising of power was done by dancing in a circle and chanting. If the ritual took place outdoors, the centre of the circle would be occupied by a small bonfire. Indoors, they worked by candlelight. They worshipped the Goddess and the God as the ancient powers of primordial nature, going back into unknown depths of time.

Cochrane impressed me as he had impressed my friends and most of the people who met him. He had that intangible quality which nowadays is known as 'charisma'. He believed in getting close to nature as few 'Gardnerian' witches at that time seemed to do. I entirely agreed with his preference for working outdoors – an idea which Gerald Gardner had never seemed really interested in, probably because of his insistence on ritual nudity, which is seldom a practical proposition in the sort of weather we get in the British Isles. Cochrane told me that they had their own places in the countryside near his home, which they knew of but which they kept strictly quiet about. In fact, they kept strictly quiet about the very existence of their coven, in contrast to the constant publicity-seeking of Gerald Gardner and some of his followers. Consequently, they had never encountered the sort of trouble with the sensational press that I have described in a previous chapter.

I felt that Cochrane was telling the truth about his tradition, and he impressed me with his personal sincerity in his devotion to the Old Religion. Looking back on these memories today, I still feel that he was sincere in that devotion and that he wanted to promote a better form of the old faith than that which Gerald Gardner had publicized. But was he telling the truth when he said that the tradition had been handed down in his family? Frankly, I do not know. He was not precise about just who had passed the tradition on to him, though he once showed me an old photograph of an elderly man sitting on a park bench or garden seat and told me that this was his teacher. I think he said that the man was his great-uncle on his mother's side.

Cochrane had led quite a varied life and at one time had lived on one of the old narrow-boats or barges which plied the network of Britain's canals. These waterways were once an important part of the nation's communication system, but in time they became neglected and almost lost as modern roads took their place. Nowadays, I am glad to say, many of them have been cleared and restored and the narrow-boats move up and down them peacefully again, though today these are more often used as houseboats or for holidays than for the trading and commercial purposes they once served.

The narrow-boats and the people who lived on them had a lore all their own. The boats were drawn by a massive cart-horse of the variety known as shire horses, which walked slowly along the tow-path beside the canal. Inside, every inch of space had to be utilized, as in the old gypsy caravans, to contain the household necessities of the family who lived in it. It was a peculiarity of the narrow-boat dwellers to ornament their possessions with brightly coloured patterns of decoration, the favourite one being roses and castles. Why this decoration should have been so important to them, I do not know; but Cochrane hinted that it had something to do with the Old Religion.

Cochrane had also worked as a blacksmith, another profession which has a good deal of folklore surrounding it. According to old belief, all blacksmiths are natural magicians. The magic of the horseshoe is still believed in, and horseshoes are often seen over the doors of old houses; though to be really lucky, the horseshoe has to be found and not merely bought. Also, it has to be nailed over the door with its ends pointing upwards 'or the luck will run out'. The only one who is entitled to hang the horseshoe up with the ends pointing downwards is the blacksmith or farrier himself, 'to pour out the luck upon the forge'. A farrier is distinct from a blacksmith in that he specializes in the skilled job of shoeing horses, whereas a blacksmith is a general worker in iron who may or may not have this special skill. In olden days, when horses were the chief means of transport, of course the blacksmith would also be a farrier; but this is not necessarily so today. Even so, the blacksmith has his own special skills in wrought iron, and the forge has its own special magic, which can still sometimes be found in the British countryside. A horseshoe nail which has been hand-wrought by a working smith and made into a finger-ring is renowned for its magical properties. Today one sometimes sees costume jewellery made of such nails.

It was because of his work as a blacksmith that Cochrane called his coven 'The Clan of Tubal-Cain', who was traditionally the first smith. He preferred the word 'clan' to 'coven' as he regarded the latter word as being nowadays usually associated with the followers of Gerald Gardner, whom he detested. He maintained that traces of the Old Religion were to be found all over Britain in the folklore of the old crafts such as smithcraft and in such communities as those described above, the people who worked the old sailing barges on the canals. Folk-songs were full of allusions to the old faith, he said.

Cochrane had little sympathy for what he regarded as the shoddy and sleazy society of his own day. The pursuit of money and status held no attractions for him. He once said to me: 'I can tell you what is wrong with the world today in one word – greed.' I think he was not far from the truth. However, when I first met him he had given up working as a blacksmith and was employed in a large modern office as a designer. I think he had been compelled to seek more lucrative work because he had a wife and a small son to support; but I do not think he was happy there, although his employers regarded him as being highly talented.

His home was in a modern estate and outwardly no different from its neighbours, but it was not far from the beautiful woodland known as Burnham Beeches, and there were other woodland places he knew where his small coven could secretly meet. They also held rituals in his home. The neighbours probably thought he gave rather noisy parties, as did many of the young married people on the estate.

Robert Cochrane was the anonymous writer of an article printed in the Spiritualist newspaper *Psychic News* on 9 November 1963, which appeared under the headline: '"GENUINE WITCHCRAFT" IS DEFENDED.' He asked the editor not to publish his name and address, as he had a wife and child to consider. He wrote in protest at the 'tirades' against witchcraft which had been appearing at various times in the national press. Whether or not they published his contribution in full I do not know.

The article begins: 'I am a witch descended from a family of witches. Genuine witchcraft is not paganism, though it retains the memory of ancient faiths.' Cochrane goes on to claim that witchcraft is '. . . the last real mystery cult to survive, with a very complex and evolved philosophy that has strong affinities with many Christian beliefs. The concept of a sacrificial god was not new to the ancient world; it is not new to a witch.' Further on, he states: 'I come from an old witch family. My mother told me of things that had been told to her grandmother by her grandmother. I have two ancestors who died by hanging for the practice of witchcraft.' (As I have said previously, Cochrane told me that his teacher was a male member of his family. He did not name the alleged witch ancestors who had been hanged.)

In my opinion, having known Robert Cochrane, the most significant passage in this article is the following:

> One basic tenet of witch psychological grey magic is that your opponent should never be allowed to confirm an opinion about you but should always remain undecided. This gives you greater power over him, because the undecided is always the weaker. From this attitude much confusion has probably sprung in the long path of history.

> Nothing about witchcraft is ever stated definitely. It is always left to inference and your judgment. Consequently nothing written about witchcraft can ever solve it or confirm or deny its existence.

This is typical of Cochrane's love of mystification for its own sake. He was an even more devious person than Gerald Gardner, but he justified his deviousness by the sort of 'psychological grey magic' described above. Others, of course, give this sort of thing harsher names. For instance, one acquaintance of his, who was not a member of his coven, described Cochrane as 'an expert on everything and the biggest liar in town'.

Cochrane pulled poor Justine Glass's leg unmercifully and shamelessly admitted to me that he had done so. Justine Glass was the author of *Witchcraft, the Sixth Sense – and Us*, published in 1965. Robert Cochrane was the Magister or 'high officer of the Craft' who co-operated with her in the production of his book, which has subsequently been reprinted in the USA. Unfortunately, the original book seems to have been got out in a hurry and teems with misprints and statements which in my opinion are sheer nonsense. Cochrane's attitude did not help. When I remonstrated with him, saying that Justine was a nice, well-meaning woman and it was unfair to treat her as he did, he just laughed. Basically, I think, he despised women, in spite of his devotion to the goddess of the witches.

I understand that Robert Cochrane still has some fervent followers in the USA who revere his memory as a real traditional witch. Among them, I am told, the picture contained in Justine Glass's book of a copper platter bearing the figures '1724' and allegedly a witch heirloom handed down in its owner's family for 'several hundred years' has become something of a cult object. I am afraid I have a nasty shock for them. I bought this copper dish for Robert Cochrane in a Brighton antique shop. He asked me to try to find him something suitable to use for the ritual meal of cakes and wine, as Brighton, my home town, is famous for its large number of antique shops. I thought this dish was rather nice, and I purchased it for him. The shopkeeper told me it actually came from an old house called Shelleys, somewhere in Sussex.

When I saw the illustration in Justine's book, I was amazed. I tackled Cochrane about it, because this claim was sheer invention and I was not prepared to go along with it. He had the grace to look a little shamefaced. Then he tried to tell me that it was the fault of the publishers, who had 'got the captions to the pictures muddled up'. It was the other dish, he said, with the pattern of intertwined oak leaves upon it, illustrated on a further page, which was really the dish that had been in his family for hundreds of years. However, the detailed claims in the first caption make it obvious that this is not so.

By the time this incident took place, however, I had already become sceptical about Robert Cochrane's claims and rather disillusioned about him generally, so it was not such a shock to me as it would have been earlier in our acquaintance. At first, I really thought that in him I had discovered a genuine hereditary witch. I was delighted when he invited me to join his clan, small as the group was. It consisted of himself and his wife, whom I will call Jean, together with three other men. He told me that there had been another woman member, called Diana, who had died and was much missed. Later two other new women members beside myself were invited to join.

I travelled to his home and met the rest of the group. I underwent a simple ceremony of initiation and was taught the basic beliefs and ideas upon which they worked.
The main one was that they rejected nearly all the 'Gardnerian' practices (in fact, I
believe it was Cochrane who invented the word 'Gardnerian' – originally as a term
of abuse). They did not make use of ritual nudity but instead wore a plain black
hooded robe. This enabled them to work outdoors much more conveniently than
the insistence on ritual nudity.

Like 'Gardnerian' witches, Cochrane's coven used ritual tools. These consisted
mainly of a knife, a staff (or 'stang'), a cord, a cup (preferably made of horn) and a
stone. The stone had to be a natural piece which was capable of being used as a whet-
stone to sharpen the knife. Cochrane recalled to me the fact that carefully carved
whetstones had been found preserved as grave-goods in old burial mounds. The stang
had a forked top which represented the horns of the Horned God. The other end of
it was pointed, so that it could be stuck upright in the ground when a ritual was held
outdoors. Sometimes the pointed end was shod with metal to strengthen it for this
purpose. It resembled the old-fashioned thumbstick used by walkers in the countryside and could have been disguised as this if necessary.

The cup was used at the full moon Esbat to drink a ritual toast to the Old Gods.
It was an important part of this ritual that the full moon should be reflected in
the wine with which the cup was filled, before the toast was drunk. To do this, the
priestess held up a small mirror to reflect the moon's light into the cup, while
the coven paced nine times deosil around her. Then the priest stepped forward, with
a lighted lantern in his left hand and the ritual knife in his right. He spoke a form of
words to the priestess, to which she answered. Then he ritually sharpened the knife
upon the stone, plunged it into the cup and stirred the wine three times around with
the blade. He took the knife out of the wine and splashed the drops on it to the four
quarters, east, south, west and north. He kissed the priestess, drank from the cup
and then passed it deosil round the circle to the rest of the coven. Another woman
handed round the cakes on a platter.

There were various versions of the words used. One was as follows:

> In the Old One's name we eat this bread,
> With great terror and fearful dread.
> We drink this wine in Our Lady's name,
> And She'll gather us home again.

As in Gerald Gardner's version of the Craft, the Old One, the Horned God was
the ruler of death and what lies beyond, as well as the power of male fertility,
whereas the Goddess was the giver of life. Hence the 'great terror and fearful dread'.
But in Cochrane's rituals the emphasis on the Old One as the Lord of Death seems
to me, on re-reading them, to be much more obsessive than it was in Gerald
Gardner's. I remember Cochrane's telling me that he had once had a vision of the
Old God as a being vastly ancient, massive like some great and ancient tree in a dark
forest, brooding yet all-sentient, smelling of dead leaves and newly turned earth. He
was lying in bed at night when he became aware of this great presence in the room.
He was not frightened, but awed and unable to move until it faded away. 'He was
so *old*,' he said to me, 'old from the beginning of the world.'

At another time he told me that he had first felt the presence and reality of the Goddess when he was a small boy. He had been upstairs alone in an old house at night. It was full moon, and the wind was blowing high. He had gone to the window to look out at the moon and had seen the clouds flying past in the broken moon-light, while the wind screamed over the roof and soughed in the trees. Suddenly, something had happened. He could not tell me what. He scarcely knew himself. But, he said, he knew that the old gods were real and particularly that the goddess of the moon was real and alive. This numinous experience had stayed with him for the rest of his life.

Cochrane's coven used a circle with the four quarters marked at north, south, east and west; but their allocation of the quarters to the four elements was different from that used by Gardner, who adopted the correspondences generally used in the Western Mystery Tradition, namely air at the east, fire at the south, water at the west and earth at the north. These correspondences, according to the rituals of the Order of the Golden Dawn, are derived from the nature of the prevailing winds from those quarters. (That is, their nature in the British Isles; in other countries they might well be different.)

Cochrane kept to the convention of the Four Castles or Watchtowers, as described previously, which are visualized at the four quarters. However, he regarded the east as the place of fire, the west as the place of water, the north as the place of air and the south as the place of earth. He represented this allocation of the four elements to the four quarters as being part of his secret tradition; but I discovered subsequently that it is the same as that given by T.C. Lethbridge in his excellent books on dowsing (see *The Essential T.C. Lethbridge*, edited by Tom Graves and Janet Hoult). In this book, Lethbridge is quoted as saying that his book about witchcraft, which was published in 1962, produced a number of pen-friends who were '. . . representatives of the old Witch religion. There are still some of these, who are quite distinct from the modern imitative covens.' Was one of these pen-friends Robert Cochrane?

Incidentally, I do not know whether or not Lethbridge realized it, but his findings by dowsing as illustrated in his drawing of a 'rose' of forty divisions, worked out from the different pendulum 'rates' he discovered, correspond at the four quarters very closely to the colours given by the old Celtic traditions of the 'Four Airts' of east, south, west and north – that is, purple-red at the east, blue-green at the west, white at the south and black at the north. The actual colour given by the old Celtic writers for the west is 'dun', which is rather hard to describe; it means dusky or shadowy. The other three colours are identical.

The rituals as performed by Robert Cochrane and his coven were less formalized than those of Gerald Gardner's followers. Today they would probably be called 'shamanistic'. Eventually I could not escape the feeling that Cochrane was making them up as he went along. This, of course, would scarcely matter if the rituals were effective. However, the point was that Cochrane claimed to be the hander-on of time-honoured traditions. On the strength of this, he began very much to play the 'Magister', which he told me was the traditional title of the male head of a coven. He told Justine Glass that in his group the male was the head of the coven because this symbolized the esoteric truth that this outer world is a reflection or mirror image of the true inner world and, 'What is seen on the external must be the opposite of the inner reality.' In other words, he was the head on the outer plane to signify that the Goddess was the head on the inner plane. Personally, I think the reason was much less mystical than that; in fact, it was not mystical at all.

However, I have to give credit to Robert Cochrane for having given me the opportunity to take part in some of the best outdoor Sabbats I have ever attended. One in particular I remember, which we held on the Sussex Downs at Hallowe'en. We assembled quite a crowd of people, though not all of them were regular coven members. Cochrane had what I considered to be the odd habit of inviting sympathetic people to attend the Sabbats, because he said that it was the old tradition to invite people as guests. I and some others in the coven objected to this, and our objections grew stronger as time went on; but we said nothing against it at first, until people began to be invited whom we considered unsuitable. At that early Sabbat, however, we were all good friends and worked in harmony.

We had picked out a location on the Downs where we thought we could celebrate safely; and we made sure of this by doing a preliminary daylight reconnoitre. We had all assembled at my flat in Brighton, where most of the company subsequently bedded down rather uncomfortably in the sleeping-bags they had brought with them. But we did not mind a bit of hardship in order to have a really good Sabbat in the traditional way. We went by car to the site and parked our vehicles in a place previously looked out, off the main road. Then, carrying discreet lanterns and torches, we set off up a wooded hill to the higher part of the Downs. It was quite a long climb, and the night was dark, but we made it without mishap and set down our gear at the top.

We had brought the traditional black-hooded cloaks to wear, together with our ritual tools and a small cauldron. We also had food and wine with us and the materials for a bonfire, or at any rate enough to get one started. There was more dead wood lying around on the site. We lit incense in a censer and wafted it around the circle, which had to be of a wide circumference in order to accommodate our dance. If I remember rightly, the circle was outlined with a ring of fine ash, which Cochrane had brought with him in a bag. (Ash and soot are traditional materials to outline a witches' circle. They can be supplemented with brushwood, as their only purpose is to show where the bounds of the circle are. It is the ritual consecration which actually gives the circle its power.) The four quarters of the circle were marked by candles, protected from the wind by being placed in lanterns.

The scent of the incense mingled with the woodsmoke from the fire and the odours of the fallen leaves and the earth we danced upon. Above, the stars shone intermittently through the clouds, and the wind blew gently, with the chill of approaching winter. We were in a hollow, to screen the fire from any watchful eyes; so we could not see any lights of the surrounding countryside. The modern world seemed to have faded away and left us in a sort of timelessness.

We raised the stang to signify the presence of the Old God and placed the cauldron beside it to symbolize the Goddess. Into the cauldron we poured some water we had brought with us and mingled it with wine. Then we put the cauldron by the fire to heat and steam. The cauldron is a fitting emblem of the great mother of nature, because, being a hollow vessel, it represents the womb; and it involves the four elements of life, because it needs fire to heat it, water to fill it, the products of earth such as green herbs to put in it (some scented herbs were mingled with the wine and water), while its steam arises into the air. Moreover, it fulfils a practical purpose because at the end of the rite the fire can be ceremonially quenched with the contents of the cauldron. (For the benefit of anyone who may want to perform a rite like this, it should be said that care is necessary to handle a hot cauldron and its contents. The vessel should not be too big, hence witches prefer the small cauldrons called gypsy-pots because they heat quicker and are less heavy to lift. Sometimes witches prefer to use a ladle to take the liquid from the cauldron. This does not have to be actually boiling, just fragrantly steaming, sometimes with strange spirit-shapes seeming to rise up in the steam.)

Then we danced deosil around the bonfire, slowly and purposefully, chanting as we went – slowly at first, because we meant to conserve our strength and keep up the dance as long as we could. This particular dance was called 'the Mill', because it resembled the continuous grinding of an old millstone or the steady turning of the sails of a windmill, round and round until the corn was ground. We wanted the Old Religion to live and grow again, and so we danced and ground out our will as a mill grinds corn. But eventually, as excitement arose, we danced faster, with loud shrieks and yells.

We felt that we were not alone on those wild hills. People from the past were with us, invisible but there. It seemed to me that the circle was growing lighter. A kind of green fire seemed to be spreading and sparkling over the ground. I saw this phenomenon distinctly, whatever may have been the cause of it. Later I recalled an account of the witches of Forfar, Scotland, in 1661, one of whom confessed that she had taken part in a witch-meeting in the old churchyard of Forfar at midnight, when, 'They daunced togither, and the ground under them was all fyre flauchter.' Margaret Murray quotes this and suggests that the witch was describing the effect of flickering candle-light. I know different!

Eventually we fell exhausted to the ground and lay there, getting our breath back. There was nothing but the night and the silence, broken only by the soughing of the wind and the crackling of the bonfire. We had raised power and we knew it. Satisfied, we brought out our food and drink and distributed it. It was probably very much like the provisions the witches of old had taken to their Sabbats: bread and cheese, cold meat, bottles of wine, apples, small loaves with butter – anything easily portable that would not spoil. To us it tasted like a true feast, eaten round our bonfire under the stars.

As the night wore on, it was time to go. We ceremonially closed our circle and bade the old gods farewell. Then we gathered up our possessions, carefully extinguished the fire and made our way again down the hill and through the dark hanging wood. Before we reached the cars and so-called civilization, we removed our black hooded cloaks in the hope of looking like a group of observers of nature by night, which was to be our cover-story in case we were questioned. But in the event no one saw us leave, and we returned to my home to sleep what was left of the night and have a good breakfast before we dispersed.

This experience of a Sabbat gathering was repeated several times upon the Downs. We also held Esbat meetings at full moon in a wood near Robert Cochrane's home. These were much smaller, being only for the actual coven. It is one of these meetings that I described in my book *Witchcraft for Tomorrow*, when we ran whooping and shrieking through the woods, playing the Wild Hunt. It is a wonder that we aroused no suspicion, but the gods who inspired us must have also protected us on that crazy night.

When the weather made it impossible to go out, we would meet indoors at Cochrane's home. These meetings, too, were enjoyable; but events were gathering which would cast a dark cloud over the whole affair. For one thing, Cochrane was becoming more and more authoritarian in his attitude, both toward other covens and toward the members of his own coven. He was starting to do what Gerald Gardner had done before him, namely to pose as the great authority. But he added to this a characteristic which Gerald had never shown; that is, a tendency to threaten anyone who opposed or even questioned him. He had also started a liaison with one of the new women members.

I have seen more covens break up over this one cause than any other. In fact, I would say that, so long as a coven has a functioning pair as High Priest and High Priestess, that coven can work magic; but as soon as that magical relationship is broken by infidelity, that coven is as good as finished. This, unfortunately, is what broke Robert Cochrane's clan in the end, though it was not the only reason for the break-up. Cochrane had thought that Jean would accept the situation. I knew that she would not, and I did not blame her. She left him and started divorce proceedings; and in my opinion the true magical power of the coven went with her.

Before these unhappy events occurred, I had already broken with Robert Cochrane and ceased to work with his coven; but friends told me what was happening. The immediate occasion of our parting was that I had grown increasingly unhappy with Cochrane's authoritarianism and with his frequently expressed hatred of 'Gardnerians'. I was happy to be working a form of witchcraft different from that which I had known with Gerald Gardner; but I saw no reason to be at enmity with others who remained followers of old Gerald's ways. It seemed to me that there was room for ways of working other than Cochrane's, when they were being pursued by sincere and well-intentioned people. Cochrane, however, thought otherwise and threatened all who dared to differ from him with fearful occult vengeance.

Now, I am not a person who reacts very well to threats. Consequently, one day when he was holding forth about how he relished the prospect of having what he called 'a Night of the Long Knives with the Gardnerians', I rose up and challenged him in the presence of the rest of the coven. I told him that I was fed up with listening to all this senseless malice and that, if a 'Night of the Long Knives' was what his sick little soul craved, he could get on with it, but he could get on with it alone, because I had better things to do.

Awful things were supposed to happen to me as a result; they didn't. I continued to work with other friends in the Craft, and nothing very dreadful happened to them either. Someone had defied the Magister openly and had not fallen blasted on the spot.

In retrospect, I think this must have had a very deleterious effect upon Cochrane's standing in the eyes of the rest of the coven. I had had no intention of breaking up his clan, simply of stating an honest opinion about what was happening; but the break-up began. My act of defiance was followed by Jean's walk-out, and the effect of the latter was devastating. From that point, the coven virtually ceased to function.

I must back-track on this story a little to explain the background against which Cochrane's fury against the 'Gardnerians' had been building up. It will be remembered that Gerald Gardner had died in February 1964. On 1 October that year the *Daily Mail* had published a full-page article under the headline 'WITCHES: BUBBLE, BUBBLE, TOIL AND TROUBLE SPLIT THE MAGIC CIRCLES IN BRITAIN.' The article was inspired by an interview with a friend of Robert Cochrane's who was trying to start what he called the Witchcraft Research Association. The ostensible purpose of this association was to bring together what we were told were the warring factions within the Craft of the Wise in Britain.

Now, it was quite true that the majority of Britain's witches had been very unhappy over Gerald Gardner's choice of the people to whom he left his museum and the collection it contained. In view of the fact that these people subsequently sold the entire collection to Ripley's (of 'Believe It or Not' fame) in USA, many might feel that this disquiet was justified. Others claim that it was because Gerald's heirs were virtually boycotted by the rest of Britain's witches that they were unable to run the Witches' Mill as a paying concern and were consequently forced to sell up. Be that as it may (and I take neither side here but merely state the facts), witchcraft in Britain in 1964 was left leaderless as far as the public was concerned. Nevertheless, there was no conflict except that which, in my opinion, was deliberately stirred up.

I welcomed the idea of the Witchcraft Research Association, as did many other witches. Its founder, according to the *Daily Mail* article, was 'A 36-year-old London Press Relations consultant who uses the pseudonym John Math'. We were told that he was in touch with the followers of Gerald Gardner and also with some older traditional witches and that he was trying to bring the two sides together. He was starting a quarterly witchcraft magazine called *Pentagram* and planning a dinner at a London hotel to launch the association.

This duly took place on 3 October 1964 and was very successful. It was attended by 'precisely 50 subscribers and their friends', according to the subsequent description in *Pentagram*, and I had the honour of giving the opening speech. Of course, a few news-hounds came sniffing around, discovered that no orgy was involved and departed disappointed.

I stated in my speech that, 'The best answer to attacks upon witchcraft is for all of us, whatever branch of the Craft we belong to, to stand together, to be united in a common constructive purpose . . . The things which unite us are very much bigger and more important than the things which divide us.' This remains my opinion to this day. I did not then realize that, whatever the intention of John Math in founding the Witchcraft Research Association, Robert Cochrane and the other 'representative of the older tradition' with whom he was in contact had no intention whatsoever of working for unity and co-operation. On the contrary, they were venomous in their denigration of everyone except themselves and their personal followers.

This venom soon began to appear in the pages of *Pentagram* and proved ultimately to be counter-productive. It is hard to respect the opinions of a writer who hides behind a pseudonym in order to vilify others. Personally, I am of the rather old-fashioned belief that, if a person cannot summon up sufficient moral courage to sign his name to what he writes, he should at least have the decency to keep a civil tongue in his head. Not so 'Taliesin', the other 'hereditary witch' beside Cochrane who used the pages of *Pentagram* to express his views. His attacks upon 'Gardnerians' became so offensive that I and some of my friends set out to discover just who this self-appointed authority was.

The result was rather amusing. I will not detail here the steps by which we arrived at the discovery that, in spite of his professedly ancient Celtic lineage, his name proved to be very unCeltic indeed. Nor, in spite of claiming to represent 'a traditional group in the West Country', did he prove to live in the wilds of Devon or Somerset. In fact, he lived in the Thames Valley, not all that far from Robert Cochrane's home.

Moreover, we discovered that, in fact, he was an ex-Gardnerian himself, having been initiated into Gerald's coven at the old 'witch's cottage' in the woods, described previously. This he admitted, but he said that he had done it on the orders of his clan. In view of what I had found out, however, I felt that it was legitimate to enquire of John Math, the editor of *Pentagram*, whether he had any proof that this alleged clan really existed, beyond Taliesin's word for it. John Math was, I think, rather embarrassed by the question; but by this time it was academic, because both the Witchcraft Research Association and *Pentagram* were upon the point of expiring. People had become so sickened by all the vilification that they simply turned their backs on the whole thing. *Pentagram* survived as a witchcraft review for five issues and then ceased publication. One more issue appeared in a different format; but, to its readers' surprise, it contained nothing about witchcraft. As witchcraft was what people had been buying it to read about, it promptly sank without trace. If, then, this episode was a power bid by Cochrane to take over the leadership of witchcraft in Britain (and I was told that it was), it did not succeed. Taken in conjunction with Cochrane's personal troubles, I have no doubt that it caused him considerable chagrin. In fact, he became desperate to re-assert his authority over his followers.

Another element had also intruded itself into the scene – a very dangerous one. Both Cochrane and Taliesin had a considerable interest in hallucinogenic drugs. In one of his contributions to *Pentagram*, Taliesin had mentioned that he had once asked Gerald Gardner what he knew of the mushroom Fly Agaric (*Amanita muscaria*). According to him, Gardner had replied that he knew nothing of this mushroom and did not believe that its use had ever formed part of the Old Religion. Taliesin quoted this to show how ignorant Gardner was. I could have told him differently. Gerald Gardner well knew about the properties of Fly Agaric and other herbal hallucinogens, and so did the old New Forest coven. That he did not choose to discuss them with a newcomer showed that for once he had used discretion.

Cochrane became obsessed with this question of the ritual use of herbal psychedelic drugs. I used to tell him that personally I would rather get my tea from the grocer's than drink any brew he offered me, so the use of such things did not arise when I was working with him. However, after I had left his group I was told a horrifying story of his reckless use of herbal substances. A young couple who were members of his coven wanted to have a witch 'handfasting' ceremony as well as a regular legal marriage. Cochrane agreed to preside over this, and a ritual was arranged to take place in a privately owned wood which was lent to them for the occasion by a friend of the writer Justine Glass. As the climax of the ritual, they were each given a large dose of the berries of Deadly Nightshade and told to drink it '. . . to see if the Gods would accept or reject them'. If they were rejected, they were told, they would die! Fortunately, the amount given was such a gross overdose that its effect was to make them violently sick, which probably saved their lives.

When I heard this story, I felt furious with Cochrane. How dared this man wantonly endanger the lives of two young people in such a manner? The truth was, however, that by this time Cochrane's own mental balance had become disturbed. So if there is any excuse for his conduct, that must be it. Eventually he became unable to continue in his job, and his employers released him on sick leave. He was treated by a doctor for depression and prescribed drugs.

Justine Glass had become a close friend of mine through her book on witch-craft, and I saw quite a lot of her. One day she told me that Robert Cochrane was telling his followers that he was going to commit ritual suicide at midsummer of that year, 1966. This date was still quite a long way away, and apparently no one was taking the threat very seriously, including Justine herself. By this time she too had become somewhat disillusioned with Cochrane. 'It's just Robert talking,' was her reaction.

I felt very uneasy when I heard this. 'Look,' I said, 'I think you should take it seriously. I'm not saying that Robert means to commit suicide; but I'm horribly afraid that he might stage some stunt which could go very wrong. I believe a lot of people die like that. They don't really mean to kill themselves; but things go too far and get out of hand. Please tell the persons who told you this to keep an eye on Robert.' Justine promised to do so.

Time went on and I heard no more of the suicide threat. But I remembered the story of the Divine Kings and sacrificial victims of olden times. Was this what Robert Cochrane had in mind? In view of his mention of midsummer as the selected time, I feared that he might be brooding on some such idea as this. However, I heard that he was meeting with his friends and apparently seeming quite cheerful. I hoped that it might indeed have been 'just Robert talking'.

Then in June of that year I had a recurrence of an old health problem which sent me into hospital for an operation. All went well, but I had to stay there for a while. While I was convalescing, I had quite a normal and pleasant letter from Robert Cochrane. He told me that he was sorry for his previous arrogant behaviour, as he put it, which had alienated me. He hoped that we could be friends again. He did not know that I was in hospital when he wrote, as my husband brought the letter in to me. I was very glad to hear from him, especially in such a friendly manner. I promptly replied in a similar way and said I hoped to see him again. I did not tell him where I was, as I knew I would soon be returning home, so I put my home address on the letter. I find people who insist on talking about their ailments and operations very boring, so I said nothing about mine.

I duly returned home to a scene of domestic chaos. There had been some mishap in the premises upstairs which had caused water to come pouring down the stairway and under my front door. My carpets were soaked and my poor husband was desper-ately trying to clear things up before I returned. Although I felt very shaky after coming out of hospital, I told him not to worry and gave him a hand with the cleaning-up. Then we sat down for a well-earned cup of tea and my husband said, 'Oh, by the way, there's a letter up there on the mantelpiece for you. It's been there a couple of days, but I didn't bring it in because I've been busy getting things straight here and, anyway, I knew you would be home soon.'

I opened the letter. It was from Robert Cochrane. It told me that by the time I received it he would be dead. And it had been posted several days previously.

I realized that it was the middle of June – midsummer.

There was no telephone in our flat. I forced myself, groggy as I felt, to go out to a call-box and ring my friends in the West Country who had first introduced me to Robert Cochrane. 'Yes,' they said, 'it's true. Robert's passed over. They took him to hospital, but he never regained consciousness.'

Apparently Cochrane had swallowed a lethal mixture of some narcotic herbs (I believe Deadly Nightshade) combined with the sleeping-pills prescribed by his doctor, which he had been saving up for this purpose instead of taking them as the doctor intended. He had been found the next morning and rushed to hospital deeply unconscious. It was too late to save him.

On the previous Saturday, he had met some of his followers at a London pub. He had seemed quite cheerful, and no one had been worried. He had even made an arrangement to meet some of them the next Saturday. So what had happened?

One suggestion was that he had tried something like the 'magic potion' he had ordered the young couple to drink, as described above, with the idea of finding out if the gods would accept or reject him. But which alternative constituted acceptance and which rejection – survival or death? Alternatively, was he trying to play the role of the Divine King who died a ritual death as a sacrifice for his people?

Or was the whole thing a ploy which went tragically wrong? If Cochrane had posted that letter to me fairly early in the day, he would have had reasonable expectation that I would receive it by the first post next day (our Post Office was more reliable in those days, before the heavy hand of 'progress' fell upon it). Then if he had taken the potion late at night, at midnight perhaps, he knew me well enough to know that as soon as I received the letter I would have been on the telephone to the police and the ambulance service. Only it did not work out that way. One does not play games with the powers of life and death.

I do not pretend to know the answer to these questions. There was, of course, a police investigation and an inquest. It returned a verdict of 'Suicide while the balance of the mind was disturbed'. Fortunately there was no mention of witchcraft. If the authorities suspected anything, they may have kept it quiet for the sake of the family.

Robert Cochrane's death was a great blow, not only to me but to all who knew him. He was perhaps the most powerful and gifted personality to have appeared in modern witchcraft. Had he lived, I believe he would have been a great leader. Ironically, it was precisely because he wanted so much to be a leader that he died so prematurely. Time and experience would have mellowed him – he was tragically young when he died. When we are young and enthusiastic for a cause, we tend to see things in black and white. Age teaches us differently. We become more tolerant as we grow older and a little wiser. Cochrane was a highly intelligent man as well as a talented one; he would have learned judgement and patience as the years went by.

Had he lived, the history of modern witchcraft might well have been different. As it is, we have only his memory. Some of his followers still remember him and try to carry on the best of his tradition. Not long ago, some of them went to the place on the Sussex Downs where he used to hold our Sabbats. It was at midsummer and they gathered at the foot of an oak tree and lit a candle there to the memory of Robert Cochrane.

I wrote a short poem about his death and entitled it 'Elegy for a Dead Witch'. It runs as follows:

> To think that you are gone, over the crest of the hills,
> As the Moon passed from her fulness, riding the sky,
> And the White Mare took you with her.
> To think that we will wait another life
> To drink wine from the horns and leap the fire.
> Farewell from this world, but not from the Circle.
> That place that is between the worlds
> Shall hold return in due time. Nothing is lost.
> The half of a fruit from the tree of Avalon
> Shall be our reminder, among the fallen leaves
> This life treads underfoot. Let the rain weep.
> Waken in sunlight from the Realms of Sleep.

As his writings which I still have show, Robert Cochrane was a firm believer in reincarnation. I share his belief. I think he will return to us to finish his work. As for the 'fruit from the tree of Avalon', this is the apple. Cut an apple in half across its width and you will see the sign of the pentagram, which in one of its meanings is the figure of the Goddess of Life standing with arms outstretched. She gives rebirth in due time, until we need this world and time no more.

Chapter 25

Evan John Jones and Doreen Valiente

THE NATURE OF THE RITES

■ from **WITCHCRAFT: A TRADITION RENEWED**, London, 1990, pp. 47–68

E VAN JOHN JONES (B. 1936) was brought into the Craft in the early 1960s by Robert Cochrane. Cochrane was more influential as a teacher and ritualist than writer, but during the 1990s Jones expanded and enlarged on Cochrane's and his associates' work in several books, anthology contributions, and numerous articles in *The Cauldron,* a long-running British witchcraft magazine. He lives in Brighton on the southern English coast, where his co-author Doreen Valiente also lived.

This chapter lays out a gentler version of Margaret Murray's claims of an enduring pre-Christian Old Religion (e.g. Murray, 1929, reprinted in this volume)— here called the Old Faith—persisting despite the nominal Christianization of England, "the fanciful picture of a pious peasantry as painted by the Church chroniclers of the time." This description of Merry Old [Pagan] England, with Robin Hood as coven leader and the rules of the Plantagenet dynasty seen by the people as sacred kings, owes a great deal to Murray. But it is balanced by another, more theological claim, similar to that of Robert Graves, of a universal worship of the Great Goddess in different times and places throughout human history—at least in Europe and the Mediterranean world.

In Cochrane's witchcraft religion, these and other symbols were condensed into the "stang," a forked pole or two-tined pitchfork. No longer is the Old Faith hierarchical, the writers claim: it has now become an egalitarian mystery religion, "fluid and dynamic," focused on the cycles of nature.

For further discussion of Cochrane-style Witchcraft, see Jones and Cochrane (2001) and Jones with Clifton (1997).

Chas S. Clifton

References

Jones, Evan John with Chas S. Clifton (1997) *Sacred Mask, Sacred Dance*. St. Paul, MN: Llewellyn Publications.

Jones, Evan John and Cochrane, Robert (2001) *The Roebuck in the Thicket: An Anthology of the Robert Cochrane Witchcraft Tradition*, ed. Michael Howard, Milverton: Capall Bann Publishing.

Murray, Margaret (1929) "Witchcraft," *Encyclopedia Britannica* 23: 686–8.

I N THE BEGINNING THERE WAS chaos, and out of that chaos came order. With order came life, in all its many and varied forms. The culmination of this life was humanity. Human beings, thinking, feeling and evolving in what to them was a hostile environment, surrounded by the ill-understood forces of nature, to whose every whim they were a prey.

These first human beings sought for a meaning to all this in the relationship between themselves and their surroundings. Dimly at first, but with growing certainty and understanding, they realized that they were at one and in harmony with the very forces of nature which seemed hostile to them. The divinity of nature was there and was recognized; and within humanity itself a spark of that same divinity resided.

As humanity developed from the hunting existence to the more settled agricultural way of life, people became even more dependent on the forces of nature, personified as benevolent spirits. While they were still in the hunting stage, people felt that by the use of the re-enactment of a successful hunt they could, by a form of sympathetic magic, appeal to and influence the great guardian spirit of the deer, bison or whatever animal they were hunting, to send some of these animals to the hunters. Gradually, people adopted certain animals as being related to them in some way. In dark and secret places they put the bones of these animals in a ritual pattern as a thank-offering for a successful hunt. In time, groups of people began to associate more and more with a certain breed of animal. The animal in question then became increasingly associated with the guardian spirit of that group, clan or tribe. Thus one step in humanity's spiritual awareness and development was taken.

However, when a more settled life-style came about, due to their being tied to the land and the growing of crops, people found themselves ever more at the mercy of the elements. Nature in the form of the seasons had to be understood and the spirits of those seasons placated. People's very existence depended on the benevolence of nature. A bad year meant starvation, a good year life. It was little wonder that people should try to interpret and adapt the still-remembered rituals from their hunting past to meet the needs of their new circumstances.

Gradually they began to see in the seasons a mirror image of human life. As the man's seed planted within the woman grew, so the seed planted within the earth grew, matured and eventually ripened for harvesting. In the year's span from planting to harvesting, human beings could see their own lives reflected – birth, youth, maturity, old age, death and finally rebirth through the planting of new seed, as they who were once children became the parents of the next generation.

In the case of the female, she was the mysterious one, the one with the future within her. She was the child, the maiden, the mother and eventually the old barren woman who held the secrets of the tribe. As the carrier of life within herself and the deliverer of that life by giving birth, it was little wonder that people began to regard nature and the earth as a female, a Mother Goddess. Turning their eyes to the heavens, they saw the female cycle mirrored in the lunar phases. The waxing and waning of the moon were like the growing and weakening of the female fertility cycle.

Also within the phases of the moon could be seen the life cycle of humanity in general. There was the new moon, symbolic of birth and youth; the full moon, symbol of maturity and strength; the waning, the time of old age and a weakening of that strength; finally, the dark of the moon, the hidden time when no one knew where she was. Yet after the dark time, there came rebirth in the shape of the new moon. Did this symbolize the passage of the soul through life to death and then to rebirth? The evidence of grave goods being found buried with the bodies in prehistoric graves points to a belief in a separate entity or soul surviving the finality of death, and perhaps needing these goods in some way in the afterlife.

To ensure fertility in the woman, male participation was needed as well. But who would be a fitting consort for the moon, the lady of the night? Man had a symbol of himself in the sun. Like himself, at the beginning of life it held the promise of strength. By midday or mid-life, the sun was strong and at its hottest. Yet as the day progressed it grew weaker, until at sunset it was gone, leaving only the lady of the night to show her face to the waiting people.

During the year, in the seasonal changes, man saw his life mirrored. Spring was the time of youth, summer the time of maturity, winter the weakness of old age, only to be reborn in the spring again with renewed strength. Thus there were balance and harmony together, the mother, the father and the child. There was the old king, then the young king superseding the old one, only to be replaced himself by the newborn young king of the spring rebirth.

Of course, this is a simplistic approach to what in fact is a complex and many-sided aspect of humanity's growing spiritual awareness and involvement. Equally varied are the names and aspects of the Goddess and her consort and child, by whatever names they are known. Be it the rites of Adonis, the Egyptian Osiris or the European Corn Goddess myths, the sacrifice of the Divine King remains the central theme; not only remaining central to the concept but also evolving from it into the actual ritual sacrifice of a human representative of that king as a yearly tribute to the Great Mother.

Time and new thinking reduced or modified the actual ritual murder aspect of the Old Faith to where the sacrifice became the exception rather than the rule, until today the only traces of it can be found in some folk dances. For an example of this, one only has to look at 'the killing of Jack-in-the-Green' in the grounds of Hastings Castle. The dancer who plays the part of 'Jack' is dressed to represent a green bush. He dances through the town and is eventually pushed over to release the spirit of summer, or the killing of the old God-King to let the new one reign.

Times change, and with them the nature of people's religious observances. With the passing of time, the now formalized deities became the tutelary gods and goddesses of the new city states. As they did so, the old simplicity and involvement within the act of worship became lost to the congregation. Intercession with the gods could be sought only through the medium of a priest. The simple faith was formalized into empty ritual in which pomp and display became the order of the day.

Finally, with the establishment of the relatively new Christian faith as the official state religion of the Roman Empire in the year 330, the temples of the gods were gradually deserted or taken over. This is not to say that Christianity as we know it became overnight the mainstay of the empire. The Roman emperor Constantine and his successors still maintained the fundamental maxim of Roman law that the care of religion was the duty of the magistrates. By the Edict of Milan in 313, in 325 at the Council of Nicea where the Nicene Creed was ratified and later, in 484, at the Council of Constantinople, the death knell of the schismatic Churches within Christianity was sounded. By imperial decree, orthodoxy was established throughout the Roman Empire, and the sects of the Donatists, Arians and others were declared heretical. By this action, the foundation was laid for the future persecutions of all those who dared to think in unorthodox ways.

Even though paganism in all its varied forms was defeated or, where its customs or usages were too strong, absorbed, a powerful element of the worship of the Mother Goddess was still carried on in the hidden places of the Old Faith. The Mother still had her devoted followers, even though they were isolated from each other. The fact that the rites had to be practised in secret meant that the more bloody aspects of the faith had to be forgone. Instead of the sacrifice being done in the open, it was performed in the secret glades, a token one, the libation of drink poured in the name of the Goddess.

Because of the secrecy of the worship, the mystical side of the Old Faith was restored. No longer was there a line of powerful priests or priestesses controlling the rites and interpreting the will of the gods. It was a handful of lesser mortals practising the half-forgotten rites of their ancestors, and by doing so moving away from the established ritual to a simple involvement in the worship of the Goddess, and through her the Horned King of the woodland glades, *Rex Nemorensis*.

Later persecutions damaged the old ways even more. Belittled and abused, the Old Faith appeared to degenerate into nothing more than small groups, usually of old, spiteful women casting malign spells on neighbours' cattle or stopping horses until a toll had been paid, and so on. But hidden within the cycle of nature was the Goddess. Forbid her worship, deny her the congregation, yet she will still be there, for her spirit is the very spirit of the land itself. Battered, fragmented, yet never quite finished, the knowledge of the Lady still lingers on. Her rites are still observed; not only observed, but with a growing number of worshippers.

To many, the orthodox faiths have lost their fire, have become enmeshed in liturgy and are failing to meet the needs of the age. Just as the Roman Catholic Church by its own actions gave birth to the Protestant movement, which in turn, when established, led to the appearance of the Nonconformist movements, so the worship of the Goddess and all that is involved by following her cult is attracting new followers. Slowly more and more people are hearing her call, because to some she is an alternative to today's orthodox faiths.

To follow her ways is to attune oneself to the rhythm of nature, to tap into and try to understand the forces within oneself as well as being able to respond to the external forces that are part of the mystic cosmos; to rediscover the almost lost senses that were the Old Gods' gifts to humanity. The power to be able to look into the future in all its forms; the ability to foresee the results of any word, deed or action and to prophesy the outcome. To be able to reach back into the past and see our present time as part of that past; to be able to recognize and know that existence is like a spiral, and that it will take many lifetimes to travel in and at last to find the truth behind the many faiths.

By following the ways of the Lady, her consort and the young Horned King, we are turning to something that is instinctively part of our heritage. As it is part of the cycle of life itself, we must be part of that cycle as well. From the moment of birth to the moment of death, we are involved in that cycle.

Part of the magic of the Old Faith is the knowing and accepting of this. To accept life, in some cases to be an instrument of destiny within that life; sometimes to try to change the rhythm of that life in some small way. For to change life, one must change oneself also, which in turn can lead to greater understanding and involvement. Only by seeking, understanding and involvement will the Old Faith yield up its secrets of inspiration, understanding and evolvement within oneself and one's chosen group. By giving, one receives, and the balance is maintained.

History and myth

Having read this far, by now the reader must be thinking, 'Hold on – this isn't witchcraft as I know it!' In this, they are correct. These rites do not follow the generally accepted picture of witchcraft. Yet, at the same time, the inspiration that went into the creating of these rites reaches back to a tradition far older than the one generally written about. From time immemorial, there has been a faith or cult devoted to the concept of the Goddess. Call her Diana, the Magna Mater, the Corn Goddess or the Great Earth Mother, to many cultures she was the living Goddess and was worshipped as such. Time itself, plus the gradual male dominance of religion, unseated the priestess from her pre-eminence. Conquest and subjugation of tribal groups brought about change and modification of the concept. The gods of a beaten people became the population of the underworld to the conquerors. The living faith changed to suit the times and situations.

Today people look towards the Celtic pagan faiths or beliefs as a source of inspirational tradition, in much the same way as others have looked to the East for their inspiration; in some ways rightly so, mainly on the grounds that the Celtic myths have been examined, explored and written about. In fact, they represent the main root-source of modern British paganism. Yet, as they stand, they are not English witchcraft. The true English witchcraft spanned the gap between the old Anglo-Saxons and the general acceptance of Christianity by the population as a whole.

This is the faith that was lost. Belittled and scorned by the Church, preached against and its god turned into a devil. This is the knowledge that was shattered; and with it, part of the spirit of both race and land. For in the spirit of the land were the rhythms of the English roots.

What is known of the faith was written by its enemies; and, through a long catalogue of pain and suffering meted out to those who dared to think differently, there are glimpses of the faith they died for. Unfortunately, there is not enough to form a sound basis to build upon. Instead, whether as a group or as individuals, each of us must find our own way or path to the portals of the castle. What is written in the following pages is our way of doing so. It works for us, and what more can you ask than that?

One of my favourite myths concerning the origins of the Craft is the story of Aradia, the daughter of Diana, fathered upon the Goddess by her brother Lucifer. Diana, seeing the suffering of the poor and weak, instructed Aradia in the arts of the Craft and then sent her to earth to form and instruct the secret gatherings of witches. This Aradia did; and among the secrets she passed on to her followers were the secrets of poisons, the raising of storms (a charge which was to figure prominently in later witch trials) and how to curse those who refused to help their fellow men and women.

When the time came for Aradia to rejoin her mother, one of the instructions she left behind was that the followers of witchcraft should gather at the full of the moon to pay homage to Diana, with feasting, dancing and music, hailing her as the Queen of the Heavens. In exchange for this worship, Diana would gradually instruct them in the unknown arts of magic. Of course, this is only the bare bones of the story, as given by Charles Godfrey Leland in his book *Aradia: or the Gospel of the Witches*, first published in 1899. However, enough has been mentioned to establish a connection between Diana as the lunar goddess of witchcraft and the witch faith; also to establish the sacred dance, music and the feast as part of the rites, and, above all, the reason why some witches consider themselves to be part of 'Diana's darling crew, who pluck your fingers fine'.

In reality, behind the rather light-hearted myth of the origins of the Craft, there is a darker side of the Goddess. What her name would have been in some other and less literate cultures, we will never know. The Greeks knew her as the goddess Hecate, and from their description of her, she is recognizable to us today. Ancient Hecate, older than the Olympian gods themselves, with her triple powers extending to the heavens, the earth and the underworld. With her three aspects reflected in the phases of the moon, she is the Young Maid, the Mature Mother and finally the Old Hag in the form of the Pale-Faced Goddess. A place where three ways meet is sacred to her as the Triple Goddess.

Within the faith, and certainly one of its most basic tenets, is the cult of the Horned God, or the Dying God in the shape of the sacrifice of the Divine King. It was this living representative on earth of the God that became 'the Devil', since, by accepting kingship, he had accepted the fate that was the lot of the Divine King and Incarnate God, namely that of a sacrificial death.

As the faith became more broadly based and organized, on an extended tribal/mini-state basis, the idea of the divine substitute became established – the mock king paying the price for the true king. In this way the cult gradually evolved into a more recognizable state pantheon, such as was found in Greece and Rome. At the same time, the division between the gods and man became more pronounced. The price once paid with human blood on the altars of the gods was now paid with animal blood, a substitute life for the human one. Even then there was the recognition that in some ways a king was set apart from the rest of humanity and reigned only by the grace of the gods as a servant of the gods. Only when called to power through the blood royal, the tokens of office given to him by a priesthood, could a man become the king, and to raise a hand against him became sacrilege. To strike the gods' anointed one was to strike at the gods themselves. Thus a long line of priest-kings would come into its own.

It must be realized that Christianity, when it became the recognized faith of the western world, was nothing more than a very thin veneer overlaying a predominantly pagan population. In many cases, a kingdom was Christian only for the lifetime of a particular ruler. Many of the so-called Christian kings in fact held dual allegiance, with altars to both the Christian God and the pagan gods. At the same time, the bulk of the population would still carry on the customs and faith of their ancestors. There was very little the Church could do about it. The organized Western Church at that time simply was not strong enough. Not only that, but Rome had to deal with the schisms within its own ranks first.

Rather than the fanciful picture of a pious peasantry as painted by the Church chroniclers of the time, the reality was that of a peasantry gathering at night with the old priesthood of thirteen, to worship the Horned God and, through him, the Goddess. The priesthood or covens of priests and priestesses in any given district would have been led by the Incarnate God, the horn-wearing living representative of that Horned God. Each coven in that given district would have been led by their own representative of the god. In the forms of the Magister of the coven, and helped by the Maid of the coven, he would lead the group in the rites of worship. This was the 'Devil' that the Church would later have to deal with.

It was not until the hereditary ruling classes became firmly committed to the new Church that Christianity was able to start the long-drawn-out battle against European paganism. Until then, the Church had to compromise and settle for an outward conformity. In fact, there is some evidence to suggest that a few of the Anglo-Norman kings were Christian in name only and that other notable historical figures could also be suspected of being members of the Old Religion. For instance, King William Rufus, Joan of Arc, Gilles de Rais, the Fair Maid of Kent and Edward III, just to name a few mentioned in the books of Dr Margaret Murray, *The Witch Cult in Western Europe*, *The God of the Witches* and *The Divine King in England*. If the evidence is correct, this shows just how high into society the old faith must have reached.

In the first of the witch trials,[1] it was only the humbler members of the faith who were brought to trial, and it is from these records, biased though they are, that a picture of the organization of the faith can be built up. In the first instance, a few villages would each have its local witch, male or female, and it was these who could make up the coven for a small area. These covens in their turn would be part of a greater gathering of a district. Over all these interconnected covens would be the Incarnate God on earth, the Grand Master. It was in his name that the whole gathering would be summoned for the Sabbats, and for these the leaders of the individual covens would act as officers for the meeting. It also meant that the Grand Master, in his position as the Incarnate God and through the network of covens, had his finger on the pulse of his area. He knew what was going on, who was doing what and selling what, and where to find a willing buyer. He could then use the old ploy of, 'Go to a certain place and there you will meet a short dark man who will offer you such and such' for whatever it was that was being sold. Also, he would be in the position to know who was being laggard in paying due respect to the Master and the priesthood, and very soon that person would find their crops damaged overnight, and so on. In short, until the system was broken up, the countryside was largely under the sway of the followers of the Old Religion.

In looking at the witch trials, and ignoring the ecclesiastical elaborations in the evidence, it is possible to re-create some of the rituals and feelings that were held by members of the faith. Also from these trials, it can be seen how the following of the Old Religion became more and more isolated, fragmented and eventually reduced to a handful of covens or groups practising half-forgotten rites, and because they had to be inward-looking, keepers of fragmentary bits of the knowledge that was once the wisdom of the old faith.

In spite of what the Church said, these people were not 'devil-worshippers', as made out at the trials. Their God was far older than the Christian God. Nor was the Old Religion in any way oppressive, unlike the Church with its tolls and tithes. In fact, what does shine through from the trial records is that witches enjoyed being members of their faith and looked forward to the meetings.

In a practical sense, the witch, having knowledge of herbal medicine, would be the village healer. In a spiritual way, the witch was the only force available to deal with localized crime. The magical powers held by witches gave them the ability to 'smell out' wrongdoing, in much the same way as the African witchdoctor does. On another level, they were able to deal with ghosts, demons and the evil spirits that haunted the minds of early men and women. In times of trouble, it was the witch who was turned to, because the witch priesthood had the power and the knowledge to deal with things. People became witches because they wanted to, rather than conforming to a religion out of fear.

One thing that is noticeable from the trial records is that membership of the faith was, something that was handed down through the family. Another is that most of the witches brought to trial were female. The reason for this is simply that in the days when the magician-prophet was an honoured and accepted member of any royal Court, as in the case of Merlin, the male witch tended to be the adviser on the more important aspects of Court life, especially politics. The female witch dealt with the more homely and domestic things. She was more or less the healer-priestess of the hearth and home. Christianity eventually meant that the old magician-prophet lost his position in the royal Court, being replaced as adviser by high-ranking clerics. The female witch as a priestess-healer to the ordinary person took a lot longer to root out and destroy.

One of the reasons for this intense hatred of the female witch was her claim to be a priestess. In the time when the Church regarded woman as unimportant and a mere chattel of her husband (only a male priest would call the pains of childbirth 'kindly'), for a woman to claim the title of priestess struck at the very roots of orthodox society.

Another reason to be considered is that women are often the most faithful followers of any religion. When men leave the churches and temples half empty, it is women who still carry on the worship. Hence, while the male witch lost his position as Court adviser-cum-astrologer, the woman still fulfilled her role as priestess of the Old Gods. In a way, it is through women and their devotion to the faith that it survived the persecutions, battered and fragmented though it is. It was the devotion of women to the Goddess and to the incarnate figure of the Horned God that has carried the knowledge down through the years. It is also the reason why in our rites we have given a place of honour to the woman as the Lady and priestess of the coven.

In the same train of thought, yet still within the basic philosophy of the faith, we have re-aligned our thinking concerning the role of the Incarnate Horned God–leader of the coven. Historically, the leader of the coven was always considered to be the living representative of the Sacrificial Divine God-King. Within this person there was the manifested essence of the Godhead, the spirit of the God in living form on earth. Sacrificed in his prime, the spirit of the God would then transfer itself to the body of the Young Horned King. In this way, the incarnate spirit of the God was kept strong. An old and weakened king was in effect an old and weakened god.

As the concept of the cult changed, the actual sacrifice of the king was replaced with the appointing of the willing Divine Substitute, the Mock King. This concept of the substitute ruler was still manifesting itself in classical times through the festival of the Lord of Misrule, the Saturnalia, with the slaves becoming the mock kings and their owners the servants. Sir James Frazer has given us a detailed description of this, and many other matters connected with the sacrifice of the Divine King, in his famous work *The Golden Bough*. There is still a trace of this concept in the Church, with the celebration of the custom of having a 'Boy Bishop' for a day.

Later, the idea of the substitute human sacrifice was modified to that of an animal sacrifice, usually the living representative of the totem spirit of the group. In the sense that the Magister of any coven is the direct descendant of the sacrificial living God, it can be understood how the seven-year cycle of office with the substitute animal sacrifice at the end of it came about. Also, and to a greater degree, how the office of Magister has lost its Divine King overtones and has now come to mean the priest-leader of the coven. In a sense, he is still the 'Devil', but the god-like attributes have reverted back to the mystical spirit-form of the Old God and his mother-consort, the Goddess.

No longer is the Magister the Incarnate God of the coven. To us, the Horned God is represented by the coven stang, the horned ash staff which stands outside the portal or gateway of the circle. Thus invoked, he is the guardian spirit of the entrance to the realm of the circle. He is the spirit of the countryside, in the guise of the Oak King and the Greenwood Lord, the reincarnated spirit of the Old God reborn within the body of the new one at the May Eve rites. He is also the old leader of the Wild Hunt, Herne with his hounds, carrying off the souls of the dead into the underworld. All these ideas are bound up in the symbology of the stang, insofar as the stang becomes the icon of the God.

With the placing of the priestess once again at the head of the rites, many of the duties that once belonged to the Magister are now hers. Where once the Magister and the Maid would have charged the cup, it is now the Lady and the Officer of the East who do it. In the past, the masked, horned figure, with a candle set between the horns, would have presided over the rite and the feast afterwards. Now the stang serves the same purpose. With a lighted candle between the prongs of the pitchfork head, and the animal mask below them, the stang recalls the memory of the Horned God and the Totem Spirit who was the sacrificed guardian of the coven.

In the same way, the crossed arrows mounted on the shaft of the stang recall the old magical workings of the rituals for good hunting. There is one aspect of the Goddess that is very often overlooked, and that is Diana the Goddess of the Hunt.

It was to that aspect of her that the horned, masked figure of old would dance his sacred dance and make his ritual offerings, in the days when the people depended on hunting for their food. (Incidentally, a pair of crossed arrows is the symbol of the pre-dynastic Egyptian goddess Neith.)

By transferring the now symbolic attributes of the Incarnate God-leader of the coven to the coven stang, in effect the human who was once recognized as the living God on earth no longer has to pay the old demanded blood price, with either his own blood or that of a substitute. In this sense, even though the rites have moved away from the primitive workings, the concept of who and what the Horned God stood for has not altered. By invoking him in the spiritual sense, rather than by worshipping the living representative, it means that the more authoritative form of coven leadership is done away with. No longer should any one person be able to say, 'I am the Master. What you learn, you learn from me, as I choose to show you.' Instead, with our way of working, there is no great secret to be passed on. There are only our rites of worship, and these are open to all who wish to follow our ways.

Each and every one of us must seek to develop their own self; to discover within themselves what they want to gain from the faith; and, above all, to realize that within the faith they are perhaps looking for an answer to certain unfulfilled longings. To what extent the faith serves to fulfil these longings is up to the individual. Only by joining in the worship of the Goddess can a person get a glimpse of what it all means. To stand on a hilltop on a moonlight night, opening yourself up to the Goddess – only then can you get the feel of the forces around you, the aura of the powers that seem part of the very air itself.

In time, and with the correct frame of mind, you can and will become as one with this power for a short while, and in that joining there is the feeling of linking up with the past. In that linking comes understanding, and with that understanding the realization that this is something you have experienced before. In this way, the echoes from the past become linked to the realities of today, and both in turn lead to a growing awareness of the future lives that will have to be lived in the lifetimes to come. Above all, in that growing awareness is the express belief that each of these lives should bring us closer and closer to the realization of some of the awesome and eternal splendour of the creation and re-creation of life and nature that is to be found in the concept of the Godhead. Only by understanding of self – and, if need be, the changing of self – can there be the opening-up and blossoming of the individual soul under the influence of the external power that is the inspirational wisdom of the Goddess.

One of the great disappointments concerning the history of the Old Faith is the lack of written records. By this, I mean records written by members rather than by the opposing forces of orthodox Christianity. Yet because the Old Religion was the religion of nature and the countryside, a lot of old country lore and fireside tales contain within them fragments of what was once a large body of matter pertaining to the craft. Accelerating changes in life-style, from the rural to the urban, mean that this lore is being lost faster than ever; and with this loss, there is the loss of some of the understanding, logic and knowledge that are the inheritance of the craft. What is left can be worked on; but in most cases any conclusions arrived at must be treated as supposition or probability, in the light of existing evidence. It is a matter of re-examining certain events and persons in the light of your own knowledge of the Old Faith.

To illustrate this point, one only has to look at the story of King Richard II and the Peasant's Revolt of 1381. The young King met the common people and their leaders at Smithfield, where, according to contemporary reports, the rebel leader Wat Tyler came to the King 'in a haughty fashion'. The upshot of this meeting was that Tyler was mortally wounded. The King rode across the green towards the mob, crying, 'Sirs, will you shoot your King? I am your captain, I will be your leader. Let him who loves me, follow me!' Instead of a flight of arrows and a slaughtered royal party, Richard turned his horse and led the rebels into open country. A hastily gathered relieving force later found the King in the Clerkenwell fields, still sitting on his horse, surrounded by the leaderless rebels and arguing with them.

At this point there are questions raised that have to a certain degree been answered, though not all that convincingly, in an orthodox way. Only days before, this same mob had had the most powerful and richest lords and clerics in the land cowering behind strong walls in fear of them. In the first meeting between the King and the insurgents at Mile End, in spite of royal promises of reform, the mob was still posing a threat to the established order. Yet a few days later this same young King, with just a few words, took over a now uncontrolled and leaderless army of rebels. How? Knowingly or unknowingly, the young King Richard had by his words 'I will be your leader' placed himself in the position of the Divine King, head of the Old Religion. Even if Richard, brought up as he was to see himself as a Christian prince, may not have known the heritage he was claiming with his words, there were many amongst the crowd with enough knowledge of the Old Faith to realize that in the eyes of that faith he was now the God on earth, and that by killing the King they would be killing that living God.

To accept this means accepting the fact that England was not the Christian country that history would have us believe. There are few scholarly works on the witch trials of Britain, and in most standard history books witch trials and the Old Religion receive no mention at all. All we get is a picture of a pious peasantry which in 1381 rose against their masters, burned manors and priories and executed Simon of Sudbury who was both the Primate and the chancellor of England, and also the Lord Chief Justice – hardly the actions of a God-fearing Christian people.

In the person of Richard Plantagenet, they had the descendant of a line of kings whose family were reputed to have claimed, 'From the Devil we came and to the Devil we go.' Looked at again in the light of the 'Devil's' being the God of the Old Religion, what was being said in reality was, 'From a long line of Divine Kings we came, and to the Old God whose representatives we are, we return in death.' By saying, 'I will be your leader,' Richard took upon himself the mantle of his ancestors, the divine Plantagenet kings.

Instead of reading official or accepted history as a single subject, then reading the history of the witch trials as another subject, both must be read as complementary to each other, because they are two different sides of the same coin. Only by combining the two can what is left of the matter or lore of England be rediscovered.

In the same train of thought, there are many other things worth looking at again. Among these are definitely the tales of Robin Hood. On the surface, they are a collection of straightforward stories concerning an outlaw who lived in a forest and led a band of jolly fellow-outlaws. Superb archers to a man, they used their prowess with the longbow to rob the rich and help the poor. The outlawed leader of the band had at some time suffered an injustice which had stripped him of his rightful place in society. Outlaw though he was, his loyalty and that of his men was to the king. In most stories the king in question was reputed to be Richard the Lionheart.

One thing that must be recognized is that the ballads of Robin Hood as we know them were first written down some time in the fourteenth century, though stemming from a long oral tradition. It should also be noticed that attached to the mainstream of this tradition are various historical persons. In this sense, Robin Hood and his band of men became not so much a living group of people, as an ideal, a hope or, if you like, an earthly saviour and defender of the common people.

Throughout history, there have been many attempts to give a name to the man behind the legend: Eustace de Foville, Fulk Fitzwarin, Adam Bell and, strangely enough, one Robin Hood who was known to have held land in Wakefield, to name but a few. Another view is that Robin Hood is derived from Hodskin, the old Anglo-Saxon wood sprite who later became Robin Goodfellow. It should come as no surprise to find that the same Robin Goodfellow is none other than the Green Man or the spirit of spring found in many old morris dances. The Green Man whose effigy was carved by masons on a boss in the cloisters of Norwich Cathedral, in the transept of Llantilio Crossenny church in Monmouthshire, among the decorations of Rosslyn Chapel near Edinburgh and in many other sacred edifices. The Green Man whose smiling face appears among the carvings on the front of one of the oldest inns in Sussex, at Alfriston. The same Robin whom the General Assembly of the Church of Scotland petitioned King James VI in 1577 and again in 1578 to ban, in connection with the performing of plays featuring Robin Hood, King of the May, on the Sabbath day, mainly because of the unseemly ribaldry of the vulgar people on these occasions.

This was a recognition by an established Church that there was more to these tales than just a straightforward story, fictional or otherwise; more to Robin Hood than just a band of outlaws living a merry life in Sherwood Forest. One generally accepted theory regarding the story is that the common people saw Robin as the law-defying, anti-establishment hero, recognizing in him a natural champion of those who had suffered injustice at the hands of both State and Church.

At the same time, in these stories no blame is laid on the king for these injustices, only on the royal officials. In fact, the one strong theme running through the whole of the saga is the individual loyalty to the king shown by the common people. This was in a time when (unlike today when government and throne are separate institutions) the king and the state were more or less one and the same thing. Yet at no time is any blame for the corruption of the royal officials laid at the feet of the King who appointed them. Also noticeable is the devotion shown to Holy Mother Church, with special reverence being shown to the Virgin. Yet at the same time it was the wealth of Holy Mother Church that was being heisted by Robin, and it was the spiritual leaders of that same Church who were being held hostage, ridiculed and held to ransom. Moreover, we are asked to accept that these people could see Holy Mother Church as an abstract concept separate from the activities of its leaders, without realizing that by robbing the Church the outlaws were in fact robbing St Peter of some of his pence. As the saying goes, 'If you will believe that, you will believe anything.'

Just supposing Robin and his band of merry men are re-examined in the light of the Old Religion, what then? Firstly, you have a full coven, including the Maid in the shape of Marian, the only woman who receives any mention by name as a member of the band in the ballads. In spite of her living in the forest with a gang of healthy, virile males, there is no record or tradition of any sexual relationship. Far from it; in fact, Marian was placed on a pedestal and treated more as the Queen of the Greenwoods than anything else.

In the battle for the hearts and minds of the ordinary people, Robin comes out of it as hands down the clear winner. People living in grinding poverty could have grown rich by turning him in; but they didn't. Part of the loot taken by the band was reputed to have been passed on to the needy. Perhaps in Robin there was a personification of the commoners' resentment of the ruling classes; resentment against a system that was alien to them, a system in which the faith of their ancestors had become 'the cult of the Devil'. Instead of being able to share in the rituals of their faith with understanding and knowledge, they had to attend a church in which the articles and mysteries of faith had to be preached to them, usually by someone little better in status than they.

Perhaps at some time there *was* a Robin Hood – or, considering the number of place-names connected with him, a number of Robin Hoods. But instead of being outlaws in the conventional sense, they were outlaws because they were the priestly followers of the Old Religion and the Old God. Then it became understandable why they were sheltered, aided and even a hidden part of the peasant's life. For it would be to them that he would turn to placate the evil spirits and demons that haunted the minds of medieval people. When he or his animals fell sick, the herbal remedies needed to heal them were part of the old witch lore and knowledge. It was either the old wise man or woman to whom he would have to go. At that time, Mother Church, mainly through the monastic orders, certainly had a knowledge of herbal medicine; but how far down the class lines it would have extended no one really knows. In most cases, I suspect, not very far. It would be to the old wise man or woman whom the peasant would turn for his healing and that of his family. So more especially would his wife, when she was having a baby. Can we imagine celibate monks and nuns being very good at midwifery? But there was an old saying: 'The better the midwife, the better the witch.'

Sometimes hard cash would be needed, to pay off the hated heriot and other tallages. Only by going to the Lord of the Greenwoods could the peasant get the money – that self-same cash taken from the Church or from wealthy traders. Who can blame him when, instead of looking to the Christian God in heaven for help, except in a token conformity, he turned to his old God on earth, the horned, masked figure of the coven leader?

Little wonder that the peasant, wrapped up in his knowledge of his God in a recognizably human form, saw in Robin the God that was human. Outlawed and forced into the greenwoods, the living representative of that God and the priesthood were still there, to serve the congregation as they always had. To the knowing, singing the ballads of Robin Hood was not just singing songs about an outlaw and his merry men cocking a snook at the establishment. It was an expression of belief in the old ways, a way of passing on a memory of the old ways; and in others, like the slave who spat in the master's food before serving it, a secret act of defiance, something to be kept hidden from *them*.

Even though the stories, when written down, gradually lost their meaning over a long period of time, there was and still is an element of magic in them. Through books and later films and television, the story of Robin Hood lives on. Indeed, it not only lives on but has spread through a far wider audience; for wherever the Anglo-Saxon race went, the story of Robin Hood went with them. Hidden in that story and travelling with it, are still to be found the few remaining hints of the ideals of the Old Religion. Even in the death of Robin there are echoes of the mourning for the sacrificed Divine King. Only this time, instead of awaiting the joyful spring rebirth of the new Young King, only the stories remain, and hidden within them are the memories of the old priesthood of the beloved Old Religion.

There are endless stories from the past that can be re-examined with knowledge of the Old Religion as a new way of seeing them. The one thing, of course, is that this is purely speculative and should be treated in the light of 'possibly', 'could be' or 'maybe'. But what this sort of research does indicate is that the faith now called the Old Religion *is* old, not just something thought up by a handful of cranks. Though the Goddess is known by as many names as there were different cultures, the basic concept of her worship – and, through her, that of the Horned God and the Young Horned God-King – was a universal concept enshrined within the death and resurrection cycle of both humanity and nature.

Also, and perhaps the most important point, the faith was a fluid and dynamic one, able to absorb changes of emphasis on certain aspects of it while remaining true to the basic theme. One has only to look at the way in which the theme of the Horned Sacrificial God came to be the Incarnate God on Earth to later covens. Yet, at the same time, behind him was another figure, half hidden, half forgotten perhaps; but she was still the Goddess, queen of both night and the heavens, and worship was still paid to her through the Horned God-King of the coven or clan.

In a modern sense, the aims, aspirations and reasons for worshipping the Goddess have changed. In the past, many of the followers were members because to them it was a familiar part of their lives and was as natural to them as eating, drinking and breathing. Without a doubt, most of us are conservative in nature – that is, conservative in a non-political sense. Even today, many people who are not regular church-goers in the accepted sense still marry in church, with all the trimmings, including the white wedding-dress, even though they may have been living together for years before the ceremony. In the same way, they have their children baptized, as something that is 'done'. In short, they are 'wheeled Christians' – pushed to church in the pram, driven in the bridal car and then carried to church in the hearse. It was this inbuilt conservatism in the past that would have made people turn to the familiar rather than to the new-fangled Christian Church.

At the same time, there were those who joined and remained members of the Old Religion through choice, in spite of all the laws to the contrary and the appalling danger they placed themselves in by doing so. They remained staunch and true to their gods and their faith. Even in the face of a rising tide of zealous Christian persecution, they and their children remained true, as the witch trials prove; and now that being a practising witch is no longer a matter of law-breaking in a civil sense, those who call themselves witches have picked up their mantle.

However, when picking up this mantle we must remember that we are not the same people as they were. Our aims and ideas are different. What we look for in the faith and what we hope to gain from the faith are different from their aspirations. Unlike them, we have no helping hand to take us through an age-old and hallowed initiation. Instead, we have to find our own way and build on the work of others. No longer do we look for the same things in the faith as they did. Times change and so do aspirations; and in this sense we are not bound by a long and traditional form of worship or thinking. Instead, we are free to build our own castles; free to create our own concepts and understanding.

In most cases, we know what we look for in the faith; and though differing from the hopes and aspirations of past witches and followers, we still subscribe to the same broad concept of the Goddess, the Old Gods and the rites as they did. Like them, we look to the Goddess for our inspiration and spiritual understanding. To what extent we find this is more or less up to ourselves. We can work at one level, not advancing from there, with total satisfaction; or we can look to the rites to give us that little extra that crosses the borderline between merely working and inspirational working; the knowledge that behind what is being worked on one plane is another plane – and, beyond that, still another.

Perhaps it is the quest for what lies beyond this plane that is the inspiration which drives people to look beyond the workings of this world and urges them to explore the sacred drama, the wordless rite and spell that are the magic of illusion. It is in these first steps beyond the basic rites that another corner of the veil is lifted, and the illusion becomes reality itself.

Note

1   Early records are naturally scanty, and it would be impossible to say with certainty what was the date of the first witch trial. However, according to Montague Summers in his *Geography of Witchcraft*, the earliest recorded witch trial in England took place in 1209. This is confirmed by C.L'Estrange Ewen in *Witch Hunting and Witch Trials* and its sequel *Witchcraft and Demonianism*.

Chapter 26

June Johns

A MAGIC CHILDHOOD

■ from **KING OF THE WITCHES: THE WORLD OF ALEX SANDERS**, New York, 1969, pp. 18–26

THIS EXCERPT FROM *KING* of the Witches should be regarded largely as fiction, the story of a witch's growth to adulthood as it ought to have been, complete with wise mentor and a temptation by the "dark side." Other accounts of Alex Sanders (1926?–88), written after his death, give a very different story of a thirtyish man seeking initiation into several Gardnerian covens, being turned away, and creating his own lineage of 'Alexandrian' witchcraft instead, based on the Gardnerian version but with a larger portion of ceremonial magic. This published version of Sanders' childhood, however, is significant in that it provides today's Pagan witches with a handy slang term: a "grandmother story," meaning a highly embellished account of one's hereditary magical lineage, designed to improve one's image as a witch or magician.

In this original grandmother story, given by Sanders to journalist June Johns in the 1960s, the 7-year-old Alex has walked into his grandmother's kitchen, only to find her standing naked in a magic circle. She has initiated him on the spot, nicking him behind the scrotum with her sickle-shaped knife and proclaiming, "You're one of us now, and all the power of heaven and earth will strike you if you break your promise [not to tell what she has done] . . . You'll live to thank me for this. I'll teach you things you never heard of, how to make magic and see the future." Now the fictive child witch must began to learn his magical lessons.

Described by some as a "born showman," Sanders, after Gerald Gardner's death, was the most visible "media witch" in Britain, together with his second wife, Maxine. A middle-aged English journalist, Stewart Farrar, who came to interview him in the late 1960s for a magazine article, joined his coven, married a fellow initiate, and produced one of the better witchcraft books of the era, *What Witches Do*. As a team, Stewart and Janet Farrar produced numerous other books on modern witchcraft (e.g. 1971, 1984), and they later discovered that Sanders had claimed as his own work various pre-existing magical works. Nevertheless, they said, "like the Joker in a pack of cards, he had a role to play," and continued on good terms with him until his death in 1988. In the final chapter of *Sacred Mask, Sacred Dance* (1997), Evan John Jones raised a similar question about his own Craft teacher, Robert Cochrane: "Was he a real magician of the old tradition, or was he just another magical trickster?" Like Jones, the Farrars decided that Sanders' positive legacy outweighed his personal failings: "There are many excellent covens working today which would not exist but for the Sanders." As with both Gerald Gardner and Robert Cochrane, Alex Sanders might have fudged the evidence, but his legacy is greater than himself.

Chas S. Clifton

References

Farrar, Janet and Farrar, Stewart (1984) *The Witches' Way*. London: Robert Hale.
Farrar, Stewart (1971) *What Witches Do: The Modern Coven Revealed*. New York: Coward, McCann & Geoghegan.
Jones, Evan John with Chas S. Clifton (1997) *Sacred Mask, Sacred Dance*. St. Paul, MN: Llewellyn Publications.

L EFT TO HIMSELF, Alex might have ended his foray into witchcraft there and then, but family circumstances forced him into contact with his grandmother almost daily and before long he found himself becoming interested and then totally absorbed in the secret teachings. A quick learner—he had been able to read at the age of three—he was never fully extended by his school work and had no difficulty maintaining, his place at the top of the class. After school, when he had finished peeling potatoes and running errands for his mother, he would ask to go to Gran's for his lessons in Welsh. Hannah was sadly out of practice herself and was glad that her son was so keen to speak a second language.

Alex did in fact have Welsh lessons—but only for half an hour. After that the witch regalia was brought out and the boy was taught the meaning of each item; the runic symbols dating back thousands of years when prophets cast sticks into the air and, from the pattern they made in landing, foretold the future; the inscriptions on the witches' dagger—the kneeling man, the kneeling woman, the bare breasts touching, the arrow speeding through the wheel of life down into the pointed blade, ready to strike at its owner's bidding; the miniature whip, a harmless substitute for the earlier weapon with which members were scourged, sometimes to the point of death; and the glistening crystal, which fascinated him most of all.

He learnt by heart the meaningless chants in a long-dead language, and at the end of the lesson he would take a small brass bowl of water and darken it with ink. He squatted on the floor by the light of the fire, the bowl before him. At first he could see only the flickering reflection of the coals, but Gran urged him to have patience. "It will come," she said confidently. And it did. One day, long after he had given up hope of ever seeing anything, the reflections seemed to mist over. When they cleared, his mother was looking up at him from the ink. She was lying on a bed and beside her leg, splashed with blood, was a new-born baby, its umbilical cord uncut. Three months later Hannah Sanders gave birth to her fourth child, Patricia.

Visions did not always confine themselves to the bowl. Alex was playing in the schoolyard one day when another boy suddenly appeared to him to have a double image, as if out of focus, and the fainter image revealed the boy's left leg in plaster.

"You're going to break your leg," Alex exclaimed. The boy, who was bigger than Alex, didn't take kindly to this and promptly thumped him. Several weeks later he fell off a swing—and broke his left leg.

After that Alex was careful to hold his tongue when his friends appeared in his visions. Once, for instance, a "picture" appeared in his mind of a schoolmate's mother being taken to hospital in an ambulance, but there was little he could do to warn her. Not long after she had to have an appendix operation.

On another occasion he saw a white-haired man whom he had never met. Weeks later he and two friends, Alan and David, raided a local soft-drinks factory. They climbed up a back wall, crawled across a steeply pitched roof and dropped into the inner yard where the crates were piled ready for delivery. The three boys each grabbed a bottle and made off the way they had come. Once in the street, David told Alex to go back and fetch another bottle. But Alex was less careful this time. He missed his footing on the roof and crashed through a glass skylight, gashing his leg. With difficulty he got back on to the roof and as far as the top of the wall but then he began to feel faint. Two young men were passing and Alex called to them for help. That was all he remembered until he woke up to find the white-haired man of his vision bending over him. He was a doctor and he was stitching the cut.

Alex's growing belief in witchcraft, reinforced by each experience of clairvoyance, did not conflict with his regular attendance at Sunday School. His gran had explained that there was only one God but that he was known by many names. It was easy, too, to accept that the Virgin Mary was the moon goddess in disguise.

Alex's childhood heroes took on new aspects when Gran re-told their stories. There was Robin Hood, previously just the leader of the merry men, but now revealed in his real role as a witch who used his powers to direct money where it was most needed, and to escape his pursuers. And Joan of Arc, who was really the Witch Queen of France and unashamedly declared it by her dress in an age when witches were the only females who would wear men's clothing. The terror Alex had felt when he first heard of her dying in the flames was allayed when he learnt that condemned witches were usually helped by their companions at liberty. If drugs like dwale or foxglove could not be smuggled into gaol, then witches in the crowd round the pyre would use their powers to hypnotize the victim and deaden her pain when the flames reached her.

Love potions, good-luck charms—Gran's remedies were all absorbed by the enchanted child. He hardly ever saw a blade of grass in his world of concrete, but he learnt how to recognize wild thyme, rosemary and pimpernel from the book in which his grandmother had pressed leaves, ferns and flowers during her youth in the foothills of Snowdon. As a girl she had belonged to a coven of four witches who were ardent chapel-goers—in Bethesda anyone who missed a service without good reason was ostracized by the other residents. At night the coven used to climb part-way up the mountain to a small lake reputed to have belonged to witches since the

Middle Ages. Stepping-stones led to the small island in the centre which was the circle where they performed their rituals, and in the inky black waters they studied the moon's reflections and conjured up the future.

When he was nine, Alex was allowed to take part in his first full-moon ceremony. Gran had no difficulty in persuading his mother to part with him for the night, for she was delighted with the progress he had made in Welsh and grateful to her mother for having taught him.

As the moon rose, Gran opened the kitchen curtains and let its light flood the kitchen. She had banked up the fire with small coal to deaden its glow and now she led Alex into the centre of the circle. The air was heavy with incense burning in four bowls placed at intervals round the perimeter. She handed him his own athame and told him she was going to consecrate it. The boy had to lie flat on his back, the dagger on his bare chest; then she lowered herself on to him, muttering incantations he had never heard before. He felt peculiar, his bare body pressed close to hers, but she was deadly serious and already he firmly believed in her magic. When they rose, she led him outside into the yard where she told him to raise his athame to the moon and repeat the words of the ritual. It was his first "calling down the moon" ceremony.

Although magic, witchcraft and the ever-increasing affinity he formed with his grandmother filled most of his childhood, Alex was usually able to lead an entirely separate life at home. He was very close to his sister Joan, two years his junior, but though he often longed to tell her his secrets, there was scarcely ever the time or privacy required. At one stage he was getting up at five o'clock every other morning to take a pillowcase to the local bakery where a new bread-slicing machine was having teething troubles. The first half-dozen loaves of the day were deformed and Alex could buy them for threepence.

Boyish rivalry sometimes stretched the promises he had made to his grandmother. When a classmate boasted of a Spanish rapier his father had bought, Alex could not resist mentioning his grandmother's swords.

"Go on, you're a liar!" jeered his classmate. Alex was too small and thin to fight, so he marched his friend to Gran's house, told him to keep quiet, and led him into the empty kitchen. He knew how to operate the double-lock on the chest. As he was turning the key, Gran came in. She had been in the front room and had seen them coming up the street. She fetched him a clout across his head that made his ears ring.

"You're never to bring boys in here again, do you hear?"

Alex nodded silently, and when his companion had gone, Gran made him promise never to open the chest again without her permission.

Alex did not forget, but not long afterwards his school was performing a play and one of the props needed was a ceremonial sword. Alex immediately told the master in charge, who was his favourite, that he had just the thing. "It's gold and it has huge rubies in it, I'll bring it in," he volunteered.

Gran was horrified and told him that he certainly could not borrow it. Even though it was only gilded and the "rubies" were coloured glass, it was a consecrated piece of regalia and not to be handled by non-witches.

Chastened, Alex went to school the next day and explained the matter to the master. "I'm a witch, you see, and non-witches aren't allowed to use such weapons."

The master threw back his head and roared with laughter and Alex could never really like him again.

Now that he had an athame of his own he began to take part in the rituals within the circle which Gran performed to cure the sickness of neighbours who had petitioned her. Then he embarked on the next step of his training; he started to make his own copy of the *Book of Shadows*, the witchcraft manual containing basic chants, recipes and instructions for various magic rites. Almost unaltered over the years, the book had been copied by every witch in his or her own handwriting so that if arrested in the era of persecution, one could not implicate another.

Carefully Alex copied every word of his grandmother's tattered volume into an exercise book, and promised her that when she died he would destroy her copy and keep only his own.

This was a major development in Alex's training as a witch, and with it came new powers. Instead of gazing into a bowl of ink, he was now allowed to use his grandmother's crystal.

"Don't clutch it—you'll mist it over," she scolded, the first time he tried. "Sit in a relaxed position and half close your eyes. Now, tell me what you see."

Alex gazed in shock and amazement. There were aeroplanes falling out of the sky and crashing into houses. The side wall of one house had been torn away, exposing a cross-section of tilting floors. Flames were licking at buildings; people with terror-stricken faces were running wildly through the streets, carrying their screaming children. Five years later, in 1940, he would gaze again at the identical scene.

He now had his own witch-name, Verbius, and he called his grandmother by hers, Medea. Sometimes he used it when his brother and sisters were there and he had to pretend it was a nickname. He revelled in Gran's favouritism; he loved his mother, even his father, but Gran was someone very special.

"What would have happened," he once asked her, "if I had not interrupted your ritual that day? Would you have let me go on as a non-witch?"

She did not know; for her, Alex's unscheduled appearance that day had been the work of fate. None of her own three daughters had ever discovered her secret; even her own mother had not known, although she herself had been a witch's daughter.

Gran was certainly proud of her apt pupil; he had mastered the rituals, he knew how to draw the magic circle, how to call down the power to work for him, how to conjure up spirit children he could play with. Gran understood all this of old and smiled indulgently, but she impressed him with the need for utter integrity. She warned him that if he abused the power, used it for selfish ends, to the harm of others, it would destroy him.

For Alex at this point, it was all somewhat exasperating. He dreamed of riches, even of gaining a few extra inches to make him as big as other boys his age. And his rapidly developing gift of clairvoyance was not always welcome. Hours before his mother and father had a quarrel he would hear the words they were going to use against each other. Near to tears, he would bury his head in the pillow and wait impatiently—the sooner the quarrel began, the sooner it would be over.

His grandmother wasted no sympathy on him, and told him to think of the good he could do. Without letting her neighbours know she was a witch, she worked to cure their ailments, both physical and mental.

"If I can help others, why can't I help myself?" Alex once asked her. He was referred to his *Book of Shadows* and told to attend to the basic rules—ask, never command; be grateful for what you get even though it is not exactly what you want.

Now as it happened, Alex for once knew exactly what he wanted. He worked out a series of incantations, and dreamed of a pair of magnificent brown boots. Three days later, on his way to school, he saw a splendid second-hand bicycle on sale for fifteen shillings. However, he didn't have one shilling, let alone fifteen, and his mother, who regarded debt as only one step removed from theft, refused to try to borrow the money. The next day he was told of a newsagent looking for a delivery boy. Alex got his mother's permission to proposition him: he, the employer, should buy the bicycle and for the next thirty weeks keep sixpence out of Alex's one-and-sixpence-a-week wage to pay for it. Alex would save up his remaining pay for the brown boots. Sure enough, before three weeks were out, he saw in a pawnbroker's shop the very boots he had dreamed of—priced at three shillings!

A by-product of his new job was that it absolved him from the punishment meted out by his father, who was fond of making an errant child stand upright at the table for two or three hours at a time. The offence might be as small as making a noise while Father was listening to a symphony concert on the radio. Now that Alex was a wage-earner, his mother demanded that he be spared such treatment.

When Alex was eleven he won a scholarship to William Hulmes Grammar School, but it never crossed his mind to use magic to make his parents accept the award. Already there was a fifth child in the family and much as Alex longed to be a doctor, taking up a place at grammar school was out of the question, even for a witch. His father was now working in a floor-tile business, but they had had to leave the house in Chorlton and were renting a large old house in Old Trafford, No. 23 Virgil Street. Times were hard. Alex himself was going through a bleak period—all his visions spoke of sorrow and loneliness, there was no one he could turn to. When he asked his grandmother to interpret them she refused. It was his future; no one else could read it for him.

Chapter 27

Michael McNierney

THE STOIC WAY OF NATURE
A pagan spiritual path

■ from **THE POMEGRANATE** 7 (February 1999): 13–27

A S MICHAEL MCNIERNEY, A former lecturer in Humanities at the University of Colorado, here points out, the ancient philosophy of Stoicism lives on today in many unrecognized forms, including the twelve-step programs pioneered by Alcoholics Anonymous and its imitators. In an essay first published in the Pagan studies journal *The Pomegranate*, McNierney not only argues for Stoicism's value as a guide to dealing with life's ups and downs, but places this Pagan philosophy on an equal plane with Buddhism and Taoism, when its cosmological roots are considered.

For further discussion of Stoicism, see Hazlitt (1984) and Long (2002).

Chas S. Clifton

References

Hazlitt, F.K. (ed.) (1984) *The Wisdom of the Stoics: Selections from Seneca, Epictetus, and Marcus Aurelius*. Lanham, MD: University Press of America.

Long. A.A. (2002) *Epictetus: A Stoic and Socratic Guide to Life*. Oxford: Oxford University Press.

S TOICISM DOESN'T HAVE ALL the answers. It doesn't even have all the questions. But it has some very good answers to some important questions— sensible answers to questions people still ask today, in spite of two thousand years of Christianity and a century of psychotherapy. Like most Pagan and polytheistic world views, Stoicism, as developed by the ancient Romans, does not claim to be the only true path or to be suitable for everyone. Nor does it claim to be an easy path. It does not require a doctorate in philosophy or years of immersion in the obscurities of an esoteric system. It simply claims to be a sensible path for active people in everyday life. I believe that it is a spiritual path particularly suited to modern Pagans.

With its keen understanding of psychology, somewhat rare in the ancient world, Stoicism is a hard-headed, practical view of how to live. It is concerned with the acceptance of things as they are, not as they were or might be. This practicality is both grounded and given a rich spiritual dimension by the Stoics' profound intuitive grasp of Nature and her eternal cycles. The ideal of the Stoic path is to live in harmony with the Universe and thereby maintain one's soul or deeper self in a calm state of grace regardless of circumstances.

"Nature is sacred—that is, from nature we draw our inspiration, our teachings, and our deepest sense of connection." This statement reflects the core of ancient Stoic belief and practice, yet it comes from a recent Pagan book (Starhawk, *et al.* 1997: 6). "I am the soul of nature that gives life to the universe. From Me all things proceed and unto Me they must return." Every Pagan will recognize that these words are from a version of the Charge of the Goddess, but they could have been spoken by the Divine Fire—one of the many names by which the Stoics knew the Ultimate Reality. In our age of spiritual turmoil and change—which mirrors the syncretistic religious development in the later Roman Empire—the Roman Stoics speak to modern Pagans across the millennia with a clear and relevant voice.

Although Stoicism is a creation of the Graeco-Roman world and largely unknown to most people today, the Stoic approach to life and some of its ideas will have a familiar feel to contemporary readers. This is not surprising since Stoic thought has probably had a more powerful and lasting influence on the way people live their lives than any other philosophy in western culture (Dilthey, 1975: 7). It is only in our own century that this influence has been forgotten.

In an article of this length, it is impractical to do more than point out a few places in the fabric of our culture where Stoic threads can be found. The most important patch of the fabric is Christianity. As the religion spread outside of Palestine and early church writers developed a Christian theology in the successful attempt to appeal to educated Pagans, they borrowed liberally from Stoic thought. These Stoic strands are still with us, woven into Christian scripture and dogma. As one example among many possible ones, the cosmic "Word" of the Prologue to the Gospel of John was adapted by its philosophically minded author from the first principle of Stoicism, the *Logos*. We shall see later that "word" is only one of the many possible translations of *Logos*. In fact, it is this translation that makes the Prologue so mysterious, and once its Stoic context is understood it becomes less enigmatic, though no less profound.

Elements of Stoicism are embedded in many contemporary psychological and self-help regimes. The widespread Twelve-Step programs have many Stoic ideas at their core. Reinhold Niebuhr's famous Serenity Prayer: "God grant me the serenity to accept the things I cannot change, the courage to change the things I can, and the wisdom to know the difference", for example, which is recited at virtually every Twelve Step meeting, is pure Stoicism. Cognitive therapy, a highly successful treatment for depression popularized by Dr. David Burns in a best-selling book, appears to be based on the Stoic principle of *apatheia*. Burns' statement that "your emotions result entirely from the way you look at things" is not a bad beginning at a definition of *apatheia* (Burns, 1980: 29).

"Basing our happiness on our ability to control everything is futile," says Stephen Covey in his time-management book. "While we do control our choice of action, we cannot control the consequences of our choices. Universal laws or principles do. Thus, we are not in control of our lives; principles are" (Covey, *et al.*, 1994: 13). Substitute fortune or the gods for principles, and you have a statement that no Stoic would repudiate. Exactly how Stoic ideas have turned up in self-help and time-management books in the late 20th century I do not know, especially as I find no evidence that the authors have read or even heard of Stoicism. It is perhaps the ultimate tribute to the influence of Stoicism that many of its ideas have simply become part of the Zeitgeist of our times. It would be an interesting exercise in the history of ideas to trace the development of certain Stoic concepts from the ancient world to our own popular culture.

Since I am interested in Stoicism as a western, Pagan, spiritual path, another very different reason for Stoic ideas being familiar to contemporary readers is more important than the issue of influence. This is that Stoicism has some affinity with several eastern spiritual paths—particularly with Taoism and Zen—that westerners are likely to be familiar with and perhaps have also practiced. Ideas such as following Nature and living in the present are now commonplace in our culture. We have brought these and other powerful ideas home from the East, yet they have been present in our own western spiritual tradition for over two thousand years.

Here at home, however, these insights are allied with a respect for and faith in the power of our minds to find truth and happiness without eschewing reason as does Taoism and without requiring years of practice in meditative techniques as does Zen. This is not to say that intuition plays no part in Stoicism or that meditation is incompatible with it. It is simply that Stoicism offers some of the things we have found appealing and fruitful in the East without requiring the radical abandonment of familiar and useful western assumptions about reality that is often necessary to wholeheartedly follow an eastern path—and that is often the cause of westerners turning back disillusioned from the East.

I have learned much from the East and plan to continue doing so. But exclusive concentration on eastern thought and practices leaves me feeling rootless, homeless, ungrounded, and disoriented (pun intended). C.G. Jung asked of what use are the insights and wisdom of the East to us ". . . if we desert the foundations of our own culture as though they were errors outlived and, like homeless pirates, settle with thievish intent on foreign shores?" (Jung, 1962: 114). I believe that my true Self or Soul is somehow part of a community of spiritual brothers and sisters, extended back in time rather than space, and if I turn my back on the West, on my home, I cut connections with this community and am worse off for it.

Gnosis editor, Richard Smoley, wrote in an editorial (Winter 1994) that "today we assume we must seek truth as far afield as possible" and reminded us that "teachers with real insight" often urge us to "recognize and develop the strengths of our own traditions." But this can be difficult, since outside the institutional monotheistic religions and Native religions (which are often inaccessible to outsiders), teachers to pass on traditions are few and far between. People exploring western spirituality outside the mainstream seldom have a living link with the past, so they turn to books to find, recreate, or create traditions. As poet Gary Snyder writes, "In this huge old occidental culture our teaching elders are books. Books are our grandparents!" (Snyder, 1990: 61). We are fortunate to have such grandparents as the works of the Roman Stoics.

The adjective "stoic" elicits in most people's minds the idea of simply not showing one's emotions. This attitude is unappealing to people in our age who have been constantly enjoined to "get in touch with your feelings," and it is downright politically incorrect if you are a male. But this usage does not do justice even to the dictionary meaning: "indifferent to or unaffected by pleasure or pain; impassive; enduring; brave," which itself barely hints at the richness of ancient Stoic thought.

Misuse of the word is one reason why Stoicism is little known today. Another is an understandable misapprehension of its true nature as a spiritual path. The best-known ancient Stoic today is Marcus Aurelius Antoninus (121–180 CE). His *Meditations* have been in print since the 17th century, and most educated people today have heard of him, yet few have read him. The problem is that in libraries and bookstores his book will he found under the heading of "philosophy," and that word drives people away with its connotation of ivory-tower, logic-chopping irrelevancy or intimidates them with the idea that, even if it is relevant, it is too difficult to understand. A recent paperback edition of the *Meditations* carries the information on the front cover that this "is the book on President Clinton's bedside table." Perhaps Clinton will do for Marcus what a former president did for Tom Clancy. Or, even better, perhaps Marcus will do for Clinton what Stoicism did for Marcus.

But philosophy to the Romans meant something very different from what it means today. For them it had a meaning much closer to what we think of as religion. They even spoke of being "converted" to a particular philosophy. Most of the things we moderns turn to religion for—spiritual practice, moral guidance, comfort, insight, and encouragement in time of suffering—educated Pagan Romans found in philosophy, not religion. "Philosophy!" Marcus Tullius Cicero (106–43 BCE) exclaims, "the guide of our lives! Had it not been for your guidance, what would I ever have amounted to?" (*Tusculan Disputations* 5:2). Marcus Aurelius writes: "Where, then, can man find the power to guide and guard his steps? In one thing and one alone: Philosophy. To be a philosopher is to keep unsullied and unscathed the divine spirit [*daimon*] within him" (*Meditations* 2.17). And Lucius Annaeus Seneca (c. 4–65 CE) writes to his friend, "Without it [philosophy] no one can live with courage or serenity" (*Ad Lucilium Epistulae Morales*, 3 vols., Harvard UP, 1917: 25; all translations from Seneca are mine unless otherwise noted).

To literate Romans, "religion" was synonymous with ritual that one performed out of patriotism and respect for tradition. It had little to do with ethics or the soul. Divinity and one's personal, as opposed to public, relationship to it—whether in the form of gods and goddesses, a philosophical One, or one's personal daimon—was a matter of philosophy.

Earlier, in the more circumvented world of the city states of Classical Greece (5th and 4th centuries BCE), philosophy had had a broader meaning. Plato and Aristotle, while never forgetting that philosophy meant "love of wisdom" which included guidance on how to live, also developed speculation on the nature of reality into elaborate systems of metaphysics, ethics, politics, and natural science.

After the death of Alexander the Great in 323 BCE and the division of his empire into the smaller, warring empires of his successors, the world changed radically. This new Hellenistic world was now much larger and more diverse and in an almost constant state of political and social upheaval. Life became profoundly disorienting.

> Both individual freedom and responsibility were undermined by the massiveness and confusion of the new political world. Personal destinies appeared to be determined more by large impersonal forces than by individual volition. The old clarity no longer seemed available, and many felt they had lost their bearings.
>
> (Tarnas, 1991: 75)

Although Plato and Aristotle were still studied, the times demanded something different and more down-to-earth. New philosophical schools arose, whose inspiration "arose less from the passion to comprehend the world in its mystery and magnitude, and more from the need to give human beings some stable belief system and inner peace in the face of a hostile and chaotic environment" (Tarnas, 1991: 76). If philosophy originally began in wonder, as Aristotle said (*Metaphysics* 982b.12), these new Hellenistic philosophies surely began in confusion and suffering.

Among them was Stoicism, founded by Zeno of Citium in Cyprus (335–263 BCE). Zeno (not to be confused with Zeno of Elea, author of the famous paradox bearing his name) taught in Athens at a well-known site, the *stoa poikile*, the painted colonnade or porch—hence the name of his school. We could perhaps translate the name of this school as Porchism and refer to its followers as Porchers, but somehow these words don't quite have the proper ring of dignity. He and his successors as head of the school, Cleanthes (*fl. c.* 263 BCE) and Chrysippus (*fl. c.* 233 BCE), taught a stern ethic proclaiming absolute virtue as the only way to happiness. They also apparently developed theories of logic and cosmology, but so little of their work survives that reconstructing their systems is largely speculation.

The later Stoics modified and softened the early dogma and were much more interested in practical applications of Stoic ideas than in systematic philosophy. They never ceased, however, to speculate and wonder about the universe. While Stoicism maintained a continuous tradition from Zeno onwards through the Hellenistic period, the Roman Republic, and into the Empire, when it was the dominant philosophy of educated people, it is three Stoics of the first two centuries CE who are most important today: Lucius Annaeus Seneca, a politician and virtual head of the Roman state during Nero's youth; Epictetus (55–135), a freed Greek slave; and Marcus Aurelius, an emperor and general.

Since I am more interested in showing the relevance of the Stoics to people today than in providing a balanced history of Stoicism and do not have the space to consider all three in equal depth, I will concentrate on one philosopher—Marcus Aurelius. This is to some degree an arbitrary choice reflecting my personal taste; I don't mean to slight Epictetus and Seneca. Far from it. They are both worth repeated reading and study, and both have been more important than Marcus in transmitting Stoic ideas to later centuries. But there are practical reasons for this choice also. Marcus' *Meditations* is much more easily available in translation than any other Stoic work. It is a short and compact book that bears repeated reading and can serve as the Pagan equivalent of Thomas à Kempis' *Imitation of Christ*, to which it has often been compared. Epictetus' ideas are often reflected accurately in Marcus, since the emperor considered the former slave his spiritual master. Touching only lightly on him will not, therefore, distort the picture of Roman Stoicism unduly. Some consideration of Seneca, however, is indispensable, even though his work is uneven and scattered among numerous essays and plays and 124 letters. His Stoicism is warmer and more poetic than that of the emperor and contains some profound insights into social psychology. He is useful as a balance to the austerity and solitariness of Marcus. A portion of Epictetus' work is available in *The Enchiridion*, T.W. Higginson, trans. (Macmillan, 1948). A selection of Seneca's letters can be found in *Letters From a Stoic*, R.C. Campbell, trans. (Penguin, 1969).

Marcus Aurelius wrote, as far as we know, only one literary work, his *Meditations*, although some of his correspondence has also survived. And he wrote only for himself. The *Meditations* are apparently a personal, undated journal he kept with no idea of its ever being made public. The title is not his but was added later. The readers' attention is directed to *Marcus Aurelius: A Biography*, by Anthony Birley (Yale UP, 1987). Emperor from 161 to 180, Marcus spent most of his time away from Rome defending the Danubian frontier against various Germanic tribes in the Marcomannic wars, which have been compared for their horror and barbarity to the First World War in the same area. Compared to most Roman emperors, Marcus lived a life of hardship and extreme stress. There can be no doubt that he followed his principles. He felt it was his sacred duty to personally supervise the defense of the empire, although he could have, as many emperors did, sit in luxury in Rome and delegate the dirty work to someone else. At the age of 59, he virtually died in the saddle, worn out by the rigors of almost constant campaigning.

If you live with Marcus and his thoughts for a period of time, you begin to feel a kinship and even friendship with him as a living spirit—an uncle, say, or grandfather, who always has a word of counsel when it's needed. He is not a remote mind delivering the word of god or some other form of putative absolute truth. He is a human being with his own doubts and failings as well as virtues. Marcus can sometimes be depressingly melancholy and annoyingly inconsistent, but his courage, wisdom, and humanity shine through every page.

En archê ên ho logos. "In the beginning was the Logos." Thus begins the Gospel of John, and thus begins Stoicism also. The word *logos* is untranslatable by any one English word. "Word" is only the commonest of its meanings. It also denotes universal mind, explanation, meaning, measure, universal reason, purpose, plan, providence, inner structure, divine law, divine archetype. It is a vague, encompassing, and powerful word, sometimes seeming to carry an even mystical weight. One thing that can be said with certainty about it is that it is the opposite of randomness and chaos, and that it is the ground of all being. Perhaps it is best thought of as the divine archetype of the universe, both the plan, the creation, and the substance of things together. A suggestive and fruitful analogy is the equally untranslatable Chinese word *Tao*. Logos is probably the closest word in a western language to Tao. Tao is often translated as "way," and it is suggestive that Christ, who is the Logos in the Gospel of John (14:6), says "I am the way and the truth and the life."

Marcus sometimes uses Logos interchangeably with the words god, the gods, Nature, the Universe, Fate, Necessity, and even Zeus. For modern Pagans, as I will discuss later, there is no inconsistency in adding Goddess to the list. The most important thing to bear in mind is that the word "God" has none of the connotations of the word in monotheistic religions: "If Greek philosophers speak of 'god' in the masculine singular, this is generally to indicate everything encompassed by the divine or to distinguish a supreme god from lesser divinities; no formal commitment to monotheism is implied" (Long 1989: 136). (Although the word is capitalized in all the translations, I will use it in lower case to attenuate this association.) To us his most exotic term for this primordial creative principle is "Mind-Fire" or "Active Fire" (*pyr technikon*), a concept going back to Heraclitus (*c.* 500 BCE). To the Stoics, the Logos or Mind-Fire or god is both the creator and the substance of the universe. It is in everything, and everything is in it, and everything is destined to return to it.

The Stoics are technically classified as materialists, since they believed that the Logos, and therefore everything else, is ultimately made of "matter." But *hylê* (matter) has such a rarefied meaning by the time of the late Stoics, that translating it by the English word 'matter" is gravely misleading. Matter to us means something that solidly fills space, can be touched, has weight and mass, etc. We will be much closer to the Stoic understanding of the word if we think of the fundamental substance of the universe as energy. (After Einstein, of course, we realize that matter is energy in frozen form.)

Each human soul is a particle of the Logos. "Sunlight is all one, even when it is broken up by walls, mountains, and a host of other things. Soul is all one, even when it is distributed among countless natures of every kind in countless differing proportions" (12.30). This concept implies a deep interconnectedness of everything in the Universe, and although the Stoics only occasionally express a passionate relationship with the deity, their "deepest religious intuitions are founded on their doctrine that the human mind, in all its functions—reflecting, sensing, desiring, and initiating action—is part and partner of god" (Long 1989: 149). This relationship points the way to right action for each human being.

The end of human life for the Stoics as for most ancient philosophers is happiness. (*Eudaimonia*, the Greek word for happiness, literally means "blessed with a good daimon, or inner god." Hence the English, "to be in good spirits.") Happiness is to be found in virtue (*virtus* in Latin, *aretê* in Greek), and virtue for the Stoics means living courageously in harmony with Nature. This does not necessarily mean living in Nature, retiring to a Roman Walden Pond for instance, although something like that was often a dream or fantasy of many Romans, including Marcus (4.3), Seneca (Ep. 28), and Horace (Odes 3.29). Cicero, like other wealthy Romans, had his country estate as well as his house in Rome. (I am indebted to Richard Smoley for pointing this out to me.) Living according to Nature first of all entails realizing that one is as much a part of Nature as wild animals or the wind. God or the Logos is present in everything in the Universe. In life as a whole it is manifest not only in the turn of the seasons or the march of the years but also in the actual course of events, the way things happen, the way things are here and now on both a personal and impersonal level.

What is, is God or Logos or Nature. There is no recourse to a Platonic realm of ideas or a Christian afterlife. As historian of philosophy Frederick Copleston says, "The Stoics rejected not only the Platonic doctrine of the transcendental universal, but also Aristotle's doctrine of the concrete universal. Only the individual exists and our knowledge is knowledge of particular objects" (Copleston 1962: 386).

"[T]he interest of every creature lies in conformity with its own constitution and nature," writes Marcus (6.44). Trees, lions, and people all have their place in the great woven fabric of Nature. Our place and purpose are determined by the form the Logos takes in us: a rational soul. Reason had a much broader meaning in antiquity than it does now. The Stoics' "commitment to rationality as the essence of what is divine and good includes the love of wisdom, *philosophia* . . . The Stoics did not, as is frequently supposed, set up as their ideal one whose wisdom excludes all emotion or feeling. Rather, they extended the notion of rationality so that it included desires and 'good feelings' (*eupatheiai*), in contrast to the passions and mental perturbations that characterize a soul whose reasoning faculty is disordered" (Long 1989: 146).

Since the seventeenth century, we have split off our reasoning capacity from our emotional capacity, seeing them even as warring opposites. It's notable that recently even empirical science is beginning to recognize that this is a dangerous error: the "absence of emotion appears to be at least as pernicious for rationality as excessive emotion. It certainly does not seem true that reason stands to gain from operating without the leverage of emotion. Emotion may well be the support system without which the edifice of reason cannot function properly and may even collapse" (Damasio 1994: 144). The more holistic view of the ancients is being confirmed by neurobiology.

Marcus says that the qualities of the rational soul include "love of neighbors, truthfulness, modesty, and a reverence for herself before all else" (11.1). If my soul and your soul are ultimately the same, then it follows that self-love (not selfishness) leads directly to love of all humankind. Marcus Aurelius, Seneca, and Epictetus proclaim the doctrine of "love thy neighbor as thyself" so often that it is superfluous to cite specific examples. It's not difficult to see why the Church Fathers found such useful allies in the Stoics. This strain is strongest in Seneca, which explains why, if not how, the legend of his correspondence with St. Paul arose.

Living in conformity with one's own true constitution, which is the same as following the Way of Nature, leads to the state of *autarkia*—self-reliance. Self-reliance brings inner freedom when one realizes that one can only truly rely on oneself when that self is recognized and felt to be part of and in harmony with the universal whole. Stoic self-reliance and the serenity or happiness that follows from it derive from a total acceptance of things as they are. Pain, loss, and death itself are all as natural as the change of the seasons. To resist or resent them is as futile as trying to stop a hailstorm. Everything is in constant change. "We shrink from change," Marcus writes to himself, "yet is there anything than can come into being without it?" (7.18). Change is Nature's way, the only way. "Out of the universal substance, as out of wax, Nature fashions a colt, then breaks him up and uses the material to form a tree" (7.23, 25).

Fortuna, Imperatrix Mundi, Fortune, Empress of the World, seems to dispense her goods and ills without regard for a person's character. Often, the just suffer, and the unjust prosper. In the parlance of a modern best seller, why do "bad things happen to good people?" Every philosophy and religion must ultimately come to terms with this problem of theodicy, defined by the dictionary as "the vindication of divine justice in the face of the existence of evil." For a monotheistic theology that holds that there is one transcendent, omnipotent, omniscient, and good God, the problem is simply insoluble. Augustine spent much of his life in the unsuccessful attempt to prove that evil doesn't really exist in and of itself but is merely a lack of good.

The Stoic, like the Taoist, sees the question differently. Neither falls into dualism: the practice of seeing good and evil as separate entities at war with each other. Both, being followers of the Way of Nature, see them as opposite but complementary, each necessary for the other's existence, like day and night, summer and winter, life and death. The universe could not exist without these contraries. Alan Watts' description of the Taoist yin-yang principle could have been written about the Stoic Logos or World-Fire: "being and nonbeing are mutually generative and mutually supportive the somethings and the nothings, the ons and offs, the solids and the spaces, as well as the wakings and the sleepings and alternations of existing and not existing, are mutually necessary" (Watts 1975: 23–25).

As far back as Chrysippus, the Stoics had maintained that one of a pair of contraries cannot exist without the other. If any twentieth-century person knows what the Universe and the World Fire is like at the most fundamental level, it must be a quantum physicist. One of the greatest, Niels Bohr, had emblazoned on his coat of arms the motto: "*Contraria non contradictoria sed complementa sunt.*" Opposites are complementary not contradictory. Seneca would have agreed: "Eternity consists of opposites. To this law our souls must adjust themselves" (Ep. 107.8–9).

"The picture, then, is of a world in which everything ultimately fits together according to a divine pattern" (Long 1989: 148). Following nature "involves contemplation of nature's ways, recognition of their fitness, and perception that all of them are 'good' in the sense of being essential to the pattern as a whole" (Blofeld 1978: 10).

If you realize this in your bones, you will be able to "keep a straight course and follow your own nature and the World-Nature (and the way of these two is one)" (5.3), and you will find "peace of mind under the visitations of a destiny you cannot control" (3.5). Stoic happiness lies in accepting and flowing with things as they are, not wasting energy fighting against things you can't control, and realizing that you are usually powerless to change people, places, and things. What the Serenity Prayer requests, the Stoic strives for: "the serenity to accept the things I cannot change, the courage to change the things I can, and the wisdom to know the difference."

Although we cannot control most external events, we can decide what our attitude toward them will be. From this insight rises the infamous Stoic virtue of *apatheia*, which does not mean apathy or not feeling, but rather not being thrown about and controlled by our emotions, either positive or negative. The Stoic does not deny or suppress the emotions but recognizes them as reactions to external events and not as parts of the essential self and also as not necessarily accurate evaluations of the external world.

"If you are distressed by anything external," Marcus says, "the pain is not due to the thing itself but to your own estimate of it; and that you have the power to revoke at any moment" (8.47). "Subtract your own notions of what you imagine to be painful, and then your self stands invulnerable" (8.40). "[T]hings can never touch the soul, but stand inert outside it, so that disquiet can arise only from fancies from within" (4.3). Seneca tells his friend Lucilius that once he has tested his powers of *apatheia* by dealing with the whims of Fortune he will know that "true spirit will never allow itself to come under the authority of anything outside ourselves" (Ep. 13.1). Epictetus enjoins us, when faced with something unpleasant, "to examine it by those rules which you have; and first and chiefly by this: whether it concerns the things which are within our power or those which are not; and if it concerns anything beyond our power, be prepared to say that it is nothing to you" (Enchiridion, I).

Copleston concisely describes the rewards of *apatheia*: "happiness depends on that which alone is in our power and independent of external conditions—namely our will, our ideas concerning things, and the use we make of our ideas" (Copleston 1962: 435). In this insight lies the Stoics' greatest contribution to psychology (Peters and Mace 1967: 7:4), one of the things that makes their philosophy directly relevant to active existence today.

Love and respect for all fellow human beings as well as other creatures follow from the premise that we are all part of the same unity. There is no doubt that the Stoics tried to practice as well as preach this truth, Marcus Aurelius seems to have had a particular problem with impatience and anger, compounded by his position as Emperor. He had the power to do a great deal of damage to a great number of people, but he was aware of the temptation and constantly admonishes himself to remember "the closeness of man's brotherhood with his kind; a brotherhood not of blood or human seed [a tacit acknowledgment of class differences] but of a common intelligence; and that this intelligence in every man is God, an emanation from the deity" (12.26).

Seneca wrote passionately against the stupid cruelty of gladiatorial games (Ep. 7) and the degradation of drunkenness to which the Romans were particularly susceptible [he was a teetotaler] (Ep. 88). Incredibly, and as far as I know, uniquely in the ancient world, Seneca also proclaimed the equality of the sexes and demanded that conjugal faithfulness in a husband be interpreted every bit as strictly as the honor of the wife (Ep. 94).

He is especially passionate on the subject of slavery: " 'They are slaves.' No! They are human beings. 'They are slaves.' No! They are comrades. 'They are slaves.' No! They are unassuming friends" (47.1). "We treat them not as human beings but use and abuse them as if they were beasts of burden" (47.5). "I'd like you to think of this, that the one you call your slave comes from the same human stock as you, has the same skies above him, breathes, lives, and dies exactly the same as you" (47.10). Seneca's influence led directly to the improvement of the legal status of slaves in the Roman Empire.

Nature, the Universe, and the gods were not just abstractions to the Stoics. Although they used these and many other words almost interchangeably, this was a matter of mood, of context, or perhaps of recent personal experience. When writing in a mode of logic, they may reduce all spiritual reality to the One—the Mind-Fire or god—but Stoicism was not a systematic philosophy nor a doctrinaire religion. The gods may ultimately be manifestations of the unity of the Universe—just as you and I are—but that does not make them any less real. The Stoics were polytheists with all the tolerance, open-mindedness, and acceptance of ambivalence that makes

Paganism increasingly appealing to spiritual searchers today. I can make an offering to Hekate at a shrine in the woods and still be a Stoic. Like Taoism and Zen, it is compatible with other spiritual beliefs and practices. I can do *zazen* on my cushion everyday and still be a Stoic.

No one reading the Stoics carefully can doubt that much of what they write is based on personal spiritual experience, not just ideas. Listen as Seneca, in his famous forty-first letter, describes just such experiences:

> If you have ever come on a dense wood of ancient trees that have risen to an exceptional height, shutting out all sight of the sky with one thick screen of branches upon another, the loftiness of the forest, the seclusion of the spot, your sense of wonderment at finding so deep and unbroken a gloom out of doors, will persuade you of the presence of a deity. Any cave in which rocks have eroded deep into the mountain resting on it, its hollowing out into a cavern of impressive extent not produced by the labors of man but the result of processes of nature, will strike into your soul some kind of inkling of the divine. We venerate the sources of important streams; places where a mighty river bursts suddenly from hiding are provided with altars; hot springs are objects of worship; the darkness or unfathomable depth of pools has made their waters sacred.

How many readers have felt something like this? I know I have. Unmistakable experience of the Holy in dark, quiet places in the Rocky Mountains was one of the things that led me away from Christianity as a teenager and into Paganism as an adult.

If they can overlook the fact that the ancient Stoics—from the slave Epictetus to the Emperor Marcus Aurelius—were born, lived their lives, and died in a patriarchal society, and that they were all, through no fault of their own, members of the much maligned society of DWMs (Dead White Males), modern Pagans or Neo-Pagans may find in them congenial spiritual ancestors.

Starhawk, probably the best-known modern Pagan writer, says in *The Spiral Dance*: "The Goddess does not rule the world; She is the world. Manifest in each of us, She can be known internally by every individual, in all her magnificent diversity." And further, that:

> all things are swirls of energy, vortexes of moving forces, currents in an ever-changing sea. Underlying the appearance of separateness, of fixed objects within a linear stream of time, reality is a field of energies that congeal, temporarily, into forms. In time, all "fixed" things dissolve, only to coalesce again into new forms, new vehicles.
>
> (Starhawk 1989: 23, 32)

Since I have taken the liberty of adding the Goddess as one of the names and forms of the Stoic Universe or Mind-Fire, I find these words of Starhawk's completely compatible with Stoicism. There is nothing in them with which Marcus or Seneca would disagree, and perhaps they wouldn't even object to my addition of the Goddess. Men of their time also worshipped the Goddess. Although he was a

Platonist, not a Stoic, Apuleius (*c.* 123-? CE) wrote in his *Metamorphoses or The Golden Ass*, a beautiful and powerful prayer to the Goddess in the form of Isis, of which this is a small part: "Neither day nor any quiet time of night, nor indeed any moment passes by that is not occupied by your good deeds. You roll the globe, you light the sun, you rule the world the stars answer to you, the seasons return, the godheads rejoice, the elements serve you. At your nod, breezes blow, clouds nourish, seeds germinate, seedlings grow" (*Metamorphoses* 11.25). As a Platonist, Apuleius would not of course identify the Goddess with the world as would pantheistic Stoics and modern Pagans, but his delight at and reverence for the connection between divinity and the natural world is common to both.

Stoicism is an ancient spiritual path that can help us on our journey today. This is not an empty statement. As an instructor of humanities, I have had the privilege of teaching the *Enchiridion* to university students and have heard from several that studying Epictetus changed their lives. The man who was Ross Perot's running mate in 1992 is a Stoic. Vice-Admiral James Stockdale was a prisoner-of-war in Hanoi for eight years during the Vietnam War. What kept him and many of the men for whom he was responsible alive was Stoicism. He had previously found Epictetus so appealing that he had memorized much of the philosopher's work. From the moment he was captured, he began to apply his internalized Stoicism and thereby saved his sanity and his life under some of the worst conditions and treatment imaginable (Stockdale 1993).

Stoicism is western and thus lies at the roots of our culture and traditions, yet it offers wisdom that many have struggled through the esotericism of the East to find. It offers in concentrated form psychological insights that can lead to a life of serenity, insights that are scattered throughout much modern psychological literature but without the deep spiritual dimension of Stoicism. Above all, it is a way of Nature and wholeness, a way of realizing our unity with all living things and with the Universe itself.

Every day I pray—and try to live up to the courage it requires—a passionate, beautiful prayer written for himself by Marcus Aurelius Antoninus seventeen centuries ago:

> All is in harmony with me that is in harmony with you, O Universe. Nothing is too early or too late if it is in due season for you. All that your seasons yield is fruit for me. You are all things, all things are in you, and to you all things return.
>
> (384.23. My translation)

Works cited

Blofeld, John. *Taoism: The Road to Immortality*. Boulder: Shambala, 1978.
Burns, David D. *Feeling Good: The New Mood Therapy*. New York: New American Library, 1980.
Cicero. *Tuscan Disputations*. M. Grant, trans. Penguin, 1971.

Copleston, Frederick A. *History of Philosophy, Vol. 1: Greece and Rome.* New York: Doubleday, 1962.

Covey, Stephen R., Merrill, A. Roger and Merrill, Rebecca R. *First Things First: To Live, to Love, to Learn, to Leave a Legacy.* New York: Simon & Schuster, 1994.

Damasio, Antonio R. "Descartes' Error and the Future of Human Life," *Scientific American* 271:4 (October 1994).

Dilthey, Wilhelm. quoted in F.H. Sandbach, *The Stoics*, New York: Norton, 1975.

Jung, C.G. *The Secret of the Golden Flower.* Richard Wilhelm, trans. New York: Harcourt Brace Jovanovich, 1962.

Long, A.A. "Epicureans and Stoics" in A.H. Armstrong, ed. *Classical Mediterranean Spirituality.* New York: Crossroad, 1989.

Marcus Aurelius. *Meditations.* M. Staniforth, trans. Viking Penguin, 1964.

Peters, R.S. and Mace, C.A. "Psychology," in *The Encyclopedia of Philosophy.* New York: Macmillan, 1967.

Seneca. *Ad Lucilium Epistulae Morales.* Harvard UP, 1917.

Snyder, Gary. *The Practice of the Wild.* San Francisco: North Point Press, 1990.

Starhawk. *The Spiral Dance: A Rebirth of the Ancient Religion of the Great Goddess*, 2nd ed. Harper: San Francisco, 1989.

Starhawk, M. Macha NightMare, and The Reclaiming Collective. *The Pagan Book Of Living and Dying: Practical Rituals, Prayers, Blessings, and Meditations on Crossing Over* Harper: San Francisco, 1997.

Stockdale, James Bond. *Courage Under Fire: Testing Epictetus's Doctrines in a Laboratory of Human Behavior.* Stanford: Hoover Institution on War, Revolution and Peace, 1993.

Tarnas, Richard. *The Passion of the Western Mind: Understanding the Ideas That Have Shaped Our World View.* New York: Ballantine, 1991.

Watts, Alan. *Tao: The Watercourse Way.* New York: Pantheon Books, 1975.

Chapter 28

Heather O'Dell

THE SOLO WITCH

■ from Chas S. Clifton (ed.) **THE MODERN CRAFT MOVEMENT**, St. Paul, MN, 1992, pp. 133–47

D ESPITE THE COMMON IMAGE of witches meeting in covens (which may range in size from two to the traditional thirteen people—or more), many contemporary Pagan witches, in fact, do not belong to covens. A senior executive at Llewellyn Publications, the largest American publisher of books on Paganism, has estimated that as many as 70 percent of today's Pagan witches are "solitaries," not members of regular groups. That observation would square with the high sales of two books by the late Scott Cunningham, one of Llewellyn's most successful authors, *Wicca: A Guide for the Solitary Practitioner* and *Living Wicca: A Further Guide for the Solitary Practitioner*. In fact, before the efforts of such writers as O'Dell and Cunningham, virtually all Wiccan authors assumed that all witches found or founded covens. It is probably no coincidence that the same volume that included "The Solo Witch" also contained "An Insider's Look at Pagan Festivals," by a New Mexico witch who herself had helped to organize several. The huge growth of American Pagan festivals in the 1980s and since may well be at least partially attributed to the fact that they allow these often-solitary practitioners to be part of a temporary community.

Chas S. Clifton

References

Cunningham, Scott (1990) *Wicca: A Guide for the Solitary Practitioner*. St. Paul, MN: Llewellyn.

Cunningham, Scott (1993) *Living Wicca: A Further Guide for the Solitary Practitioner*. St. Paul, MN: Llewellyn.

UNDER A FULL MOON THE woman crosses the meadow, listening to the swish of silvered grasses as they brush against her legs. She stops in a circle of oak trees, her whole being focused on muted sounds, on the smell and feeling of night air against her face. The Moon spills its milky light on her shoulders; she begins to move in a circle. Slowly, heavily, as if rooted within the Earth she moves, singing softly, creating a magical space around her . . .

In a city miles away a man walks into a sanctuary he has created, closing the door behind him. Incense obliterates city smells; street sounds diminish. Finally there is only the sound of his breathing. Candles illuminate his ritual tools: athame (ritual knife), chalice, and other objects arranged before him on an altar. In the flickering light he moves through the phrases of his ritual: "This is a time that is not a time, in a place that is not a place . . ."

In cities and rural areas everywhere women and men go alone to celebrate the Pagan festivals. Solitary Witches by chance or by choice, we practice our religion just as coven members do. In some ways we must work a little harder, explore some blind alleys, fight some personal demons along the way, but the result can be worth the extra trouble.

You do not have to belong to a coven to acquire the knowledge you need to be a Witch, to work magic, create powerful rituals and experience the wonder of a life lived in celebration. You can explore the mysteries of the cosmos and of your psyche, returning with treasures of self-reliance and self-knowledge. And far from being lonely, you can use your strengths to form connections of friendship and service, building a community around you.

Certainly there are disadvantages. If you are already a practicing solitary Witch, you are well aware of them. For example:

You do not have a ready-made group with which to celebrate rituals. With a group, a feast can be more festive. There are more voices to sing, more bodies to dance, more colors, laughter, hands to touch and usually more wonderful plates of food from which to eat afterwards. If everything is working right, a tremendous amount of power is generated; you know that magic is in the air.

You lack the special companionship that covens can offer. Of course you want to share your thoughts and experiences with others who "speak the same language," who know just what you mean when you describe your plans for Candlemas or how you found your athame or exactly how you felt the circle build around you that last time. You may want to seek or give advice that is not couched in the terms of someone else's religion or the newest psycho-babble. You may simply long for the heightened bond that can exist between individuals who share Wiccan spirituality as well as other facets of life.

You cannot rely on someone else for motivation. Left on its own, your enthusiasm can be all but extinguished under the weight of everyday stress and cares, illness or just plain boredom—just when you need it most. The intellect is willing, but the spirit has taken a vacation; it is easier to turn on the television or curl up with a novel than to create a ritual. A group's psychic energy can jump-start your flagging enthusiasm, get you started when you thought you would never start and keep you going when it seems like an uphill struggle.

You may find it difficult to be objective. As Witches we are constantly exploring uncharted areas: the realms of magic and the mind. What we find sometimes confuses us or even scares us. It helps to have others to furnish us with an objective viewpoint or an experience against which to compare ours. On our own we face a risk of getting lost in tangles of subjectivity.

There is no Craft teacher right there with you. If you are alone and new to the Craft, you may be overwhelmed by all that you think you must learn. The many books seem to present a bewildering array of information to the newcomer and—especially when it comes to the specifics of ritual—may seem to contradict one another. No one can blame you for wanting to join an experienced coven, to have a safe haven where you can practice and learn under the direction of others who have integrated and used all this information in a way that works.

For all the problems of going it alone, however, being a solitary Witch has some advantages. Consider the compensations afforded solo practitioners:

You are better off on your own than in the wrong coven. Suppose you are drawn to the feminist traditions and find the only coven available in your area to be one led by a dogmatic high priest whose practice—in your eyes—is patterned too closely on one of the patriarchal religions. (Covens like these do exist!) What if you prefer to improvise your rituals while other coveners never deviate from the procedure set down in someone's *Book of Shadows,* or conversely what if your preference for form and continuity is constantly sabotaged by those around you who seem to thrive on anarchy? Or what if you simply have nothing in common other than your religion with other Pagans in your community? In the intimate, family-like coven setting, this can be a real drawback for the "different" member. Alone, you can work and celebrate as you please, when you please and (assuming you like yourself) in congenial company.

You are not bothered by distractions. Most people find it easiest to concentrate when alone, and concentration is vital to good magic. But even in the most harmonious company you may find yourself swayed from your intention by the sheer force of group energy or interrupted in your mental imagery by a comment or inadvertent noise from someone else.

You can always act when the time is right. In magic as in sex, timing is all-important. The time of day, your own special rhythm, Moon phase or weather may be crucial to accomplishing your magical intention, and rarely will a group's timing perfectly match your own. Inspiration, the kind that suddenly dissolves all boundaries, is fragile and elusive as a minute. If you ignore it until your group finishes discussing last month's ritual or the appropriate way to "call the quarters," you may lose it.

You learn to rely on yourself. Working alone in the Craft—searching for answers within yourself and from outside, striving to integrate your spirituality into your daily life and relationships, learning to trust your perceptions, intuitions and reactions—you can develop a degree of self-reliance that is hard to attain within the shelter (and confines!) of a group. The admonition, "Know thyself," is timeless and universal. As Ralph Waldo Emerson said in his essay "Self-Reliance," "Nothing is at last sacred but the integrity of your own mind." Knowing ourselves, relying on ourselves, we develop inner reserves from which to draw when we or others need to. Witches are reminded how important self-reliance is when we repeat the Charge of the Goddess:

> And thou who thinkest to seek for me,
> know thy seeking and yearning
>   shall avail thee not
> unless thou knowest the mystery:
> That if that which thou seekest
>   thou findest not within thee,
> thou wilt never find it without thee.
> For behold, I have been with thee
>   from the beginning
> and I am that which is attained
>   at the end of desire.

Living the craft as a solitary

When you blend your spirituality with the cadence of your life and live the Craft from day to day, you come to appreciate solo practice's benefits and minimize its shortcomings. The quality of our Craft derives more from what we put into it— commitment, work, a sense of wonder, a willingness to share what we have learned—than from any coven affiliation.

If you are new to the Craft and alone, or if you are already practicing but find something missing, here are some suggestions for solitary practice. First, read. Read books on understanding dreams, astrology, meditation techniques, parapsychology. Read about the history of Witchcraft and its practice today, about myths from different cultures, and herbal medicine. Read fact and read fiction: let one source lead you to another in a treasure hunt for knowledge. I will admit to a personal prejudice here: I cannot imagine my world without books. But beyond that, I have found that most people drawn to the Craft are addicted to reading. It is rare to find a modern Witch without also finding a houseful of books.

Keep a dream journal and record everything you remember about your dreams: color and feeling and waking associations as well as the dream sequence itself. Look to your dreams for messages and inspiration. Play with your dreams. Act out the parts of various dream images, both animate and inanimate. Draw a picture of your dream; transform it into your personal myth; build a ritual around it. Not only will you learn from your dreams, but you will find that close attention to that other world you enter in sleep will imbue your waking hours with an aura of enchantment.

If you want to work magic you must learn mental discipline. Choose the meditation technique that suits you best and practice it daily. Learn to find that quiet place inside yourself where wisdom speaks—and listen. Cultivate the art of visualization. Without the ability to visualize, your rituals will be merely theater, not complete magical workings.

A Witch must learn to hear his or her inner voice through dreamwork and mental exercise, but the physical senses need exercising too. The Craft, after all, is an earth religion. We work with powers of Air, Fire, Water and Earth: observe these forces as they occur in the world around you so that you will know them in your heart. Notice how sounds travel on the wind, and how the air changes day to day, place to place. Take a long, slow breath.

Open your palms to the Sun's heat. Watch its light fill hidden corners of the landscape and change the color of the sky. Wade in a stream or the ocean and feel the water's force. Watch it move.

Gather a handful of soil and feel its temperature and texture against your skin. Smell it when it is wet; compare that to its smell when dry. Gardening is a great way to observe all the elements. Plant some herbs and watch them sprout and grow, responding to light and water. (If you have no garden, plant them in pots.) Feel their leaves; smell them. Taste them. Learn their uses in magic and in healing.

Remember that your body is sacred too and attend to its well-being. Swim, run or walk. Practice T'ai Chi or Hatha Yoga. Move as much as you are able. Choose nourishing food and prepare it with love, then savor it.

Practicing solitary witchcraft

Solitary ritual work does not have to be dreary. Alone you can carry out ritual that is powerful, effective and just right for you. You may choose from a script in a book, re-enact one you learned or create your own. The beauty of solo ritual lies in your freedom to fashion it just as you want.

In adapting a group ritual to solo, you will probably want to simplify it and make it less wordy. In a group, the theatrical presentation is usually more effective, so when working alone, you may find it better to substitute intense visualization for much of the speaking and action of group ceremonial. But if you wish to add a poem, chant or dance, you can. Search within yourself to find what your deepest Self responds to. Lift aside the curtain of your dreams. Listen to your body and your heart; translate what you hear into motion. You may this way touch the sacred more surely than you could in all but the most developed group simply because you have put more of yourself into your magic.

However you decide to carry out your ritual and spellcasting, you will probably want to follow the basic structure of modern Craft ceremonies. What follows is a short description of ceremonial structure, followed by a solo self-initiation ritual. If you are standing at the threshold of declaring yourself a Witch, you may wish to study this part carefully, then perform it at the first good opportunity.

Purification. Before you start any ritual, set aside time to shed emotional baggage that will distract you from total involvement. No magic works when you enter your circle burdened with leftover anger or worry; this is one of the most important principles. To symbolize your purification, try bathing by candlelight, adding cleansing herbs such as sage, cedar, rosemary or lavender to the water. Or lie in a rushing stream, or build a sweat bath and burn sage. However you purify yourself, you must feel all preoccupations "washed away." Follow that with a short meditation until you feel the quiet place inside you where there is only serenity.

Casting the circle. The circle marks the area for ritual working. It sets off the mundane world from the timeless, spaceless point that becomes magic's setting. The power you build in ritual, gaining intensity as it spirals around you, is contained by the circle. Traditionally a Witch moves clockwise when casting a circle, the direction in which the (Northern Hemisphere) Sun appears to move above us, denoting a gathering-in of power. The circle is oriented to the four cardinal directions which in turn symbolize the magical elements of Air, Fire, Water and Earth.

Invoking the Goddess and the God. In invoking the Goddess and the God we become them for a time. We experience that part of ourselves that is divine. We call for the feminine and masculine powers—dark and light, generating and dying, searching and sheltering—that each of us contains, repeating in our ritual the act of creation made by the joining and separating of these divine forces. When that power is felt, whether you have invoked it by words, thoughts, songs, dance or mental imagery, then magic can be worked.

Self-initiation

Through initiation we express our commitment to the Craft (and in groups, a formal acceptance by the coven). Initiation is an essential step the solo practitioner should not skip. It becomes a powerful expression of your transition into Witchcraft.

Initiation takes you from death to your old life to rebirth in a new one. You die to some old attitudes and ways of being in the world and are born to living the Craft. You enter the darkness of your unconscious, listening for the voice of inner direction, relinquishing dependence on old authorities as you move toward the light of your own true nature. Carefully planned and carried out, your personal initiation ceremony can effect a powerful transformation in your life.

A close friend of mine, who carried out a ritual similar to the one below when he decided as a young man to follow the Craft, described it as more powerful than he had expected merely reading the printed words beforehand. As he moved through the ritual, he said, he was unexpectedly hit by an uneasy feeling that white-bearded Jehovah would indeed be angered by his defection and strike him dead, even though he had not consciously considered himself a Christian for a decade. But by the time he had finished the short ritual, he knew he was a Witch, with all vestiges of his childhood religion's "authority" put away from him. He has never turned back.

That which follows is a simple self-initiation ritual. Use it as a starting place from which to build your own.

To define your ritual area, place candles at what will be the north, east, south and west points of your circle. Place an altar candle on a flat surface such as a rock or table. Near the altar candle arrange a small container of anointing oil (either prepared ritual oil or simply pure olive oil), another of incense or fragrant herbs to burn, and some wine in a cup or chalice. If you have other personal items that are important to you, such as your athame (ritual knife), magical jewelry, or a "medicine bag," put them on the altar too.

If possible, schedule this ritual at the full Moon on a day when you can be alone. Spend that day quietly, perhaps walking outdoors or listening to music—some activity that will encourage a meditative state. Then prepare for ritual by slowly bathing in water to which you have added the appropriate herbs and/or oils. When you leave the bath, leave all preoccupations—along with your clothing—behind. Nude ("skyclad," as Witches say), enter the ritual space as though you were entering a world you have never known before.

Light a candle and take a few minutes to feel its warmth on your body and to watch its moving light. Ignite your incense.

Carrying the anointing oil, move to the east quarter and light the candle there. Touch the it to your forehead, your eyelids, lips, hands, breast, genitals and feet, saying in turn, "My mind, my eyes, my lips, my hands, my breast, my sex, my feet." Visualize a wind from the east breathing life into each of the body points you have anointed.

Move to the south quarter, lighting that candle. Repeat the anointing and self-blessing, visualizing the Sun's heat from the south building vitality and passion at each point you touch.

Move to the west quarter and light that candle. This time, feel the fluids in your body as they flow through each of the spots you anoint.

Move to the north quarter and light that candle. As you repeat the anointing and self-blessing, visualize the earthy, enduring substance of your body at each of the spots you touch.

Returning to your altar, anoint your body as before one more time, very slowly and consciously. As you do so, say:

> Be with me, Goddess and God.
> With my mind and imagination
>   I will seek to understand Your mysteries.
> With my eyes I will see the beauty of the Earth.
> My lips will speak of You
>   in music and language,
>   and my hands will do Your work.
> With my breast I will give comfort;
>   my sex will express joy in new life.
> And always in Your ways my feet will travel.

(You may substitute any divine names you wish.)

Slowly drink the wine from your chalice, savoring it. Then hold the chalice up in front of you and say, "I, (give your Craft name if you have chosen one), am a Witch."

Community. Just because you are a solitary Witch does not mean you must be a lonely one. You are neglecting an important part of the Craft if you hug it to yourself, turning your energy always inward instead of allowing it to radiate into the world around you. Remember, the Craft is an earth religion: everyone and everything is sacred. Contribute to and partake of this sacredness by sharing your gifts and knowledge. The people around you can benefit from your abilities as an astrologer or an herbalist or a storyteller or a carrier of groceries. Every person you meet can use your compassion at one time or another, as can plants, animals and the Earth that supports you. Strengthen your connection with the Goddess and God by strengthening the bond between you and the world.

You have a community, and it is all around you. You almost certainly will encounter people, both Craft and otherwise, who share your interest and possess similar talents. Others will be able to fill in where your knowledge is weak. In associating with these people and with those who need your help you will learn and grow, just as you would in any coven. In fact, as a solitary Witch you will be unlikely to fall into the habit of confining your "community" to fellow coveners. By opening your circle of friendship you will discover that there is indeed richness in diversity.

When you want to make contact with others in the Craft, you will find it is increasingly easy to do so. Pagan festivals are proliferating all around the United States and some foreign countries. The best way to find them is through Pagan publications. (. . .) Bring your tent and some food and be prepared to meet like-spirited people who just might become lifelong friends.

One day when I was a child, I sat on a grassy bank in the woods, listening to a symphony played by robins and wood thrushes, rustling maple leaves above me and the rush of Willow Creek below me. It was late spring and the smell of new vegetation was sweet on the air. No one else was there to distract me with words; this one time everything I saw, felt, smelt and heard was there for me only. It was one of the happiest moments of my life. Later I painted the scene as I remembered it: a solitary girl in the woods. I titled it "Alone." The painting won first prize in a school contest, which pleased me, but some viewers' reactions did not. "How sad," they said. "She looks so lonely." It seemed futile to protest this misconception, and so I did not, just as now I ignore those coven Witches who think my life is somehow less complete than theirs. Instead, I find joy as a solitary practitioner, knowing that while it may not be the best for everyone, it is the only way for me. I can be a Witch alone. And so can you.

Chapter 29

Judy Harrow

INITIATION BY ORDEAL

Military service as a passage into adulthood

■ from Chas S. Clifton (ed.) **MODERN RITES OF PASSAGE**,
St. Paul, MN, 1993, pp. 129–63

THE AMERICAN MILITARY, AT least, is a more supportive place for
Pagans than at one time. Much to the surprise of some social conservatives, an
attempt to pressure the US Army not to permit an open Pagan worship group at
Fort Hood, Texas, was resisted by the (largely Christian) Army Chaplains Corps to
the highest levels. Ironically, some of the anti-Pagan contingent tried to use the writings of certain prominent Pagan pacifists, such as Starhawk, to show that Pagans
were theologically ill-equipped to be soldiers. But as Judy Harrow argued in this
1992 essay, Paganism follows a "high-choice" ethic that does permit military
service, and most American Pagans adhere to their own version of the "just war"
doctrine rather than to pacifism. In fact, the on-post Pagan group at Fort Hood had
as its high priest a retired Army major.

The Pagans that Harrow interviewed for this chapter, however, were all veterans
who assessed their military experience, both good and bad, as a form of initiation
into adulthood. As one of them told her, you must make your commitment to the
initiatory process and complete it before you can say whether it was false or real.
And despite their mixed experiences, these veterans did regard their service as form
of initiation into adulthood, a rite of passage that contemporary society does
not generally provide to its young adults. As Harrow noted, where the military
"initiation" fell short was in failing to provide the third stage of the classic separation–liminality–reintegration initiatory process. Military veterans are too often
sent home unprepared to be reintegrated into civilian life: "When we fail to bring
our warriors back into the civilian community, we place them—and ourselves—at
serious risk."

Also see Harrow (2002) and the Military Pagan Network website.

Chas S. Clifton

References

Harrow, Judy (2002) *Spiritual Mentoring: A Pagan Guide*. Toronto: ECW Press.
Military Pagan Network: http://www.milpagan.org

BUDS SLEEP IN WINTER. As the sun slowly returns, they gradually swell. Then, one sudden, surprising morning, we find every tree on the street covered with tiny, tender leaves. Human growth is like that: seasons of gradual change punctuated by moments of sudden breakthrough. This is how Tony remembers his experience on the "confidence course" during Air Force Basic Training:

"The obstacle is called the 'weaver.' Two telephone poles are set at a 30-degree angle to the ground, connected by tie bars about every three feet. You go sideways over the first bar and under the second, then continue alternating till you reach the top, about seven feet off the ground, and drop off.

"I found it impossible at first. My back muscles just weren't toned for the reverse push-up movement it required. I dropped off after the third tie. The training instructor told me to start again. I dropped off a second time.

"He had me stand at attention while he yelled at me. He said he didn't believe I had actually tried. He said that I could do it if I let myself get angry enough. If I couldn't, he said, he'd send me home to my momma. And then, he told me that I could drop off, if I wanted, at the red tie bar, about 2/3 of the way up, where the women recruits would drop off. The concession was what really did make me angry. I started again.

"I realized halfway through that I was actually doing it. When I reached the red tie, the instructor asked if I wanted to get off. I shouted 'No, sir!' and went to the top.

"Later I was astonished—astonished that I had done it at all, and that I had refused his offer of an easy out. Astonished that muscles I never knew I had could hurt so much. And, yet, now I knew they were there, and I knew I could use them again at need without a training instructor there to goad me on. Years later, the knowledge stays with me, literally ingrained into my body as well as my mind."

These days, we postpone marriage and vocation long past the advent of adolescence. The old puberty rites may still change us from children to youths, but not to grownups. Folk wisdom says joining the Army will "make a man of you." And so for some young men—and young women—military service makes and marks the delayed passage from youth to adulthood.

Here's a classic description of initiation into adulthood:

> "The term 'initiation' in the most general sense denotes a body of rites and oral teachings whose purpose is to produce a decisive alteration in the . . . status of the person to be initiated. . . . To gain the right to be admitted among adults, the adolescent has to pass through a series of initiatory ordeals; it is by virtue of these rites, and of the revelations that they entail, that he will be recognized as a responsible member of the society. . . . In philosophical terms, initiation is equivalent to a basic change in existential condition; the novice emerges from his ordeal

endowed with a totally different being from that which he possessed before his initiation; he has become another. . . ."[1]

Eight Pagan military veterans shared their memories and reflections with me. I am grateful for their frankness and generosity. All eight had enlisted voluntarily. Their enlistment dates range from 1952 through 1987. Two were in the Army, two in the Navy, three in the Air Force, and one in the Marines. Two saw combat. All have now returned to civilian life. Two intend to re-enlist; one has refused to accept his veteran's benefits. But all, even he, believe that their military experience moved them into adulthood.

They enlisted for a variety of reasons. Bob quit high school to enter the Marines as an escape from his dysfunctional family. Paul, as a youngster, had been fascinated by his stepfather's dog tags, hanging on the bedpost. Phyllis was looking to "get out of the nest and see the world."

Fritz said, "I finished high school in 1956. I knew better than to do what other people of my economic class in my hometown did, which was just get a job in the mill. Most of the young fellows who had gotten those jobs were already missing fingers. It was a miserable existence. The only way I knew that a poor person could get out of my dismal town was to join the military, so I did. I joined the Air Force."

As Ben told it, "I joined the Navy in 1979 as a hard-hat diver. I was 23. I went into the military because of a combination of blind and irrational hormones and just dealing with the day-to-days of a working-class kid trying to cut academia and pay the bills. It just got to a point that I felt a need for some kind of adventure."

For Paul, "Something wasn't right in my life. Finally, I decided to go check out the recruiting officer. We talked and we talked. He suggested that I wait for an opening in some technical specialty. But the nearest one was about nine months away on a delayed entry program. I didn't want to wait that long. In my life, I needed the change. So, in 1987 I signed up for infantry against everybody's advice, including the recruiter's."

In retrospect, some can identify deeper needs and motivations. Fritz reflected, "I was in the grips of what I now recognize as the need for an initiatory experience. I intuitively knew that unless there was something life-threatening or some small risk, even, of life-threatening activity, it wouldn't count. Now, you may ask why I didn't accept the challenge of working in the steel mills or coal mines, which was certainly life-threatening enough—and it was because there was no element of heroism in it, no adventure."

Paul, one of few who already knew he was Pagan at the time of his enlistment, recalled, "I always worshiped a hunter-gatherer God, and so I saw no problem going into the military and being a Pagan. Most of my Pagan friends were highly anti-military. My priestess at the time tried to talk me out of it, but my priest was more supportive."

Departures

Rites of passage often consist of three major phases: separation, transformation and re-integration.[2] Looking closely, we could see Basic Training as a passage in itself, an initiation into military life. The duration and intensity of military Basic Training, and its underlying structure, are similar to traditional, tribal initiations. Or step back a bit, and look at the several years a youngster will spend in the military as an extended initiation into adult life. In that view, Basic Training can be understood as a very strong method of separation. Sharply and suddenly the young recruit leaves behind all that was familiar.

Ex-servicemen and women report indelible and poignant memories of leaving home, leaving family, and of their first moments of contact. Paul: "I got up early on the day I left for training. I tried to wake my brother up to say good-bye. He barely woke, said, 'Yeah, good-bye,' and went right back to sleep. That was kind of disheartening. Then I left. I remember waiting for the bus, feeling so alone for the first time in my life. Like I was finally, totally on my own. It was an odd feeling, like a step into manhood."

Brett: "My Dad dropped me off at the Academy, and that was it. I was alone in the middle of the drill field with my suitcase. Since that day, I've never taken any support from my parents. It was just very much a setting free. That in itself was a rite of passage, of being on your own, because you can't go back."

Phyllis: "They make sure that you arrive in Texas in the dark, at night, tired. So they've got you right there. They've disoriented you completely. They've got you exhausted and they've got you in the dark. And then they start yelling at you almost immediately. You know: you will do this and won't do that. They just take you right over."

That shocking first contact, like the traditional "Guardian at the Gateway," serves as the first challenge to the neophyte. Bob: "I joined the Marines to see if I could do it. I got off the bus and I said, 'I made a mistake.' I knew I had got myself in over my head. I still had to prove to myself that I could do it. I lasted it. It was seventeen weeks of Hell."

Basic Training—separation from childhood

"During their time of separation from the community, the initiates experienced a ritual death and rebirth. Boys passed away and men emerged. In order to evoke the virtues of courage and strength, this transition involved ordeals of danger and self-denial. In psychological terms, the ordeal served to evoke the archetype of the hero . . ."[3]

Basic Training normally includes intense physical fitness training, instruction in military terminology and etiquette, training in the use of weapons, and more. But it is not just like going to any trade school. All instruction is presented in the context of powerful psychological techniques that are also part of classical initiation processes around the world. At the core of Basic Training lies intense, carefully delivered, psychological stress.

Training instructors deliberately use humiliation and verbal abuse. Fritz: "It was really a big surprise. I had the idea that the service would treat us in some sort of chivalric fashion. I was very surprised at how rude and rough they were with us, how mean they felt it necessary to treat us."

Phyllis: "Eventually, you get to know a routine and you know what is expected of you, so it's not as disorienting. But it can be just as frightening, because they won't give you any inch. They try to keep you a little bit off balance the whole time." A series of confusing, apparently irrational demands adds to the stress level. At the Merchant Marine Academy, Brett recalls, plebes walking the building corridors are required to stop and do a "face turn" at every corner.

With behavior so strictly controlled, eventually every recruit is caught making mistakes. Punishments increase the pressure. They do not simply humiliate. They are also designed specifically to deprive the recruit of recreation and of sleep. Brett: "At the Academy, your day was planned so that you got up at 5 a.m. and got to bed at 10 or 10:30 p.m., so you'd always be tired. There was never enough time to do everything you had to do by way of shining your shoes, your buckles, your buttons, your pins, etc., to be ready for inspections. So, it would be 10:30 at night, after lights out, and you'd get out the flashlight and start shining your shoes.

"To add to the pressure, they would give you extra duty for things that seemed inane and trivial. Once, I had to guard the head (bathroom), several days in a row, with my rifle. I had to challenge everybody that entered to identify himself as 'friend,' 'foe,' or 'Communist subversive cockroach.' This was during time that the rest of the section had free to do whatever they wanted."

Paul: "They had me on a lot of extra duties. I was doing fire guard in the middle of the night every single night. On a seven-hour night, I had to get up for a two-hour shift in the middle of the night, every night except Sunday. And I also had to do extra details in the platoon, plus I had to maintain my own stuff. So, I wasn't getting enough rest, which created more problems because I fell asleep sometimes when I shouldn't have. I lost every single day pass that came up."

Peer pressure, too, was deliberately engendered. Bob: "They would pit you against other people. If someone was overweight, for example, it was up to us to whip them into shape. They would turn us against each other. They'd say, 'I'm coming back in five minutes, and if he doesn't have this done by then, you're all going to get it.' One time somebody didn't take a shower, and a group of guys jumped this guy and scrubbed him down with scrub brushes."

Phyllis: "When you had somebody who wasn't quite pulling it together, everybody suffered. If one girl screwed up, you all got your privileges taken away, or you all got jumped on. So you all kind of made sure everybody else was toeing the mark. And you became responsible for one another, which you might not do as a young person out doing a job. You learn that you're affecting other people's lives."

Training instructors do not actually hate young recruits. Their exaggerated hostility, ridicule, and anger are a role assigned to them by the training model. Eventually, most recruits see through the act, and this gnosis removes much of the sting. Fritz: "The drill instructors used a lot of psychological violence against us. It took me a couple of weeks to pick up on the fact that their hearts really weren't in it. Most of them didn't believe it would work. They would occasionally just walk away from an encounter, disgusted, I think, with themselves. And, after a while, they just gave it up. I think the whole thing might have been an act."

Brett: "They put you under severe stress, and they don't let you realize at the time that it's all false. It's all fake. There's nothing real there, really. I mean there's no real threats, but they seem like real threats to you at the time. They do it so that, when you are presented with a real threat, a real stress situation, you won't break."

After Basic—assessing the changes

Basic is tough. But those who complete it are not just glad it's over. They report a rueful kind of pride, a firm basis for bonding, and greater confidence in their own strength and capability. Paul: "You get proud of it, and you laugh at it afterwards, because you do get by. And they do let up after a while, but you've got to earn that."

Brett: "Because I went through all that crap, now I can deal with almost anything. Right now, I'm under a lot of stress in my life. When my wife left me, I only missed one day of work. I was broken up and everything, but by the second day, I was able to pull myself together enough to go to work and do the bare minimum requirements of my job. I wasn't excelling at it, like I usually do, but I was functional. It's because of my military background that I was able to do that."

Paul: "They want to get you to the point where you will crack, and then cut it off there. They don't want you to crack. They want to push you to your limits to make you harder and stronger, more able to take it. They don't want to push you past that point."

Bob: "What I still have is the camaraderie and the bonding. Whoever made it, we can say we've been through that, we can go through anything together. You know going into any situation that somebody who can handle things is watching your back."

Phyllis: "We all knew that we'd all gone through it, and we could relate to each other at least on that level. You know, we were all terrified and we were all thrown off. We were all screamed at, treated like morons, generally humiliated. When you got done, you know that, if you could get through that without going crazy, you could handle anything. You also knew that the people around you had that same kind of stamina."

Ben: "Basic Training hardened me physically and also in a lot of terms mentally. Along with the physical conditioning goes a technique of resolve that where you can't quit, you won't quit. There is no response except success, and no excuses. How to deal with a stark reality, and making rapid choices, in an instant, a split second."

Brett: "After going through the artificial stress at the Academy, I went to sea. Whether it was on merchant ships or when I was on active duty with the Navy, there were always things that you had to decide that could be somebody's life depending upon it. On an oil tanker: who's going to go out on deck and close the tops of the tanks that you've been washing when you get into heavy weather? Who's going to do what with which lines when you're docking? There are some dangerous jobs that if a line parts, the guy's dead.

"A lot of the things that people find stressful in business life, somebody that's been through a military experience isn't going to find stressful. People come screaming into my office now, saying something or other is an emergency. I sit there relatively calmly. It frustrates them to no end. I say, 'What's the emergency?' They say, 'We could lose half a million dollars if this computer doesn't start working in the next ten seconds.' I just go about my business, and they want to know how I can do that. But there's nothing there that's that important, no emergency, no one's life depends on anything. You know, it's only money. What is money?"

Ben: "In my teens and my early twenties, I was the lost youth, that confused, James Dean-kind of figure. I was given a focus. Still to this day, when I need to sit down and focus, I can do it. I can sit down and deal with a problem for twelve hours at a time if necessary."

Paul: "I learned something else in the military which carries over to civilian life. I always accomplish my task, my mission. I may leave other things by the side doing it. But, for example, at work, I do things that nobody else can get done. I will get the job done, period. Sometimes we get too many orders in and my boss starts to panic. I say 'don't worry, I've never not gotten it done.' He always leaves me alone to do it, finally, and I always get it done."

Fritz: "The other thing that I noticed years later, when I moved to Canada and became a back-to-the-land hippie, was that you could sure tell which guys had been in the service and which guys hadn't just by looking at their woodpiles. It wasn't just that it was tidy; it was big."

I used to be opposed to conscription on simple political grounds. Listening to the veterans, I came to understand the gritty reality of their experience. I became convinced that military service is a valid initiatory path. Now, as priestess and counselor, I am appalled that anyone was ever forced into it. Such a path should only be undertaken by free and careful choice. And, as with any valid path, one who has willingly begun should not easily be diverted.

Ambrose: "In the military, you cannot leave if you don't like something. So, you are forced to go through the experience. As you know, life itself does this. That, I think, is valuable."

The veterans I spoke with are all Pagans, all used to thinking in terms of ritual. Most agree that in Basic they experienced a true initiation.

Phyllis: "Basic is definitely a rite of passage. You either make it or you don't. In the real world you might not take having somebody get right up in your face and scream at you, but there you've got to, or you know you can be sent right back to day one and start all over again. They'll put you through it and put you through it, until you get it."

Ambrose: "Military Basic Training rids people of false timidity. I think a lot of the timidity of people is not real: it's a habit or something that's a presumption on their part. They're not really that timid, but they don't know it because they haven't experienced yet the things that they're shying away from. Once they do, a lot of that falls away, and they become no longer timid, but careful."

Brett: "It's the difference between being a child and a man, almost immediately. If you're not a man by the time you report in, you're certainly a man by the time you're done with Basic Training. Actually, it's an experience that I think everybody should go through. I had a lot of hell at the Academy, but it's an experience that I would not give up for anything."

Fritz, although he appreciates what he learned in the Air Force, had to wait a few more years for his true initiation: "Basic definitely did not make me a man. It made me more clever and conniving. It taught me to keep my head down. It made me lose my respect for the people in authority. All those things are valuable, but I don't think they contributed to my manliness."

Non-combatant assignments—a day job in a uniform

Even during a war, only a minority will actually participate in combat. Most perform support services. Phyllis was an aircraft mechanic in Germany: "You go to work and you come home. That's it. You work your shift. While you're at work, you do your job. When you get off, off comes the uniform, and you're on your own."

The Air Force trained twice as many radar technicians as it needed in 1957, so Fritz painted signs in Portland, Oregon, and lived as a civilian: "I had a room in the barracks, which I never slept in. I stayed with friends downtown in their college-type communal houses. I'd come back out to the base on the bus every morning, take a shower, eat breakfast, go to work in my uniform, leave work, eat supper, take the bus into town, and hang out, party, study. I started taking college courses in the evenings. I just put in a very minimum effort in the service for my remaining two years."

Simple enough, but there was no active combat during those years. Others that I spoke to had noncombatant assignments during wartimes, while friends from training were in danger. Safety, in such circumstances, was not at all comfortable. Ambrose: "I wanted to fight, and I was trained for it. But I didn't actually go to Korea. I was in Seattle, at Pier 91, boarding the ship. I was probably halfway up the gangplank. I remember it struck me so. Somebody came around with a clipboard. Fifty names out of the five thousand of us were being taken out and reassigned. I was one. I was given a different assignment, on this continent.

"I was very pissed. I didn't like it at all. My adrenaline was up. I was packed and dressed and well into it. I was really prepared, prepared to take a wound if necessary. I was all dressed up for the party and the party was canceled. The disappointment lasted a couple of years.

"My second reaction came when I heard of the first person that I knew personally that was killed. I wondered why I wasn't there. I wanted to know if I had any personal responsibility there. Did I do anything at all to not go when I should have gone? That's what I had to clear up."

Bob: "I was never in combat. People that I trained with died in Vietnam. I felt I should have been there, with my friends. The Marines did nothing to help me handle my guilty feelings about not being there.

"I felt bad until just a few years ago when I met another Marine veteran in a bar. He told me it was not my fault. I had followed orders. It's not like I copped out and got myself ordered to Guam, so I'd be safe. But I still have the feeling like I should have been there to help my friends."

Combat—the Warrior's initiation

All proper initiations force us to face critical issues in our lives, to make choices and commitments, to set our course for the next period of slow and incremental growth. But just as not all people are the same, neither are all initiations. Different issues are presented along different initiatory paths. The military initiation, besides being a general initiation into adulthood, is a specific initiation into the way of the Warrior. Those who enter the military must face, directly or indirectly, the question of violence. All know that they maybe ordered into combat at any time. All are trained in combat skills.

Ambrose: "What they learn about violence is going to have to be supplemented a bit, because they don't learn the morals of violence. They learn courage and accuracy. They learn how to operate in violence."

Draft boards used to frequently hit applicants for Conscientious Objector status with this hypothetical question: you are walking down the street with your aged, infirm grandmother. A gang of muggers approaches. Would you defend her? If you say you will, your application for CO status will be denied. By current legal standards, whoever would defend their elderly grandmother is required to kill without question anyone the government points them at. Pagan ethics point to a very different kind of standard.

"If it harm none, do what you will," says the Wiccan Rede, the core ethical statement of our religion. A few of us interpret the Rede as an absolute, a mandate for Gandhi-style pacifism. Other Pagans may avoid all military participation because the high-tech nature of modern warfare is ecologically devastating, intolerable even to those Nature worshipers who would, at need, draw sword.

For others, the Rede is a statement of situational ethics. The grandmother/mugger hypothetical demonstrates that in real life absolute harmlessness is often impossible. That realization relativizes the Rede.

If muggers attack your grandmother, somebody is going to be harmed. Belief that you are absolutely forbidden to harm the muggers may impel you to let the mugging take place unhindered. Your passivity could harm your grandmother emotionally at least as much as their aggression harms her physically. In such a situation, you can only choose whom you will harm. Still you are responsible, as always, for the outcomes of your choices. The Rede provides no guidance, but natural loyalty does, and so does a normal sense of justice.

We can also set beside the Rede our heritage of Warrior God/desses and hero myths from almost all Pagan cultures. These model fair and honorable combat. They teach us that we have the right and obligation to defend ourselves, our communities, our sacred ways and, most of all, our sacred Earth.

Bob: "I want to know how to kill so I can protect myself and my loved ones. I don't want to assault, I want to defend. Everybody should know how to defend themselves and their loved ones. The important thing for a true Warrior is not knowing how to use the sword, but knowing when to use the sword."

Contemporary Paganism, drawing on many sources, supports what has been called a "high-choice" ethic. A statement by the First Officers of Covenant of the Goddess made during the 1991 Gulf War reads in part: "It is CoG's policy to support individual matters of conscience. We understand that devotion to the Goddess may either direct individual members to participate in war, or to conscientiously object to participating in a war. We pray that the wisdom of the Goddess guide all members of our faith who face such a decision."[4]

So, conscientious Pagans handle the question of violence just as we handle any other truly important issue. We find out as much as we can about any given situation, apply our values as well as we can, choose on a case-by-case basis, and accept the consequences of our choices. In legal terms, this is called the "selective Conscientious Objector" position, and it is not recognized as a valid legal option. The "all-or-nothing" standard of the draft laws infringes on Pagan religious teachings, which insist on our right and responsibility to choose. By so doing, it also violates the American Constitution and the freedom the American military purports to defend.

Paradoxically, whoever chooses to enter the military by that very decision chooses to give up most other choices during his or her term of enlistment.

Ben: "Discipline is everything. It ain't *Star Trek* where they talk about motivation or initiative. The first and last issue is discipline for an enlisted man. You're told to do something, and you're expected to perform."

For Pagan youth, trained to a high-choice ethic, the military emphasis on taking orders will be especially challenging. But when you have chosen of your own free will to fight for a cause you truly believe is just, your moment-to-moment actions need to be coordinated with the rest of the team. Proper coordination both maximizes effectiveness and minimizes risk.

Furthermore, total obedience during the initiatory period is another classic characteristic of tribal initiations. "Between instructors and neophytes, there is often complete authority and complete submission. . . . The authority of the elders is not based on legal sanctions; it is, in a sense, the personification of the self-evident authority of tradition. . . . The passivity of neophytes to their instructors, their malleability, which is increased by submission to ordeal, their reduction to a uniform condition, are signs of the process whereby they are ground down to be fashioned anew and endowed with additional powers to cope with their new station in life. . . ."[5]

Military obedience does carry that initiatory quality. Bob: "We were constantly being told what to do. You were never allowed to think for yourself. There was never a choice. It was part of trying to break you down mentally. Once they have you broken down and pliable, then they make you into who they want you to be. They want you to do what they tell you without stopping to think about it."

Ambrose: "But this discovery makes you a more limber and more adaptable person. When your pride gets battered, it turns you in on yourself in—I think—valuable ways, and brings out a maturity. The ability to take orders, even from someone that you feel is stupid, is valuable. It loosens up unnecessary stiffness in the personality. When you resist, that's when you hurt. Pain comes from resistance."

Phyllis: "You have to have a certain amount of willingness to bend. But, it taught me some things about myself and about other people that were good."

Historically, recruits enlisted in the military for "the duration" of a particular conflict. They committed themselves to causes they knew they could, with good conscience, support. But modern weapons technology requires far longer periods of training. An army can no longer be called up, trained, and fielded within a few weeks. Now, people enlist for a period of years, not knowing what conflicts may arise during their term. The military emphasis on obedience to orders remains necessarily unchanged in this changing circumstance.

Ambrose: "The point of military training is not the particular weapon that you're using at the time; the point is that you use it when you're told to."

The idea of battle, of glory, carries a certain romantic allure. Paul, whose assignment was noncombatant, holds this dream: "War is like nothing else in the world. You change, you transform by the idea of war. There is nothing else like it on the face of the world. Not martial arts training, not the Guardian Angels, nothing. From those, you go home at night. This is your life, twenty-four hours a day. And you accept it and thrive on it. You become a soldier, a Warrior, a servant of the people."

For some, it really is like that. Ambrose: "I was in South America as a mercenary soldier. I thought it was a just cause, and so I went. I still think that it was a freedom fight.

"Combat causes things that nothing else does. It's the shock of dealing with somebody that wants to kill you and the realization that you're going to have to kill them in order to live. I can't describe what that does to one very well.

"The intensity of the teamwork. Not the camaraderie, but the teamwork itself. Gung ho, in Mandarin Chinese, means working together, and that's what it is. You learn gung ho at high intensity when your life is at stake. That brings people to their maximum efficiency. The violence, the facing of death, the baptism of fire. That's what's unavailable anywhere else, and I'm glad I had that."

Others felt the same intensity of focus, the same quality of teamwork, but remember these as evil seductions. Ben: "Down south, I had to deal with killing people. It was that wonderful word, an 'insertion.' That's what a short-term conflict is called: the team is inserted into a situation. When you think about it, it's like a rape.

"We were mining a harbor . . . and we ended up hitting a couple of little bases there to make sure everything was going to go smoothly for the mining vessels . . . and we hit a refinery . . . and from what we could tell at the time and from what I suspect looking back, I think we took out a village at the same time. I think that's what really flipped me out.

"Even while I was there, I was having dreams of my grandfather saying, 'What in the hell are you doing, man?'

"But there's this kind of trance-like state in motion that you exist in, and you just follow it through until you come to the end. The one issue with all these specialty teams is 'no excuses, no retreat, you do it.' Very much like Thor, its all or nothing. You don't even question it, because you have been programmed. There's a kind of a wild cross between joy and aggression. As a natural adrenaline rush, it's incomparable. It's about as hard as a methamphetamine rush.

"Your team goes through training together, so by the time you get out of UDT school, you are set up in your team structures. That team is very much like a pack of African wild dogs. There's a commitment to the group. No matter what, you're committed to help. If somebody's a little behind, you pull them through. You do it.

"So, I managed to get through it. But the time comes when you get off the adrenaline drive. And then—I just couldn't handle it. I went into this really heavy guilt reaction. I spent the five days coming back on a ship just in a ball. I kept coming back to what had I done? What is this? Why is this? What am I doing here? This no longer is where I'm coming from. The adventure's over. This is the adventure: blood on my hands. Like Lady Macbeth, I was trying to wash the blood from my hands. It can never be done.

"I have destroyed everything I ever had from them. As far as I am concerned, I am not a vet. I was a thing. And I wish nothing to do with it. I have refused my veteran's benefits."

Only one thing distinguishes Ben's account from Ambrose's. Ambrose believes he fought in a just cause. Ben does not. And the only opinion that counts for this purpose is their own. Certainly, orders must be given and taken for any combat team to survive and prevail. And yet, we remain responsible for the consequences of our acts. A Pagan ethic still requires autonomy and personal responsibility. As many of these veterans see it, these also constitute the honor that distinguishes the soldier from the Warrior.

Ambrose: "To teach people to kill people they don't know, on the orders of someone else they don't know, in a place they have never seen before—this thing is alien from the Warrior. The Warrior does not fight for other people. The Warrior does not kill strangers unless the strangers are invading. The Warrior does not fight for national interest in other lands. The Warrior does not go to a war because he's told to go to a war."

After his term in the Air Force, Fritz actively opposed the American invasion of Vietnam. He draws a distinction: "I have never been against war. I was against that war. I never had anything against the Warrior archetype or Warrior energy. I now know that I was striving very hard to manifest archetypal Warrior energy. I sought it out in the service. I couldn't find it there. So I went and found it somewhere else.

"I have tried always to manifest the Warrior's line-drawing capacity, the ability to say, 'That's okay, and this isn't okay. It's okay to go to war against Hitler, but it's not okay to go to war against the people of Vietnam.' Draw the line and say, 'This far and no further.' Call that anti-war or anti-military if you want, but it's certainly not anti-Warrior."

As polytheists, we understand that, just as there are many ways to be Divine, there are many ways to be human. For some of us, the Warrior archetype stays in the background, lending a certain quality of boldness and determination to whatever it is we do. Others see themselves primarily as Warriors. This is their lifetime calling, their spiritual path.

Ambrose: "By the time I was 12, there were a couple of things that I knew to be true. One is that there is a war and I am a Warrior. I knew I was on that Path. It wasn't the war people around me were talking about. It wasn't World War Two. It wasn't 'the war within.' I didn't know what war it was. And I knew I am an artist—mine is a double Path. And I knew the Supreme Being to be female, and the planet to be a live being. And I felt a bond to the Earth and into the past.

"I have learned that my real war is the war against evil, or the war against some agent of evil that's responsible for the killing of this planet. It can be won, I think."

Re-entry—the failed phase

Step back again, a moment, and look at the whole term of military enlistment as a classic, three-phase initiatory experience. The first part, Basic Training, elegantly accomplishes the separation from adolescence, carrying the new recruit to the limen, the threshold at which transformation can happen. Combat training and for some the experience of combat give the neophyte an intense experience of aggression and violence. The young person discovers and defines her or his relationship with the Warrior aspect. This self-confrontation very effectively fulfills the transformation phase.

But the third phase of initiation is to return the candidate, changed, to the community, to occupy new roles and receive new status based on the new wisdom that initiatory changes have created. Only with re-integration is the initiatory process complete. And this is the moment at which the military fails. In contrast to the intense weeks of Basic, there is maybe a day, maybe two, to do paperwork and return equipment. Then, with no psychological preparation and no demarcatory ritual, the new adult civilian is back home. Each has to work out his or her own re-adjustment and re-integration, usually without guidance or support. It's never easy, and it's not always successful.

When we fail to bring our warriors back into the civilian community, we place them—and ourselves—at serious risk.

"Those who become warriors must of necessity assume a changed psychological state in order to kill the enemy and win victory. . . . After battle, the community may recognize the need to return the warrior to a new role and identity in the culture. The warrior identity must be transformed into a new identity that demands maturity and responsibility. Failure to achieve this transformation of the warrior identity may lead to alienation and the assumption of a victimized state . . ."[6]

Brett felt a loss of focus when he returned to a less structured civilian environment: "The hardest thing for me to deal with was deciding what am I going to wear? I was used to a set routine, at the Academy or on ship. I didn't have that routine anymore. Without it, without knowing what I was going to wear, and stuff like that, I've become somewhat slack in certain aspects of my life.

"I've gotten slack about the way I keep my home. If I kept my quarters at the Academy or on ship the way I keep my home—forget it! I've also gotten somewhat slack in the way I take care of myself, my body. I used to keep myself in better physical shape, exercise in some form every day.

"Some of it is that there are just so many more things that can catch my eye. I tend to spread myself thinner than I did previously. I was going through life with a bigger set of blinders."

Phyllis went all the way back home again. Faced with the old expectations and the old reinforcers, her newer self eroded: "For a while I was changed. I had more confidence in myself. No one could tell me that I couldn't do something. People couldn't act up around me. For instance, my sister and I drove cross-country with some friends. The husband and wife started to fight out in the middle of nowhere. I just got out and said, 'Now, everybody knock it off. You shut up and get in the back, and you get in the front. I'm driving.' I took charge of the situation. My sister said she didn't know it was me.

"I'm more reserved now. I wouldn't jump into an argument between a husband and wife now. I'm not sure why I lost that. I wish I hadn't. Perhaps it was because when I got out, I went back into my parents' home. I fell back into the whole pattern of being the dutiful youngest daughter. I also went right back to my old job. I had taken a military leave of absence. When you come back, they have to give you your old job back. It was like going back to square one. It might not have been a very good idea, but that's what I did.

"I think I can probably get it back if I thought real hard on it."

Paul made a premature ritual gesture of separation, and lost what was for him as a child an important symbol of adulthood: "I let my priestess convince me to chuck my dog tags. I was having real trouble integrating back into civilian life. She suggested, 'If you really want to make a break, do a symbolic magickal thing. Chuck it off of the back of the Staten Island ferry, like leaving it behind you.' I've always regretted that. I've only myself to blame for listening to her." Similarly, Tony, all alone in his new apartment, put one of his uniforms into the dumpster as an intentional symbolic statement.

A slick return to *status quo ante* did not work, and neither did a superficial gesture of separation. The transition out of military life is every bit as complex and demanding as the transition into it. The absence of any structure for making the shift makes it much harder to work through the process, but in no way lessens the need to do so. It is hard, but it can be done. It has been done.

Fritz: "When I came out of the service, I was a fire-breathing enthusiast for the military and all it stood for. Fortunately, I had some friends. One of them suggested that I go spend the winter on a Quaker communal farm in Canada. This was my real debriefing. They were all pacifists there, and they were real eager to talk with me about my military experience.

"That's when I started getting into psychological trouble. I could see that the military wasn't the solution to the world's problems, because it was hopelessly fucked up. But I thought some sort of physical power was necessary to straighten the world out. What these people did was put me on the path that it might be some sort of spiritual power that was necessary to do the job that I knew needed to be done.

"When I left there, I started my actual journey. I went around the West looking for work. I ended up in Los Angeles just in time for the world's first Peace March on Easter Day in 1961. I went from there to Berkeley, where I got recruited to go on the Freedom Ride.

"I'd learned in the military to go out and get what I wanted on my own. The military wasn't going to give it to me, but it did teach me that I could do it, myself, and so I did it. I went to Mississippi. I went to prison. I went around all the places in the South doing voter registration. I was actually for the first time being effective in a life-threatening situation, what I'd been looking for from the beginning.

"That summer of 1961 was a noticeable rite of passage. All of a sudden, I was grounded. I was rooted. It was like I had a tattoo on my forehead that said 'initiated.' I became a person that had lots and lots of friends and lots of things to do and lots of wonderful adventures. I was no longer adventureless. I no longer had to make my own adventures. I was welcomed into the society of people who were having adventures.

"That's what I wanted out of the service. I think I got it because what I learned in the service was that's not where to go for it, and I can get it myself, and here's how to do it. I came out of the service self-propelled. I came out of jail in Mississippi an initiated person, ready to go to war, which I did.

"My revolution got under way in '61, and caught fire in '63 at Berkeley. That was the year of the Free Speech Movement and all that sort of stuff. My original involvement with the movement against the Vietnam war was street theater: demonstrations in Berkeley and at the draft board in Oakland. Later, I moved up to Mendocino. There we got in touch with some Methodists who were moving draft resistors up to Canada. I helped with that for a couple of years.

"It truly took a Warrior's self-discipline to choose to stay out of the military, and to make all the moves that were necessary to get your ass to Canada. A lot of the people who set their foot on that path didn't continue because they lacked Warrior energy."

It is hard, but it can be done. Even under the most challenging of circumstances, it has been done.

Ben: "The military expects you to perform. And they give you all the training you need to perform. But when your term is up, they don't deprogram you. When you're dumped out, that's part of the problem. You get all this really weird, nasty shit that just goes through your system. Someone just may trigger it, and you lash out. Just like a wild dog.

"It got so at least I learned not to go to bars. I'd rub up against some working-class character and there'd be a scuffle, and people would be hurt. Who needs all the hot water and the chats with the cops? In recon, special forces, UDT, the Seals, two-thirds of the guys that go through it come out psychically wounded.

"I went back to school, spent two years failing as a human being there, feeling un-human, or like a troglodyte or something. Isolated and not clean—spiritually just filthy. I realized I couldn't go on. I was tired of not being around people, having people not want me to be around. What am I going to do about this? Am I going to go through it all my life, or is there something I can do about it?

"You could talk about some kind of shamanistic experience where that person was left behind. You can use the image of the snake shedding its skin. This shedding of skin took five or six years. I kind of walked into being somebody else. I feel much better every day now. It's probably still ongoing. Only recently now I want some bits and pieces back from the warrior that I was before.

"I got into the Navy because it was a great lovely game. I think a lot of people all had the same mindset. We make absolutely horrible, terrible mistakes in our lives. That's what this was. And then, here we are. This is where it's at. You're in crisis, and you've got to turn it around. Either the lever's going to break or the rock's going to move. I guess I was lucky—the rock moved.

"In a lot of ways, you're just a kid until you get to a decision like this in life. And then, here's your initiation to adulthood. I may find out as I go through all this that what happened to me back then may have just been a key crisis in my life where I was forced to make a decision on my humanity. Can I just go through life sliding and not making a decision?"

We are the civilian religious community to which Pagan veterans return with their initiations often so painfully incomplete. Our job starts here. We can and should provide spiritual counseling and ritual services to mark the process of rein-tegration. As Paul's experience shows, this cannot be a one-shot ritual, no matter how beautifully designed. Rather, we need to organize peer support groups, perhaps facilitated by elder veteran peer-counselors, in which veterans can face and work through their bad memories, assess and celebrate their learning and growth, and assist each other to relearn civilian lifeways. Following the Native American model, larger rituals should mark when such a group begins and ends its work. This demon-strates to veterans that their families, covens and community respect them and support their efforts.

They will not be returning to us unchanged—to expect they would is foolish and destructive. For our own benefit as well as theirs, this needs to be recognized with new roles and status for returning veterans. Those who have learned that their life lies along the Warrior path are already in places taking on the role of providing security at our gatherings. Others may use their new-learned ability to function under stress as public spokespersons. Many will want to advise younger people about what the military experience might mean for them.

Many of us are not veterans, but still want to help. The advice the veterans give us about how best to be helpful is simple and common sense. Don't rush them. Don't pry. Listen. Don't judge. Whatever they did, you've never walked in those shoes.

Ben: "They have to do it in their time, and not in anybody else's. Just be absolutely supportive. They're going to go through a lot of stuff. You can't stop anybody from doing anything, but just stand by them. Give them a lot of room. If they're feeling dirty, all you can do is just wait for them to open. Make sure everybody in the community is there to catch them when they fall."

Ambrose: "When they come back, don't ask them what they did. Don't ask them what it was like. Let them talk, be prepared to listen, but don't probe. Let them pace it."

Ben: "Make it absolutely clear that, whatever has happened, that they're okay, that they're part of the community. They're a good person, even if they've gone through all this.

"You look at the Vietnam experiences. The guys were already coming back guilty. Telling them that they're a rotten dirty shit just doesn't help either. Then they're not even accepted back into their communities, and then they're lost. You see so many of them lost and on the street."

Informed consent—how shall we advise the young?

Some of you reading this may be thinking about entering the military. What advice would I give you? Others may be parents of teenagers, or relating to teens as priest/esses, teachers, elder friends. What advice would we offer them? I don't believe we can just tell them "go," or "don't go." As Pagans, we believe that the choice and the responsibility rest with them. And if we have raised them well, to be autonomous and self-responsible, they wouldn't listen. As trusted elders, all we can do is to guide them through a decision-making process. It starts with being sure they have a realistic picture of what to expect.

Ben, on the basis of his civilian skills, was promised assignment as a diving instructor. After his name was on the line, his assignment was changed. He says: "When somebody is contemplating the decision, be completely honest with them. Recruiters are never going to tell you the whole truth because they are in need. So they're going to paint a very rosy picture of the situation.

"Make sure they know that whatever is put on that paper isn't worth the stuff that comes off the round tube beside the toilet. An enlisted man is nothing but a piece of meat. They own your ass. They really own your ass, no ifs, ands, or buts about it. If you're willing to accept that, okay. You have no power, absolutely none."

After the reality check comes the ethical check. When this country had a draft, those who sought Conscientious Objector status were required to write an essay defining the religious and philosophical reasons for which they declined to participate in the military. That was a fair requirement, as far as it went. The problem was that it carried a built-in assumption that whoever could not give a good reason against it would enter the military.

But joining the military is not trivial. All who do will undergo a severe and serious initiatory process. Some will later be commanded to kill or die on somebody else's say-so. Wouldn't it be wiser to ask all youngsters, regardless of whether they do or do not enlist, to write an essay outlining the pros and cons, and giving the reasons for their choice?

Writing such an essay, clarifying their thoughts and feelings, would also be, for all of them, a step into maturity.

Ambrose: "In primitive society, the young are not presented with a choice about initiations or rites of passage. In our society, the decision is a phase. It is part of the initiation."

From a Pagan standpoint, what they finally decide is far less important than that the decision be made with full knowledge and full consideration, Fritz: "Life's a dance. Your dance may take you to Canada, or to a grave in the sand. It may also take you to the war and safely back. You have a lot of choice about what your dance is, but don't make any moves without thinking them over real carefully. Sometimes, if you're going to be a Warrior, the right thing to do is to go to war. And sometimes, if you're going to be a Warrior, the right thing to do is to stay away from a war. The best way to find out is to find out as much as you can about the war, because all wars are not the same. Go do your dance, but do it mindfully."

Ambrose: "If anyone were asking me what should they do, and they're 17, I would recommend the military training experience without a war. However, there is that risk. There hasn't been a war since World War Two that in my opinion was right, that anyone should have gone in. And I see nothing coming up either. There's no threat to this country from another country."

Because modern military enlistment is for a term of years, I believe all potential recruits who take responsibility for their choices and actions ought to research current world affairs and American foreign policy. There's still a lot of disagreement about various recent incursions, so let's use the genocidal Indian Wars of the last century to demonstrate that our country is not morally infallible. Pagans, who do not give oath lightly, need to look before they leap. Although no one can predict events perfectly, recruits should be satisfied that in any reasonably predictable conflict, the American military will fight on the side that they feel is just.

The risk of being caught between your conscience and your given oath can be minimized, but it can never be completely eliminated. Fritz: "Almost anything worthwhile requires some sort of time commitment and some sort of release of authority to an Other. This may be a real initiator or a false initiator. There's almost no way to tell except through the experience. So signing up for a military term, knowing full well that during that period you may be ordered to do something against your conscience, is entering a potentially initiating situation."

Ben's story, like so many others, shows that killing people in violation of your own conscience puts your very sanity and soul at risk. This is the final, awful, possibility that faces every member of the military. No young person should enlist without at least acknowledging this risk, and considering what his or her response might be.

Let the last word come from Ambrose: "If I were talking to a person, I would begin with what the military does for them, and see whether they could get that anywhere else these days. If they could find it somewhere else, they should. It's a prickly decision."

Taken at face value, that sounds like an anti-military statement. But I say much the same thing to young seekers after Wiccan initiation. "Don't do this unless you have to." It's the advice of initiates to seekers on all Paths, in all lands, at all times.

Suggestions for further reading

On initiation

Eliade, Mircea. *Rites and Symbols of Initiation: The Mysteries of Birth and Rebirth*, New York: Harper, 1958.

Mahdi, Louise Carus, Steven Foster, and Meredith Little, eds. *Betwixt and Between: Patterns of Masculine and Feminine Initiation*. LaSalle, Illinois: Open Court, 1987.

Raphael, Ray. *The Men from the Boys: Rites of Passage in Male America*. Lincoln, Nebraska: University of Nebraska Press, 1988.

On the Warrior archetype

Bly, Robert. *Iron John: A Book About Men*. New York: Addison-Wesley, 1990.

de Vries, Jan. *Heroic Song and Heroic Legend*. Oxford: Oxford University Press, 1963.

Gilmore, David D. *Manhood in the Making: Cultural Concepts of Masculinity*. New Haven: Yale University Press, 1990.

Moore, Robert, and Douglas Gilette. *King Warrior Magician Lover: Rediscovering the Archetypes of the Mature Masculine*. San Francisco: Harper, 1990.

Pearson, Carol S. *Awakening the Heroes Within*. San Francisco: Harper, 1991.

On return to civilian life

Imber-Black, Evan, Janine Roberts, and Richard Whiting, eds. *Rituals in Families and Family Therapy*. New York: Norton, 1988 (especially Section 1: "Defining and Designing Rituals").

Krippner, Stanley, and Benjamin Colodzin, "Multi-Cultural Methods of Treating Vietnam Veterans with Post-Traumatic Stress Disorder." *International Journal of Psychosomatics* 36 (1989): 79–85.

Metzer, Deena, "Re-Vamping the World: On the Rebirth of the Holy Prostitute," in Zweig, Connie, ed. *To Be a Woman: The Birth of the Conscious Feminine*, Los Angeles: Tarcher, 1990.

Wilson, John P. *Trauma, Transformation, and Healing: An Integrative Approach to Theory, Research, and Post-Traumatic Therapy*. New York: Brunner-Mazel, 1989.

Acknowledgement

Special thanks to Fred Lerner—"Fred the librarian"—for helping me find many of these resources and for every much else—JH

Notes

1   Mircea Eliade, *Rites and Symbols of Initiation*, (New York: Harper & Row, 1975), x.

2   Victor Turner, "Betwixt and Between: The Liminal Period in Rites of Passage" in Louise Carus Mahdi, Steven Foster, and Meredith Little, eds. *Betwixt and Between: Patterns of Masculine and Feminine Initiation*, (LaSalle, Illinois: Open Court, 1987), 5.

3   Fred R. Gustafson, "Fathers, Sons and Brotherhood" in Mahdi, *et al.*, 170.

4   *Covenant of the Goddess Newsletter*, 16:2, (Imbolc, 1991).

5   Turner, 9–11.

6   John P. Wilson, "Culture and Trauma: The Sacred Pipe Revisited," in John P. Wilson, *Trauma, Transformation, and Healing* (New York: Brunner-Mazel, 1989), 42.

Chapter 30

Tony Kelly

PAGAN MUSINGS

■ first published in **THE WAXING MOON** under the title 'Pagan Movement', 1971

I N THE LATE 1960S and early 1970s, Gardnerian Wicca, which required that a candidate be formally instructed and initiated, was the best-known face of the Pagan revival. Its very visibility, in fact, helped to bring in new seekers who, in turn, could not always locate a coven to train them. In response, in 1969 several British and American witches from different traditions created a set of "outer court" training rituals for new Pagans. The Pagan Way (Kelly, 1994) was envisioned as an accessible form of Paganism with no membership requirements. In a sense, it was a predecessor of the later Pagan Front and Pagan Federation.

One of the Pagan's Way's founders was the poet Tony Kelly, author of the essay "Pagan Musings." Others were Ed Fitch, Joseph Wilson, Thomas Giles, Fred and Martha Adler, John Score (known as "M," editor of the British newsletter *The Wiccan*), and the American journalist Susan Roberts, author of *Witches U.S.A.* (1971). Spread from California to England, they rarely met face to face but formed a "committee of correspondence."

Kelly at the time lived in the Selene Community in Wales, an "intentional community" which, among other activities, produced *The Communes Journal*. His own utopian vision had a distinct Pagan cast: "We must create a Pagan society wherein everyone shall be free to worship the goddesses and gods of nature." As a manifesto of the growing Pagan revival, "Pagan Musings" was widely circulated in the 1970s and subsequently reprinted in small journals; and it now may be found in numerous locations on the World Wide Web.

Chas S. Clifton

References

Kelly, Aidan (1994) "The people of the woods: Some history of the Pagan Way tradition," http://www.oldways.org/paganway.html (accessed 29 December 2002).
Roberts, Susan (1971) *Witches U.S.A.* New York: Dell.

W E ' R E   O F   T H E   O L D   R E L I G I O N , sired of Time, and born of our beloved Earth Mother. For too long the people have trodden a stony path that goes only onward beneath a sky that goes only upwards. The Horned God plays in a lonely glade for the people are scattered in this barren age and the winds carry his plaintive notes over deserted heaths and reedy moors and into the lonely grasses. Who know now the ancient tongue of the Moon? And who speaks still with the Goddess? The magic of the land of Lirien and the old pagan gods have withered in the dragon's breath; the old ways of magic have slipped into the well of the past, and only the rocks now remember what the moon told us long ago, and what we learned from the trees, and the voices of grasses and the scents of flowers.

We're pagans and we worship the pagan gods, and among the people there are witches yet who speak with the moon and dance with the Horned One. But a witch is a rare pagan in these days, deep and inscrutable, recognizable only by her own kind, by the light in her eyes and the love in her breast, by the magic in her hands and the lilt of her tongue and by her knowledge of the real. But the wiccan way is one way. There are many; there are pagans the world over who worship the Earth Mother and the Sky Father, the Rain God and the Rainbow Goddess, the Dark One and the Hag on the mountain, the Moon Goddess and the Little People in the mists on the other side of the veil. A pagan is one who worships the goddesses and gods of nature, whether by observation or by study, whether by love or admiration, or whether in their sacred rites with the Moon, or the great festivals of the Sun.

Many suns ago, as the pale dawn of reason crept across the pagan sky, man grew out of believing in the gods. He has yet to grow out disbelieving in them. He who splits the Goddess on an existence-nonexistence dichotomy will earn himself only paradoxes, for the gods are not so divided and nor the magic lands of the Brother of Time. Does a mind exist? Ask her and she will tell you yes, but seek her out, and she'll elude you. She is in every place, and in no place, and you'll see her works in all places, but herself in none. Existence was the second-born from the Mother's womb and contains neither the first-born, nor the unborn. Show us your mind, and we'll show you the gods! No matter that you can't, for we can't show you the gods. But come with us and the Goddess herself will be our love and the God will call the tune. But a brass penny for your reason; for logic is a closed ring, and the child doesn't validate the Mother, nor the dream the dreamer. And what matter the wars of opposites to she who has fallen in love with a whirlwind or to the lover of the arching rainbow.

But tell us of your Goddess as you love her, and the gods that guide your works, and we'll listen with wonder, for to do less would be arrogant. But we'll do more, for the heart of man is aching for memories only half forgotten, and the Old Ones only half unseen. We'll write the old myths as they were always written and we'll read them on the rocks and in the caves and in the deep of the greenwood's shade, and we'll hear them in the rippling mountain streams and in the rustling of the leaves, and we'll see them in the storm clouds, and in the evening mists. We've no wish to create a new religion for our religion is as old as the hills and older, and we've no wish to bring differences together. Differences are like different flowers in a meadow, and we are all one in the Mother.

What need is there for a pagan movement since our religion has no teachings and we hear it in the wind and feel it in the stones and the Moon will dance with us as she will? There is a need. For long the Divider has been among our people and the tribes of man are no more. The sons of the Sky Father have all but conquered nature, but they have poisoned her breast and the Mother is sad for the butterflies are dying and the night draws on. A curse on the conqueror! But not of us, for they curse themselves for they are nature too. They have stolen our magic and sold it to the mindbenders and the mindbenders tramp a maze that has no outlet for they fear the real for the One who guards the path.

Where are the pagan shrines? And where do the people gather? Where is the magic made? And where are the Goddess and the Old Ones? Our shrines are in the fields and on the mountains, in the stars and in the wind, deep in the greenwood and on the algal rocks where two streams meet. But the shrines are deserted, and if we gathered in the arms of the Moon for our ancient rites to be with our gods as we were of old, we would be stopped by the dead who now rule the Mother's land and claim rights of ownership on the Mother's breast, and make laws of division and frustration for us. We can no longer gather with our gods in a public place and the old rites of communion have been driven from the towns and cities ever deeper into the heath where barely a handful of heathens have remained to guard the old secrets and enact the old rites. There is magic in the heath far from the cold grey society, and there are islands of magic hidden in the entrails of the metropolis behind closed doors, but the people are few, and the barriers between us are formidable. The old religion has become a dark way, obscure, and hidden in the protective bosom of the night. Thin fingers turn the pages of a book of shadows while the sunshine seeks in vain his worshippers in his leafy glades.

Here, then, is the basic reason for a Pagan Movement; we must create a pagan society wherein everyone shall be free to worship the goddesses and gods of nature, and the relationship between a worshipper and her gods shall be sacred and inviolable, provided only that in her love of her own gods, she doesn't curse the names of the gods of others.

It's not yet our business to press the law-makers with undivided endeavor to unmake the laws of repression and, with the Mother's love, it may never become our business for the stifling tides of dogmatism are at last already in ebb. Our first work, and our greatest wish, is to come together, to be with each other in our tribes for we haven't yet grown from the Mother's breast to the stature of the gods. We're of the earth, and sibs to all the children of wild nature, born long ago in the warm mud of the ocean floor; we were together then, and we were together in the rain forests long before that dark day when, beguiled by the pride of the Sky Father, and forgetful of the Mother's love, we killed her earlier-born children and impoverished the old genetic pool. The Red child lives yet in America; the Black Child has not forsaken the gods; the old Australians are still with their nature gods; the Old Ones still live deep in the heart of Mother India, and the White Child has still a foot on the old wiccan way, but Neanderthaler is no more and her magic faded as the Lli and the Archan burst their banks and the ocean flowed in to divide the Isle of Erin from the land of the White Goddess.

Man looked with one eye on a two-faced god when he reached for the heavens and scorned the Earth which alone is our life and our provider and the bosom to which we have ever returned since the dawn of Time. He who looks only to reason to plum the unfathomable is a fool, for logic is an echo already implicit in the question, and it has no voice of its own; but he is no greater fool than he who scorns logic or derides its impotence from afar, but fears to engage in fair combat when he stands on his opponent's threshold. Don't turn your back on Reason, for his thrust is deadly; but confound him and he'll yield for his code of combat is honorable. so here is more of the work of the Pagan Movement. Our lore has become encrusted over the ages with occult trivia and the empty vapourings of the lost. The occult arts are in a state of extreme decadence, astrology is in a state of disrepute and fears to confront the statistician's sword; alien creeds oust our native arts and, being as little understood as our own forgotten arts, are just as futile for their lack of understanding, and more so for their unfamiliarity. Misunderstanding is rife. Disbelief is black on every horizon, and vampires abound on the blood of the credulous. Our work is to reject the trivial, the irrelevant and the erroneous, and to bring the lost children of the Earth Mother again into the court of the Sky Father where reason alone will avail. Belief is the deceit of the credulous; it has no place in the heart of a pagan.

But while we are sad for those who are bemused by Reason, we are deadened by those who see no further than his syllogisms as he turns the eternal wheel of the Great Tautology. We were not fashioned in the mathematician's computations, and we were old when the first alchemist was a child. We have walked in the magic forest, bewitched in the old Green Thinks; we have seen the cauldron and the one become many and the many in the one; we know the Silver Maid of the moonlight and the sounds of the cloven feet. We have heard the pipes on the twilight ferns, and we've seen the spells of the enchantress, and Time be stilled. We've been into eternal darkness where the Night Mare rides and rode her to the edge of the Abyss, and beyond, and we know the dark face of the Rising Sun. Spin a spell or words and make a magic knot; spin it on the magic loom and spin it with the gods. Say it in the old chant and say it to the Goddess, and in her name. Say it to a dark well and breathe it on a stone. There are no signposts on the untrod way, but we'll make our rituals together and bring them as our gifts to the Goddess and her God in the great rites. Here, then, is our work in the Pagan Movement; to make magic in the name of our gods, to share our magic where the gods would wish it, and to come together in our ancient festivals of birth, and life, of death and of change in the old rhythm. Well print the rituals that can be shared in the written work; we'll do all in our power to bring the people together, to teach those who would learn, and to learn from those who can teach. We will initiate groups, bring people to groups, and groups to other groups in our common devotion to the goddess and gods of nature. We will not storm the secrets of any coven, nor profane the tools, the magic, and still less, the gods of another.

We'll collect the myths of the ages, of our people and of the pagans of other lands, and we'll study the books of the wise and we'll talk to the very young. And whatever the pagan needs in her study, or her worship, then it is our concern, and the Movement's business to do everything possible to help each other in our worship of the gods we love.

We are committed with the lone pagan on the seashore, with he who worships in the fastness of a mountain range or she who sings the old chant in a lost valley far from the metalloid road. We are committed with the wanderer, and equally with the prisoner, disinherited from the Mother's milk in the darkness of the industrial webs. We are committed too with the coven, with the circular dance in the light of the full moon, with the great festivals of the sun, and with the gatherings of the people. We are committed to build our temples in the towns and in the wilderness, to buy the lands and the streams from the landowners and give them to the Goddess for her children's use, and we'll replant the greenwood as it was of old for love of the dryad stillness, and for love of our children's children.

When the streams flow clear and the winds blow pure, and the sun never more rises unrenowned nor the moon ride in the skies unloved; when the stones tell of the Horned God and the greenwood grows deep to call back her own ones, then our work will be ended and the Pagan Movement will return to the beloved womb of our old religion, to the nature goddesses and gods of paganism.

Chapter 31

Asphodel Long

THE GODDESS MOVEMENT IN BRITAIN TODAY

■ from **FEMINIST THEOLOGY** (1994) 5: 11–39

IT IS SOMETIMES HARD to place Goddess Spirituality. Is it a Pagan movement or a Jewish one, or a post-Christian one? Is it something unique or is it a bridge between existing religious possibilities? Perhaps it allows women and men who are neither entirely satisfied nor completely dissatisfied with their existing religion to stay while attempting to effect change in themselves and others. Certainly, the movement is a diverse one, and much of it is explicitly Pagan. Asphodel Long has been an important member (activist, writer, teacher and devotee) for many years and is greatly and deservedly respected.

Her chapter surveys the origins, nature and state of the Goddess Movement in contemporary Britain. Written in the early 1990s, it provides a valuable insight into the important matters then and now. It demonstrates the plurality of understandings of 'the Goddess' within the movement (and much the same could be said for other Paganisms), the diversity of motivations, experiences and future-visions. It tackles the question of essentialism, refers to a number of similarly important writers and artists, and cites ancient literature and contemporary women's experiences as authorities.

Asphodel Long is the author of *In a Chariot Drawn by Lions: The Search for the Female in Deity* (London: Women's Press, 1992). Her website (http://www.asphodel-long.com) includes or refers to more of her important work, including 'The One and the Many . . .'. In addition to the literature cited in the article, Carol P. Christ (1998, 2003) is highly significant.

Graham Harvey

References

Christ, Carol P. (1998) *Rebirth of the Goddess*. London: Routledge.
Christ, Carol P. (2003) *She Who Changes*. New York: Palgrave/St. Martin's Press.
Long, Asphodel (1992) *In a Chariot Drawn by Lions: The Search for the Female in Deity*. London: Women's Press.

Introduction

A RECENT PROPOSITION THAT we have reached 'the end of history'[1] has been widely nodded through. Fukuyama suggested that with the collapse of Communism in Eastern Europe and the former Soviet Union, there is no longer any real confrontation of ideas—in the West at least.

My suggestion is that this overlooks a growing philosophy that is attracting more and more interest, one that poses as fundamental a challenge to established ways of thought and action, to methods of living and relationships between individuals, as did the very different assaults from Marxism–Leninism.

Socialism and Communism based their theories on an economic view of society, but made it clear that a substantial trickle-down effect to the realm of ethics and morality was their theoretical justification.[2]

Indeed those ethics and that morality—the hope of a world family that could live in peace, justice and equality—took the place of religion during this century for millions of the world's disadvantaged, as well as of its leading thinkers and activists. It became, in fact 'the soul of soulless nations, and the heart of heartless people'.[3]

Because of the power of this dream, many today still cling to the out-moded Marxist concepts, despite the proof of their total disintegration in practice.

The new philosophy, which I propose to discuss in some detail, is that of spiritual feminism. This understands that a major cause of the failure of the socialist aspiration is the banishment of a spiritual dimension; but it is important to emphasize that such feminism does not seek merely to introduce a novel or renewed religious faith or practice. Rather, it gives due weight to the religious factor, which it sees as fundamental to all aspects of the human being in society. The world-view which it seeks to replace has been grounded in religions as they have been expounded and practiced—a world-view that supports male dominance in every sector of human life, and relies on tradition and texts which until today have disseminated this belief.

Spiritual feminism declares that this is a false picture; that in both human and divine terms the female is as much the norm as the male. Women's needs and opinions therefore are as valuable as men's. Women's values, where different from men's need adequate expression and action. Above all, the history and religions that have inflicted the traditional viewpoint of the contrary case are deficient and need correction.

This form of feminism differs from the classic types in that it places the onus for change in society, firmly on the recognition of the spiritual as a major element, and claims for women a right to their autonomous spirituality, not mediated through men's views and actions. The result of this change of thinking can spread into every sector of social and political action, as well as into intellectual endeavour and human relationships. It even spins off into the newly appreciated need for the world's peoples to change their methods of living on this planet.

Such spiritual feminism is commonly tagged as something to do with 'the Goddess', and I propose to discuss various aspects of this perception, as I have understood them. It is important at this point to state that there is no consensus, no credo and what I write is from my own experience. Indeed part of the 'Goddess philosophy' is the autonomy of each individual's thinking and religious faith and practice.

It is my own part in and knowledge of the Goddess movement in Britain over the period of the last eighteen years which has led me to assess the general phenomenon in the way in which I introduced this paper. Much has been written elsewhere of the US picture. I shall only refer to that as it affects my own experience and perceptions.

Who or what is the Goddess?

> Blessed Queen of Heaven . . . you who wander through many sacred groves and are propitiated with many different rites . . . I beseech you, by whatever name in whatever aspect . . . you deign to be invoked . . .
>
> Apuleius[4]

One of the heritages of monotheism is enthusiasm for a supreme deity. This is particularly exhibited by researchers into 'other' religions by anthropologists, ethnographers and the like, even where practical evidence indicates that the many names and varying characteristics of deities in the religions studied can easily mean that the question of the 'One' does not arise. The same difficulty arises when we come to look at today's 'Goddess' phenomenon. Those outside it, and certainly many who first approach it are in a sense conditioned to seek for the One and only, and to take for granted the term 'the Goddess' must mean a female equivalent of the traditional God of Judaism, Christianity and Islam. In fact, 'the Goddess' is a shorthand term for a much more varied set of concepts, which I will try and describe as I have experienced their development in Britain. I see that they come from three major sources:

(a)   the feminist movement itself;
(b)   paganism or neo-paganism to which can be connected New Age thinking;
(c)   forms relating to Judaism and Christianity.

First, the Goddess as she has developed in feminist thinking in the UK. I have written accounts of this subject at various times, and will summarize here. The Matriarchy Study Group, London, which I joined as a founder member, in London in 1975 started as an offshoot of the London Women's Liberation Movement. I remember a notice in the newsletter put out from the Women's Liberation Movement's then headquarters near London's Leicester Square. This had stated that the group would question the assumption that God had always been perceived and addressed as a male (Lord, Father, King, Son, etc.), no matter how often it was stressed that God is beyond gender. It denied the current thinking that women had always been 'the subordinate sex' and linked this thinking to perception of the female in divinity. Basically it set out to research this area in as scholarly a way as possible.

The Matriarchy Study Group published a number of pamphlets and magazines setting out the results of each women's research. The editorial in the first of these 'Goddess Shrew' (1977) set out our thinking of that time:

(a) 'There was a time when society was organized on the basis of a woman-led culture. The Goddess was worshipped not only in terms of fertility and survival, but as a way of life in which the feminine and the female were considered preeminent. Great civilisations were built on these cultures.

(b) We do not wish merely to contemplate the past. Our aim of understanding the past is to influence the present. We see the part that male-based religion has played in demeaning and exploiting women. In exposing this, we want to share our regained confidence in ourselves with other women . . .

(c) Further, we see that such control of the spirit as well as of our bodies will extend the possibility of change in society . . . we move from the importance of feminist social demands to total re-appraisal of patriarchy in politics generally.'

It will be seen that the question of defining 'the Goddess' did not arise. The Goddess to our thinking then, and in the thinking of our respondents, was the perception that the divine could be female—and consequently women too could be part of or represent in some way the divine. Further it was part of the excitement that not only did we wish this to be the case, there was ample evidence to argue that for long periods of the past, this was actually accepted as the case. In some ways the terms 'the Goddess' was a synonym for a woman with newly regained self-worth. 'I am in the image of the divine; I am acknowledged. I have, all this time been told a lie. I am not—and never was—inferior, subordinate.' This was the thinking. Later one woman summed it up for me: coming across and reading this and similar material was, she said 'like a pinhole in the darkness'.

Eventually, and in the other areas, as we shall see, the thealogy[5] of the Goddess became more important. But not only at that time, but ever since and up until today, the work I do in adult education, women's workshops and the like evokes a similar response among women who are at the introductory stage of the subject.

What is *not* important to them is whether the Goddess is a supreme deity, or is one deity. In fact the question arises only after some time, when people are well advanced into Goddess culture and action and are interested in debate on the subject. It actually bothers very few seekers in terms of definition.

While this is still the case, a similar comprehension of 'the Goddess' was described in the early days of the movement by two US writers—Carol Christ and Merlin Stone.[6] In the keynote address at the University of California conference on 'The Great Goddess Re-Emerging', spring 1978, Carol Christ's reflections on 'Why Women Need the Goddess' became part of the received theory. She started by quoting the famous sentence from Ntoshange's play 'For Coloured Girls who Have Considered Suicide when the Rainbow is Enuf': 'I found God in myself and I loved her fiercely'. She comments that the speaker is saying that the divine principle, the saving and sustaining power is in herself, and she will no longer look to men or male figures as saviours (p. 277). Carol discusses whether the Goddess is only within ourselves or is also 'out there'. Three major answers are discussed. They comprise:

(1)   the belief that 'the Goddess is a divine female, a personification who can be invoked in prayer and ritual;
(2)   the Goddess is a symbol of life, death and rebirth energy . . .
(3)   the Goddess is a symbol of the affirmation and beauty of female power' (p. 278)

Further, the Goddess is to be recognized in many aspects of female life, which have been denigrated—menstruation, childbirth, etc. This essay has a profound effect in Britain since it summed up, for many, the ideas and feeling that were so powerful but for which no real discipline had been discovered. Merlin Stone, also at the same conference, set out her three aspects of Goddess spirituality. The feminist movement's acceptance of the Goddess is motivated, she wrote 'by much the same feeling that has encouraged us to rediscover and reclaim female artists, writers, scientists, political leaders . . . affording us . . . a broader view . . . a perspective which allows us to look into the past to see further ahead' (p. 2). Next, because of this, women can 'confront the many tangible and material issues of the blatant inequalities of society as we know it today', while thirdly, a Goddess viewpoint allows us to examine specific ways in which male religions have a maintained a subordinate status for women and helps us to challenge this. It will be seen from both these authors that the question of exactly 'who' is the Goddess was hardly addressed. Much more important was the effect of such a concept on women themselves.

However, in Britain, one woman did take up this problem and has had a powerful effect on the movement here. Monica Sjoo,[7] a Swedish artist who settled in Britain, has written widely, as well as exhibiting major paintings on the subject. An early pamphlet—a precursor of a book to be written with US poet Barbara Mor and published fifteen years or so later—states her position. The Goddess is the Greatest Cosmic Mother of All, from her womb the universe was created.

Monica's view is that creation and creativity spring from the woman who is herself a representative of the Mother Goddess, who is both light and dark and whose motherhood is essential to her status. She also emphasizes that the 'rebirth of the Goddess' is also about the renewal of women's own creativity and powers. This period of the Goddess movement in Britain has been covered in depth by Ursula King who also notes my own dissent from Monica's views on the identification of the Goddess and creativity totally with motherhood.

In the meantime, the Matriarchy Study Group produced two more publications, one a full-scale journal entitled *Politics of Matriarchy*[8] and in the same year a pamphlet called *Menstrual Taboos*. The former ranged widely over prehistory, for example, goddesses in Crete and Anatolia, but concentrated more particularly on the effect of Goddess understanding or 'matriarchy' on the lives of women today. In particular, major articles on women's sexuality and a 'matriarchal manifesto' set out the full-scale change of values in ways of living and being together that were involved.

It became clear here, and this understanding was replicated widely elsewhere that the question 'Who or What is the Goddess' did not particularly refer to any entity, being, concept, personification or Greater Being 'out there' somewhere.

Rather, it specifically brought forward a complex of ideas centred on an identification of women's lives and received values with something 'more', something 'divine', which was understood as 'The Goddess'. Further, such a view of 'The Goddess' could be attached to any known names of goddesses, and as study and research proceeded, it could be seen that some goddesses in the known past could be related to specific aspects of life.

Increasingly, women began to feel that not only were there goddesses 'out there', but the concept of 'the Goddess within' was immensely important. She was us and we were Her. My own formulation over a long period has been 'In raising Her we raise ourselves; in raising ourselves, we raise Her'.

After a time it became clear that the major groupings of Goddess research and understanding could be categorized. For example, the following list provided a start:

> The Lady of the Beasts/Mistress of Nature
> The Triple Goddess/The Moon/The Fourth Aspect
> The Goddess and sexuality
> The Goddess and the landscape/Sacred sites
> The Goddess and the Bible/Judaism, Christianity
> The Goddess in literature
> The Goddess in cultures other than those based on Judaism and Christianity including contemporary forms, for example, some Native American religions, South American Indian, etc.

There were other categories: in *Politics of Matriarchy*, for example, one writer from New Zealand gave an account of the Goddess in contemporary Maori culture as she had experienced it.[9]

Obviously it is impossible in this space to describe this work in any detail but since that time a great number of books have been published (see selected list at end) and on the whole, although they come from diverse sources, much of the understanding is similar. All I can do here is point to the various threads that build up the Goddess web that continues to inspire more and more women.

> As Mistress of Nature and Lady of the Beasts, the Goddess is . . . well-
>   founded earth, mother of all,
> eldest of all beings, she feeds all creatures that are in the world . . .[10]

The study group agreed with M.J. Vermaseren who continues 'The Earth Goddess encompasses the mystery of every woman. The Goddess is the beginning and end of all life on earth' (Vermaseren 1977, p.10). She is identified with wild beasts, particularly lions and leopards while the bull is her special creature dedicated to her service. His survey emphasizes the power of this Goddess religion in its appeal to women.

Elsewhere goddesses were portrayed sometimes as human women, sometimes as women with animal characteristics. One of the latter, native to Britain, can be seen in the Colchester Museum, Essex, where a strong woman with many breasts has her lower part as a lioness, and she has the wings of an eagle. She is holding in her (human) arms the head of a dead soldier. We are entitled to infer from looking at this sphinx that the female is proud and dignified, symbolized by the royal beasts; she is not distinct from the animal creation, but part of it, as is her human form; she nurtures the living with her many breasts, and she cares for the dead.

In triple forms the Goddess relates to the phases of the moon. The new and young moon are seen to be her 'maiden' mode and perhaps linked with Artemis, Kore (Persephone). The full moon, the celebrant of life is Aphrodite; her waning form, is Hecate in touch with the mysteries of age, death and hereafter. However it is pointed out strongly that these three aspects are parts of each other and not separate. Kore becomes Queen of the Underworld, and interchanges with Hecate, for example. We are warned that when we meet Aphrodite, when we start a new love affair, for example, we are to remember her sisters, the autonomous women who will not be cowed by men, and the wise woman who knows the beginnings and the end of all things.

The fourth aspect relates to the dark moon: what happens then? Some point to anger and rage, some depression, some to the role of darkness in creativity. For myself, I usually find the need to emphasize that the dark of the moon is a phase, and that when we women go into depression or despair, as so many have done and still do, we are entitled to remember that we are aligning with the moon itself, who withdraws from view and her light is not seen for a while. But we must remember that the new moon will rise and that we will shine with it.

To indicate metaphors within other major aspects of Goddess understanding, it seems that the best way is to imagine a picture of a standing woman. At her feet is the earth, from which comes renewal, but which we as human beings have exploited and polluted almost to disaster. For too long, religion denied the earth any identification with the divine. To resacralize the 'material', the ground on which the mother-mater stands will surely indicate how different must be our approach both as individuals, communities and societies. The Goddess was researched in the landscape, in the form of 'sacred sites' and standing stones where it is believed she was venerated—for example at Avebury, Silbury Hill, Glastonbury, Bath, etc; some women have formed groups to endeavour to protect such sites from exploitation and misuse, or she is felt to be in the landscape in the changing of the seasons, which are marked with seasonal rituals (see below). At the feet of this imaginary female, in addition, we can postulate our physicality and perceive it as part of the divine, our bodies, no longer 'dirty', our menstrual cycle no longer a 'curse'. Rites-of-passage for childbirth, menarche and menopause are instituted. Sexuality is understood as a celebration of life, and has inherent sacrality. Since much evidence from the past shows that sexuality was much freer in prepatriarchal societies, this aspect is taken up joyfully, but within sacred confines. Lesbian and bisexual spirituality grow naturally within this concept. One of my own observations over the long period I have been working in Goddess terms is that our groups are among the few where women of different sexuality find little difficulty in working together (see section on Lesbian sexuality below).

Perhaps at this point I should say formally that there is total disagreement with the conventional view that the goddesses signify fertility only. Restoring sacrality to sexuality does not mean restricting it in this way.

If we move from the feet to the head of the woman we are looking at, and to the heart, we can seek out the Goddess of Wisdom, Lady of Intelligence and Insight.

In doing this we can attempt to reclaim our intellects as well as spiritual and physical needs from intervention by patriarchal concepts.[11] This is a vast area that covers feminist research in biblical and related texts, its aim being to regain and restore some female presence, and to understand what has been obscured. One current aspiration is to build up a spirituality for women that denies the grasping materialism that has dominated the past decade or so, and that reinterprets life styles in more modest and holistic forms.

If we look at our imaginary woman's arms, and ask 'what does she do?' we find ourselves in the world of ritual, of healing, of spiritual praxis. Before entering that world, I will summarize the major effects of the feminist spirituality so far described. Based on research and on gender politics, a Goddess view of the world meant changes in the way we view and live our lives. Nature is to be respected and not exploited; as are women's bodies and physical functions so often downgraded alongside nature. Aspects of the moon or of the Goddess do not indicate a changeability or a fickleness associated with women, but a many-sided appreciation of the whole of life. Conventions of women's subordination and lack of ability in various intellectual spheres are seen to be nonsense.

Material emanating from scholars of various disciplines (theologians, archaeologists, prehistorians, anthropologists, etc.) indicated that there was a respectable case for at least some, and probably many, Goddess-oriented early societies to have been organized on reasonably egalitarian lines between women and men. The word gylany (Gimbutas, Eisler, Orenstein)[12] was introduced from the US to describe this relationship. While the word has not come into general use in this country, the ideas are certainly prevalent, some of them perhaps veering too emphatically into a 'golden age' dream. However, there is certainly a force of sentiment that believes that things were better organized in the past and that we can learn from those societies to help reorganize our own.

In particular, the suppression of acknowledgment of the female divine, the negating of the Goddess was understood to be part of a 'great lie' which entangled every part of human life in its web. Consequently from whatever angle one tried to cut through this web, and free the female divine, one was also freeing the divinity in ourselves and helping to heal the world. Now we can attempt to answer the question 'what does she do?' We enter the world of ritual, neopaganism and magic.

The Goddess and paganism (or neo-paganism)

An excellent survey appears ma recent issue of the US magazine *Circle Network News*[13] of today's phenomenon of the resurgence of paganism and the development of neo-paganism. A number of writers discuss 'pagan world views'.

Dennis Carpenter sets the scene in an essay of paganism's 'spiritual contours'.[14] He defines its spirituality within the context of postmodernism—a theme which also attracts other writers in the survey—and selects major themes for examination. Among them are 'inter-connectedness, the immanent/transcendent dimension, animism and spiritism, monotheism/polytheism . . . and the concept of magic'.[15] All these headings are essential elements; perhaps the first two, inter-connectness and the immanent/transcendent dimension were the first to be connected clearly to the feminist Goddess movement. Carpenter quotes a full panoply of modern sources including Starhawk: 'The Goddess is around us and within us. She is immanent and transcendent . . . the Goddess represents the divine embodied in nature, in human beings, in the flesh . . .'[16] Many writers have dwelt at length on the inter-connection between the divine and the earthly, and on the same inter-connection between all parts of the universe. Carpenter sums up this area: 'Pagans maintain immanent and pantheistic perspectives in which the divine is dispersed through Nature and is Nature'.[17]

Another writer in the survey, Kathleen Starnes, discusses witchcraft within the setting of a nature religion and within the concept of related immanence and transcendence.

> One need not deny the materiality of the Divine in order to accept the power and spiritual manifestations of the Divine. The Goddess is evident in all forms around us . . . For the Witch, the Earth and Stars are the visual tactile aspects of the Divine in Union . . . herbs, crystals, trees and stones are all part of the Craft. But the visionary and transcendent application is what makes a spell work.[18]

Until American views started becoming important in the British Goddess scene, spiritual feminism and witchcraft or paganism had hardly met. Spiritual feminists did not identify as witches until the early and mid-eighties and then only a minority did so. The work of Starhawk and Z. Budapest[19] had a startling effect, and came at a time when such feminist researchers and those interested in their work were demanding more than just 'cerebral activity'. In Britain of course, there existed the pagan and witchcraft movement, which did not and indeed today still does not in any way define itself as feminist. By an interesting paradox, the US, usually West Coast feminist witches looked to Britain for age-old pagan and craft traditions, and bound these inextricably it seemed into their Goddess movement. There was, it appears to me, very little interest from the US in actually identifying the British pagan and witchcraft scene in its proper context. Age-old mysteries of Albion were more or less taken for granted. However, more recently there have been a number of extremely helpful studies into this subject.[20] The provenance of today's witchcraft and the Wicca movement is open to scrutiny. Some of the questions include their origin. For example, are modern Wicca and its relations a construction based on the work of Crowley, Gardner, Sanders in the middle decades of this century? Do they contain some elements of village magic, and some hereditary witch families? While Margaret Murray's theories of witchcraft's prominence in the history of England from the Dark Ages to the Enlightenment[21] have been rejected by academics, is there something of substance that has been overlooked in this area of her work? Many pagan researches are set within a description of paganism as a religion, and allow little sentimentality. It is clear that Wicca and paganism are defined as the religions of 'the God and the Goddess' in the context set out by Carpenter.

How then did the Goddess movement become so involved in it? Another look at the *Circle Network News* survey can help us. Susannah McBride writes:

> The concept of the divine feminine is one of the greatest selling points of modern Paganism. Women in conventional spirituality are bombarded

with images of our sex as imperfect, as less than whole, as unclean. Yet in Wicca and most forms of Neo-Paganism we are Goddess—divinity incarnate.[22]

Rhiannon Asher in the same survey adds a further cogent argument. Calling her article 'Drawing down the Gods through Sexual Ecstasy', she speaks of the freedom of casting away the conditioning of shame and guilt about sex and identifying sexual experience with the sacred.

I am a woman in a violent sexually repressed motherless world, a world in which women are raped and beaten and used to sell products . . . that glorifies war and reveres the taking of life. It is vital that the act which created life be returned to its honourable place in worship.[23]

Sacred sexuality, she says is worshipping the Gods through the act of sexual loving. (It will be noted that 'the Gods' are presumably meant to include 'the Goddess or Goddesses,' an indication of the lack of awareness of feminist thought.)

However, once the ideas of neopaganism reached feminists it is obvious that there was an immediate attraction. Women could be restored to their divinity or recognise the Goddess within; all the sexual denigration could fall away.

Further, there was exposure to the rhythms and rituals of the pagan movement, and the identification of these as belonging to one's own relationship with the Goddess—and with one's own self-growth. Seasonal celebrations depended a great deal on Robert Graves' celtic calendar:[24] Samhain (Halloween), Winter Solstice, Imbolc (Candlemas), Spring Equinox, May Eve, Summer Solstice, Lammas and Autumn Equinox mark the sacred points of the year. Rituals developed in the spiritual feminist movement which were created fairly spontaneously from the research available. 'Let's do that age-old ritual we invented last Friday night' said one woman in a sentence that re-echoes. They were simple ceremonies of aligning oneself with the season, with the elements, relinquishing baggage that had become inappropriate such as conflict, depression, under-valuing oneself, etc. and affirming one's hopes and identity. In such rituals goddesses were not named or invoked in any way, although someone would usually tell stories, myths and legends in perhaps a homiletic manner.

Neo-pagans, however, do not care for such informal structures. Calling upon whichever tradition they have been trained to follow (and there are several), they carry out a series of rituals, attended by both women and men, which probably include invoking the 'Goddess and the God'. As the US involvement with the 'craft' spread to Goddess feminism in this country, new groups started a women-only development named the Dianic Craft. This was composed solely of women, who invoked the Goddess or Goddesses only. Training groups were set up and often included women who had been introduced to Goddess material through women's groups, in addition to those who wanted spiritual experience without political base. In fact, although some ridicule has been poured upon the latter women by feminists generally, there can be no doubt that exposure to the ideas of Goddess veneration has a marked effect in raising self-value, and providing a spiritual dimension not otherwise possible.

It is important here to mention Lesbian spirituality groups. As has been said for many women, the freeing of sexuality meant that Lesbians, heterosexuals and celibates could work together in amity. But those Lesbians who wanted their own privacy and space turned to Lesbian spirituality groups. It has been commented that such groups tend to be political, because of the social situation that Lesbians find themselves in; and they also tend to be among the few in the feminist spirituality movement which have attracted black women. (As I write in mid March 1993 I am happy to hear of a widening of interest generally by women of colour, mediated perhaps through the renewal energy in the traditional religions.)

Of course this is a huge subject. There is no doubt that the general movement is composed of highly educated white women, though a large number live in conditions of some poverty. The early matriarchal feminists were not wholly Eurocentric in their work; and I have told elsewhere[25] my own dilemma in being offered a postgraduate course in which I could present a thesis on African goddesses which I refused, because I did not want to take up a 'colonialist' position—a refusal I still regret and am not sure even now, ten years later, if my decision was the right one.

In the early days, we understood there was a huge legacy of African, South American and pre-patriarchal, traditional religions and we imagined something of their influence on the European scene. But as time went on, the current shifted strongly to, 'home goddesses'—those of the Celtic world, goddesses of Britain and of northern Europe and of course those embedded deeply in biblical texts. The latter were understood to be very much part of a woman's culture that had been despised and swept away, thus needing to be reclaimed. At the same time, the material that became available from the world of scholars and other researchers bought back the Roman and Greek Goddesses and their festivals, while Diane Wolkstein's collaboration with Samual Noah Kramer in the translations of Inanna texts[26] brought this ancient Near Eastern material closely to the surface of feminist consciousness and has been much discussed and used as an experimental resource.

It is to the shame of the spiritual groups of this country that little was done to understand why so few black women joined the movement and little attention was paid to the furore in the US on this subject.[27] Where such groups did form, knowledge and veneration for Goddesses from African and West Indian cultures were introduced, and interest was taken for example in the Yoruba culture following the appearance of material on this subject. At Greenham Common too, black women joined others, often, but not only in groups who had turned to Goddess spirituality as an element in their struggle against American missiles there. Various studies of the Greenham experience have been made, and common to all is emphasis that women of all ages and cultures found there a consciousness of their own power and autonomy, and this included freeing both of sexuality and of religious experience. Consequently two different, but related programmes were going on there: the first and overt activity was a political struggle against missiles and for peace in the world; the second that 'just grew', involved a forceful spiritual feminism which overlapped into the political. In fact, one of the major components of paganism, outlined by Carpenter (above), that of magic, came to the fore.

The dimension of magic in neopaganism has of course attracted much specious comment and meretricious headlines. Some explanation of its place in spiritual feminism is needed. If we return to Wicca for a moment, it is generally assumed that the word itself means to shape or to turn, and the process of magic within Wicca is, as I understand it to use our energies to shape the world—ourselves, our situation, personally and in society for the better. Prurience and scare material concerning Satanism, devil worship 'black magic' and so on have no place here. Some women at Greenham sought to re-shape the world by calling upon and practising 'good-magic', and in the first place needed to learn what this might be and how to go about it. The works of Z. Budapest and Starhawk were much used. At the same time, people looked around to find indigenous beliefs and praxis that could help. Inexorably they moved towards the 'western tradition', which I understand to rely heavily on Celtic mythology and on mysticism, as well as strands from the Kabbalah and European magic.

A resurgence of acknowledgment of the part the witch hunts played in women's history became prevalent. If the intention of the witch hunters was to silence women, well, women have not been and will not be silenced. Patricia Beer summed up a strong current feeling, in her poem 'The Witch'. The last lines read: 'By the light of my long burning, I will see justice done'.[28] Invoking the memories of the persecuted witches who were understood to be strong women who may or may not have been oriented towards the 'old religion' of paganism, went together with aligning oneself with the earth and seasons, 'grounding and centring'. (There is a growing literature on this subject, see book list.)

A spiritual path, indeed a religion, began to build up. Central to it was the concept of the 'Goddess' or Goddesses, many named, many, or One who contains the many; who is immanent within the world and within us all, in nature and in the universe. To reach her and thus reach our innermost selves, women must undergo some psychic training. It will include meditation, divination and the use of beneficent rituals for cleansing and purifying. Journeys of the imagination or path working on which an individual may to a lesser or greater extent travel through consciousness to reach one's deepest self, with the help possibly of spiritual guides, are important. They will be set in Goddess myth and landscape. A significant theme is the journey on which one takes an offering to Her and receives a gift—a gift one keeps and uses daily in life.

Magenta Wise, who has been a Goddess activist working through psychic methods since the early 1970s, gives classes on psychic development. Her underlying philosophy is to do with the concept that 'we create much of our own problems unconsciously. Through developing intuition and by visualization we can bring much of this to the surface, and we can then consciously decide what we want to happen.' There are two sides to the process. Describing the first, she labels it 'getting information about the problem'. This can be done by all sorts of psychic means— developing meditation and visualization, employing divination such as Tarot, Palmistry, etc. Using path working, one can try to identify the problem. Then, by 'giving out' one can visualize and define what one wants to happen.[29] Healing, whether physical or psychological, can be affected in this way, as can healing this planet itself. Starhawk has described in detail how similar magic has been used to attempt to change US policy in Central America and elsewhere.[30] By these means, energy is raised and its force is directed—visualized—towards the person, object or situation that requires to be healed.

It is clear that when women meet for this purpose, freeing themselves, healing themselves and others, and attempting also to direct 'good energy' into the world itself, seeing the planet as sacred and in some way as a manifestation of the Goddess, they discard their inbuilt sense of guilt and inferiority. They find strength within themselves. Their own creative faculties are reinforced and the new confidence can help them take a surer place in the world.

The Goddess and psychotherapy

As we have proceeded on this path, it has been becoming increasingly evident that such 'magical' practices have a good deal in common with psychotherapy. Indeed post-Jungian writers Whitmont, Pereira, Neumann, Harding, Bolen, Cashford and Baring have influenced a considerable section of the Goddess movement. Jung's theories of the collective unconscious and of timeless archetypes and of individuation of the personality allowed a mythology which brought forward ancient goddesses and gods, and in particular the Great Goddess who was understood to have existed in a wide variety of cultures. She is the Feminine who must balance the Masculine in all of us. Whitmont[31] writes, for example:

> The awakening call of the new conscience in our time is the call to selfhood or individuation, as Jung has called it. It is the call to be what you are. But Dionysus-Azazel cannot come alone. He is the god of the Feminine, the consort of the Great Goddess. She was banished with him and with him she must also return. The way of the phallus alone, without the personalizing and integretative attitude of the Feminine, its sense for wholeness and containment would fail to satisfy our growth needs.
>
> (p. 118)

In this passage we have a justification for Jung's influence on the women's spirituality movement, and also for many of us, its objectionable character. The Masculine and the Feminine are each given specific characteristics, and although the point is always made by Jungians that each personality will contain both of these categories, yet as Whitmont has pointed out (p. 142): 'male trends predominate in men, female ones in women'. These 'male' and 'female' trends suppose that the Masculine is to do with the intellectual, analytic, explicit, active, etc. and the Feminine is perceptive, receptive, sensuous, intuitive and diffuse. For myself, I reject this type of thinking as being sexist; Gloria Orenstein (1990) has recounted her own journey from Jungian ideas to an understanding of their deficiencies. In particular she makes the point that

> The Jungian hypothesis of a collective unconscious . . . leads to a historical and transpersonal conclusions that simply erase specific historic and cultural contexts. I would also argue that the Goddess image as it appears today . . . symbolizes not just nature-fertility and cosmic creation motifs, but also a new unification of women's roles, both as procreator and creator of culture (e.g. artist). The prevalence of the re-emergence of

the Goddess today . . . can be seen to stand for a conscious reclamation of a world view whose ethics, spiritual values, and social organisation are deemed superior to those of today's dominating technocratic non-ecological androcratic systems.

(p. 20)

Much of the objection to ideas of women's spirituality and the Goddess movement has centred on the eager acceptance by many women of Jung's ideas of 'the Feminine', disregarding his own overt sexism. Many still today believe that the Feminine and thus women are more sensitive, caring, perceptive, intuitive and so on, and yield to the Masculine the areas of intellectual thought and activity in the professional world.

My opinion is that this is not only mistaken but is dangerous. There is within it, a covert sexism that, keeping traditional ideas of 'women's place', appears to allow some power and autonomy.

Various forms of psychotherapy, and therapies associated with complementary and holistic medicine have much in common with the practices to be found in neo-pagan circles, in terms of underlying hypotheses about the need for a different way of living in society and in the world at large. Of course, much help is given to people in trouble, and much understanding of one's personal problems can be achieved. However my own inclination is to argue firmly with the older feminist movement that 'the personal is the political'. Helpful methods of dealing with one's psychological and physical aches and pains should not be confused with what misogyny and sexism have done and are doing. The emergence of 'the Goddess' as a powerful force in women's consciousness should not be used to entrench them in traditional attitudes. Men can be perceptive and women can use their intellectual powers; each may have to be trained to discard ideas that they are deficient in these attributes. A move away from sentimental notions of the femininity of the Great Goddess can include information of the female divine as intellect and wisdom as a power figure in society at the very least.

Other objections to the women's spirituality and 'matriarchy' movement centre upon involvement with the occult, and the association of this with right-wing politics. That Hitler and the Nazis were involved with pagan occult mythology and endeavoured to put the most androcentric version of this into practice, is becoming common knowledge as is the fact that German women of the period were, in part, seduced by the concept of their 'goddess-hood' provided it was expressed in the 'feminine' virtues. In the neo-Nazi movement and the other right-wing groups in Europe today some similar tendencies have been glimpsed and are the subject of much discussion in feminist spirituality circles there. For myself, as will have become obvious, I have no great desire to work with the occult, or with magic. But it is important to distinguish between the male supremist, genocidal, xenophobic cults which focus on hierarchy and on obtaining 'power over' the world at micro and macro levels, and holistic, ecology-minded neo-paganism. Particularly as taken up by spiritual feminists the latter becomes part of a world-view which understands that all creation is sacred, all its parts of creation are connected, and that one works towards a situation where non-aggression and 'power within' people is the norm. Possibly the fascination of occult experience and praxis overtakes gender politics among some groups, but it is very rare indeed for the women involved to forget the basic principles of achieving self-worth and throwing off the consequences of long drawn out misogyny.

The Goddess movement and Judaism and Christianity

Readers of this journal do not need me to point to the material that encompasses feminist theologians. I will touch only briefly on the subject in this area, picking out themes that seem to me to be gathering importance.

For a long time there appeared to be little convergence between 'goddess women' and those in Judaism or Christianity who were struggling to bring about a change in their religious traditions and practice that would challenge misogyny and acknowledge the female in the divine. The original Matriarchy Study Group included one such radical Christian woman who confessed she felt uncomfortable but saw, long before many others, that there was similarity in the struggles and that there was no need to continue traditional hostilities.[32] These, of course, were based on the deeply-embedded suspicion on both sides (and in this I am able to class Jewish and Christian women together) that the 'other' camp represented the negation of the most deeply-held faith and moralities. Goddess women would point to monotheism as misogyny; those in the traditional faiths saw polytheism and paganism as worse.

To some extent, this is still the case, but the differing viewpoints have converged in a sense, in practice. Christian activists for the ordination of women found among their opponents clerics who held up Scripture and tradition to deny the female in the divine; among them were those who promulgated a kind of misogyny that would not have been amiss during the period of the witch hunts. Others, pursuing theological research found material abounding which could be seen to open up huge new areas of understanding.[33] The possibility of the female nature of God, the place of the Virgin Mary in doctrine and in popular perception, a new appreciation of the figure of Wisdom, and the possibility of a Jesus-Sophia figure, themes that could be drawn from Gnostic material, are among the many areas that showed Christian women that 'Goddess' need not be a word of fear. Jewish women joyfully met the Shekinah, re-worked Kabbalism, and in many ways introduced, particularly in the US, an attitude to Judaism that could talk freely of 'the Goddess' and carry out amended ritual and ceremonies still based upon tradition. In this country, the Ruach Chavurah movement gathered together large numbers of Jews, women and men, who had moved away from their religion. They happily saw in this new appreciation something that restored their roots appropriately today.

The major question that both divides and unites both sides has been explored by Judith Plaskow and Carol Christ in their recent compilation of essays on feminist spirituality.[34] Published in 1989 it comes over a decade after their previous collaboration *Womanspirit Rising*[35] which inspired a whole generation of women on both sides of the Atlantic.

The new work *Weaving the Visions* sums up in its preface one of the most important themes that presents itself to us today. Beginning with the statement that intellectual and religious commitments have drawn each of the editors away from each other during the past ten years, they say that 'Carol has now more deeply embraced the Goddess and nature spirituality, while Judith has clearly committed herself to the transformation of Judaism' (p. v). These differences, while at times extremely difficult to bear, did not stop them 'affirming friendship and mutual commitment to feminism and to the feminist transformation of religion that now spans almost twenty years'. They point out that although they no longer speak with one voice, their personal struggles 'have taught us the importance of working with and learning from differences in feminist theologies and thealogies' (p. v).

Here, I think, we have the nub of our movement today. It is possible to explore differences and to reach similar goals. Of course this raises the second great struggle, and one which is chronicled to a major extent in various issues of the *Journal of Feminist Studies in Religion* (see n. 27). This is the struggle and perception of black women, of Hispanic women and women from other world cultures, all of whom have their own experience, who properly reject white 'Anglo' didacticism, and who are struggling for their spiritual identities as part of feminist and social autonomy.

Ada Maria Isasi-Diaz writes of the struggle to name her Hispanic feminist community.

> Feministas Hispanas have been consistently marginalized in the Anglo feminist community because of our critique of its ethnic racial prejudice and lack of class analysis. Though Anglo feminists have worked to correct these serious shortcomings in their discourse, in my experience their praxis continues to be flawed.

She presents the term *mujerista* to describe a theology of liberation for Hispanic women which includes a religious perspective. *Mujerista* theology 'is a process of enablement for Hispanic women, insisting on the development of a strong moral agency and clarifying the importance of what we think and what we do'.[36]

In the same 'round table', Lourdes Arguelles and Raven-Anne Rivero emphasize that a Lesbian dimension must be acknowledged and celebrated. 'Mujerista theology must not only confront heterosexism as one of the most fundamental oppressive processes but must encourage change in fundamental attitudes concerning our place in the natural order'.[37]

These Latina women in their concern for the ecology of the world speak from within Christianity, and join the critique made by such writers as Anne Primavesi[38] who seek to re-establish a more harmonious working together of all creation. The emphasis on ecology links them strongly with Christian and non-Christian women from many parts of the world who are also involved in this struggle. Although the Latinas in their material discussed do not explore a Goddess option, yet the Goddess as nature and as a means of re-establishing such harmony is an option for many.[39]

We see then that the paths of those who may be called God women and 'Goddess women' who would expect to diverge in fact fall in with each other and lead in similar directions. Exploring differences but being united in vision, universality and particularity combined is the strongest trend I perceive. It may also be germane here to note that where Goddess women have in the past appropriated rituals and deities from every source available, there is now a move to condemn 'cultural theft'.

This discussion is still in its early stages. In essence it applies a 'colonialist' judgment to those who eclectically adopt whatever sacred concept or practice that appeals to them, without permission, and usually without much knowledge of its history and background. At the same time, there is also appreciation that such ideas of the sacred have much to teach us. Is the answer one of attitude, of equality and of harmony between differing groups? Of honouring the other's place, of believing in the other's integrity?[40]

Conclusion

Today the women's spirituality movement is growing steadily, and newcomers often have little sense of its history, believing it to be more or less New Age or neo-pagan in its entirety. Happily there are some signs that with all the new scholastic research becoming available, some interest is being taken in actual sources and in the work of feminist scholars and theologians.

The advent of women's studies courses in feminist theology and spirituality (though the latter are scarce) brings the subject into the 'respectable' world of academia. Difficulties arise there since the material is so inflammatory, however handled, that the usual cool so-called objective approach is extremely difficult. However, ultimately there can be no doubt of its impact. We are at the centre of the confrontation of ideas referred to at the beginning of this paper. From the physical, to the social, from economic to the sexual, and above all in perception of the spiritual, the old ideas simply will not do. It is not a question of making improvements here and there—though these are certainly welcome. A whole new way of understanding our life together in society is being placed before us.

Sometimes it is possible to mediate changes that, while radical, still allow the establishment to stay in place—as in the case of the ordination of women rabbis and priests. But in my opinion, this too will eventually have a revolutionary effect— and to some extent the process has started.

We are looking at a new morality that declares that the mainspring of the past has been distorted to produce a mechanism that is inherently faulty. The pressure is growing for it to be taken apart, renewed, repaired and verified. This is the core of the message of the Women's Spirituality Movement.

In this overview, I have been able only to pick out some of the major concepts and practices that make up the Goddess movement in Britain today. All—and others—need to be explored in greater depths. Key questions arise in the search for women's spirituality. They concern justice, as well as a challenge to today's materialism.

We have seen that the advent of a spiritual dimension to feminism expands its parameters. Assuring women of their basic self-worth and providing historical precedent, it offers an exceptional affirmation of confidence. Younger women, in particular, who have been influenced by media denigration of feminism welcome its approach to their problems and find that it can bring earlier attitudes into new understanding.

Diverse groups from historically adversative settings find similarities, in appreciation of the need for change in our attitudes—to our relationships, to ourselves, to other peoples of the world and to the earth itself.

The Goddess movement is still an uncharted land; no geography and no maps have been agreed. We start by challenging at least two thousand years of Western thought and action, precisely positing misogyny as underlying deficient Western civilization and the spirituality within it. Those with their roots in the Bible as well as some who look elsewhere agree on Gen. 1.26, 'imago dei' as a starting point. Lines from the 'Orphic Hymn to Nature' may inspire the latter group and are acceptable to most of the former. So it is in a spirit of conciliation and progress that I end my account with this ancient invocation:

> O Nature, mother of all, artificer mother,
> Celestial, venerated, goddess of richness, sovereign.
> Leader, accomplisher, life-giving, all nourishing maiden
> Goddess of earth, air and sea . . .
> All-flowing, circular in motion, shape shifting . . .
> You are deathless, are everlasting life and know the future . . .
> Goddess, we pray you in good season, lead us to peace, health and increase of prosperity.
>
> ('Orphic Hymn to Nature', no. 10; trans. Asphodel Long and Miriam [Diana] Scott.)

Acknowledgements

I am indebted to Magenta Wise who read the draft and encouraged me throughout the work, to Alex Sutherland and Daniel Cohen for their suggestions and to Daniel also for help with book research. Grateful thanks to Louise Hart and Liv Livingstone for major exploration of ideas and information and, as ever, to Robin Thodey for her encouragement as well as her help in putting the work on to a word processor. Special thanks to Lisa Isherwood who emboldened me to write this paper.

Notes

1   F. Fukuyama, *The End of History and the Last Man* (London: Hamilton, 1992).
2   For example, V.I. Lenin, *The Emancipation of Women* (Moscow: Progress Publishers, 1965); V. Kolbanowski, *Communist Morality* (Current Books, 1947).
3   K. Marx, 'Religion is the soul of a soulless society, the heart of a heartless nation, it is the opium of the people'. (Criticism of Hegel's *Philosophy of Right*, 1864).
4   L. Apuleius, *The Golden Ass* (trans. R. Graves; London: Penguin, 1950), p. 269.
5   I use the word 'thealogy' in common with increasing practice among feminist theologians. Carol Christ notes in her introduction to *Laughter of Aphrodite* (1987), p. xvii that the term (which of course derives from Greek *thea* meaning goddess) was first suggested by Naomi Goldenberg.
6   C.P. Christ, 'Why Women Need the Goddess'; M. Stone, 'The Three Faces of Goddess Spirituality'; both in the journal, *The Great Goddess Heresies*, NY (Spring 1978), pp. 8–13 and 2–4 respectively.
7   M. Sjoo, 'The Ancient Religion of the Great Cosmic Mother of All' (privately published 1975). See also M. Sjoo and B. Mor, *The Great Cosmic Mother, Rediscovering the Religion of the Earth* (San Francisco: Harper & Row, 1987).
8   (London, 1978).

9   P. Henderson, 'Matriarchal Values in Maori Culture', in *Politics of Matriarchy*, pp. 50–4.

10   'Homeric Hymn XXX', in M.J. Vermaseren, *Cybele and Attis* (London: Thames & Hudson, 1977), p. 9.

11   I have discussed this theme in detail in my book, *In a Chariot Drawn by Lions* (London: The Women's Press, 1992).

12   R. Eisler, *The Chalice and the Blade* (San Francisco: Harper & Row, 1987); G. Orenstein, *The Reflowering of the Goddess* (Oxford: Pergamon Press, 1990); M. Gimbutas, *Goddesses and Gods of Old Europe* (Thames and Hudson, 1982).

13   *Circle Network News* 46 (Winter 92/93), pp. 14–22.

14   D.D., Carpenter, 'Spiritual Contours of the Contemporary Pagan World View', in *Circle* above.

15   D.D. Carpenter, 'Spiritual Contours of the Contemporary Pagan World View'.

16   Starhawk, *Dreaming the Dark* (Beacon Press, 1982), pp. 8–9.

17   D.D. Carpenter, 'Spiritual Contours'.

18   K. Starnes, 'The Divine in Witchcraft', p. 19, in *Circle* above.

19   Z. Budapest, *The Holy Book of Womens Mysteries* (2 vols.; Oakland, CA, 1982) and other works by this author.

20   See book list below.

21   M.A. Murray, *The Witch Cult in Western Europe* (Oxford: Clarendon Press, 1921) and others by this author.

22   S. McBride, 'Images of the Goddess and God', *Circle*, p. 20.

23   R. Asher, 'Tantra Wicca: Drawing down the Gods through Sexual Ecstasy', *Circle*, p. 20.

24   R. Graves, *The White Goddess* (London: Faber & Faber, 1948), *passim*.

25   A. Long, *Letter: From the Flames*, 8 (Winter, 1992–93), p. 20.

26   D. Wolkstein and S.N. Kramer, *Inanna, Queen of Heaven and Earth* (New York: Harper & Row, 1983).

27   *Journal of Feminist Studies in Religion* 5.1 (Spring 1989); 5.2 (Spring 1992) and 8.2 (Fall 1992).

28   *Collected Poems* (Carcanet Press, 1988).

29   M. Wise, forthcoming book on the philosophy of the Tarot, to accompany current video 'How to read the Tarot cards'.

30   Starhawk, *Truth or Dare* (San Francisco: Harper & Row, 1987), pp. 18–19. The concepts of 'power over' and 'power within' have become currency in feminism and in the alternative culture. Starhawk's description (*Dreaming the Dark*, 1982, p.3) contrasts power-over, which is domination, ultimately the power of the gun and the bomb with 'the power, we sense in a seed . . . we feel writing, weaving, working . . .' She points out the latter has more to do with the Latin root *podere* 'to be able'. It is, she says, the power that comes from within which can also be understood as spirit, or even immanence. It is in utter contrast to domination.

31   E. Whitmont, *Return of the Goddess* (Routledge & Kegan Paul, 1983).

32   E.g. the works of Phyllis Trible, Elizabeth Schüssler Fiorenza, Rose Arthur, Elaine Pagels, Marina Warner, A. Pirani, *The Absent Mother Mandala* (1991).

33   A full bibliography is available in my book *Chariot* (see book list).

34   C.P. Christ and J. Plaskow (eds.), *Weaving the Visions: New Patterns in Feminist Spirituality* (New York: Harper & Row, 1989).

35   New York: Harper & Row, 1979.

36   A.D. Isasi-Diaz, 'Mujeristas: Who We are and What We are About', *Journal of Feminist Studies in Religion* 8.1 (Spring 1992), pp. 105–6.

37   L. Arguelles and R.-A. Rivero, *Journal of Feminist Studies in Religion* 8.1 (Spring 1992), pp. 122–3.

38   A. Primavesi, *From Apocalypse to Genesis: Ecology, Feminism and Christianity* (London: Burns & Oates, 1991).

39   See for example the moving account of the work of Indian women and the goddess of the forests in Shiva, Vandana, *Staying Alive* (San Francisco: Zed Books, 1988).

40   This discussion is currently taking place in issues of *From the Flames*, a small journal produced by a Women's Spirituality Group in Nottingham. On a much larger scale the whole spectrum of reciprocity and appropriation was made visible and discussed in depth in a session of the Women and Religion Section at the 1991 Annual Meeting of the American Academy of Religion. The papers presented there are published in the Fall 1992 issue of the *Journal of Feminist Studies in Religion* 6.

Selected book list

British pagan tradition/women's spirituality

Crowley, V., *Wicca: The Old Religion in the New Age* (Aquarian Press, 1989).
Farrar, J. and S. Farrar, *Eight Sabbats for Witches* (Robert Hale, 1981).
—— *The Witches Way* (Robert Hale, 1984).
Green, M., *Magic for the Aquarian Age* (Aquarian Press, 1981).
Hutton, R., *The Pagan Religions of the British Isles: Their Nature and Legacy* (Blackwell, 1992).
Jones, P. and M. Caitlin (eds.), *Voices from the Circle* (Aquarian Press, 1990).
King, U., *Women and Spirituality: Voices of Protest and Promise* (Macmillan, 1989, revised and updated, 1993).
Matthews, C., *Elements of the Goddess* (Element Books, 1989).
Matthews, C. (ed.), *Voices of the Goddess* (Aquarian Press, 1990).
Matthews, C. and J. Matthews, *The Western Way* (2 vols.; Arkana, 1985, 1986).
Medici, M., *Good Magic* (Macmillan, 1988).
Valiente, D., *An ABC of Witchcraft* (Robert Hale, 1974).
—— *The Rebirth of Witchcraft* (Robert Hale, 1989).

US pagan resources

Adler, M., *Drawing Down the Moon* (Viking, 1979; revised and updated, Beacon, 1986).
Fox, S. (ed.), *Circle Guide to Wicca and Pagan Resources* (Circle: Madison, 1980).
Gawr, R. (ed.), *Pagan-Occult New Age Directory* (Berkeley, 1980).

The Jungian dimension

Bolen, J., *Goddesses in Everywoman* (Harper & Row, 1987).
Cashford, J. and A. Baring, *The Myth of the Goddess* (Viking, 1992).
Harding, E., *Womens Mysteries, Ancient and Modern* (Rider, 1971).
Neumann, E., *The Great Mother: An Analysis of an Archetype* (Princeton University Press, 1963).
Perera, S., *Descent to the Goddess* (Inner City Books, 1981).
Whitmont, E., *Return of the Goddess* (Routledge & Kegan Paul, 1983).

African heritage

Amadiume, I., *Afrikan Matriarchal Foundations: The Igbo Case* (Karnak House, 1987).

Bernal, M., *Black Athena: The Afro-Asiatic Roots of Classical Civilisation* (2 vols.; Free Association Books, 1987 and 1991).

Gleason, J., *Oya: In Praise of an African Goddess* (HarperCollins, 1987).

Teish, L., *Jambalaya* (HarperCollins, 1985).

General: Goddess books

Gadon, E., *The Once and Future Goddess* (Harper & Row, 1989).

Gimbutas, M., *Goddesses and Gods of Old Europe* (Thames & Hudson, 1982).

Long, A.P., *In a Chariot Drawn by Lions: The Search for the Female in Deity* (The Womens Press, 1992).

Pirani, A. (ed.), *The Absent Mother: Restoring the Goddess to Judaism and Christianity* (Mandala, 1991).

Starhawk, *The Spiral Dance* (Harper & Row, 1979).

Sjoo, M. and B. Mor, *The Great Cosmic Mother: Rediscovering the Religion of the Earth* (Harper & Row, 1987).

Chapter 32

Marion Bradley

INITIATIONS

■ from **THE MISTS OF AVALON**, London, 1984, pp. 157–8, 202–3

PAGANISM'S SOURCES AND EXPRESSIONS include not only serious academic debates but also fantasy and historical fiction. Marion Bradley's *The Mists of Avalon* is probably one of the most popular books among Pagans. It is on the shelves of Goddess Feminists, Druids, Wiccans and many others. Like similar works, it re-imagines the Arthurian epic tales, this time in ways that are recognizably Pagan.

The first short extract concerns the initiation as priestess of Morgaine, situated within an evocation of the service offered to the Goddess. This bears comparison with the description of initiation among Wiccans (see, e.g., Crowley, 1989, 1990; or Starhawk's 'Initiation' in *Spiral Dance*, 1989). There are, of course, differences from what Wiccans and other contemporary Pagan initiates undergo.

The second short extract concerns the initiation of Arthur as king as seen in a vision by Morgaine. While this finds no parallels in the regular rites of any Paganism, it has inspired a number of Pagans – especially those attracted by the 'Men's Movement' or 'Male Mysteries' (e.g. Stewart, 1991) – to construct imaginative hunts or races with the wild. Although these may not be typical events, they do demonstrate the creative playfulness of Paganism. Perhaps, too, the importance of ritual in Paganism underlies the shift away from Protestant Christian stress on correct belief towards a more indigenous stress on action and performance – something also seen in Judaism and in many other religions.

Among the many other recent works of fiction and fantasy of importance to Pagans, see the works of Robert Heinlein, Alan Garner, Ursula LeGuin, Susan Cooper, Marge Piercy, Brian Bates, Terry Pratchett, Guy Gavriel Kay, Robert Holdstock, Tom Holt, Philip Pullman, and many others. The influence of J.R.R. Tolkien is, of course, inestimable. Some of this literature and its place in contemporary Paganism are discussed in Graham Harvey (2000, 2004).

Graham Harvey

References

Crowley, Vivianne (1989) *Wicca: The Old Religion in the New Age*, London: Aquarian.

Crowley, Vivianne (1990) 'The Initiation', in Prudence Jones and Caitlín Matthews (eds) *Voices from the Circle: The Heritage of Western Paganism*, London: Aquarian, pp. 65–82.

Harvey, Graham (2000) 'Fantasy in the study of religions: Paganism as observed and enhanced by Terry Pratchett', in *Diskus*, 6. http://www.uni-marburg.de/fb03/religionswissenschaft/journal/diskus/#6

Harvey, Graham (2004) 'Discworld and Otherworld: the re-enchantment of nature in Paganisms', in Lynne Hume and Kathleen McPhillips (eds) *Popular Spiritualities: The Politics of Contemporary Enchantment*, Aldershot: Ashgate.

Starhawk (1989) *Spiral Dance*. San Francisco: Harper & Row.

Stewart, R.J. (1991) *Celebrating the Male Mysteries*. Bath: Arcarnia.

HOW DO YOU WRITE OF THE making of a priestess? What is not obvious is secret. Those who have walked that road will know, and who have not will never know though I should write down all the forbidden things. Seven times Beltane-eve came and went; seven times the winters shrivelled us all with cold. The Sight came easily, Viviane had said I was priestess-born. It was not so easy to bid it come when I willed and only when I willed, and to close the gates of the Sight when it was not fitting I should see.

It was the small magics which came hardest, forcing the mind first to walk in unaccustomed paths. To call the fire and raise it at command, to call the mists, to bring rain – all these were simple, but to know when to bring rain or mist and when to leave it in the hands of the Gods, that was not so simple. Other lessons there were, at which my knowledge of the Sight helped me not at all: the herb lore, and the lore of healing, the long songs of which not a single word might ever be committed to writing, for how can the knowledge of the Great Ones be committed to anything made by human hands? Some of the lessons were pure joy, for I was allowed to learn to play upon the harp and to fashion my own, using sacred woods and the gut of an animal killed in ritual; and some lessons were of terror.

Hardest of all, perhaps, to look within myself, under the spell of the drugs which loosed the mind from the body, sick and retching, while the mind soared free past the limits of time and space, and to read in the pages of the past and the future. But of that I may say nothing. At last, the day when I was cast out of Avalon, clad only in my shift, and unarmed save for the little dagger of a priestess, to return—if I could. I knew that if I did not, they would mourn me as one dead, but the gates would never again be opened to me unless I could bid them open at my own will and command. And when the mists closed around me, I wandered long on the shores of the alien Lake, hearing only the bells and the doleful chanting of the monks. And at last I broke through the mists, and called upon her, my feet upon the earth and my head among the stars, stretching from horizon to horizon, and cried aloud the great word of Power . . .

And the mists parted and I saw before me the same sunlit shore where the Lady
had brought me seven years before, and I set my feet on the solid earth of my own
home, and I wept as I had done when first I came there as a frightened child. And
then the mark of the crescent moon was set between my brows by the hand of the
Goddess herself . . . but this is a Mystery of which it is forbidden to write. Those
who have felt their brow burned with the kiss of Ceridwen will know whereof
I speak.

. . .

She lay as if lifeless, but a part of her went with them, raced with them, speeding
down the hillside, racing with the men of the tribe, flooding after the Horned One.
Barking cries, as if they were hounds, sped after them, and a part of her knew that
the women were crying out, speeding on the chase.

Higher in the sky the sun rose, the great Wheel of Life spinning in the heavens,
fruitlessly speeding after her divine consort, the Dark Son . . .

The life of the earth, the pounding tides of the spring, flooded and pounded in
the hearts of the running men. Then, as the ebb followed the flow, from the sunlit
hillside the darkness of forest closed over them and swallowed them, and from
running they moved swiftly on noiseless feet, imitating the delicate step of the deer;
they *were* the deer, following the antlers of their Horned One, wearing the cloaks
which held the deer spellbound, the necklaces signifying life as endless chain, live
and feed and bear and die and be eaten in turn to feed the children of the Mother.

. . . hold thy children, Mother, thy King Stag must die to feed the life of her Dark Son . . .

Darkness, the inner life of the forest closing around them; silence, the silence of the
deer . . . Morgaine, aware now of the forest as life and the deer as the heart of
the forest, cast her power and her blessing through and over the forest. A part
of her lay on the sunlit hillside, tranced, exhausted, letting the life of the sun flood
through her, body and blood and inner being, and a part of her ran with deer and
men until both were one . . . blending into one . . . the surges of life that were the
quiet deer in their thicket, the little does, smooth and slender, the life racing in them
as it raced in her body, the surges of life that were the men, slipping silent and intent
through the shadows . . .

Somewhere in the forest she felt the King Stag fling up his head, sniffing the
wind, aware for the scent of an enemy, one of his own, one of the alien tribe of life
. . . she did not know whether it was the four-footed King Stag or the two-legged
one she had blessed, they were one in the life of the Mother Earth, and their lot was
in the hands of the Goddess. Antlers answered the toss of antlers, the sniffing breath
taking in the life of the forest, searching it for alien, for prey, for predator, for rival
where there could be none.

Ah, Goddess . . . they were off, crashing through the underbrush, men fleet
behind them only more silent, running, running till the heart throbs like bursting in
the chest, run till the life of the body overwhelms all knowledge and thought, fleet,
searching and being sought, run with the deer who flee and the men who pursue,

run with the spinning life of the great sun and the surge of the spring tides, run with the flow of life . . .

Lying motionless, her face pressed into the earth and the flooding sun burning her back, time crawling and racing by turns, Morgaine began to see—and from very far off it seemed that she had seen this before, in vision, sometime, somewhere, a very long time ago—the tall, sinewy youth, gripping his knife, falling, falling among the deer, among the slashing hooves—she knew she screamed aloud, and simultaneously knew that her cry had rung everywhere, so that even the King Stag paused in mid charge, appalled, hearing the shriek. There was a moment when everything stopped, and in that terrible moment of silence she saw that he scrambled to his feet, panting, charging with his head down, swinging his antlers, locking head-on, as he swayed and struggled, wrestling the deer with his strong hands and young body . . . a knife slashed upward; blood spilled on the earth, and he was bleeding too, the Horned One, blood on his hands, blood from a long slash on his side, the blood spilling on the earth, sacrifice spilled to the Mother that life should feed on her blood . . . and then the blood of the King Stag went over him in a gush as his blade found the heart, and the men around him rushed in with their spears . . .

She saw him carried back, covered in the blood of his twin and rival, the King Stag. All around him the little dark men were slashing, putting the raw, warm hide over his shoulders. Back they came in triumph, fires rising in the gathering dusk, and when the women lifted Morgaine she saw without surprise that the sun was setting, and she staggered, as if she too had run all day with the hunt and the deer.

Chapter 33

Wren Sidhe

DRAWING DOWN THE MOON AND CANDLEMAS RITUAL CAKE

■ from Wren Sidhe, self-published, nd

PAGAN DIVERSITY INCLUDES DIFFERENCES of opinion about gender. In 'Drawing Down the Moon', Wren Sidhe offers a humorous but pointed response to those who insist that the central rituals of Wicca can only be performed where there is a gender balance and, indeed, that gender polarity is not merely cultural but cosmic. Her writing is rooted not only in Goddess Spirituality but also in Lesbian Eco-Feminist Spirituality. It exemplifies the kind of Paganism celebrated by many deterred by workshops, elaborately crafted rituals and hierarchies with unusual names. Nonetheless, the language of Pagan ceremony is recognizable here, as is the purpose – broadly speaking – of Paganism as a nature religion: namely, communion with the living world around us. If 'drawing down the moon' typically refers to an initiation with Wiccan mysteries, here it refers to self-initiation into delight in the beauty of the world.

Wren Sidhe's second piece, 'Candlemas Ritual Cake', arises from the problem of children and ritual. There have been times and places that have made it foolish or dangerous to permit children to participate in Pagan events (as, for example, during the 1990s at the height of accusations about 'satanic ritual abuse'). However, with the diminishment of that kind of opposition, and with increasing numbers of children born in Pagan families, it has become necessary to consider ways of including children. The inner-Pagan dimension of this problem is that most Pagans prefer to offer their children complete freedom of choice in the matter of their spirituality. However, most Pagan festivals offer plenty of opportunities to elaborate on popular customs and folk traditions as part of the celebration of seasons and places. Wren Sidhe here offers another playful version of a Pagan event that can be meaningful to all participants. This playfulness is itself a characteristic of Pagan ritual and celebration.

Graham Harvey

Drawing Down the Moon

IT IS SOMETIMES SAID THAT the ritual of Drawing Down the Moon can only be performed onto a High Priestess by a High Priest whose training has included wandering in the wilderness for seven long years with nothing but an old grey cloak, a staff and a lamp for company. Maybe he also should have crossed rough and tossing seas, read the omens in the migratory patterns of birds, learnt the language of the marsh marigold and then gone on to win the hand of the King of Spain's daughter. However, I drew down not just the moon, but the whole sky, bit by bit in my own back garden last week without ever having done these things. It only took two days and didn't include anyone using their male polarity to bring out the divine essence in my female polarity although some previous Craft writers have said this is a strict necessity. I did it by myself, inspired by the creative divinity in another woman. The Gardner/Valiente Book of Shadows states that 'woman and woman should never attempt these practices together, and may all the curses of the Mighty Ones be on any who make such an attempt'. Reading this I firmly returned these curses whence they came and gave thanks to She-Who-Mightily-Loves-Her-Twin for the many blessings She has brought. Didn't She say 'All acts of love and pleasure are My rituals'?

In Londinium and Aquae Sulis they have some nasty and unnatural practices in how they pass on information. They make up workshops about spirituality and charge people too much money for things which in a matrifocal society would be included freely in the sum of human knowledge. However, it is possible to Draw Down the Moon for next to nothing. Here's how.

CASTING THE CIRCLE. Put your oldest clothes on because this is an unusually mucky way of casting. Get a sturdy spade and start to dig a deep round hole in the garden in whatever dimension is pleasing to you, although digging on the astral will not have the required effect. This is hard work but I found that the resulting mound of earth brought my animal familiars to join me in rooting out worms, slugs and forgotten one pound coins, and their company considerably eased the task. Maude the All Devouring Mother who was taking a break from the Royal Chicken Shed to holiday and gossip with me was especially delighted. She is not a vegetarian and neither does she have the good grace to wait for her meat to be dead before she eats it, so she tucked in with a great vigour, cooing and clucking at each new titbit the turning of the earth revealed.

After a while you will be standing in a hole and will probably have noticed that where once the ground was flat you now have both a circular hollow and an unshapely mound. Forget the mound. The transformation is done. The circle is cast.

Say any appropriate ritual words and drink a can of lager or a cup of tea, remembering to pour a libation. Rest.

RAISING THE POWER. Each of you will have to choose your own preferred method. Mine was to hold in my hands the writings of a woman who told how the moon comes to her nightly in a Mercedes the colour of apricot-yoghurt. Together they rumple and swathe her bed in the sheeniest shiniest sheets the colour of a night by water. Oooh, mmmm, I thought, I like her, I thought. When I went on to read her description of death sleeping inside our cheekbones I immediately adopted the Pose of the Corpse, in love with her writing, her vision, her craziness, her grief and I sent my skeleton away to clack out a bone dance of cart-wheeling life before her. I'm sorry to say that the raising of the power turned me into a right show-off.

WORKING THE MAGICK. I let my fingers do the walking and phoned several local garden centres to see if they had the necessary magical tool. One did, for 16.99, a large sheet of thick black plastic. I didn't quibble. On the box was written GUAR-ANTEED FOR THREE YEARS with a big cross through it, and beside it a yellow sticker boldly proclaimed NOW GUARANTEED FOR FIVE YEARS! This is the first time that I can give my magic a time guarantee, and believe me, it's a weird and wondrous feeling.

The work you are now going to do is to make a pond. I recommend if possible that you get one of these plastic pondliners rather than rummaging through skips to find old pieces of carpeting, though of course it is perfectly possible to line a pond that way. If you get a box like I did you'll notice an ironic discrepancy between the suddenly small liner the box actually contains and the illustration which shows a Grecian Goddess fountaining water into what can only be described as a lily-covered-lake-in-the-grounds-of-a-stately-home. You will NOT be able to replicate this. Line the hole that you have dug. Fill it with water, fish, plants. Edge it all round with large flat stones which slightly overlap the sides of your pond. Mention to any famil-iars that you might have that it is not appropriate either to eat the fish for breakfast, or to worry any plants between their teeth as if they had a half dead rat by the short and curlies.

The hardest part of doing magical work is sometimes to actually notice that you have done it. So stop, take your time and look at your pond. Move around it, peering in and see how each part of the sky scuds across it. You have effected a great trans-formation. Where once the land was flat and monodimensional, you have introduced depth and complexity such that looking in the pond will not only take you to the bowels of the earth but at the same time reflect the sky and Draw Down the Moon. Be amazed.

(For those without gardens a saucer of water placed on a windowsill will also Draw Down the Moon.)

Candlemas Ritual Cake

Ingredients

3 children
1 mother
a mirror
a bundle of straw
a five-candled candle crown woven with reeds and snowdrops

a bowl of milk which has been warmed with a teaspoonful of honey and
mixed spice
the words of a Bridget chant (provenance unknown):

> Like the phoenix of the flame
> Bridget has risen again
> breathing life into the earth
> tis the time of rebirth

a general despondent feeling that the world has been dull and grey for
too long and that it will probably never be any different
any animal familiar cuddly toys, and plastic farm toys.

One

Light a fire in the hearth, wait until evening comes, which at this time of year will
not be arduous. Then put all the ingredients together in a darkened room. Sprinkle
on an air of expectancy and begin to cast your circle, with the children calling the
quarters in and placing an appropriate cuddly toy in each direction. I have found my
children have a particular affection for a little black bull in the north, panda bears in
the east, lions or pussy cats in the south and dolphins and seals in the west. These
Guardians of the Watchtowers will give familiar safety and protection in order to
begin the magical work.

Two

Sit around the fire and talk about what the natural world is like now. Remind each
other how at each Turning of the Wheel of the Year the world looks different and
we feel different. Think about the miracle of change, and wonder at She-Who-
Causes. Remember back to the promise that the new born baby Sun-King made to
us at Yule, that although he was only little, he was going to grow bigger and stronger
every day.

Three

Begin to call upon Bridget, 'Brede, Brede, come to my house!' Lay out a little bed
of straw for her to nestle in when she arrives, for doesn't she love the cows and the
ewes, and the smell of their warm breath in the byre, and the milk that she pours
from their teats? She needs a familiar place to come to. Arrange the cows and ewes
in the straw.

Four

Get up and dance around the room singing the Bridget chant to raise power. Then
light the candle crown, and place it upon each child's head in turn, letting them look
in the mirror. Have the mother whisper in each child's ear, 'See how beautiful you
are!' Let the children have all the time they need to gaze upon their transformed

faces, both publicly with everyone noticing their loveliness and also privately. At this point the children can send out their wishes and hopes for change in the world, that there be no more war, or that someone will give them a £5 note — whatever is their deepest wish.

Five

Sit around the fire again drinking warmed milk like you have never tasted anything like it before in your life. Feast, chat, enjoy one another's company until bedtime. Open the circle, give thanks to the Guardians and go to bed with one of the cuddly toys.

Six

Next morning hurry down to see if the bed of straw has been lain in. I have never found it undisturbed. Send the children to school full of hope and mystery and have the mother get on with her ordinary life.

Chapter 34

Chas S. Clifton

NATURE RELIGION FOR REAL

■ from *Gnosis* 48 (Summer 1998): 16–20

I N   T H E   L A S T   F E W decades Pagans have been reassessing their origin myths, distancing themselves from what was once academic fact and rediscovering deeper roots in particular landscapes and communities. The old 'facts' included folkloric and early anthropological notions of the survival of ancient religions in popular prac-tices, Murray's assertions about early modern 'witches' as a surviving fertility cult, and archaeological demarcations of the boundaries of 'Celtic' culture. Much of this is now rejected by academics and Pagans alike. But the Pagan traditions that evolved within such understandings still produce literature that looks to some kind of golden age, usually somewhere in Europe, in which people lived in harmony with nature. If 'Native American spirituality' remains popular (even among Australians, Kiwis and other Euro-descendants who might be expected to valorise more local indigenous traditions), this is rarely rooted in engagement with the contemporary realities of Native life. Like Murray's hypothesis, the appropriation of Native religiosity is rooted in evolutionist Victorian theorizing. Happily, it does not predominate among the ways in which contemporary Pagans practise and develop their traditions. In this chapter, Chas Clifton provides an expert discussion of the problematic ways in which Pagans might define themselves and source their ideas. But he does so as a preface to an incitement to engage in 'Nature Religion for Real'.

Eschewing racialism and romanticism, Clifton encourages the embedding of Pagan life in bioregional particularities. He suggests the putting down of roots in the places where people actually live and celebrate. Thus, this chapter powerfully exemplifies the diversification of Paganisms that take note not only of ancestral and communal authorities, but also of the authority of place and the power of belonging. It resonates well with Barry Patterson's chapter (Chapter 36) and other writings arising from the more explicitly 'eco-Pagan' turn. What makes Clifton's article important is its recognition that the definition of Paganism as a 'nature religion' could not be predicted with certainty from earlier sources. It might instead have evolved as a more inward-looking, esoteric or mystery religion. The trajectory by which the nature celebration side of Paganism became predominant will be traced in Clifton's book *Her Hidden Children* (2003).

Graham Harvey

Reference

Clifton, Chas S. (2003) *Her Hidden Children*. New York: Altamira Press.

S INCE MY FIRST INVOLVEMENT with Neopagan Witchcraft in the mid-1970s, I have been told that ours is a religion of nature. Occasionally people say — erroneously — that we "worship nature."

In fact contemporary Witches and other Pagans have tossed the term "nature" around for years without seriously examining what it means to them or reflecting on its history. We should realize that if we sat down to supper with Thomas Jefferson at Monticello, for example, and said over the soup course that we practiced "nature religion," his understanding of this term would be considerably different — perhaps something quasi-Masonic — from that of a person today.

Examining what we mean by "nature" is more than a scholarly exercise. For Wiccans, for environmental activists, for hunters, gardeners, and other outdoor people, the definition of nature involves our definition of ourselves.

More importantly, I believe that we as practitioners must clarify our definition of "nature" in order to create a religious tradition that is a true "nature religion" or "earth religion." To do so, we must first examine the several positions towards which we tend to move when declaring ourselves to be practicing "earth religion." As a point of clarification, let me say that in this essay, I speak primarily for and to North Americans; since I live in the U.S., that is my frame of reference. But I hope that what I say will be applicable elsewhere.

On the surface, North American Neopagans seem to be stuck between two approaches to "earth religion," both of which are untenable in the end.

The first approach is merely to transport European practices to North America. At its worst, this attitude leads towards ethnic exclusivism: "You must be of Scandinavian ancestry to worship Thor." (Or Yoruban to worship Xangó. Or Lithuanian to worship Perkunas.) At best, it's merely a poor fit.

This strategy has been attractive, however, because Pagans, like other varieties of *homo religiosus*, tend to value the old. Witches in particular have been referring to themselves as "the Old Religion" since at least the 1950s. Our British coreligionists got a lot of mileage out of identifying themselves with embattled Britain in World War II — ancient ethnic Paganism battling the "invader from the East," a dazzling rhetorical conflation of the Wehrmacht with Christianity!

Seeking a revitalized spiritual path, North American Pagans have likewise made an end run around the culture that most of us were raised in and sought Old World, Old Time models. It would take pages and pages to list all of the books and articles written, with greater or lesser degrees of historical care, on what is presented as "the Old Religion." One might read *Ancient Ways: Reclaiming the Pagan Tradition*, or *The Arthurian Quest: Living the Legends of Camelot*, or *Glamoury: Magic of the Celtic Green World*, or *Northern Magic: Mysteries of the Norse, Germans, and English*, or *Ways of the Strega: Italian Witchcraft: Its Legends, Lore & Spells*. And those titles are only from one publisher's catalogue (Llewellyn's, for April 1998).

These titles demonstrate one thing: authors, publishers, and Pagan book buyers often believe that the real power, magic, knowledge, and "juice" is Over There rather than here in North America. They give up their own power or any chance of having their own "earth religion" in favor of the imported article — or perhaps more accurately, in favor of a domestic product that is presented as an imported article. (Truth-in-labeling laws are nonexistent when it comes to "Celtic magic.")

The second untenable position is to appropriate other people's traditions — to be, as one writer put it, a member of the "Wannabe Tribe." If the North American Pagan searches elsewhere for authenticity, his or her gaze is likely to fall upon the "noble savage," the idealized creature dubbed the "Eco-Indian" by the iconoclastic ecofeminist Mary Zeiss Stange.

Stange writes in her book *Woman the Hunter*, "The problem with such idealized representations as ecological gurus, of course, is that they in no way realistically portray original Native American life. The Eco-Indian has been a vehicle for that ambivalence towards wilderness which is as old as the Euro-American cultural imagination."[1] In the "Eco-Indian" we see the cherished notion that the older inhabitants of this continent lived in an ecological and spiritual paradise, never made mistakes, and were imbued each and every one of them with an innate wisdom and a talent for speaking philosophically about it.

Setting aside for the moment Stange's phrase "ambivalence toward wilderness," which is important and which raises issues that I will return to later, I can only agree with her that these idealized Eco-Indians are not real Indians, who are as diverse and complex a group of people as anyone. Nevertheless the Eco-Indian has become a cultural icon, and of course some contemporary Indians are completely capable of exploiting the stereotype both to gain acceptance in the Anglo world and to exert moral influence on their own people.[2] "After the movie *Dances with Wolves* we've had a lot of people with Sioux blood using that as a springboard to line their own pockets," admitted the prominent Lakota Sioux journalist Tim Giago.[3]

Although this practice has a long history going back at least to the 1600s, anyone from "outside" attempting to participate or learn from Native spirituality will be hammered with the accusation of "cultural appropriation." Stange approvingly quotes Carol Christ, who said, "We can't just take off what we want from Native American culture and assimilate it, which is a typical imperialist posture of Americans."

Yet even this is a matter about which the tribal peoples of North America do not speak with one voice and never have. For every Indian who guards the mysteries, there is another one willing to share them — and yet another who has converted to Mormonism. As Stange goes on to say:

> The boundaries of human culture, and consciousness, are not so readily
> demarcated in fact, as they appear in any "I/Other" (Anglo/Indian,

human/nonhuman, male/female) scheme. This has led some environmental philosophers to argue for a model of human culture as a "mosaic of ever-changing and yet recoverable parts that can be reintegrated into the present." Such a model would make it possible to recognize affinities with the Paleolithic past, and with modern hunter-gatherer societies as well, in order to "fashion an old-new way of being."[4]

In other words, cultural appropriation is a valid charge, insofar as it means putting on the dress of the Eco-Indian without engaging modern Indians' lives. Yet Stange also criticizes those who romanticize Indians as noble savages, genetically capable of a relationship with the natural world that is unknown to Anglos. Even if your ancestors have only lived on this continent for twenty or five or two generations, you hurt yourself by acting as though it is impossible to establish any sort of relationship with it. What is the point of such high-minded hand-wringing? At its worst it leads only to complete passivity.

Most Neopagan Witches in my experience proudly distance themselves from the charge of cultural appropriation. In print, in person, and on-line I have encountered numberless variations on the theme of "we have no need to steal the spiritual practices of Native Americans, for we have our own roots." Modern Pagans are often quick to sign on with the Culture Police and denounce members of the Wannabe Tribe.

But to my mind there is something hollow about many North Americans' assertions of these Old World roots. They "smell of the lamp," as nineteenth-century critics used to say; in other words, they owe more to scholarship than lived experience.

We must realize, for example, that we do not own a single text written by a Pagan Celt other than very brief inscriptions. No anthropologist ever sat down to interview a Druid; even the Roman historians whose descriptions of the Celtic Gauls are quoted endlessly were not above treating them as "noble savages," the better to critique perceived lacks in their own society.[5] Even a great number of the Western European "Pagan survivals" and folk customs owed more to antiquarian landlords and nationalistic movements of the past two centuries than to any genuine Pagan heritage.[6]

Likewise, the "Murray hypothesis," the idea of an unbroken secret Pagan practice passed down from pre-Christian times, which passed as gospel in the British Craft and its American offshoots until perhaps the mid-1970s, is in my experience now mostly ignored by the majority of North American Craft elders except as a soul-stirring myth. Most of us accept the fact that the "witches" burned or hanged in centuries past were for the most part Christians who went to their deaths with the Our Father or the Hail Mary on their lips. And if an Englishman of the seventeenth century spoke of the "Old Religion," he meant the Catholic Church upheld by the Stuart dynasty.

While some Pagan writers do continue to hint at an unbroken "Goddess tradition," they increasingly craft their language so that it alludes to more than it claims, and in private tend to defend what they have written by saying in effect that it is a "noble lie" in Plato's sense.[7]

Now we stand at the threshold of a new century, and for all that the calendar is merely an arbitrary calculation based on a bad guess about the birth year of Jesus of

Nazareth, those three zeros that we will soon be writing will have their own enormous mythic power. The new century will be — is already being — promoted as a time for new beginnings. So here is my modest suggestion for North American Pagans of all varieties: learn to be truly *North American* Pagans.

Picking pantheons out of comparative religion books or based on one's ancestry or on some imagined affinity will become more and more unsatisfactory in a changing cultural matrix. At least we are spared the problem recounted to me by several Swedish students at my university, who said if they showed too much interest at home in the old Norse religion of the Vikings, they would run the risk of being called white supremacists by their peers. Among European countries, that problem is not unique to Sweden.

The charge of cultural imperialism made by thealogian Carol Christ and many others keeps most North American Pagans from wholesale adoption of Native religious traditions, although it fails to address the fact that those traditions have themselves changed over time and that cultural adoption runs in more than one direction. No one "owns" the ideas of drumming, firelight, chanting, trance work, sex magic, meditation, or the symbolism of knife, cup, staff, or anything else.

Instead, let the 21st century be the century when we admit that we live in North America, not in Neolithic Europe. We have no Stonehenge. We have nothing to go back to. So let's make a virtue of that fact and start literally at the ground level. In order to have "nature religion," let's start by understanding nature.

Many modern Pagans idealize prehistoric times, as depicted fictionally in works such as Jean Auel's *Clan of the Cave Bear*. One thing we can say about those people is that they knew their landscape well. Yet I meet many followers of "earth religion" who have no idea of the source of their drinking water and no knowledge of the history of the land where they live — either its human history or its wild, nonhuman history.

Would not there be a connection between the symbolic element of water and the water that we drink? Shouldn't people who name themselves after hawks and wolves and bears at least look one of those animals in the eye outside of a zoo? And how come no one ever has a white-breasted nuthatch (for example) as a power animal? Is it because there is no such bird in a box of animal crackers? Have the people who claim those names really connected with the animal in its habitat, or are they just projecting onto it their desires for power?

One answer might come in questioning what we really know about where we live. Back in 1981, the magazine *CoEvolution Quarterly* (now known as *Whole Earth Review*) published a quiz on basic bioregional knowledge called "Where You At?"[8] A "bioregion" is a loose term for a watershed or an ecological zone with common characteristics. Some bioregions are fairly easy to envision, such as the Florida Everglades. Other zones might require subdivision, such as the High Plains/short-grass prairie or the entire Great Basin.

Almost no one, including me, could answer all the questions on the quiz without some research and thought. But one characteristic of modern Pagans is that we are not averse to the scientific way of knowing. We take it and blend it with the knowledge that we gain in other ways. Thus knowing that my soil series is Larkson stony loam can enrich and add texture to what I think about the symbolic element of Earth.

Loren Cruden, one of the clearest writers on "neoshamanism," observes in her book *The Spirit of Place*: "There is a spirituality indigenous to every land. When you move in harmony with that spirit of place, you are practicing native (not Native) spirituality. . . . Ancestry gives form and continuity to spiritual practices; place gives immediacy and manifestation to power."[9]

You don't have to live on a farm to find the answers; in fact this knowledge will do a great deal to help a city person to "connect with the Earth," a stated goal in most Pagan spirituality. At least one coven in New York City and one in Seattle have adopted the "Where You At?" quiz in their training programs for prospective initiates.

Some of my coreligionists may object to the collection of such basic scientific data as precipitation or soil series. You cannot find such data at the average metaphysical bookstore. When I took a "spirits of nature" workshop once from Michael Harner's Foundation for Shamanic Studies, we communed with rocks, but no one asked just what sort of rocks these were or how they came to be where they are. Our only focus was on what the rocks were "telling" us for our personal anthropocentric good. An uncharitable outsider might have said that we were merely projecting our wishes onto the rocks.

Rather than trying to be revived ancient Somebodies-or-Other, rather than trying to adapt or adopt Native spirituality (which is itself inconsistent and in a state of flux), I would rather see my fellow Pagans focus on becoming rooted. I am not proposing some agrarian fantasy of instant peasanthood here, nor am I ruling out people's needs or desires to move around occasionally. But when we are in a place, let's be in it. Let us truly learn from it and learn about it. Let us feel its tides and changes in our lives. I think that someone who knows the flow of water, the songs of birds, and the needs of grasses has a basic store of knowledge that puts flesh on her claim that the earth is sacred.

As I have argued elsewhere, North American Neopaganism owes at least as much to the old Boston Transcendentalists as it does to the Western Hermetic tradition.[10] And it was Ralph Waldo Emerson, the most notable of Transcendentalist writers, who wrote in the conclusion of *Nature*, "When I behold a rich landscape, it is less to my purpose to recite correctly the order and superimposition of the strata than to know why all thought of multitude is lost in a tranquil sense of unity." Yet I would hate to see Emerson's call for transcendental unity manifest itself in our common "geography of nowhere," where all the streets look the same, all the lawns are bluegrass, and all sense of place has been obliterated. To be Pagan is to be particular.

So that is my modest proposal. If you would practice "nature religion" or "earth-centered spirituality," learn where you are on the earth and learn the songs of that place, the song of water and the song of wind. Yes, Western science is flawed, but it is our way of knowing, so take what it offers: its taxonomy, its lists, its naming. Start there then build a richer spirituality from that point. When you understand something about the relationship of the fire and the forest, the river and the willow grove, or the accidental history of the tumbleweed, then you begin to inhabit where you are; then you are *paganus*.

Notes

1   Mary Zeiss Stange, *Woman the Hunter* (Boston: Beacon Press, 1997), p. 100.

2   The "Eco-Indian" as spokesman for the environment has a long and complex history, ranging from the Anglo interpreters who put words in the mouths of such leaders as Tecumseh and Spokane to such modern interpreters of the idealized Indian way as Oren Lyons of the Iroquois Confederacy, not to mention the well-meaning white Protestant who concocted the famous "Chief Seattle" speech in the early 1970s.

3   Quoted in "Phonies Causing Problems for Modern-day Medicine Men," *Colorado Springs Gazette-Telegraph*, Oct. 30, 1994, p. B9.

4   Stange, pp. 128–9. She is quoting from Max Oelschlaeger, *The Idea of Wilderness: From Prehistory to the Age of Ecology* (New Haven, Conn.: Yale University Press, 1991).

5   Examples include historians of the Roman Republic and Empire, such as Posidonius (*c*.135–*c*.50 B.C.E.), Strabo (63 B.C.E.–*c*.21 C.E.), and Diodorus Siculus (fl. 60–30 B.C.E.). Stoics such as Posidonius liked the idea of Druids as sages and philosopher-kings in Plato's mold.

6   This idea is developed at length by the English historian Ronald Hutton in his recent book *Stations of the Sun: The Ritual Year in Britain* (London: Oxford University Press, 1996).

7   Plato, *Republic*, 3.414b. He suggested that the rulers of his ideal society perpetuate the idea that its social structure was ordained by the gods rather than created by humans, lest both subsequent rulers and citizens be tempted to tamper with it.

8   Originally published in *CoEvolution Quarterly* 32 (Winter 1981), the quiz was compiled by Leonard Charles, Jim Dodge, Lynn Milliman, and Victoria Stockley. The original version is also given in *Whatever Happened to Ecology?* by Stephanie Mills (San Francisco: Sierra Club Books, 1989), p. 100. . . .

9   Loren Cruden, *The Spirit of Place* (Rochester, Vt.: Destiny Books, 1995), p. 3.

10 Chas S. Clifton, "What Has Alexandria to Do with Boston: Some Sources of Modern Pagan Ethics," in James Lewis, ed., *Magical Religion and Modern Witchcraft* (Albany: State University of New York Press, 1996), pp. 269–76.

Chapter 35

Chas S. Clifton

WHAT HAPPENED TO WESTERN SHAMANISM?

■ from **WITCHCRAFT AND SHAMANISM**, St. Paul, MN, 1994, pp. 73–91

S HAMANISM HAS BEEN GAINING ground as a style of Paganism and as a reinvigoration of existing Paganisms. Clifton's discussion begins with a playfully evocative hint of the shamanic roots and uses of the Cinderella story, traces elements of shamanism in classical and European cultures and literatures, and then discusses the similarities and differences between Wicca and Shamanism. He makes it possible to consider whether Mircea Eliade's 'techniques of ecstasy' have much in common with Wicca energy raising, visualization and meditation.

As ever, the book from which the extract is drawn (Clifton, 1994), is an important source for further consideration of these issues. Further discussion of the activities and world-views of shamans worldwide – and academic study of them – is available in Harvey (2003) which includes Pagan material such as Gordon MacLellan's 'Dancing on the edge: shamanism in modern Britain' and Robert Wallis's 'Waking ancestor spirits: neo-shamanic engagements with archaeology'. Jenny Blain's *Nine Worlds of Seid-Magic* (2002) is also of exceptional importance as a study of contemporary Heathen shamanizing. For a wider survey and discussion of shamans in various Western contexts, see Wallis (2003).

Graham Harvey

References

Blain, Jenny (2002) *Nine Worlds of Seid-Magic: Ecstasy and Neo-Shamanism in North European Paganism.* London: Routledge.

Clifton, Chas S. (1994) *Witchcraft Today, Book Three: Shamanism and Witchcraft.* Minnesota: Llewellyn.

Harvey, Graham (2003) *Shamanism: A Reader*. London: Routledge.
Wallis, Robert (2003) *Shamans/Neo-Shamans: Ecstasy, Alternative Archaeologies and Contemporary Pagans*. London: Routledge.

CINDERELLA WAS A SHAMAN—or at least she started out as one. That may come as surprise to anyone who has heard only the more recent versions of her story. In those, she appears only as a passive girl, a mannequin who never complains, gets a makeover from her fairy godmother, and wins the handsome prince without actually doing much. Yet her story conceals a more interesting past, and it says much about shamanism's course in the Western world. Like a river meeting the sea and splitting into numerous branches, it divided and changed. Some parts kept flowing, but now they were different than they had been. And others slowed and spread out into wide wetlands where the wild ducks flocked and swam, and only a faint, slow current persisted to suggest the former river's flow.

A single shoe floated in that slow-moving water. It may have been a glass slipper, or a fur slipper, or a simple sandal, or an Asian horseman's boot.

To follow some portions of this river, we might start in ancient Greece. Although some modern Pagans work with the Greek or Roman pantheon, Wicca claims mainly Western European roots. I myself long resisted studying ancient Greek religion for ideas to bring forward into my present practice. I placed too much emphasis on my Anglo-Irish family heritage and not enough on the Greek spiritual and intellectual heritage that screams out every time we use a word like "pantheon."[1] Eventually I ended up reading Plato for a new perspective on shamanism, an approach not often found in introductory philosophy courses.

Tracing one stream of Western shamanism through chiefly Greek materials has several advantages. If we include its archaic forms, written Greek is more than three thousand years old. Scanty as they are, "very few texts, a few inscriptions, a few mutilated monuments, and some votive objects,"[2] we can still read large amounts of ancient Greek Pagan material unfiltered by a Christian or other worldview. And compare the advantage of the enormous amount of literary material (even though epics like the *Iliad* were written down after having been told orally for generations) that was then quoted and commented on by generations of literate persons seeking ancient roots for their own "modern" understanding of divinity, the soul, the afterlife.[3] (The so-called Dark Ages, the decline in urban life and formal learning that marked western Europe, never happened in the Eastern Roman Empire.) That continuity was lost with works like the Old English *Beowulf* or the Old Welsh *Mabinogion* that only reach us having been copied—and who knows how censored—by monastic scribes of the Middle Ages. Many Irish tales were not even collected until the nineteenth century, for example. Only with some of the Celtic tales, Norse sagas, and a few Old English magical fragments can we see bits of the Western European Pagan past unedited; and folklore, while fascinating, is not as pure a conserving force as people often believe.

Thanks to the time-binding effects of ancient Greek literature we can see some familiar patterns emerge. A diffuse polytheism of many local cults and local forms of the gods is countered by a growing skepticism and an attempt to speculate rationally on the physical world—is it made up of tiny bits called atoms, asked the philosopher Democritus (C. 460–362 B.C.E.). Is it ultimately composed of air, fire, or something else? Where do souls go after death, and how much of reality is an illusion? This is not to say that the Greeks and only the Greeks asked such questions. No doubt they have been asked around the world. The Chinese and the Indians, for instance, asked similar questions and likewise wrote them down, the difference being that their thought entered Western civilization much more recently and has only had a significant impact since the nineteenth century.[4]

Because ancient Greek religion had many centers, many stories, and its cults and initiations were not necessarily in conflict with one another, modern Pagans can feel an affinity with it that we cannot feel with the exclusive, judgmental, and dogmatic scriptural traditions. Often, reading the classical thinkers does not give the same sensation one gets nowadays of a divorce between the intellectual life, the life of feeling, and the mystical life.[5] The same persons who coolly discussed philosophy might well also have drunk the mind-altering potion some researchers believe was passed out at the climax of the Eleusinian Mysteries—and they kept the secrets required of initiates.[6] Even in Plato, whose writings (which include the ideas of his teacher, Socrates) seem so rational, some scholars discern a cross-fertilization of "Greek rationalism with magico-religious ideas whose remoter ideas belong to the northern shamanistic culture."[7]

The phrase "northern shamanistic culture" refers to two shadowy cultures, those of ancient Thrace and particularly ancient Scythia—shadowy because all we can do is speak of them by geographical region, so many changes have transpired there since those times. "Thrace" refers to an area now divided between Greece, Bulgaria, and European Turkey; it was at various times part of the kingdom of Macedonia, the Roman Empire, and the Byzantine Empire before coming under Turkish control after the fall of Constantinople in 1453. Scythia was a catch-all term for the land north of the Black Sea, and "Scythian" likewise was applied to various horse-riding pastoral nomads ranging from Hungary to Turkestan, including some of the peoples referred to as Huns.[8] Greek and later Roman writers sometimes referred to Scythia as Hyperborea, the land "behind the North Wind," which could be understood simply as "way up north." The names of two famous shamanistic Greek spiritual figures, Orpheus and Pythagoras, are intriguingly connected with these areas.

Shamanic ideas and practices that originated in central and northern Asia may well have come south through the Black Sea trade route, becoming embedded in the spiritual traditions of Orphics and Pythagoreans. Previously, Greek religion had been largely a here-and-now affair with only a shadowy concept of the afterlife. "The abode of the dead, the dark and gloomy Hades, was somewhere far away beneath the earth."[9] Central Asian shamanism may have added the idea of a preexistent "spark" of soul within the body that could leave it in dreams or in a shamanic trance. (The Greeks, however, did believe that people received messages from the gods in dreams.) "Such an ontological self [existing separate from the body] appears to have started as a shamanistic idea, which migrated south from Scythia and Thrace into Greece during the fifth century before the Common Era."[10] Not surprisingly, the idea of a wandering soul fit well with teachings of reincarnation by Orphics and Pythagoreans.

The legendary shaman Orpheus has several connections with this area. Classical Greek stories set his life one generation before the Trojan War, in other words, "long ago," and made him the son of a Thracian king. (His mother was said to be one of the nine muses while in other versions of the story his father was Apollo.) A musician of miraculous talents, he joined the Argonauts, the crew of the hero Jason, who sailed in their ship *Argo* into various adventures on the coasts of the Black Sea during the quest for the Golden Fleece. But his most famous exploit was his descent into Hades itself to bring back his wife Eurydice. His harp-playing charmed the guardians of the Underworld into letting him pass even though he was not dead, but his quest was ultimately unsuccessful. In one version, he broke the prohibition against looking at Eurydice on the return journey, causing her to vanish and him to kill himself. In another, he left without her. In a variant version of his death, he was murdered by a mob of Thracian women.

By the sixth century B.C.E. a large body of mystical poetry was attributed to Orpheus including stories of the world's creation, the genealogy of the gods, and the soul's journey after death. One famous passage, speaking of those souls who travel after death by the "path of the well-head that is beside the white cypress" was incorporated by the English magician and author Dion Fortune into her rituals of Isis.[11]

In addition, an Orphic movement arose. Its members ate no meat, beans, or wine, and practiced no violence—a notable contrast to their countrymen, whose religion included animal sacrifice and whose warfare shaded off into piracy.[12] Several writers, including Plato, described Orphics as wandering magicians. They fasted, worked wonders, and undertook shamanic journeys. "Beggar priests and seers come to the doors of the rich and convince them that in their hands, given by the gods, there lies the power to heal . . . if a misdeed has been committed by themselves or their ancestors . . . and they offer a bundle of books of Musaios and Orpheus . . . according to which they perform their sacrifices [to deliver people from evil in the afterlife]; anyone who declines to sacrifice, however, is told that terrible things are waiting for him," wrote Plato in his *Republic*.

The man Pythagoras, by contrast, can be more confidently dated to the sixth century B.C.E.; he was born on the Greek island of Samos and lived mainly in the Greek colonies of southern Italy. While he is best remembered for teaching mathematical ideas—everyone learns the Pythagorean theorem in geometry—his mathematics was originally combined with many mystical ideas that the schoolbooks leave out. "The pre-Platonic testimonies point to a rather strange mixture of number symbolism, arithmetic, doctrines of immortality and the afterlife, and rules for an ascetic life."

Whether by followers of the Orphic mysteries, Pythagoras's ascetic philosophy, or initiates of the Dionysian mysteries, which also had shamanic elements, Greek ideas of the soul began to be transformed in a nondogmatic way. Plato, who lived from about 427 to 347 B.C.E., not only pursued the implications of having a preexisting, eternal soul, but moved further to asserting that ideas have a truer reality than their physical counterparts and manifestations and that the soul longs to move from the material plane into this realm of archetypes. "Through Plato reality is made unreal in favour of an incorporeal, unchangeable other world which is to be regarded as primary," wrote the historian Walter Burkert.[13] "The ego is concentrated in an immortal soul which is alien to the body and captive in it. 'Flight from the world' is a watchword which actually occurs in Plato."[14]

Yet an alternative view suggests that Plato's "separate reality" was the gift of his experience at Eleusis, where a psychoactive preparation, similar to LSD, derived from ergot (*Claviceps purpurea*), a fungus that grows on rye, could have been used to heighten the spiritual effects of the ritual presentation of the story of the grain goddess Demeter, her daughter Persephone, and Persephone's sojourn in the Underworld—which brings us back to our theme.[15]

From Plato's time on into the early centuries of the Christian era was the heyday of the Mediterranean mystery religions: those of Orpheus, Isis, Jesus, Mithras, Dionysus, and the rest. It was a time of increasing urbanization and the concentration of political power in the empires of Alexander the Great, his successors, and then the Romans. No longer were all people content merely to sacrifice to the gods and then get on with farming, trading, or whatever; fascinated with the quasi-shamanic ideas of the soul, they sought forms of private practice involving ecstatic journeys. The parallels with our world are obvious!

In the minds of Jewish and Christian Gnostics these ideas became still more world-denying. Thus we arrive at a tremendous irony: what started as shamanism was modified by philosophy and influenced by Iranian, even Hindu and Buddhist ideas to produce the dualistic outlook blamed for much of what is wrong with the world today, the complex of associations in which body/female/material world is somehow "bad" and mind/male/spiritual world is "good." Thus one stream of shamanism becomes a stagnant swamp covered by a Gnostic mist.

But the streams flowing from primordial shamanism led other directions as well. From Scythia or Hyperborea another flows into Celtic Europe—it might be traced by the similarities between the "animal style" or zoomorphic Scythian art and Celtic interlaced animal figures. Carlo Ginzburg, an Italian historian whose works such as *The Night Battles* and *Ecstasies* represent the most original thinking on the witch-trial era (the Burning Times) in a generation or two, suggests that Asian Scythian and European Celtic animal style art represents a continuity of shamanic practice: "Indeed it has been proposed that in the struggles between animals, real or imaginary (bears, wolves, stags and griffons), portrayed by the art of the nomadic peoples, we should recognize a representation of the struggle between souls, transformed into animals, fought by the Eurasian shamans (alongside whom we might place, in the European sphere, the Hungarian *táltos* or the Balkan *kresniki*)."[16] Using Ginzburg as a guide, one may follow his linkages of "Siberian hunters, nomadic shepherds of the steppes of Central Asia, Scythians, Thracians, and Celts" to connect Central Asian shamanism with the nocturnal "flights" and the "flying ointments" attested by the witch-trial documents.

In *Ecstasies: Deciphering the Witches' Sabbath* Ginzburg exhaustively examines the lore of the "wild hunt" or "Diana's army," a throng of the dead (and/or the spirits of sleeping witches) who fly through the sky or pass through houses on their way to their rites and feasting. One of the earliest and most-quoted records of "Diana's army" was the *Canon Episcopi*, an ecclesiastical legal document of unknown origin often cited as evidence that pre-Christian Paganism coexisted with Christianity into at least the early Middle Ages. First publicized in about 906 by Regino of Prüm, Abbot of Treves (or Trier, a city in western Germany), who claimed that it had originated in the fourth century, the *Canon Episcopi* passed into the body of religious law. In essence, the canon stated that witchcraft, as commonly imagined, was a delusion and that it was *belief* in the reality of witchcraft, not witchcraft itself, that constituted heresy.

Its most famous passage reads:

> It is also not to be omitted that some wicked women, perverted by the
> Devil, seduced by illusions and phantasms of demons, believe and profess
> themselves in the hours of the night to ride upon certain beasts with
> Diana, the goddess of Pagans, and an innumerable multitude of women,
> and in the silence of the dead of the night to traverse great spaces of
> earth, and to obey her commands as of their mistress, and to be
> summoned to her service on certain nights . . . For an innumerable multi-
> tude, deceived by this false opinion [of those women], believe this to be
> true, and so believing, wander from the right faith and are involved in
> the error of the Pagans.

The period Ginzburg examines, stretching from the tenth to the eighteenth centuries at its extremes, included many such reports, however. In literary texts, he
notes, processions of the dead were led by legendary male figures (such as King
Arthur or King Herla, the origin of "harlequin," possibly identified with Woden/
Odin) while the ecstatic women were led by a female figure.[17] But the witch trial
documents (to whatever degree they are trustworthy, considering the circumstances)
complicate the picture. "In some cases we find men who in ecstasy visited the Queen
of the Elves (in whom we have recognized a variant of the nocturnal goddess);
women who, like the *benandanti* of Friuli, watch the processions of the dead in
ecstasy; men who . . . participated in the battles for the fertility of the fields."[18]
Ginzburg traces variants of the Wild Hunt back to Roman times, but in areas of Celtic
population, and suggests that this "Celtic pulp in a Roman rind" included a surviving
cult of the Celtic goddess Epona, who was associated not only with horses and
stables but with the world of the dead, and also a continuation of the cult of "the
mothers," usually portrayed as three seated goddesses, whose statues were found
throughout the northern Roman empire: Britain, Gaul, and the lower Rhineland.[19]
Ultimately, Ginzburg suggests, the nocturnal goddess who leads the processions may
be traced back to the "mistress of the animals" divinities found in many areas.
"Moreover," he adds, "the ecstasies of the followers of the goddess irresistibly call to
mind those of the shamans—men and women—of Siberia or of Lapland."[20]

Many explanations for the Burning Times have been offered: they represented
a war against women midwives and healers, a war against an actual surviving Old
Religion (the Margaret Murray theory), the growth of an actual Satanic religion
(suggested by historian Jeffrey Burton Russell), and so forth. But I think it is unde-
niable that "psychotropic herbalism" played some part, simply because some of the
recipes for "flying ointments" contained known psychoactive ingredients in addition,
some of these plants were potentially deadly in large doses, unlike the more benign
peyote or psilocybin mushrooms. Consequently, it seems likely that some sort
of tradition(s) for their safe preparation and use must have existed—but what this
tradition called itself we cannot say.

The elements of midwifery and psychotropic herbalism come together in one
particular instance, if the knowledge of how to safely prepare *Claviceps purpurea* had
been passed down from ancient times. (Eating bread baked with ergot-contaminated
rye can cause convulsions, cramps, and gangrene in the limbs, and the burning feeling

associated with this poisoning led to it being referred to as "St. Anthony's fire.") In addition, ergot stimulates labor in pregnant women; midwives knew this, giving them the ability to hasten a difficult birth or to abort an unwanted baby, an action condemned by ecclesiastical (and sometimes civil) law.

And what about Cinderella? Her story makes an intriguing footnote to the quest for shamanistic elements in medieval, Renaissance, or early modern Europe. Beginning with an observation by the anthropologist Claude Lévi-Strauss, Ginzburg devotes a chapter of *Ecstasies*, "Bones and Skin," to the common theme of bodily asymmetry in shamans, gods, or spirits who move between this world and the world of the dead. This asymmetry may, for example, take the example of lameness, an injured foot or heel, or the loss of one shoe or sandal. For instance, the legendary Greek warrior Achilles, hero of the Trojan War, was (in one common story) dipped by his semi-divine mother in the river Styx, which flows through the Underworld. She held him by his heel, and that was the only place on his body where an enemy's weapons could hurt him. And, Ginzburg adds, although Achilles is normally thought of as wholly Greek, a Greek poem from the seventh century B.C.E. identifies him as "lord of the Scythians."

In a Christian context, consider how in *Genesis* 32 the patriarch Jacob wrestles all night with "a man" (conventionally described as an angel but possibly to be understood as the Hebrew god Yahweh himself), winning the contest at the price of a dislocated thigh. In his novel *King Jesus* Robert Graves gives Jesus the same affliction as a sign of his sacred kingship: Graves also has much to say about lameness in *The White Goddess*, connecting mushrooms and the ecstatic god Dionysus, whose cult began in Thrace.[21]

In a ritual context, wearing one shoe or sandal also expresses the idea of being between two states, hence the admonition in some secret societies and magickal lodges that the candidate should be presented neither barefoot nor shod. Beyond that, "It is thought that the custom of wearing a single sandal was connected with ritual situations in which, through more immediate contact with the ground, the attempt was made to achieve a relationship with the subterranean powers [for example, in invoking Hecate]."[22]

Having discussed numerous other examples of "monosandalism," Ginzburg suggests that all fairy tales involving journeys and quests are shamanistic at their roots; that is, they are based on journeys to the world of the dead. "Anyone who goes to or returns from the nether world—man, animal, or a mixture of the two— is marked by an asymmetry," he asserts, even Cinderella. Her story (which in variations was told from Scotland to China) follows a classic sequence. She is forbidden to attend the prince's ball, gets help from a non-human source (her fairy godmother or an animal, depending on the version told), goes to the ball anyway and flees at midnight, leaving a slipper behind. After she is discovered and recognized as the only woman whose foot the slipper fits, she sees her step-sisters destroyed and she marries the prince. "Cinderella's monosandalism is a distinguishing sign of those who have visited the realm of the dead (the prince's palace)."[23]

But from "shamanistic elements" to shamanism is a long jump. Even if we could collect all the shamanistic elements in historic European witchcraft traditions, would that make modern Wicca a form of classical shamanism? I do not think so. In fact, as more Neopagan Witches study shamanism, some fundamental differences between Wicca and traditional shamanism emerge, not only in what operations are performed, but in their conceptions of the universe.

In *Shamanism: Archaic Techniques of Ecstasy*, his important cross-cultural study of shamanic patterns described in "Shamanism and Neoshamanism," the historian of religion Mircea Eliade described a cosmology common to a number of the northern and central Asian peoples, including the tribes who gave us the word "shaman." Among them is usually found a supreme sky god or creator, but this Supreme Being has become over centuries a *deus otiosus*, a distant and detached divinity.[24] Eliade's technical term comes from the Latin word *otium*, meaning leisure. The only access through him is through intermediaries: "spirits," "messengers," "sons," and so forth, to whom the shaman must "ascend." (In the mythical past, this Supreme Being was closer to humans, but something happened to change this Golden Age relationship— so goes the frequent pattern.)

Another important figure, "the only great god after the Lord of the Sky," is the Lord of the Underworld, with whom shamans also communicate.[25] In Eliade's view, over centuries Asian shamans became more occupied with acquiring helpful spirits, being possessed by spirits, struggling with evil spirits, and dealing with a variety of divinized ancestors and lesser divine beings while the original Sky God was of less everyday concern. "In a general way, it can be said that shamanism defends life, health, fertility, the world of 'light' against death, diseases, sterility, disaster, and the world of 'darkness.' "[26]

Like the protohistorical Indo-European culture, these Central Asian shamanic cultures had few goddess figures: "The Turko-Tatar and Siberian peoples know several female divinities, but they are reserved for women, their spheres being childbirth and children's diseases. The mythological role of women is also markedly small, although traces remain of it in some shamanic traditions."[27]

As Eliade and numerous other researchers have demonstrated, shamanic traditions usually picture the cosmos divided into levels to which the shaman "descends" (via a tunnel or cave, for example) or "ascends" to by climbing a magical tree, being carried by an eagle, and so on. And as we have seen, such concepts were carried into the folklore of Western Europe, where travelers visit the Faery Folk "under the hill" or ride through the night with the goddess Diana.

But in Wicca as it has developed over the past half century, such ecstatic travel was downplayed in favor of ritual forms based on the circle, the four quarters, invocations of the deities, the sexual imagery of the central rite, and the working of magick appropriate to the time, followed by a ritual meal. That is not to say that trance work, with or without psychoactive agents, has not been part of twentieth-century Wicca. As Evan John Jones points out in "Sacred Mask and Sacred Trance," some potentially dangerous experiments were made in this century based on old witch-trial records. But as it has evolved, Wicca has been more about the sacrality of sexuality and the immanence of deity in the here-and-now than about ecstatic travel to other dimensions. "The great emphasis on sexuality in the rituals . . . is neither hedonistic nor exploitative, but genuinely sacramental, since it arises out of a search for communion and for community."[28] Some modern Witches strike an almost pantheistic note, for example, Starhawk in her metaphor-loaded descriptions of the Goddess and God of the Craft:

To a Witch the world itself is what is real [as opposed to the Platonic reality of archetypes]. The Goddess, the Gods, are not mere psychological entities, existing in the psyche as if the psyche were a cave removed from the world; they too are real—that is, they are ways of thinking-in—things about real forces, real experiences.

"Would you like to have a vision of the Goddess," I ask groups when I speak in public. When they nod, I tell them to turn and look at the person sitting next to them. The immanent Goddess is not abstract.[29]

Another contrast was noted by a Witch who commented in a recent discussion of shamanism as compared with the Craft, "It seems that shamans do much more of their work on the other planes while the Craft works more on this plane. We tend to call our Guardians, Watchers, Deities to our circle, rather than wander out to meet them."

In fact, many Witches celebrate and do magickal work without the use of trance or ecstasy at all, merely a state of heightened inner awareness while within the sacred circle. But few would deny the importance of a sacramental interpretation of sexual energy, whether that is expressed symbolically, allegorically, or in the flesh.[30] Before the neoshamanic renaissance, modern Witches were more likely to characterize Wicca as a reborn fertility religion, although in an overpopulated world the fertility aspect was frequently understood to apply to mental "children" and to other aspects of life and Nature.

The interplay of sexual energies seems by contrast to play little part in traditional shamanic practice—which is not to make a comment about the sexual natures of the shamans themselves. The traditional shaman's important journeying and curing is performed alone; he or she primarily interacts alone with the spirits or the gods—even if the goal is fertility. Some Siberian shamans used to describe their relationships with "female" spirits in sexual terms, but, "The sexual relations that the shaman is believed to have with his *ayami* [tutelary spirit] are not basic to his shamanic vocation. For on one hand, sexual possession in dreams is not confined to shamans; on the other hand, the sexual elements present in certain shamanic ceremonies go beyond the relations between the shaman and his *ayami* and form part of well-known rituals intended to increase the sexual vigor of the community."[31]

I suspect that the eagerness with which many Neopagan Witches have embraced the equation of the Craft with "European shamanism" has more to do with claiming primordial roots than with actually comparing their similarities and differences. This claim was first made, to my knowledge, in the 1970s, an era when the renewed—and wholly justifiable—political struggles of American Indians combined with one of our nation's periodic "back to the land" movements, producing as a side-effect a renewed interest in "the noble savage" and an upsurge in superficial interest in Native religions. (Likewise, one contemporary Witch and writer recently admitted to me that she knows how part of her present interest in shamanism can be traced back to the "cowboy and Indian" movies she saw as a young girl.)

But Witches, more than anyone, should be aware how allure and danger are combined in the "noble savage" stereotype, for "witch" is a very similar stereotype. Modern people have often viewed both tribal people and witches with a mixture of fear, respect, and ridicule. The witch is ridiculed for "pretending" to magickal powers and for being "primitive" and "irrational," but at the same time many people desire or fear those powers. As anthropologist Michael Taussig wrote of colonists' attitudes toward the Peruvian and Colombian tribes of the Upper Amazon, "Going to the Indians for their healing power and killing them for their wildness are not so far apart."[32] Modern Pagan Witches share the cultural stereotype of the "noble savage" because we were born into these times, yet, having sometimes been on the receiving end, we ought to be more aware of it than most people. Saying that Wicca is shamanism—which it is not although it may contain shamanic elements—is merely an attempt to grab something that has slipped through our fingers. It may serve as a political statement, as one way for the new, twentieth-century Old Religion to outbid Christianity, but it is not a defensible claim from the point of view of actual practice and cosmology

Still, Wicca is nothing if not eclectic and open to borrowing. And, as Mircea Eliade noted, shamanic ecstasy is a primary phenomenon. No one owns it. While shaped by historical influences, it is every culture's property. It is recoverable and reusable. The investigations of Felicitas Goodman and her students, summarized in "Shamans, Witches, and the Recovery of the Trance Posture," are just one example of the gains to be made by looking at old material with new eyes.

At the same time, the larger Pagan movement is growing so fast that at least some sympathetic observers believe it may be the fastest-growing religion in North America, even though relatively small in absolute numbers.[33] The growth in regional and national festivals, whose size and numbers zoomed upward in the 1980s with no end yet in sight, is one indicator that the coven of a dozen or fewer people is no longer the primary group model of Pagan practice. True communities are evolving, and a lively debate has arisen over whether and how Pagan clergy should be paid for their functions as planners, managers, counselors, ritual specialists, and religious functionaries. With this size comes an increasing division of the community into specialists and nonspecialists. Some people, for all their commitment to a Pagan worldview, do not wish to participate in the frequent, intense, small-group magico-religious practice of the Witches' coven.

This growth and this division are creating a niche for a Wiccan type of shamanism as the "techniques of ecstasy" are rediscovered and updated. (It has been suggested that computer-generated virtual reality, now used primarily for pilot-training and entertainment, could be used to mimic a shamanic journey or even the soul's journey after death, thus preparing people for that inevitable experience.) The Craft's increasing appeal and rapid growth cause some Witches to fear losing the intensity small groups generate; quite possibly, shamanic work will become a new method for increasing that inner experience as organizational forms expand around it.

Somebody is picking up that floating sandal and finding that it fits.

Notes

1   "Pantheon" comes from the Greek words for "all [the] gods." Some modern psychologists see the Old Gods reflected in the elements of the self.

2   David Carrasco and Jane M. Swanberg, eds., *Waiting for the Dawn: Mircea Eliade in Perspective* (Boulder, Colorado: Westview Press, 1985), 48.

3   The philosophical schools of Athens, rooted in Classical Paganism, although developing in many different directions from it, lasted until 529 C.E. when Emperor Justinian suppressed them.

4   This is not to disallow individual exceptions. Buddhist monks, for example, may have reached Alexandria or other parts of the eastern Roman Empire, but their influence was not widespread.

5   One reason it is easy to over-emphasize the rational side of ancient Greek life is visual. We are so used to seeing all those chalky-white marble statues and buildings and their whiteness seems "cool" and "rational" in our symbolic vocabulary. But originally both the statues and the buildings were colorfully painted and gilded, something that the later Europeans who revived Greek and Roman styles did not realize at first, the paint having long since weathered away.

6   R. Gordon Wasson, Carl A.P. Ruck, and Albert Hofmann, *The Road to Eleusis: Unveiling the Secret of the Mysteries* (New York: Harcourt Brace Jovanovich, 1978). This large public religious event, held every two years at a sanctuary near Athens, began in the remote past and lasted at least until the fourth century C.E.

7   E. R. Dodds, *The Greeks and the Irrational* (Berkeley: University of California Press, 1951), 209.

8   Asiatic in origin, the Huns absorbed other races to the point that they had no definite ethnic or linguistic identity, particularly in their Western ranges.

9   Martin P. Nilsson, *Greek Folk Religion* (New York: Harper and Row, 1961 [1941]), 9.

10   Harold Bloom, *The American Religion: The Emergence of the Post-Christian Nation* (New York: Simon and Schuster, 1992), 51.

11   Dion Fortune, *The Sea Priestess* (New York: Samuel Weiser, 1978 [1938]), 221.

12   Consider how the hero Odysseus, homeward bound after the fall of Troy, first stops to raid and plunder the city of the Chicones, a Thracian people.

13   Walter Burkert, trans. John Raffan, *Greek Religion* (Cambridge: Harvard University Press, 1985), 299.

14   Burkert, 322.

15   Wasson, *et al.*, 20.

16   Carlo Ginzburg, trans. Raymond Rosenthal, *Ecstasies: Deciphering the Witches' Sabbath* (New York: Penguin, 1991 [1989]), 215.

17   To complicate the issue, processions of the dead were sometimes acted out—the origin of Halloween trick-or-treating by bands of "ghosts" and "witches."

18   Ginzburg, 102. For his study of the *benandanti* of Friuli, see his book *The Night Battles: Witchcraft and Agrarian Cults in the Sixteenth and Seventeenth Centuries* (New York: Penguin, 1985 [1966]).

19   Ginzburg, 104–5.

20   Ginzburg, 136.

21   Robert Graves, *The White Goddess* (Farrar, Straus, and Giroux, 1966 [1948]), 330–3.

22   Ginzburg, 232–3.

23   Ginzburg, 243.

24   Mircea Eliade, trans. Willard R. Trask, *Shamanism: Archaic Techniques of Ecstasy* (Princeton: Princeton University Press, 1964), 504–505. Through a series of connections, the *deus otiosus* may become the "god who disappears," causing a breakdown in the processes of life itself, creating the "wasteland" of Grail stories.

25   Eliade, 10.

26 Eliade, 508.

27 Eliade, 10. Anyone who thinks from this conclusion that Eliade must have been merely a limited, "patriarchal" thinker should then read the Great Goddess portions of his *A History of Religious Ideas* (Chicago: University of Chicago Press, 1978).

28 Aidan A. Kelly, *Crafting the Art of Magic Book 1: A History of Modern Witchcraft, 1939–1964* (St. Paul: Llewellyn Publications, 1991), 40. In the furor over Kelly's alleged betrayal of secrets and his suggestion that the rituals of Gardnerian Wicca reflected the sexual needs of its founder, Gerald Gardner, many critics ignored this more important fact: twentieth-century Wicca is a new religion based on sacred sexuality.

29 Starhawk, *Dreaming the Dark: Magic, Sex, and Politics* (Boston: Beacon Press, 1982), 73.

30 For an introduction to the topic of sexual activity within a Wiccan framework, see Valerie Voigt, "Sex Magic," in Chas S. Clifton, ed., *Witchcraft Today, Book One: The Modern Craft Movement* (St. Paul: Llewellyn Publications, 1993), 85–108.

31 Eliade, 80–1.

32 Michael Taussig, *Shamanism, Colonialism, and the Wild Man: A Study in Terror and Healing* (Chicago: University of Chicago Press, 1987), 100.

33 Aidan A. Kelly, "An Update on Neopagan Witchcraft in America," in James R. Lewis and J. Gordon Melton, eds., *Perspectives on the New Age* (Albany: State University of New York Press, 1992), 136–51. Kelly estimated the American Neopagan population to be about 300,000 at the beginning of the 1990s.

Chapter 36

Barry Patterson

FINDING YOUR WAY IN THE WOODS
The art of conversation with the *Genius Loci*

■ from http://www.redsandstonehill.net/espirit/woods-fulltxt.html

PATTERSON'S CHAPTER IS A further exploration and encouragement of earthy contact – and conversation – with places and those who live there. He expertly blends the tested and working structures of ceremony and magic with intense environmental knowledge and experience, to provoke adventurous approaches to natural places. Some of his writing unsettles neat distinctions and easy approaches. For example, having said that the *Genius Loci* (spirit of a place) might be experienced in ways similar to Spiritualist encounters with 'subtle beings', he writes that they might also be studied by ecology, geology, archaeology and history. He is not confused here but insistent that the 'art of conversation' be rooted in a kind of objectivity rather than a projection of fantasy. To some, this might be a radical move. Patterson's project, however, arises from his work as an environmental educator with intense and profound religious experience and motivations (see his website at http://www.redsandstonehill.net).

If Patterson's writing clearly expresses an eco-centric and activist kind of Paganism, it can also be read as a further elaboration of the principles of magic that would be familiar in more ceremonially focused styles of Paganism. This makes it useful in considering magic, eco-magic, environmentalism and the more earthy and located Paganisms that are now of growing importance.

Graham Harvey

Introduction

I AM NOT WRITING THIS AS an expert or authority other than as someone who has derived great benefit from my contact with Nature on many levels and in many ways since an early age. I am someone who might say: "It is Imagination" rather than "It was *just* imagination." Neither is this an academic essay with references – I am sure that you will form your own associations. Neither is this intended as an explanation of meditation or magical techniques and although some suggestions are given for exercises it is assumed that the reader has some previous familiarity with a system of some kind. If at any point you do not understand my terminology I recommend that you take steps to clarify the matter before you proceed.

I believe that ultimately we all should get out into our world and learn to *feel* it again in a primordial way. I am not prescribing a belief system, a tradition (a word which hides a multitude of sins) or a set of practices which are repeatable with predictable outcomes like scientific experiments. This is the Way of Adventure, the Lover's Way. Don't ever expect to have rewarding conversations in a warm safe pub about this with your friends. No one can predict the result of *you* taking *your* meditation or magical practice out of doors in the ways that I am going to suggest.

Wherever you may be the question will always remain – what is the truly Wild and how can we learn to live with it again? The *Genius Loci* is the "spirit" of a "place". You may experience this in the way that a spiritualist would as a subtle being who lives somewhere, but initially it is better to set out with a more open-ended model. A good one is to see the *Genius Loci* as a composite, a complex – an ecosystem with feelings. They may be constelled within space – as energies, structures and relationships – in time as events, or in other, imagined dimensions. For convenience I will refer to such a complex as a "Glade", although of course the general principles of this essay are entirely applicable to a mountain top, a moor, a desert or anywhere else you may happen to find yourself.

This kind of structure can of course be studied by such disciplines as Ecology, Geology, Archaeology and History. If you want to form some kind of healing relationship with the Glade or if it has already affected you, then the study of these subjects to some level or other, however simple, is essential. The establishment of a rapport that will be more than just sentimental, nostalgic, escapist or parasitic is dependent upon objectivity. Anyone (most of us) may get lost in the forest of their own projections

As far as defining anything is concerned, belief is unimportant. What you do and how you do it are. Definitions are part of the practice – the game rules if you like. Make them. Change them when necessary but not too regularly. What are *you*?

Orientations

If you already have a place or area in mind to work you don't have to be 100% faithful to it. If you begin to feel compulsive or obsessed then give it a rest. This should always be your first response to any problems or discomfort in this kind of work – meditate at home and sort out your everyday life a bit more. If you work in more than one area then understand the geographical, geological or historical relationships that exist between the places that you visit. This said, it is very important that you do visit some sites fairly frequently so that you become more familiar with the lie of the land, the other people that use them, the wildlife and the sensations, moods and events which you can find there.

If you haven't got a good place in mind then lucky you! Explore! You are free to discover whatever the Land will show you or guide you to. An Ordnance Survey map, even of urban areas can be useful. There may be more green bits than you expected! Accessibility is important, however, and I don't recommend trespass. Unless you have easy access to a genuine wilderness area, other human beings are probably going to be your biggest initial distraction in this kind of work.

Whatever situation you may be starting from, there is, in my experience, only one way to start. Go there simply for the sake of it for as long as you can. Give your relationship with the place a chance to stabilise and deepen in an uncontrolled way. What I mean is, don't just say: "Oh that's a good place, I went there last Wednesday, let's do Beltane there." Just wander around to see what you can see, feel what you can feel, hear whatever you can hear, smell, touch etc. The subliminal is a vital foundation and you may be unaware of things that will later become important. Get books on tree, bird or wildflower identification from your local library and try to keep nature notes. Watch the seasons changing, try it in different weather conditions.

Don't start by going around and searching for something particular unless you really have need, at least at this stage. Wandering about as aimlessly as you can is a nice exercise. How did it affect you to do so? What happened after a couple of hours wandering in the wood? Did you get lost or disorientated? Good! Did you end up back where you had started when you didn't expect to? This is the polite way to start a conversation. Ask hir about hirself, show interest in hir and forbearance with your trips. In the initial stages don't take anything home unless you are certain that it is intended for you. I might have suggested a rather abstract, impersonal sounding model, but behave as if you were actually someone's guest.

Other basic orientations to make are obvious. The four, six, eight or ten directions. The dominant life-forms. Shade and temperature in different parts of the site at different times. You will possibly be doing lengthy meditation or ritual on occasions. Where are the best places to do so? Why? Where are the best entrances, exits and straight or circuitous routes through the site?

Tuning in

By the time that you can give an interesting guided walk to a friend for about an hour without getting lost, running out of ideas or getting tangled in the briars and stung by nettles with wet feet then you are starting to tune into the Glade. The next stage, rather than pursuing some objective straight away, is to proceed by making offerings. Offerings may be material or non material, formal or informal. They are an important part of the positive mental approach that you want to engender towards and within the Glade. Immaterial offerings which are both easy and powerful to make are your attention, gratitude and love. Glades are very sensitive to human beings and many of them actually need us. Much can be achieved with a simple gesture from the heart. Material offerings may include food, drink, tobacco, essential oil, objects of personal significance or some kinds of creativity and hard work. Remember as well that what you think of as an offering might be litter to someone else and that it might not look so pretty in a day or two's time. It is important to be as sensitive as possible to the nature of the site when making material offerings.

In terms of meditation a good idea is to start with something simple with which you are already familiar. Try not to force contrived visualisations onto your surroundings though. Is that mantra appropriate? Would that particular being feel at home here? Try standing or sitting very still in one place for as long as you can. You need to be able to change track from being excited, expectant or bored into an open relaxed state which monitors what is actually going on, both within and without. If you are very distracted by thought patterns then try to concentrate on the sensory information which is coming in: light and shade, colour and tone, sounds or smells. It isn't difficult to meditate in this way for a while and to forget all your head-trips. This is a good way to see the indigenous wild animals too.

Whatever you do, keep an eye on yourself. Even at an early stage you may make conscious contact and find yourself on the receiving end of a barrage of impressions from the Glade's human dimension. This could take the form of sudden changes of mood or strong dreams or visions of events taking place there. Ghosts are not necessarily the souls of dead people with nothing better to do than hang around interfering with our lives but sometimes they certainly seem to be! It is natural for you to anthropomorphise some of the Glade's more abstract structures and to key in to energies that have something to do with your own species. However, if at an early stage you regularly leave the area with feelings of relief, escape, pursuit or you repeatedly get a headache or some other bodily symptom, then stop and give it a rest. Maybe the chemistry is just plain wrong. It is useful to have some kind of grounding and/or purification practice to hand in case of such hangovers, or a good witchdoctor you can trust to put you straight without power tripping you or interfering with the energies of the Glade.

All cases of haunting or "psychic attack" are primarily dependent upon our own state of paranoia. Not that they are all entirely psychological but they are reliant upon our state of mind and physical health in order to manifest themselves. In my opinion, many methods of so-called "psychic self defence" are merely methods for blocking out or screening what you don't like. 99% of the time this will be something about *yourself* which you'd rather not face up to. Instead of building walls that you'll need to climb or knock down someday – if in doubt, Invoke. I mean this in the proper sense of the word. Take a good long look at your reasons for doing this work and assert your highest principles every time you visit, preferably out loud.

We all have predispositions towards certain kinds of altered state of consciousness or "psychic" experience, and must at all times recognise the way in which we contribute our own energies and expectations to them, no matter what kind of meditation or magical work we are engaged in. This is a vital part of a healthy and happy rapport with the Glade. The ability to distinguish one's own stuff and to ground or earth excess or unnecessary energies is vital. Other recommendations are given later on such matters, but to simply visualise whatever we want to "earth" as passing from our body into the ground where it is then harmlessly absorbed and/or recycled is a simple but effective way of "calming things down". Check out self purification processes such as smudging, ritual bathing and yoga, too.

Another thing to remember is that there may be other people to whom the site is important. Are you going to avoid them all like the plague or feel uncomfortable if someone sees you hugging a tree? Think about it. Try to have a positive and helpful relationship with your local naturalists trust. Some people will be able to show you more about the site in one afternoon than you could discover by yourself in weeks. It is also a good idea, if possible, to be involved in active conservation work in the area, even if this does not extend beyond picking up litter every time you visit.

It is not the intention of my writing this to suggest that you should do things my way. The suggestions which have preceded this section and the ideas which follow are simple, practical and positive with regard to our relationship with the Glade. If you are already practising then you may need to adapt your practice to outdoor situations. Candles and incense may not be practical. You may need to be more covert on some occasions. Sensible clothing and something to sit on are vital. New materials are also all around you and you may discover that you are guided to certain places. A balance must be struck between what is intended and what is really possible. Do you for instance cancel or postpone because it's raining? Do you plan something and then impulsively change your plans once you get there? Do you work in a group? How do other group members relate to your place? These can be vital factors which it is easy to fall foul of.

Once you have arrived in the general area in which you have planned to do something don't just walk straight to your place, set up and get going. Try to follow a circuitous route and wander about to judge the conditions and make little offerings when and where appropriate. If you have a clear plan in mind then do your best to stick to it, but retain a degree of flexibility and don't rush in. Sometimes this initial stage is as important as the work itself – the waiting room is also, often, an audience chamber. Try to be open – sometimes the Glade will guide you to where you're meant to be in its own time. You may also achieve just as much on an informal ramble, hugging a tree which you are particularly fond of, talking to an animal, a plant or another human or sitting quietly observing in a nice spot than you could have by attempting something more formal. As your familiarity and relationship with the Glade grow, you will find that there are some aspects of your visit that you don't, or even can't plan in advance and you will get used to following your intuitive feelings.

This said, there are also going to be times when your clarity and resolve may be tested by distractions – this is a subtle aspect to this kind of work – the degree to which, in order to get in tune with the energy of that particular place and time, you need to compromise. Sometimes, whether as a result of your own lack of clarity or a disposition of the Glade, you may need to politely point out that you aren't at all interested in what is being suggested or shown to you. In particular be wary of imperious demands or pretty promises that may result from your contact. Many Glades have a colourful, atavistic or playful side that can cause complications.

Basic practice

If you have followed the orientation and attuning processes suggested above, you will probably have a wealth of ideas for both formal and informal, shorter and more lengthy rituals, visualisations and meditations that are possible. Nevertheless I include below brief accounts of some techniques that are both simple and powerful and which can be developed into more sophisticated forms if you desire.

The horizon

Find a place where you have a wide circular view of the surrounding area. Turn slowly and scan the skyline. Which direction you turn in and when or whether you change direction can vary as you see fit. Become stationary, whether standing or sitting. Close your eyes or focus them on the foreground. Visualise the ring of horizon all around you. Don't try to build it out of individual landmarks as if it were a jigsaw – feel it first and trust that it is all there before your mind's eye. This is difficult but resist the temptation to check the "bits". Now feel your own presence as a small creature or whatever – maybe a point or a symbol at its centre. Imagine an axis, like a straight line of infinite length passing through that centre from deep above through to deep below. Make the whole a sphere. Try to turn the sphere of your perceptions on its axis in an appropriate direction. What is moving?

Trees

Trees are often the dominant life form, or at least the largest and most noticeable. They may form a large proportion of your early work with the Glade. There are many ways of selecting a tree to work closely with and many possibilities for practice. Try pacing slowly around it in either or both directions for a period then lean your back against the tree where it is appropriate or comfortable to do so, either sitting with your legs flat on the ground or standing. Face or hug your tree. Stroke it slowly with the palms of your hands. A tree, too, can be an axis (see above). Trees contain vertical flows of energy and materials. Visualise upward streaming on your in-breath and downward streaming on your out-breath. Alternate these movements as you breathe until the movements come alive for you. Then try to visualise both as continuous. This "visualisation" may be visual, auditory or both. Try doing it visually until you can "hear" the flows. One direction may predominate. This will vary with the season and time of day. It may also vary with your own state. You may choose to concentrate on only one direction for a particular purpose such as earthing an energy, which can be very important. Don't, please don't become a tree parasite! Always ask permission or test the situation in some other way. Some trees are emphatic with their "NO". This is a most positive sign – well at least you heard it! A tree talked to you! and you understood what it said!

With permission and at your own discretion try a bit of tree climbing. Don't forget that getting down can be harder than getting up! Nowadays there are quite a lot of expert tree climbers associated with anti-road protests. Go down to your local camp, give them some support and they may teach you some stuff!

Magical Mystery Tour

Suitable mainly for larger areas. Enter the area. Meditate openly, standing. Wait for a guide. It may be a birdcall. It may be some other stimulus. Follow it until its influence wanes. Repeat this process. Do you end up somewhere? Is there some significance in the journey of however many stages which you have made? Do this regularly. What patterns emerge? Are there familiar and reliable guides? Are you often led to the same place? Do you get unexpectedly lost? Do you find new places or things that you haven't seen before? Are there places and guidings that you can't trust?

Going underground

Study local geology and soil types. While sitting or lying on the ground imagine that you travel down through the layers. Use all possible senses to enhance this, go as far as you feel comfortable. What do you find down there? What do you feel like? The deeper you go, the older the material through which you are passing. Don't forget to come back up at the end, or to find an exit! It's a good idea to practise this at home before you go out. If you live on the fourth floor like I used to you can go down through the walls and foundations. You can also send a root or tentacle down there which can be a useful earthing device.

Creativity

Draw, paint, sing, make music or love in the glade or its vicinity. How consistent are your creativity or inspiration? Do you get a response? Do recognisable patterns begin to form on which you can base further explorations or ritual work? The possibilities are of course endless. The more time, attention, study and activity that you give to the Glade, the more you will come to understand why you are there at all.

Danger and discovery

There is great potential for discoveries of all kinds in this work. There may be new self knowledge, enhancement of certain mental, emotional and perceptual abilities or any number of opportunities for self development. Thus, too, I hope that it goes without saying at this stage, that there are dangers.

Apart from the dangers of obsession, paranoia and mental instability that can arise from mishandling the contact – the avoidance of which I have already made reference to, there are physical dangers as well. Climbing trees, mountains or cliffs, entering caves or wandering through wilderness or wasteland without due care and attention can kill you. It happens all the time. Don't think that you are immune because you regularly frequent a particular area. Even in an urban park, for instance you may run the risk of physical attack. Try to be aware of all the possible dangers or traps associated with each expedition or piece of work that you undertake. Don't do trance work unless your feet or bottom are well and truly on terra firma!

But there is another side to this too, *fear!* Don't kid yourself that you're okay if the truth is . . . you're shitting yourself.

You may set out on a visit to a physically safe suburban wooded park with a feeling of anxiety or dread. You may feel this because what you are doing is both meaningful and powerful to you. You wonder if you will return with all your limbs and marbles or whether you will return at all. Usually, by the time you get to your destination you'll be alright. Partly this is just "normal" insecurity but it is also a vital part of the work. To pile cliché upon cliché (a cliché is in the mind of the beholder!) it has to be a good day to die if your path is to have heart.

There may be times, however, when you are really, really scared. The first rule is to recognise and accept that fact. The second rule is not to make any sudden moves. This includes an abrupt halt to what you were already doing. If you are by yourself, or even in company perhaps, don't talk out loud about feeling fear. If you can pass through such an experience you will never be the same again and your relationship with not only the Glade but your whole existence will have changed. By doing this work we are choosing to be funny little animals in a wide and complex world again. But we are doing so in order that we can come to a greater understanding of our struggles and the wider world which puts our little drama into perspective.

If this puts you off, or you think that I am using tired clichés, then just forget that you ever read this. If it excites you and you can't wait to peer into the slavering jaws of Monster Time then grow up and come down before you get involved in this endeavour. Easy for me to type into my machine, but vital. Take it easy, and don't, as I have already said more than once now, try to force things. How you handle an encounter with fear, the terrible guardian(s), the ring-pass-not, Chapel Perilous or whatever you want to call it is up to you, and it will be highly personal. It demands self knowledge and paradoxically it is the source of self knowledge. Yes, I have been there. Maybe you have already, too. Try to remember:

> *Is what is ugly or terrifying or horrible necessarily evil?*
> *What is the worst thing that could happen?*
> *Do you really believe that it will?*
> *If it does, so what?*
> *Your body is tense — but can you relax your mind?*
> *Is this going to affect your performance at work or play tomorrow?*
> *Isn't this just what you wanted anyway?*
> *Is this not just a psychological projection?*
> *How many times have read about this?*
> *How many times have you imagined this?*
> *How many times have you spoken about this?*
> *Isn't this strangely familiar?*

These glib little questions are not meant to reassure you and will not get you back home safely. What I am trying to say is that how you interpret an experience is very much up to you. Think about the little list above, think psychology, now and rehearse such encounters with the great unknown. True Invocation, as I suggested earlier is a powerful response to doubt or fear. Assert your highest principles and be clear regarding your true intentions. Concentrate on the questions that what is happening raise for you. Answers and explanations are two a penny. This is happening to you now. A good question is worth a million answers – crystallise what is happening into a powerful and meaningful question. Stick to it. Shout it out. Don't accept all these answers! The question is what counts! There are folk traditions about this, but it works both ways. You may need to be prepared to answer a question with a question or solve some kind of riddle to get free.

Hey, all you geet hard magicians! Don't knock this approach, it works! The kinds of beings that may manifest for you in the Glade and all the varieties of possible experience are part of the work. They are a "pointing out instruction". They have a function and that function is the success of the work and your self realisation. The realisation that will free you from a strangleloop or an intense and disturbing encounter is the recognition that you are the operator – that you are being tested or that you have finally found out how to plug yourself in the mains and discovered how to do this! Who or what are you anyway? Ultimately if you are capable of meeting, say, a horrible monster, then you are capable of manifesting yourself as something more powerful than it is. Or of surrendering to it, of course, which is also an option.

Acting under fear is courage. Try to challenge or touch an object of your loathing. Does it need your love in order that it can be free or unnecessary? Is it a joke? Try laughter as a response – it is a very potent release energy – even more so if you can see the genuine humour in your circumstances, and if you can't perhaps it will put you in touch with it! Shout "FUCK OFF!" as loudly as you can – jump up and down and scream and shout. The intruder probably will go away, but you can guarantee that if you do this you may return to this space again. Exorcism, despite its popularity among the craven and superstitious, is a very limited technique and can cause as many problems as it seems to solve.

None of these comments contradict the basic common sense which I have tried to propound in earlier sections. This won't just happen to you out of the blue unless you're ripe for it in one way or another. It may never happen. It may be years before such an experience overtakes you (so much for that so-called initiation) and you'll get plenty of warning that something is brewing – that discovery/danger is around the corner. And there is always an opt out clause. Sadistic horror movies in which there is no escape are expressions of the most sublime ignorance and are manufactured, for the most part, for the titillation of people who wouldn't be seen dead in the woods at night. No pun intended!

So far I've avoided using the word shaman because it is so trendy right now to describe an experience as "shamanic" but remember that despite our romantic notions about shamanic experience, a shaman is someone who makes regular use of experiences that would completely freak out most of the people who sit proselytising at weekend seminars and who will be trying to sell you something else when the fashion changes.

Some people think that to practise powerful magic means to precipitate crises and push themselves to their limits. It is possible to use such methods but it is very easy to delude yourself, particularly if you have got used to such things and your palate has become jaded. To contrive some kind of crisis or confrontation and then believe that you've really been there is sad. There are far simpler and less exciting ways of discovering and exploring your limitations that are, in the long run, more valuable, but they seem boring to the dilettante.

It would also be completely misleading of me to suggest that the only experiences with real potential for self development are the trials and traumas of facing your primal fears. True self knowledge comes with time, maturity (I don't mean age!) and patience. The person who complains that they never saw a spirit in their lives and that they don't get amazing messages from the Glade is actually in a very positive position – there's less to get confused and mixed up about for a start! I'm not suggesting that we all go out into our local woods or commons every week in order to complicate our lives with a new form of cerebral entertainment. The mental health service is already overworked and under-funded!

Gifts from faery

Sooner or later you will start bringing things home with you from your visits to the Glade. Twigs, stones, feathers and so on are likely finds. Remember that in searching for or accidentally finding "power objects" there are pitfalls.

A profligate collector may end up with an assemblage of objects which together add up to something greater than their sum, but more than likely the things which they bring home will end up having less meaning and power just because there are so many of them and their purpose is unclear. This is why I refer to them as gifts. It is useful to do so and also to maintain a gift protocol in your attitude as well as your behaviour. I have known people to be so proud of their "magic stone" which they took from the site of a ritual but to be rushing back to return it a week later. Errors of this kind can cause illness, mental confusion and relationship difficulties with those close to you amongst other things. You should be in no doubt as to whether a gift is intended for you. To have seen it in a vision previously is a good sign (as long as you're clear about the vision's significance) as is a pun, synchronicity or a positive alteration of your emotional, mental or physical state as a result of contact.

On originally finding it, give thanks and ask for guidance as to its potential function. It may be little more than a souvenir (lest you forget something important) or you may discover that it has certain properties or other significance at a later date. You will also have to decide whether it is immediately ready for use or whether it will require ritual purification or charging before you make use of it. Some kind of purification is usually advised for reasons of hygiene if nothing else, although you sometimes may make the mistake of "purifying" away the very reason that you found it in the first place. Salt is a good standby.

Sometimes something will come to you for a particular reason and when that has been realised will either go of its own accord or require appropriate disposal. Sometimes the loss of a much loved stone will signify a change in the air, but I am not in any way encouraging people to become blindly superstitious. The answer to the question "Why?" is always "because" and simple cause and effect explanations don't have a place in my kind of magic.

Giving away such objects to people should be done with either great caution or complete randomness. Question your motives for doing so. Maybe the object "told you". The strong attraction of a friend to one of your things may become a common experience. That is why many practitioners keep their gifts under wraps. It is best not to give away just because someone asked you or on the spur of the moment. A common experience of mine is of an object, say a nice fossil, requiring transport to somewhere else. This can be a very powerful experience – to know that you are placing this thing where someone else will find it or where it will never be seen again by human eyes.

Another subject that should be considered very seriously is that of the collection of live wood from trees. This should never, in my opinion, be done casually, or even informally if you are engaged in conversation with the Glade, which is a sensitive matter. Question exactly what you need and why you need it. A twig or piece of dead wood that you pick up from the ground may serve your purpose just as well. The so-called "power" in a "power object" such as an ash wand is entirely dependent upon your own capacity. Don't let the live wood snobs con you into thinking that you have to do it their way or that a certain (maybe very expensive?) object has any intrinsic power of its own independent of the Glade from which it came or the practitioner who uses it.

It is absolutely necessary if you take living wood from a tree for magical purposes that you have a positive relationship with the tree and preferably with its Glade. This can mean a considerable amount of preparation. Even then, prior to selection and/or removal of the wood ask permission or do some kind of divination regarding whether or not you should do the deed. I may seem to be overstating my case here but it is essential that we leave behind the consumer attitudes which are so prevalent in society today – regrettably even among so-called "pagans". I offer my blood in a gesture of thanks and bonding to all trees from which I take living wood.

Greater gifts of the Glade are visions, healings, respite and love. The greatest gifts of the Glade are the most difficult to accept. They are knowledge and wisdom, which brings us to the heart of the matter.

The heart of the matter

A Glade is no more a closed system with discrete edges than is any ecosystem, plant community or, for that matter, human being. When you enter a Glade you become one of its parts. Remember that property of a hologram by which any part contains the information to make the whole thing? The Glade experiences itself through you in a number of different ways and energy exchange takes place in a variety of dimensional contexts, some of which human thought and language cannot categorise.

Many people are motivated to have a relationship with non-human dimensions but once their conversation has reached a certain level of familiarity or they have got certain practical results they cease to be adventurers, preferring the role of caretaker, lover, healer or symbiont. As such they miss out on one of the most important implications of the Glade experience. The Glade exists in relationship to its peers on a particular organisational level. Likewise it is a unit in a larger composite, as well as being a collective entity itself. The Land is Glade, the Earth is a Glade, the Solar System is a Glade, the Galaxy is Glade. Yes! You are a Glade – there are more symbiotic organisms in your gut than there are human cells in your body. What are you?

The point of all this is simple. The heart of the matter is the meaning of life. Relationship(s). Relativity. The "Unified Field". The nature of reality. The discovery and manifestation of timeless essential being. Our True self, our secret heart – God or Goddess if you insist on religious terminology. I don't mean the realisation of any concept or myth – I mean the bare-faced brilliance of this NOW – usually obscured by conditioning, alienation, mental habits and the repression of true emotion. Our culture has replaced true E-Motion with a safer vocabulary of thought forms (love, hate, happy, sad) but it can still really move us if we allow it to. In the long run we need to relearn how to relate. How can we "be in harmony with", or "save" or "heal" a world which we seem to be constantly denying, fighting and struggling to escape from?

Chapter 37

Gordon MacLellan

ENTERTAINING FAERIES

■ from **WHITE DRAGON** 19 (1998): 4–7

I F PAGANISM HAS BEEN caught between attending to this-worldly or other-worldly matters (playing out its own unique version of the dynamic inter-play of immanence and transcendence), faeries have often been met at the borders. Some may conceive of them, as the Victorians did, as cute flower-people, aiding the re-enchantment of gardens and childhood. Others see them as the dangerous denizens of strangely inhuman worlds, tricksters who steal brides and lovers. Perhaps, in truth, faeries are essentially ambiguous: neither from here nor unknown here, neither moral nor immoral, thoroughly sensual but hard to touch, elusive but inviting, human-like but hardly humane, natural but far beyond the everyday. Perhaps Paganism could exist without deities, elementals, the fey, and other allegedly metaphysical persons – it could celebrate a world inhabited only by beings known to the most secular of scientists. But common Pagan experience seems to demand assent to the existence of neighbors, co-inhabitants of the world, persons of power whose presence may inspire awe or terror, celebration or caution. Often, of course, Pagans share the broader culture's diminished view of the 'lords and ladies' (as one traditional circum-locution names them in an attempt not to invite their presence). Gordon MacLellan (or 'the Toad') invites careful consideration and bold adventuring to see if the world is indeed a richer place than has been imagined. There are no 'ten steps' or 'DIY' programmes on offer, but some clues as to the habitat and habits of those who might be encountered.

Actually, this chapter is not only about the most powerful of the other-world beings who some Pagans take to be more than folklore, more than childish tales (although others do take them to be just that, but enjoyable all the same). It suggests that our homes too are, or could be, part of the sacred ecology, the diversity of which Paganism attempts to enhance and celebrate. It suggests that while we might encounter much that is strange 'out there' in the woods and wildernesses, we might also attempt to make space in our busy human lives to attend to those who live alongside us. MacLellan is another environmental educator (his website shows what he does: http://www.creepingtoad.org.uk/toadhall.html) whose earthy Paganism is part of the trajectory marked by labels such as 'shamanic' and 'eco-activist' as well as 'eco-magician'. His publications include MacLellan (1996a, 1996b, 1997, 1999).

Graham Harvey

References

MacLellan, Gordon (1996a) 'Dancing on the edge: Shamanism in modern Britain', in Graham Harvey and Charlotte Hardman (eds) *Pagan Pathways*. London: Thorsons, pp. 138–48. Reprinted in Graham Harvey (ed.) (2003) *Shamanism: A Reader*. London: Routledge, pp. 365–74.

MacLellan, Gordon (1996b) *Talking to the Earth*. Milverton: Capall Bann.

MacLellan, Gordon (1997) *Sacred Animals*. Milverton: Capall Bann.

MacLellan, Gordon (1999) *Shamanism*. London: Piatkus Books.

> So you want to meet the Faeries?
> Tell me, O, tell me do:
> Why should the Faeries ever want to meet with you?
> Because you are a witch? a magician? shaman? powerful? beautiful? earnest? honourable?
> Because we are all alive?
> Because it might be fun?
> Because you might be . . . tasty?

So we go prancing off, looking for Faeries in our best right-on, elegant, new-modern-pagan way and our voices echo back, unanswered, from the empty places. Our calls at the edge of the day in wood and glen go all unheeded. The stories tell us of The Departure, of the Good People gathering and withdrawing into the Hollow Hills, the doors closing and leaving us cast aside on the bleak strand of our progress. And we are left wondering if it was all true and we talk anew of a golden age when the hills were alive with the Little People, now gone beyond reach because they will not answer when we call.

And it seems that we are left in an empty world.

An empty world that is quite likely sniggering beneath the rocky ledge we stand on. Or licking its lips.

But maybe we are going about this the wrong way, maybe reaching out to Faerie[1] is not the process we envisage. Almost nothing else in Faerie is quite what we think it will be, so why should knocking on the door conform to our ideals either?

This article is an invitation to you to go on another journey and maybe on the way you will meet Faeries. Or maybe you will just meet yourself. Hopefully, one way or the other, you will not be quite the same person at the end of it. Is that a good thing? Who knows? If you go into faerie hoping for only *good* things, then you have not read your folklore!

Western society seems to have pursued a severance from wonder with a ferocious determination and an equally determined sense of tragedy. We grow up in a dream of separation – cast out from Eden, evolved beyond the measure of other animals, enchantment banished by reason and forsaken by our heroes (Arthur is asleep, Merlin lost in a cave, or a tree, or a crystal, or some such thing; Thomas is in Elfland, all of them out of reach). Even our fiction has been full of "the Age of Man . . .", the end of magic, the elves have sailed beyond the edge of the world.

> All the wild witches, those most noble ladies,
> For all their broomsticks and their tears,
> Their angry tears, are gone.[2]

This is changing now: we are taking a much more positive view of the world we live in, more active and less nostalgic. The stories we spin seem more hopeful again. But there is still so much of separation. . . . Even when we describe ourselves as "Pagan" and reach out anew to a living world, we bring that culture of estrangement with us and this is still reflected in much of what we do. I wonder at the amount of language of our ceremonies that speaks of crossing distance. We "draw down the Moon", invoke the Directions, invite the Presences of This or That or The Next Thing to join us. Maybe the living Goddess is already here and do we really think that the Powers of the Four Directions are waiting for us to speak? Are they not always sweeping across the land in pulsing tides? Maybe the words of our rituals should turn inwards and call the change within us that opens our senses to the eternal presence of the Old Stone Woman, to the tide of the West moving across our little circle? The sharp answer is that, "Of course, that is what our invocations really mean and all that 'reaching out' language is actually, of course, you know, metaphysical. Or is it metaphorical? But you know what I mean, don't you? Don't you? Stop licking your lips." Nice answer. Very neat. Very trim. Forget it.

This is Faerie, remember, and the first step on your journey is to say what you mean: words are a power, they describe and define and the wrong words can throw you flat on your face. "No, we Faeries will not touch this thistle that hides the gold." (You did not say anything about the hundred other thistles in this field, though, did you?). "Me Myself is hurting me!" Listen to what you say and only play word games when you are very sure of yourself. Say what you mean or shut up. You don't get a chance afterwards to say "I didn't mean that!"

Because the second step on this journey is a realisation: Faerie is still there. Still watching. Fairly pissed off in some places, bruised and battered in others and in still others downright hostile. But very definitely there. And now, at last, more of us are saying that we want to talk, to listen, to learn, to share. And then we go stamping off into the sacred places carrying our enthusiasm like a placard and our humility like trumpets and wielding field guides to "Fairies I Have Known". We do all that and then feel disappointed when the doors do not open and the Shining Ones do not come cascading out like a swarm of cheerleaders. . . .

We need to remember our Faerie lore: to read the old stories again. Not necessarily the latest sweet and powerful interpretations that turn our images of Faerie into handy archetypes and thought forms, but the simple stories. The old stories of people living with the Good Neighbours down the road, by the stream, in the Hollow Hill. That is where we might learn the etiquette that guides contact and advice on who we might encounter, and what they might do to us. The world is changing and both ourselves and the people of Faerie with it. We who are Pagan seek a different relationship with the world than our more recent ancestors and can share a different set of friendships with Faerie. With this in mind, be brave and be strong: if we are Pagan then we already talk to a world similar to that Faerie and, hopefully, are less likely to be shocked, dismayed or brow-beaten by a simple Faerie presence and, again hopefully, are more likely than some of our contemporaries of Entertaining faeries. We know we are earth-children, just as they are – just as we all are! Faeries delight in pushing humans, testing us, seeing how far we can be stretched, what they can get away with. Modern Pagans should have the personal confidence and enough of the touch of magic to stand up for themselves and treat with Faerie as fellow children of a singing Earth. So be brave: we are Pagans, we can reclaim old relationships with Faerie (our ancestors may have been Christian but do not dismiss their lore and their understanding) and we should have the strength to shape new relationships, too.

In our recent myth, Faeries tend to be the people of the wild places: strange and noble figures of lowering cloud and blowing snow, of white water, deep pool and green moss. And indeed some are, but simpler stories remind us that they are just as often people of hedgerow, field and lane, farmyard, barn, house and home.

We need to think about who we hope to meet and why. We need to be very careful of those romantic associations. Why are you sitting here at the crossroad hoping the Faerie Queen will notice you as She rides out at Midsummer? What do you think She is going to do? Grant you three wishes? Often the people of those wild places who we long to meet so much are themselves wild and fierce. Maybe by our modern reading they are meant to be so: beings of power, yes, with grace and wisdom and a certain stern dignity but essentially good and pure and noble. Very angelic? It sounds lovely, and maybe I just live in a grubbier world, but the Faeries I meet have not read those books. They may be all those things, at times, but they are far more than that. The Shining Ones, the People of the Heights are all of the above and might freeze the marrow in your bones if they actually noticed you at all. Nuckelavee, part human, part horse and all skinless, haunts the windswept beaches of the western coasts, while Redcap now favours the ruins of Border castles and the empty hills where the reivers once rode. Jenny Greenteeth, Peg Powler and the Kelpie all haunt deep, dark pools and will gladly introduce you to those depths. The people of the wild places are not all so grim, but their nature reflects their homes and the wild and lonely places where they live mark their characters.

We need to recognise your desires in seeking Faerie: are we looking for a magic equivalent of a "wilderness experience", a walk in the high places simply because it is the "best" one to have, because it *is* wild, because it threatens us, offers danger and credibility? Why do we want these things? It may sound much more dramatic to have encountered the People of the Moor and Mountaintop than the Brownie who lives next to the coal scuttle, but which is more likely to happen, which are you more likely to learn from, and come out of it unscathed? If we hope to meet Faerie, maybe we should go looking for contacts who we can develop an ongoing relationship with, grow into Good Neighbours with, one with the other. The danger is still there and the unpredictability. Anyone who says that the lowland, farmland people are harmless is, maybe conveniently, forgetting the Boggarts that can haunt a life out of all joy and hope and the cold Woman with the White Hand who drifts through birch groves and leaves you mad or dead.

So who do you go looking for? Or do you actually look for someone, or do you just wait and see who comes visiting?

There are various classifications of the Faerie world. Yeats talks of The Sociable Fairies, "in the main kindly . . . These creatures who go about in troops, and quarrel, and make love, much as men and women do . . ." and The Solitary Fairies, "full of all uncharitableness . . . These are nearly all gloomy and terrible in some way. There are, however, some among them who have light hearts and brave attire".[3] Scottish tales separate the Seelie (more or less pleasant) and Unseelie (more or less unpleasant) Courts. More recent accounts talk of Faeries as elementals, memories of lost races and decaying gods. This does not necessarily help the traveller on a Faerie road much: you do not get much time to whip out your guidebook and work out the nature of the laughing, horsy thing that has just jumped on your head and left you spluttering in the ditch.

In general, I would disagree with Yeats and suggest that often the solitary people are actually more approachable that the trooping Faeries. You stand more chance of having a one-to-one conversation with a solitary Faerie than being viewed as a gift for some rare jest. Many of the solitaries also hold old associations with people: most of the household and farmyard people are solitaries: Brownies, Hobs, Boggarts, Fenodyree, Gruagach, even the alarming Banshees.[4] It is true that those old associations are not always amiable: some are definitely "marginal" and others downright unpleasant. Boggarts swing in and out of charm with delicious uncertainty and Banshees (the name simply means "Faerie Woman", but let's hang onto the wailing spectre bit) are chilling, but still part of family life like a rather shocking relative who only ever turns up at funerals. Of course, with the Banshee, she turns up to let you know of the funeral in advance. Hedley Kow and his Pouca relatives may be annoying but are mostly harmless while the Black Shuck or Padfoot coming up behind you of a dark night is another matter.

> I listen. In the fields dark furrow, my pelt is invisible. Their fingers have felt my coat and tugged at my neck. They have dealt with the Death-Dealer and there is no going back.[5]

But these are also the local people: these are the ones who have overlapped with human lives for years: as involved with house and hearth and home as a place's human inhabitants. Often they are still around, warier now, but sometimes approachable.

Why bother anyway? Where does this leave us – realising that Faerie is still there, a world of wonder and enchantment but maybe out of reach? Some would say, "Good! And the further away the better!" and they will stay safe within the walls of a human world and miss some of the thrills of a wider life. For to touch Faerie, be touched by Faerie is a thrill! To invite Faerie back into our lives is to open a door to a chaos of light and glitter, of glimmering mornings and screaming nights and the sudden clatter of hooves on the roof. It is a world of wild and strange people with their own codes and rules, and their own agendas and we will have to learn again the old rules for these Good Neighbours. And we, both humans and Faeries, will all have to learn some new ones as well for just as we are not the people our ancestors were, neither are the Faeries we meet now quite the same people we were dealing with in the past. These are all good things, too: things that break our egocentric, humanocentric world and magic, things which teach us how to live and let live within that wider world without being passive and acquiescent but as equals in a fiercely dynamic interplay of laughter and trickery bouncing to and fro between the worlds.

But the journey still awaits and the seven-league boots are fretting by the door. The adventure beckons and, here, I keep telling you not to go away to the high hills. The adventure may as readily be at your own hearth so put on your fluffy slippers and potter about at home. If you go away to hunt the Faeries you may find nothing, or, more likely, you will find your over-eagerness, or your arrogance, or your conceit and self-importance, twisted and thrown back at you while the hills lie empty but laughing around you.

Take it easy. Work to create spaces where They know They are welcome: a home with occasional dusty shadows, a deep corner in a warm room, as near such hearth as your house may have, a garden with an overgrown corner, an old bench with room for you and a friend. An old comfy chair. Food set out on the step or bright gifts hanging, glittering in a birch tree or hawthorn. Grow the flowers that invite the People in – oak, ash and elder, bluebell, foxglove and thyme. Have a pond – or even just a small, dark bucket of water that will reflect the stars in your backyard and grown about with ferns.

Practise your stillness. Expect nothing. Demand nothing. Offer friendship and the company of silence and one day you may turn around and find someone beside you on the bench. A shape, a face, or simply a presence: a space where a character is. Faeries are not bound to particular physical shapes: the forms we meet are usually a compromise between what the Faerie feels she should look like and the images that our dreams offer her. Often the more human contact a Faerie has had, the more independent he is of our personal preconceptions – he has a bigger repertoire of images to work with. So open your eyes with care: try to welcome whatever shape the Faerie chooses to wear, and if this one shocks you, see that as something you need to go away and think about. If you *feel* someone who is pleasant but *see* someone who alarms you, try having a conversation with your "eyes", inner or outer, closed!

The simple point here, is not to expect things – not to try to define who should come, who you want to meet, who should turn up in this setting. . . . That person may no longer be here, may never have been here, but you can be fairly sure that *someone* is and if they feel their welcome and your comfortable, self-assured warmth they are more likely to pop in and have a look . . . but who is it that may come calling?

Traditional settings for Faeries are rural or wilderness ones, but they are here in our cities too. Sometimes there are beleaguered groups of woodland, pool or grassland people hanging on in a park or nature reserve, protecting their memories and the dream of their home in a world that seems out to devour it. Bring your strength and your human support to those situations. Find the old wells and clean them of debris and rotting leaves. Love the place. Those People are often very wary and very elusive and you may never meet them, but if you are there with graceful support, you will feel their presence and a smile on your back as you clear the rubbish from under a bush.

There are new People too; Faeries not described in the old stories, strange stilt-legged spirits who stalk the lamplit streets late at night, boggarts of stone and bin-lids and those odd forgotten spaces between the terraced houses.

> She would see them in the twilight when the wind was right, roly-poly shapes propelled by ocean breezes, turning end-over-end along the beach or down the alley behind her house like errant beach balls . . . Sometimes they would get caught up against a building or stuck on a curb and then spindly little arms and legs would unfold from their fat bodies until they could push themselves free and go rolling with the wind again.[6]

This draws us back to the question of "what are Faeries?" and to their answer "We are". Humans talk of "memories of older races", "decaying gods of earlier cultures", "projections of our subconscious", "elemental forces". I suspect that it might be a bit of all these – accumulated dreams that humans and Land have shared over the years. But Faeries are also just Faeries: they are there because they are there. Often they do belong to places, draw their strength from, grow from? the place where they live – hence maybe the new shapes they wear in cities? "I am the luck of the farm", the dream of the wood, fairy folks are in old oaks. They walk out of the need of rock and root for a voice. But not all are bound by place or a roving feature like wind or rain or storm. Faeries are Faeries. Do not go on this journey having decided what you will find, how they will behave and where they have come from. I have met very few humans who can explain where *we* have come from and why *we* are here (if there is any reason at all, other than "to live") – why should we expect every-thing else to be set here for a purpose? There is often an implicit bit of human arrogance in such thoughts as well: "why are you here?" often carries an assumption that "you are here to serve us (humans)" – or "you are here because we want you to be". Oh, such a delight for the Faeries! What a juicy tidbit to chew over and tempt and taunt and lure into a long walk along a short pier!

So. Another step. Walk away from needing answers and know that Faeries are Faeries and will be so whether we like it or not. Or whether we believe in them or not: that Tinkerbell syndrome may well be the wrong way round. When we stop believing in Faeries, *we* disappear from *their* world, Faerie will go on being Faerie. The Earth it grows from is being battered and waylaid and in many places Faeries struggle to hold safe their homes, but Faerie is part of the Earth's Dream. It persists. And Faeries are out there when we walk in the woods, when we tend a garden, when we walk home late at night through empty streets.

The journey that we take towards Faerie also takes us into ourselves. It calls for much from us: those seven-league boots might be strides across your personality. Almost all that is called for is about recognition: of ourselves and our attitudes and of Faerie right to do what Faeries will, and our right to make sure they do not do it to us! We are not prey. If we are not swift, and clear and humorous we might become so, but we do not enter Faerie as victims. Read the stories, remember the tricks and know that if you are calm and confident in being "me, myself" you just might be respected enough to be talked to and not tricked, to become a friend and not just a neighbour.

This article has been a rambling one, like the "bonnie road that lies across the fernie brae", the road that leads to Elfland and the journey it describes only touches the first steps you might take towards Faerie. In the end there are not steps I could teach you for they are as unpredictable as the Faeries themselves and what I tell you might just be a will-o-the-wisp to take you into a bog. I do not apologise for that: Faerie is wild and strange and fierce and delightful and in the end you will have to find your own way in.

When I was thinking about this article, however, I was standing in a flooded field where the River Mersey in Manchester had spilled out through a willow wood.

. . .

> Tell them to go and find the places where the water is still, where the water reflects the trees and the reflections hold mystery. It does not matter where it is. Listen for the silence. Listen for the mystery. Where the shadows under the trees are still in the fiercest storm, that is where we are.

Notes

1   Faerie: both the "land" and the people are called "Faerie" and swarms of Faeries are sometimes also just called "Faerie". "Faerie", the land, is not really a separate country, although it is often easier to talk as if it were. It is the other side of the land we walk on everyday: the hidden side of things. The shadow behind the door, at the back of the wardrobe.
2   Yeats, W.B., from the poem "Lines Written in Dejection".
3   Yeats, W.B., *Fairy and Folk Tales of Ireland*, Colin Smythe, 1973.
4   See Katherine Briggs' novel *Hobberdy Dick* for a wonderful retelling of Hob and related lore of the farmland peoples.
5   Gordon, John, *Catch Your Death, and Other Ghost Stories*, Magnet, 1985.
6   de Lint, Charles, *Dreams Underfoot*, Tor, 1994. de Lint writes wonderful books about a new magic, a modern pattern of human and Faerie.

Further reading

Paganisms have been studied in various ways by many scholars of various academic disciplines. This guide to further study is intended to suggest some books and other resources, the value of which this *Reader* intends to enhance. It is not intended to be a complete bibliography of all that has been published but merely an introduction to core texts and resources that should be key to any academic engagement with Paganisms.

It should be obvious that some of the readings provided here are drawn from books and/or journals that may provide further important insights and discussions. For example, when referring to some sources for engaging with Feminist or Goddess Spirituality below, we will not repeat advice on the importance of Asphodel Long's article. We also assume that students will search the Internet for related discussions and material – once again, for example, Asphodel Long's website should be easy to find through any good web browser.

The editors have written and/or edited several books that are important to the study of Paganisms. Chas S. Clifton edited the four-volume *Witchcraft Today* anthology series for Llewellyn Publications: *The Modern Craft Movement*, 1992a; *Modern Rites of Passage*, 1993; *Witchcraft and Shamanism*, 1994; and *Living Between Two Worlds*, 1996. He is also the author of *The Encyclopedia of Heresies and Heretics* (1992b) and of a new history of Paganism in the United States, *Her Hidden Children* (2003). He edits *The Pomegranate: The Journal of Pagan Studies*, which includes a wealth of articles, reviews and discussions at the cutting edge of the academic study of Paganisms. He is also central to the 'Nature Religions Scholars Network', a web-based gathering of scholars of many disciplines interested in these and related phenomena. Their website also provides a valuable and growing bibliography (http://chass.colostate-pueblo.edu/natrel).

Graham Harvey has written an introduction to the various Pagan traditions or paths that includes discussion of Pagan environmental ethics, theologies and much more. In the UK and Australia it is entitled, *Listening People, Speaking Earth: Contemporary Paganism* (1997) while the North American edition is called *Contemporary Paganism: Listening People, Speaking Earth* (1997). With Charlotte Hardman he co-edited *Pagan Pathways* (2000). This covers much of the same ground but includes articles by scholars and practitioners of particular styles of Paganism. Although out of print, it should be available in many libraries. He is also co-editor, with Jenny Blain and Doug Ezzy, of *Researching Paganisms: Religious Experiences and Academic Methodologies* (2004), which brings together significant scholars within the various academic disciplines interested in Paganisms. This book will be part of AltaMira's important new series (edited by Chas S. Clifton and Wendy Griffin) on Pagan Studies. He has also written and edited books about indigenous religions and shamanism (e.g. *Indigenous Religions: A Companion*, 2000; and *Shamanism: A Reader*, 2003) which raise interesting questions about the sometimes parallel trajectories taken among some indigenous communities and some Pagan ones.

Margot Adler's *Drawing Down the Moon* (1986) remains the classic introduction and discussion of North American 'Witches, Druids, Goddess-Worshippers and Other Pagans'. While not a scholar in the strictest sense of the term, Adler certainly provides an important text that should not be ignored in any academic consideration of Paganisms.

A five-volume series called 'Religion Today: Tradition, Modernity and Change', co-published by the UK's Open University and Ashgate, includes *Belief Beyond Boundaries: Wicca, Celtic Spirituality and New Age*, edited by Joanne Pearson (2003). This would work very well alongside this *Reader*, as would other volumes in the series, either by providing further discussions of similar topics or by examining the broader religious and cultural context in which Paganisms thrive. Joanne Pearson is also co-editor with Richard Roberts and Geoffrey Samuel of *Nature Religion Today: Paganism in the Modern World* (1999). The term 'nature religion' seems to have arisen independently both as a term used by Pagans for their own religion and in Catherine Albanese's (1990) discussion of an important trend (wider than Paganism) in North American religiosity. This illustrates two important matters: first, the way in which labels operate within academia and beyond, and second, that Paganisms arose and continue to develop as elements of broader cultures. Sometimes they match and illustrate truly popular and widespread trends, at others times they are counter-cultural or alternative to both elite and popular cultures. A similar point is made evident in the work of Steven Sutcliffe and Marion Bowman (2000).

The works of Ronald Hutton are the most significant discussions of the historical and pre-historical contexts in or from which contemporary Paganisms arose. *The Pagan Religions of the Ancient British Isles* (1991) discusses the available evidence on ancient British pagan religions. It argues for limited but interesting continuities between earlier historical movements and the Paganisms that arose in the twentieth century. Hutton's *The Triumph of the Moon* (1999) focuses specifically on the creation and evolution of modern witchcraft (mostly in Britain but with some reference to North America, Australia and elsewhere). In 2003 Hutton published *Witches, Druids and King Arthur* which discusses the recent history of the Druidic movements. All these are complemented by *The Rise and Fall of Merry England* (1994) and *The Stations of the Sun* (2001), concerned with the ritual year.

There are, of course, other historical treatments of the precursors, sources and origins of contemporary Paganisms. These include those by Diane Purkiss (1996), and Ken Dowden (2000). The titles of these books clearly indicate the quite different interests of the authors. It may be interesting to read Hutton and Dowden's books alongside that of Prudence Jones and Nigel Pennick (1995), another book by scholarly insiders.

An American scholar, Aidan Kelly (1991), was the first to apply biblical textual criticism to the Gardnerian Book of Shadows. Kelly was perhaps the first Pagan scholar to openly suggest that Wicca represented a new religious movement, a fresh creation on older roots.

Sociology provides another academic perspective on the question of the nature and development of Paganisms. York (1995) suggests an interesting perspective on sociological patterns evident among New Agers and Pagans. Many scholars (some far less careful than York) conflate the two movements under the label 'New Age' as if that was unproblematic and self-evident. Some (such as Sutcliffe and Bowman noted above) prefer instead to class both as parts of a larger group of 'alternative religions'.

Wendy Griffin, a sociologist and Professor of Women's Studies, edited a wide-ranging anthology by women in contemporary Paganism and the 'Goddess movement', both inside and outside of academia (2000). Also see Helen Berger's book (2000) based on ten-years of participant-observation of the practices, structures, and transformations of Pagan groups and festivals in the eastern United States.

Gini Graham Scott (1980) and Susan Greenwood (2000) offer two anthropological studies of contemporary Pagan Witchcraft. The former examines the California-based New Reformed Orthodox Order of the Golden Dawn, a playfully named Witchcraft group, as it existed in the late 1970s, while the latter book examines how magical rituals designed to facilitate contact with the other-world affect magicians' notions of identity, gender and morality. Loretta Orion (1995) examines in particular how and when contemporary Pagan Witches use magical methods of curing. Jone Salomonsen (2002) provides a ground-breaking dialogue between anthropological and theological approaches to the study of religions. The book is also important as a discussion of the Reclaiming tradition growing around Starhawk's work. It is, therefore, also an important discussion of Feminist Goddess-centred spirituality. Similarly, Kathryn Rountree (2003) provides a fascinating discussion of such spirituality and activities in New Zealand. Lynne Hume is another anthropologist interested in southern hemisphere Paganism. Her (1997) book represents the first significant study of Australian Paganism. This may be complemented by a collection of practitioner accounts of Australian witchcraft edited by the sociologist Doug Ezzy (2003).

Ethnographic research among Pagans has not only enriched understanding of these religious traditions themselves, but also operates at the forefront of developments in academic reflection. Two good examples are Blain (2002) and Wallis (2003). Both of these, but particularly the former, discuss Heathen or Ásatrú shamanic practice and performance. Both challenge researchers and teachers to be more thoroughly reflexive, dialogical and experiential. They are, thus, important models of how academia might evolve. Similarly, Sarah Pike (2001) discusses an important dialogue between nature-respecting religions and the rising academic interest in embodiment and selfhood.

Complementing such ethnographically rooted studies are works such as that of Evert Hopman and Bond (1996) which collects interviews with a number of public figures in the American Pagan movement, including Margot Adler, Starhawk, Oberon G'Zell, Don Frew, and others. Similarly, Prudence Jones and Caitlín Matthews (1990) collects articles by leading British Pagans. One of those voices is Vivianne Crowley (a psychologist of religion), whose own books (1994, 1996) are important.

A recent reference book is *The Encyclopedia of Modern Witchcraft and Neo-Paganism* (Rabinovitch and Lewis, 2002) with entries ranging from 'Ásatrú' to 'Wyrd' and including a useful appendix on the methodological issues of trying to determine the size of the North American Pagan population. Lewis (1996) provides another useful anthology with more of a religious studies perspective.

If theology is under-represented among scholarly approaches to Paganisms, there are some powerful contributions. Salomonsen's theological training certainly informs her approach in *Enchanted Feminism* (2002). Michael York (2003) proposes that the term 'Pagan' includes not just 'Neo-' and Classical Paganisms, but also could be interpreted as a general form of religious behaviour which may be found in other religions as well. It will be interesting to see how Pagans and other scholars respond to this incitement to consider Paganisms in the company of other religions rather than as a separate and new Western phenomena. Long (1992) exemplifies recent feminist theological and historical research. This is also another example of the permeability of boundaries: not only Pagans but Jews, Christians and others are concerned and inspired by such interests. Billington and Green (1998) is useful alongside this.

An important contribution to feminist re-imagining of how theology might be done in a feminist manner, i.e. as 'thealogy', is Raphael (1996). Her *Introducing Thealogy* (2001) provides a good introduction to this area. While the list of Pagan thealogical, Goddess-respecting and feminist writings is extensive, growing and exciting, the works of Carol Christ (e.g. 1995, 1998, 2003) must take pre-eminent position among them.

Alongside these, the study of Paganisms should not only consider scholarly texts (albeit describing and discussing experience-rich and dynamic events and activities). Books such as Monica Sjöö and Barbara Mor's *The Great Cosmic Mother* (1987) and Elinor Gadon's *The Once and Future Goddess* (1990) enrich academic study by bringing together art, narrative, discussion and passionate commitment.

Last, but far from least, there are myriad sources and resources for the study of Paganism made available by Pagan writers, artists, web-managers, musicians, poets, and performers of all kinds. The list is endless. Not all study need be face-to-face with Pagans engaged in rituals or celebrations of the seasons. Reference to books, websites and other resources is also invaluable. We encourage readers to examine 'insider' accounts alongside the largely scholarly texts noted above. Consider whether the topics that Pagans think it important to foreground and debate are the same as those of interest to academics. For example, among the best accounts of British Witchcraft is Valiente (1989). Two excerpts from Valiente's book are included in this volume along with other important material that, we hope, will greatly enhance and further the study of Paganisms.

References

Adler, Margot ([1979] 1986) *Drawing Down the Moon*. Boston: Beacon Press.

Albanese, Catherine (1990) *Nature Religion in America: From the Algonkian Indians to New Age*. Chicago: University of Chicago Press.

Berger, Helen (2000) *A Community of Witches*. Columbia: University of South Carolina Press.

Billington, Sandra and Green, Miranda (eds) (1998) *The Concept of the Goddess*. London: Routledge.

Blain, Jenny (2002) *Nine Worlds of Seid-Magic: Ecstasy and Neo-Shamanism in North European Paganism*. London: Routledge.

Blain, Jenny, Ezzy, Doug and Harvey, Graham (eds) (2004) *Researching Paganisms: Religious Experiences and Academic Methodologies*. New York: AltaMira.

Christ, Carol (1995) *Odyssey with the Goddess: A Spiritual Quest in Crete*. London: Continuum.

Christ, Carol (1998) *Rebirth of the Goddess: Finding Meaning in Feminist Spirituality*. London: Routledge.

Christ, Carol (2003) *She Who Changes: Re-imagining the Divine in the World*. Basingstoke: Palgrave Macmillan.

Clifton, Chas S. (ed.) (1992a) *The Modern Craft Movement*. St. Paul, MN: Llewellyn.

Clifton, Chas S. (1992b) *The Encyclopedia of Heresies and Heretics*. Santa Barbara, CA: ABC-Clio.

Clifton, Chas S. (ed.) (1993) *Modern Rites of Passage*. St. Paul, MN: Llewellyn.

Clifton, Chas S. (ed.) (1994) *Witchcraft and Shamanism*. St. Paul, MN: Llewellyn.

Clifton, Chas S. (ed.) (1996) *Living Between Two Worlds*. St. Paul, MN: Llewellyn.

Clifton, Chas S. (2003) *Her Hidden Children*. New York: AltaMira Press.

Crowley, Vivianne (1994) *Phoenix from the Flames: Pagan Spirituality in the Western World*. London: Thorsons.

Crowley, Vivianne (1996) *Wicca: The Old Religion in the New Millennium*. London: Thorsons.

Dowden, Ken (2000) *European Paganism: The Realities of Cult from Antiquity to the Middle Ages*. London: Routledge.

Evert Hopman, Ellen and Bond, Lawrence (1996) *People of the Earth: The New Pagans Speak Out*. Rochester, VT: Destiny Books.

Ezzy, Doug (2003) *Practising the Witch's Craft: Real Magic under a Southern Sky*. London: Allen & Unwin.

Gadon, Elinor (1990) *The Once and Future Goddess*. Wellingborough: Aquarian.

Greenwood, Susan (2000) *Magic, Witchcraft and the Otherworld*. Oxford: Berg.

Griffin, Wendy (ed.) (2000) *Daughters of the Goddess*. New York: AltaMira.

Harvey, Graham (1997) *Listening People, Speaking Earth: Contemporary Paganism*. London: Hurst; Adelaide: Wakefield. Also published as *Contemporary Paganism: Listening People, Speaking Earth*. New York: New York University Press.

Harvey, Graham (ed.) (2000) *Indigenous Religions: A Companion*. London: Continuum.

Harvey, Graham (ed.) (2003) *Shamanism: A Reader*. London: Routledge.

Harvey, Graham and Hardman, Charlotte (eds) (2000) *Pagan Pathways*. London: HarperCollins (previously entitled *Paganism Today*, 1995).

Hume, Lynne (1997) *Witchcraft and Paganism in Australia*. Melbourne: Melbourne University Press.

Hutton, Ronald (1991) *The Pagan Religions of the Ancient British Isles: Their Nature and Legacy*. Oxford: Blackwell.

Hutton, Ronald (1994) *The Rise and Fall of Merry England: The Ritual Year 1400-1700*. Oxford: Oxford University Press.

Hutton, Ronald (1999) *The Triumph of the Moon: A History of Modern Pagan Witchcraft*. Oxford: Oxford University Press.

Hutton, Ronald (2001) *The Stations of the Sun*. Oxford: Oxford Paperbacks.

Hutton, Ronald (2003) *Witches, Druids and King Arthur*. London: Hambledon and London.

Jones, Prudence and Matthews, Caitlin (1990) *Voices from the Circle: The Heritage of Western Paganism*. Wellingborough: Aquarian.

Jones, Prudence and Pennick, Nigel (1995) *A History of Pagan Europe*. London: Routledge.

Kelly, Aidan (1991) *Crafting the Art of Magic: A History of Modern Witchcraft 1939-1964*. St. Paul, MN: Llewellyn.

Lewis, James (ed.) (1996) *Magical Religion and Modern Witchcraft*. Albany, NY: State University of New York Press.

Long, Asphodel (1992) *In a Chariot Drawn by Lions: The Search for the Female in Deity*. London: The Women's Press.

Orion, Loretta (1995) *Never Again the Burning Times*. Prospect Heights: Waveland Press.

Pearson, Joanne (ed.) (2003) *Belief Beyond Boundaries: Wicca, Celtic Spirituality and New Age*. Aldershot: Open University and Ashgate.

Pearson, Joanne, Roberts, Richard and Samuel, Geoffrey (eds) (1999) *Nature Religion Today: Paganism in the Modern World*. Edinburgh: Edinburgh University Press.

Pike, Sarah (2001) *Earthly Bodies, Magical Selves*. Berkeley, CA: University of California Press.

Purkiss, Diane (1996) *The Witch in History: Early Modern and Twentieth-Century Presentations*. London: Routledge.

Rabinovitch, Shelley and Lewis, James (eds) (2002) *The Encyclopedia of Modern Witchcraft and Neo-Paganism*. Sacramento: Citadel Press.

Raphael, Melissa (1996) *Thealogy and Embodiment*. Sheffield: Sheffield Academic Press.

Raphael, Melissa (2001) *Introducing Thealogy*. Cleveland: Pilgrim Press.

Rountree, Kathryn (2003) *Embracing the Witch and the Goddess: Feminist Ritual-makers in New Zealand*. London: Routledge.

Salomonsen, Jone (2002) *Enchanted Feminism: The Reclaiming Witches of San Francisco*. London: Routledge.

Scott, Gini Graham (1980) *Cult and Countercult*. Westport, CT: Greenwood Press.